Avant-Doc

Avant-Doc

INTERSECTIONS OF DOCUMENTARY AND AVANT-GARDE CINEMA

Scott MacDonald

OXFORD
UNIVERSITY PRESS

OXFORD
UNIVERSITY PRESS

Oxford University Press is a department of the University of Oxford.
It furthers the University's objective of excellence in research, scholarship,
and education by publishing worldwide.

Oxford   New York
Auckland   Cape Town   Dar es Salaam   Hong Kong   Karachi
Kuala Lumpur   Madrid   Melbourne   Mexico City   Nairobi
New Delhi   Shanghai   Taipei   Toronto

With offices in
Argentina   Austria   Brazil   Chile   Czech Republic   France   Greece
Guatemala   Hungary   Italy   Japan   Poland   Portugal   Singapore
South Korea   Switzerland   Thailand   Turkey   Ukraine   Vietnam

Oxford is a registered trademark of Oxford University Press
in the UK and certain other countries.

Published in the United States of America by
Oxford University Press
198 Madison Avenue, New York, NY 10016

Library of Congress Cataloging-in-Publication Data
Avant-doc : intersections of documentary and avant-garde cinema : an oral panorama /
Scott MacDonald.
pages cm
Includes bibliographical references and index.
Includes filmography.
ISBN 978-0-19-938870-7 (cloth)—ISBN 978-0-19-938871-4 (pbk.)—ISBN 978-0-19-938872-1
(updf)—ISBN 978-0-19-938873-8 (epub)   1. Documentary films—History and criticism.
2. Experimental films—History and criticism.   3. Motion picture producers and directors—
Interviews.   I. MacDonald, Scott, 1942- interviewer.
PN1995.9.D6A947 2014
070.1'8—dc23
2014006115

{ CONTENTS }

{ ACKNOWLEDGMENTS }

Various individuals and organizations have helped make *Avant-Doc* possible. Oxford University Press editor Brendan O'Neill had faith in this project from early on and was persistent in his support.

Thanks to Autumn Campbell and Jeremy Rossen, then directors of the Cinema Project in Portland, Oregon, for arranging for me to interview Todd Haynes, a public event co-sponsored by the Northwest Film Center; to Steve Holmgren of UnionDocs, the center for documentary filmmaking in Brooklyn, New York, and to Dennis Lim of the American Museum of the Moving Image for helping to arrange for me to interview Michael Glawogger as a public event at UnionDocs; to Rebecca Meyers at Studio7Arts for facilitating my interview with Robert Gardner; and to the Flaherty Film Seminar for providing me with an opportunity to interview Susana de Sousa Dias.

My teaching has supported my interviewing, and I am grateful for the teaching opportunities offered by Hamilton College (thanks especially to Patrick Reynolds, Deborah Polinski, Patricia O'Neill, Peter Rabinowitz, Nancy Rabinowitz, Bret Olsen, and Heather Johnsen), by Harvard University (special thanks to David Rodowick, Alfred Guzzetti, Robb Moss, Dominique Bluher, Heidi Bliss, and Clayton Mattos); and by Colgate University (thanks to John Knecht and Lynn Schwarzer).

The Academy of Motion Picture Arts and Sciences named me an Academy Scholar for 2012; their grant was for another project, but it enabled me to finish this volume more quickly than I would have been able to without the Academy's support.

Others who have assisted me in one way or another include J. J. Murphy, who read an early draft of the book and made valuable suggestions; Mara Campione, Brittany Gravely, David Pendleton, Graham Swindoll, John Paul Sniadecki, Stuart Liebman, and of course, my wife Patricia Reichgott O'Connor, who has been endlessly supportive. Thank you.

Earlier and/or condensed versions of some of the interviews in this collection appeared in journals: "From Underground to Multiplex: An Interview with Todd Haynes," *Film Quarterly* 62, no. 3 (Spring 2009): 54–64; "Indonesia in Motion: An Interview with Leonard Retel Helmrich," *Film Quarterly* 63, no. 3 (Spring 2010): 35–41; "Perception as Transcendence: Interview with Paweł Wojtasik," *Film Quarterly* 65, no. 2 (Winter 2011): 52–58; "An Interview with Alfred Guzzetti," *Millennium Film Journal*, no. 55 (Spring 2012): 70–83;

"Personal Effects: Ed Pincus on His Magnum Opus *Diaries (1971–1976)*," *Moving Image Source* (June 2012), an on-line journal (http://www.movingim-agesource.us) sponsored by the Museum of the Moving Image in Queens, New York; "Knots in the Head: An Interview with Michael Glawogger," *Film Quarterly* 65, no. 4 (Summer 2012): 40–49; "Interview with Susana de Sousa Dias," *Film Quarterly* 66, no. 2 (Winter 2012): 25–34; "Cine-Surveillance: 3 Avant-Docs" (interview with Jane Gillooly), *Film Quarterly* 66, no. 4 (Summer 2013): 28–29, 36–40; "Ruminating on Sweetgrass: An Interview with Filmmakers Ilisa Barbash and Lucien Castaing-Taylor," *Framework* 54, no. 2 (Fall 2013): 259–330; "Castaing-Taylor and Paravel on *Leviathan*," Framework 54, no. 2 (Fall 2013): 325–330; and "Remaking a Found-Footage Film in a Digital Age: An Interview with Jen Proctor," *Millennium Film Journal*, no. 57 (Spring 2013): 84–91. I am grateful for permission to reprint the portions of those interviews included here.

Avant-Doc

Introduction

In the spring of 2009, I was invited to be a keynote speaker at a conference sponsored by the graduate students in the Department of Comparative Literature and Film at the University of Iowa, called "Avant-Doc: Intersections of Avant-garde and Documentary Film."[1] I accepted the invitation, partly because I had begun to realize that when my Hamilton College students decided to take my course, Facing Reality: A History of Documentary Cinema, having already taken Critical Cinema: A History of Avant-Garde Film, I was, increasingly, asking them to re-see a good many films: Peter Kubelka's *Unsere Afrikareise* ("Our Trip to Africa," 1965), for example, and Stan Brakhage's *Window Water Baby Moving* (1959) and *The Act of Seeing with One's Own Eyes* (1972), William Greaves's *Symbiopsychotaxiplasm: Take One* (1972). This was not a problem in itself, of course (these films deserve multiple viewings), but it posed a dilemma: given my students' limited awareness of independent cinema, repeating these films meant that I could not show others. And when in one instance I was asked to teach both courses during the same semester at Harvard, I was embarrassed to find that I needed to ask the department to rent some of the same films twice, at different points during the fall term. The fact that an "Avant-Doc" conference had been organized helped me realize that my growing sense that these two histories were converging was more than a personal pedagogical issue.

"Avant-garde film" and "documentary" not only designate different film histories, they are different kinds of terms. "Avant-garde" originally referred to the leading edge of a military attack; it was adapted to film from the other arts, particularly from modernist painting, first, to identify that body of cinema created during the 1920s by painters (and poets and photographers) interested in the potential of film, and in the 1960s and 1970s, to represent

---

[1] The "Avant-Doc" conference was sponsored by the graduate students in the department. The conference description: "Avant-Doc: Intersections of Avant-garde and Documentary Film seeks to explore the historical and contemporary intersections of documentary and avant-garde film and media. While the categories of avant-garde and documentary have been used to designate separate modes of filmmaking and institutional frameworks, in practice, filmmakers, theorists and spectators have experienced and understood the two as malleable and interactive categories. Avant-Doc foregrounds the relationships between avant garde and documentary modes in order to open examinations of their productive intersections and the historical and theoretical questions which emerge from them."

the idea that "avant-garde" filmmakers have often devised new approaches to cinema that have been exploited by commercial moviemakers and television advertisers.[2] The logic of "avant-garde" in a cinematic context has always been questionable, since it is obvious that without the evolution of commercial film, the means for producing avant-garde film would never have developed.[3] However, as the term is currently used, at least in the United States, "avant-garde" includes an extremely wide range of approaches to cinema, everything from Oskar Fischinger's forays into "visual music" to the "psychodramas" of Maya Deren and Kenneth Anger, to John Waters's early "Trash" films, to Tony Conrad's *The Flicker* and the "slow cinema" of Peter Hutton, James Benning, and Sharon Lockhart. Indeed, the current value of the term is its inclusiveness, rather than its designation of any particular approach, though generally speaking, the films included can be understood as explicit or implicit critiques of commercial media and the audience that has developed for it.

"Documentary" has traditionally referred to films that make a "truth claim." Of course, any estimable commercial narrative film, like any estimable novel or poem, can be said to offer truths, or a Truth, about human nature and human life—though, unlike documentaries, fiction films do not claim to provide actual documents, as opposed to dramatizations, of the people and places represented. "Documentary" was first used by John Grierson to refer to Robert Flaherty's *Moana* (1926): Grierson said the film had "documentary value," meaning, presumably, that Flaherty had documented aspects of the life of a distant culture (the Samoans) that no one else had.[4] Of course, we know now that during the production of *Nanook of the North* (1921) and *Moana* Flaherty asked the Inuit and the Samoans to reenact elements of their current and/or previous ways of life; basically, he was "documenting" a fabrication. Nevertheless, these reenactments were produced in collaboration with real Inuit and real Samoans, and were filmed in their actual environments.

Of course, there are those who are suspicious of any definition of "documentary." Trinh T. Minh-ha has said, "There is no such thing as documentary—whether the term designates a category of material, a genre, an approach, or a set of techniques. This assertion—as old and as fundamental as the antagonism between names and reality—needs incessantly to be restated,

[2] For some, "avant-garde" has continued to have a more specifically political emphasis, denoting films that are meant to confront the implicit/explicit politics of media in service of global capitalism, and while this sense of "avant-garde" is certainly not irrelevant to the idea of "avant-doc," or to the filmmakers interviewed in this volume, it was not the primary meaning of "avant-doc," at least as I understood it, at the Iowa conference and is not the primary meaning in what follows.

[3] I remain indebted to Morgan Fisher for this insight.

[4] Grierson made this comment in a review of *Moana* in the February 8, 1926, *New York Sun*; the review was reprinted in Lewis Jacobs, ed., *The Documentary Tradition* (New York: Hopkinson and Blake, 1971), 25–26.

despite the very visible existence of a documentary tradition."[5] Perhaps the most useful definition of what Trinh admits is a "documentary tradition" comes from the French nature filmmaker Jean Painlevé: for Painlevé a documentary is "any film that documents real phenomena or their honest and justified reconstruction in order to consciously increase human knowledge through rational or emotional means and to expose problems and offer solutions from an economic, social, or cultural point of view."[6] Obviously, this definition has its own problems—how do we know a documentary is "honest" or decide it is "justified"—but it has the advantage of including most all of the films that have usually been considered documentaries.

The ongoing debates about the terms we use to designate these two particular strands in the weave of film history will not be put to rest here, but I think it is fair to say that in general "avant-garde film" and "documentary" are primarily useful in a pedagogical sense: that is, if one teaches a course in avant-garde film, students can expect that course to cover certain films, filmmakers, and concepts; and the same is true of a course in documentary film. What is also clear, and most relevant here, is that within this pedagogical sphere, overlaps and imbrications of the territories designated by the two terms have become increasingly interesting to students of cinema for a variety of good reasons. As I thought about "Avant-Doc" in preparation for the Iowa conference, I began to realize the obvious: that the histories of avant-garde film and documentary have been intersecting in a wide variety of interesting ways since the dawn of cinema. These intersections are evident within both the history of filmmaking and the history of alternative exhibition.

Historical Intersections—A Brief Sketch

An intersection of an avant-garde artistic practice and a documentary impulse occurred before, and helped to instigate, cinema itself. When Eadweard Muybridge and Etienne-Jules Marey were discovering and exploring the possibilities of photographic motion study, they were certainly the photographic avant-garde of that moment. And their subject was the documentation of the motion of animals, birds, and human beings, presumably so that we could know, more fully, the truth about this motion.[7] The Muybridge motion study photographs and Marey's chronophotographs were formative in the

[5] Trinh T. Minh-ha, opening lines of "The Totalizing Quest of Meaning," chapter 2 of *When the Moon Waxes Red: Representation, Gender and Cultural Politics* (New York: Routledge, 1991), 29.

[6] See Jean Painlevé, "The Castration of the Documentary" (1953) in Andy Masaki Bellows, Marina McDougall, Brigitte Berg, eds., *Science Is Fiction: The Films of Jean Painlevé* (Cambridge, MA/San Francisco: MIT Press/Brico Press, 2000), 149.

[7] An excellent source for information on Marey and Muybridge is Marta Braun's *Picturing Time: The Work of Etienne-Jules Marey (1830–1904)* (Chicago: University of Chicago Press, 1992).

improved efficiency of assembly-line industrial production and in the technological development of manned flight and, at the same time, were aesthetic and technological breakthroughs that instigated, or at least predicted, new forms of serial aesthetics. Beginning in the 1960s, avant-garde filmmakers—Hollis Frampton, Robert Huot, and Morgan Fisher, for example—were drawn to Muybridge's serial photographs as a model for cinematic structuring.[8]

It has long been assumed that Muybridge's development of the Zoopraxiscope, his device for synthesizing drawings of his motion-study photographs into the illusion of motion, and his use of Zoopraxiscope projections as part of his lectures, were developments that led toward Thomas Edison's Kinetoscope and, finally in 1895, to the Lumière Cinématographe. At the moment when W. K. L. Dickson perfected the Kinetograph and Kinetoscope and the Lumière Brothers perfected the Cinématographe and the projected motion picture, they in turn became the photographic avant-garde, and as was true for Muybridge and Marey, their primary fascination was the documentation of motion, specifically human activity, first, in the world around them and soon, in the case of the Lumières, across the globe.

The early street films of the Lumière Brothers, the Edison Studio, and other producers revealed a fascination with the modern city—a fascination particularly relevant to the business of cinema, which requires concentrations of population—that paved the way for films that proposed to interpret city life.[9] The most important premonition of what came to be called the City Symphony is probably *Manhatta* (1921) by photographers Charles Sheeler and Paul Strand, which intercuts between inventively composed images of lower Manhattan and poetic evocations of the city adapted from Walt Whitman

---

[8] Frampton wrote about Muybridge in "Eadweard Muybridge: Fragments of a Tesseract," in *Circles of Confusion* (Rochester, NY: Visual Studies Workshop Press, 1972), 69–80; he satirized Muybridge's "Animal Locomotion" photographs in his "Vegetable Locomotion" series (made with Marion Faller); and the central section of his *Zorns Lemma* (1970) seems informed by a serial logic inspired by Muybridge. Huot's *Turning Torso Drawdown* (1971) is an homage to Muybridge; and Fisher worked with Thom Andersen on *Eadweard Muybridge, Zoopraxographer* (1975), and his own *Documentary Footage* (1968) evokes Muybridge.

[9] Bill Nichols, who remains the leading scholar of documentary, has argued for a distinction between document and documentary. For Nichols, making a *document* of a cultural moment or practice is not making a *documentary*, since a documentary requires the filmmaker's formation of an intellectual argument: that is, an interpretation of the subject, based on whatever film documents have been recorded or whatever information the filmmaker has discovered. While this is a useful distinction, one problem with it is that even the basic recording of documents implicitly reflects a filmmaker's vision. Dziga Vertov's *The Man with a Movie Camera* (1929) certainly offers what Nichols would call an interpretation of modern life in urban Russia in the late 1920s, but is Vertov's celebration of industrial modernization and modernity really all that different from the single-shot Lumière documents of street scenes and arriving trains made in 1895–96? The Lumières may not have been promoting any political position, but we can easily read the Lumière films as representative of an implicitly capitalist and modernist point of view.

See chapter 2 of Nichols's *Introduction to Documentary* (Bloomington: Indiana University Press, 2001) for a useful discussion of the various ways in which "documentary" can be defined.

poems. A full-fledged City Symphony documents a composite day in the life of a city, usually a city that is representative of a particular culture. The early masterworks of the form include *Rien que les heures* ("Nothing but Time," 1926), Alberto Cavalcanti's depiction of Paris; Walther Ruttmann's *Berlin: Symphony of a Big City* (1927), the film that gave the form its name; and *The Man with a Movie Camera* (1929) by Dziga Vertov, a meta-city symphony that combines documentary footage of several cities into a vision of modern post-revolutionary urban life in Russia.

The City Symphonies have regularly been claimed by the histories of both documentary and avant-garde film. While documentary history focuses on the city as subject and on the filmmakers' ways of seeing cities as reflections of particular ideologies, in avant-garde history, the City Symphonies are crucial early instances of cinema's potential for experiment, for developing new forms, for moving beyond the commercial marketing of narrative melo-drama, and for making an exploration of the cinematic apparatus the subject of film. Dziga Vertov's self-reflexive experimentation in *The Man with a Movie Camera* has been an inspiration for many documentary and avant-garde film-makers, and the City Symphony genre has continued to evolve over the past eighty years as part of both histories. Robert Gardner's *Forest of Bliss* (1986) is usually understood as a documentary (though Gardner himself would prefer a broader sense of the film),[10] while Rudy Burckhardt's numerous City Symphonies of New York and Pat O'Neill's Los Angeles City Symphony, *Water and Power* (1989), tend to be understood as part of avant-garde history.[11]

The late 1920s also saw the emergence of a new kind of "avant-doc," a small set of films that did not exemplify either of the two major approaches to docu-mentary that had developed by then (the depiction of far-flung, preindustrial cultures and the City Symphony) and were also unlike the Dadaist and sur-realist works of European artists-turned-filmmakers—Man Ray's *Retour à la raison* ("Return to Reason, 1923), and *Un chien andalou* ("An Andalusian Dog," 1929), are representative instances—as well as the abstract flights of rhythm, chiaroscuro, and color, produced by Hans Richter, Walther Ruttmann, Viking Eggeling, and Oskar Fischinger. These new films—Ralph Steiner's *H2O* (1929), Joris Ivens's *Rain* (1929), and Henwar Rodakiewicz's *Portrait of a Young Man* (1931)—were early instances of the use of the motion picture camera as a means of retraining perception and producing what Steiner called "a visual

[10] In conversations with me, Gardner made clear that he prefers "filmmaker" to "documentary filmmaker," and indeed, recent celebrations of his work at Anthology Film Archives and at Bard College reflect this preference.

[11] I discuss a few of Rudy Burckhardt's many New York City Symphonies and his other New York City films in *The Garden in the Machine: A Field Guide to Independent Films about Place* (Berkeley and Los Angeles: University of California Press, 2001), 154–159. Of course, the City Symphony has grown beyond both these categories: In the same volume I argue that Spike Lee's *Do the Right Thing* is this country's most remarkable and insightful City Symphony.

poetry of formal beauty."[12] Like the City Symphonies, these films have been claimed by both avant-garde and documentary history.

Using the skill with composition that he had developed as a photographer, Steiner's focus in *H2O* is water, though by the end of the film, the film's dry, scientific title has become ironic. *H2O* is a montage that begins with relatively mundane shots of water being pumped, flowing over dams, and the like, but gradually moves in the direction of visual mystery: near the end, Steiner's shots of reflections on the surface of water become so abstract that viewers often have trouble believing that what they are seeing was not generated by animation.[13] Joris Ivens's *Rain* depicts the coming and going of a rainstorm in Amsterdam. While it is a city film, its focus is not so much on city life, as on the ways in which the storm transforms the look of the city. *Portrait of a Young Man* is, as Rodakiewicz suggests in his film's first intertitle, "an endeavor to portray a certain young man in the terms of the things he likes and his manner of liking them: the sea, leaves, clouds, smoke, machinery, sunlight, the interplay of forms and rythms [sic], but above all—the sea." The resulting 49-minute film presents an array of lovely sequences, a premonition of the films of Peter Hutton.

For all three of these filmmakers the motion picture camera was a means of demonstrating that each of us is capable of seeing much more in our daily surround than we normally allow ourselves to notice—an idea that would be elaborated by Stan Brakhage and many other avant-garde filmmakers a quarter of a century later. And for all three, the arrival of the Great Depression and the changing political climate in Europe were transformative, moving them away from a focus on the aesthetics of vision and toward an involvement in new forms of politically oriented documentary. Steiner contributed cinematography to Pare Lorenz's *The Plow that Broke the Plains* (1936), Sidney Meyers and Jay Leyda's *People of the Cumberland* (1938), and *The City* (1939), which he also co-directed with Willard Van Dyke; Rodakiewicz was one of the writers for *The Wave* (1936, directed by Fred Zinnemann) and *The City*; and he directed *One Tenth of a Nation* (1940). Ivens, of course, became and remained until the 1980s among the most revered makers of political documentary.

During the 1940s the most important development for independent cinema in the United States was the emergence of a full-fledged film society movement. The leading contributors were Frank Stauffacher's Art in Cinema Film Society in San Francisco and Berkeley, founded in 1946; and

[12] Ralph Steiner and Leo Hurwitz, "A New Approach to Film Making," *New Theatre* (September 1935): 22.

[13] All Steiner's "effects" are a function of his careful perception and his imaginative framing. Even the most fantastic image in *H2O* reveals its basis in reality: as we are noticing an essentially abstract image, a sliver of wood is sure to float into the frame.

Cinema 16, founded by Amos and Marcia Vogel in New York City in 1947, and programmed by Amos Vogel and Jack Goelman until 1963. Both Art and Cinema and Cinema 16 were remarkably successful. At the height of their popularity, Art in Cinema attracted audiences of 600 in both San Francisco and Berkeley; and Cinema 16 filled a 1,500-seat auditorium twice a night for its monthly programs. Both film societies used similar programming strategies, reviving classic films that had been out of circulation for decades and showing classic or recent films from foreign countries. But the essence of both Art in Cinema and Cinema 16 was an inventive mixture of documentary and avant-garde film. The first Art in Cinema series of programs focused on the history of avant-garde filmmaking in Europe as a means of creating a context for Stauffacher's commitment to support American, and particularly Bay Area, avant-garde filmmakers. But documentary was represented during the first season by the seventh program, "Fantasy into Documentary," which included *Rien que les heures, Berlin: Symphony of a Big City*, and *The City*. In subsequent years, Stauffacher's programming often included documentaries in what Bill Nichols has called "the poetic mode": *Rain*, for example, and Basil Wright's *Song of Ceylon* (1934), Sidney Meyers's *The Quiet One* (1948).[14]

At Cinema 16 Vogel consistently used documentary and avant-garde film to contextualize each other within dialectically arranged programs (Vogel was a great admirer of Eisenstein's theory of dialectic editing). Cinema 16's first program included five films: *Lamentation* (1943), a study of Martha Graham's interpretive dance; Douglas Crockwell's hand-painted abstraction, *Glens Falls Sequence* (1941); Sidney Peterson and James Broughton's surrealist riff, *The Potted Psalm* (1946); *Monkey into Man* (1938), Stuart Legg's documentary on ape behavior; and Phillip Stapp's political animation *Boundarylines* (1945). The second program presented *The Feeling of Rejection* (1947), a documentary on the effect of childhood emotional ties on the behavior of adults; *Five Abstract Film Exercises* (1941–44) by the Whitney Brothers; *And So They Live* (1940), a documentary on an Appalachian family by John Ferno; and *Hen Hop* (1945) and *Five for Four* (1945), animations by Norman McLaren made by painting and scratching directly on the filmstrip. A special program of "Damned Films" presented in 1953 offered the quintessence of Vogel's dialectic of documentary and avant-garde: after a revival of Carl Theodor Dreyer's *Vampyr* (1931), Vogel presented Kenneth Anger's psychodrama, *Fireworks* (1946) (fig. 1a), and then *Le Sang des bêtes* ("The Blood of the Beasts," 1949) (fig. 1b), Georges Franju's beautiful and visceral depiction of Paris slaughterhouses.[15]

---

[14] See Bill Nichols, *Introduction to Documentary* (Bloomington: Indiana University Press, 2001), 102–105.

[15] The same dialectic mixture of the two histories characterizes Vogel's *Film as a Subversive Art* (New York: Random House, 1974), essentially a research report on his experiences programming Cinema 16.

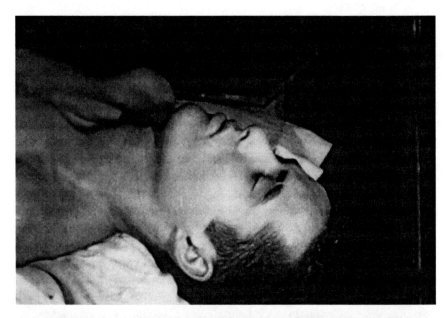

FIGURES 1A AND 1B *(above) Kenneth Anger as dreamer in his breakthrough* Fireworks *(1947); (below) the rite of animal slaughter, in Georges Franju's* Le Sang des bêtes *(1949)— shown together in Amos Vogel's special Cinema 16 program, "Les Films Maudits: An Evening of Damned Films."*

Source: Courtesy David E. James; courtesy Amos Vogel.

The development of lightweight cameras and tape recorders, more flexible microphones, and faster film stocks during the late 1950s created new options that simultaneously drove documentary filmmaking and avant-garde filmmaking further apart, *and* created a different kind of intersection between them. The opportunity to do sync-sound, "cinema-verite" shooting gave documentary filmmakers the option of avoiding an earlier reliance on the use of narration and music; and while many filmmakers continued to make films in the older, expository mode, cinema-verite shooting made more experiential forms of documentary possible.[16] These technological advances functioned not only to expand the options available to filmmakers committed to documentary, they provided new opportunities to create cinematic entertainments that could compete with, while simultaneously functioning as critiques of, the forms of entertainment marketed by Hollywood and early television. Drew Associates, D. A. Pennebaker, Frederick Wiseman, and the Maysles Brothers were able to fashion engaging melodrama out of real life in *Crisis: Behind a Presidential Commitment* (1963), *Don't Look Back* (1967), *High School* (1968), and *Salesman* (1968).

During the moment when cinema-verite shooting was transforming documentary history, avant-garde filmmakers, most of whom could not afford sync-sound technology, were producing different forms of cinematic engagement by abjuring sound altogether and/or by exploring new non-sync approaches to sound. The resulting films could hardly have been more different from the cinema-verite films, but from a later perspective, we can see that their fundamental mission was identical: the cinematic confrontation of convention-bound commercial media.

Of the filmmakers who refused sound altogether, Stan Brakhage is the best-known: committed to the idea of cinema as a *visual* art, Brakhage provided remarkable confrontations of visual taboo—*Window Water Baby Moving* (1959), *Three Films: Bluewhite, Blood's Tone, Vein* (1965), *The Act of Seeing with One's Own Eyes* (1972)—exploring with gestural, hand-held camera many of those aspects of the body-as-process that society (and conventional cinema) had censored, as well as many dimensions of perception that our acculturation within a consumer culture tends to erase. While Brakhage was

---

[16] In *Documentary: A History of Nonfiction Film* (New York: Oxford University Press, 1974), Erik Barnouw defines two basic approaches: "direct cinema" (i.e., fly-on-the-wall observational filmmaking); and "*cinéma vérité*" (i.e., films in which the process of shooting instigates interesting situations that are recorded as they unfold)—the accents and italics reflect the fact that *cinéma vérité* was a French translation of Vertov's *kino-pravda* (see the first two sections of chapter 5, "Observer" and "Catalyst"). In *Introduction to Documentary* Bill Nichols called these two approaches the "observational mode" and the "participatory mode" (I would prefer "provocational mode") (34), which avoids the confusion between filmmakers, who tend to refer to all sync-sound shooting as "cinema-verite," and scholars who need to distinguish between various documentary approaches, a confusion reflected in spelling. "Cinema-verite," like "*cinéma-vérité*," is often used to refer to the provocational forms of cinema-verite shooting instigated by Jean Rouch.

Page 10 Introduction

not the first avant-garde filmmaker to choose silence (the 1943 silent version of *Meshes of the Afternoon* by Maya Deren and Alexander Hammid might have been an inspiration), he liberated a generation of filmmakers who didn't have the economic resources to work in sync sound or the inclination to work in an approximation of it.

Peter Kubelka was also a crucial figure in exploring ways of working with sound other than conventional sync, in his interpretation of a big-game hunting safari in the Sudan: *Unsere Afrikareise*. Kubelka used image and sound in a dialectic arrangement that allowed him to lay bare the colonialist and racist assumptions of the Austrian businessmen who had organized the safari and had hired Kubelka to document their exploits, thinking the result would be a typical travel diary they could share with their admiring colleagues and friends. Like Brakhage's *Window Water Baby Moving* and *The Act of Seeing with One's Own Eyes, Unsere Afrikareise* has, in recent years, been recognized by many scholars and teachers as a documentary, as well as a canonical avant-garde work.

In 1955, Francis Flaherty, Robert Flaherty's widow, hosted a symposium of filmmakers to honor her husband's filmmaking oeuvre and to promote his commitment to filmmaking "without preconceptions."[17] Within a few years, "the Flaherty," as the symposium came to be called, was attracting dozens of filmmakers, programmers, scholars, teachers, students, and other cine-aficionados for week-long immersions in a program of screenings and discussions. By 1963 the Flaherty had become so identified with documentary that it could provoke an aesthetic guerilla action by avant-garde filmmakers Jonas Mekas and Ken Jacobs, who wanted to present Jack Smith's *Flaming Creatures* (1963) and Jacobs's own *Blonde Cobra* (1962) at the seminar. Mekas documented their cine-guerilla invasion of the seminar and later depicted the experience in the "FLAHERTY NEWSREEL" section of his *Lost Lost Lost* (1976).[18]

---

[17] Francis Flaherty's emphasis on the idea of "non-preconception" continues to inform the modern Flaherty seminars (e.g., films are presented at the seminars without introduction) but the idea that one can approach a film, or a subject, with no preconceptions seems of questionable value even in a context of Robert Flaherty's work (clearly when he returned to northern Canada to make *Nanook*, he had preconceptions about what to film), and all those attending a Flaherty seminar bring with them their assumptions about cinema and the world.

[18] Later, in his September 12, 1963,*Village Voice* column (reprinted in Jonas Mekas, *Movie Journal: The Rise of a New American Cinema, 1959–1971* (New York: Collier, 1972), 94–95), Mekas remembers his experience at the 1963 Flaherty seminar: "This year. . . [the Flaherty seminar] was devoted to a retrospective of the so-called cinéma vérité, the documentary-like cinema. The work of Leacock and the brothers Maysles took a prominent place. A number of filmmakers and film critics were gathered from Canada, France, the U.S.A. The very fact that a retrospective of this sort could take place reminds us that the cinéma vérité is only one passing stage of cinema and that some people are already beyond it. . . .

We took *Flaming Creatures* and *Blonde Cobra* to the seminar, two pieces of the impure, naughty, and "uncinematic" cinema that is being made now in New York. The only cinema that I think is doing something new and good today. It was a late midnight screening. Midnight screening in Vermont!

By the end of the 1960s the nearly exclusive focus of the Flaherty seminars on documentary was under attack. Programmers D. Marie Grieco and
Willard Van Dyke instigated a substantial invasion of West Coast avant-garde
filmmaking in 1968, and during the following two years Adrienne Mancia
and Van Dyke maintained the new balance between documentary and
avant-garde. In more recent decades Flaherty seminar programming has continued to reflect an implicit debate about the correct balance between documentary and avant-garde film. Documentary has remained the Flaherty's
primary commitment, but a number of programmers—Bruce Jenkins and
Melinda Ward (the 1983 seminar), Richard Herskowitz (1987), Ruth Bradley
and Kathy High (1992), Ed Halter (2002), Susan Oxtoby (2004), and Irina
Leimbacher (2009), among them—have maintained a substantial presence of
avant-garde film at the Flaherty.[19]

For a time avant-garde filmmaking and documentary understood the
"personal," at least as cinematic subject matter, in quite different ways.
Since the 1940s, avant-garde filmmakers have found ways of exploring the
personal, first by psycho-dramatizing their inner disturbances (Deren
and Hammid's *Meshes of the Afternoon* and Kenneth Anger's *Fireworks* are
landmark instances), and later by filming the particulars of their personal
lives. Brakhage documented dimensions of his personal life in many films,
as did Jonas Mekas, in *Reminiscences of a Journey to Lithuania* (1972), and
Lost Lost Lost (1976), and Carolee Schneemann, in her Autobiographical
Trilogy: *Fuses* (1967), *Plumb Line* (1972), and *Kitch's Last Meal* (1973–78). By the
1980s, Su Friedrich and Alan Berliner, both of whom identified themselves
as avant-garde filmmakers, were using their filmmaking to directly engage
struggles with their family histories. *The Ties that Bind* (1984) and *Sink or
Swim* (1990), Friedrich's films about her relationships with her mother and
her father, respectively; and *Intimate Stranger* (1991) and *Nobody's Business*
(1996), Berliner's films about the maternal grandfather he never knew and his

My God, we felt like underground even at Flaherty's. But a few souls saw our work and were shaken
by it. Others just walked out and slept peacefully, dreaming cinéma vérité. Nobody should disturb
those who sleep, unless it is a fire or something. We'll disturb you some other time. . ."

[19] The ongoing debates about programming avant-garde film at the Flaherty reflect a more fundamental debate about Robert Flaherty himself. Was Flaherty a documentary filmmaker? While
they are usually categorized as documentaries, his films create experiences that are generally quite
distinct from what became conventional documentary practice in the 1930s and remained standard
through the 1950s; Flaherty's finished films do not feel like lectures or polemics. What distinguishes
Nanook, Moana, Man of Aran, and *Louisiana Story* is the way in which Flaherty worked with indigenous groups and with non-actors over substantial periods of time, without screenplay or script, to
produce romantic evocations of particular places and times. This experimental narrative approach
has as much in common with avant-garde film as with the forms of documentary that were popular
in Flaherty's lifetime, and it remains very much alive in films by filmmakers usually identified as
avant-garde: for example, Sharon Lockhart's *Pine Flat* (2006), Naomi Uman's *Unnamed Film* (2008,
part 1 of her "Ukrainian Time" project), and Ben Russell's *Let Each One Go Where He May* (2009) feel
something like contemporary Flaherty films.

relationship with his father, incorporate material gathered from a variety of sources into composite forms that function as therapy for some of the frustrations the filmmakers have experienced as a result of family traumas.

What has come to be called "personal documentary" (basically, the use of cinema-verite filming to explore issues of family and friends) was instigated in the early 1970s by Martha Coolidge's *David: Off and On* (1972), Miriam Weinstein's *My Father the Doctor* (1972) and *Living with Peter* (1973), Jeff Kreines's *The Plaint of Steve Kreines as Recorded by His Younger Brother Jeff* (1974), Amalie Rothschild's *Nana, Mom and Me* (1974), Alfred Guzzetti's *Family Portrait Sittings* (1975), and Ed Pincus's *Diaries* (filmed from 1971 to 1976; completed in 1981). By the 1980s, several of Pincus's students at MIT were contributing to this approach, among them, Robb Moss (*The Tourist*, 1991) and Ross McElwee, whose *Backyard* (1984), *Sherman's March* (1986), *Time Indefinite* (1994), *Six O'Clock News* (1996), and *Photographic Memory* (2011) represent a major contribution.

Though these forays into the personal were occurring more or less simultaneously, the various makers worked generally in ignorance of each other's work and in rough concert with approaches familiar from earlier developments within the particular history they saw themselves part of. In *The Ties That Bind*, for example, Friedrich interviews her mother by scratching her questions into the film emulsion (we only *hear* her mother's responses), a formal tactic related to Brakhage's scratching titles and filmmaker credits into the emulsion of his films; and Berliner punctuates *Nobody's Business* with heavily edited moments of precisely organized montage, sometimes evocative of the precision editing in *Unsere Afrikareise* (Berliner studied with Kubelka during the 1970s). The personal documentaries, on the other hand, depend on candid, sync-sound recording of the interaction between the filmmakers' family members, and friends. However, the filmmakers from both traditions recycle their family home movies into their films as a means of situating present struggles within family history, and they reveal how the filmmaking process itself has become an intrinsic dimension of their relationships with family members, sometimes in very similar ways. Both McElwee and Berliner, for example, struggled with their fathers' disapproval of their filmmaking careers—a major theme in both *Time Indefinite* and *Nobody's Business*.

As the archive of cinema accumulated, decade by decade during the twentieth century, this archive became raw material for new kinds of film, and beginning with Esfir Shub in *The Fall of the Romanov Dynasty* (1927), films made as documents for one purpose began to be recycled into new films that redirected and sometimes reversed the implicit/explicit messages of the original documents. By the 1980s "recycled cinema" had become an important approach in both documentary (NBC's *Victory at Sea* series, 1952–53; Frédéric Rossif's *To Die in Madrid*, 1962; Emile de Antonio's *Point of Order*, 1964; Jayne Loader and Kevin and Pierce Rafferty's *Atomic Café*, 1982) and avant-garde film (Bruce Conner's *A Movie*, 1958, *Report*, 1963–1967, and *Crossroads*, 1976; Ernie Gehr's *Eureka*, 1974). One might argue that by the 1980s, recycling had become the most significant and productive approach among independent filmmakers of all kinds, many of them working in what could be seen as the territory between avant-garde and documentary: Yervant Gianikian and Angela Ricci Lucchi, in their films from *Karagoez—Catalogo 9.5* (1981) and *From the Pole to the Equator* (1986) through *Pays Barbare* (2013); Alan Berliner in *The Family Album* (1986), Peter Forgács in the Private Hungary Series (1988 on), and in *Meanwhile, Somewhere* (1994), *The Maelstrom: A Family Chronicle* (1997), and *Danube Exodus* (1998); Gustav Deutsch in *Adria* (1989) and *Film ist. (1–6)* (1998); Penny Lane, in *Our Nixon* (2013). . .

One final confluence of avant-garde and documentary cinema (clearly there are others) has particular import for interviews in this collection. Among the most interesting recent accomplishments of filmmakers working out of both the documentary and avant-garde traditions is a burgeoning cinema of Place. Globalization and the standardization of so many dimensions of modern life, as well as threats to the environment, have created a desire on the part of many filmmakers to contribute to what has come to be called "eco-cinema." This urge has informed various forms of documentary, including "ethnographic film" and "nature film," and is behind a considerable body of recent avant-garde work.

The ethnographic documentaries of pioneers such as John Marshall, Robert Gardner, Timothy Asch, and the McDougalls are, of course, attempts to depict preindustrial cultures on the verge of or in the process of transformation, but the depictions of peoples in these films are embedded within particular landscapes that are often as informative and interesting as whatever social practices seem to be the focus. More recently, the depiction of people-in-place is the subject of what has come to be called "sensory ethnography": that is, attempts to use filmmaking, not as a way of illustrating written ethnography, but rather to evoke the sensory experiences of certain kinds of lives in particular places. Ilisa Barbash and Lucien Castaing-Taylor's *Sweetgrass* (2009) and Stephanie Spray and Pacho Velez's *Manakamana* (2013) are exemplary instances. Nature film and television, perhaps the most popular and ubiquitous genre of documentary, is often as fully engaged with place as with the wildlife that is the ostensible focus. In *Microcosmos* (1996), a film that helped revive the theatrical exhibition of nature documentary, Claude Nuridsany and Marie Pérennou provide an in-depth look at the diversity and complexity of life within a French meadow; and in *Ice Bears of the Beaufort* (2010), Arthur Smith sees the polar bears on the islands of the Beaufort Sea as a community of peaceful neighbors within the spectacular environment of Alaska's North Slope. Since the 1970s, cinematic contemplations of Place have also been a significant dimension of American avant-garde filmmaking. Larry Gottheim (*Fog Line*, 1970; *Horizons*, 1973), James Benning (*11 X 14*, 1976; *Deseret*, 1995;

13 Lakes, 2004; *Small Roads*, 2011), Nathaniel Dorsky (*Hours for Jerome*, 1982; *Song*, 2013), Peter Hutton (*Landscape (for Manon)*, 1987; *Study of a River*, 1996; *At Sea*, 2007), Sharon Lockhart (*Double Tide*, 2009), and a good many other filmmakers have created a remarkable range of avant-docs about Place.

The Shaping of *Avant-Doc*

Although our traditional categories and terminology for independent film-making are increasingly stressed, they remain embedded in the minds of many filmgoers and cineastes, as well as within systems of distribution and exhibition. Canyon Cinema and the New York Film-Makers' Cooperative distribute avant-garde film, while Documentary Educational Resources distributes ethnographic documentary; and other independent distributors have carved out their own niches. "Views from the Avant-Garde," a sidebar to the New York Film Festival, has focused on avant-garde work, while the main festival is devoted to feature narrative and documentary. Within film scholarship too, the distinction between avant-garde filmmaking and documentary is still generally accepted. The Visible Evidence conferences focus on documentary and the books in the impressive Visible Evidence series, edited by Jane Gaines, Faye Ginsburg, and Michael Renov, announce documentary as their primary interest. No scholars have collaborated to offer a series of books on avant-garde film comparable to the Visible Evidence series, but conference sessions at the Society for Cinema and Media Studies (SCMS) focusing specifically on avant-garde film have become increasingly popular, and that stalwart, *Millennium Film Journal*, edited by Grahame Weinbren and Jessica Ruffin, continues to maintain its focus on avant-garde film and video art.

In recent decades there have been significant exceptions to this pattern within scholarship. In 1999 Catherine Russell published *Experimental Ethnography: The Work of Film in the Age of Video* (Duke University Press), which explored a remarkably diverse set of films from both the documentary and avant-garde traditions. Russell's chapter, "Zoology, Pornography, Ethnography," for example, includes discussions of Bill Viola's *I Do Not Know What It Is I Am Like* (1986), Peter Kubelka's *Unsere Afrikareise*, Ray Birdwhistell's *Microcultural Incidents in Ten Zoos* (1969), Martin and Osa Johnson's *Simba: The King of Beasts, A Saga of the African Veldt* (1928), and Su Friedrich's *Hide and Seek* (1996). Indeed, throughout *Experimental Ethnography* Russell defies conventional distinctions between types of film as a means of revealing commonalities and distinctions that would not be apparent otherwise.

Other scholars have worked across the documentary and avant-garde distinction in various ways. Patricia R. Zimmermann in *States of Emergency: Documentaries, Wars, Democracies* brings together a wide range of films and videos that tend to straddle or incorporate aspects of the documentary and avant-garde traditions, particularly work that is in rebellion against corporate power and conservative politics, in order to offer "a historical reclamation" and "a rerouting of the commodification" of the term *independent film*.[20] In his remarkably thorough *The Most Typical Avant-Garde: History and Geography of Minor Cinemas in Los Angeles* (Berkeley and Los Angeles: University of California Press, 2005), David E. James explores Los Angeles as a nexus of avant-garde and documentary film and video practices, counter-cinemas that form an aesthetic and political context for the Hollywood industry. Other scholars—Chris Holmlund and Cynthia Fuchs, in *Between the Sheets, In the Streets: Queer, Lesbian, Gay Documentary* (Minneapolis: University of Minnesota Press, 1997); Paul Arthur, in *A Line of Sight: American Avant-Garde Film since 1965* (Minneapolis: University of Minnesota Press, 2005); Jeffrey Skoller, in *Shadows, Specters, Shards: Making History in Avant-Garde Film* (Minneapolis: University of Minnesota Press, 2005), and Michael Renov, in *The Subject of Documentary* (Minneapolis: University of Minnesota Press, 2004), for example—have brought various documentaries and avant-garde films together within a variety of conceptual frameworks. There is also my own *The Garden in the Machine: A Field Guide to Independent Films about Place* (Berkeley and Los Angeles: University of California Press, 2001).

Avant-Doc is meant to provide a different kind of engagement with the intersection of documentary and avant-garde filmmaking by focusing on the commentaries, conjectures, and memories of filmmakers who have been influenced by and have contributed to both histories in one way or another. Of course, filmmakers' comments on their films can never be the final word; as Hollis Frampton said, long ago, "it's obvious that there are things that spectators can know about a work, any work, that the person who made it can never know."[21] Nevertheless, since filmmakers, and especially the documentary and avant-garde filmmakers interviewed for this volume, often think seriously about the work they make and the ways in which this work relates to the traditions within which they are working, interviews can serve as a resource for those interested in exploring non-industrial movie-making and the various debates it has engendered. The interviews in *Avant-Doc* reveal a panorama of ways in which documentary history and avant-garde history have intersected, overlapped, become imbricated—and food for thought for cineastes, students, and film scholars interested in the wide world of independent cinema.

[20] Patricia R. Zimmermann, *States of Emergency: Documentaries, Wars, Democracies*, Visible Evidence Volume 7 (Minneapolis: University of Minnesota Press, 2000), p. xix.

[21] Hollis Frampton, in Scott MacDonald, *A Critical Cinema* (Berkeley and Los Angeles: University of California Press, 1988), 57.

Despite whatever theoretical arguments have been used to distinguish between documentary and avant-garde cinema, the experiences of making these films have often brought the filmmakers into meaningful contact, and in *Avant-Doc* I am at pains to expand recognition of this dimension of film history. Many film artists usually categorized as documentary filmmakers have learned from their avant-garde colleagues: Alfred Guzzetti learned from Peter Kubelka and Bruce Baillie; Nina Davenport, from Peter Hutton; Paweł Wojtasik, from Stan Brakhage; Ilisa Barbash and Lucien Castaing-Taylor, and other filmmakers connected with Harvard's Sensory Ethnography Lab, from James Benning, Peter Hutton, and Sharon Lockhart.

Filmmakers, programmers, and scholars who have identified themselves with the traditions of avant-garde cinema have often seemed less open to the accomplishments of documentary, sometimes ignoring cinematic achievements closely related, even potentially useful for their own filmmaking/curating/writing. Nevertheless, a range of direct and indirect interconnections have been at play between individual filmmakers. Stan Brakhage collaborated with Robert Gardner on a commentary track for the 2008 DVD release of Gardner's *Forest of Bliss*. Jim McBride and L. M. Kit Carson did a good bit of research on cinema-verite filmmaking during the 1960s for a book to be published by the Museum of Modern Art, but when they came to make their breakthrough faux documentary, *David Holzman's Diary* (1967), in order to critique the (implicit and sometimes explicit) claim that cinema-verite films were more *real* than other forms of documentary, the inspiration for their protagonist, the struggling personal documentarian David Holzman, was avant-garde filmmaker Andrew Noren, whose candid, personal (and silent) evocations of his daily life were part of the avant-garde tradition exemplified by Brakhage.[22] McBride himself appears in Ed Pincus's *Diaries (1971–1976)*.

The interviews in *Avant-Doc* are arranged in a rough chronology, not in the order in which they were conducted, but so as to suggest how earlier careers have impacted later ones and how recent careers have worked to redefine the cinematic traditions they have inherited. My selection of interviewees is driven primarily by my admiration of the work these filmmakers have done and by my sense that each of their careers, and many of their films, are meaningful contributions to the evolving liminal zone between documentary and avant-garde. I see the category of "avant-doc" not so much as a theoretical conclusion, but as a means for bringing the work discussed in these interviews more fully into the larger conversation about cinema and media.

Of course, I am well aware that this panorama of filmmaker conversations cannot pretend to represent all the worthy achievements of what I am

---

[22] See L. M. Kit Carson's introduction to the screenplay for McBride's *David Holzman's Diary*, published by Farrar, Straus & Giroux in 1970.

calling "avant-doc"—even the worthy achievements I am presently aware of. In recent years, no area of cinema has expanded more energetically and more internationally than documentary, and the films and filmmakers worthy of attention here have become almost too numerous to name. It will be obvious that my survey focuses primarily on recent filmmaking in the United States (and within this country, on work that has a connection to Cambridge, Massachusetts). One can only do what one can, and I must fall back on Flannery O'Connor's sense that "to declare a limitation" can be "a gateway to reality."[23] The limitations in this (already, perhaps, over-long) volume will be obvious to anyone aware of recent documentary production—and yet, I am confident that the filmmakers I have talked with and the films that are discussed here raise a good many of the issues that documentarians have struggled with throughout history and continue to struggle with around the world.

In all likelihood, those who find their way to *Avant-Doc* will pay scant attention to the organization of the volume, and may or may not read this introduction—in our Web-surfing era, most people engage a collection like this one in ways reflective of their particular interests and largely unpredictable to the author. Nevertheless, in assembling the interviews included, I have been concerned to provide a structure for those readers who do, still, read books in the traditional way—though the structure here is less conventionally academic than implicitly provocational, less like a lecture and more like a film society presentation. My "programming" is meant to maximize the value of the individual interviews, as well as to exploit their many levels of contrast and interconnection.

Avant-Doc begins with my interview with scholar/writer/teacher/editor Annette Michelson. Michelson has made a significant impact on independent cinema, and more generally on the field of modern art, in a variety of ways, the best known of which, at least in recent decades, is her 35-year editorship of the journal *October*, which she and Rosalind Krauss founded in 1976. Michelson has been a champion of independent filmmaking since the 1960s and her sense of independent cinema has always been broad. She was powerfully drawn to Russian filmmaking during the era of Constructivism—particularly to Eisenstein and Vertov—and to the North American structural film moment during the 1960s and early 1970s. For Michelson these were companion interests: Vertov had generally been thought of as a documentary filmmaker and structural film as an avant-garde movement, but both Vertov and the structuralists use the cinematic apparatus to re-present reality in a cine-reflexive manner that has both aesthetic and political implications.

[23] Flannery O'Connor, "The Regional Writer," in *Mysteries and Manners* (New York: Farrar, Straus & Giroux, 1961), 54.

The Michelson interview is followed, first, by interviews with five filmmakers who worked—and in three instances continue to work—in Cambridge, Massachusetts (I have argued elsewhere that Cambridge is the fountainhead of American documentary filmmaking).[24] At the time when Michelson was exploring the commonalities between the Russian avant-garde of the 1920s and the American avant-garde of the 1960s and 1970s, the Cambridge filmmakers were understood as representatives of forms of filmmaking quite distinct from the avant-garde, at least as "avant-garde film" was being defined in New York and San Francisco during those years.

Robert Gardner found his way into ethnographic filmmaking by doing short films about the Kwakiutl on the Northwest coast of British Columbia (one failed project was a collaboration with avant-garde filmmaker Sidney Peterson) (fig. 2), then returned to his native Cambridge to study anthropology and become the first director of Harvard's Film Study Center, working with John Marshall on the !Kung San films Marshall had shot in the Kalahari Desert in southwest Africa. A series of Gardner's own poetic ethnographic films followed; *Dead Birds* (1964) is the best known. In 1972 Gardner created *Screening Room* (1972–1981), a late-night television interview show during which he presented a wide range of film—avant-garde, documentary, animation—to a considerable audience in the Boston area and discussed the films with their makers. Anthology Film Archives honored Gardner and *Screening Room* with its Film Preservation Award in 2008. During the 1980s Gardner's filmmaking focused on ritual in far-flung cultures and on art making in Western societies, and Gardner himself provided support to independent filmmakers (including avant-garde stalwarts Peter Hutton, Sharon Lockhart, and Robert Fenz) through his Studio7Arts. Gardner died, a still-active 88 years, in June, 2014.

Ed Pincus studied philosophy at Harvard before becoming part of the documentary filmmaking scene in Cambridge, borrowing one of John Marshall's cameras in order to document civil rights activity in Natchez, Mississippi, for what became *Black Natchez* (1967, co-made with David Neuman). Hired by MIT to teach filmmaking, Pincus teamed up with Richard Leacock to form the MIT Film Section. Pincus's decision to document his open marriage with Jane Pincus resulted in the breakthrough personal documentary *Diaries (1971–1976)* (1980) and Pincus's entry into the personal directly and indirectly influenced a generation of Cambridge filmmakers—Ross McElwee, Steve Ascher, Ann Schaetzel, Miriam Weinstein, Robb Moss, Nina Davenport, Alexander Olch—who went on to play a major role in the emergence of what has become one of the most common genres of modern documentary.

[24] See my *American Ethnographic Film and Personal Documentary: The Cambridge Turn* (Berkeley and Los Angeles: University of California Press, 2013).

FIGURE 2 *Sidney Peterson and Robert Gardner in Kwakiutl outfits sometime in the early 1950s during the early stages of an unrealized collaboration on a film: a love story between a Kwakiutl princess and an Anglo settler.*
Source: Courtesy Robert Gardner.

Like Pincus, Alfred Guzzetti was an early contributor to personal documentary with his *Family Portrait Sittings* (1975), which focused on the ways in which a family envisions and defines itself through its ritual stories. But Guzzetti's filmmaking took him in other directions too. Powerfully influenced by the avant-garde films he had seen at Fred Camper's MIT Film Society in the late 1960s, Guzzetti began making contributions to avant-garde filmmaking with *Air* (1971). Later, having grown increasingly concerned about American involvement in the political life of Nicaragua, he teamed with Richard P. Rogers and photographer Susan Meiselas to make the documentaries *Living at Risk* (1985) and *Pictures from a Revolution* (1991). And still later, his early fascination with the poetic documentaries of Marshall and Gardner (with whom he had studied) led him to collaborate with anthropologist Ákos Östör to make *Seed and Earth* (1994). One of Guzzetti's deepest aesthetic commitments, however, has been to sound; and this eventually led him to video. In the early 1990s, he began exploiting the advantages of video—a level of sound quality not possible for 16mm optical sound and a fast-developing facility with visual text—producing what has become a series of videos that explore the relationships of image and sound in ways that bear comparison with Kubelka's *Unsere Afrikareise* and the recent, silent, 16mm films of Nathaniel Dorsky.

These days, the best known of the Cambridge filmmakers interviewed for this volume is Ross McElwee, whose rejection of both the personal detachment of observational documentary as well as the distrust of narration shared by his MIT mentors, Pincus and Leacock, led to new forms of personal documentary that are often deceptively simple in the way that Hemingway's fiction can be. McElwee remains best-known for *Sherman's March: A Meditation on the Possibility of Romantic Love in the South during an Era of Nuclear Weapons Proliferation* (1986), and while *Sherman's March* may be McElwee's most entertaining film, the accomplishment of his work is fully evident only to those who have explored the personal saga he has created during the past thirty years. If at one point, this saga seemed to conclude with the achievement of a happy and stable family life, recent films reflect the transformation of McElwee's domestic circumstances. I interviewed McElwee for *A Critical Cinema 2* (University of California Press, 1992) in 1987, before he completed his masterwork, *Time Indefinite* (1993). My decision to talk with him again was instigated by the accomplishments of *Time Indefinite* and *Six O'Clock News* (1996) and of his most recent films, *In Paraguay* (2009) and *Photographic Memory* (2011).

Nina Davenport, who studied with McElwee—she can be seen in a McElwee filmmaking class in his *Six O'Clock News* (1996), on which she served as an assistant editor—has undergone her own personal evolution, which has taken her from *Hello Photo* (1994), a travel film about India inspired primarily by Peter Hutton's work and supported by Robert Gardner, through *Always a Bridesmaid* (2000) and *Parallel Lines* (2004), films closely related to McElwee's approach, to the breakthrough *Operation Filmmaker* (2007), in which Davenport's attempt to record the experiences of a young Iraqi man living in Europe is transformed into a personal documentary by the young man's insurgency against her plans.

The five interviews that follow my conversations with the Cambridge filmmakers reflect the diversity of approaches to "avant-doc" demonstrated by filmmakers working in the United States, in Europe, and in Indonesia. For Dutch-Indonesian Leonard Retel Helmrich life is movement and cinema is the art of movement; and from early in his career, Helmrich has worked—as fully though differently from Marie Menken and Stan Brakhage—to free the camera and the film experience from stasis. The development of high-quality digital video has made it possible for Helmrich to explore the potential of continuous shooting-in-motion and the most impressive result has been a trilogy of features—*The Eye of the Day* (2001), *Shape of the Moon* (2005), and *Position among the Stars* (2010)—focusing on a family in Indonesia forced to adjust to continual changes in their personal, political, and environmental situation.

Jonathan Caouette's first feature, the personal documentary *Tarnation* (2004), has the visceral, confrontory impact of films normally identified with certain forms of avant-garde filmmaking: *Flaming Creatures* (1963, Jack Smith), *Scorpio Rising* (1963, Kenneth Anger), and John Waters's early features, for example—though like Waters, Caouette has not been willing to consign his work to the margins and to a coterie audience devoted to formal experiment. *Tarnation* is a surreal bildungsroman, a harrowing, but ultimately triumphant trip through the filmmaker's troubled young life with a bipolar mother, abusive foster homes, and loving but bizarre grandparents. In 2012, after working in a variety of ways in and around the media industry (acting in television commercials; working on a feature about the All Tomorrow's Parties rock concerts; and in 2010, finishing a short surrealist film, *All Flowers in Time*), Caouette completed *Walk Away Renee*, a second personal documentary, focused on his mother. If *Tarnation* is the horror film of personal documentary, *Walk Away Renee* is one of the suspense thrillers.

Paweł Wojtasik is also the product of a troubled childhood—in Wojtasik's case the "trouble" was growing up in Poland during the Cold War. Wojtasik's emigration to New York, his discovery of meditation, and his subsequent entry first into painting, then into digital video provided him with a means of working through the troubling psychic residue of depression to directly confront his most fundamental fears. *Dark Sun Squeeze* (2003), Wojtasik's contemplation of sewage treatment, and the videos that have followed, have been devoted to intense, often beautiful depictions of elements of our social surround that we avoid or that we have little perceptual knowledge of (for example, the creepy naked mole rats in *Naked* [2005] that have the longest lifespan per pound of any mammal). *9 Gates* (final version, 2012) is a powerful contribution to a mini-genre of avant-garde film that begins with Willard Maas's *Geography of the Body* (1943) and includes Yoko Ono's *Fly* (1970). Wojtasik's digital videos are simultaneously creepy and exhilarating, fundamentally celebratory of what Wojtasik sees as cinema's ability to provide forms of psychic transcendence through cinematic perception.

Austrian Michael Glawogger, who studied avant-garde filmmaking at the San Francisco Art Institute, directed both feature narratives and documentaries, though in Glawogger's case, feature filmmaking tended to be a vacation from the work involved in making documentaries. For each of the films in his Globalization Trilogy—*Megacities* (1998), *Workingman's Death* (2004), and

Whore's Glory (2012)—Glawogger spent years finding his way into the experiences of working people doing difficult and dangerous jobs, then documenting their labors. Glawogger was not a detached observer of this labor; it is obvious that his filmmaking was as close to participatory as he could make it. Glawogger died in April, 2014, while filming in Liberia.

Having grown up in the wake of the Carnation Revolution, which developed during the years following the death of António de Oliveira Salazar in 1968 and toppled his dictatorial regime in 1974, Susana de Sousa Dias became fascinated with the forms of filmmaking sponsored by the regime during its forty-eight years in power. Since 2000, when she was first allowed to explore the Salazar regime's official archive, de Sousa Dias has struggled to find cinematic forms that can do justice to the realities of oppression within what has often been seen as a relatively benign dictatorial system. For *Still Life* (2005) de Sousa Dias found ways of recycling moments from propaganda "documentaries" so that they reveal the seeds of the regime's collapse; and in *48* (2009) she focuses on the mug shots of the regime's political prisoners and on the memories of those who endured the regime's brutality, within a cinematic form closer to Andy Warhol's *Screen Tests* (1964–66) than to most documentary cinema.

Each of the next seven interviews is focused on a single inventive film. My hope is that together, this montage of conversations begins to suggest the wide variety of approaches that filmmakers working in the cinematic territory between avant-garde filmmaking and documentary have developed and the varied kinds of achievement these approaches have produced.

In the wake of the German reunification following the collapse of the Soviet Union, Amie Siegel grew fascinated with the brief history of the DDR (Deutsche Demokratische Republik, what Americans called East Germany), which was established in 1949 and walled off from the West in 1961. She was particularly intrigued with two aspects of DDR history: the massive surveillance program that with 91,000 full-time staff was the DDR's largest employer and the emergence in East Germany of a form of the American Western that reversed the assumptions of the genre. Siegel's *DDR/DDR* (2008) is simultaneously conventional and unconventional in its use and critique of the rhetoric of traditional informational documentary, as well as observational and provocational cinema-verite. If her explicit focus is life in East Germany before the *Wende* (the German word for the transformation of the DDR after the fall of the Berlin Wall) and the *Wende* itself, Siegel's implicit focus is the United States up to and since 9/11.

Alexander Olch, who unlike Nina Davenport rebelled against the focus on documentary at Harvard when he was a student there, nevertheless came to make a feature "documentary" about the lone Harvard filmmaking instructor who supported his goal of making fictional narratives. When Richard P. Rogers died of cancer at 57, his wife, photographer Susan Meiselas, asked Olch to help her sort through Rogers's archive and perhaps produce a tribute to her husband. Working with footage Rogers had shot for a personal film he never completed, with actors Bob Balaban and Wallace Shawn who had been close friends of Rogers, and with a diary Olch himself wrote *as if he were* Rogers, Olch spent seven years making "Rogers'" personal documentary, *The Windmill Movie* (2008).

Arthur and Jennifer Smith live, year round, off the north coast of Alaska, where they film the local polar bear community that lives in and around the largely Iñupiat village of Kaktovik. Their *Ice Bears of the Beaufort* (2009) is a stunning work that argues the beauty of Alaska's north slope and the complex community life of the bears—in the hope that a broader understanding of the reality of this ecosystem might help stem the tide of offshore oil drilling set in motion by the George W. Bush administration's opening of the Arctic National Wildlife Refuge to oil prospecting. While their mission may seem Quixotic, *Ice Bears* is a tribute to their courage and an impressive demonstration of visual gifts reminiscent of avant-garde filmmakers Peter Hutton and Sharon Lockhart.

Betzy Bromberg's beautiful *Voluptuous Sleep* (2011) is an impressive contribution to a tradition of filmmakers (including most obviously Stan Brakhage, whose 1974 film *The Text of Light* is close in concept and related in execution to *Voluptuous Sleep*), for whom filmmaking is a means for transforming light moving in time (to evoke a William Wees title) into Light. Jennifer Proctor's *A Movie by Jen Proctor* (2012) is a shot-by-shot remake of Bruce Conner's *A Movie* (1958), that simultaneously foregrounds the fifty-year gap between Conner's entry into cinema and Proctor's into video and erases that gap by creating a digital experience that retrieves the mixture of horror and humor that must have been the experience of the original audiences for Conner's breakthrough recycling of documentary and commercial material.

In *Suitcase of Love and Shame* (2013) Jane Gillooly works with auditory documents—primarily reel-to-reel tapes recorded in the early 1960s during a secret love affair—to evoke the end of an era in American culture. Through her deft editing of the tapes and by contextualizing what we hear with a range of visuals that are resonant of avant-garde approaches of the time, Gillooly creates an engaging (and often harrowing) listen into the most intimate moments in two private lives. In *Visitors* (2014) veteran avant-doc filmmaker Godfrey Reggio (*Koyaanisqatsi*, 1984; *Powaqqatsi*, 1988) returns to filmmaking, and his periodic collaboration with composer Philip Glass, to provide a stunning reflection on contemporary life, by combining close-up portraits of individuals (reminiscent, like the mug shots in De Sousa Dias's *48*, of Warhol's *Screen Tests*) and documents of the results of Katrina in his native Louisiana.

The final interviews in *Avant-Doc* represent a kind of yin/yang. My decision to include Todd Haynes in this volume, despite the fact that Haynes may seem closer to the commercial industry than any of the other interviewees, is a function of his imaginative, sometimes avant-garde ways of dealing with historical realities. His *Superstar: The Karen Carpenter Story* (1987) is a faux documentary about the singer's battle with anorexia, made with Barbie dolls instead of live actors. My original decision to interview Haynes was a result of my seeing *I'm Not There* (2007), which is something like a bio-pic about Bob Dylan, or around the idea of Bob Dylan, that depends on our recognizing Haynes's continual allusions to the new kinds of film that were emerging during the 1960s as Dylan moved from acoustic folk music to rock, including cinema-verite documentary—D. A. Pennebaker's *Don't Look Back* (1967), in particular—and various forms of avant-garde filmmaking.

Avant-Doc concludes with a five-part interview that focuses on Harvard's Sensory Ethnography Lab (SEL), a remarkable attempt to revive ethnographic film, but in a way that recognizes the limitations and particular advantages of the cinematic documentation of Other cultural groups. The films emerging from the SEL simultaneously reinvigorate ethnographic documentary and challenge traditional distinctions between documentary and avant-garde film by joining documentary subject matter with a level of formal experiment usually understood as avant-garde. I talk with Ilisa Barbash and Lucien Castaing-Taylor about *Sweetgrass* (2009), which depicts the end of a century-old tradition of herding sheep into the mountains near Yellowstone National Park for summer pasture; then with Castaing-Taylor about his image-sound installation work and the thinking behind his development of the SEL (which in recent years has nurtured a cadre of skilled young anthropologist/filmmakers); and finally with Castaing-Taylor and Véréna Paravel, about *Leviathan* (2012) and with SEL veterans Stephanie Spray and Pacho Velez, about *Manakamana* (2013)—each, as perfect an instance of an "avant-doc" as one can imagine.

A word about my methods seems in order. Interviewing filmmakers has been my passion since the 1970s, and my method has changed little during the intervening years.[25] Having studied the films of filmmakers whose work I admire, I record conversations with them at length and in as much detail as seems feasible. Then, using my careful transcriptions of the interviews as raw material, I rework these conversations into finished interviews, often playing fast and loose with the particulars of the original conversation. I try to remain in touch with the filmmakers throughout this process—often edited versions of our conversations pass back and forth between us, as we add, subtract, correct, over a period of months and sometimes years—so that, in the end, they and I can feel that the result represents both what I have understood through talking with them and what they have meant to communicate.

[25] My earlier interviews are collected in the five volumes of *A Critical Cinema: Interviews with Independent Filmmakers*, published by the University of California Press: volume 1 in 1988; 2, in 1992; 3, in 1998; 4, in 2005; 5, in 2006; and in *Adventures of Perception: Cinema as Exploration—Essays/ Interviews* (Berkeley and Los Angeles: University of California Press, 2009).

Each of my books of interviews has been shaped in part by chronology and in part by my sense of the crucial issues in independent filmmaking during a certain period. At a certain point, it becomes clear to me that my interviewing seems to be dealing with particular developments and, insofar as I can do so without compromising my sense that the films I want to interview filmmakers about must be formally accomplished and ideologically significant, I pursue these issues and developments in the hope of assembling a book that does some justice to a productive, energetic, and engaging moment in the modern history of cinema—a book that can be useful (and enjoyable to read) for both those who teach and study cinema and for cineastes in general. Ultimately, of course, I mean to honor the filmmakers I interview and to draw new audiences to their accomplishments.

Annette Michelson

Whereas early documentary filmmakers could find corporate and/or government support for their work and beginning in the 1950s found television networks willing to present their films, avant-garde filmmakers have generally had far less dependable resources for their filmmaking—and have needed champions. Especially since the Second World War there have been champions of many kinds. In this country, Maya Deren's energy and persistence in creating an audience for her own films helped to inspire Amos and Marcia Vogel to create Cinema 16. Vogel and his San Francisco colleague Frank Stauffacher at Art in Cinema became champions of many forms of avant-garde and documentary cinema. In the 1960s Jerome Hill, operating relentlessly under the radar, provided angel financial support for many crucial films. Of course, Jonas Mekas championed what he called the New American Cinema in his widely read and influential column first in the *Village Voice* and subsequently in the *Soho Weekly News* and was a prime mover in the creation of the New York Cinematheque, Anthology Film Archives, and New York's Filmmakers' Cooperative. Bruce Baillie, Chick Strand, and their Bay Area colleagues founded Canyon Cinema, which became exhibitor, publisher (of the *Canyon Cinemanews*), and the most dependable distributor of avant-garde work.

There have also been pioneer scholars. Sheldon Renan's *An Introduction to the American Underground Film* (Dutton, 1967) was an important early foray into the vast cinematic territory of avant-garde filmmaking, as were Gene Youngblood's *Expanded Cinema* (Dutton, 1970) and P. Adams Sitney's *Visionary Film* (Oxford University Press, 1974). And Amos Vogel's *Film as a Subversive Art* (Random House, 1974) was a visually exciting, politically astute, widely influential survey of many forms of avant-garde and documentary film.

Among the most important early champions of many forms of formally inventive avant-garde and documentary cinema was teacher, scholar, critic Annette Michelson. After establishing herself as a capable fiction editor working for various French publishers and then as an art critic, Michelson returned to the United States in 1965 and quickly found her way into the burgeoning avant-garde film scene. She began writing essays on film for the new journal *Artforum*, and during the early 1970s was given the opportunity to edit two issues: the September 1971 issue focused on filmmakers (Hollis

Frampton, Joyce Wieland, Ken Jacobs, Paul Sharits, Michael Snow) who had become identified with what P. Adams Sitney called "structural film"; and the January 1973 issue, which was called "Eisenstein/Brakhage." Those of us who came across Michelson's writing in *Artforum,* and in particular those two special issues, found them a powerful confirmation for our excitement about this new and rapidly expanding cinematic territory; they provided a fledgling avant-garde movement with a level of caché just at the moment when cinema studies was entering academe and many of us were rethinking what the experience of cinema was and could be. In 1974 she edited the catalogue for her breakthrough show, "New Forms in Film," presented in Montreux, Switzerland—an early collection of writing on a range of avant-garde film and experimental documentary, introduced by her influential essay, "Film and the Radical Aspiration."

Michelson's passion for Dziga Vertov would help to revive interest in *The Man with a Movie Camera* and would lead to her editing *Kino-Eye: The Writings of Dziga Vertov* (Berkeley: University of California Press, 1984). Michelson has continued to make important contributions to the study of independent cinema throughout her distinguished career, as a lecturer and through her editing of *October.* It is no accident that the screening room at the New York University Film Department, where she inspired students for decades, is named after her.

I talked with Michelson about her personal and educational background, and about her championing of avant-garde cinema and experimental documentary, in January and again in August of 2011; the interview was refined by phone and mail. I am grateful to Melissa Ragona for making the suggestion that I interview Michelson—I shouldn't have needed the prodding!

MacDonald: You've become well known as a defender of American avant-garde cinema. Were you always interested in film? And when did you begin to be interested in experimental forms of cinema?

Michelson: I had, as a child and young person, the sort of experience that any middle-class American had before the advent of television. I was taken to the movies. Only on rainy days, however, for "one should not," my mother believed, "waste the sunshine."

Of course, the first films I saw were silent comedies, which were considered *suitable* for children. These experiences were for me, however, terrifying beyond any other enduring memories of my childhood. In one film, trained animals (dogs, I think) were dressed, seated and feasting like humans at table. A second film produced the nightmare of a chase through the labyrinth of Chinatown (I've never tried to identify the source, although one might easily do so; my guess would be a Harold Lloyd or Lloyd-type production). There was one other silent "comedy" of a slightly later period—with a traumatizing sequence. I did not remember it in any detail, but I knew the film's title and the director's name. Indeed, I had so strongly retained the memory of violence in this particular film that when it was widely re-released in the 1950s, I waited a year before re-seeing it. It was Chaplin's *City Lights* [1931] and the traumatizing sequence, a drunken battle fought between two men with streams of champagne aimed from opposing bottles!

One other film of a completely different genre must be included in these early, fragmented screen memories, because it was truly my introduction to screen magic. I was taken, in secret, by my piano teacher to see Garbo's second sound film, *Romance* [1930]. It had not only the glamour of "unsuitable" fare, the magic and beauty of its star, but another, quite different sort of magical effect: the transformation of the falling snow that surrounds Garbo's lover as he walks, pensive and alone through the city streets, *into countless falling white silhouettes of Garbo's profile*. Reflecting on this, many years later, I came to see it as my introduction to that "special" kind of effect that first astonished and delighted a Parisian prestidigitator's spectators in 1896.

Before going to Paris, I'd had almost no contact with what is called avant-garde or experimental film, what I came to see as truly independent, artisanally made cinema. What I did see—and they were correctly called "experimental" at the time—were the British films *Night Mail* [1936] and *Coal Face* [1936], both with sound in verse by W. H. Auden (I came only recently to read the titles in verse Auden wrote for the distribution in England of Vertov's *Three Songs of Lenin* [1934]); his contribution to the two British films had particular interest for me: I cared passionately for Auden's work, had attended his lectures on Shakespeare [Auden's lectures were given in 1946 at The New School for Social Research in Manhattan]. I'd seen a few other British documentaries, including Basil Wright's *Song of Ceylon* [1932]. But no Flaherty, no Riefenstahl or Lorentz, no Russian or other Eastern European or Far Eastern films. Other, more assiduous filmgoers certainly saw more than I did.

MacDonald: Where were you seeing the British films?

Michelson: At the Museum of Modern Art—though I did not, at that time, see much else there, apart from *The Cabinet of Doctor Caligari* [1920]. For a time, when I was in middle school and then at Hunter High (I was between 12 and 14 years old), we lived on the Upper West Side, only two streets away from the New Yorker theater. I did a lot of my early film-going there, and at the Symphony Theater, where I saw my first Hitchcock, *The 39 Steps* [1935], and at the Loew's 82nd Street, where I saw my first Sternberg, *The Scarlet Empress* [1934]. That one, I found both thrilling and somewhat terrifying, but deliciously so. It gave me a first inkling of the fuller range of cinematic possibility, including the use of a distinct and emphatic style.

I could not have described very well what Astaire-Rogers and Busby Berkeley brought to cinema or even what I saw and felt experiencing their work—but in that I'm sure I differed not at all from the millions who had the same strong, inarticulate reactions to the work of these artists.

As a teenager, I went to see everything French that I could find. At that time for 35 cents you could see a French double feature at the Apollo on 42nd Street. To many, those films seemed very advanced and I particularly remember the article that the *New York Times* ran on *Les Enfants du paradis* [1945], presenting it to us as the *ne plus ultra* of film art. And it is, of course, a splendid work. It was only many years later, in thinking about industrially produced film, that I could see it as also, in the complexity of its script, camera work, decor, lighting, and the brilliance of its cast, not only the sign of a national cinema's emergence from the bitter years of war and occupation, but the French industry's prodigious response to *Gone with the Wind* [1939].

MacDonald: Did you come from an artistic family? How were you educated?

Michelson: My mother's parents were Hungarian Jews, born under Franz-Joseph's reign; their first language was therefore German. I was not close to my paternal grandparents, who were Yiddish-speaking Romanian Jews, originally from Ukraine: my father's mother did not speak English and his father did not appear interested in his grandchildren. I did have a close and affectionate relation to my maternal grandparents, who were quite remarkable people, but not "artistic."

I had no introduction to the visual arts at home and certainly not in school, but began, when 13, to take life classes offered free of charge by the Brooklyn Museum, and both the instructor and students there were extraordinarily kind to the child I still was. I had begun, before that, when I was about 11 or 12, to walk through Central Park to the Metropolitan Museum and, three years later, to the Museum of Modern Art and to the Guggenheim in its pre-Frank Lloyd Wright era. At MoMA, by the way, I frequently saw a striking young woman with long, curly hair, dressed in Batik dresses, striding about in Mexican sandals. I knew nothing about her, but did think, "When I grow up, I'll know people like her." However, despite my regard for Maya Deren, for her courage, intelligence and her work in film and its theorization, for the energy of her defense and illustration of a filmic avant-garde, I doubt that had we met—in her latter days—we would have got on well.

I also discovered later that by simply asking for a pass to MOMA's library you could enter gratis, go up by elevator to the fifth floor, then later take the elevator down to the basement, where the film theater was located and enter for the screening since no tickets were then required. Among the readers I remember seeing in the library was a man busily at work, who had constructed, with manila folders, a triple-sided screen that protected both his face and his work from view. I never knew who he was, until Jay Leyda told me, many years later, that this was Siegfried Kracauer, and that scribbled on the inner panels of the screen were notes for *From Caligari to Hitler* [Princeton University Press, 1947]!

Although there had been no introduction to the arts at home, my grandmother gave me a piano when I was 9, and I started to have lessons and to develop the passionate interest in music which has lasted all my life. In fact, Noël Carroll told me once that music, not film, was my life's true passion, and he may have been right, but it contends for that title with painting, sculpture, and literature, and. . .—well, I can't possibly rank things in that way. In any case, later on, my musical education was extended in Paris, as it was for so many others, by the work of Pierre Boulez as composer, animator, conductor, and educator. Although I would later recognize the interesting relation between the "structuralist" film and the music of the minimalists or "*les repetitifs*," I've remained a *Boulezienne*, rather than a *Glassicist*.

As for my formal education, it was, as you can tell, largely by the City. I went to Hunter High School and then to Brooklyn College—I was tired of the all-girls schools I'd attended until then. Brooklyn College was an excellent institution, full of bright young students and boasting a number of scholars, refugees from Nazism, whose courses were pitched on a level of sophisticated analysis and research; they were exciting, and crowded. In my sophomore year I discovered the New School for Social Research, even more exciting; it seemed to me a sort of intellectual heaven, for at that time it was small and a refuge for even more European intellectuals from a greater variety of backgrounds—*and* it was possible to attend any course gratis.

Very near the New School was the Fifth Avenue Playhouse, a venue that S. J. Perelman unforgettably described as the theater in which you could see a double bill of *Blood of a Poet* [1930] and *The Fall of the House of Usher* [1928], to be followed next week by *The Fall of the House of Usher* and *Blood of a Poet*. Perelman's witticism actually demonstrated the limits of avant-garde repertoire at the time. Of course, these *were* two important films that could justify attendance to repetitive viewings for those interested in an expansion of existing filmic possibilities.

MacDonald: These experiences at Brooklyn College and the New School are happening when?

Michelson: During World War II. When I began to work, I saved money for Europe, and when the war was over, my reading, my interest in music, art and history, the theater, and so much else made of me another of the young intellectuals still drawn to Paris.

MacDonald: What did you work at that allowed you to save the money?

Michelson: I was a part-time salesgirl in two different department stores, but then got a full-time job at the Brooklyn Public Library and shared an apartment in the Village with a friend. The job didn't pay well, but I managed, after a couple of years, to have enough for passage by ship and a few months in France. The exchange at that time was massively in favor of the American dollar.

In the meantime, I had registered at Columbia for a year of studies in art history and was very excited by my reading and research there. I took baroque painting, a seminar in Giotto, and Carolingian manuscripts with

Meyer Schapiro, whose lectures on modern art I had heard at the New School. Schapiro, brilliant as he was, was always responsive to one's questions and, invited to lunch at the end of the academic year, I told him that I was going to Paris and would return in six months. When he learned I'd been working fifty hours a week at the Library, he was shocked but said, "When you return, there will be a fellowship for you." Of course, I didn't return; I stayed for fifteen years, with a visit to New York every five years.

I left for Paris at the height of the Rosenberg Affair, and on my first trip back to New York, found the climate dominated by McCarthyism. I returned gladly to Paris; I had developed personal relationships in Paris that meant a good deal to me. I had lost any desire for a doctoral degree and, in any case, had never strongly wished for an academic career.

It was not until ten years later (in 1965) that I felt a return was, from a political point of view, possible. The Cold War was on and we were in Vietnam, but I'd had an inkling of the existence of the student movement. Sartre had refused an invitation to lecture at Cornell University because of our Vietnam venture, but I thought he was wrong and that his contact with the students might have been mutually beneficial.

MacDonald: You'd studied French here before you went to Paris?

Michelson: I'd had two years of French and Latin in high school, and continued with both, but I'd begun to read in both languages on my own, and by the time I'd got to France, I could speak somewhat decently, although my vocabulary, gleaned from reading Baudelaire, Marot, Flaubert, etcetera was totally lacking in the sort of words and idioms that you really need in daily living. I had to learn to read a restaurant menu, to clarify my choice of this over that product in a department store, and when necessary, how to tell someone to "get the hell out!"

I do have an ear for music and, more generally, for sound and speech, and by the time I reached France, I sounded more fluent than I really was. I felt, somehow, that French was inside me; it just had to be brought out. But hanging out with the natives made for much improvement. Within a year, I was a bit more fluent and could write simple expressive letters in French. Eventually, I began to publish articles and essays in both languages. Extensive reading, a life-long proclivity, was essential for that, of course.

MacDonald: You're so busy reading, you haven't unpacked your books from your move to this apartment!

Michelson: There are too many of them! I never knew *how* many until the moving man told me—they're accustomed to making estimates. Getting the books unpacked and shelved is my project for the summer.

MacDonald: Could you tell me what their estimate was?

Michelson: Ten thousand, to which I've since added another thousand, perhaps—not a great number really. There are many much larger private libraries in New York and in every city in every country one could name.

MacDonald: So in what ways did film begin to factor more fully into your education?

Michelson: Before leaving for Paris, something happened that was to open me more fully to film: I had read, in the *Times Literary Supplement*, the review of a French film that seemed as though it might be interesting and had thought, "Hmm, when I get to Paris, I'd like to see that film." Fortunately, when I arrived in Paris in 1950, it was playing in a Latin Quarter revival house: Bresson's second film, *Les Dames du Bois de Boulogne* [1945]. My first viewing had the profound and ineffaceable effect of conversion: through Bresson, I began to think about technique, but it was the grace and economy of the work that captured and enraptured me. And I was very fortunate to have arrived in time to see all the subsequent films as they arrived on screen.

MacDonald: When did you begin to come in contact with avant-garde work?

Michelson: Well, one might say that my first experience of that somewhat broad category of work was also through a French film: Genet's *Un Chant d'amour* [1950]. I'd come to know Genet and attended a screening, among many arranged by Henri Langlois to spur the possible purchase of prints by wealthy, gay American tourists. Of course, I was at the Cinematheque all the time.

In 1955 I met Noël Burch and we remained close friends for many years. I remember going to see von Stroheim's *Greed* [1925] with Burch and Kenneth Anger and had the sense, after the screening, that Kenneth was angry with me. I asked Burch what I had said that had disturbed Kenneth, and he replied, "It wasn't *what* you said, but rather that you said anything at all!"

I first saw Kenneth's films at a private screening in someone's apartment. I liked them and was touched by his first film [*Fireworks* (1947); Anger's earlier films are lost], the work of the gay teenager entranced by his discovery of film, of Cocteau, of ritual, and the pleasure of the anonymous, sado-masochistic sexual encounter. Of course, Kenneth's reputation in Paris was based largely on his book of Hollywood gossip [*Hollywood Babylon* (San Francisco: Straight Arrow Books, 1975)], which was translated, published in France in the late 1950s and often quoted as a *reliable* text on the dreamland that meant so much to everyone!

We saw films by Len Lye and some by Europeans whose work was not what we were hoping for (we were not yet familiar with the films of Richter, Duchamp, and the remarkable earlier generations of avant-garde filmmakers). But when we saw Robert Breer's work, we recognized it as something else entirely! Breer, who had been showing painting at the Denise René Gallery, *the* gallery for hard-edge abstraction, knew the work of those earlier generations, learned from it and admirably went his own way, evolving from the humor of rapid-fire collage to drawing in motion, to pure color abstraction and beyond. Breer lived in Paris for quite a number of years, had his first child there, and I saw him and his wife often.

There was not much other independently made, artisanal cinema to see in Paris. However, I cared not only for Bresson but also for the early Resnais and for Godard. Burch and I had gone to see the first screening of *Breathless* [1960]; we'd heard it was going to be interesting and though we did find that to be true, technically (we walked out of the theater in admiration of the cutting, saying, *"you don't do things like that"*), it was not, on the whole, a film that deeply interested us. Godard's great period started after this film, and to it I remain deeply attached, as I do to almost all of Tati, and to many others in France and elsewhere. I was never able to adopt a critical position of wholesale exclusiveness, not even for tactical reasons.

MacDonald: How did you support yourself during the years in Paris?

Michelson: I published a lot of art criticism, wrote catalogue texts, the Paris Letters for *Arts* and *Art International*; I acted as Art Editor (the sole reviewer, really) for the international edition of the *Herald Tribune* and worked in publishing as editor for a project on modern European sculpture published by George Braziller. I also was a reader/consultant for what the French publishers called *la literature anglo-saxonne*. One day a manuscript by an 18-year-old girl arrived at René Julliard. Everyone there liked it, and *Bonjour Tristesse* was published within a bit more than a month (European publishing continues to go more rapidly than ours) and sold millions of copies throughout the world. Sagan continued to be very productive.

Julliard asked me to read English-language books submitted for translation and publication, but they also said, "We know that there are some American writers living here; could you find something interesting for us?" I spread the word, and Jimmy Baldwin brought me the typescript of his first book, *Go Tell it on the Mountain* [published by Knopf in 1953], which they rejected!

Later, they asked, "Are there any published American writers we might pursue?" I said, "There *is* a young writer who interests me. He's published one book so far; it's not very long (which would mean lower translation fees). It offers the reflections of a man in a state of suspense and general uneasiness, due to be called for military service." This was Saul Bellow's *Dangling Man* [published in 1944 by Vanguard], parts of which I'd read in *Partisan Review*. They passed on Bellow, too—and missed having a Nobel Prizewinner on their list.

MacDonald: You came back to the states in 1965?

Michelson: I came for a visit on April 1st of that year. With the art scene changing direction, and with performance, postmodern dance, and Happenings still in development, I felt that someone like myself who had lived between languages and artistic media might have work to do here. Soon after my return, I became aware of what was also happening in film. Earlier, I'd read the text of a symposium on poetry and cinema with Arthur Miller, Dylan

Thomas, Willard Maas, and Maya Deren, and I thought Deren was brilliant and heroic in that moment [the text of the discussion to which Michelson refers, which took place on October 28, 1953, is available in Scott MacDonald, *Cinema 16: Documents toward a History of the Film Society* (Temple University Press, 2002), 202-212; P. Adams Sitney recently told me that he had transcribed that discussion and is not confident his transcription was as accurate as it might have been].

MacDonald: The men look like buffoons next to her.

Michelson: Except Arthur Miller, strangely enough, who had something really sensible to say. So I knew there was interest in cinema in New York, but until I moved here, I had no sense of the amount of exciting work being done.

MacDonald: How did you find your way into the film scene?

Michelson: I'm not sure I quite remember! Once I was back to New York, the friend with whom I was staying before finding a place of my own knew the film of a man named Peter Emanuel Goldman [*Echoes of Silence*, 1965], and she thought I should see it. I did see it and this could have been my first experience at Jonas Mekas's Cinematheque in the Wurlitzer building on 41st Street, where I began to see so many films that excited me.

Of course, by that time, Breer had already resettled a small distance from New York, so I'd go up to see him and look at his work. He had a barn in which he could do his sculpture and cut his films and so on. Visiting him was always a great, great pleasure, and remembering this leads me to make a confession: I have never written on Bob Breer, whose work I loved and continue to love. This was a great mistake on my part, something that I very much regret. I hope you will publish my saying so.

I came to know Warhol, too, and I knew the Studio in its heyday—although for the most part I didn't go to the parties; I went to look at the work . . . for the most part. The parties *are* nonetheless reflected in what I've written and published about Warhol [Michelson's essay on Warhol is included in Michelson, ed., *Andy Warhol* (Cambridge, MA: MIT Press, 2001)], just as the aluminum-papered walls of the Factory reflected what went on there.

I began to spend time with Jonas; we talked and went to a couple of concerts together and to the visiting Japanese NŌ theater. And I came to know P. Adams—a delight—and through him became aware of the film and performance worlds here, including what Michael Snow called "the Chambers Street Brotherhood," a group of filmmakers living Downtown (not all were interesting). That was an exciting time, *and* there were two consequences: first, I was finding developments in independent film much more exciting than most of what was happening then in painting and sculpture—by that time the art world was beginning to be dominated by the market; and second, I was finding the milieu of the independent film world more interesting. I was very pleased that my art world friends were selling pictures and so on, but an earlier sense of community was gone. What I *now* had was a sense of the

FIGURE 3 *Annette Michelson with Peter Kubelka during the filming of Jonas Mekas's* Reminiscences of a Journey to Lithuania *(1972).*
Source: Courtesy Anthology Film Archives.

fascinating community of the *filmmakers* and eventually, through teaching, of the young film lovers as well.

One thing I found *very* interesting was that Jonas finally had the theater of his dreams for Anthology Film Archives, The Invisible Cinema, designed of course by Kubelka. I was very supportive of Anthology Film Archives and The Invisible Cinema; I think I bought the first two subscriptions, one for me and one for Babette Mangolte, whom I had invited to stay with me for a while in New York. She stayed for six months, and both she and Chantal Akerman were very excited by the films they saw at Anthology (figure 3).

The art world and the film world were at this point quite separate. The only artist I knew who came regularly to see the Anthology Film Archives collection was Richard Serra.

MacDonald: He made some nice films.

Michelson: Indeed! Some excellent films.

MacDonald: Under-recognized now, even by the art world, I expect.

Michelson: I think you're right. For me, Serra's films were very important and I talked about them and questioned him about them; his films might be due for another *October* piece, though film doesn't seem what he's preoccupied with now. But in any case, as you say, for the most part the art world never really looked with any intensity at Serra's films.

MacDonald: Were you asked to be on the Anthology committee that selected the "Essential Cinema" repertory?

Michelson: No, you were supposed to be a filmmaker, and in any case I was still quite a newcomer. P. Adams apparently had made one film—I don't know if anyone has seen it! But whether it exists or not, I'm glad he was on the selection committee.

I owe to Jonas Mekas and P. Adams so much of my education in film in general, and my support of a truly independent cinema emerging, for the most part, from an artisanal mode of production. Their knowledge, both deep and vast, of that cinema was offered with a generosity for which I shall always be grateful. And it is not for that cinema alone but also for their installation at Anthology of a canon of works from the larger history of cinematic production. One could quarrel (as many did) with their choices, but the recurring cycle of the "Essential Cinema" allowed one to refresh and intensify one's knowledge of the work of Bresson, Keaton, and so many others. Mekas and Sitney are gratefully remembered by many for providing access to the excellent Anthology library and for the general climate of welcome to visitors: together with several generations of doctoral level students, I enjoyed the hospitality Anthology extended to successive years of my seminars.

MacDonald: You found this new cinematic milieu interesting and exciting, but it's a step from there to deciding to bring that work to the forefront in *Artforum*, which must have been a struggle.

Michelson: It was.

MacDonald: There had been no serious attention to this work, particularly in periodicals that had a broad readership. *Film Culture* was important for the comparatively small readership that had found its way to avant-garde work; and of course, Jonas was writing in the *Voice*.

Michelson: Which was *very* important.

MacDonald: Yes, there's never been anybody to take the baton from Jonas.

Michelson: Never.

MacDonald: So how did you convince *Artforum* to take film, and in particular avant-garde film, seriously?

Michelson: Let me go back a bit. I was extremely well-received in New York when I came as a visitor from Paris in 1965, because I had worked for *Arts* magazine and after that for *Art International*. Everybody in New York was very kind and very hospitable. Someone I knew had a party at which I met Barbara Rose, and when I mentioned to her that I was about to take my first trip to California, she said, "There's this new magazine out in California and the editor is really smart; you should go and see Phil Leider while you're there."

When I got to California, I went to see Phil and he too was very nice and responsive, and asked, "Will you work for us?" I told him I hadn't quite decided if I was going to stay in Paris or move to New York, but when I did decide to settle in New York, I informed him, and wrote my first long piece for *Artforum*. It appeared in a special issue on surrealism (with a splendid cover by Ed Ruscha). My piece, "Breton's Surrealism: The Peripeties of a Metaphor or, A Journey through Impossibility" [*Artforum International* 5, no. 1 (1966): 72], was dedicated to André Breton for his seventieth birthday—I had come to know Breton in Paris.

I began reviewing gallery shows for *Artforum*, which was a pleasure because *Artforum* writers were allowed a bit more space than you might find elsewhere, and we could illustrate the pieces. At first, my writing about film was very limited. Then, in 1968 I saw *2001: A Space Odyssey* [1968], and this film blew my mind. I went back to see it twenty-three times. In fact, the New York representative of MGM, who had produced the film, got wind that there was this mad woman who was coming back to see *2001* all the time and asking for the same seat in the third row: 102, I think it was.

MacDonald: Were you seeing it in Cinerama all these times?

Michelson: Yes. This was its first run, in Cinerama.

MacDonald: What an experience that was.

Michelson: Ah, it was amazing.

MacDonald: Somehow I thought Cinerama would always be around and so I procrastinated re-seeing *2001*, to my continuing regret. I didn't make the same mistake with *Avatar* [2009].

Michelson: I worked on a piece on *2001* for a whole year, produced a very long text; and a fairly sizable section of it was published in *Artforum* ["Bodies in Space: Film as 'Carnal Knowledge'," 2, no. 6 (February 1969): 54-63]. I approached the film as someone interested in the avant-garde and the future of film.

Phil Leider was a marvelous guy, but he had no particular interest in film and he didn't really understand my writing on *2001*. I remember sitting down with him for three hours and going over the piece sentence by sentence, explaining to him why someone who was interested in avant-garde cinema— he didn't really know it at that point—would be interested in *2001* and when I'd finished, he said, "Okay, I do understand, and we'll publish the piece." *Then* he said, "Maybe I ought to see some of the films you're so interested in," so I sent him to Anthology, and he became truly and intensely enthusiastic.

I also received an invitation from Kubrick to come and follow the shooting of his next film—presumably on Napoleon, to be shot in Yugoslavia—but the box-office for the first year of *2001*'s release was so low that Metro cancelled the project.

My *2001* piece was written partly in anger at the whole film-critical establishment, including Andrew Sarris, who just dispensed with the film, didn't understand it. The only film critic I'd found interesting, starting when I was probably a teenager, or at least by the time I was 17 or so, was Manny Farber, whom I read in *The Nation* even before I went to Paris. I think Phil developed some sort of friendship with Manny, who published film reviews in *Artforum* for a time.

In 1968 Manny went to see *Wavelength* and it captured him; his sense of the film was very different from mine. In his essay Manny referred to the loft on Chambers Street in which *Wavelength* had been filmed, in a sentence that I thought was wonderful: "Michael Snow's *Wavelength*, a pure, tough forty-five minutes that may become the *Birth of a Nation* in Underground films, is a straightforward document of a room in which a dozen businesses have lived and gone bankrupt" [Farber, "Canadian Underground," reprinted in Manny Farber, *Movies* (New York: Stonehill, 1971), 250–255]. I had always thought of *Wavelength* not as about a room or *place*, but a *space*. For me Michael's film was really about the traversal through a space, as well as the way in which that traversal, slightly complicated by some unrelated and undeveloped actions, was the paradigm for suspense film. Manny didn't think of it that way at all.

MacDonald: When did you get to know Stan Brakhage's work?

Michelson: Before I met Stan, I had a vision of him as a skinny, somewhat querulous type, but when we were introduced—he was in New York for one of the early meetings of Anthology Film Archives and then to do a screening at Yale—I was greeted by this tall, handsome, very charming guy! I accompanied him to Yale; Jay Leyda came to that screening and was thrilled to meet him, as I had been. From then on, when Stan came to New York, we'd go to events together. Part of shepherding him around was my attempt to make his New York stays more pleasant, because he always dramatized New York as dangerous and hostile. One evening we went to the top of the RCA Building in Rockefeller Center and he filmed; he later sent me the film. That was the only time I saw Stan at work.

We even went to the movies once, a film about country music.

MacDonald: *Nashville* [1975]?

Michelson: *Nashville*, yes! And we enjoyed it!

Early on, it seemed to me that essentially Brakhage was doing abstract expressionism in film, and I didn't think that that was really the thing to do. At that point, I hadn't thought deeply enough, consistently enough about his films and in time, I realized that really they were something else.

I was asked to talk at the University of New Mexico, a fascinating place. I did a desert tour, then went up to Colorado for a visit with the Brakhages, where I met the family. They had a wonderful trailer as a guest room and it was a memorable visit.

MacDonald: "Film and the Radical Aspiration" was an inspiring essay for me, for many people, I'm sure.

Michelson: Oh, there are things wrong with it, *really* wrong with it. I'm sorry now that it was so widely circulated.

I'd had a call from a guy who was working with the New York Film Festival, asking did I know a man named Panetsky, and I said no; he explained that this Panetsky had written an article on film and I realized he meant Panovsky: they wanted Panovsky to give a talk at the Festival (at that time the Festival made a more serious effort intellectually). He'd said no, so they asked me, and I gave the talk, "Film and the Radical Aspiration."

Soon after this, I had a call from Pauline Kael saying there were certain people that she knew from California who might be of interest to me. The one I remember is Bruce Baillie, and indeed I've always found Baillie very interesting, though I haven't—I *should have*, but haven't—written about him. There are *so* many people I *should have* written about! But the Soviets and Russian language took me off track.

That was the first and last talk I ever had with Pauline Kael. When I reviewed the third volume of Bazin's essays, which had been translated and published by University of California Press, I opened by saying that nobody had written in any interesting way about this book, particularly the reviewer in the *Times*. I didn't name Pauline, but if she read me, she must have detested what I wrote. I was setting out to remake the level of criticism and theory by contesting the writer at the *New York Times*.

When Pauline died, *Artforum* asked if I would write about her, and I said, "I don't think you want to publish what *I* would write about Pauline Kael," but then I had an idea and called them back. I'd read her from time to time over the years because I subscribe to the *New Yorker*, and in my essay for *Artforum*, I offered an analysis of what having to produce copy on a regular basis can do to a critical mind ["Prose and Cons—An Appreciation of Pauline Kael, *New Yorker*'s Film Critic" includes Michelson's essay; see *Artforum* 40, no. 2 (March 2002): 128, 165].

MacDonald: When did you begin teaching at NYU?

Michelson: 1967. What I brought to film when I first started teaching was essentially my art-historical background. The first course that I taught was "Modernism and the History of Film"; it was about the relation of film to the successive Modernist adventures: Expressionism, Constructivism, Surrealism, and so on.

When I first suggested to my chairman at that time—George Amberg, a very nice man—that it would be interesting to have a course entirely on contemporary avant-garde films, he said, "Okay, but maybe not too many of them!" But I taught a whole semester course and continued to teach it. Being able to do that course was wonderful because I was able to induce the department to buy a certain number of prints, and Ted Perry, who succeeded Amberg as chairman, got us the money to buy films by Stan, Warhol, Conner, Breer, Anger, and others, allowing my students and me to really get to know this work.

MacDonald: What led to your doing that 1971 *Artforum* issue that focused on new formalist film, a very exciting issue [*Artforum* 10, no. 1 (September 1971)]?

Michelson: When Phil Leider left *Artforum* in 1971, he was replaced by John Coplans.

Between Phil's leaving, and John's arriving, there was going to be an interval of one month, and Phil said, "Perhaps you'd like to do an issue that's completely film," and I said, "Absolutely!" I had a wonderful time. The essays were written in great part by my students at NYU, who for several years had been taking my seminars and attending Anthology and having drinks with me after classes. The filmmakers put their films at our disposal when and if we needed them, and I think we produced a very good issue. Of course, the filmmakers were delighted with it.

So by the time John Coplans arrived, *Artforum* had developed something of a tradition of publishing film criticism, and although at first I think John felt uncomfortable about that, after his arrival I was able to write on Vertov, the first piece I ever published on Vertov [" 'The Man with a Movie Camera': From Magician to Epistemologist," *Artforum* 5, no. 7 (March 1972): 60–72]; and I had a free hand with the visual design of the piece.

MacDonald: And not long after that came the "Eisenstein/Brakhage" issue [*Artforum* 11, no. 5 (January 1973)].

Michelson: Exactly. Another exciting experience, again working with my students and others, for a good issue, I think.

MacDonald: When did you first see the Russians, particularly Vertov and Eisenstein?

Michelson: I'd hardly seen them at all until I came back to America and started teaching. I'd seen a Pudovkin in Paris at the Cinematheque; I'd seen *Ivan the Terrible* [1943, 1946], but had not yet seen *Potemkin* [1925] or *October* [1928]. I'd not read Eisenstein's writings or Pudovkin's. In Paris I had asked Noël Burch if I should be reading Eisenstein, and he said, "Oh, absolutely not. Forget it." And I did forget it for quite a while because I was very busy exploring other aspects of cinema, and especially Bresson.

When I heard that the Museum of Modern Art was about to receive a hundred Soviet films, I thought I would like to see them and to see if perhaps one might teach a course on them—I was already very interested in the avant-garde painters of the revolutionary generation: Kandinsky, Malevich, and the others. There had been a first important book on that period by Camilla Gray, which came out in New York during the early 1960s [Camilla Gray, *The Great Experiment: Russian Art 1863–1922* (New York: Abrams, 1962)].

So I sat in the MoMA theater through a whole summer, looking at these Soviet films with Adrienne Mancia—I forget who else was there—and I was quite overwhelmed by a lot of what I saw. I decided to invent a course, so then I did read Eisenstein and did more work on the art historical context of the films. In 1976 I went to the Soviet Union for the first time, and everything I was interested in, everything I was curious about, increased while I was there—I was much helped by Naum Kleiman, the scholarly editor and curator of the Eisenstein archive, who has been a resource for many researchers, filmmakers, and assorted intellectuals who have gone to Moscow. We became fast friends.

MacDonald: You discovered Vertov that summer?

Michelson: I don't remember! But I know that whenever I did first see Vertov, I was excited—to put it mildly. I discovered that you could rent a 16mm print of *The Man with the Movie Camera* [1929], and I ordered it for my NYU Soviet course (I seem to remember that it was Tom Luddy who had made the film available in 16mm to whatever company was distributing it—a great and wonderful deed). When we had the print, I got to really look at this film and found it just incredibly, extraordinarily stimulating, like no other film I'd ever seen. I learned that the film had been available for several years but that there had been only *two* rentals before mine—there were years when *nobody* rented it!

There was virtually no literature on *The Man with a Movie Camera*. Of course, Jay Leyda had written about it in his *Kino* [*Kino: A History of the Russian and Soviet Film* (Princeton: Princeton University Press, 1960)], but it was not a film that he was particularly struck by. He thought it was unusual and in certain ways extraordinary, but didn't quite know what to make of it. As I came to know Jay, I became suspicious that he didn't like Vertov *the man*. Leyda had originally been assigned to work with Vertov when he went to Moscow as a student, but that didn't last very long. Jay became a student of Eisenstein, and eventually Eisenstein's devoted friend and translator. I imagine that Vertov's attacks on Eisenstein, or really on the historical drama, might have been part of Leyda's resistance to *The Man with a Movie Camera*. It was well known that Vertov and Eisenstein didn't get along particularly well. I attempted to re-convert Leyda back to Vertov, and I think I did succeed in some measure, but he was finally an Eisensteinian.

Eventually, the Soviets offered MoMA an exchange. They said, "You can keep the hundred prints if you will give us what you have of Eisenstein's Mexican film." What the Museum did *not* acquire were prints of other Vertov films; those were eventually acquired by Kubelka when he was co-director of the Cinematheque in Vienna; he had brought Madame Vertov (Svilova), Vertov's editor, to Vienna and had the films in his collection. Without letting it be known, Kubelka got copies made and so I was able also to write about *Three Songs of Lenin* [1934], a fascinating film. I had enormous pleasure in writing about Vertov, though I could never write the book on him that I'd have wanted to write. John McCay at Yale, a fine Vertov scholar, has spent much time and effort studying Vertov and his Russian is fine—all those who care for Vertov's work await the publication of his research.

I taught Soviet film for quite some time, and I do think my enthusiasm was communicated to my classes.

MacDonald: The "New Forms in Film" catalogue was published in 1974 [Lausanne Museum of Art, Montreux, August 3–24, 1974]; it helped confirm the status of avant-garde film, implicitly conferred by those *Artforum* issues.

Michelson: The Guggenheim had asked me to do something on the avant-garde and I put a series together, and everybody was very happy with it, even the Guggenheim people. After that show, a well-known art critic in Switzerland thought there ought to be a similar show in Switzerland, and it turned out to be in Montreux, just before their annual jazz festival. This was a terrific opportunity because we could do a catalogue; new prints of everything we showed were made and given to the filmmakers after the event, plus all of their transportation and expenses were covered. The filmmakers were very happy about the show, with the exception of Ken Jacobs who at some point during the planning for that occasion demonstrated such gratuitous ill temper that I decided that no matter what wonderful films he would produce from then on, he was somebody I didn't want to see! Of course, that passed and we're on very good terms, have been for years. I think his work is still remarkable.

MacDonald: He's been remarkably prolific these past few years.

Michelson: It's fantastic.

By the time of the Montreux show, Ken was teaching, which produced *Tom Tom the Piper's Son* [1969, revised 1971], one of the most visually sumptuous films. One of his students had come to NYU and was my projectionist in Montreux.

MacDonald: Helene Kaplan [now Helen Kaplan Wright].

Michelson: Yes. The Swiss, who were very generous to me and very proper, were politely surprised at Helene's coming in and out of the screening room never wearing any shoes! In any case, she was a fantastic projectionist. The series didn't attract quite as many people as I had hoped, but those who did attend were enthusiastic, and I was very pleased that it worked out so well for the filmmakers.

This was, I think, Ernie Gehr's first public appearance, and he was tremendously nervous. Michael Snow was there. Paul Sharits arrived late and the hotel may have given out his room. I remember him sitting down on the floor in the screening room, saying, "I really don't know what's wrong with all you people, but things have been so difficult for me here!" Of course, the event was *Swiss*, all *absolutely* well-managed, punctual, etcetera, and I realized that Paul was somebody with whom I never wanted again to be engaged in any practical way. P. Adams had warned me about Paul's behavior, but I thought, why not bring him? I admired his work.

I don't think I saw Paul again until years later when he came to my loft in New York. By that time, he was well-installed in Buffalo; it might have been

Gerald O'Grady who arranged our meeting. I remember Paul saying to me, "You probably think I'm terribly self-destructive," and my responding, "Paul, I don't care if you *are* self-destructive, but your so-called *self*-destruction involves the destruction of so many other people, and *that's* what I don't care for." It obviously hit home.

My relation with Paul remained as limited as I could make it, though I enormously cared for, and do care for, his work.

MacDonald: I wonder if you know that in her film *Kitch's Last Meal* [various versions 1973–78] Carolee Schneemann takes a shot at you.

Michelson: Really!

MacDonald: It's indirect, but I know from talking with her that a particular reference is to you. It was based on her hearing that you had slept through a program of her films and on her assumption that you didn't care for her work.

Michelson: What does she say?

MacDonald: She says, "I met a happy man/a structuralist filmmaker," who tells Carolee that she is "charming/but don't ask us/to look at your films/we cannot/there are certain films/we cannot look at/the personal clutter/the persistence of feelings/the hand-touch sensibility/the diaristic indulgence/ the painterly mess/the dense gestalt/the primitive techniques." When I interviewed Carolee in 1979, she explained that she was paraphrasing not you, but what was reported to her by your students.

I'm sure you've seen *Fuses* [1967] and I wonder what you think about it.

Michelson: Well, I should go back a little further than that. I first saw Carolee in Paris, at the American Center, which had a couple of studios available to American artists and sometimes hosted events. The American Center is one of the places where Burch and I first saw Breer's films.

A Happening had been scheduled, the first Happening I ever saw. The event itself was very interesting. Carolee was in it, and she was terrific. I didn't see her again for years, when one day she asked if she could come to see me. I said, "Of course!" And she came, bringing with her, Anthony McCall, who had just arrived in New York. Anthony was not yet really making films but he'd conceived of his first important film, *Line Describing a Cone* [1973], on the boat on the way over. I didn't pay too much attention to Anthony, who didn't talk.

Carolee sat across from me and when she crossed her legs, her short dress traveled up to her thighs, and she was absolutely magnificent. Carolee had *the* most famous body and she used it very well. She was right; I *didn't* care about the films, didn't really think much about them.

Earlier, when I'd first read David James's writing on Brakhage in *Film Quarterly*, I'd thought, "God, I wish *I'd* written that!": his was another way to think about Brakhage. So, when David's book [*Allegories of Cinema: American Film in the Sixties* (Princeton: Princeton University Press, 1989)] came out, and I saw that he had discussed Carolee's work, I thought, "Oh, god, why is *she* there? Maybe I should take another look," *except* that I also remember David having totally off-the-wall views of several things: for example, he included Slavko Vorkapich in his account of the avant-garde in Los Angeles [*The Most Typical Avant-Garde: History and Geography of Minor Cinemas in Los Angeles* (Berkeley: University of California Press, 2005)]. I mean *really!*

I realize that I *should have* taken a more careful look at Carolee's work, and the Filmmakers' Cooperative is now just a few blocks away from me. I've been looking at a couple of things again, and since you remind me, I'll put Carolee on the list. One factor in my original reaction to David's attention to her work had to do with the fact that I suspected that he felt forced to add a stronger feminist component to that book. That may have been so—but it was ungenerous of me not to take another look at her work, and I will.

MacDonald: At *Artforum* and in your teaching, you championed many filmmakers, including Yvonne Rainer. Later you even performed in her *Journeys from Berlin/1971* [1980] (figure 4).

Michelson: I published a long piece on Yvonne in two successive issues of *Artforum* ["Yvonne Rainer, Part One: The Dancer and the Dance," 12, no. 5 (January 1974): 57-63; and "Yvonne Rainer, Part Two: 'Lives of Performers,'" 12, no. 6 (February 1974): 30-35], which, by the way, you weren't supposed to do; *Artforum* was not supposed to publish pieces that long.

FIGURE 4 *Annette Michelson as therapist in Yvonne Rainer's* Journeys to Berlin/1971 *(1980).*

Source: Courtesy Yvonne Rainer.

Before I came back to New York in 1965, Ileana Sonnabend, who had not yet opened her gallery in New York, told me there were some interesting things going on at Judson Church on Washington Square and that I might want to take a look. I went and saw Yvonne and Bob Morris (I'd missed their historic performance in the nude). I was amazed by Yvonne's work and was shocked, truly shocked, at the lack of response to it—except by the very fervent Judson crew. She and I quickly became friends and saw a lot of one another, up to a certain point. She was probably the first performance artist in whom I became interested.

I thought the Whitney should be using the Museum space for performances, because at that time performances were happening only in a few places Downtown. And so a number of performances were done at the Whitney; I even got Pierre Boulez invited, when Boulez was first appointed at the Philharmonic, to do a lecture and demonstration; and Yvonne did a performance of *Grand Union* [1971], which I had a small part in. It was interesting for me and for Yvonne to see her work with a different audience.

Then, of course, she began to make films. Just when she was beginning, I showed her some films that I was crazy about, and one of them was a Godard—it could have been *Two or Three Things I Know about Her* [1966]. I remember her saying, "Oh, *that's* a film *I* would have made!" She kind of took possession of Godard.

MacDonald: What was it like working with her on *Journeys*?

Michelson: I have vivid memories of *Journeys from Berlin/1971*, which was made in London. Noël Burch was present one time when Yvonne was shooting. She was working with a professional crew, and at one point she went up while the cameraman was filming, or in between shots maybe, talked to him, and indicated something with her hand on the camera. Noël was shocked; he said, "In Paris you do *not* do that! The director *never* lays a hand on the camera!" Union rules, presumably.

The way Yvonne worked on *Journeys* was comparable to the way Sternberg worked, which is to say that she took *total* control of everything, including the positions of one's head, hands, and body. In my role as an analyst, I was seated all the time, but even the slightest movement of my arm, my hand, my head, my body was controlled. When you look at Dietrich in *Shanghai Express*, you can practically hear Sternberg saying, "No, no, no! An inch to the right!" That was the way Yvonne worked in this film and it was altogether a very interesting experience.

MacDonald: I know you were interested in Hollis Frampton's films early on, and that you and he became close. How did you get to know him?

Michelson: I was living on the Upper West Side, at the beginning of Film Forum. In those days, Film Forum did not show films or host events all week long; it might have been just a couple of times a week, maybe even one time every two weeks.

MacDonald: This is when Peter Feinstein ran Film Forum?

Michelson: Yes. I was a faithful attendant, and one week Hollis brought his films.

I don't even know if I'd seen Hollis's films before then, perhaps not. Of course, I was very struck by them. There was the usual question and answer period after the screening, and at one point I raised my hand and asked a question about *Lemon* [1969]. Now, I don't really remember the question, but I do remember the *beginning* of the answer: "Ah, you must be Annette Michelson!" What response could have been more flattering! And what voice more seductive, what response more complete? And that was how I met Hollis.

We talked a bit after that session, and during the coming months we got to know each other fairly well. This was around the time he moved to central New York State, which was a pity, because, once he'd moved, we no longer got to see each other all that frequently. *But* each time he came to New York, there was a wonderful and very fruitful conversation. When he left my place, which would generally be at about three in the morning, there would be an ashtray *full* of stubs, an ominous portent. He would see me anytime he came to New York, and I think he made a few visits especially so we could talk. It was always a joy to see another film of Hollis's and to think about it. I was at the first screening of *Hapax Legomena*—an extraordinary experience.

Hollis and I had a wonderful time together in Edinburgh as invitees of the Edinburgh Festival. *Then* I realized that Hollis had never been to Paris, so we went to Paris for two or three days and I took him around.

I went to see Hollis when he was dying, and later, for the funeral [Frampton died in 1984].

I have *never* recovered from Hollis's death. I've had very few intellectual companions like Hollis, very few friendships like this one (and it *was* an *intellectual* friendship). I continue to miss that, and him, terribly.

As soon as possible after Hollis's death, as soon as there was enough material gathered, I did an issue of *October* on Hollis [no. 32 (Spring 1985)] and we published another one, recently [no. 109 (Summer 2004)], on the twentieth anniversary of the first.

MacDonald: What led to your leaving *Artforum*?

Michelson: Eventually I felt it was time to do another issue, on relatively new avant-garde work—not only on film but also on performance and music. I was interested in Stockhausen and other new musicians. I was planning to do an article on interrelations of music, film, and performance. Of course, Ken Jacobs was doing performances like mad and Hollis had done some, using Michael Snow as his voice. There were others, of course.

I sent off a letter to everyone, telling them what they would receive for contributing to the issue, giving them deadlines and all of that, and *then* John Coplans tells me, "No, no, no, no. I've decided we can't do that." I said,

"Why?" And he said, "Well, you know, that's not the source of the magazine's lifeblood." What he meant was that the advertising money, which had always produced the relatively luxurious (and now even thicker and more luxurious) *Artforum*, came from advertising for galleries, most of which had no stake in film or performance or experimental music.

I was very disappointed and decided to leave *Artforum*. I took with me Rosalind Krauss, who at that time was a young, but very brilliant member of the *Artforum* editorial staff, and she and I founded *October* in 1976. By now *we're* an ancient journal. *October* was founded precisely in contradistinction to two major publications: *Artforum* and the *New York Review of Books*, which didn't then, and still doesn't, do anything particularly new or interesting with film.

Quite frankly I don't feel that we at *October* who are interested in film, which means Malcolm Turvey and myself, do enough, and we feel we *can't* do enough, because when we look for younger people to write about film, we don't find them. I'm translating a wonderful article by a French curator at the Beaubourg on Anthony McCall, and occasionally something will come into us, but we'd like to have more of a group on whom we could call more regularly.

MacDonald: I assume the recent Frampton issue was an attempt to generate some energy in younger scholars [Melissa Ragona, Federico Windhausen, and Michael Zryd contributed].

Michelson: Yes, in part, but I would like scholars and others who can explore more recent work. *October* is very special—we know that—and not everybody is going to submit to us, but I think there must be a certain number of people who could make important contributions.

Robert Gardner

Robert Gardner is still best known as the pioneering ethnographic filmmaker who made *Dead Birds* (1964), *Rivers of Sand* (1974), *Deep Hearts* (1981), and *Ika Hands* (1988). A controversial figure, even within the field of ethnographic film, Gardner's commitment as a filmmaker was always less a matter of providing anthropologically useful information about the peoples he depicted, than of offering his own poetic visions of their lives, visions that often have a good deal to do with Gardner's sense of his own culture. The fascination of *Dead Birds*, for example, is that, despite the fact that the basics of a comfortable existence—food, shelter, clothing—were available in abundance, the Dani people of central New Guinea were constantly at war with neighboring groups. That the film was made during the Cold War, an era when both NATO and the Soviet Bloc were committed to a nuclear arms race and much of the world was living under what seemed a very real threat of nuclear annihilation, is no accident. *Dead Birds* is simultaneously an engaging report on Gardner's experience of a culture on the verge of major transformation and his mordant rumination on the surreal nature of the human species.

In any case, while Gardner established himself as an accomplished filmmaker with his ethnographic work, he did not see himself as a specialist. And while *Dead Birds* has often been understood as a canonical ethnographic film, its impact went beyond anthropological circles. Indeed, the film's first audience, at the home of Robert Penn Warren in Connecticut, included Mike Nichols, Lillian Hellman, and William Styron. Further, before and during the years when his canonical ethnographic films were being made, he was also engaged in quite different projects. For a time, he and avant-garde filmmaker Sidney Peterson worked toward a never-realized fiction film about a Kwakiutl princess pursued by a love-struck non-native-American man. One of Gardner's earliest completed films is a portrait of the painter Mark Tobey (*Mark Tobey*, 1952), a subject he would return to years later in *Mark Tobey Abroad* (1973). Gardner has always been fascinated with artists and artists-at-work. In *The Great Sail* (1966) he documented Alexander Calder installing his *La Grande voile* at MIT. More recently, in *Dancing with Miklos* (1993), Gardner documented filmmaker Miklós Jancsó shooting his film *The Blue Danube Waltz* (1992); in *Passenger* (1997) and *Scully in Malaga* (1998), the

FIGURE 5 *Man rowing along the Ganges in Benares/Varanasi, India, in Robert Gardner's* Forest of Bliss *(1986).*

Source: Courtesy Robert Gardner.

painter Sean Scully at work; and in "It's Stupid" (part of the compilation *Nine Forsaken Fragments*) and in *Deus Ex Boltanski*, Christian Boltanski installing new work.

Gardner's most powerful and memorable film is probably *Forest of Bliss* (1986), his magnificent depiction of the holy city of Benares, India, where pilgrims come to access the holy waters of the Ganges, and where dying men and women receive final blessings and their bodies are burned on the banks of the river or are released into the river itself (figure 5). For Gardner, Benares is the ultimate exotic—a place of great spiritual and emotional power, but unlike virtually any other place on earth: one of the most ancient cities in the world, but one where age-old rituals remain vital. Gardner does not pretend to understand Benares; rather, he allows viewers an extended moment to see and hear the multitude of activities going on along the banks of the Ganges. *Forest of Bliss* is among the most impressive modern instances of the "City Symphony": that is, a film that depicts a composite day in the life of a major urban center. Like Ruttmann and Vertov, Gardner sees the city he depicts as the quintessence of a culture; but in this instance, not the filmmaker's own.

In addition to his considerable achievements as a filmmaker, Gardner has functioned in a variety of other roles. He was the first director of Harvard's

Film Study Center, and for decades functioned in that capacity—first in the Peabody Museum and subsequently at the Carpenter Center for the Visual Arts—not only as a researcher and as an early teacher of filmmaking and film history, but as a film producer. He became one of the owners of Boston's Channel 5, and beginning in 1972 hosted *Screening Room*, a late-night television talk show that focused on independent filmmakers and presented their work, sometimes controversial work—Brakhage's *Window Water Baby Moving*, for example, and sections of Michael Snow's *"Rameau's Nephew" by Diderot (Thanks to Dennis Young) by William Schoen* (1974)—to an audience of hundreds of thousands.

Always fascinated by writers, Gardner has spent much of his time in recent years seeing the written diaries of his filmmaking expeditions to far-flung locales and peoples into print. His *The Impulse to Preserve* (Other Press, 2006); *Making Dead Birds: Chronicle of a Film* (Peabody Museum Press, 2007), and *Just Representations* (Peabody Museum Press/Studio7Arts, 2010) are engaging and revealing (and beautifully designed, by Jeannet Leendertse) records of Gardner's filmmaking experiences.

In the interview that follows I have attempted to avoid revisiting issues discussed in Gardner's own chronicles of his career as filmmaker and in previous interviews focused on his work. In 2001 the Harvard Film Archive, then under the direction of R. Bruce Jenkins, published *Making* Forest of Bliss: *Intention, Circumstance, and Chance in Nonfiction Film*, an extensive conversation between Gardner and anthropologist Ákos Östör; and as part of *The Cinema of Robert Gardner* (Berg, 2007), co-edited by Ilisa Barbash and Lucien Castaing-Taylor, Barbash interviewed Gardner about his films. My interview is a supplement to these conversations. Gardner and I met at his Cambridge studio, Studio7Arts, to talk about his work in the fall of 2007, and again during the winter and spring of 2010; subsequently, we corresponded by phone and email. Our "discussion" of *Nine Forsaken Fragments*, included at the end of this interview, was adapted from the video record of Gardner's presentation at the retrospective of his work hosted by Bard College in October 2009.

MacDonald: You've been involved in filmmaking and film exhibition here in Cambridge for more than fifty years. I'm wondering how you got here and into your position as filmmaker-director of the Film Study Center, and what your early days, helping to build a film scene in Cambridge/Boston, were like.

Gardner: I came here from Seattle in 1953 and entered grad school at Harvard in anthropology. I came carrying the baggage of what I'd learned about film on the West Coast during two years in Seattle and before that.

MacDonald: How early did you become interested in film?

Gardner: At an early age I was the projectionist for family screenings of mostly Chaplin and Our Gang kinds of comedy. I especially liked the seeming plausibility of the Our Gang episodes.

MacDonald: You're from an old Boston family, a family long involved in the arts. Isabella Stewart Gardner is a legend. How exactly are you related to her?

Gardner: She was my great aunt by marriage. She died the year before I was born so I never knew her. I was born in her summer house (Green Hill) in Brookline and was a frequent visitor to Fenway Court (now the Gardner Museum) in Boston. I was also saturated with her aesthetic: objects and decorative elements that she did not include in Fenway Court surrounded me in the house where I was born and grew up.

MacDonald: When you were growing up, was your family much involved in the arts?

Gardner: My father was an investment banker but also an engaged member of the boards of the Museum of Fine Arts and the Gardner Museum. He was also something of a prose stylist, a classmate and friend of T. S. Eliot, who would occasionally visit our family. My father wrote about sailing and the sea, as this was his real enthusiasm. He was a great admirer of Sarah Orne Jewett and thought her an unacknowledged prose giant.

Grosvenor was my mother's name and is my middle name. Her brother was an excellent sculptor. One nephew (William Congdon) was a very accomplished, internationally known painter. Late in his life, Brakhage showed me the work of a painter he thought was great: it was by this first cousin of mine! Another nephew of my mother is Robert Grosvenor, the sculptor.

MacDonald: Were you artistic as a child?

Gardner: No.

MacDonald: You were an undergraduate at Harvard. Was there a Harvard film society? Were you involved in making films?

Gardner: Not at all as an undergraduate. The only "filmmaking" I had done was to record athletic events at my high school—when I wasn't involved myself.

As an undergraduate at Harvard, I was a roommate of Jack Lemmon. We were great pals, and we continued to see each other right up until he died of prostate cancer. We acted in college plays together. In fact, we went out to California together to try to get into the movies—mostly, as I remember, through girls who were also trying to find their way into the industry. It's not a very long story: Jack and I spent a summer looking for work. I ended up being an assistant to a man who mopped the floors in the Rexall Drug Company in Beverly Hills, and Jack gave up and went back to New York after accompanying silent films on piano at Chicken in the Basket—and not being offered even a screen test. Jack returned to Hollywood by way of some acting lessons from Uta Hagen. I think Uta was the reason Jack always wanted to act on the stage.

As it turned out, believe it or not, I was asked to try out for the role of Mark Trail in a projected TV series based on the comic strip. I was offered a role in a pilot but declined. I don't think the series was ever made. But in the end, I came back to the East Coast for a while, and then went out to Seattle.

MacDonald: You taught medieval history at the College of Puget Sound; then you studied anthropology at the University of Washington. That's a substantial change in direction. Did you get a degree in anthropology?

Gardner: I did not. I studied just long enough to be smitten by Ruth Benedict and Bronislaw Malinowski.

I remember no anthropologists of any interest at the University of Washington, but there were history teachers I quite loved and admired, one in ancient history and the other in European history. It was the age of Toynbee as I recall and much was made of him.

MacDonald: In your introduction to *Making* Dead Birds: *Chronicle of a Film* you talk about meeting Sidney Peterson. What was he doing in Seattle?

Gardner: His wife was the sister of the woman who was married to my psychiatrist!—can you follow that? My therapist, who had the implausible name of S. Harvard Kaufman—he loved to call himself "Harv"—told me about this guy from San Francisco who was the cat's meow as far as independent film was concerned. I said, "I gotta meet him!" When Sidney came up to visit, I got to see *The Lead Shoes* [1949]! Well, pow! I had never seen *anything* like *The Lead Shoes*. [laughter]

MacDonald: I still love to surprise my students with it.

Gardner: I thought, what is this guy *doing*! How much liberty does he think he can take with my willingness to suspend . . . not disbelief: *belief*. I could probably talk all day about Peterson, but I won't. I knew him *extremely* well, probably better than anybody else knew him at a certain point in his life.

MacDonald: You and Peterson apparently thought about making a feature narrative about the Kwakiutl.

Gardner: Yes, a film about a Kwakiutl princess a white man wanted to marry. We went to Vancouver Island and started filming in a place called Fort Rupert. Peterson was shooting black and white with a 35mm Arriflex he had discovered in a second-hand camera store. He was totally incompetent; the negative had to be slowed to half-speed in the laboratory in San Francisco in order to eke out an image. Our sound was awful too. Our plans for the film fell to pieces in no time. But while on Vancouver Island I visited a place called Blunden Harbour, an old Kwakiutl fishermen's village, which became the subject of the first film I edited and wrote for.

You know, I did a *Screening Room* with Sidney Peterson. Stan Brakhage begged me to do it.

MacDonald: It's not one of the episodes in distribution.

Gardner: There are probably copies somewhere.

Sidney was the one who got me into Maya Deren. In fact, I met Maya Deren, right after she had come back from shooting her Haitian footage. At the time, I was running a tiny film distribution company called Image Resources in Seattle. It wasn't a successful business, but one of the things that Images Resources did was distribute Maya Deren's films (I don't know whether she had other distributors at the time; it's likely she did). She was traveling and had decided to check up on her distribution. She depended on rentals of *The Private Life of a Cat* [1947] and *Meshes of the Afternoon* and various other films. I don't think she was making much money.

I don't remember whether Maya stayed with us or not, but I think she was around for a couple of days. I do remember her wanting to kill a chicken one night at my house and show me some Vodun. I was very struck by her and her films.

I found my way into a tiny scene around a film society that showed films at the University of Washington's Henry Gallery. I would go there whenever they had a show, and saw wonderful films—films that, as an undergraduate at Harvard, I'd never heard anything about: Dovzhenko, Eisenstein, Riefenstahl. I saw all of Maya Deren, some of Brakhage. I worked through a repertoire of what I think of as independent cinema. Obviously *The Battleship Potemkin* [1925] is not an independent film, but it was independent of the kind of thing that you saw at movie houses in those days, and Eisenstein—and Dovzhenko, Riefenstahl, Deren, Brakhage—were all as marginalized as they were inventive.

By the way, years later, I met Leni Riefenstahl on a beach in the Balearic Islands. She was a piece of work, full of herself and telling endless stories of her past life as a victimized artist—her screed until the end.

MacDonald: Do you remember who ran the film society? Was it students or faculty?

Gardner: The series was informally organized by patrons such as myself. A bunch of us became steady attendees and so whoever did the booking just listened to what we wanted to see.

MacDonald: You directed *Blunden Harbour* and *Dances of the Kwakiutl*, both finished in 1951. *Blunden Harbour* feels like a late 1940s early 1950s film society film. The narration of the Kwakiutl story at the beginning reminds me a bit of Willard Maas's *Geography of the Body* [1943], and sometimes the compositions remind me of Frank Stauffacher's *Sausalito* [1948]. All in all, it's an impressive first film, with much lovely imagery.

Gardner: When the project with Sidney collapsed, I felt obliged to retrieve something from the wreckage. I sent William Heick and Pierre Jacquemin to Blunden Harbour, asking them to collect daily-life footage. Heick was a student of Peterson's and Jacquemin was a friend of Heick. When they came back, I edited the work print into what is now *Blunden Harbour*. I also wrote the commentary and asked a young poet (Richard Selig) to voice it. He died not long after—cancer, I think.

MacDonald: Where was *Blunden Harbour* shown?

Gardner: Here and there, in festivals of one kind or another.

MacDonald: Heick also shot *Dances of the Kwakiutl*, which is an early instance of your interest in the ways in which the spread of modern life has transformed traditional indigenous rituals.

Gardner: Yes, I didn't learn to shoot until later. *Dances* was mostly a record of dancing done at a late stage in the modernizing of Kwakiutl life, which was celebrated for its color and complexity by numerous writers, including Ruth Benedict and Franz Boas.

MacDonald: When did you see Edward Curtis's *In the Land of the Headhunters* [aka, *In the Land of the War Canoes*; 1914]?

Gardner: I was familiar with Curtis's still photographs of American Indians, and did see the film in Seattle at some point, but didn't like it much.

There were other elements of my experience in Washington of greater importance than anthropology. Before I went to Seattle, I was told there were two people to meet there: the painter Mark Tobey and the poet Theodore Roethke, who taught English at the university and who I came to know well. I quickly decided the poet's view of the world was one I wanted to emulate.

I think absorbing all this poetry, painting, and independent film left me never wanting to be literal about filmmaking—I don't mean "literal" in the actuality sense, but in the sense of conventional storytelling or straight observational documentary. In Deren's work and Brakhage's, in Dovzhenko's and even in Riefenstahl's, I'd come in contact with lyrical filmmaking and the lyrical documentary, and I remained very much drawn to this kind of thing, rather than to the hard-edged, cinema-verite style of truth every 24th of a second that soon came to dominate everybody's attention. I came to feel that there was *no* truth in most of the cinema-verite films, and even if there was, then I was more interested in what *wasn't* that sort of truth, what was beyond that "truth."

In Seattle, I also saw a lot of Grierson's rather grim and pedantic GPO [General Post Office] British public relations films—institutional filmmaking. I admired some of them, but thought that they were confined by their goal of teaching the audience: when film does teach, it doesn't do it because the filmmaker means to, it does it because it can't help it. For me the documentaries that mattered were *Night Mail* [1936] and *Song of Ceylon* [1934]. I like to think my work can be considered as part of that tradition.

In the long run I came to feel that if film was going to be what I thought poetry was (and I was constantly thinking about their similarities and differences and talking to poets about these issues), it had to be poignant, it had to touch people, it needed to call forth one's own anxieties and hopes and despair. . . *everything*, just like poetry does.

MacDonald: Mark Tobey seems to have been an enthusiastic participant in your film about him. You and he are both narrators in the film. Did each of you write the text that you read?

Gardner: I wrote most of the lines, but Mark wrote some too.

MacDonald: There's very nice city imagery in *Mark Tobey*, and the color holds up. The film does feel a bit over-narrated, which was not unusual for 1950s independent films; I see this as a case where sound distracts somewhat from the quality of the imagery.

Gardner: I wholly agree, but at that time I was under the spell of word-smiths like Auden (I'd watched *Night Mail* maybe twenty-five times) and Roethke.

MacDonald: Your two Kwakiutl films and *Mark Tobey* predict your later filmmaking career, which, generally speaking, has "intercut" between lyrical documentaries about indigenous cultures and rituals and documentations of particular modern artists.

Gardner: Those little films were all that I had to show for my three years in Seattle—except for my marriage and a child (early in *Mark Tobey* there's a shot of my wife and child in a gallery).

While I was in Seattle, I tried to support myself by starting a little company I called New Dimensions and another called Orbit Films. I made a couple of commercial films, then gave it up. I felt some shame about quitting, as if I were a wastrel, a prodigal son, so I came back east to gain some respect-ability—as a graduate student of anthropology at Harvard.

MacDonald: Who were your teachers at Harvard?

Gardner: Two I remember well: Clyde Kluckhohn and Earnest Hooton. Kluckhohn was a cultural anthropologist; Hooton, a physical anthropologist--both trained in classics.

MacDonald: Did film play any role in their thinking about anthropology? Did their teaching later inform your filmmaking?

Gardner: No. Film played no role at all in their practice of anthropology, though Kluckhohn was intellectually supportive.

MacDonald: What did you find in the way of a film scene in Cambridge, once you got back?

Gardner: I've sometimes jokingly referred to the film activity around Harvard during the mid-1950s as being confined to an interesting biologist who was using film to make records of bats catching insects in flight (he had a research grant from the Navy), and Timothy Leary, who was using film to observe people undergoing various psychic transformations, psychedelic experiences, and so forth. At that time, Leary's work was not well-known, but it wasn't hidden; I knew about it either because I'd met him or because he was working nearby—I'm not sure which.

Beyond these very specialized kinds of things, what was there? Not much. WGBH was doing some documentary work in a fairly conventional way.

Almost immediately upon my return, somebody heard that I knew something about film, or at least that I had made some films, and said, "We have this project going on at Harvard that doesn't know quite what it's doing; maybe you can offer some advice." They got me involved with the Marshall family, John Marshall's father and mother, incredible people who took their son and daughter to the Kalahari Desert and put them, and themselves, to work, as a way of building a stronger family life.

MacDonald: You worked on the editing of what became *The Hunters* [1957]. What was it like working with John, and what dimensions of that film reflect your involvement?

Gardner: I came into the *The Hunters* when the film had been edited to about forty-five minutes with the help of some commercial film people. My influence was to rethink the film as edited to that point and help move the project to a new and longer edit. It got to be seventy-five minutes, I think, by the time John and I had finished (figure 6).

Working with John was important for me, but what *I* most wanted at that time was to get into Boston's community of making—I don't mean just filmmakers, but people working in all the arts. And I did get to know painters and

FIGURE 6 *John Kennedy Marshall (left foreground) and Robert Gardner working on Marshall's* The Hunters *(1957) at Harvard's Film Study Center.*

Source: Courtesy Robert Gardner.

poets: Donald Hall, Philip Booth, Ted Hughes, Robert Lowell and his circle, including of course his wife Elizabeth Hardwick, Phillip Rahv, and Sylvia Plath. That was the community that I gravitated to. We traded dinner parties and cocktail parties when visitors came from elsewhere. All my memories of those days are good. I remember gossip in abundance—I think all writers are practicing gossips; it's the substance of their verbal invention.

I had friends who knew Robert Frost, who was living three streets away from me in Cambridge, and I told my poet friends, "I'd like to meet him because I'd like to make a film about him," so they said they'd see if they could arrange for me to go see Frost. A time was arranged and I went over to Brewster Street, and there was the old guy, sitting in this big chair. I was frightened, didn't really know what to say, but I blurted out that I had made a couple of little films and that I thought it would be wonderful if he would let me make a film about him.

He harrumphed a little and said, "Well, I don't know, it would just be more *me*; I'm sick of me, me, me, me, me!" And of course, he *wasn't*—this was the most egotistical man I had ever met; there was never enough *me* for Frost.

I could see that he was trying to put up some defenses against this young squirt trying to get into his life—though I think he would have gladly done the film if I'd played my cards right. He said, "Well, what would it mean? What would I have to do?" and I said (you're going to laugh at this): "Let me just suggest what might be a good analogy. You could pretend that you're Nanook, and I'll pretend that I'm Robert Flaherty, and we'll just start from there."

Frost found this absolutely hilarious and chortled over the idea of being Nanook, with all his little Eskimo wives. After that, he didn't take me seriously I think, but I was sincere in wanting to make a film about a man who made things, a man who was an extraordinary figure in many ways; I wanted to look at what he surrounded himself with.

MacDonald: You'd already worked with Mark Tobey in this way.

Gardner: Yes. But I've always been, still am, in awe of writers. Among the things that I brought back from Seattle was the indelible memory of watching *Night Mail*, with Auden's words, and *Song of Ceylon*, with the words of Robert Knox, spoken I believe by Lionel Wendt.

I did feel that if there were to be a filmmaking scene in Cambridge or Boston that *I* could be interested in, it would involve independent filmmaking of an innovative nature. I wasn't interested in joining any commercial efforts, either Hollywood narrative-type feature filmmaking or local advertising work.

So who else was here? Robert Flaherty, who died in 1951, was very important to the Boston situation as I found it, and to me personally—through his foremost champion, Francis Flaherty. I never met Robert, but in the mid-1950s Francis was an important figure in the documentary environment in and around Boston. In fact, I think she exerted her influence more in Boston than anywhere else. Francis was not part of the social scene here, but she would come down from Vermont from time to time.

Francis was an incredible person. She and Robert must have been an astonishing pair. I don't know how they operated together, because they both had their own force, their own great energy. Francis had only one desire after losing Robert, and that was to memorialize him, to enshrine him and to engrave his name in film history. She did that extremely well. I immediately became devoted to her and to the Flaherty method as she espoused it—not as it's being espoused these days.

MacDonald: How do you mean?

Gardner: I don't think Flaherty advocates are sufficiently open to storytelling. There's too much dependence on the camera (always video now) as the vacuum cleaner of actuality; there's no subtlety and little if any style.

I went to the first so-called Flaherty Seminar up at the little Flaherty farm in Brattleboro. Francis had said, "You've got to come up! You've got to come up!" I remember Robert's brother, Tim, a thin little guy who ran the projector and was very quiet and nice (and completely at the mercy of Francis), and there were a few other people I didn't know and don't remember.

To my everlasting regret, in 1960 I was asked by WGBH to do a TV piece of Francis talking about her husband. She could talk about Robert *so* well; she had her presentation *completely* nailed, and during the interview she spouted this monologue. I felt like a total jerk, just sitting there, nodding my head. I'm told that "interview" is still available. I'd hoped that all the tapes had burned up in the great fire that consumed most of WGBH's earlier efforts.

MacDonald: I saw that interview at the 2009 Flaherty seminar! Francis comes across just as you describe her.

Gardner: I was under her spell. But in time I began to carve out more independent ideas of who *I* was and, for that matter, who Flaherty was. I found I liked the Flaherty films that other people didn't like, more than the films that everyone thought were so wonderful. I liked *Man of Aran* [1934] better than *Nanook* [1922], and I didn't like *Moana* [1926] at all. I think it was the way *Man of Aran* was shot that caught my attention. Flaherty is often listed as "co-photographer," whatever that means. What is sure is that he spent a lot of time on the Aran Islands and found a pretty compelling cast. It really is an enacted piece, what with shark fishing already abandoned when Flaherty decided to make a film with that as an important part of the story. All of Flaherty's films were enacted to some degree, and his widow's assertions notwithstanding, they really have to be taken as he intended them, as made-up stories, not the "un-preconceived" works Frances insisted they were.

MacDonald: How did you become involved with the Film Study Center?

Gardner: I established the Film Study Center in 1957, maybe 1956, as an adjunct project within the Peabody Museum, where I had been working with John Marshall.

MacDonald: You began to teach a seminar on film around then.

Gardner: Yes. While I was still a graduate student, I was given the opportunity to head a little seminar at the Peabody, not just on filmmaking, but on film-cum-studying culture; basically it was an early visual anthropology course, possibly the first ever—even though I didn't call it that.

The seminar was under the supervision of Jo Brew, John Otis Brew, the director of the Peabody—a really nice roly-poly guy who made everybody feel good, including himself (he drank himself out of a job I'm afraid). Jo Brew had a lot to do with the Peabody Museum being where it is now, in terms of its leadership in the area of photography and film. He had a lot of help, particularly through his friendship with Laurence Marshall, John's father, who lived on Bryant Street in Cambridge and was a big donor to the Peabody. Laurence contributed all of the Kalahari materials to the Film Study Center.

I think the seminar was Anthro 214—something like that. Anybody who had an interest in learning about the connection between anthropology and filmmaking was welcome. The very first group I taught—really it was just a dialogue with interested folks—included the poet Stanley Kunitz, who I had come to know quite well, owing to his friendship with my sister Isabella Gardner who was also a poet. I remember Stanley telling me that his mother took him to a double feature every day as he was growing up in Worcester, and that he gained much of his appreciation of the world through film.

I was a graduate student in the Department of Anthropology. I took my Ph.D. orals once and failed them, then took them again and when I passed, breathed a sigh of relief and said to myself, "Okay, *that's* over; I've not failed *completely* to do what I'm expected to do, and I can now leave academe. I know I'm not going to adopt the life of an academic, so why go further? Start making films, Gardner." My career path changed at that point. I was awarded an M.A. degree in anthropology, but that's as far as I went.

MacDonald: In 1957 you went to the Kalahari with the Marshalls. "A Human Document," your portrait of an old woman, came out of that trip, but what else can you tell me about your experiences there?

Gardner: It was a fine opportunity at the time and I got plenty out of it, including building some skill as a cameraperson. Much of my attention went into watching the Old Lady, as I referred to an ancient person who lived in our midst. I shot film about her and wrote a piece published in *Daedalus* [*Daedalus* 89, no. 1 (Winter 1960): 144-150]. Fairly recently, the film I shot has resulted in the short piece that is one of the "forsaken fragments," a group of unfinished films [*Nine Forsaken Fragments* (2009) was assembled for an event honoring Gardner, sponsored by Bard College].

Other than my fascination with the Old Lady, I was intrigued by the whole situation of these huge trucks borrowed from the US Army by Laurence Marshall, grinding their way to these remote Bushmen. I always felt that there was a New Yorker profile waiting to be written about Laurence Marshall. He was a singular man and had a singular family: a wife who made herself into an ethnographer, a daughter who could write with real ability, and a son who could shoot and edit film.

MacDonald: During the early 1960s the Film Study Center moved to the Carpenter Center.

Gardner: The Carpenter Center was under construction even before I'd left for New Guinea in 1961. I remember going over the plans and deciding how things would be laid out, at least in my area. I had been put in charge of film and photography. When I got back, the three of us—Edward Steckler, a very methodical Viennese architect who was in charge of studies; Mirko Basaldella, a wonderful Italian sculptor and a really cool guy who died much too young, headed sculpture and painting; and I was in charge of "Light and Communications" (which I thought was a way of bringing together all the different kinds of art-making that had to do with light). We called ourselves a troika—a popular way of describing autocracy! We were up and running by 1964.

MacDonald: Were all the offerings at the Carpenter Center production courses, or were history and theory included?

Gardner: The course I taught always included a little history, but it was mainly production. My first class at the Carpenter Center used little Bolex 8mm reflex cameras. One of the students in that class, the first filmmaking class ever given at Harvard, was Alfred Guzzetti. Alfred is still at Harvard, very august and determined to continue teaching celluloid filmmaking.

MacDonald: Was the original mandate the formation of a production program, an exhibition program, or an academic program—or a combination of these?

Gardner: I understood it to be a combination, with an emphasis on practice.

Getting this program started involved an enormous amount of work. Each of the three of us was free to make things happen just the way we wanted them to happen in our own little bailiwicks. I was constantly trying to make the Carpenter Center available to filmmakers of the kind that I admired. Of course, we were all acting in our own self-interests, but it seemed to me that our *self-interests* created a lot of good attention.

My colleagues and I were on what was called the Committee on the Practice of the Visual Arts, and I held true to what was implicit in that title as long as I possibly could. In recent years, here and pretty much everywhere else, things have gotten tipped in another direction—maybe not disastrously at Harvard, I don't know; I don't go there often any more. Slowly but surely, the academics got hold of the program, arguing, "We've got to become a regular department." Everyone but me seemed to think there were benefits to the change: sabbaticals and I don't know what else. My colleagues didn't want to be thought of as fundamentally different from the Department of Romance Languages or the Department of English, and as a result, we were transformed into the Department of Visual and Environmental Studies, a very odd designation. I tried my best to keep that from happening, but in the end, I couldn't; there was just too much pressure to do what had become the conventional thing.

All along, *I* felt that our becoming a department would take the emphasis away from *practice* and redirect that energy into more academic kinds of activities: theses, for example, like other departments required—*theses*! All this borrowed detritus from other departments was brought in and I believe it has overwhelmed the *practice* of the visual arts at Harvard ever since.

MacDonald: How much were you teaching in the early days at the Carpenter Center?

Gardner: Ridiculously little. Only one course. Now, you wouldn't get away with that; you'd have to teach two courses each semester.

My students were wonderful and I hear from them all the time—though I wasn't Mr. Chips: students didn't come back wanting to pal around with me.

MacDonald: You brought a number of people to the Carpenter Center to work and lecture.

Gardner: One of the first was Dusan Makavejev, who came over from Yugoslavia and taught brilliantly; he was absolutely what Harvard needed, in so many ways. He made his mark and even did some film work while he was here. Miklós Jancsó, one of the greatest filmmakers alive, came for two or three years. That was the flavor of filmmaking at Harvard, and I think it was tasted throughout Boston, if not further. I don't think there was any place that had more interesting filmmakers or a more independent spirit than we had.

When I was designing the basement of the Carpenter Center, I wrote "Cinematheque" on the blueprint—and that was the start of the Harvard Film Archive. The Archive made available an incredible program of film watching. We just threw everything up on the screen.

MacDonald: Did you do all the programming at the cinematheque?

Gardner: Certainly not. It was a combination of people and interests. Stanley Cavell was an important voice in it all.

By the way, I didn't just bring filmmakers to the Cinematheque, but other contributors to the contemporary art scene. I came to know Emmett Williams and persuaded him to do the first "Happening" at Harvard.

MacDonald: I'm a fan of Williams's visual poetry, and I suspect he (especially through his alphabet performances) was an influence on Hollis Frampton's *Zorns Lemma* [1970]. For a few years I pretended I was a concrete poet and for me, Emmett is the best who ever worked in that form, and *THE*

VOY AGE [Stuttgart, Hansjörg Mayer, 1975 (limited edition)], the most engaging and brilliant of all visual poems.

Gardner. He was an important influence on the way that I looked at the world. I knew him intimately, and I know his partner Annie Noël as well.

Emmett's performance at the Carpenter Center was amazing; I just turned him loose. Nobody knew who he was or what he was doing. I think he also gave one course, or maybe he was on some kind of fellowship that gave him access to the Xerox machine—he loved the Xerox machine: he Xeroxed the alphabet a hundred times, at the end of which it was completely transformed, but still the alphabet.

MacDonald: Who else did you bring to the Carpenter Center?

Gardner: They came one after the other, from Brakhage to Kubelka to Breer and other animators. You've not asked about animation, but for years, Boston was an epicenter of independent animation. I put animation into the program at the Carpenter Center from the very start. I tracked down the man who made the Oxberry; it turned out he was a Harvard graduate. I convinced him that he should give an Oxberry to Harvard. Of course, the moment you get something that big into a building, you almost have to use it, so right away, I began bringing in the best animators I could find: the Hubleys for example—John Hubley was our first animator. Almost every animator of moment in American and European animation has taught at Harvard.

I found Derek Lamb in London; I remember drinking a Guinness with him in a bar in Piccadilly Square, trying to persuade him to come to Harvard. He was working for John Halas at the time; Halas and Joy Batchelor did *Animal Farm* [1954].

George Griffin, Caroline Leaf, Jan Lenica all taught here, and we brought John Whitney in for a screening. The films that were made here set a standard for independent animation that not even the National Film Board of Canada has come up to.

I was especially taken with Lenica's work, couldn't get enough of him. Lenica is clearly the greatest poster painter there ever was, or at least the best Polish poster painter there ever was, and was one of the foremost animators of all time. When Jan was teaching here, Dick Rogers was teaching photography or was working as an assistant. I said, "Hey, Dick, you're a filmmaker; you should make a film about Jan making a film." And he did: *Moving Pictures* [1975].

MacDonald: You stayed close to Rogers his whole life.

Gardner: Yes, we did a lot together--a *lot*. I miss him. And, of course, knowing Dick brought me into contact with his widow, Susan Meiselas, who is also a close friend.

MacDonald: I wonder how much contact you had with other filmmakers who have become identified with Boston and Cambridge. At what point did you become aware of Fred Wiseman?

Gardner: The first time I ever saw Wiseman, he was engaged in *The Cool World* [1963] with Shirley Clarke. I think he thought he was going to be a feature filmmaker, but then of course he went into actuality filmmaking in his own distinctive way.

MacDonald: Did you have much interaction with him?

Gardner: It was pretty minimal other than the occasional tennis match.

MacDonald: Did you have much interchange with Ricky Leacock, once he came to MIT?

Gardner: Not so much. As you know, Ricky arrived on the filmmaking scene with *Louisiana Story* [1948]. He got a lot of mileage out of his collaboration with Flaherty. I don't think he had anything to do with the editing on that film; in fact, I don't think Ricky's ever had much to do with editing, but he certainly was an advocate of lyrical documentary, so we had that in common. After his work as a journalist filmmaker with Bob Drew at NBC and with Pennebaker had petered out, he needed a job and he got one teaching at MIT. That's what people who want to make films independently usually have to do, get a job teaching. During his years at MIT, of course, he had great influence on a generation of filmmakers.

MacDonald: It's always struck me that MIT was a strange place to have a film department.

Gardner: I remember how that developed. There was a sudden convergence across the Humanities at MIT that permitted Minor White, who was one of the looniest and most mystical photographers of his generation, to teach. I'm sure he taught the subject in a very compelling way, but his thinking always had to do with the Beyond or the Jungian. György Kepes ran the arts at MIT and it was through him that Minor White could slip in through the cracks, and later Ricky. György was a fascinating person and a brilliant Hungarian painter, also a conceptualist and a prolific writer (he wrote *The Language of Vision* [1944]).

When Ricky was at MIT, he used to tell me, "You know, when I studied at Harvard"—he went to Harvard; I don't know if he graduated—"I studied physics and wanted to become a physicist, so now I'm happy; I'm finally going to combine engineering and filmmaking in a way no one ever has!" So Ricky went around doing something that he probably came to regret, which was to invent his Super-8, sync-sound editing system. It didn't really work the way he wanted and didn't get out into the world and make him a pot of gold.

Of course, Ricky had already played a role in perfecting the independent sync-sound capability of 16mm: he and Pennebaker, and the Frenchman André Coutant, who was really at the bottom of it all. Coutant was a camera specialist, the manufacturer of the Aaton. Coutant's cameras are the best in the world and his sync inventions were the ones that we all fell back on.

Ricky and Pennebaker and others went around saying that this new sync-sound capability was a great boon for filmmaking, that it produced a distinct way of looking at the world and resulted in extremely revealing films, and so on. I think they were perfectly justified in saying all those things, but I also think their method was something of a dead end. I did make one sync sound film [*Marathon* (1965, co-made with Joyce Chopra)]—in fact, I asked Pennebaker to come up and help shoot it. It was a project I assigned in one of the last filmmaking classes I taught.

MacDonald: Did you know Ed Pincus?

Gardner: Ed, Ricky's colleague at MIT, was completely his own person; he and Ricky hung out a lot, but they were never collaborators, except as colleagues in the MIT Film Section. Early on, Ed, who got his undergraduate degree in philosophy here at Harvard, was interested in still photography.

So MIT was a hotbed of a certain kind of filmmaking that was being taught by Ed and Ricky, and was absorbed—and greatly improved upon as time went by—by the likes of Ross McElwee.

MacDonald: What was going on, film-wise, at other Boston area universities?

Gardner: Tim Asch taught at Brandeis for several years.

MacDonald: I can't teach without *The Ax Fight* [1975], which was completed at Harvard.

Gardner: Tim was a student of Margaret Mead's at Columbia. When I was no longer able to work with John Marshall, I had to find somebody who *could* work with him, so I contacted Margaret Mead to ask for suggestions. Margaret said, "Tim Asch; he's a really nice person and he would love to help." So I got Tim up from New York, and for a while he became the glue that held John together—because John was abusing alcohol and had all kinds of problems. He could never finish anything, which was the reason that I had originally been asked to help him on *The Hunters*.

I think I arranged for Tim to teach in my absence one semester. Later, he went off with Chagnon, partly I think because he wanted to get away from Marshall. He and Chagnon got their Yanomamo thing going, and Tim busied himself with that for a long time. Then John needed him again, and they got back together and edited some great little films about the Bushmen.

Still later, Tim and Patsy Asch went off to Bali. Tim ended up at USC [University of Southern California] where he was the head of whatever they had going in documentary. Tim was very naïve, very, very naïve, but also very sweet, a truly earnest person who really cared about teaching. I think much of his energy was devoted to communicating principles of anthropology in a visual way; he was definitely a proponent of teaching good anthropology, and far more interested in that than in entering into filmmaking as a way of being an artist, or as a way of communicating to a world beyond anthropology departments.

I didn't know Tim well for the last twenty-five years of his life, but I knew him well at the start, and he was dependable and conscientious. He deserves a lot of credit for keeping John as sober as he did and at work.

MacDonald: When I was first getting into the history of independent film-making during the early 1970s, one of the transformative experiences for me was an event sponsored by an organization called the University Film Study Association, which was run, I believe, by Peter Feinstein.

Gardner: Yes, I knew Peter.

MacDonald: Each summer for a number of years they offered one-week intensive courses, taught by a wide variety of people. I took a course in ethnographic filmmaking, taught by John Marshall. What I remember most about his course is that the first film he showed was Peter Kubelka's flicker film, *Arnulf Rainer* [1960]. I remember being surprised by what seemed Marshall's broad sense of what film could be; I had expected him to stay pretty much within a conventional ethnographic framework.

Gardner: Well, I never detected in John any particular interest in experimental cinema, and I knew him well. He was interested in some of the films I was interested in, and of course, we would look at things together, but I never knew him to engage with experimental work either in his aesthetic judgments or in his filmmaking style.

I used to show *Le Sang des bêtes* [1949] at the beginning of my courses or sometimes Deren's *A Study in Choreography for the Camera* [1945]; these seemed essential works to me. They may even be included in the Anthology Film Archives Essential Cinema collection.

MacDonald: They are.

Gardner: A lot of things *should* be part of that listing that aren't, and a lot of things *are* that shouldn't be!

MacDonald: What led to your deciding to try television with the *Screening Room* series: it was, still is, unusual.

Gardner: *Screening Room* helped to fulfill a promise on the part of those of us who had won the right to run Channel 5 in Boston—after lengthy litigation, all the way to the Supreme Court.

MacDonald: What was the litigation about?

Gardner: A few of us thought that there was a chance of acquiring the license of Channel 5 from its then-present owner, which was a local newspaper. It had been discovered that the newspaper's publisher had had an ex parte meeting with the chairman of the FCC, and that opened the door to litigation. A bunch of us got together and I was chosen—I don't know why; I think it was because I was at Harvard and teaching something about the visual arts—to be in a group that would challenge the then-current owner's right to have the station. I was a director of that corporation on the basis of a modest investment—I think I put in $10,000 when the group was formed in the middle to late 1960s. Also, they wanted a mixture of ethnicities in the group and a range of talents. Many in the group were Jewish lawyers, and I was something else. A Protestant? A Buddhist?

Very interesting people were owners of that corporation. Oscar Handlin, a great historian at Harvard, was recruited early (he did editorials for the station); and Gerald Holton, one of the most famous physicists to ever teach at Harvard; and John Knowles, one of my undergraduate roommates at Harvard, who was then director of the Massachusetts General Hospital.

In presenting our case, we had to promise, or at least to outline in some fairly convincing terms, what we would do should we become the operators of the channel. It is the public's "need, interest, and convenience" that must be served in the awarding of these licenses. Of course, it all depends on what you mean by "need" and "convenience." As a director of that new ownership group, I had considerable power to influence the kinds of things we would do were we to get the station, and as part of the proposed programming, we included a show on film and filmmaking.

Our company was named Boston Broadcasters Incorporated, and we operated as a corporation with the station as our only asset. We had a very good manager who was able to get a lot of advertising. The station grew and soon it was as if it had a license to print money! Pretty quickly, great wealth was available to all of us who had any percentage of equity in Channel 5.

Once we got the license, *Screening Room* became possible. I knew I could do the show because I had all the contacts and knowledge I needed to produce a program. I was excited that a much larger group of people could see kinds of work that, until that time, was only available to a few students and at out-of-the-way screening rooms. As you remember, those were the days when Stan Brakhage or whoever else would put a few 16mm reels in his suitcase and drive around showing the work.

MacDonald: That's still pretty much the way it's done—though it's more likely to be DVDs and hard drives, now.

Gardner: Each week, I would ask a different filmmaker to come and show work and talk about it. The only rule governing how I was to conduct interviews was that each show had to be less than fifty percent film—because the moment you use more than fifty percent of your airtime to show films, you're no longer considered to be originating locally. So all the *Screening Room* shows are more talk than screenings, although many complete works were shown for the first time to a very astonished audience.

MacDonald: The first show was in November of 1972, with John Whitney, Sr. as the guest.

Gardner: That sounds right (figures 7a, 7b).

MacDonald: You showed films on *Screening Room* that I can't believe you were able to broadcast. Brakhage, who was a guest in June 1973, at the end of the airing of *Window Water Baby Moving*, says, "Well, there it is, *Window Water Baby Moving* on television for the first time!" Rouch's *Les Maîtres fous* [1955] was aired in July 1980.

FIGURES 7A AND 7B *(above) Robert Gardner (left) with Stan Brakhage and (below) Peter Hutton, during episodes of* Screening Room.

Source: Courtesy Robert Gardner.

Gardner: Screening Room aired from midnight to 2:00 a.m., the graveyard slot, because the station manager knew perfectly well that in prime time, we would be offending people. I'm not sure if they ever got any advertisers for our show.

Because Boston was what it was (and still is): a university town, there were numberless students in the area who would switch on *Screening Room*. At one point we did a survey and found that 250,000 people were watching this program! The station didn't really know who we were reaching, but we knew it had to be a younger crowd. I'm sure a lot of the movies we broadcast were seen through a haze of marijuana smoke. When I announced we were going to end the series, I got many letters begging us to stay on.

MacDonald: Were there repercussions from your showing any of the films?

Gardner: In Michael Snow's *"Rameau's Nephew"*, excerpts of which we showed when Snow was a guest, there is a shot of a man and a woman, both standing, peeing into buckets. I remember getting a call around two o'clock in the morning from the head of the station: "Jesus, Gardner, are you trying to get our license taken away! A movie with somebody peeing in a bucket!" I said, "It's a work of art!" He thought that was a big joke.

MacDonald: On the DVD of that show there's a black rectangle covering the midriffs of the man and woman.

Gardner: The station must have done that before the show aired, but you still *hear* pee hitting the buckets—of course, *"Rameau's Nephew"* is *about* sound!

There have been recent repercussions involving Brakhage. Marilyn Brakhage is at my throat for letting the Brakhage *Screening Room* shows be seen. She feels that the films don't look their best, that the prints we showed weren't good enough. I'm disappointed with her reaction because I think that there's something to be gained from looking at the films within the context of the show. Maybe you don't see the best version of those particular films, but you can get the Criterion DVD and see a better version if you want. During his *Screening Room* visits Stan talks passionately about his work.

I said to Marilyn, "*I* didn't ask him to bring those prints that you don't like; *he* brought those prints and *he* knew what condition they were in, and *he* knew they were going to be seen by 250,000 people, so blame *him*." But she just says, "Nobody should see any of the films with so many scratches."

I do think that she has finally succumbed to the idea that these shows *are* available; and so, if somebody asks for a *Screening Room* with Brakhage, it will be sent to them. I'm not *promoting* the product in any vigorous way; I'm just taking the position that this is part of the public record and should be available.

MacDonald: Were you able to pay filmmakers to be on *Screening Room*?

Gardner: Yes. Nobody programming independent film had much of a budget in those days, but I had something like a thousand dollars to pay each filmmaker, plus money for their travel expenses; they were put up in a hotel; and they were paid a per foot rental fee for the films we screened. They could usually walk away with fifteen-hundred or two-thousand dollars.

MacDonald: A lot of money then.

Gardner: I had no trouble recruiting people for the shows. I wish I'd done more, but at least we did about a hundred.

MacDonald: You said earlier that you destroyed some of them.

Gardner: In the end I felt that some just didn't deserve to exist, so I got rid of them. I should never have done that. I held out maybe thirty as being worthy of archiving, and that's what we've got on DVD.

MacDonald: Early on, you sometimes had both a filmmaker and a guest—Stanley Cavell, Rudolf Arnheim, Gerald O'Grady. Later you gave that up. The extra person often feels a little cumbersome—is that why you stopped?

Gardner: Well, my reason for inviting a scholar was just a lack of courage on my part; I felt I needed somebody with me to help me through the ordeal. Then it got so that the shows were pretty easy to do, and I didn't feel I needed help. But it's true, often the extra guest wouldn't add much.

MacDonald: I found O'Grady on the Bruce Baillie show impossible.

Gardner: Well, Baillie was even more impossible!

MacDonald: There might be four minutes of him actually talking!

Gardner: That's because he was late for the show! For a while there was just an empty chair! It's lucky Gerry *was* there. [laughter]

MacDonald: Often, what's interesting about these shows now is not so much what anybody says, but the way in which the interviews reference a certain moment when many of us were struggling to deal with new work. I remember watching the Yvonne Rainer piece and empathizing with your discomfiture. It took me almost twenty years to figure out what Yvonne was doing.

Gardner: *I* couldn't figure her out for the life of me! And I wonder what she would make of her attempts to explain herself nowadays. She certainly became a voice that was listened to.

MacDonald: I think the *Screening Room* episodes that work the best are the ones where you show relatively short films. I think the John Whitney program is a very good one, partly because his work comes across really well on TV. And now after the digital revolution, his early pioneering work with computer imaging is fascinating.

Gardner: That's true.

MacDonald: The Broughton show worked really nicely.

Gardner: Breer I liked too.

MacDonald: Was *Screening Room* aired every year?

Gardner: The shows were done in groups of thirteen. Thirteen might have been budgeted for a certain year and then not budgeted for the next year, but for the year after that. They were all made between 1972 and 1981, but there may have been years when I didn't do any and there may have been a year when I did twenty-six instead of thirteen—I have absolutely no memory of the details.

The only existing record of all of the *Screening Room* shows is the D-2 copies that were made by the Museum of TV and Radio in New York, and some Beta SPs that the station made of each program. They're either upstairs or at the Harvard Film Archive—certainly all those that survived that first severe cut, and probably a few others.

MacDonald: Did you edit the versions now available on DVD?

Gardner: They were edited under my supervision by Grace Fitzpatrick, a very nice woman who understood the project and knew what was worth cutting and what was important to keep. Basically, she cut out all the commercials and all the interruptions of the program by the station. Plus there were a few places in the programs when something really dumb was said or when something happened that marred the flow. I don't know whether notes were kept of what was eliminated, but we have the original and we have the result of Fitzpatrick's editing.

MacDonald: You've mentioned a couple already, but are there other shows that you think back on as disasters or as triumphs?

Gardner: I think my biggest disaster was Les Blank [January 1973], because although I'd known Blank for years, I'd never been able to talk to him. As you know, when you're doing something on television, you have only that 90 minutes to work with. *Screening Room* was not live television, but almost live, because you couldn't do repeats; you couldn't say, "Let's erase and start over"; there wasn't the studio time for that. I could get fairly impatient with somebody like Les, who didn't want to talk.

I had a really nice time with Standish Lawder; I had a nice time with Robert Fulton both times he was on the show. Rudy [Rudolf] Arnheim was on the first Fulton show; he didn't contribute much, but it was just nice to have him there: such a brilliant man and such a strong moral agent for film. He died at a hundred only a couple of years ago. An amazing person.

MacDonald: Both he and Cavell, it seemed to me, were so wedded to commercial film that they had trouble computing Fulton and Lawder.

Gardner: Cavell has never been open to much on the experimental side; he *is* open to documentary. Arnheim took a very purist view of things. For him cinema *was* an art, as is clear in his *Film As Art* [Berkeley: University of California Press, 1971], but I think the only place he ever came in contact with avant-garde film was at Harvard.

MacDonald: That book was important to me because of his argument that limitation is the generator of creativity. He was one of the people who argued that the lack of sound forced 1920s filmmakers to be visually experimental, so I've always been surprised that he couldn't see that avant-garde filmmakers struggled with the limitation of having no money, and despite this, and perhaps because of this, produced amazing film experiences. That's been one of the glories of avant-garde film.

Gardner: Screening Room seems to have a long half-life; various episodes are continually being bought by film departments and individual film lovers. In fact we are recently experiencing a surge in orders for the whole series of thirty programs, now available for $750.

MacDonald: Was Robert Fulton your student? You collaborated with him on many projects.

Gardner: I would say that I was more Bob's student than he mine. I'm writing a book about him now. I have it mostly in mind and I'm collecting all the stills of him I can find. I want not only his face, but the content of his mind to be known by a larger group of people, because *anyone* who ever rubbed against Bob got so much from it. He was astonishing. And this despite the fact that he wrote some of the most opaque English I've ever tried to read!—though when you did begin to understand what he was getting at, it was always memorable and amazing.

Bob was a major influence on my aesthetic, right from the time I first met him, which I think was 1971 when he was a student at Harvard for one semester. He got kicked out for failing a course the historian Seckler gave. Later, he showed me some of his film work, and when I was looking for somebody to teach in the department, I mentioned him to Seckler. Seckler had maybe seen one of his films and couldn't have had much of an opinion of Bob, but to his credit he said, "Well, fine, if you want to recommend him, we'll give it a try." So Bob came and I think he liked being at Harvard, and many loved him being here and got a lot out of his instruction and his example.

MacDonald: You first worked together on *Mark Tobey Abroad* [1973], which is a lovely film.

Gardner: That was our first modestly large undertaking.

MacDonald: On the end credits of *Mark Tobey Abroad* "Robert Fulton" comes first, then, after a pause, "Robert Gardner."

Gardner: Bob did more of the photography than I did.

MacDonald: It seems a bit like a homage.

Gardner: Indeed.

MacDonald: In *The Impulse to Preserve* when you're talking about *Deep Hearts* [1981], you mention that Fulton is doing "reasonably well considering his fragile mind/body situation. The slightest jarring can have catastrophic consequences." What are you referring to?

Gardner: Bob's nerves were drawn so tightly, his perception was so exquisitely tuned that it seemed as if a sudden noise or disturbance could really shake him. You might be driving down the street and another car might appear, and there would be this really fast reaction, sort of a fright reaction. Loud noises were abhorrent to Bob and ganged up on his nerves. But he was generally able to go with the flow in ways that few other people I've ever known could. A case in point is when we walked to the sacred lakes to film Mama Marco in *Ika Hands* [1988].

The sacred lakes are very high and getting there involves a tough journey. Stupidly, I didn't bring enough food, we didn't have enough clothes, and Bob was already coughing. He was living in the men's house in the village, which was all smoke and coughing. We walked up to the lakes and spent a few days there with Bob really sick, yet he carried on, really carried on, and made fine shots, including a couple that I'll always treasure. We left immediately after that trip, both of us just absolutely exhausted. It took Bob a long time to get well; he had pneumonia.

Bob shot several gorgeous time-lapse sequences both among the Ika and for *Deep Hearts*, time-lapse sequences that I would like to pull together sometime and show as a group. They're hard to work into films and yet I always wanted to include Bob's vision if it was possible to find a place for it.

MacDonald: We've not talked about your own films of the 1960s through the 1980s. They have a surreal dimension that's not often commented on.

Gardner: I wish that dimension of the films were more obvious to more people.

MacDonald: The society in *Dead Birds* is crazed in its very coherence—as ours is in a different way.

Gardner: Well, that's right. When I set foot in the Baliem Valley, with very little preparation, I found myself on a different planet.

MacDonald: *Dead Birds* is not *so* different from *The Lead Shoes*! [laughter]

Gardner: True, it couldn't get more improbable! "Sticking those penis gourds in the face of the public!—what are you *doing*, Gardner!"

MacDonald: The opening sequence of *Forest of Bliss* is a kind of surreal montage.

Gardner: Oh absolutely. It's meant to be.

MacDonald: And that dog being killed is like the slicing of the eyeball at the beginning of *Un Chien andalou* [1929].

A question about *Deep Hearts*. In *Rivers of Sand* [1974] you're dealing with gender in the sense of the man/woman division of labor in Hamar society; it's as if you're bringing your own concerns about gender to bear on this very distant group. It strikes me that from its opening moments, *Deep Hearts* is dealing with what has come to be called "Queer," meaning a destabilization of the idea of gender. It would make a fantastic double feature with Jenny Livingston's *Paris Is Burning* [1990]. I'm wondering if, at the time when you decided to film the Bororo, you had this in mind.

Gardner: I had a dear friend who was married to a Bororo, a beautiful Parisian who told me all about them. I certainly knew that the Bororo were gender provocative. In our culture men can't make up with rouge and lipstick without suggesting certain meanings, but these meanings are not at all the same in Bororo culture. I do think the Bororo are playing with gender, but from what I could learn about them, heterosexual prowess was their object in life. Each man wanted to be a bull and get on with the business of having intercourse with young women. In fact, the young women were required to service the young men.

MacDonald: This past week I was looking at *Altar of Fire* [1976] and *Deep Hearts*, films made right after one another. *Altar* is far more conventional than *Deep Hearts*, in large measure I assume because the Bororo Fulani piqued your imagination more powerfully than the Nambuduri Brahmins— and even though the films are more or less the same length (actually *Altar* is longer), you don't even mention *Altar* in *The Impulse to Preserve*. Could you talk about the differences in these two films as expressions of your interest and commitment?

Gardner: *Altar of Fire* was made at the request of some close friends. It was supposed to be a record of an infrequent ritual. I hated the task and the result. It was a film that could not really be made since the rules of pollution prevented me from being close to the action. I was a pollutant. *Deep Hearts* came about through my long interest in the people of the Niger Sahel.

MacDonald: The Film Study Center produced a number of your own films, as well as films by other filmmakers, including several by Dick Rogers. Once the Film Study Center was at the Carpenter Center, it seems to have become fundamentally a film production organization.

Gardner: That's right. But that is what it was always meant to be. In fact, lately it has been required to spend what I think is too much money and time on other than pure and innovative actuality filmmaking, which was its mission.

MacDonald: You were either the Executive Producer or the Producer on all the films funded by the Carpenter Center. How did that work? Were you the academic version of a Hollywood mogul in the sense that you decided what projects got funded?

Gardner: I'm afraid so. And it worked for a while, though in the end there was an inquiry as to what the Film Study Center *was*. And why it even existed. And who *is* Gardner, and what do he and the people associated with him think they're doing? Making the films *they* want to make?! Not doing peer reviewed scholarly articles?!

It was an enormous investigation, by apparatchiks of the administration coming in and asking questions and putting me on the spot. I told them, "The Film Study Center is something I set up years ago to make good films." "Who's to say they're good films?" "I don't know, I guess the public, the audience. But certainly the attempt is being made to find people who are making good films, and give them a chance to do something." "Is it open to *everybody* on a fair and equal basis?" Finally there was a report. I was never able to see it—although I was promised that I would see it when it was done. Guzzetti was very much involved in that report as a good soldier in the department.

Then a committee was formed to vet all the requests for film production money and to make awards to people. Maybe this was necessary, a way to take power out of the hands of one person and put it in the hands of a group of people who were more representative of the whole constituency of the faculty. And I think they wanted it to be possible for graduate students to get money, and other faculty members too: Ross McElwee has gotten money, as has Robb Moss.

So the Film Study Center comes and it goes, or it comes and changes and keeps going. It has a bunch of money. Scott, a lot of what the Film Study Center did all those years would never have been possible if my investment in Channel 5 had never happened. I mean the only reason I had money was because I was a lucky winner in that improbable event of taking over a television station. Every single thing that I've ever done at Harvard, including your coming here as a visiting professor, was possible because I lucked out and came into serious money, which I immediately began giving away. I felt it wasn't really *my* money; it was the public's money and should be returned to the public in some fashion. Some of that money went to bring guest artists and teachers; some of it went into the Archive's purchase of prints. All of that money got recycled into a variety of enterprises at Harvard. I'm not sure I'd do the same thing again, but I don't think it was badly spent.

MacDonald: Recently, Michael Hutcherson sent me *Nine Forsaken Fragments*, the presentation you did at Bard College last year. I understand that you don't really consider this a finished work.

Gardner: When Peter Hutton invited me to Bard as a tribute to my work, I thought there might be some purpose in at least my looking at, and maybe other people looking at, films that I began and never completed. As you've seen, the individual fragments are quite varied, but they do relate to each other in two ways: one is their focus on the fragility of human beings. All that we have to mitigate our fragility is our culture, our beliefs, our faiths. The other cohering notion is the idea of finding one's way. I've always been interested in people's need to find their way, to try and identify and take the right path; this is a need that has been met by people by doing everything from reading rats' entrails to peering at dried scapulas.

You mentioned Michael Hutcherson, who has become my technological wizard. He made *Nine Forsaken Fragments* possible on the technical side, as well as by providing me with all kinds of good advice.

MacDonald: The first "forsaken fragment," "Tide," reminds me of Flaherty and Vittorio De Seta, and at times of Baillie's *Valentin de las Sierras* [1968], his portrait of a Mexican village.

Gardner: In Nova Scotia I met a fisherman who went to fish "his weir," as they say up there, *in a wagon*. I was interested in the idea of a person who was controlled by the tides and who could find himself in the position of getting lost in a fog and having to escape before the tide got too deep for his horse to pull the wagon. I shot in 35mm, hoping this could be a substantial work, but the man died before I could finish the film.

MacDonald: "It's Stupid" could hardly be more different from "Tide."

Gardner: Christian Boltanski, the subject of that piece, is a remarkable artist, sort of the Marcel Proust of his moment. I found that, at the end of whatever he did or whatever he was talking about, he would say, "It's stupid." Of course he didn't mean it; he's very proud of and committed to what he does, but at the same time, he thinks that, because we're all so frail, our work and our lives are, in some sense, pointless, kind of *stupid*. This film wasn't finished because I just didn't shoot enough at the time; I didn't forsake it so much as decide to wait until I had an opportunity to do something more.

MacDonald: Both "Creatures of Pain" and "Healing" are like filmic companions of journal entries you included in *The Impulse to Preserve*.

Gardner: "Creatures of Pain" is a piece that I salvaged from material shot in Nigeria where I had gone in hopes of doing a completely different project. By the time the original plan fell through, I had heard about this ritual. For a time, I was very interested in the issue of pain, how much humans can give and how much they can bear. I even visited a man in Eau Claire, Wisconsin, who ran a place that dealt with absolutely unbearable pain. Actually, "Creatures of Pain" was the title I originally wanted to use for *Rivers of Sand*, though better heads prevailed.

"Healing" was salvaged from some material that I shot in the town of Lei in Ladakh in 1978, where I had gone in the hope of making a film about a pilgrimage by a Buddhist healer—another project that fell through.

MacDonald: Peter Hutton has told me that you've urged him to make a film in the area where you shot "Salt." Actually, "Salt" reminds me of Hutton's work.

Gardner: In 1968, I wanted to make a film about a journey from the highlands of Ethiopia to the Denakil Depression and then back up to the highlands. I never really got enough material to warrant a full and finished film, but yes, I am doing my best to persuade Peter to make the film I didn't make [Hutton's *Three Landscapes* (2013) includes imagery filmed in the Denakil Depression in 2013].

MacDonald: "Policeman" is quite different from your other work, in both topic and mood.

Gardner: During the years when I was involved with Channel 5 and *Screening Room*, I suggested to the station manager that we do some *non*-commercials. I told him, "We have lots of commercials, but why don't we try having *non*-commercials? That is to say something that lasts just a minute but doesn't sell anything!" I remember the blank stare I got, but in the end I was allowed to make a few. "Policeman" was one which aired, and people must have been very perplexed by it; there were calls to the station, asking, "What was *that*!?"

FIGURE 8 *Gardner's photograph of "the Old Lady."*
Source: Courtesy Robert Gardner.

My plan was to make little films about people doing their jobs; I thought this was something that the average television watcher might be entertained by. I made one of a farmer scything a field, which worked out pretty well, and one of a carpenter sawing some boards, and one of a lobster man taking in a catch. The non-commercials didn't last long. By the way, that policeman was later killed by a car at the very place where I filmed him.

MacDonald: "The Old Lady (AKA A Human Document)" is a film version of your essay, "A Human Document" (figure 8).

Gardner: My film portrait of the Old Lady was the first filming I did after I had left Seattle. While I was in the Kalahari with John Marshall, I got fascinated by the woman. To me, she represented vast age, just extraordinary age and persistence and fragility, all rolled up into one remarkable body. The title "a human document" is probably a little pretentious, but we *are* documents: our faces are documents; our figures are documents; everything about us documents what we've been through and who we've become. And this kind of document is particularly accessible through photography and film.

MacDonald: "Finding the Way" is a triptych about people using different kinds of oracles to find their way. There's the sandal oracle from *Rivers of Sand*

and the bubble oracle from *Ika Hands*, plus your own consulting the *I Ching* with Octavio and Marijo Paz.

Gardner: Paz knew all about the *I Ching*. He had used it with many people, including John Cage. Fulton was also conversant with it.

MacDonald: Fulton is your partner and ultimately the focus of "It Could Be Good It Could Be Bad," the final section of *Nine Forsaken Fragments*.

Gardner: Bob and I had gone to Chile to make aerial shots of glaciers and peaks in the Chilean Andes for a project of his; he was an accomplished aerial filmmaker. This was not a very safe thing for us to be doing in a tiny plane, my first airplane, a little Cessna with one small engine.

This piece has special meaning for me because of Bob, who was perhaps my dearest friend. He was killed in 2002 when he flew into a hellacious storm cell. "It Could Be Good It Could Be Bad," is a tiny tribute to him.

MacDonald: These days, I feel like a Greek underworld character, not exactly Sisyphus, but a person who the older he grows, the more interests he has and the less time there is to explore them.

Gardner: Of course! The more you know, the more questions you have, and the more doors there are to go through.

MacDonald: What are you working on these days?

Gardner: More projects than I can name: writing projects and film projects. I'm trying to make a film I'm calling "Still Journey On"; it will have a lot of endings of my films in it; actually, it will have endings from a lot of films— if I can bring myself to deal with the issues around appropriating work.

Ed Pincus (and Jane Pincus, Lucia Small)

I don't remember precisely when or where I first saw Ed Pincus's *Diaries (1971–1976)* (1980), but I do remember being astonished by the film—by its openness, its honesty—and simultaneously envious and frightened of the open marriage that is the focus of the first half of the film. The willingness of Ed and Jane Pincus to work at rethinking their marriage—and it did seem *work* to do this—was impressive, and the five-year-long experience the film documents seemed full of surprises, both in terms of the personal relationships that are the ostensible focus of the film and in terms of how the footage was shot and edited—though my fascination with the film was so much a function of the melodrama of the Pincuses' personal lives that it was not until much later that I realized that *Diaries* is also a beautiful film, both in its sense of family life and in its inventive sense of composition and subtle editing.

During the decades between my first seeing *Diaries*—I assume on the film's initial release in 1981, in New York City—I wondered about Pincus and the film, which had made something of a splash and then, along with its maker, seemed to disappear. Of course, Pincus's colleagues at MIT, where he had taught since 1968, and his friends and family were aware of what had happened to him; it is one of the stranger episodes in the annals of American cinema.

As Pincus was beginning to consider himself a filmmaker (he was a philosophy student at Brown University, then at Harvard), a neighbor of his in Cambridge, Dennis Sweeney, suggested that he go to Natchez, Mississippi, to film the civil rights struggle going on there; Pincus and his friend David Neuman jumped at the suggestion. As the years went by, Sweeney, who appears in Pincus and Neuman's documentary, *Black Natchez* (1967), became increasingly delusional and by the 1970s was threatening the lives of both the Pincus family and civil rights activist Allard Lowenstein (who had been Sweeney's mentor at Stanford). The Pincuses moved to a mountaintop in rural Vermont where they began a flower-raising business, and Ed struggled to maintain a low profile at MIT and as a filmmaker. On March 14, 1980, Sweeney killed then-US Congressman Lowenstein in his New York office, turned himself into police and was sent to prison. Pincus would not return to filmmaking in earnest for a quarter-century, until he teamed up with Lucia Small in the aftermath of Hurricane Katrina to shoot what became *The Axe in the Attic* (2007). After Pincus was diagnosed with a virulent form of leukemia in 2012, he and Small teamed up to make a second film, about the next phase of Pincus's life and his imminent confrontation of mortality; *One Cut, One Life* was finished in 2013, not long after Pincus's death.

This interview is presented in three parts. The first section, focusing on Pincus's career up through *Diaries (1971–1976)*, began in April of 2009 when Pincus and Small were guests in my history of documentary class at Harvard, and was expanded first in a personal interview session with Pincus and later, online. In October 2010, I interviewed Jane Pincus when she and Ed Pincus presented *Diaries* at Hamilton College. For all the obvious reasons, I wanted to speak with Jane about her role in *Diaries*. When I learned that she had also been involved with a different film, perhaps the first film to deal openly with abortion, I decided to begin our conversation with her participation in that project—she and I refined our conversation online. The final section, my conversation with Ed Pincus and Lucia Small about *The Axe in the Attic*, began during the class visit in April 2009, and was refined online. In the parts of the interview originally recorded during class, I have sometimes indicated when people other than Ed Pincus and I ask questions or make comments.

MacDonald: You were a philosophy major at Harvard. Did that influence your becoming a filmmaker, and in particular, the kind of filmmaker that you are? My sense is that Cambridge's importance in the development of documentary cinema has something to do with the fact that Pragmatism developed here and has had an abiding influence.

Pincus: There is a strong relationship between the work I did in philosophy and my approach to documentary film. As a student, my interest was in epistemology, in theories of constructing knowledge. How do we know? What is the basis of knowledge? But my sympathies were much more with David Hume, than with John Dewey and William James. My sensibility came out of English empiricism, though there were always limits to empiricism, I felt, which is why I was always interested in Kant: like Hume, Kant felt that the world of sensation was the basis of knowledge, but he thought that that sensation was empty without concepts.

Anyway, that move from Hume to Kant pretty much became the arc of my filmmaking. At the beginning, with *Black Natchez*, my interest was more or less in whatever happened in front of the camera; and David Neuman, my filmmaking partner at the time, and I felt that editing should be invisible so that all attention would be on what the camera saw. By *One Step Away* [1968], our film about a hippie family in San Francisco, David and I were critiquing that approach and deciding that while what happens in front of the camera does have primacy, editing should *not* be invisible—though we did continue to do invisible editing within particular sequences. By *One Step Away* we wanted to make clear *in* the film that the film was edited, that what happened in front of the camera was later conceptually constructed by the filmmaker.

Observation of reality can only take you so far. For example, you could watch every baseball game ever played—sandlot, major league baseball, triple A—but no matter how many games you saw, you wouldn't be able to be sure of the rules of baseball just by observation. I came to realize that no matter how careful an observer I was with my camera, more was necessary, and that "more" was a conceptual framework.

MacDonald: How did you go from being a Harvard philosophy student to making *Black Natchez* and how did you and David Neuman get into the middle of the black debates about the civil rights struggle in Mississippi?

Pincus: That's *such* an interesting question. *Black Natchez* was shot during a unique historical moment, a moment when *no* black crew could have had the access we did. A black crew would have had to take a side in the controversy we document; we didn't. In the black community we were looked upon as beneficent apparitions (filming the *white* community was a whole different story!). People just figured we were good people and made us welcome. A year later, or a year earlier, things might have been different.

Just before we decided to do the film, Jane and I were living on the corner of Western and Putnam in Cambridge; diagonally across the Charles River a railroad roundhouse was being torn down and there were all these sculptural forms that I loved to look at. I took out a still camera that I had gotten when I was 13 years old, and hadn't used since, and recorded some of these forms. That got me started (figure 9).

When the Carpenter Center opened, I decided to take a still photography course. Len Gittleman, who was teaching the course, asked if I wanted to be his teaching assistant, and I said sure. I remember Bob Gardner asking me if I was interested in film, and my saying, "Not at all!" But soon after this, I saw the Maysles Brothers' *Showman* [1962], and while I wasn't so taken with the film itself (it was about Joseph Levine, the movie producer), there were moments when the Maysles shot into window light or in some other way that produced flares on the lens and visible grain. I was struck by the tactile qualities of these shots, and I began to think more seriously about film.

I had wanted to go down South and do something in the civil rights move-ment, and had begun to hear stories about how the movement was finished and that all the civil rights workers were burned out and were spending their time in bars. But other people were saying, "No, it's happening now! All these freedom schools are being started." In December of 1964, Dennis Sweeney and J. D. Smith, who lived up above us and who knew I was inter-ested in Mississippi and that I had done a short fiction film based on Camus' short story "The Adulterous Woman," said, "We can raise money to do a film about freedom schools in Mississippi. Will you do it?" I said yes. At the time, J. D. was working for David, who was making sandals in a leather shop in Brattle Square. David was interested in writing scripts, which I wasn't

FIGURE 9 *Ed Pincus, early in his career.*
Source: Courtesy Ed and Jane Pincus.

interested in, but he was about the only person I knew who was interested in film, so I said, "Do you want to do this with me?" He said, "Sure!" In the end, freedom schools played no part in *Black Natchez*.

One of the important ways in which documentary has changed over the years has to do with how it's financed: the cost of starting a documentary in the era of film was exorbitant, but *finishing* a film wasn't that expensive. With the advent of digital shooting, the equation has changed: now, starting a film is very cheap, but finishing—if you outsource it—is more expensive than it was for film. In the end, a digital film costs about the same as an emulsion film.

I felt we needed a good camera, and the best was a camera that you could buy off the shelf, and then have modified by Mitch Bogdonavitch. If you ordered this camera, it was two years before you got it and the cost was exorbitant, something like $16,000, probably $120,000 in today's money. I had a friend who knew John Marshall, who had one of these cameras. My friend introduced me to John, and John said he'd rent the camera to us for a thousand bucks. I asked John for some instruction and he said, "Put it on your shoulder and push the button; you'll do fine." [laughter] That was all the instruction I had. David had about the same amount of instruction for taking sound. We had to figure things out from scratch.

We came back from Mississippi with forty hours of footage—at that time, a lot for this kind of film—and in order to do the editing we had to call up a friend who worked at WGBH and have him come over and show us how to load a Moviola. The fact that we were so inexperienced didn't mean we didn't have very strong ideas about how to make a film—though, of course, a lot of our ideas just exploded in our faces. David and I argued a lot, but got along well both in the field and during the editing.

MacDonald: In early observational films like *Monterey Pop* [1967, by D. A. Pennebaker] and *Hospital* [1969, by Frederick Wiseman], the filmmakers can seem invisible, in part because most of the people they film were involved in their own lives and probably not paying much attention to the filmmakers, but you and David had to be totally visible: northern white boys with a camera in the middle of a southern black social struggle.

Pincus: We gave the process a lot of time. *Panola* [1970], the short film we made from footage we shot while we were shooting *Black Natchez*, includes scenes of kids playing in an alley. Those scenes required us to spend a couple of hours a day for weeks and weeks, until we were no longer the most interesting thing in the alley. Also, we had very laid back personalities; we never said much, and basically people got bored with us.

MacDonald: How long were you in Natchez?

Pincus: A little over two months, I think. A long time in those days for that kind of filming.

MacDonald: Were you hassled by whites?

Pincus: We were. When we first got to Mississippi, we knew hardly any-body. We had rented a house in a black subdivision outside of Natchez, and there was a three-mile stretch of deserted woods between the town and that subdivision. One night we decide to go to this black, fast-food chicken place. We pull up and two minutes later this white cop car pulls in and just sits there watching us. We had no idea what to do. Finally the chicken comes and David says, "Well, let's just get in the car and see what happens." I'm about to get in the car when this black guy in the car next to me says, "Don't worry, I'll follow you home." That was the total conversation. We say thanks and pull out, then this guy's car pulls out, and the cop car pulls out. We get across those three miles back to the apartment without incident, but two days later the black guy shows up and tells us that the cops stopped him and took him to court, where the judge said, "Stop agitatin'" and gave him a small fine, which we paid. But that was the general atmosphere. It was the first time I'd ever been in the United States *not* feeling that the police might afford some protection.

MacDonald: I went to graduate school in northern Florida and the minute you were outside Alachua County, where the University of Florida is, you were in the Deep South. I remember the fear of being a white boy with long hair—in those days that signaled your politics.

Pincus: We wanted to be as invisible as we could, so we arrived with short hair, in white short-sleeved dress shirts and khaki pants. And we had southern license plates. But we didn't have southern accents, and once, when we stopped in Vicksburg to have dinner—David, his girlfriend, and me—we noticed that everybody in the restaurant was looking at us hostilely. David said, "Let's get out of here," and we hopped in the car and sped off. We were followed by some of the people from the restaurant, but they didn't catch us; we were going like a hundred miles an hour.

MacDonald: Are you sure you didn't see this in *Easy Rider* [1969]?

Pincus: [laughter] That *is* the way it was.

MacDonald: In the finished film we see an older approach to dealing with whites that no longer seems to be making any difference—it's represented by Charles Evers; and also a newer approach represented by group of activists who want to take to the streets. James Jackson, who we hear in voice-over, seems to represent a third option: in a back room several men are creating an anti-Klan guerilla group.

Pincus: It was called Deacons for Defense. At the time we thought that the NAACP was giving short shrift to the people on the front lines: basically, women and teenagers who had no representation were doing all the footwork. We saw the black businessmen as trying to emulate white businessmen, and while we felt that they had a totally justified claim to equality, it seemed to us that they were representing *their* interests as bourgeois business people and not the interests of the poorer blacks and the younger blacks. In retrospect

I think the film gives Evers shorter shrift than he deserved—but we were young.

MacDonald: What led to the choice of Jackson as a narrator?

Pincus: We got to know him and really liked him, and we liked his friend Otis. David, who was very mistrustful of the white civil rights workers, romanticized James and Otis, saw them as the future of the movement.

We would have preferred not to have a voice-over, but we wanted the film to have a viewpoint that was neutral between the young turks and women on one side and the tax-paying black bourgeoisie men on the other side. Jackson's voice-over was a compromise—as you've said, a third option.

We had our point of view, and we thought that our brand of observational cinema was strong enough to allow viewers to see what we saw and either disagree or agree with us. What we weren't going to do was to curb the truth to support our particular viewpoint.

MacDonald: One black woman, who seems to be the NAACP secretary, is very eloquent in dressing down the businessmen about not representing the entire community.

Pincus: If you look at the film again, notice how the women in the film gesticulate: the black women were powerful both within the black community—they led households—but also by virtue of working for white people and *knowing* white people in a way the men didn't. As nannies, for example, the women had a certain amount of power and as a result weren't as constrained within space as the men were. This wasn't in the forefront of our consciousness as we shot; we realized it in the editing room.

Black Natchez premiered at the New York Film Festival. There was a large, predominantly black crowd. In fact, the theater was so crowded that we sat outside during the screening. The audience seemed to see a lot of comedy in the film. *We* knew there was comedy and were happy that the audience was getting it, but the subsequent response to *us* was a surprise.

By the time of the New York Film Festival, we had just finished shooting *One Step Away* and at the *Black Natchez* premiere we looked like hippies in tweed suits. Anyway, when we walked out onto the stage for the Q & A, a gasp went through the audience; I guess they'd been sure we were a black crew because it was clear that we'd had such intimate access to the black community. The hostility in the room was thick, and a lot of people walked out.

This was a time of retrenchment for the black movement. On one hand, there was the tradition of Martin Luther King, and, on the other, Malcolm X (in fact, *Black Natchez* was premiered with a short about Betty Shabazz). But there were new developments too. Stokely Carmichael had proclaimed "Black Power," and whites had gotten excluded from SNCC [Student Nonviolent Coordinating Committee]; there was obviously a feeling of betrayal on the part of the black community and maybe that was reflected in our audience that night.

Black Natchez turned out to be quite controversial. We had taken a chance by calling the film "*Black* Natchez"; "black" was still kind of a dangerous word. The NAACP threatened to sue when the film showed on *NET Journal*, the closest thing then to public television. The film shows clear class differences that are reflected in the kinds of action people were willing to take, and at that moment a lot of black activists didn't want to show divisions within the black community: under the umbrella of Black Power, you weren't supposed to say there were differences.

Also, *Black Natchez* does not confirm the civil rights workers' view of the efficacy of nonviolence. Patrick Moynihan saw the film and said, "Aren't you afraid that the movie will create a Sinn Féin?" The film did become very popular in what was called the "Kitchen Cabinet," and if Bobby Kennedy had lived, we would probably have been able to do the series of films about community organizers that his people had proposed to us.

I did have one wonderful experience with feedback. I was taking a cab from LaGuardia to Manhattan the day after *Black Natchez* played on NET. Feeling expansive, I was talking to the cab driver, who had been in the merchant marine, wondering out loud if there was a *film* to be made about the merchant marine. The driver stops at a traffic light, turns around and says, "Sonny, I have to tell you about this great film I saw last night. It involved drama and politics and conflict," and goes on to describe *Black Natchez*, telling me I should do a film like *that*, not something on the merchant marine. I couldn't wait to tell him *I'd* done that film, but when I told him, he couldn't have cared less: for him films didn't have makers; they just happened.

MacDonald: In the interview you did years ago with G. Roy Levin [*Documentary Explorations* (New York: Doubleday, 1971), 329–371], you talk in some detail about *One Step Away*, but Levin's book is out of print, so I want to come back to that film.

What's interesting to me at the moment, since I've just been studying *Diaries*, is the parallel between *your* satirically documenting the hippie lifestyle and what you reveal about your own life in *Diaries*. The folks in *One Step Away* are a little scary—letting the baby inhale smoke from a joint seems outrageous now—but your and Jane's open marriage in *Diaries* strikes my current students as pretty scary, too.

Pincus: David and I did think the lifestyle in *One Step Away* was scary, but not as scary as people would later make out. At that time in straight culture nursing mothers would drink beer to put their babies to sleep, so Leslie's blowing smoke from her joint into her baby's face may seem more outrageous than it was.

For us, *One Step Away* was a bit like a Beckett novel. The first line of *Murphy* is "The sun shone, having no alternative, on the nothing new." That's what we came to feel about hippie culture, that it wasn't a change in the relationships between men and women and between people in general; rather, it was a somewhat grotesque exaggeration of conventional relationships. If we had realized this at the beginning, we might not have done the film. At the beginning we thought that there really was something new there. The finished film has the feel of the disappointed lover.

MacDonald: The sardonic intertitles communicate that.

I assume you went to a commune with the idea that you'd be there for a while.

Pincus: Yes.

MacDonald: But the commune came apart as you arrived?

Pincus: That's right. I remember David describing to Harry, the commune leader, the level of access we wanted. David says, "Of course, we don't want to film you shitting or anything like that," and Harry says, "Why not?!" and launches into this whole Norman O. Brown theory. Remember Brown's *Love's Body*?—it's about how American cultural habits are created in the privacy of the bathroom.

Harry saw *Black Natchez* and understood exactly what we were interested in, and he gave us total access to everything. The result was a wonderful confluence between observational cinema and the ideology of no privacy. Actually, we did a wonderful film which has never been released, called *Harry's Trip* [1969], which creates exactly that confluence. Basically, we put Harry in a room by himself, turned the camera on, and went and had coffee. The result is sort of like Beckett's *Krapp's Last Tape*.

The big thing about hippies, from an ideological point of view, was their belief that we were living in a postindustrial society, where nobody should have to work. This was totally different from the world I believed in and was used to, and that you see in *Diaries*.

MacDonald: The similarity I see is in the openness of the relationships.

Pincus: There's been a total change of consciousness since the Fifties. During the Fifties, it was radical to say that everything was about sex. Now, everybody assumes that everything *is* about sex. That's a big change. And, of course, it turns out not to be true!

By the way, you should know that, so far as I know, before *One Step Away*, nobody had ever done this kind of film in color. We weren't sure you *could* do it in color. You could do *Monterey Pop* in color. But to film interiors in color was new.

One Step Away was done with money from PBL [the Public Broadcast Laboratory], a precursor of PBS. The story goes that Fred Friendly was at CBS and wanted to broadcast Kennedy's testimony before the Foreign Relations Committee and instead, CBS put on a re-run of an *I Love Lucy* show. Friendly was infuriated, went to the Ford Foundation and got money to start an alternative network, the Public Broadcast Laboratory.

In 1967, when we finished *One Step Away*, television was ideologically not too far out of the Fifties, when you couldn't say the word "pregnant" on air.

So there were a lot of battles around *One Step Away*. David and I showed the film to the executive board at PBL, and they *loved* it. They said things like, "This is really gonna turn this network around," and "I want to show this to my wife and children!" We walk out of the meeting on cloud nine, and then start hearing other things: the executive of the studio, who I think had come to PBL from the sports section of ABC, is feeling queasy about the film. Then, when we're in an office negotiating to do another film for PBL, *Portrait of a McCarthy Supporter* [1968], David sees a notebook on this executive's desk and it's the script of *One Step Away* intercut with commentary by two sociologists, probably the only two sociologists in the country who love hippies, and they *hate* our film. We hit the ceiling.

Soon after this, there was some kind of collapse at PBL, and LBJ appointed a new guy to head it up. Somebody at the network showed this new guy *One Step Away*, and he said, "This is the best film I've ever seen!" (apparently somebody else said, "It's the *first* film you've ever seen!"). Anyway, we'd bought back the rights to the film, and when we reopened negotiations, we had to deal with a lawyer who absolutely hated it. He said that during *One Step Away* ninety-eight felonies were committed and to make matters worse, the filmmakers had not reported these felonies to the police. The film was never shown on television. Later, Leacock/Pennebaker did some theatrical distribution.

We were offered money to shoot *One Step Away* in 35mm. This would have meant much heavier, more cumbersome equipment and more than likely, theatrical distribution. We talked about renting a house and using hidden cameras to catch what Harry and the others did, but finally decided the idea was too disgusting: We were imagining reality TV!

David had wanted to do a film on Woodstock. He had raised half the money, and the rights to film there were open until a few weeks before the concert. I told David, "It'll never make money." Later, when *Woodstock* [1970] was a big hit, David said, "Aha! See, it made *a lot* of money!" and I said, "Yeah, that's because Wadleigh shot the *performers*." What *we* would have done was shoot the pig farm and the people attending the concert; Jimmy Hendricks would have been this little figure you could barely see, like Icarus in Pieter Brueghel's *Landscape with the Fall of Icarus* [c. 1558]. Neither of us had a talent for making the kinds of films that make money.

MacDonald: Tell me about how MIT decided to have a "Film Section." Were you the first hire?

Pincus: I was, yes. It's the Sixties, 1966, 1967, and film is in the air. A group of Humanities teachers at MIT, Lefties who were really interested in film, saw *Black Natchez* and said, "Let's start a film section." There was some resistance from the administration, but in the end, I was hired: my first appointment was half in Humanities and half in Architecture.

MacDonald: Kind of a strange mix.

Pincus: Yes, Jerry Wiesner [then president of MIT] thought that engineers and scientists could relate to spatial arts. He had already brought Minor White to MIT, and Wiesner thought that film would also fit. Eventually my appointment was just in Architecture, not in Humanities.

It turned out that MIT liked what I was doing. They rented my editing studio in Central Square and students found their way over there. The very first undergraduate class I taught at MIT included Terry Malick, the art critic Rosalind Krauss, and Judith Wexler, the art historian. An amazing group.

Then Wiesner decided that they would expand the department, so a series of people gave lectures and for various reasons Ricky Leacock was chosen.

MacDonald: Can you say the reasons?

Pincus: We all liked Ricky and his films, but I think the real reason was that Ricky had worked for Wiesner and Jerrold Zacharias doing educational films about physics. I suspect his appointment was pre-decided, and they just waited for me and some other people to fall in line.

Of course, Ricky was a key cameraman in the development of cinema-verite, but he wasn't much of a teacher. He was usually in a crisis in his life. David Neuman told me that one time he asked Ricky, "What do you do at MIT?" and Ricky said, "I come in with a list of my girlfriends and I start at the top and work down the list."

But he became the face of the department and attended all the faculty meetings. I was *so* grateful; I *hated* the faculty meetings. Ricky worshipped physics and physicists and he wanted them to love film, so he worked very hard to keep us legitimate in MIT's eyes.

This was the time of the anti-war demonstrations at MIT, and Wiesner had this idea that cinema-verite film could bring about a reconciliation between the faculty and the radical students, so he gets Ricky to film the faculty and he wants me to film the student movement. I bridled at this, which caused a certain amount of friction. Ricky did film the faculty meetings, but as far as I know never did anything with what he shot.

As things worked out, Ricky's being at MIT gave me protection to do what I wanted, and I've always been grateful for that.

One of Ricky's major projects was designing a sync-sound Super-8mm camera rig that would be cheap and easy for people to use. What he was trying for became available with the digital camcorder. For me the major problems with film were not technical, so we disagreed there, but basically we agreed not to argue about our differences.

We had *incredibly* talented students and MIT was a wonderful place to study filmmaking. If you were interested in doing a film, we would give you all the support we could, even if you had no institutional affiliation. I've never encountered another place like this in my life. Of course, we thought it would last forever, but it was part of that moment in the early Seventies when so many things seemed possible.

Once we had developed the program fully enough to have graduate students, we had Ross McElwee and Robb Moss, Jeff Kreines and Joel DeMott—lots of good people: Ann Schaetzel, Carolyn Schwartz, Claude Chelli, Michel Negroponte. I can't remember them all.

MacDonald: Who else taught with you at MIT?

Pincus: Over the years there was John Terry, Ann McIntosh, Gloriana Davenport, and others I'm not remembering.

I also taught at Harvard from 1980 to 1983 and I remember one class of twelve people, eleven of whom became serious filmmakers. Pretty amazing. The class divided into the good guys and the bad guys. The good guys made a film about workers on the night shift; the bad guys did a film about spring break.

The spring break class had nine days to shoot, and Marco Williams, who was my teaching assistant, went down with them to oversee the shooting. After three days, I called to see what was happening, and Marco says, "We haven't shot anything yet"; they were waiting for a wet T-shirt contest! I thought, "This is not okay," and flew down. What a *weird* scene; there was nobody over thirty; everything was about cigarettes, beer, and sex, but nobody was actually making it. You'd walk along the beach and there would be groups of males and groups of females. Rooms would have twelve people in them. I remember yelling at the film students—I almost never yell—and giving them twenty suggestions about what they could film, but they came out with a mediocre film, which one of them parleyed into a job at MTV; another bad guy went to work for *Hustler*; and another did a movie called *Joe's Apartment* which caused a bidding war between two studios. If I remember the story right, it was about a guy who moves into an apartment in New York City where there are singing cockroaches!

In those days there was a lot of interest in filmmaking at both MIT and Harvard, and lots of go-getters, but most of them weren't interested in the kinds of filmmaking that mattered to me.

MacDonald: *Diaries (1971–1976)* is your magnum opus, not just in the sense that it's your longest film, but because of the nature of the project. I was surprised to learn that in setting out to make *Diaries*, you gave yourself five years to shoot and five years to edit.

Pincus: The deal I made with all my subjects was that I would be filming for five years and then would wait five years more before releasing a finished film. "Magnum opus"—that's exactly what it was. It was meant to be epic, though in retrospect, I wish the result could have been epic in *under* two hours!

MacDonald: It's not that much of a stretch to watch the film.

Pincus: You're older so you're part of a generation that's more patient, but the three-plus-hour length limited theatrical distribution; *Diaries* was a tough film to sell.

MacDonald: Did you in fact shoot for the five years and edit from 1976 to 1980?

Pincus: No. The footage sat in the can for four or five years. The editing wasn't that difficult. Recently, the Pompidou Center in Paris did a show on early cinema-verite, which ended with *Diaries*. I told them I thought that the film was finished in 1981, and they said, "No, it says 1980 on the film, and it's important for us that it *be* 1980." So I said, okay. But I'm not sure—I think actually it was finished in 1981.

MacDonald: You must have looked at the material as you shot it, just to see what you had.

Pincus: Steve Ascher did the syncing up. I'd ask if the exposure was okay and that's about it.

MacDonald: I sometimes play a trick on my class in history of documentary the first night of the course by showing *David Holzman's Diary* [1967]. Though the McBride film is a fiction, the character of David Holzman is, in a general way, quite close to your persona in *Diaries*. Like you, David wants to use filmmaking as a way to understand his personal life. I was surprised to see that Jim McBride actually has a credit on *Diaries* and appears in the film. Did you know him, and did his film have any influence on *Diaries*?

Pincus: So far as I remember, *David Holzman's Diary* didn't have any influence on me. Jim was a friend of David's. [John Terry, Pincus's colleague at MIT in the late 1960s and early 1970s, remembers a screening of *David Holzman's Diary* in Pincus's studio when it was serving as the meeting space for the Film Section, and that he and Pincus much admired the film.]

MacDonald: *Diaries* chronicles your marriage with Jane (figure 10). How long had you been married when you started *Diaries*?

Pincus: We were married in 1960, and I started *Diaries* in 1971, so it was eleven years—but it felt like six thousand!

MacDonald: Whose idea was the open marriage, and does what we see in the film accurately represent its trajectory?

Pincus: The notion that no one person could fulfill another's needs (whatever that meant) was in the air. Most of our friends split up—we stayed together.

MacDonald: Were you in fact the first to have an affair—it seems as if this is the case in the film?

Pincus: No.

MacDonald: And did Jane's involvement with the Our Bodies Ourselves collective play into the open marriage?

Pincus: I don't think so, but sometimes I think a better title for *Diaries* would have been "What Happened When the Winds of the Women's Movement Blew Open My Front Door." Especially at the beginning I wanted to film what Jane was doing with the Our Bodies Ourselves collective, but they said, "No way!" Now they all regret it.

In the early years of cinema-verite, because of the expense of putting a crew out in the field, films had to be shot in a week or two; a month was a long

FIGURE 10   *Ed and Jane Pincus during the filming of* Diaries *(1971–1976 (1980).*
Source: Photo by Edna Katz. Courtesy Ed and Jane Pincus.

time. So when something meaningful happened during a shoot, the filmmakers would feel the equivalent of "gotcha!" That kind of shooting could not create my vision of how people change or try to change. A very important part of the *Diaries* project was my wanting to see what changes happened over a five-year period in people's lives, in the tenor of their politics, and perhaps in the way a filmmaker shoots.

MacDonald: In a way *Diaries* is a film about Jane. The opening is her talking about how she feels manipulated by the camera and is afraid of how the camera will reveal her. By the end of *Diaries* she's grown accustomed to the camera, and all the distractions from earlier in the marriage seem to have faded. The film charts the emergence, or re-emergence I guess, since it starts eleven years into the marriage, of your respect for Jane and for your relationship.

Pincus: You're correct. *Diaries* is really a love story.

The film was meant to be uncompromising, but it did have small compromises. The structuring you've described wasn't entirely true to the rushes. I made Jane the heroine in the film, and I made myself the villain, though "villain" is a bit of an exaggeration. Let's say I prettied Jane up a bit to make this distinction work. That's the most serious distortion in the film—and it's not *that* serious. If you looked at the unedited rushes, I think I would have come off a little better and Jane would have come off a little worse. Not a whole lot.

I thought it was important to get *Diaries* down to a single sitting. The last time I looked at it, I thought I could probably cut twenty minutes, maybe thirty. But I do love the different pacings in the film; they embody the way time changes and the way different episodes of your life go quickly or slowly. The film becomes about memory too and how sometimes you have intense memories about something and then blanks, then semi-intense memories, and so on. To shorten the film definitely would be to give up something.

MacDonald: Have Sami and Ben watched the movie? Have their reactions evolved over time?

Pincus: A wonderful question. Sami has a hard time with the movie, and I don't really know why. When Ben went off to college, one of his college chums said, "How does it feel to be in one of the most important movies ever made?" [laughter] I think that predisposed him to like *Diaries*. I think he still likes it. His wife looked at the first forty-five minutes, cried, and didn't want to see anymore.

You see the seeds of Sami's reaction to the film *in* the film; you almost never see her except when she's performing. In some sense she always wanted to be in control of how she appeared. Ben didn't care.

MacDonald: Sami has a poignant scene at the end, where she tries her hand at conflict resolution when Ben is upset. She tells you to quit filming him because it makes him worse.

Pincus: That's one of my favorite parts of the film.

MacDonald: Did the presence of the camera affect you? Did you feel that documenting your experiences changed the way *you* dealt with things?

Pincus: Well, I was hoping it wouldn't. When I began, I didn't think I was going to be in the film at all—what a naïve thought *that* was!

To put some of this in historical perspective, the women's movement had come and there was this notion that the personal is the political, and there was also this feeling that you shouldn't be filming the Other. It was important to examine your *own* life. Also, previous to the women's movement, there was a branch of SDS, the Weathermen, whose slogan was "The pig is in us." We were supposed to look inside.

So all of a sudden I found I had to be a subject. Up until *Diaries*, I had never *talked* while I filmed, and I had to start talking. Ideally you learn to work with the camera in such a way that it becomes part of you. You have good days, you have bad days, but on a good day you're not thinking of color balance or whatever, you just *do* stuff. For this film I had to use that ability *and* be able to talk as a human being and interact with my friends while filming. That was a struggle. At the beginning of *Diaries* you can hear a kind of strangeness in my voice that later disappears (you wouldn't pick it up if you didn't know me, but I can hear the changes).

I didn't think at all about a finished film while I was shooting; the shooting itself *was* the experiment. At the beginning filming was easy, then it became a burden. There's a section called "Small Events of Days at Home" in which I make a commitment to shoot something for thirty days in a row. I think half of what's in that section was shot at 11:59 at night, because I'd forget to shoot or couldn't find anything I wanted to shoot.

It may seem that I was shooting all the time, but in fact there was relatively little footage shot for *Diaries*. In five years I shot something like thirty-two hours; for *The Axe in the Attic* Lucia [Small] and I shot 180 hours in sixty days.

When I edited *Diaries*, I was trying to hold onto the feeling of rushes, of dailies, of unedited footage, while shortening the film. In the end I thought that I *was* true to the footage, not that the viewer cares about that, but it mattered to me.

Amazing things happen in the editing room when you look at rushes, things that couldn't have been preconceived, natural juxtapositions that end up having meaning. Of course, it's in the nature of human consciousness to see connections and there are many amazing connections in *Diaries* that are *totally* happenstance.

MacDonald: You found a way to have a voice in the film without being a conventional narrator, in two different ways. One is that you periodically say something, usually as a transition from one sequence to the next or as a set-up for the passage that follows. And in other instances you use text, which we first see in *One Step Away*. Had you seen Jonas Mekas's diary films? He found intertitles very useful.

Pincus: I might have seen his diaries, but Godard was probably the influence on my use of text. In *One Step Away* David and I wanted to structure the film as a series of anecdotes. And we thought titles were the perfect way to do that. In *Diaries* the chapter titles are meant to be a fun way of distancing the intimacy a bit. That's the way I saw Godard using titles: as a distancing device.

I think it's in Rousseau's letter to D'Alembert, where he talks about how the problem with art is that people go to the theater and feel all the right emotions, and then they go home and they're the same old sons of bitches they've always been. To me that's always been the dominating question for me in documentary on social and personal issues: how do you close the gap between what you feel in the theater and what you do when you've left the theater? Godard tried to cope with that gap through the use of titles, and by having people talk to the camera.

Have you ever seen Lucia's film, *My Father the Genius* [2002]? The first time I saw it, I told her, "You used everything but the kitchen sink." Lucia says I said it sarcastically, and maybe I did. In my films I was always trying for a kind of purism; I was trying to get by with as little as possible, but after *One Step Away* text did become at least a minimal part of my vocabulary.

MacDonald: *Diaries* is a beautiful film; the shots near the end of your family in Vermont during the winter are stunning. You seem to always have had great confidence in your shooting.

Pincus: Thank you. But when you say I have confidence in my shooting, it's really more that I have confidence *in the world*. I trust that if I'm prepared and have good equipment, the world will provide me with something interesting to record and something good to look at.

MacDonald: During the five years when you were shooting what ended up being *Diaries*, was that the only shooting you were doing? And did you always know when you were shooting for that film?

Pincus: Well, definitely I always knew when I was shooting for *Diaries*. I shot and edited *Life and Other Anxieties* [1977] between the end of shooting *Diaries* and beginning the editing. And I'm sure I must have done some pick up shooting, though I've never done much camera for hire.

MacDonald: It's interesting that you edited *Diaries* after *Life and Other Anxieties*, since *Life* loops back and picks up where *Diaries* ends, with David Hancock's illness and death. Then it seems to revisit the first section of Jean Rouch's *Chronicle of a Summer* [*Chronique d'un été*; 1961].

Pincus: That's interesting, I'd never thought of *Life* as Rouch-ian. Where he's on the streets asking people if they're happy, we ask what aspects of their lives people want us to shoot.

MacDonald: What instigated *Life and Other Anxieties*?

Pincus: I spent a semester as a visiting filmmaker teaching in Minneapolis, and the next year, they asked, "How would you like to come back and shoot a film in Minneapolis, any film you want." I'd never gotten an offer like this before. When PBL wanted us to do a film, we had to pitch the film; and to do *Diaries* I had to write applications for grants (I don't want to make a big thing of it; they were one-page proposals), but here was a film I didn't have to pitch or write proposals for. I decided to do a film about nothing and everything, to see how far you could get with that.

I didn't even think about doing the film by myself; I asked Steve Ascher if he wanted to work with me and he said yes. He and his wife Jeanne Jordan are very good filmmakers. They did *Troublesome Creek: A Midwestern* [1995], about Jeanne's farm family, and more recently, a film about ALS, Lou Gehrig's disease [*So Much So Fast*, 2007]. Steve was already a very good filmmaker back then.

MacDonald: Was all the material about David Hancock's dying and funeral shot with the idea that it would be part of *Diaries*?

Pincus: Yes. David was younger than me and the *healthiest guy*. All of a sudden he had terminal cancer and it was shocking. He wanted me to do a film about what was happening to him, but I was shooting *Diaries* and told him I couldn't also do a film entirely about him. But I tried a few times, so there's a little bit about David in *Diaries*. Then, when I was shooting *Life* in Minneapolis—and thinking what the fuck am I doing in Minneapolis!?—I realized that that's where David grew up. And there I was, going around, asking people what part of their lives they wanted me to film, just what I *wasn't* able to do for David. In retrospect, *Life* seems, on one hand, a form of expiation, and on the other, a response to mortality.

MacDonald: Often *Life* seems like two filmmakers in search of a subject—in the dead of winter.

Pincus: Not just winter—*Minnesota* winter. There was a stretch of twelve days when the temperature never went above minus 20°. It does get to be minus 20° in Vermont, but just for a couple of hours during a whole winter.

MacDonald: Was the film an equal collaboration?

Pincus: I think I did all the shooting; if I didn't do it all, I did ninety-five percent. Steve and I edited *Life* co-equally.

MacDonald: Between 1981 and 2005, so far as I know, you didn't make a film. Why did you disappear from filmmaking for so long?

Pincus: Well, part of the story is in *Diaries*. Basically, Dennis Sweeney, who I knew during my *Black Natchez* days, had begun to threaten my life, Jane's life, and my son's life. Dennis had become delusional, paranoid, and dangerous. To do the kind of film I was doing, you had to make personal appearances and that put my family at risk. Once Dennis began to threaten us, we made a permanent move to Vermont in order to hide from him. We de-listed our telephone number and told everybody not to tell anyone where we were. A psychologist who had seen Dennis suggested that I use a different route to work every day (I was still teaching at MIT, but commuting from Vermont) and that I avoid being alone. Basically I created the life of a paranoid—for six years.

Dennis was not only stalking us, but other people, including the civil rights and anti-war lawyer Allard Lowenstein, who Dennis shot and killed in 1980. Afterward, Dennis was put away in a mental institution. [Found not guilty by reason of insanity, Sweeney served eight years in the Mid-Hudson Psychiatric Center, New York State's maximum security mental hospital, and later was moved to a lower security facility; he was released from custody in 2000.]

Though Dennis was the main reason why I stopped making films, there were other reasons. *Diaries* took a lot out of me, and it accomplished everything I wanted to do in film at that time, especially in seeing how far you could go with observational cinema when you had good access to the people you filmed over a long period—and what the limitations were.

But since these people were my family and friends, *Diaries* revealed a great deal about all of us. Believe it or not I'm a very private person. In order to make the film, I had told myself a little fib: that after ten years I wouldn't care what was revealed in the footage. I expected to be pilloried for having done the film, but in fact, the press reaction was incredibly favorable. I was totally surprised, and pleased on one hand, but it was also very difficult for me, and still is, to be so visible. Lucia recently reminded me that when I showed *Diaries* at a film festival a year ago, ten minutes in, I turned to her and said, "I'm so embarrassed! Let's get out of here!"

MacDonald: What is it that embarrasses you?

Pincus: I have a mescaline trip at Jim McBride's house [laughter]. It has its function in the film, but it's embarrassing. So many things in the film embarrass me that it's pointless to try and name them all.

You know, I did feel privileged to make *Diaries*. I had a teaching job and didn't have to worry about income; I got a series of grants; I didn't have to release the film for ten years. At the time, I was committed to the idea that part of the payback was that I had to be absolutely honest in the film. That was what I owed society for allowing me the rare privilege of ten years of not having to finish anything.

Actually, your pointing out earlier that the film is beautiful—*that's* really what I cared most about. *Diaries* was meant to be beautiful, in a tactile sense, and that's why I've never wanted to show it on television. It was always meant for large-screen projection.

Dominique Bluher: I have a twofold question. First, to my knowledge *Diaries* is one of the very first personal documentaries, and it has given birth to many others, not just in Cambridge, but all over the world. Second, is there any connection between this documentary approach and the experimental film approach to the personal that developed a little bit earlier?
Pincus: Well, at the time that I made *Diaries*, there was zero conscious connection. Looking back, there was this notion of the camera stylo and the idea of the filmmaker as a kind of creator; that certainly was shared. But to me the possibility of capturing life had to do with sound, and most of those early experimental filmmakers, what used to be called the New York Underground, made silent films.

I remember getting into a big argument with Stan Brakhage at a conference on autobiographical film that Gerry O'Grady organized in Buffalo [in March, 1973]—an interesting event. Robert Frank was there and a group of New York experimental filmmakers. I felt totally out of place. Brakhage had said, "Everything you see on the screen is exactly what happened"—I think he was talking about *Scenes from Under Childhood* [1967–1970]. I argued that understanding the world has to do with other senses, and in particular sound.

Granted, most of the things that people say are stupid. During the editing of *Diaries*, I would think, "God, did *I* really say *that*? Did *she* really say *that*?" But stupid or not, what we say is an essential part of who we are, and to pretend that you're capturing reality in a silent film is a fantasy.

The development of personal documentary had to do with technology. Éclair had come out with a new camera that was relatively small—it weighed ten pounds rather than eighteen pounds—and just as important, there was this little tape recorder (the Nagra SN) that you could fit into a pocket or a purse. I had Stuart Cody design a wireless connection so I could turn the tape recorder on and off from the camera. Without this equipment, I couldn't have done *Diaries*. When the possibility of shooting intimately and making a film that looked *and* sounded good arrived, so did the option of making *Diaries*.

Lucia Small: Also, there was the practical issue of your leaving home for long stretches of time to make films. You and Jane were both artists, and you had to deal with the inevitable power struggles about who would be available to take care of the kids. All of that fed into your deciding to make a documentary about your personal life.

Pincus: Definitely.

MacDonald: During the years just after you finished *Diaries*, you weren't making films, but you (and Steve Ascher) did make an important contribution to cinema in 1984, with the publication of *The Filmmaker's Handbook*. Your films are remarkably unpretentious. Indeed, it's easy to forget, when watching *Diaries* or *Life and Other Anxieties* that you were a distinguished and well-known academic. But when one looks through *The Filmmaker's Handbook*, it's obvious that your knowledge of filmmaking was/is remarkable. Could you talk a bit about how that book evolved? Along with Lenny Lipton's *Independent Filmmaking* [Simon and Schuster, 1983], it became the canonical filmmaker self-help book in English.

Pincus: In 1967, I wrote *Guide to Filmmaking*, published in 1968 by Simon & Schuster as a mass market paperback. This was the first technical book to deal with the new filmmaking technology. It eventually became the basis of the first edition of *The Filmmaker's Handbook* that Steve and I co-wrote. Subsequent editions have been written by Steve without my help.

MacDonald: One of the things that I've seen happening in documentary in the last few years, or at least in people's writing about documentary, is that the distinction between documentary and avant-garde film has been disappearing.

Pincus: I think of some of my documentaries as experimental films. In fact, experimentation has been more important to me than any traditional sense of documentary. When I was growing up, the practical function of documentary was to interrupt the boredom of public school, but the documentaries we saw in school created another kind of boredom. I *hated* those documentaries, and even once I was older, it didn't seem to me that some of the famous documentaries were from life. Even in *The Plow that Broke the Plains* [1936] there seemed little connection between what you saw and heard and people's real lives. WPA photography was much more influential on my thinking and my films than the 1930s documentaries. Even though some of the same people who did those documentaries were WPA photographers, there seemed to be a difference in how they were imaging life in photographs and how their imagery was used in the films.

Ricky used to love to quote a line from Jean Renoir about the change in film brought about by sync-sound shooting: Renoir said that traditionally the camera has been this altar that you had to bring reality to; and now all of a sudden, you had a camera that could go into reality itself. I thought that was a perfect metaphor. All of a sudden in the Sixties there was a possibility of providing people with information about what was happening in real lives. Novelists use their real experiences when they write novels; why couldn't film have that same sort of grounding? A series of technological innovations—light-weight cameras, sync sound, and so forth—made something new, and *not* boring, possible.

Jane Pincus, on *Abortion* and *Diaries (1971–1976)*

MacDonald: You were a founding member of the Our Bodies Ourselves collective, which did important feminist political work. Could you talk about your early involvement in political issues?

Pincus: Let's see, I had my daughter in 1965; my son, in March of 1969, and in between those years Ed and I were doing civil rights work, I think with CORE [Congress of Racial Equality]. We'd go and look at an apartment and then a black couple would go to visit that apartment—to test whether the landlords discriminated. We did that a few times, and we marched against the Vietnam War, and I was involved in a rudimentary kind of draft counseling for young men who didn't want to go to Vietnam. In general Ed and I were in amongst people doing political work.

And women were getting together to talk about themselves—it was in the air. Around 1969 I became involved with two groups. One was what I thought of as my personal group; the other was "The Doctors Group," which held huge meetings of women at MIT. A number of us had had babies or other experiences with medical care, and we wanted to understand the care we were getting. At some of the gatherings at MIT, we'd hand out a questionnaire, and we learned that we knew more about ourselves than we thought—often, we knew more about ourselves than our doctors did! During May of 1969 there was a women's conference that included a workshop called "Control of Our Bodies." A fairly large group of women who attended that workshop decided to meet in the fall to talk further about our experiences. I wrote down what I knew about pregnancy, and if a woman had had an abortion, she wrote her experiences down. We'd meet and ask each other questions; and then in January of 1970 we offered what we called a course, at MIT. The first session was on sexuality and about fifty women attended. Many had never even heard sexual words—"masturbation," "clitoris"—spoken aloud before.

Of course, this kind of thing was happening all over the country, not just in Boston.

MacDonald: How did you happen to be meeting at MIT?

Pincus: A number of us had husbands who were professors at MIT; that was our entrée into the male bastion.

There were two women attending our course who worked at the New England Free Press, a radical press in Boston; they decided the information we were gathering should be expanded and given to lots of other women, though it took them awhile to convince the *men* at the Free Press that this *was* a political issue. We got our information together, wrote it and rewrote it, and that turned into *Women and Their Bodies*, which was published by the Free Press in 1970.

Our group incorporated in 1971, as the Boston Women's Health Book Collective, and that's when I started to work on the re-write, which became the 1973 Simon and Schuster edition of *Our Bodies, Ourselves*.

MacDonald: Ed mentioned to me that he wanted to film the collective for *Diaries*, but wasn't allowed to.

Pincus: Nobody wanted to be filmed by a man at that point. And it's too bad. That was a huge part of my life and it's not included in *Diaries*. I regret that.

MacDonald: During this time you also helped to make *Abortion*. How did that project get started?

Pincus: I'll never forget listening to the radio as men in the Massachusetts Legislature talked about abortion! They had *no* understanding of what women go through. I can't remember the details, but I was shocked, and some of us demonstrated at the Legislature in favor of choice—abortions were illegal then. During 1970–71, I made the abortion film with Catha Maslow, Mary Summers, and Karen Weinstein. We were the third group of women to get together to make a film about abortion and the first group to finish one. We were able to use the MIT Bolexes to make our film; we sent our footage out with the MIT student films to be processed, and we used the MIT editing equipment to finish the film.

MacDonald: How widely did *Abortion* get seen?

Pincus: Not very. When we gave it to the Newsreel people to distribute, they didn't believe it was politically important. And we ourselves didn't really promote the film. I do remember showing an early version to a large group of people in the MIT screening room.

MacDonald: Did all four of you work on every aspect of the film, or did you each take responsibility for a particular part of the process?

Pincus: We divided the work. We were an interesting group because politically we ran the gamut and we had different ideas of what a film should be. There was Catha who was heavily involved with aesthetics; I was kind of aesthetic/political; Mary Summers belonged to the Socialist Workers Party and was living in a commune; and the most dogmatically political of us was Karen Weinstein, who worked and lived in the Newsreel commune. I have a journal of our working on the film—I keep diaries, journals—in which I talked about the process in three parts. The first part is about me in relation to the film; the second, about the four of us and how well or badly we were working together;

and the third, about the content of the film itself, as we imagined it, shot it, changed things around, and subsequently evaluated the process and project.

Many issues arose as we worked together. Our names aren't on the film. Catha Maslow was Abraham Maslow's niece [Abraham Maslow was a Brandeis University psychology professor who developed a theory of "humanistic psychology" and "Maslow's Hierarchy of Needs," which sees self-actualization as the pinnacle of psychological development]; we decided her name would stand out too much, so we didn't put anybody's name on the film.

MacDonald: The film has a strange structure. The opening section, "Sue's Story Told by Five Women," is the most interesting cinematically: you use several alternating voices to tell an abortion story. Who played Sue?

Pincus: The main actress in the first section is Susan Ghirad, a friend and a political organizer. The alternating voices are all excerpted from the audiotapes that seemed magically to appear once people knew that we were making the film. By piecing them together, along with Sue's voice, we could tell one woman's story, which was really the story of so many, too many women. For the second section, we wanted a story by a woman not of our social class. A woman from East Boston told her story but did not want to be filmed, so another friend, Janet Murray, agreed to be filmed in her home. Editing the live action and Marie's voice-over together was a challenge and a joy.

MacDonald: After the second oral history section, there's a radical switch in approach, introduced by a woman with a microphone. The second half of the film is a broadside relating abortion to other women's issues. How did you four decide on this organization?

Pincus: We kept having different ideas about how the film should be structured. For the third section, introduced by Mary Summers, we chose to represent a range of women's reproductive and health concerns, so as to put the issue of abortion and choice into the wider framework. We had a certain number of still photos and used them to go with Mary Summer's voice-over.

We did experiment with sync sound; two of the women from the Health Book Collective were filmed in short sync-sound passages.

MacDonald: The film is introduced by a text that seems to have been added after the film was made. It provides some context for the making of the film. When and why did you add the introduction?

Pincus: Believe it or not, I don't remember!

MacDonald: Let's talk about your role in Ed's *Diaries*. At the beginning, it's clear that you're uneasy about being filmed . . . (figure 11).

Pincus: I *hated* it.

MacDonald: Did you ever *not* hate it?

Pincus: Yeah. Toward the middle I began to think I was a really interesting woman and why didn't Ed film me more [laughter]! I got used to it, and as you

FIGURE 11 *Jane Pincus uncomfortable in front of the camera in* Diaries *(1971–1976) (1980).*
Source: Courtesy Ed and Jane Pincus.

may remember, at a certain point in the film I turn the camera on Ed, which was great fun.

MacDonald: Ed looks as embarrassed in that shot as you look early on.

Pincus: At the beginning I was very self-conscious, and being filmed made me more self-conscious, and I hated feeling so insecure. Early in the film, Ann Popkin talks directly into the camera. I saw her as being much braver than me, at least in relationship to being filmed.

MacDonald: Had you agreed to let Ed film you?

Pincus: I felt that without consulting with me *Ed* had made the decision to film five years of our lives. He may have felt we did discuss it, but I felt that we hadn't. He continued to make decisions like that. For example, he informed me out of the blue that he was going to Minneapolis for four months to film *Life and Other Anxieties* [shot in 1976–77, completed in 1977].

Not much has changed in that regard: it was the same when he made the recent trip down South with Lucia Small to shoot *The Axe in the Attic*. I don't feel that we discussed any of these film projects beforehand. And, of course, earlier on, he had gone to Mississippi to film *Black Natchez* when I was pregnant with Sammy. I felt abandoned, which, of course, had a lot to do with my own issues.

MacDonald: Whose idea was the open marriage?

Pincus: I don't remember whose idea it was. I think what happened is that each of us had become attracted to other people, and then at a certain point in the midst of the ferment that developed after 1965, we made what we thought was a conscious decision to open our marriage. Right now, I'm not sure how conscious it was, and I'm not sure how smart it was—but I remember it as a mutual decision.

It was a complicated life. I was a young mother bringing up our kids. I would be in love with other men and still be functioning as Ed's wife and as Sami and Ben's mother; and Ed would be involved with other women—I didn't know about some of his dalliances until I saw the finished film! I struggled through jealousy and at times wished I weren't tied down with kids and a marriage. If I could do it all over, I would do things differently.

MacDonald: What would you do differently?

Pincus: In those years, in my thirties, I was going through the adolescence that I'd never had. If I could do it over, I would hope to be more mature *before* my thirties so I could pay more dedicated attention to my children from the beginning.

MacDonald: When people watch *Diaries*, they often assume that Ed was filming all the time.

Pincus: He always says he shot twenty-seven hours of material.

MacDonald: That's not a lot, over five years.

Pincus: It seems like practically zero now. But at the beginning it did feel like a lot. And there were struggles about when he should be filming and when he should be involved with the family. When Ben got his finger smashed in the door, I think at first Ed was going to get his camera, but then decided not to. He had to make decisions like that all the time, which I'm sure made him uncomfortable.

After a while, I was happy to see him film. I even remember asking him if he would film certain things, but Ed had his own agenda—and he was shy too and hesitant to ask people if he could film them.

MacDonald: There's a startling sequence, shot during the summer of 1972, where you and Ann and another woman are lying in a kiddie pool nude. . .

Pincus: [Laughter] Ann Popkin was lovers with Trudy Barnett, the third woman. That was an amazing summer; it felt so free and easy going. We would run water from the washing machine through a hose into the kid's swimming pool and lie in the sun; it was all very happy.

MacDonald: In the film you seem to have a big struggle with your father. He doesn't take you seriously as an artist.

Pincus: Oh yeah. That footage when we're in the country and I make him sit and listen to me was one of the most startling experiences of my life with him; when I looked at the footage of that visit—parts were cut out for *Diaries*—I could see that he actually did listen to me, for the first time. Up until then, when he would visit, he'd say, "How are you?" and then just talk about himself. My stepmother would say, "Paul, you asked them about themselves, now be quiet and listen to their answers!"

MacDonald: By the end of *Diaries*, Ed's other relationships have moved to the background and you and the kids, and your domestic life in Vermont, have emerged as the foreground; the film becomes a kind of love letter to you.

Pincus: People say that to me, but I don't feel that. Actually, when I watch the film (and I don't look at it often, except for the "Freeze Tag" section with the kids), I get *so* upset with myself for rambling on and on.

I remember that one time when Ed was asking me questions and filming me at the kitchen table, I was thinking, "Everything I'm saying here is not exactly true." I can't remember now what I was thinking about—it might have been about Bob, this man I love, who I wish had appeared in the film somehow—but I remember thinking, "I'm not being completely honest. I *can't* be completely honest with Ed, because he's my husband and because I have such a passionate attachment to this other person."

My marriage was a possible love, but for a long time I also needed some kind of impossible love. Maybe our marriage has survived because each of us had passionate attachments to other people at different times. We've survived for fifty-one years! And I'm not sorry. I'm glad I got to know other men; I was *so* naïve growing up in the Fifties. I didn't know how to love. I didn't know how to be married well or how to be a mother.

MacDonald: Sami is fascinating to watch because as the film evolves, she becomes a performer; it's clear that she doesn't like being on film when she's not performing.

Pincus: She made that very clear, almost from the start. I don't know if something had happened in Sami's short life that had spooked her, but she was very cautious. Ben went right along with everything.

MacDonald: Do they know the film? How do they feel about it?

Pincus: When she last looked at it, Sami found it interesting; finally she could take it in and not feel threatened by it. Ben's fine with it, but Ben's wife finds it threatening. She hasn't seen it straight through.

MacDonald: Was the open marriage experiment something that ended during the period when the film was made?

Pincus: It's complicated, because up until 1990, there were a few men in my life, men I'd loved from the 1980s on. In the mid-1980s Ed asked me not to see one of these men, and I didn't for a while. Since 1987 there's not been anyone else for me: I put myself in the middle of my marriage. Sometime after that, Ed had an affair with one of our best friends in town, which felt to me like a double betrayal, but that's in the past now too.

I think one of the things that's kept our lives together in spite of all of these outside affairs and allegiances is some wonderful, incredible bond that Ed and I share. The other thing is that throughout our marriage, I would have considered our separating as a failure, my own failure. We did sort of separate, as you see at the beginning of *Diaries*, and I remember going to

Vermont when he had moved out for a few weeks, to look for a place to live; but it didn't feel real.

I do wish that more of my life and the women's movement, which was very important to my art, could have been included in *Diaries*. But, of course, *Diaries* isn't *my* film; it's *Ed's*.

Some people have been hostile to *Diaries* and that always surprises me. Two of my oldest friends—I've known them almost sixty years—saw *Diaries* not long ago, and during the time when Ed was down South doing *The Axe in the Attic*, my friend Ruthie wrote to tell me how she *hated Diaries*, and finished with, "And if you think *that's* something, you should see what *Peter* thinks!" I was *so* shocked. Ed no longer speaks to them. It's a pity they couldn't see the beauty in the film.

Ed Pincus and Lucia Small (on *The Axe in the Attic*)

MacDonald: How did your collaboration on *The Axe in the Attic* come about?

Pincus: W. C. Fields said it was a woman who drove him to drink and he's been grateful to her ever since; I got driven to the country and at first I really loved living there, but after twenty years it got old. And this drove me back into filmmaking and into my collaboration with Lucia.

Lucia and I met at the New England Film and Video Film Festival in 2002, as judges. I hadn't wanted to participate because I'd been out of film for so long and thought I wouldn't understand the problems that filmmakers were having. Instead, I found that I *did* understand what the problems were; they were pretty much the same problems that existed in 1960. Anyway, Lucia's and my tastes were remarkably similar. We got talking about making a film and decided that when the right project came along, we'd collaborate. By the time we met at that festival, digital cinematography had advanced and could render flesh tones beautifully. Lucia had a video background; she knew this new technology. That was important to me.

From the beginning it was a great collaboration because we both knew things the other didn't. We had similar outlooks, but there was enough difference between us so that each of us was able to bring important things to the film. I think that neither of us would claim that *The Axe in the Attic* was ours; it was a collaborative work. [To Small] Is that fair?

Small: Yes. I hadn't formally studied film; I'm self-taught, and when I first met Ed, I hadn't seen his work. I'd done a film about my father and had experimented with some playfulness around personal documentary filmmaking, using a collage approach. Of course, I knew Ross McElwee's films, and Robb Moss's and Jeannie Jordan and Steve Ascher's, all of whom had worked with Ed. Soon after we met, I got a VHS copy of *Diaries* and watched it, and related to the rawness of Ed's work.

Personal documentary is one of the most challenging forms, at least for me; you're constantly considering how much you can reveal about your family and about yourself. I've produced and directed other, more traditional cinema-verite films, but *The Axe in the Attic* created an unusual mix of the public and the personal, and was one of the most challenging things I've done.

Pincus: We tried to have two viewpoints in the film and to create a sense that these viewpoints were not those of experts, but of people with the same complex relationship to life that viewers have.

Small: When you're working in observational cinema, you usually understand what the filmmaker feels and how *you* should feel while watching the film. We wanted to challenge that safe space in a *social* documentary. Of course, tackling the subject of Hurricane Katrina and the diaspora it created, by inserting ourselves into our film about the disaster, was very risky. We met a hundred and fifty people, many of whom were in an acute state of crisis. But we felt that within this context it was important to look closely at the relationship between filmmakers and subjects. We wondered if you could get to a greater truth by stepping out of that comfortable safe space behind the lens.

MacDonald: From the opening tracking shot, *The Axe in the Attic* declares that while it's going to deal with a painful public issue, it's also going to be a *visual* film.

Pincus: Lucia just finished an amazing eight-minute film made up of just her tracking shots [*Lower Ninth Ward*]; it's included on the DVD of *The Axe*.

Small: It was certainly a pleasure to work with *Ed's* cinematography—not bad for not picking up a camera for 25 years!

It took us two years to find a camera Ed felt comfortable with; we finally decided on the JVC GY100 HDV camera, which fits nicely on the shoulder. I think some of the beautiful cinematography in *The Axe* came from the grace with which Ed can move with the shoulder camera.

MacDonald: How did you divide up the work? Did you both shoot?
Oh, I can see that this is an issue for you!

Pincus: Let's say it's a point of tension.

Small: We had talked about doing a two-points-of-view film, and I thought it was very important for both of us to shoot. For me, there is power in being behind the camera. Ed and I have a different opinion about this. He thought both of us shooting would be redundant; we would probably end up shooting the same things. I felt that while that might be true in general, the important exception was that Ed would also be shooting *me*. I would become a character.

I remember about a week into the shooting, realizing that when I picked up the camera, Ed did *not* pick up the sound gear. I thought, "Oh, we *do* need a division of labor; I guess he thinks I *hear* better!" So that became the division of labor. As a result, there's more of me in the film, and more revealed about me, than about Ed.

In the end I decided, okay, if *you* get to shoot, *I* get to edit. Even though we spent a lot of time in the editing room together, doing the bulk of the editing made me feel somewhat more securely at the helm. I had to scrape the barrel to find shots of Ed and had to work primarily with his voice. I think he did that on purpose.

I did shoot a lot with the DVX100-A, and the bulk of the tracking shots were mine.

Pincus: *The Axe in the Attic* is more highly edited than any other film I've worked on, and that was primarily Lucia. I remember looking at an early cut and thinking it was like a beautiful tapestry.

I think Lucia exaggerates the conflict; we agreed on who to film, how long to stay, where we were going to go next, what we were looking for—all really big questions.

Small: Yes, definitely.

Rosita Boland: Could you go into a bit more detail about what you brought to *The Axe in the Attic* as collaborators that you wouldn't have been able to do separately?

Pincus: Lucia is much more social than I am; she interacts with people much better than I can, and I think during our trip south she made people feel at ease. We both don't like talking-head movies, and interview films tend to be talking-head movies. I think *The Axe in the Attic* has a nice mixture of something like interview, but more conversational—because of Lucia.

Small: Of course, because I was out there interacting with people, I *did* absorb more of the situation in New Orleans than Ed seemed to. Ed has tougher skin than I do. I didn't even realize at the time that what I was experiencing is common among social workers during a crisis. It was a very deep stress, an absorbing of the pain of the people we were filming. This was a part of the collaboration that we didn't understand or talk about, and I think it caused some stress that we couldn't identify until much later.

Pincus: Working with Lucia took me to a different place, not necessarily better or worse, but a place of much more openness in editing. Each expansion of my habits, my repertoire, was something I fought. For example, I didn't want to use stock footage. There are three memory sequences in *The Axe*; they all take place on the same bridge and intercut between people's stories and stock footage from the Katrina disaster. I like the intensity of *not* cutting away; Lucia liked cutting back and forth. We argued about it, and came to an agreement to do it her way.

If each of us had done his or her own film, both films would have been very different from *The Axe*. When I first started filmmaking, I always thought of the lens as jutting into the world, a very masculine image; but I remember one of my students saying, "No, the camera *takes images in*"—a much more female image. Obviously film is both "male" and "female"; and this film is both male and female.

Small: All in all, it was an honor to work with Ed.

Pincus: The feeling is mutual.

MacDonald: Ed, *The Axe in the Attic* is the first of your films that has music on the soundtrack.

Pincus: I've always hated the way music is normally used, so I've avoided it. As a judge recently at a film festival I saw this absolutely beautiful film, *An Unmistaken Child* (2009; Nati Baratz), but it had a really bad, manipulative music track, and I hated that. I told the rest of the jury, "I think this was the best film, but because of the music track I can be convinced to vote for another." But I like what Lucia did with music in *The Axe*; she had to be very tough with the composer to get what she wanted. The music in *The Axe* never tells us how to feel; by contemporary standards, our use of music is minimal.

Something I discovered on *The Axe* is that I *love* working in 16-9 aspect ratio. I thought I'd hate it. With the wider image sometimes you have the center of the interest in the left part of the screen and then as time goes on, the right part of the screen develops interest. It's very different from working with the usual Academy 4-3 aspect ratio.

MacDonald [to Pincus]: You've usually been a collaborator. Often, your projects seem to involve your taking a trip with someone. It's almost as though your making a film has to do with going somewhere with someone. *Diaries* is really your only film that is not a collaboration with another filmmaker—though in a sense it was a collaboration with your family, and you didn't need to take a trip. . .

Pincus: . . . but even there, there's the "South by Southwest" section, where David Neuman and I travel through the Southwest. I think yours is a very good insight. Doing a film by myself seems awfully lonely and potentially a problem: I *need* to be brought back to reality and a partner helps me with that. I do a martial art, called aikido, that doesn't really have any kata—that is, standard movements you do by yourself. Aikido is like judo and always involves a partner. I just can't do things by myself—it's a personality thing.

I think collaboration is more important to me than it is to Lucia.

MacDonald: Lucia, was this your first collaboration?

Small: This is the first film I co-directed. I did *My Father the Genius* by myself, or mostly by myself. I'm much calmer as a producer than as a director. I'm a problem solver, and I enjoy helping someone create their vision.

MacDonald: I assume some viewers thought you were self-indulgently making this tragedy into your personal problem.

Small: Yes, some people have been really angry about it. I've gone through a range of emotions about this, often questioning myself, but in many ways the discourse the film created is exactly the kind of thing you *hope* for with this kind of film. We *wanted* to engender questions about our responsibility as filmmakers and as citizens in the world, both within the filming situation and in relation to the systemic problems in our country that Katrina was/is a microcosm of.

We wanted to evoke that feeling of uncomfortableness that you have when you're on a subway and someone is asking you for money: do you give or not? You know this is part of a bigger problem; how do you address it? *Do* you address it?

Pincus: Poor Lucia: she's gotten so much shit for *The Axe*. Basically, I've had very little to do with the distribution of the film, which became a big tension between us. I let Lucia do the dirty work, so she was the one who took the brunt of the anger.

In the history of observational cinema from the Sixties on, and certainly in my films, how the filmmaker relates to what he or she is recording has always been an important issue, but rarely as visible an issue as it is in *The Axe in the Attic*.

Small: I still struggle with the question of the filmmaker's responsibility. I do think being a historical witness, creating the record, is important; and I feel that this film is only going to get better with time, at least as an archive of that moment. The ethical issues that we grappled with in making this film are important.

Pincus: We had one aspiration that *didn't* pan out. The Bush administration had tried to eviscerate the federal government; they wanted to show that the federal government couldn't do anything. That's why they hated social security so much: it was and is a successful federal program. We wanted to make a film that was not overtly political, but that would help swing the pendulum back towards the necessity of big government—because, of course, nobody wants to pay taxes for FEMA unless they *need* FEMA. We had hoped that the movie would play a part in the presidential campaign, which it didn't.

Alfred Guzzetti

Given his considerable accomplishments and his longevity as a moving-image artist, it is surprising that Alfred Guzzetti remains little known among aficionados of independent cinema outside of the Boston area (he has taught at Harvard since 1968). There are at least two reasons for this. First, throughout his career, Guzzetti has been remarkably resistant to self-promotion. Though some of his films are in distribution, Guzzetti is, for the most part, his own (passive) distributor for many of his films and all of his video work.

Second, Guzzetti has worked in such a wide variety of ways that his oeuvre resists categorization. His first important film and the earliest of his films in distribution, *Air* (1971), is an accomplished, though under-recognized avant-garde image-sound montage; it was soon followed by the feature-length *Family Portrait Sittings* (1975), one of the early landmarks of personal documentary—and a film as different from *Air* as one could imagine. In 1981 Harvard University Press published Guzzetti's book-length analysis of Jean-Luc Godard's *2 ou 3 choses que je sais d'elle* (1967): *Two or Three Things I Know about Her: Analysis of a Film by Godard*. The influence of Godard, and of *Two or Three Things* in particular, is evident in *Air* and in Guzzetti's later work as well.

In the 1980s and early 1990s, Guzzetti finished two semi-ethnographic studies of early childhood—*Scenes from Childhood* (1980) and *Beginning Pieces* (1986)—then collaborated with photographer Susan Meiselas and filmmaker Richard P. Rogers on two noteworthy, politically motivated films on the Nicaraguan revolution: *Living at Risk: The Story of a Nicaraguan Family* (1985) and *Pictures from a Revolution* (1991). In 1994 he worked with Ákos Östör and Lina Fruzzetti on the ethnographic film, *Seed and Earth*.

In 1993, Guzzetti began exploring the possibilities of video art in what has become a long series of short videos, most of them designed for gallery exhibition on monitors. These videos—the four Guzzetti calls "Language Lessons": *Rosetta Stone* (1993), *The Curve of the World* [1994, revised 1999], *The Stricken Areas* [1996, revised 1999], and *What Actually Happened* (1996); and *Variation* (1996); *Under the Rain* (1997); *A Tropical Story* (1998); *The Tower of Industrial Life* (2000); *Down from the Mountains* (2002); and *History of the Sea* (2004)—are among the most under-appreciated moving-image works of recent decades. In their subtlety, their density, and their evocativeness,

Guzzetti's videos are often reminiscent of the films of canonical avant-garde filmmaker Nathaniel Dorsky.

Guzzetti continues to work in a variety of ways, depending on the circumstances: in 2009, his ongoing exploration of the possibilities of digital video resulted in the gorgeous, high-definition *Still Point,* which was followed by *Time Present* (2013). A recent collaboration with Susan Meiselas produced a DVD that includes *The Barrios Family Twenty-Five Years Later* (2011), and a remastered version of *Living at Risk* (*Living at Risk* is about the Barrios family). And in 2012, Guzzetti finished a dense, evocative short personal documentary, *Time Exposure,* an homage to his photographer father and to a range of filmmakers, including Ross McElwee, Hollis Frampton, Morgan Fisher, Su Friedrich, and Agnès Varda. Guzzetti's filmmaking and his considerable knowledge of independent film history have been and continue to be important to his filmmaking colleagues at Harvard—particularly Ross McElwee and Robb Moss—and to generations of Harvard students.

My interview with Guzzetti began in April of 2009, when we talked following a screening of *Family Portrait Sittings* at Harvard University (when it seems useful I identify questioners other than myself); it was expanded in phone conversations and subsequently by email.

MacDonald: How did you get into film?

Guzzetti: My father went to photography school before I was born; we had a darkroom in our basement, very unusual at that time in my neighborhood. My father had big 4 × 5 and 5 × 7 cameras, so that's how I learned still photography. He also made home movies. At a certain point when I was a kid, I read a book called something like "How to Make Good Movies," and made some movies with his camera and editing equipment.

When I was in college, I didn't see any way of making a living with filmmaking, but the Sixties were very tumultuous and all kinds of strange, new possibilities were appearing. Vietnam was key in putting me on the path toward being a filmmaker and film teacher. Beginning in the mid-Sixties, if you left school you would be drafted and sent to Southeast Asia. I was against the war, so I stayed in school, without much intention of becoming an academic, and by the time the draft deferments were lifted, I had raced through graduate school—I was miserable there—and had a Ph.D.

MacDonald: What was the field and subject of your Ph.D.?

Guzzetti: Seventeenth-century English literature: "Dryden's Two Worlds: Restoration Society and the Literary Past."

Once I had completed my degree, my prospects were limited, so far as I could tell, to teaching freshman composition someplace in western Canada or in a borough of New York City, teaching English at Rutgers, or starting a "media" curriculum at the Harvard School of Education (Marshall McLuhan was the man of the hour). As far as film was concerned, everything was very fluid and since it was a new field, people didn't look at credentials very much. I ended up getting a job that I'd never have gotten later, at the Harvard Graduate School of Education; I taught there for three years.

Dominique Bluher: When you were making your early films, did you have any relationship with the Carpenter Center and Robert Gardner?

Guzzetti: I admired Gardner tremendously. I was in awe of *Dead Birds* [1964] and then *Rivers of Sand* [1974], but I saw those films as very *other*, in a separate category of films about societies far from my own, and also as being governed by what I thought of at the time as existentialism: like Sartre, Gardner was preoccupied with mortality and with the idea that "all men, like birds, must die." The issue of mortality is the motive spark not only in *Dead Birds* but in the Gardner films that came later, including, of course, *Forest of Bliss* [1986]. My generation read the novels of Sartre and Camus in high school and we were influenced by their ideas, though we didn't really identify with them because we hadn't gone through the World War: existentialism was a war-generation philosophy.

I felt very distant from what the Carpenter Center was doing in film at the time. Apart from Gardner, everybody there seemed to think that design was the commanding factor in good films. They had a canon that included very few filmmakers out of all of film history, and those filmmakers didn't interest me at all: Leni Riefenstahl, whom I hated then and still do; and Charles Eames, whom I saw as trivial. I remember thinking, what about *The Grand Illusion* [1937] and *Rules of the Game* [1939]? What about *Ivan, the Terrible, Part 2* [1958]?

At the time, I felt more comfortable with MIT, where there was also an ideology of purity, but connected to a particular technology: sync sound. They felt that once you got this sync-sound machine going, it could tell you truths about society that we'd never seen before. I mixed an early film of mine (I think it was *Evidence* [1972]) at MIT because they were generous and open and ran a much looser ship than Harvard, and had attracted a group of film-makers that made MIT feel like the center of things.

Dominique Bluher: How much did you and the other filmmakers working here in Cambridge—Wiseman, for example—show your work to each other, communicate with each other? Was there a community around the Carpenter Center?

Guzzetti: I'm the wrong person to ask, because if there's a club, I tend not to be a member of it, really not to know that it even *exists*. I remember having a meal with Ed Pincus and saying in fun, "Ed, we should give what we're doing a name; look at what 'The New Wave' did for those filmmakers, and they're actually not all that similar to one another, either." We laughed and tried to think of a name, but of course, we were only kidding—we weren't interested in writing manifestos.

I do remember meeting Fred Wiseman, and I remember seeing *High School* [1969], which is about the high school that was the main rival to my own high school in Philadelphia. I hated every minute of *High School* and its unrelenting tone of condescension. Wiseman was an outsider who didn't understand the culture he was filming; he went in with an elitist attitude, and for him it was like shooting fish in a barrel. I *came* from that culture, so I knew. *High School* is an instance of what Ed Pincus used to call "the alienated documentary." Ed was against documentaries in which the subject was alienated from the filmmaker, where there was no real connection.

But despite my feelings about *High School*, I think Wiseman is the most important living American documentary filmmaker. I once drafted a letter proposing that he be given an Oscar for lifetime achievement.

MacDonald: When did the idea of studying film begin to have a place at Harvard?

Guzzetti: Gardner's cosmopolitan-ness, and his sense that the agenda of film had a priority of its own that came out of film history, rather than out of the history of design or something else, helped in developing a consensus about film at Harvard before there was any real commitment to film studies. There was moral support from people like Stanley Cavell and James Ackerman, but no programmatic support from the university. Of course, everybody imagines that at Harvard, film studies would have come first and later maybe some toying around with production—but in fact it was the other way around. Harvard started a filmmaking program and struggled to add a film studies program.

I got into a position where I was one of the people piloting the ship, and then Nick Browne introduced me to this brilliant MIT graduate student, Ross McElwee. I saw various cuts of *Sherman's March* [1986] and each time my reaction was almost exactly what my father says about my films in *Family Portrait Sittings*: "This film is great, but nobody will ever get to see it!" [laughter] That shows, among other things, that I have remarkably poor commercial judgment—but I was thrilled to be wrong. Ross got hired by Harvard, and during the 1970s, the filmmaking curriculum expanded.

MacDonald: *Air* is very accomplished.

Guzzetti: Before *Air*, I had made film sequences for theater productions, a couple of experimental shorts, an industrial film, and a two-screen documentary called *Notes on the Harvard Strike* [1969].

MacDonald: *Air* seems to come out of the history of American avant-garde film.

Guzzetti: Fred Camper ran a weekly film series at MIT and I went all the time. I saw Brakhage and Peter Kubelka, Warhol, Bruce Baillie—I loved Bruce Baillie—and crazy stuff that I liked but didn't seem to have anything to do with me: I knew I'd never make anything like George and Mike Kuchar's films.

MacDonald: It's clear that by the time you made *Air*, you'd decided that film is definitely sound-image art. It seems relevant that you were in a world where cinema-verite was the big new thing, where sound was considered essential for cinema. You also seem to have decided that sound needed to be a second complex track that worked in concert with the image track: early in *Air* we're listening to two people talking at the same time, and because of the doubling up we can't quite understand what either voice is saying. The only other film I remember from that era that puts viewers in a similar situation is Paul Sharits's *Word Movie/Fluxfilm* [1967].

Guzzetti: I would say that the elements of *Air* that come from avant-garde film come from Bruce Baillie's layering of soundtracks and the complexity of his image tracks, and from Peter Kubelka.

But where my approach really comes from is music. I came to film after composing music off and on for more than ten years. *Air* is a film opera that, like musical operas, includes passages of vocal counterpoint. Mike Figgis published a couple of pages of his scenario for *Time Code* [2000], which was written on music staffs—I think he's a jazz musician as well as a filmmaker. I used something like this method in *Air*. I started with the recorded interviews you've mentioned. I measured phrases and mapped them out on pieces of cross-hatched paper. I would hold the strips of paper next to one another and think, "If I move the second phrase of voice B five frames later, then *that* phrase will have a relationship with *this* and it will fall into another relationship *here*." I made the rule for myself that the rhythms of these passages would be composed so that you would have an ensemble, the way you have an ensemble in Mozart when people are singing different texts at the same time, with the music bringing them together, harmonizing them. I was interested in the rhythms of real speech and not in composed rhythm, though I did try working with that too: I transcribed those texts and had actors read them, but in the end, I thought this took away from what was interesting about the composition.

MacDonald: Did you study to be a composer?

Guzzetti: I studied music composition at Harvard for a couple of years. In high school I wrote incidental music for plays and I did that as an undergrad at Harvard too. At some point, Thom Babe, a college friend, and I decided to write an opera. He wrote the libretto and I wrote the music. We wrote it as a chamber opera—because one of the things I don't like about grand opera is the need for the voices to be very loud, loud enough to project above the orchestra, so loud that you can't understand the words. But like other operas, the one we composed included sections of ensemble.

It was during my senior year in college that I got interested in film. Bob Gardner was offering the first film course at Harvard, and I thought, oh, film, well, I know something about this already because of working with my father in photography and making some home movies. What drew me to film was that, like opera, it could be composed, but in such a way that once you finished composing a piece, it could stay the way you wanted it—unlike music, where any composition varies with different performances.

So that's really where *Air* comes from. Opera, rather than the string quartet or any other form, was my model, because opera has a visual line as well as music. I wanted to make a film that was composed in counterpoint, and I wanted to treat the image track as one more voice in the counterpoint, but a "voice" unlike the other voices. I also decided that I couldn't keep a high level of density going for eighteen minutes; I would have to modulate the film's complexity, so sometimes there's one element, sometimes there are duets, sometimes trios, and then toward the end you get a big ensemble, where there are four "voices" of audio and an image simultaneously.

I was frustrated at the time by the limitations of optical sound: everything you can hear on the mag [the magnetic tape version of what became the 16mm soundtrack], which was quite good, had to be compromised in optical sound. It wasn't until recently that I got around to making a video copy of *Air* and remixed the soundtrack to make it stereo and to eliminate a lot of the compromises I'd had to make. I even have a Dolby 5.1 version now.

MacDonald: I've assumed that the title is a pun relating to the film's audio-visual nature. Air is the physical substance that surrounds us, but *an air* is a musical piece.

Guzzetti: I've never thought of that. I don't think I would associate the film with a musical air, since a musical air is a simple melody with accompaniment. My model was the multiple voices of operatic counterpoint.

The title—and there's no way of knowing this from the film—comes from T. S. Eliot, the passage in *The Four Quartets* that talks about the death of the four elements. I was originally going to quote the whole line, "This is the death of air." Using just "Air" was partly a question of simplicity and partly not wanting to bring the baggage of *The Four Quartets* into the film.

I should also mention the influence of still photography. At the time I was making *Air*, I was as interested in photography as in filmmaking. I was, and still am, a big fan of Cartier-Bresson, William Klein, Lee Friedlander, and lots of other photographers.

In a sense, *Air* was my first real film. I worked on the imagery by sketching (so to speak) with my still camera. I made lots of studies, Kodachrome slides and black-and-white slides (which I loved at the time and which you had to develop yourself): images of cars, my apartment—I forget what else. I was also making black-and-white portraits of friends with a 4 × 5 camera; these were the basis for the four portraits in the film.

MacDonald: Who was/is Roberta Collinge? Is she related to Patricia Collinge, the movie actress [Patricia Collinge plays the mother of Little Charlie in Hitchcock's *Shadow of a Doubt* (1943)]? And what did you have in mind in ending the film with the sequence of her trying on outfits in front of a mirror? I assume it's a reference to the way that so many of us were "trying on" new ways of being in the world in those days.

Guzzetti: Roberta Collinge's name *is* actually Patricia Collinge. She acted with the Theater Company of Boston. Her aunt, Patricia Collinge, was the equity actress working under that name, so Patty couldn't use her own name when she appeared on the stage or in movies; she used her middle name, Roberta (figure 12).

I see the meaning of the sequence in more or less the way you've described. It's a matter of the nuances of roles that are expressed by different clothing; changing clothes in a kind of frenzy, as if looking for the correct way to look, the correct role to assume. But, of course, the sequence doesn't come to a conclusion, doesn't show Patty finding the "correct" role.

For me the interaction with the sound in that scene is important. A piano is being tuned—an effort to find the right pitch. You hear multiple renderings of the tuning at the same time, and these form a new kind of music, the music of preparation, of getting ready for something, but again, we don't experience a resolution of the process. Up to the final sequence, the film includes two elements in finished form: Patty is dressed in a certain way in each sequence in which she appears, and there is music, even piano music, played on a tuned instrument. But at the end, *Air* disassembles the earlier image and sound.

FIGURE 12 *Patricia Collinge trying on new roles in the concluding sequence of Alfred Guzzetti's* Air *(1971).*

Source: Courtesy Alfred Guzzetti.

MacDonald: At the end we see Collinge trying on clothes through the right window; a television is visible through the window on the left. The television suggests a different kind of mirror, the production of a social standard that Collinge is reacting to or trying to emulate or both.

Guzzetti: Yes, the TV is part of the theme of messages constantly intruding into our environment, bringing disturbing news into the interiors in which we live our private lives. In this way it's parallel to the earlier tracking sequence through the apartment in which we hear shortwave radio news about torture in Brazil and other things. I did think of "air" as carrying this meaning as well: things come to us over the airwaves, a medium that's transparent yet thick with meaning. In my mind, the main theme of the piece was the incomprehensible juxtaposition of our ordinary environment with the more distant world of turmoil and distress.

MacDonald: You thank the Carpenter Center in the credits; did the Center fund the film?

Guzzetti: I got the grant money myself, but used a little of the Carpenter Center's equipment and its sound-transfer facilities. The camera was a Bolex that belonged to a friend, except for the lengthy shot up the escalator, which needed the Carpenter Center's motorized Arriflex-S.

MacDonald: Has *Air* been seen much?

Guzzetti: Its big success was winning first prize in the experimental category at the 1972 Chicago Film Festival, but I was conscious that it didn't really fit in with the ongoing tradition of American experimental film (formally it has something in common with *British Sounds* [1969] by Godard, which I saw later). At that point, I didn't really know how to get films seen, and didn't worry too much about it.

MacDonald: How did you decide to do *Family Portrait Sittings*?

Guzzetti: At the time, I felt that cinema-verite documentary, which was all the rage, was nearly always superficial—I sometimes still feel this way. One reason is that people who make cinema-verite documentaries encounter their subjects in the way that Flaherty prescribed: practically without preconception. This is wonderful in one sense—it allows for certain kinds of discoveries—but on the other hand, diving into something new doesn't take you very deep, given the amount of time you have to learn about your subject and the amount of shooting time you usually have.

My approach to autobiography was less pure than much of cinema-verite, but I hoped it would also be less superficial. Here was a subject (my family) that I already knew a lot about, and I felt that this offered an opportunity to make a film that went deeper, into more detail, than the cinema-verite films, including the personal documentaries that were being made. Ed Pincus was committed to a very pure kind of cinema-verite; *Diaries (1971–1976)* [1980] is an exploration of that purist point of view.

Ed was always tactful enough not to talk about *Family Portrait Sittings*, but I suspect he didn't like it.

Another thing is that I knew I had this stash of my father's 8mm films. It seemed to me that these movies were an important archive, not just of *my* family, but of the culture at that moment.

When I was first thinking about what became *Family Portrait Sittings*, I assumed it would be a much shorter film. My models were *Night and Fog* [*Nuit et brouillard* by Alain Resnais, 1955], especially Resnais's mixture of the inaccessible past with a present; and his *Toute la mémoire du monde* [1956], another short film in which there's a contemplation of a present in relation to a past. I wanted to make the most vivid possible contrast between my footage, which would be black and white and in 35mm (I tried to get money for this), and my father's 8mm color films.

At the time, all of us were absolutely preoccupied with the Vietnam War in one way or another, and many of us—even people who were not very political, like me—were protesting. Vietnam touched all of us in one way or another. This is hard to imagine now because so few people seem to be touched by the wars in Iraq and Afghanistan. Something that played an important role in my beginning *Family Portrait Sittings* was a kind of family conversation that was so familiar that I'd always ignored it—your family is like your physical surroundings; they're so familiar that you see them without *seeing* them. My great uncle and my grandfather were always in the kitchen talking politics, mostly with each other and sometimes with the other adults. As kids we would escape to other rooms to do other things, but on this one night, long after my grandfather had died, my uncle Dominick started to talk to me about Vietnam, and I suddenly realized that he had exactly the same view of it as my friends and I, and in fact that he had a more coherent analysis than we did—he was a Marxist from the labor union movement in the 1930s.

That was the point of origin of *Family Portrait Sittings*: wondering where his ideas came from and realizing that my family and I are beings in history, in the Marxist sense, and that they have a story, a historical narrative. I didn't exactly make a Marxist film, but my impulse was to place myself in relation to my family and to place all of us in relationship to a certain class history and historical situation.

MacDonald: Family Portrait Sittings also evokes the history of the material ways in which families have been represented over the last century or two. You begin with photography of earlier generations, then we see your father's home movies, then your sync-sound home movies.

Guzzetti: I was the first generation for whom there were motion-picture records of life from before I was born. There were exceptions, like Jerome Hill's *Film Portrait* [1972]--the more wealthy families bought motion picture cameras as early as 1923--but for a working person in the 1930s, my father was unusual in his moviemaking.

MacDonald: What were some of the challenges of asking your parents questions; was anything considered off-limits?

Guzzetti: For years I'd heard my parents and other relatives telling the stories I recorded; I'm sure you've heard your family's stories over and over, too. When I was shooting, I just hoped I'd get good versions of the stories. I can't think of anything that was off-limits, because what I was most interested in was not secrets, but the ways in which we mythologize our lives by turning them into narrative, even if we don't write the narrative down or make films about it. *Family Portrait Sittings* is a study of the ways that a family mythologizes itself.

Is there another layer of truth under these stories? The answer is surely yes, but can you ever penetrate to that level? I never believed that you could, and I never tried. But I think that no matter how I might have posed my questions to my parents or to the older generation of my family, all my questions would have fed into their familiar narrative.

One of the stories my mother used to tell is a nodal point for our family during the Great Depression. She's been accepted into normal school (teacher's college) and the evening before school is starting, she's decided she isn't going to go, when Arthur Kemp, a guy from the neighborhood who has more power than my family because he's more Anglo and because his family is more assimilated into the society (his father was the city treasurer), comes by and says, "You should go; what kind of future do you have if you don't?" And so she does—and that shaped her future and the future of our family. Did such a conversation happen? I think *something* happened, that *somebody* said *something*, but what interests me is how it gets shaped into a story. During the many times that my mother told that story, Arthur Kemp became the character who said these things to her, and whose presence was the catalyst for her enrolling at normal school the next day. Was it really the next day?

I started by collecting a lot of audio interviews. The sync-sound interviews took several days in each case. I started with my uncle Dominick, then filmed my parents (figure 13). After I had recorded the interviews, I was convinced that Italy had to be in the film, that you had to see the room and the streets that my grandfather had never seen again, as well as the streets of South Philadelphia. Going back to Italy created some puzzles for me. At the time, I wondered why anybody would leave such a beautiful place to come to crummy South Philly.

MacDonald: Patricia [O'Connor], my wife, has her office down the hall from where I look at films, and she *listened* to *Family Portrait Sittings* as I was studying it. She would yell in, "I *love* this film!" Her reaction helped me realize that in *Family Portrait Sittings* the audio is at least as important, really more important, than the visuals.

FIGURE 13 *Susan and Felix Guzzetti, in Alfred Guzzetti's* Family Portrait Sittings *(1975)*.
Source: Courtesy Alfred Guzzetti.

Guzzetti: When *Family Portrait Sittings* came out of the lab, I was crushed. I thought the optical 16mm sound had destroyed the *presence* of the voices, and I had staked the hundred and three minutes of the film on that presence. Everybody that I showed it to said, "Oh, it's all right, don't worry about it," but it wasn't the movie I'd been making. When the Whitney Museum premiered the film, I re-mixed the soundtrack; the Whitney had a projector that could play a magnetic stripe, and that version was a different film. Whenever possible, I showed *Family Portrait Sittings* that way.

For what it's worth, in a musical sense, *Family Portrait Sittings* was the next step after *Air*. I'd done this extremely dense, compact thing with a lot of counterpoint, and now I wanted to make something which would be operatic in a different way, something that would use a very spare single-line against another single-line—more like *Pelléas et Mélisande* than *The Marriage of Figaro*.

MacDonald: During the sequences where you interview your parents, they're sitting in front of a mirror, but we can't see you or the camera.

Guzzetti: My mother had the pillows in a position that happens to hide the camera. I left them there and sat on a low chair where the camera and my wife Deborah and I wouldn't be reflected. Deborah agreed to be there because she hadn't heard a lot of the stories, and we thought this would motivate my parents to tell them in a more lively way. Once I decided on the framing, I didn't even look through the camera; I had a remote and just pushed the button.

My parents lived in a small row-house in Philadelphia, and since I wanted to film them in their own home, there were very few options: the living room is long and narrow; my mother had my father put in that huge mirror to make the room look bigger. If I had shot 180 degrees the other way, my parents would have been against the stairs and there was no place to sit. Ninety degrees to the left was the window, and I couldn't shoot directly against the light. And opposite the window, the living room opened into the dining room.

MacDonald: That space is the inverse of "David's" space in *David Holzman's Diary* [1967], where we're always seeing the camera.

Guzzetti: I realized that my set-up was going to create some tension, but the only other choice I could think of would have been to put the camera high enough so you were constantly seeing me and the camera within the frame. I expected to use a great deal of that footage, which I did, and I thought it would be obnoxious to have the Arriflex and me sitting there in the image.

It's interesting to compare my film to Scorsese's *Italian American* [1974], made at almost the same moment. It's a good film, an interesting film, and very Scorsese, full of stories—and Scorsese is continually visible, interacting with his parents. In *Family Portrait Sittings*, it's obvious that I'm *there*, but my interest wasn't in what my interacting with my parents might reveal, but in getting them to tell their family stories.

MacDonald: At the beginning of some of the passages where you're interviewing your parents, there's a screech.

Guzzetti: The beep is the sync mark that the Arriflex automatically puts on the audio each time it starts. I left it in because I thought that the technical procedures mattered to the meaning of the film. I deliberately started the film with a very long section, twenty minutes or so, before you hear any sync sound, so that the sync sound would seem abnormal within the context of the film; I was hoping to keep viewers aware of being in a critical relationship to the sound and image, to remind them that all the elements of the film had been constructed in one way but could very well have been constructed in another.

The more practical reason was that I'd planned to do the interviews by running audio continuously and rolling film whenever I thought necessary. I wanted to be able to do that without jumping up and putting in a clapper board every time I began to film, so I rented an Arriflex, which produced a sync mark in-camera.

MacDonald: The only other film I'm aware of where the sync marks are left in is Hollis Frampton's *Critical Mass*, which was made in 1971. Any relationship there?

Guzzetti: No. I hadn't seen *Critical Mass* when I shot the interviews in 1972.

MacDonald: When you were finally structuring *Family Portrait Sittings*, you divided it into three more or less equal parts and I've struggled to understand the logic. Part 1 is clear: it's family background up until the marriage of your parents; but the distinction between Parts 2 and 3 is more obscure. My conjecture is that Part 3 is more about issues: first gender, then American politics.

Guzzetti: That's precisely what I thought: that by the time you get to Part 3, the emphasis should shift from chronology to issues, or really, from issues embedded in chronology to issues and themes foregrounded (but not entirely overthrowing chronology). Part 3 links up with the original motive for the film, producing an explanation of what the ideas and values of my family are and where they come from.

Another thing, kind of a stupid thing but true, was that I felt that 16mm projectionists never got reel changes right and sometimes didn't even have two projectors. I didn't want to make a movie that depended on instantaneous reel changes; I made it so that if a projectionist blew a reel change, the audience wouldn't lose details. Each new reel begins with a title.

During the period when I was beginning to shoot *Family Portrait Sittings*, I seemed always to be meeting people at parties who were also making personal films—though they usually seemed to have a different take on family history than mine. An exhibition was organized at the Art Gallery of Ontario in Toronto a few years after my film was finished and by then there was a considerable body of autobiographical work [the catalogue for this show, *Autobiography: film/video/photography* was edited by John Stuart Katz (Toronto: Art Gallery of Ontario, 1978)].

In 1978, I took the film to the Edinburgh Festival, where the whole project of the autobiographical film was unheard of. For those programmers this was a strange new phenomenon from across the ocean.

MacDonald: Did you plan originally that *The House on Magnolia Avenue* [1989] would deal with two different times; the twelve-year jump from 1975 to 1987 is very dramatic.

Guzzetti: No. I began what became the first part of that film, thinking that it would be the end of *Family Portrait Sittings*, which was supposed to go up to the present. As I was editing *Family Portrait Sittings*, I realized that including the present would make the film unwieldy. Also, I couldn't represent my present life in the same mode that I used in *Family Portrait Sittings*. In the end I decided to make another film—one that would be completely talking heads. There was a perverseness in that decision: talking heads had become outré.

MacDonald: Your subjects are very articulate and fun to listen to. The film is an interesting document of that moment, just in terms of the way people were thinking about their lives and how their lives changed over time—it has much in common with Michael Apted's *Up* project, which was begun in 1964.

Was living in the house on Magnolia Avenue just an economically communal arrangement or was it communal in other senses?

Guzzetti: It was economically communal for sure and there were some things that we did together—we cooked dinner and ate dinner together every night, though I was censured for not cooking. But it wasn't sexually communal if that's what you're asking. Definitely not.

MacDonald: How long did you live there?

Guzzetti: Deborah and I moved in just after Ben was born in 1973. The first segment of the film was shot in 1975. We stayed until Sarah was born in 1979—there wasn't any room for her.

As I remember, the capital to buy the house came from Judy Herman, who was a psychiatrist and had some savings, and from us. Other people contributed different things. Hadley and Matthew belonged to a carpentry collective called "The New Hamburger Cabinet Works," which may still exist; they put a lot of work into renovating the house. In the end Judy wound up owning the house, which caught fire last year. I haven't seen the fire damage, which Judy says is considerable.

MacDonald: *Scenes from Childhood* strikes me as a film made by a young man who's fascinated with his son. The film is a way of thinking about childhood but also a way to be present as Ben is running around doing what kids do. The film begins with a quote from *Walden*: "Children who play life discern its true law and relations more clearly than men. . . ." I don't think *Scenes* actually demonstrates that, but I wonder what you thought you were revealing.

Guzzetti: I was watching *Chronicle of a Summer* [*Chronique d'un été*, by Jean Rouch and Edgar Morin; 1961] for the umpteenth time—I've probably seen that film more times than any other. There's a scene where the two filmmakers are sitting with Morin's children in a little shelter by a beach when the African student, Landry, arrives. Morin says to him, "You probably have no idea of the lives that French children lead." Landry asks the kids a couple of questions like "do you know how to cook" and tells them that at their age, he knew how to take care of himself. During that screening I remember thinking, "*Morin* probably has no idea of the lives that French children lead, either, and *I* don't have any idea of the life *my* child leads."

I'd also been reading the British psychiatrist of childhood, D. W. Winnicott, who writes in a beautiful, lucid way and has a very clear idea about childhood.

The film's relationship to the Thoreau quotation is something that emerged for me as the film evolved. I think what you see in the children's play is a jockeying for position and the effort the children expend to exert their powers over the world they inhabit. In adulthood those things exist but are usually masked; children are more naked. I understand that what Thoreau meant is a little bit different from what my use of the quotation suggests. *He* meant that adults are so preoccupied with the necessities of adulthood that they compromise their existence, and that being truly alive in the world is closer to play. Thoreau had read *The Upanishads* and wanted to separate himself from the Protestant need to achieve all the time, to ask, "What is life about?" If the mass of men *do* lead lives of quiet desperation, we certainly shouldn't aspire to that. I'm not a transcendentalist, but I do think that if you look closely at the transactions of children, there is a kind of clarity about what they do that isn't present to the same degree in adult life.

It's also true that adults interact with children in a way that Thoreau would deplore. We deal with their necessities, as parents who are responsible for them; we minister to them and we have interaction when they need things from us and when we need things from them, but what we *don't* do—and this is why I made the film—is just attend to them. If you look at these beings in themselves, they are truly strange, and yet they are us. *Scenes from Childhood* was almost an anthropological project in that sense. And it was a cinema-verite project: I used the process of filming to observe them without preconceptions about what I might see.

MacDonald: Generally you seem invisible to the children.

Guzzetti: I think they were at an age where their agenda was much more important to them than mine, so I faded away pretty quickly. I said to them a number of times, "I'm going to be busy because I'm carrying this big camera, so if you need something, I'm not going to be able to get it for you." I told the other adults the same thing. When kids are crying and I don't intervene, it's because there are other adults around. The other parents accepted that—they were all people I knew. One of the challenges was to go into the children's space; I wanted to be on their level, and that meant being very close to them. I also had the problem of sound, so I experimented a lot and in the end had the microphone hanging from the camera.

MacDonald: Was the title of *Scenes from Childhood* a reference to Brakhage's *Scenes from Under Childhood* [1967–1970]?

Guzzetti: I knew of Brakhage's films and I remember a Q&A when an irate viewer accused me of stealing Brakhage's title. I did steal it, but from Robert Schumann, not Brakhage. *Kinderszenen*, "Scenes from Childhood," is a set of thirteen piano pieces. You hear the beginning of the first one under the main title and the end of the last under the credits. I liked the slightly ironic association of the title of the first piece, "About Foreign Lands and Peoples," with the beginning of the movie, and the un-ironic title of the last, "The Poet Speaks," at the end. At one point I had planned to use fragments of all or most of the pieces throughout the film, but this turned out not to work.

MacDonald: *Beginning Pieces* is interesting now in a way that it probably wasn't meant to be. In this current climate, the nudity of children has become so poisoned as an idea that depicting the realities of childhood has become dangerous. I know that in his last years Brakhage had become very concerned about his film, *Vein* [1965], which intercuts between time-lapse imagery of the night sky and images of his young son lying on his father's lap, fiddling with his penis the way little boys do. Brakhage was terrified that this film was going to get onto the Internet as child pornography. During the Seventies, many of us let our kids run around nude and this wasn't a new thing: my parents were hardly progressive in terms of child-rearing, but there are many nude pictures of me, and of me and other children, in their photo scrapbooks.

Guzzetti: In *Scenes from Childhood* this wasn't much of an issue. When I had a cut of *Beginning Pieces*, I showed it to the parents of the kids and said, "Let's think through this." We talked about the nudity—could those scenes be left in? Of course I wanted them because the dialogue in these scenes is incredibly interesting. The parents said, "These are little kids; you've filmed what they do; we don't see a problem."

MacDonald: I moderated a discussion about *Beginning Pieces* at the Flaherty Film Seminar in 1987. It was attacked by a woman who argued that the camera-as-phallus implicitly created a parental rape of your daughter. You were shocked that somebody would see the film this way. Do you remember that?

Guzzetti: No. Are you sure this happened?

MacDonald: I am, only because I did such a bad job moderating that discussion—I was embarrassed about it for a long time. I'm relieved you don't remember!

Was the nudity the reason you took *Beginning Pieces* out of distribution?

Guzzetti: I took it out of circulation after the original distribution contract had expired (like so many 16mm distributors, this one went out of business). There was a possibility of another life for the film, and at that point, I asked my daughter Sarah, "What do you think about *Beginning Pieces* being in distribution?" and she said she wasn't comfortable with it. I didn't say, "Well, what scenes make you uncomfortable?" or anything like that. I mean if she doesn't want it out there, that settles the issue for me.

Recently I read an article about the artist Larry Rivers. Rivers made films of his daughters as they passed into adolescence; he got them to take their tops off and talk about their developing breasts and things like that. At the time, one of the two daughters was more uncomfortable with this than the other, but both apparently didn't like it very much. The issue is that those films belong to the Larry Rivers estate, which has been given to a foundation administered by somebody or other; but the *daughters* want those films back: they don't like them and feel that those are *their* films. If Rivers were alive, maybe he would say, "I didn't make these films as art" and give the films to his daughters, or he might destroy them. I certainly don't want to destroy my film, but I also don't want to make Sarah uncomfortable. I spent years of my life making *Beginning Pieces* and I hate to see all that work buried, but it may be that at the age of 40 or 50 Sarah will change her mind; she has a DVD.

By the way, this situation is also true of *The House on Magnolia Avenue*, which has not been shown.

MacDonald: Because some of the people are not comfortable with it?

Guzzetti: Right.

MacDonald: Everybody comes across so well!

Guzzetti: I thought so; I was completely blind-sided by the objection. I finished the film right at the time of the Cinema du Réal Festival; I sent it to them; they showed it, and that's only time it was shown in public. After that screening, there was a storm about it, and to keep the peace, I backed off. Later, people relented, so it's not an ongoing prohibition; but unless a film has a life at the beginning, is accepted into festivals and gets reviews, it doesn't really find a place in the world. I can't send out a 16mm film from 1987 now.

MacDonald: What led you to write your book on Godard's *Two or Three Things I Know about Her*? And how did you decide on the unusual form of that book?

Guzzetti: I was fascinated by the film. I scrounged around for money at the university and bought a 16mm print. Other people were interested in it too and a group of faculty members (plus a visiting Fellow from Denmark) started to meet on Tuesday evenings. We discussed the film a sequence at a time, usually one sequence per meeting, throughout the academic year. Can you imagine such a thing happening now? I had no thought that any publication would come out of this and neither did the others.

A few years later, someone asked me to write up my notes from these sessions for a film studies seminar involving Harvard, NYU, and SUNY-Buffalo [what was then the State University of New York at Buffalo, and is now the University at Buffalo]; and afterwards, Stanley Cavell suggested I turn these notes into a book. He had persuaded the Harvard University Press to do a series of books about film. By the time I was writing, I was often unsure which ideas had come from me and which from others, though in cases where I was sure it wasn't me, I said so in the text.

Because of the level of detail, I convinced myself early on that there had to be a full representation of the film in the book and I evolved the idea of facing pages. I was fascinated by the question of how you can talk about sound and moving image in a book, which can't represent those things directly, and thought I'd have a go at inventing a solution. The publisher was supportive, though a little skeptical, and the designer seemed to enjoy the challenge. Today the solution would involve a DVD.

The most frustrating thing, though, was that I was writing a lot about color and the publisher couldn't afford to include even a single color image. I'm not sure why the book cost so much. Was it all the typesetting of the French text? Was it all the white space that resulted from putting the analysis on pages that faced the relevant portion of script and frame enlargements? Was it the frame enlargements themselves, which were very hard to make because the print is in anamorphic Technoscope? Anyway, the book turned into a project in visual design, and like a lot of my work, blazed a path that no one followed. I'm told that David Byrne liked it, though.

MacDonald: In the 1980s, you, Dick Rogers, and Susan Meiselas got involved in the Nicaraguan revolution.

Guzzetti: I met Dick in 1968 or 1969, when he came back from England, where he had been studying, to get a Master's degree at the Harvard Education School. The admissions office sent me a packet of applications and I wrote to Dick in England, describing our program, and he wrote back in his irreverent style. A year or two later we were teaching sections of the same course.

After I finished *Air* in 1971, Dick and I drove across the country together for a month and shot *Evidence* [1972]. The plan was that we would shoot my film going west, then after we got to San Francisco, I would leave Dick and he would drive back by himself, taking another month to shoot still pictures— Dick had made *Quarry* [1970], but didn't yet think of himself as a filmmaker. He'd studied still photography at the Royal College of Art and thought of himself as a photographer. Dick had a not-very-old Volvo and we designed two camera mounts: one was welded to the right front fender and the other on the inside of the right window so it could swing out and you could shoot from the side (this one wasn't very successful).

After *Elephants* [1973], Dick shied away from making what he would call his own films, except for *226-1690* [1984]. What he told me was that he didn't have anything more to say in this personal mode. He did take commissions. He liked having to learn about the subjects of the films he agreed to make. If he didn't know exactly what Allen Ginsburg would say when he interviewed him about William Carlos Williams [*Voices and Visions: William Carlos Williams*; 1988], he knew where those comments belonged in the commissioned film.

MacDonald: The credits of both *Living at Risk: The Story of a Nicaraguan Family* and of *Pictures from a Revolution* say "directed, edited, produced by" you, Rogers, and Susan Meiselas, but I'm sure somebody must have been shooting imagery and somebody must have been taking sound.

Guzzetti: Susan had made her reputation as a photographer in Nicaragua in 1978–79; her pictures were seen internationally and became icons of the Nicaraguan Revolution. By the time the dust settled, she had put together a book of photographs [*Nicaragua: June 1978–July 1979* (London: Writers and Readers Publishing Cooperative, 1981)] that cemented her reputation. She was back and forth to Nicaragua a lot.

Her relationship with Dick was on and off, and always stormy—sometimes they had no relationship; sometimes they lived together—but I would see her when she was in Boston, and in New York from time to time too, and we were all in dialogue about what was happening in Nicaragua. Reagan had said that the Contras were the moral equivalent to the Founding Fathers of America and had put a lot of money into backing the Contra war. Reagan also said that Nicaragua was like Nazi Germany in the 1930s, and Dick, Susan, and I thought that maybe we could try to film what these "Nazis" looked like. I never had any illusion that a film we would make could have a drastic impact—but maybe we could change some attitudes.

The original idea was to focus on the internationally supervised Nicaraguan elections that would take place in 1984 (and which elected the Sandinistas with Daniel Ortega as president). Of course, we didn't know how the election would come out, and as we talked about it, the project seemed more and more amorphous: *how* were we going to make a film about the elections? Would it be just one of these voice-over journalistic films, which we didn't know how to make and didn't want to make, and probably would be refused by PBS anyway? I think I said, "How about a film that centers on a family and the elections?" Dick and Susan thought that was a good idea.

We didn't get enough money to do the project; the election came and went, and we saw that it wasn't a big issue for Americans: it only made an inside page of the *New York Times*. What remained was the idea of a film about a family, and Susan thought we could work with the family of Violeta Chamorro's brother Carlos, the Barrios family. Violeta had resigned from the government in 1980; in 1984 she was running *La Prensa*, of which her husband, assassinated in 1978, had been editor.

I liked the idea because they were a bourgeois family, not a peasant family, so we wouldn't be making one more film with generic campesinos fighting for their rights, which I didn't think would make much of an impression. What appealed to me was that the audience for the film, the PBS audience, basically white suburbanites, would be very similar to the Barrios family; they'd have pretty much the same values, the same kind of education—some members of the family went to college in the US—enjoy the same pop music.

It also appealed to us that the father, Carlos, had turned against the Sandinistas, as had Violeta: she left the coalition and finally ran against the Sandinistas and became the president after Ortega—but that was in the future; we couldn't have foreseen that. All but one of the children were Sandinistas (one brother was not), but the family was very close; they had not been driven apart by political disagreements. We thought this would make for a good film. We didn't want the film to be "politically monochrome," as somebody in the Paris audience later complained it was.

We scrambled around trying to raise money; we thought it was important to make the film as fast as possible, which for us meant a year from the raising of the money to delivering the finished prints. We did not foresee that when we got down there, Don Carlos, who had seemed enthusiastic about the film, would refuse to be in it. And we couldn't film the brother who was in opposition to the Sandinistas because he was living in Costa Rica and didn't want to be filmed. A big blow.

Then, during the year we were making the film, PBS showed a film by friends of ours, Newton Thomas Sigel and Pamela Yates, called *Guatemala: When the Mountains Tremble* [1983], and PBS got a lot of shit from Congress because it contained a recital of the coup of 1954 in Guatemala, which was largely CIA underwritten—the usual coup against a left-wing democratically elected leader being overthrown by right-wingers friendly to the US. By the time we were finished with *Living at Risk*, PBS was skittish; they didn't want to go near anything that looked partisan, and this was made worse by the absence of Carlos.

The essence of our film was that not only do these people have Christian values, values that have led them to support a government based on these values, but in order to act on what they believe and do their daily work, they have to function in the middle of a terrorist war sponsored by the United States. I don't understand how even the most neutral person in the world could fail to see the connection between what the US government did with the Contras and what everybody for the last ten years has called "state-sponsored terrorism"; what we did there *was* state-sponsored terrorism. The United States paid money for these thugs to rove around Nicaragua making attacks at night on cooperative farms and murdering the farmers in their beds, or storming into a little village in some remote area that had a Sandinista mayor and slitting the throat of the mayor and burning down the school and the health center. They didn't engage the Sandinista army, at least not when they could help it.

There *was* feeling in this country that the US involvement in Nicaragua was terribly wrong; there was the famous Boland Amendment, which said that no more US money could be used to support the Contras. That's how we got into Iran Contra-gate, because Reagan asked Ollie North, "Will nobody rid me of this problem?" and Ollie North sold missiles to Iran and used the money to pay the Contras.

In any case, PBS refused *Living at Risk*, but agreed to a second tier commitment: that is, they put it up on their satellite and offered it to their member stations. Dick, Susan, and I hired a friend to contact American television stations and try to persuade them to consider taking it down from the satellite. Enough stations did for me to feel that making the film was worth the effort—though I was never very fond of the film because of the compromises we'd had to make. One thing that alienated me was the dubbing of the Spanish voices by English voices with Spanish accents, which we felt we had to do for television. Last year, I had the chance to give the people back their own voices and subtitle what they say, so now I don't want to crawl under my seat when I watch the film.

When I was putting together the DVD a couple of years ago, the distributor wanted publicity material, and the thing that really amazed me as I went through my files is the way that life and film have changed since 1984. At that time, the film was widely written about; wherever it showed (in colleges, museums—places that showed 16mm film), it got reviewed in the press and the issues that are brought up in the film were engaged. There was even a political editorial in the *Boston Globe* about the film and American policy with Nicaragua, which is what we wanted. If you made a film like that now, nobody would write a paragraph about it; there are too many films and too little interest in politics.

MacDonald: During the making of the film, who did what?

Guzzetti: Dick did all the cinematography. That wasn't the original plan; we had agreed to alternate: Dick would shoot the first day; I would shoot the second day; and Susan would shoot the third day. I've always believed, and still believe, that the author of the images is in some sense the author of the film, and the moment Dick began shooting, I understood that having three people shooting would result in a film with three different styles.

I saw that Dick was shooting for image, rather than for image-plus-sound; he was shooting for what the scene could express; and he was doing a lot of what he always called "coverage": he would grab his master shot and go around changing angles and filming material to plug in as cutaways. After the first day, I thought we should leave the shooting to Dick. We wanted our film to be seen on television and Dick had been successful making films for public television. I knew that if I came back with the kind of thing that interested me—long takes of observational material—we'd probably end up with the kind of movie that's shown only in a museum.

In shooting film, I've always been intent on trying to disappear, so that as much as possible the reality can unfold seemingly by itself. As a filmmaker, Dick was the way he was in life: interventional. And that's the way he worked with the camera; he was an interlocutor so to speak, moving in for a close-up, crouching down for a low angle.

Also, neither Dick nor I knew Spanish; I was better with it than Dick because I knew some Italian, but we were both relying on Susan for our understanding of what was going on, and if she were shooting, what would *we* do?

MacDonald: So in the end you took sound?

Guzzetti: Yes. And Susan made the production happen; Dick and I didn't know anything about Nicaragua, and Susan knew everybody. Susan doesn't think of herself as a filmmaker; she has made a few films by herself, but her feeling was, and this comes out in *Pictures from a Revolution*, that for all of her incredible mastery as a still photographer, she's skeptical about still photography, about how it doesn't tell enough of the story. She's concerned with sociological context, and particularly in recent years, historical context.

Susan was part of all the filmmaking decisions and was part of the filming crew, but in the end she left most of the mechanics of the shooting and of sound recording to Dick and me. But not editing. All three of us were in the editing room all the time.

In the summer of 2009 Susan and I started work on a follow-up to *Living at Risk*, called *The Barrios Family 25 Years Later*. It consists of *Living at Risk*, plus twenty short films about various people who appear in the earlier film, one of them being Father Zubizarreta.

Father Zubizarreta is the priest that Miguel talks about in *Living at Risk*, though not by name, as the mentor who taught Christian values and the importance of fighting for the poor. Father Zubizarreta is still the same man, still teaching in the same school, and he still knows the Barrios children intimately. I have no doubt now that it wasn't so much Karl Marx who was behind the middle-class participation in the Nicaraguan Revolution, but Jesus Christ: Christ loved the poor; if you're going to be a true Christian, the measure of your deeds and your life is whether you do things to help the poor. That's how those kids were brought up.

MacDonald: Several years after finishing *Living at Risk*, you, Susan, and Dick decided to use Susan's photographs as a structural device to put together *Pictures from a Revolution* (figure 14).

Guzzetti: I've always liked *that* film!

MacDonald: *Pictures* has several levels of interest, one of which is Susan's reminiscences about what she did to get the original photographs and what happened to them. It also has a more general theme. When we're young, we think we can make substantial change, but often when we look back years later, we feel that our efforts have come to nothing, or mostly nothing.

Guzzetti: *Pictures* began when I said to Susan and Dick, "It's almost five years since we made the last film, and soon it's going to be ten years since the Sandinistas came in; why don't we go down to Nicaragua and ask people

FIGURE 14 *Susan Meiselas photograph in* Pictures from a Revolution *(1991) by Alfred Guzzetti, Susan Meiselas, and Richard P. Rogers.*

Source: Courtesy Alfred Guzzetti.

to tell us what's happened during these ten years. We'll make a three-and-a-half-hour film of historical testimony, like *The Sorrow and the Pity* [1972]." Susan said, "I don't feel qualified to make the film you're talking about, but remember the idea I had about finding the people in my photographs and seeing what's happened to *them*? We could do that." I said, "A much better idea!"

Dick was grumpy: "How do you make a film out of *that*?" I said, "We'll figure it out, Susan, and if Dick feels he's not on board, you and I can make the film." I wasn't trying to manipulate, but in retrospect, I guess I knew that the one thing Dick hated more than anything was to be left out. He immediately changed his mind.

For a long time, we thought of the film as being about the photographs and the people in the photographs. We didn't think Susan would be in the film. We even prepared samples for fund-raising in which she had no presence.

What haunted me was how do you get from one photograph to another? One of the things we considered was focusing on just one photograph. That way we could get rid of the problem of going from photograph to photograph. We even decided on a photograph taken in a town called San Isidro: in the center there's a woman with a floppy hat who wanted to be a tank driver, and up in the corner is a very handsome guy in a beret who looked like Che Guevara, who winds up being a factory worker in Canada. That idea seemed intriguing, but it didn't have enough range.

I forget whether Dick or I first realized that Susan *had* to talk; she would set the trajectory of the film, and the film would be about the intersections of a North American still photographer with people in Nicaragua for 125ths of a second at particular moments in history.

Susan *hated* this idea. She did not want to be in the film, didn't want *her* experiences to be front and center. I agreed with one of her reservations wholeheartedly: I did not want us to make a film about how Nicaraguan history happens to a North American, so that she becomes the person the audience identifies with and it's *her* disappointment, *her* enthusiasms, *her* fears that register everything, making this third world country the background for her experience. That happens in films all the time. In January Susan came up to Cambridge, and we taped her talking in detail about everything that had happened to her in Nicaragua—sometimes cued by the photographs, sometimes not.

Shooting involved a number of trips to Nicaragua over a period of two years, plus trips to Canada and Miami. When we got to Nicaragua, looking for and finding people became part of the film. We really didn't know whether we would find particular people or learn that they were dead, and if we did find the people, if they'd be bitter, happy, worse or better off.

MacDonald: Was *Pictures* widely seen?

Guzzetti: It was more widely seen abroad than in the United States. By the time the film came out, Reagan and the Nicaraguan revolutionaries were out of office; the news organizations had closed their news bureaus in Managua, and the *New York Times* had sent their correspondent elsewhere.

In the United States it premiered at the New York Film Festival, which was a big deal with lots of press attention, but I saw very clearly that, inside the United States, the film was a political problem. Here, the people who were interested in Nicaragua were the Left, and the Left wanted films that said a certain thing: that the Nicaraguan revolution was a splendid heroic uprising of the people that was entirely sabotaged by the United States and that's why it came to grief and why the revolutionary government was voted out of office. *Pictures from a Revolution* doesn't say that.

Abroad there was no problem and *Pictures* was shown on television in Europe, Japan, and Australia, and in fact it was paid for by the BBC. Our experience with the BBC was amazing. Within a couple of weeks, André Singer called to say, "I really like your proposal; I'm going to try and get it financed," and *two weeks later* he called back: "I've got it financed! Send me a budget." We said, "What are the restrictions?" Singer: "Well, the program is ninety minutes, so don't go over ninety minutes"! In England *Pictures* got two transmissions on prime-time Saturday night; it was featured on the cover of the BBC magazine, along with an article by Harold Pinter about Nicaragua and the film.

MacDonald: Your *América Central* [2004] is very different from *Living at Risk* and *Pictures from a Revolution*. To make it, did you revisit a place that meant something to you during those earlier projects?

Guzzetti: I can't claim much intention at all with that film. Susan and I were in Nicaragua, shooting a film called *Reframing History* [2004], a short documentary that would be on the commercial DVD of *Pictures from a Revolution*. Twenty-five years after the revolution, Susan decided to blow up eighteen of her Nicaragua photographs to six by nine feet (this is a process used for outdoor advertising on the sides of buildings) and put them up in the public places where they were taken; and I was to film the installations.

One morning, before we'd set out, we'd been watching CNN and looking at the news crawls across the bottom, and talking about how incredibly remote, and US-centric, all these stories seemed. Seeing them in the context of Managua, where everything was covered with dust, where people are desperately poor, made the things that America sees as so urgent seem incredibly far away. I was remembering that, and suddenly decided to shoot a short video of an intersection where I was waiting for Susan and include those news crawls.

MacDonald: How did you get involved in the ethnographic film *Seed and Earth* [1994]?

Guzzetti: Bob Gardner had a collaboration going with Ákos Östör and, encouraged by Bob, I think, Ákos wrote a grant application to the National Endowment for the Humanities to make a cycle of films on West Bengal. I think probably Gardner was interested in making *Forest of Bliss* [1986], but the grant application envisioned six films, one or more by Bob and the others by other people, all funded through the Film Study Center.

Ákos wanted to make a film about rice cultivation. His idea was to make it in two different places in India, a cool part of India in the north and in Bengal, where the rice cultivation and the rituals around it were very different. I talked Ákos out of the idea; comparisons in film always wind up making the two places look the same, and even if you *can* distinguish them, the audience doesn't care about the contrast; it just seems like an intellectual principle. He conceded this, and then it turned out that rice cultivation in India was no longer what Ákos had studied. He had been imagining a film that had the cycle of the seasons in it—the planting, the harvest, and the religious rituals concerned with those various moments. When we got to India, we found out that the green revolution had reached the villages of West Bengal. The Ford Foundation had encouraged farmers to plant multiple varieties of rice that came to maturity at different times of year, so the old seasonal cycle had become blurred; the villagers were constantly planting, transplanting, harvesting, and storing rice.

We were there for a month and a half.

MacDonald: You include a final sequence where many people are watching a Bollywood movie on TV; *Seed and Earth* is not an attempt to see the culture as something completely separated from modern life, the way *Dead Birds* [1964] depicts the Kurelu.

Guzzetti: Gardner is really the son of Flaherty in that respect (though he did return in recent years to document what had happened to the people of *Dead Birds*), but Ákos is an anthropologist, a scientist who's interested in seeing what's there now.

There was a rich man in the village, one of the few people who had electricity and the only one with a television. On some evenings he would haul the television outdoors and people would gather around.

MacDonald: *Air* is a premonition of the video work you began to do in the 1990s. *Variation* [1995], *What Actually Happened* [1996], *Under the Rain* [1997], *The Tower of Industrial Life* [2000] are like musical pieces.

Guzzetti: I think so.

I'd always hated videotape; I thought it was like second-rate film: the image was crude and you couldn't really edit tape in the way that you could edit film, so for a long time it didn't interest me at all, especially the idea of video as a substitute for film. In time I began seeing videotapes that did something else, though to do those things, you had to have access to high-end equipment, which I didn't have. What was available to me was not the equivalent of the film equipment I had access to.

When Susan, Dick, and I were making *Pictures from a Revolution*, Dick and I looked at the newest video gear and wondered whether we could schlep this camera around Nicaragua, and how would we edit? In both cases, the decision was that the time had not come: we were going to be in remote places, the video equipment was very delicate, and if it broke down you couldn't take your Swiss army knife, open the camera up and clean it out, the way you can with a movie camera.

Around 1992, Dick bought a Canon Hi-8 camera and went on a trip to Israel with Susan. He showed me what he had shot, on a good production monitor, and I remember pictures of the Dead Sea where I liked the intensity of the blue, and thought I could do something with the color palette: it didn't have great saturation—when it got very saturated, it bled—but in a less saturated realm, it looked subtle and interesting. I talked to Dick about that, and about Marie Cosindas, the photographer who worked with Polaroids at a time when the Polaroid palette was very limited but became interested in what you *could* do with that palette. I decided to buy the same camera that Dick had.

I came to the conclusion that video was a miniaturist medium; you show work on a monitor where the image is small, but the sound can be big—an interesting reversal of the traditional balance in film, especially 16mm film, where the image is great, but the sound is poor and you do your best to compensate for that.

I thought about ways to compensate for the poor quality of the video image, by doing things that you can't do easily with film. I got a cheap character generator that would allow me to work with visual text; and I became interested in putting one image inside of another. Also, when you'd let single images stay on-screen a long time, you became aware that the detail wasn't there, but you could move the camera through space smoothly because there was a tiny Steadicam for small video cameras—in 16mm this isn't possible without an expensive Steadicam that you need a trained operator for.

I had been through similar problems with a job I did for Polaroid in the late 1970s, where I was supposed to photograph museums with the Polaroid-made motion picture camera—did you ever hear about this?

MacDonald: No.

Guzzetti: It was an instant movie camera, silent, that shot cassettes three minutes long. The color palette was quite beautiful; it was additive color created by a lenticular screen—a very innovative technology. It became available in the late 1970s, just when VHS tape came out, so it was doomed economically. I was exploring how to move that camera smoothly through space.

Anyway, you *could* move this Hi-8 video camera. Also, I rigged up a way of doing stereo sound with the camera and two microphones—another thing you couldn't do with 16mm.

At the time, the other major liability of video was that you could only edit linearly. Filmmaking is non-linear: you snip out a piece of film and you move it to another place in the movie, but in video editing if you made a mistake and wanted to make a change, you had to remake the whole piece. This forced you into another kind of thinking. I lived with linear editing for several years—through *A Tropical Story* [1998].

MacDonald: Is linear editing the reason why you chose to do a series of very short pieces in *Variation*?

Guzzetti: No. I don't think I would have tried *Variation* early on because, even though it's only five minutes long, it has twelve sections and a lot of shots.

Slowly the technology developed. Sony put out a linear tape editor that worked in Hi-8 but had some computer memory—it cost a lot of money and is now totally useless. But it could remember the decisions you made for a hundred shots, so you could reconstitute the tape; and you could make a fresh tape by popping in all the source tapes, one at a time, and it would re-record those; basically it copied sections of the camera tapes onto a fresh tape by following the time codes stored in the computer chip. By the time of *Variation* I had that machine.

Variation was made for Ivan Tcherepnin, a composer and a good friend; we taught together for years. He ran the electronic music studio in the Harvard music department, but I knew him from before he came to Harvard. Back in 1978 he and I made *Sky Piece*. In the 1990s we had an idea for a tape, but just before we were about to start the project, Ivan was taken to the hospital with liver cancer—he died in 1998—and that collaboration never happened. I went ahead and made *Variation* as a present for Ivan.

In *Variation*, I was trying to make something that had no words but created a pure sound and image relationship that worked on a musical principle of variation. It wasn't *variations*, like the *Goldberg Variations*, because there isn't any theme; it's like variation without a theme.

By the mid-1990s, technicians were experimenting with computer control of linear editing set-ups. They had devices to edit tape that filled half a room; computers were controlling banks of tape recorders, so you could make a change in the computer program—you could say "Delete shot number two"—and the computer would take charge of reconstituting the tape without shot number two. I think the television stations had true nonlinear video editing a year or two before everybody had it. The real video revolution was Firewire.

I started editing *Khalfan and Zanzibar* [1999] in a linear way but was able to switch over to non-linear to finish the piece. *The Tower of Industrial Life* was edited on a computer: before Final Cut Pro, there was a program that allowed you to do nonlinear editing on a Mac.

MacDonald: In *The Curve of the World*, *The Stricken Areas*, and *What Actually Happened* you begin to include dream texts.

Guzzetti: I thought of those three tapes plus *Rosetta Stone* as a cycle called "Language Lessons" that should be shown together, one after the other. They all include the idea of learning a language, as well as what I thought of as the language of the unconscious, the dream language. In doing repetitions of the same image from tape to tape, I was working the way a painter might work: the painter paints something in one way, then returns to it, thinking, oh, *now* I see the way to paint it. Of course, there's no definitive way to paint anything; the process is an exploration of seeing what's in the material.

MacDonald: Are the dream texts in those tapes from real dreams (figure 15)?

Guzzetti: I kept a dream diary for many years before I started working with video. Some of the dreams in those tapes were recorded long before the tapes were made.

MacDonald: Do you think of *What Actually Happened, Under the Rain*, and *Down from the Mountains*, even *History of the Sea*, as travel films?

Guzzetti: Yes—especially *Under the Rain*, because as I was traveling in China, I was thinking of *Unsere Afrikareise* ["Our Trip to Africa," by Peter Kubelka; 1966], which was made from ordinary travel materials.

MacDonald: What are the locations in *What Actually Happened*?

Guzzetti: Mostly Rome. Deborah and I lived in Rome for half a year, and most everything in that piece was shot there. The outdoor sculpture garden, where you go around the statue, is the Borghese Gardens; one of the indoor museums is the Vatican Museum; the other is the Capitoline Museum.

MacDonald: At the end of *Down from the Mountains* there's kind of a magical shot where you're looking at a tree with the moon above it and the tree changes from winter to summer, but the moon doesn't change; it's a full moon the whole time. It's magical and reminds me of an early shot in Peter

FIGURE 15 *Urban scene with dream text in Alfred Guzzetti's* History of the Sea *(2004).*
Source: Courtesy Alfred Guzzetti.

Hutton's *Landscape (for Manon)* [1987], of a sycamore tree that begins to glow. How did you make that shot?

Guzzetti: I shot the first picture in one season; but later it occurred to me to make the season change, so I duplicated that first shot into the camera from the computer; then I brought the camera to the same place exactly, used the playback and the viewfinder of the camera to get the framing very close—it was off by a couple of millimeters, which I later corrected in the computer. The full moon doesn't land in the same place in the sky in two different seasons, so I shot another moon, then shrank it down so it matched the old moon. That shot goes back to Edward Steichen, who made a series of still pictures of a shadblow tree over a period of time.

MacDonald: It seems strange to me that these pieces are shown so infrequently, even in places where the work would seem a natural fit. They strike me as closely related to Nick Dorsky's recent films.

Guzzetti: Everybody seems to make that connection, but I don't see it.

MacDonald: There are obvious differences, of course: you're working in video with sound and text, and Nick, of course, makes silent films to be shown at silent speed. But overall, like your videos, his films are musical in structure; both of you use what Nick calls "polyvalent montage"; that is, each shot subtly refers backward *and* forward, each cut reveals both change *and* continuity within a complex, evolving montage structure.

Guzzetti: Don't get me wrong, I like Dorsky's work a lot. Scott, I've given up trying to figure out why some work gets shown and other work doesn't. Some exhibitors have found my work interesting; Abina Manning, who used to run Pandemonium in London, was very responsive, but then she took a job running the Video Data Bank.

MacDonald: Have you tried to get your videos distributed by Video Data Bank?

Guzzetti: I think I could, but they charge such high prices! Abina said she likes to get the artist as much money as possible, and I told her, "That's great, but I also like to get the work *seen*." Of course, Abina knows her business better than I do.

Isaac Julien once told me that what I should do is make twenty-five copies of each video, sign them and get a gallery to sell them for five thousand dollars apiece. I told him that I'd been waiting all my life for digital media, where you can make hundreds of copies, all of them identical to the original; and the idea of choking this opportunity off in order to profit from the art world made no sense to me.

MacDonald: You've mentioned that some of the pieces don't work if they're projected.

Guzzetti: The best video projections have been at Lincoln Center and at the Gene Siskel Center in Chicago. In Chicago the projector was better than the tapes; it was like putting them under a microscope! When I showed at those two places, I realized that projection had gotten much better, but at the same time, those big projections lost a lot of what I felt I'd been doing with color. What I missed in both theaters was my original sense of a fantasy color palette that's a bit fluorescent and very intense and brilliant and glowing.

The other thing that's been hard is that most projectors blur the scrolling dream texts, which are crisp when they move across a monitor. I'm often working in subtle ways with the graphics—for example, sometimes I like the text to be at the threshold of readability, to be *almost* unreadable—and those subtleties are lost if the projector blurs everything.

MacDonald: So the ideal way to look at these earlier video pieces would be to see them on a good monitor in a room with a really good sound system.

Guzzetti: Absolutely. A wonderful woman who worked for a time at the Whitney, Tania Leighton—she has an art gallery in Berlin now—said she wanted to do a gallery show of my work; did I have tapes besides *The Tower of Industrial Life*, which was about to be shown in the Whitney Biennial? She did a show at Location One in downtown Manhattan, and the installation of those two tapes—she chose *Under the Rain* and *A Tropical Story*—could not have been improved upon. They used a big, high-end monitor and they had terrific sound. It was all done very simply. They darkened the room and had comfortable places for people to sit. Perfect.

There have been other instances where I've not been very happy, despite a lot of effort going into the presentations. Most galleries are acoustically limited: even if they can show the image well, they're not arranged so that the soundtrack can be loud enough to keep subtleties evident. I've pretty much given up on the gallery route.

Of course, the solution is high definition, because a high definition piece absolutely withstands projection and in a theatrical situation the sound can be great. When the Museum of Modern Art showed *Still Point* [2009], it was as perfect a projection as I could have imagined and it sounded wonderful.

MacDonald: Was *Still Point* your first high-definition piece?

Guzzetti: Yes. I bought high-definition equipment (with help from a grant) in order to make it. It was premiered at the Dallas Video Festival at the Dallas Museum of Art. It uses two or three images from *Breaking Earth* [2008], the installation piece I did with Kurt Stallmann around the same time, also high definition. The other images are particular to *Still Point* (figure 16).

MacDonald: Was it also your first sync-sound video?

Guzzetti: Among the experimental video pieces, it's the first one to use "actual" sound. In the grant proposal I said that I wanted to record high-quality stereo with the images. In fact, I didn't stick to this procedure, though I tried to stick to the aesthetic. A few of the shots use the "sync" track (I guess I should call this the "production track") alone. The others either use the production track supplemented by others or a post-synchronized track where I've completely discarded the production track.

FIGURE 16 *Street advertisement in Alfred Guzzetti's* Still Point *(2009).*
Source:

MacDonald: *Still Point* is more minimal than anything else you've done—does this reflect a change in your thinking?

Guzzetti: Yes, though I wonder if it has a future. With *Still Point* I set out to make a piece out of the most spare elements I could find. It took a *very* long time and an enormous amount of trial and error. I've tried to make something that's simpler still, but I haven't gotten very far with it. *Still Point* might be the end of a road (a sunset mistaken for a sunrise, to paraphrase Debussy's remark about Wagner).

MacDonald: The title is from T. S. Eliot's *Four Quartets*?

Guzzetti: Yes, though I've done my best never to mention it lest the piece get interpreted in the context of the quote!

I think that high-definition video, even HDV, the kind that I have, which is not the best kind, is better than 16mm. I've looked at it very critically and the image is better. It's not as good as 35mm, but it's in between 16mm and 35mm. And for me, it's more than good enough. I imagine even Peter Hutton could make his work this way.

MacDonald: In another high-definition piece, *Time Exposure* [2012], you return to your parents and to that early moment in their relationship when your father was just finding his way into photography, by focusing on a photograph for which your father won honorable mention in a contest. *Time Exposure* is an homage to your parents and to the ways in which they supported your becoming a filmmaker, but it also evokes a number of other filmmakers who have focused a motion picture on still photographs and who have used narration in ways similar to your voice-over. I'm thinking of Hollis Frampton in *(nostalgia)* [1971], Godard and Gorin's *Letter to Jane* [1972], Morgan Fisher's *Standard Gauge* [1984], and even Su Friedrich's *Sink or Swim* [1990], which ends with a passage of questions similar to your questions at the end of *Time Exposure* (figure 17). Were you consciously paying homage to these films?

FIGURE 17 *Felix Guzzetti's Honorable Mention photograph of Emily Street in South Philadelphia, from Alfred Guzzetti's* Time Exposure *(2012).*
Source: Courtesy Alfred Guzzetti.

Guzzetti: I do admire Morgan Fisher's work—I've known Morgan for a long time, since we were undergraduates at Harvard. I've seen *Standard Gauge* only once, quite a while ago, but did respond to it and do remember it. And yes, I think that *Sink or Swim* is a strong, rich film. Likewise *(nostalgia)*. But I wasn't thinking of any of these while working on *Time Exposure*.

I was thinking nearly exclusively of the history I recount, struggling with writing, and with the voice-over, which I'd never done before (I got some good advice from Ross [McElwee]). I did think about *Letter to Jane* and even more of *Ulysses* [1986] by Agnès Varda. I thought also about *La Jetée* [1962, by Chris Marker], because it's nearly all still photographs and voice-over, with a single moment of movement, which I thought of in relation to the single moment of color and sync sound that I use—though I use movement three times. And of course all the work I've done with Susan Meiselas, especially in *Pictures from a Revolution* played a part in my thinking.

MacDonald: We've not talked about your teaching, but I assume you've mentored a good many filmmakers over the years. Do particular experiences with students stand out for you? I hear you're alluded to in Darren Aronofsky's *The Fountain* [2006].

Guzzetti: Darren names the Ellen Burstyn character "Dr. Guzetti." Darren was an English major and was in my class for a term, then took Miklós Jancsó's course, where he made a quirky movie called *Supermarket Sweep*. I admire Darren for always making his own movies and not directing generic Hollywood stuff.

But you've asked a difficult question; I don't know where to begin!

Damien Chazelle, who made *Guy and Madeleine on a Park Bench* [2009], was the best writer in my Freshman seminar. In another class of mine he made a very original experimental tape about Buddy Bolden, the near mythic coronetist who might be the person who invented jazz, if jazz was invented by a person, and who left no recordings. Damien married Jasmine McGlade, who was also in that seminar and also a fine writer. She's just finished a feature of her own called *Maria My Love* [2011].

About ten years ago I taught three friends from Philadelphia, all incredibly talented. Luke Fischbeck became an avant-garde composer; I hope Pablo Colapinto, whose family is from Argentina, is still making his amazingly original and atmospheric experimental films. And Gary Johnston, who had to teach himself so much about computers to do his complicated thesis, wound up working for Apple, developing Final Cut Pro.

In the late 1970s Mira Nair was in my beginning class and I remember her as charismatic even then. She had a way of communicating how much fun she was having working on the film the class was making. She still radiates this enthusiasm and makes people feel how special it is to be working together. In her senior year she made a lovely film nominally on a marketplace in New

Delhi, but actually on her identity as a young woman and an Indian. She was brilliant.

And Marco Williams, who began by making a film about his search for his father [*In Search of Our Fathers*, 1992] and now teaches filmmaking at NYU.

David DiGregorio made wonderful, evocative experimental films, and in the years after he graduated focused on composing and performing music, doing art performances with his partner Sung Hwan Kim, who was also an inventive filmmaker and who's been making a place for himself in the art world.

Josh Oppenheimer was endlessly outrageous and endlessly warm and kind. He moved to London where he's spent many years working on a cycle of films about the massacre of "communists" in Indonesia [the first, *The Act of Killing*, was released in 2013]. Shawn Hainsworth figured out that he could make movies by working stints as a highly paid computer engineer, and he's turned out documentaries that follow immigrants for periods of years, stuff that would be very hard to finance another way.

Peter Sellars was very unhappy in my beginning film class. I came across him one morning in the hallway of Sever Hall with a bike turned upside down, a floodlight, and a Bolex, shooting and looking miserable. I couldn't figure out how what he was doing related to the assignment. He confessed that he wanted to switch to my freshman seminar on Godard's *Vivre sa vie* [1962], which perhaps led to his enthusiasm for Godard. He wound up acting in Godard's *King Lear* [1987] and of course did other amazing things. I don't know where to stop!

Ross McElwee

No one is more closely identified with the personal documentary than Ross McElwee, in part because of the relative popular success of *Sherman's March: A Meditation on the Possibility of Romantic Love in the South during an Era of Nuclear Proliferation* (1986), but on a more fundamental level, because of McElwee's ability in his best films to provide the personal documentary with considerable depth and subtlety, not merely through engaging cinematography and deft editing, but through his development of a complex narrative perspective resonant of accomplished fiction. For each of his personal documentaries since *Backyard* (1984), McElwee has created a "Ross McElwee" persona, who resembles his creator in a good many ways, but is also a semifictional character whose foibles and frustrations become the director's focus. Of course, this is a common strategy in literature and in cinema. Hemingway's Nick Adams has much in common with the youthful Hemingway and allowed the writer to explore the implications of his early experiences; and the great American comedy directors of the 1920s—Keaton, Chaplin, and Lloyd—all created on-screen personae who are often versions of themselves, but at the same time, characters subject to their directorial interests.

More successfully than any other personal documentarian, however, McElwee has developed a *voice*, a deadpan way of addressing his audience—sometimes in off-screen voice-over, sometimes in on-screen monologues spoken directly to the camera—that has been much imitated and has come to seem fundamental to the genre.˙ McElwee's voice has evolved, film by film, over the past thirty years. His addresses to the camera in *Sherman's March* are wry comedy, whereas in *Time Indefinite* (1993), still the most powerful of his films, his comments create an unusually complex experience. For example, a moment of reflection in a seedy motel combines an amusingly dour monologue to the camera with a voice-over critique of that monologue as it is being delivered, to create a kind of nesting doll of Ross McElwees: the McElwee we

---

˙ For purposes of this interview and others in this volume with personal documentary filmmakers, I make a distinction between what is usually called personal documentary and "personal film": in a personal documentary the filmmaker uses sync-sound recording as a central means of exploring relationships with family and friends. "Personal film" generally refers to a variety of avant-garde strategies for revealing the personal and can include the (non-sync) voice of the filmmaker. Jonas Mekas has developed a narratorial voice-over that is remarkably evocative—but his films are not personal documentaries in the sense I am using the term here.

see talking to us is talked about by the McElwee we hear in voice-over, and when the two voices come together at the conclusion of the shot by repeating, one after the other, "It's all very complicated," we become conscious not only of the real Ross McElwee, who edited the film to create this complicated moment, but an earlier Ross McElwee, who wrote—and presumably practiced speaking—the two monologues before he recorded this scene.

McElwee is a capable cinematographer, though his commitment has always been to the combination of image and voice. In several of his later films—*Six O'Clock News* (1996) and *In Paraguay* (2009), for example—the Ross McElwee character within the film finds himself unable to proceed with what he had hoped to accomplish and spends a few moments recording moments of light and shadow that evoke such avant-garde masters of chiaroscuro as Stan Brakhage and Bruce Baillie, but it is always quite clear that these moments are, for the McElwee character, a kind of doodling, instances of his frustration that the real action of the film is on pause.

At the conclusion of *Time Indefinite*, McElwee's commitment to image *and* sound takes on a subtle (and perhaps unconscious) polemical dimension. As Marilyn Levine, McElwee's wife, is about to give birth to their son Adrian, McElwee includes a close-up of Levine's distended belly; in a moment of love and support, he reaches into the frame while filming, covering her hand with his. For any aficionado of American independent film, this shot evokes a moment from Stan Brakhage's canonical birth film, *Window Water Baby Moving* (1959): as Jane Brakhage, pregnant with their daughter, rests in a bathtub, Brakhage reaches in from outside the frame to cover her hand in a nearly identical gesture of love and support. What follows, however, is a very different depiction of the birth itself. Camera-in-hand, Brakhage can only watch the birth of his daughter. In *Time Indefinite*, however, McElwee puts his camera down so he can participate in delivering Adrian: the screen goes dark; nevertheless, we are present for the birth—we *hear* it. While Brakhage's commitment to cinema as a visual art necessitates a certain detachment from an important personal experience, at least until the birth is over (at the conclusion of the birth, Jane Brakhage takes the camera and records the new father's excitement), McElwee's approach allows him the luxury of direct participation in a crucial personal event without eliminating the desire to have the moment recorded.

As McElwee's personal documentaries developed into a saga, however, the very intimacy of his filmmaking approach came into increasing conflict with the realities of his evolving personal life. This process reached its apogee with *In Paraguay* (2009), a personal documentary about McElwee and Levine's adoption of their daughter Mariah in 1995. Completed in 2009, as McElwee and Levine were in the throes of divorce, *In Paraguay* is a love letter to what has passed, to a moment still early in the marriage when Ross, Marilyn, and Adrian handled a frustrating situation in a foreign country with remarkable patience and aplomb. After the film's premiere at the Venice Film Festival, it was removed from distribution at Levine's demand. One can hope that *In Paraguay* will ultimately find its way to audiences. *Photographic Memory* (2011), a complex, carefully crafted, and deeply moving film about McElwee's experiences traveling in France as a still photographer in the early 1970s and his current struggles with Adrian, now a young adult, is available.

I first interviewed McElwee in 1987 for *A Critical Cinema 2* (University of California Press), when we discussed his feature films from *Charleen* (1977) up through *Sherman's March*. In this more recent interview, conducted online in 2011 and 2012, we discuss his grounding in literature, his earliest filmmaking experiences, the preparation and production of his monologues, his current sense of the viability of personal documentary, and his most recent films.

MacDonald: I'm curious about your filmmaking before you arrived at WGBH and MIT. What can you tell me about your experiences shooting material for local television in North Carolina?

McElwee: I'm hesitant to call what I did in North Carolina "filmmaking"—most of the time I was standing behind a massive RCA studio television camera wearing my headset and dutifully shifting back and forth among close shot, medium shot, wide shot at the command of the director. The experience did, I guess, serve as a rickety bridge from photography to moving images. The previous year, I had traveled and worked in France as a wedding photographer's assistant. But towards the end of this sojourn, I realized that I wanted to make films rather than, or in addition to, still photographs.

I had no idea how to proceed with this. This was back in 1973, when being a documentary filmmaker—either independent or studio based—seemed a pretty obscure career, especially if you were raised in the South. There were very few role models, very little work to admire, and certainly no mentors available to me in North Carolina. But through a friend of my father's, I did manage to get a job working as a summer vacation replacement for a TV studio cameraman at WSOC, a commercial station in Charlotte. Jack Callaghan, the six o'clock news anchor, was a remarkable man—confined to a wheel chair but very much at home and in command of the studio from behind his news anchor desk.

My summer job turned into a longer stint, and after I had worked for several months at WSOC, I wrote a proposal to make a film about the plight of poverty-stricken seniors—not an especially original concept, even back then—and presented it to Mr. Callaghan, who approved a modest budget. But to my disappointment, he assigned a news cameraman to do the shooting. (I have no idea why I thought I could quickly master the ancient Auricon 16mm camera, which was a bitch to load, a horror to hand-hold, and came equipped with a reflex eyepiece/viewfinder that was like looking through a long pipe stem aimed at the midnight sky.)

The cameraman, Keith, and I began by filming a kid I knew from high school who had gotten in trouble by attempting to hold up a Li'l General convenience store in Charlotte. There was no weapon involved—only a pointed finger concealed in the pocket of a sweatshirt. The judge must have felt some compassion for this somewhat boneheaded ploy, and my friend dodged a prison sentence by agreeing to do community service working in a state-run facility for the elderly. Keith and I spent several days shooting my friend as he carried meal trays laden with rather inedible food—congealed grits and ham marinating in cold gravy, grey string beans—to the elderly residents. As often as not, my friend ended up carrying the untouched meals back to the kitchen where they were probably placed in the fridge until they could be served again the next day.

I remember feeling vaguely uncomfortable throughout our filming at the old persons' home: it seemed voyeuristic; I was an outsider with no real connection to the place. Though the film I had envisioned was to have been an advocacy piece, I felt I was, in some ways, a false advocate and very much at sea in this undertaking. If I were shooting the same situation today, of course, the focus would be not on the old folks, but on my friend Oliver—how he got into this situation, as well as what he would do after his sentence was over. But I was after a grander theme, I guess, and foolishly ignored the story that was staring me in the face. I do remember being thrilled at one shot we managed to get of empty rocking chairs painted in vibrant rainbow colors (this was, after all, the 1970s), moving back and forth on a porch in syncopated agitation, set in motion not by people, but by gusts of hot piedmont wind.

Our budget allowed Keith and me to drive for a weekend to Orlando where I had the notion that we would film in and around Disney World—an epicenter of youth culture and fun—a world out of reach for the impoverished elders we'd been filming. I imagined that we would be welcomed into the Magic Kingdom because we were making a well-intentioned documentary for a television station. One of the things I had hoped to film were the trash trucks hauling out the garbage after the tourist hordes had left—for some reason, Keith and I thought this might be symbolically useful for the film. But we were told by the PR fellow assigned to escort us around that there were "no garbage trucks in the Magic Kingdom," and even if there were, we would not be allowed to film them.

We shot one roll of footage but never bothered to process it. We then drove to the coast and managed to get some shots of oldsters with metal detectors combing the beach for treasure. This shot would become the final scene of our film. I wrote an impassioned narration urging my audience to wake up to the plight of the elderly, stuck in their wretched state-run rest homes. Over the shots of the people with metal detectors, I quoted from T. S. Eliot: "I shall grow old, I shall grow old, I shall wear the bottoms of my trousers rolled. . ."—I now cannot believe I insisted on this.

The film was, again at my insistence, entitled *Twenty Million Missing Persons*. And it occurs to me, in an equal mix of irony and dread, that as I approach the official "retirement age," whatever *that* phrase means, I'll soon be able to wear *my* trousers rolled (I've already noticed that the mermaids no longer sing to me).

In this one film, I think I managed to get a lot of things out of my system. I identified a documentary filming stance in which I was not at all comfortable—that of the invisible voyeur hiding behind a camera, pretending not to be present among his living, breathing subjects. I also had my fling with pretentiousness—embedding Eliot into the narration, seeking self-serious and symbolic footage.

Even when it was all stitched together and overlaid with voice written by me but intoned by the station's staff, the film was pretty awful, and mercifully, the station declined to air it. Kindly Jack Callaghan thought of it as a learning experience—for me, but perhaps more importantly for WSOC.

So the same year Steven Spielberg finished *Sugarland Express* [1974], his first film, I finished mine. Depressing. A few years ago, I came across the bulky 2-inch video master for *Twenty Million Missing Persons*, and with some guilt as to the ecological implications of what I was doing, unceremoniously dumped it into a trash container.

MacDonald: When we talked back in 1987 (my god, that's 25 years ago!), you mentioned that when you were at Brown University, you worked with John Hawkes for a couple of semesters. I read his *The Blood Oranges* [1971] recently, which you mentioned in another interview, and it occurred to me that what might have attracted you to Hawkes, and made that particular novel memorable, was his work with a narrator about whom we have ambivalent feelings. My Ph.D. dissertation at the University of Florida focused on narrative perspective in Hemingway's short stories; that is, the way Hemingway's choices of narrators affect the impact and meaning of the stories. Your films seem particularly literary in your complex work with narration.

McElwee: Well, you're right about Hawkes. While I was a student, I don't think I was aware of his impact on me (and on a generation of Brown students) in learning how to develop a narrative voice—a persona—in your writing. His fiction certainly seemed invested in the notion of creating an ambivalent relationship to the narrator. I remember having a rather heated discussion with him about why his view of life, as espoused by his protagonists, was so pessimistic. Now, I would describe that view somewhat differently: darkly ironic while taking pleasure in the sensual possibilities of life. This view was a little challenging to a 19-year-old, but to some degree, I've come to embrace a similar view myself.

It's funny that you mention your interest in Hemingway's narrative perspective. The very first assignment in the first course I took under Hawkes (a survey course in the American novel since World War II) was to take a personal experience and fictionalize it by mimicking a writer we admired. I chose Hemingway, of course, and wrote about traveling for a summer in Greece with a very handsome Greek friend and two beautiful Australian women. I wrote about feeling vaguely out of sync with the Dionysian possibilities of the situation, of being desirous of one of the women while acknowledging the impossibility of becoming her lover. I wrote in short terse sentences about the stark grandeur of the scenery, of how the heat of the sun, blasting off of the rocky Peloponnesian landscape, was both seductive and enervating, about how we had to stop for gas at a station which had a single pump, and how we had to clear the whitish road dust from the little windows on the pump in order to see how much we owed the attendant for the petrol. Like a good student, I was trying to fulfill the assignment, to match Hemingway's authorial attitude, but I knew as I was writing it that it was not a completely comfortable fit. It wasn't really me.

On that trip through Greece, I had in fact felt depressed by my own sexual insecurities and defeated by the adamantine heat and landscape, but even though technically I was writing like Hemingway, au fond I did not feel like a Hemingway protagonist. And that was exactly the point of Hawkes's assignment. My journey through the heat-stroked Grecian landscape should have been more an amalgamation of Herzog, Barthes, Roth, and Updike, with maybe a little Camus thrown in for existential flavoring. Those writers would come later in that course, and I felt I could more easily identify with the authorial tone of their writing, but Hawkes's lesson had an impact: you have to find your own voice.

As you suggest, there have been works in literature—especially nonfiction literature—that were influential in helping me transpose the notion of persona from fiction to the world of documentary: Norman Mailer's *Armies of the Night*, Joan Didion's *Slouching Towards Bethlehem*, Tom Wolfe's *The Electric Kool-Aid Acid Test*, and even the debauched chronicles of Hunter Thompson were all experiments in a highly subjective and authored "new journalism," and I believe they helped point the way towards other possibilities in documentary.

But perhaps even more influential was the nineteenth-century experimentation of William Wordsworth and Samuel Taylor Coleridge, both of whom were committed to the importance of autobiography (and both of whom I studied at length in college). In *The Prelude* [various versions, 1799–1850], Wordsworth charts his journey as a young man becoming a poet (the work is subtitled: *Growth of a Poet's Mind*). In it, he charts his thoughts as he travels through France, London, and northern England, musing on grand philosophical and metaphysical ideas, all the while embedding those broad-reaching musings within the simplest and most direct observations from "real life." At one point, he says, "The edge of meaning never lies far beyond the prose of ordinary experience"—a sentence that has stayed with me for decades. And, of course, *The Prelude* was, at the time of its publication [posthumously, in 1850], a completely unique work—a poetical autobiography of ideas.

MacDonald: You saw *Primary* [1960] and *Titicut Follies* [1967] when you were at Brown, and you attended student screenings at RISD [Rhode Island School of Design]. What else do you remember, cinema-wise, from those years?

McElwee: I graduated from Brown in 1971. I wasn't obsessed with cinema at the time—and certainly not with documentary—but I was keenly aware that some kind of epochal shift was occurring, mainly because of those extraordinary European films that kept washing up on American shores, where they were soon put on display by the owners of the Avon Theater in Providence. I remember being blown away by *8 ½* [1963], as well as *The 400 Blows* [1959]. I'm not sure I saw any Godard films while I was at Brown, but a few years later, while I was at MIT, I think I saw nearly every Godard film in existence at the time. And yes, seeing *Titicut Follies* and *Primary* ultimately had the greatest impact on me—but my reaction was delayed. I didn't commit myself to making documentaries until four years after I saw those two films. I was simply too caught up in my attempts to become a fiction writer and photographer and photojournalist (figure 18).

MacDonald: In 1974 you attended a summer institute at Stanford. Who did you work with there?

McElwee: Chris Samuelson was teaching the production course I took. She was (and still is) a marvelous teacher. I made my one and only fiction film there. Got a taste. Being at Stanford was like going to summer camp. Much time spent outdoors shooting. My first real experience with Mexican food prepared the way it was meant to be prepared. Fabulous weather. Interesting classmates. I also took a course from David Denby in film history. He was teaching there for the summer and had not yet established himself as the influential film critic he later became. He liked the way I wrote about film and actually put me in touch with a small local newspaper that needed someone who would write about film, but I never called; I was too excited about film*making*.

MacDonald: How did you find out about the MIT Film Section?

McElwee: I was at MIT from 1975 to 1977, when I got my MFA, and then lingered on as a TA for Ed Pincus for an additional year and a half. Mark Rance and I were the first graduate students.

I think I first heard about the program when I read an interview with Ed Pincus in G. Roy Levin's *Documentary Explorations* [Garden City, NY: Anchor, 1971]. That book also had a section on Ricky Leacock, and perhaps the fact that both of them were teaching at MIT, not far from where

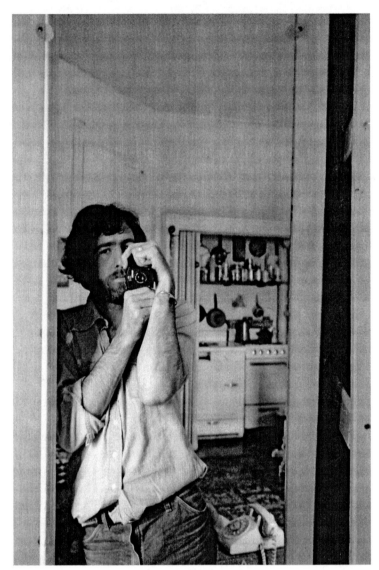

FIGURE 18 *Ross McElwee as young still photographer.*
Source: Courtesy Ross McElwee.

I lived, led me to investigate. I remember having a long conversation with Ed and Ricky, showing them some of my photographs and telling them about my work at WSOC—but being admitted into the program was a fairly informal process. There were no entrance examinations. But there was clearly a sense of an interesting experiment getting underway—and I wanted to be a part of it.

MacDonald: In the wake of Ricky's retirement from MIT and his passing, it grows increasingly clear that, like Ed Pincus, he was interested in personal forms of filmmaking. In fact, some of the work he did in his final years is diaristic—and, of course, his cinematography was always personal, engaged, capturing events from the inside. The influence of Pincus and his *Diaries (1971–1976)* [1981] and *Life and Other Anxieties* [1977] on your work seems obvious, but I wonder whether Ricky also contributed to your development of a new form of personal documentary.

Also, in our original conversation, you mentioned Jeff Kreines and Joel DeMott as important influences. Have you remained in contact with them?

McElwee: As you say, Ed was an obvious influence. But you're right about Ricky's fascination with filming everyday events—more often than not with famous people. Ricky's approach dovetailed with Ed's devotion to *his* kind of filmmaking—observational and to some degree participatory—which created a climate that enabled each of us to find a style or approach to documentary that suited us.

I believe Ricky had just finished *Visit to Monica's* [presumably made in the early 1970s, this film is not listed in any of the Leacock filmographies currently available and I can find no indication of the date]—his little Super-8 sketch of a day spent with Monica Flaherty. Monica was the daughter of Robert Flaherty, whom Ricky adored, but she herself was not famous. And to film a day hanging out with her—a day in which not much was happening— was a bit of a departure for Ricky. I also think Ricky's passion for developing a Super-8mm technology for shooting synchronous sound footage inexpensively was born of a desire to liberate documentary filmmaking, so that it did not necessarily have to be tied to big budgets, which invariably meant being tied to famous events or famous people. So yes, in that way, Ricky and Ed complemented each other.

As for Kreines and DeMott, they were at least as important an influence on me, and I'm sure on other students in the Film Section, as were Ricky and Ed. *The Plaint of Steve Kreines as Recorded by His Brother Jeff* [1974], a short film with a very long title, was the first instance of one-person 16mm documentary filmmaking I had ever seen. It was a revelation, and certainly had something to do with my decision to head down South the following summer and film my own family. But, of course, I also wanted to experiment with approaches to voice-over narration, so in that sense I was after something quite different from Jeff, who never narrated his films. I have completely lost touch with Joel, but did reconnect with Jeff at Ricky's memorial service in the summer of 2011. He has built a remarkable archival film-print scanner—a device he calls a Kinetta—which can make digitized copies of films in any format without danger to the original material.

MacDonald: What was/is *68 Albany Street* [1976]?

McElwee: 68 Albany Street is a short film I made as a student, about the last days of the old Draper Laboratory building at MIT where many important approaches and techniques were developed for inertial guidance systems. For instance, the development of the Mark 14 gun-sight that was designed at Draper during World War II enabled anti-aircraft gunners on US warships to become much more accurate in their attempts to fend off Japanese fighter planes and was credited with helping to turn the tide of the war in the Pacific. A generation later, Draper engineers developed the computerized guidance systems that enabled the Apollo 11 module to land on the moon. At any rate, Draper Lab had outgrown its humble red brick headquarters on Albany Street in Cambridge and was preparing to move all operations into a modern structure ten times the size a few blocks away. Before everyone had moved out, Draper decided to commission a little film to commemorate the illustrious structure, and contacted Ricky Leacock to see if he'd be able to direct it.

Ricky was in the habit of accepting commissions to make what he called "industrials"—short films about subjects he was himself less than interested in. But he also realized that his fledging graduate program had students (like me) who could use the money, so he would draw up a modest budget, designate one of us to take command of the film, and show up for the first day of shooting just to be sure that all was going well. I ended up with this particular commission and used it as a way to learn on the job, and on Draper Lab's dime.

We shot in 16mm, and I remember the first scene was Phil Bowditch, a brilliant engineer who had spearheaded the development of the inertial guidance systems that had been used for the Apollo moon landing, telling Ricky stories of what it was like to work on that project. Bowditch was a decent raconteur, but, of course, the film needed other sorts of material as well. I spent a few days observing the engineers packing up their instrumentation and paperwork to take to the new facility, and as a last scene, filmed the Lab's farewell Christmas party, during which the slightly besotted engineers sang their off key rendition of Simon and Garfunkel's "Sounds of Silence" as one of them played an acoustic guitar. The final shot of the film was taken from a neighboring building that night: through a window of the 61 Albany Street structure, you could see the engineers wrapping up the party as the last stanza drifted into the film's credits. Pretty corny stuff, but I loved having the responsibility for shooting the film, editing it and overseeing the making of the answer print—a kind of technical dry run before shooting my thesis film, *Charleen* [1978], that spring.

MacDonald: Your experiences at MIT seem to have created an ongoing community of makers, and a long-term support system. You've helped many filmmakers with their films; who is most useful to *you* when you're working on a film?

McElwee: I've kept in close touch with Michel Negroponte, who now lives in New York. In Boston, Robb Moss and Steve Ascher remain close friends and colleagues. Robb, Steve, and I try to get together for dinner once every few months—our filmmaker boys' night out; and I always make sure to run a cut of my films by both of them, in addition to Michel, before declaring them finished. I'm pretty sure they would say they do the same with me.

MacDonald: When we talked before, you described the chaotic scene you witnessed when you first arrived in the Kalahari Desert to work with John Marshall, and you mentioned that you could tell me "a hundred stories about the experience." I'd be grateful to hear another story or two. Also, did your experience working with Marshall have an impact on your own filmmaking?

McElwee: Where to begin with the stories? Here are two.

In 1978 John was determined to film the hunting of a giraffe, just as he had a generation earlier in 1953 for what became *The Hunters* [1958]. To do so now would be much more complicated, since the !Kung lived on what was effectively a game preserve managed by South African government officials. It was illegal for anyone—even the !Kung—to kill giraffes. I certainly had mixed feelings about agreeing to help John film this event, but from John's perspective, the giraffe hunt was an act of rebellion against the white apartheid government that ruled South Africa (at the time South West Africa, which is now Namibia, was a protectorate of South Africa). I guess I hoped the hunt would not actually succeed, that no giraffes would be spotted, or if seen, that none would be killed.

John enlisted several !Kung to form a hunting party, including a fellow named Tsamko, the son of one of the original bushman who killed the giraffe in *The Hunters*. After an hour or so, Tsamko found giraffe droppings and began following them, armed only with a poisoned-tip spear—the same type of weapon his father had used 25 years earlier. We followed the hunting party in our battered Land Rover as they tracked the giraffe. After several hours Tsamko spotted the giraffe and his spear found its mark. The giraffe began its loping run through the brush, with Tsamko pursuing it, and John and I pursuing Tsamko. John drove while I tried to film out of the window, but it was impossible to hold the camera. John was driving like a madman—40–50 kilometers per hour flat out over the veldt—smashing through thickets of small trees and through deep ruts in the sand.

The poison began its work, and after thirty minutes or so, the animal's huge heart had pumped the poison to all parts of the body. It slowed, staggered, and was clearly on the verge of falling to the ground. The Land Rover became stuck in a sandy pit, and John told me to get out and chase down the giraffe because it wasn't going to be standing more than a few minutes: "I can't run fast enough to get there in time. *You* do it, McElwee. You're young and you don't have a hangover!" I did it.

I remember how awkward it was to try to frame this immensely vertical creature in my view finder as it swayed, dazed, with the vivid blue sky behind it. It finally toppled to earth, and Tsamko approached it with his knife to begin butchering. I will never forget what happened next. John caught up with us but instead of filming with his camera, he picked up a double-edged hunting knife and began helping Tsamko butcher the beast. John was in his element, reliving his childhood, smiling broadly, wielding his knife, up to his elbows in gore, blood smeared on his cheeks, and all the while chattering away with Tsamko in the !Kung dialect. I remember specifically that he was wearing a filthy tattered white oxford-cloth Brooks Brothers shirt, splattered with giraffe blood. That image said so much about him—his patrician background and his primitive passions.

Standing next to the carcass, you got a sense of how massive a giraffe is. Like a dinosaur. Huge. It yielded a continent of meat. The hunting party carted slabs of meat back to the village. Strips of raw meat were hung from trees around the grass huts, like Christmas ornaments, until they could be cooked. The group would be able to dine on the meat for months after roasting it and drying it. They even roasted the head. I should also add that every scrap of the giraffe—it's skin, tail, the long shanks of meat, its mane, even most of the organs—were used by the village for some purpose. The only thing they left behind was the monstrous stomach. I remember looking over my shoulder as we walked away, and seeing that stomach, covered with iridescent flies, shimmering in the last of the light from the setting sun, as we left the blood soaked site of the kill. In fact, I remember how, as we drove back to the village, the whole veldt seemed to be the color of spilled blood.

In the years that followed, I would frequently see John in Cambridge at various events—usually connected with Harvard's Peabody Museum—and he always seemed ill at ease. Out of place. His place was the Kalahari. It was where he could most be himself. And he truly loved the !Kung people.

Another story: John became convinced that the South African authorities were going to confiscate the film we had shot and expel us from the country. He felt it was imperative to get the case of films—some thirty cans—to Windhoek and on a plane headed for DER [Documentary Educational Resources], his distribution company in Boston. While I was putting the camera equipment away in the tent, he hastily packed up the Land Rover and we began the seven-hour drive back to Windhoek. The first four hours were over a terrible dirt road with pot holes that would have destroyed most transmissions. But the Land Rover was able to handle it. Still, at one point we hit a particularly deep hole and suddenly the back door to the Rover swung open, and our precious case of film sailed out, along with the Nagra tape recorder. The film cans burst out of the box, and hurtled out into the dusk light, but we found them all—several of them sliced into the sand like frisbees. Amazingly, none of the cans had become untaped. Most miraculous was that the Nagra tape recorder, which had hit a sand dune on the side of the road at 25kph, still functioned! We continued our journey and got the film onto a plane to New York the next day.

One other memory: the way the lovely !Kung children mimicked my cameraman movements as I went about my work. They had it down pat: squint, stalk, kneel, stoop, glide while doing make-believe tracking shots. They fashioned battery belts out of old film ends and discarded camera-can tape. One kid had manufactured a replica of my Spectra light meter from a small cardboard box and wore it on a string around his waist. The lens was cleverly made from carefully uncoiled spirals of unused 16mm film stock which had been discarded after scratch tests. These little lenses were scaled to look exactly like the Angenieux 9.5-57 lens I used. The children held them up to their faces, making little whirring and clicking sounds, meant to sound like film passing through the camera gate. It was marvelous and hilarious. I filmed one of these little pantomimes, but I don't think John ended up using the footage.

MacDonald: Beginning with *Backyard*, you began to mine the potential of personal narration in documentary film. The opening of *Backyard*, where we see the three photographs of you and your father and listen to your comments, is a breakthrough moment. It is also—to return to an earlier topic—very literary, clearly *written*: after your father says that he has resigned himself to your fate, you say, "I didn't know exactly how to respond to this, but finally I said, 'Well, Dad, I guess I have no choice but to accept your resignation'"—a witty and amusing conclusion to the film's prologue. It's hard to believe you said this precise line, and even if you did, it is clear that you recognized the pun on "resignation."

The earliest instances of this kind of monologue I'm aware of occur in *David Holzman's Diary* [1967], which is, of course, a kind of premonition of your work. In "David's" film, these are spontaneous moments—though, of course, within *Jim McBride's* process they're not. I'm assuming that your monologues, which also seem spontaneous, are always carefully planned and practiced.

McElwee: Because that exchange between my father and me took place almost forty years ago, it's impossible for me to remember exactly what was said. I do remember telling the story of the exchange to friends over the years, and the story probably got better with each telling. I probably refined it here and there to make the delivery funnier each time. But I'm quite certain that the key word "resignation" was part of my response to my father saying that he had resigned himself to my fate.

When I wrote and recorded that voice-over for *Backyard*, I was very attentive to the rhythm and tone of the sentences, but I *always* feel I need to be aware of these matters. It's part of the writing/recording process for me. There's no formula. I just write and rewrite until what I have written seems to flow and integrate properly with the images. It always surprises me how difficult it is for me nail down the content of a given sentence and to get the rhythm and flow so that it satisfies me. When I look at a transcript of the voice-over from any of my films, I always think, "What was the big deal? Why did it take me so many versions, editions, renditions, to get it right? The ideas expressed are fairly straightforward. Nothing too poetical or philosophical. The syntax is simple. What was so complicated?" I've come to accept this problem as being related to why I decided to give up being a novelist in the first place and to make films instead. Writing was just too hard for me.

MacDonald: Do you think your voice-over has evolved over the years and through the films?

McElwee: My voice-over has basically remained the same. Perhaps content-wise, it's becoming a little more melancholy as I get older—a little less libido-driven—but that's to be expected, don't you think?

MacDonald: You and Marilyn Levine worked together on *Something to Do with the Wall* [1991], but not so far as I know on any film after that. In documentary history there are a number of couples who have collaborated: Steve Ascher and Jeanne Jordan, for example, and Claude Nuridsany and Marie Pérennou (the nature filmmakers who did *Microcosmos* [1996]). Was *Something to Do with the Wall* an experiment to see if you and Marilyn could collaborate effectively? How did you two feel about that experience?

McElwee: It *was* an experiment, and I had truly hoped that we would make other films together. Marilyn had been a reporter for the *Charlotte News* before we met and had only shot a little Super-8 at that point, but I wanted *Wall* to be something we could co-direct. She even filmed some of it—rather remarkable, given that she had never shot 16mm before.

But making the film was simply too stressful—on so many levels—personal and technical, not to mention the slight complication of the Wall suddenly coming down before we had finished the film. Plus we had just had our first child. I remember saying to Marilyn, "If our marriage can survive all of this, it can survive anything." I was wrong, of course. Steve Ascher and Jean Jordan were proof that a married couple could indeed make films, as were D. A. Pennebaker and Chris Hegedus. But for various reasons, Marilyn and I could not make it work. She went back to writing fiction, as well as trying to publish essays.

MacDonald: In some of the films there's an aspect of exposé of the South and much revelation of your family and southern friends/acquaintances. How much have your films been seen in Charlotte and around the South, and what's been the response? Did your father enjoy your films?

McElwee: "Exposé" seems a bit sensationalistic; it usually implies shining a light on something that's been hidden. I think that at times in my films the South is depicted in a way that may seem startling to outsiders—especially in *Backyard* and in *Sherman's March*. But the thing about the vignettes and portraits rendered in both of those films is that for the most part, nothing was hidden. It was all right there for anyone to see—or perhaps for any Southerner to see.

My father had various reactions to my films at various times. I remember him saying that he felt *Space Coast* [1979] was a little condescending in its view of the people we chose to film. And I now agree with him. About *Backyard*, his salient response was, "You make us seem much more wealthy than we really are," which was also true. He was a general surgeon, not a specialist, and made a good living, but we were not fabulously wealthy. However, large tracts of land and big houses were relatively inexpensive in Charlotte back in the Fifties when my father bought his house, and it must indeed seem, to my northern friends and folks who grow up in crowded places like New York or Boston or Paris, as if I grew up on an estate.

When *Sherman's March* was released, I'm sure my father had no idea what to expect. As he states quite clearly in the film itself, he was puzzled about why I spent the day filming my sister washing her dog. But when he attended the premier at the ICA [Institute of Contemporary Art in Boston], which was sold out and had a very receptive audience with much appreciative laughter at all the right places, I noticed that *he* simply could not stop laughing. After the screening, he said to someone—maybe Ricky Leacock—"I never knew he was so funny!"

After the ICA screening, he understood what this approach to filmmaking was about, and it seemed to please him quite a bit that the film was successful. Shortly after *Sherman's March* premiered, I was able to pay him back $5,250 he had loaned me to purchase film stock and processing for *Charleen*. The $5,000 was the principal and $250, the interest he charged me, god bless his Presbyterian soul. He could have afforded to give me the money, but he wanted me to prove to him and to myself that I could make some sort of a living from my filmmaking.

MacDonald: For a long time you've supported yourself both with your filmmaking and with your teaching at Harvard. Could you talk about this dimension of your life? It seems as if a good many of your students remain in contact with you, continue to use you in productive ways.

McElwee: I manage to stay in touch with a few dozen of my students and receive surprise emails from others I haven't heard from in a while. Many have found fulfilling careers as filmmakers, both in documentary and in fiction—or in bending and blending the two categories, as in the case of Andrew Bujalski. There are the high-profile alums of the VES Department— Darren Aronofsky, Mira Nair, James Toback, to name a few—and you can, I believe, see traces of the department's documentary "attitude" in much of their fiction work.

But I am especially pleased at the graduates who have made their living as documentary filmmakers—Nina Davenport, Lauren Greenfield, Kate

Davis, Amanda Micheli, Allison Humenuk, Mitch McCabe, and even a few guys: Mark Meatto, Victor Buhler, Randy Bell.

The thing I have always loved about teaching is the close interaction with my students. I teach studio courses, so the enrollments are by necessity small, and I enjoy helping students grapple—in most cases for the first time—with trying to express themselves in a visual medium. Most of them have spent their first 18 years expressing themselves verbally, analytically, rationally. Now they must learn a new set of tools for a different form of expression. It's exciting when they take to it. And frequently, it's the non-film majors who do the best work. In the class I am currently teaching, the two students who have done the best work are a senior majoring in economics and a freshman who intends to major in computer sciences. It's impossible to know for sure who will excel until they actually pick up a camera.

It's always a little painful for me to listen to an obviously intelligent student trying to convince me or the class that the work-in-progress they have just screened is working, when it's not. No amount of verbal intellectualizing, rationalizing, or contextualization can change the fact that their film is not succeeding in doing what they thought it was doing, want it to do. And conversely, when a student shares work that obviously succeeds, it raises the bar for the entire class. No extended verbal contextualization necessary.

MacDonald: I see it as an occupational hazard of personal documentary that, as the years go by, the family dynamic often changes, rendering earlier filmmaking problematic.

Further, once filmmakers have made their personal lives their topic and have revealed themselves and their family members during moments of crisis, those of us who see the films cannot *not* wonder about the makers' actual personal lives in ways that we don't wonder about the lives of other filmmakers. Understandably I think, we become nosey!

Robb Moss has struggled with showing *The Tourist* [1991] as his daughter Anna has grown up; Alfred Guzzetti has withdrawn *Beginning Pieces* from circulation because his daughter is uncomfortable with it; and recently you've had a struggle about *In Paraguay*, presumably as a result of some of the same tensions that resulted in your recent divorce—tensions that seem to me to be subtly evident in your films, beginning with *Time Indefinite*. I would be grateful to know to what extent your filming your family developed into a problem and how you dealt with this problem as you conceived and produced your films.

McElwee: I think the thing that has been most difficult for me to accept is that Marilyn simply changed her mind about supporting my approach to filmmaking. She was happy enough to go along with the whole endeavor in *Time Indefinite* and *Six O'Clock News*, but for some reason she began to feel uncomfortable being filmed—and made it pretty clear that she no longer wanted to appear in my films. In *Bright Leaves,* a 107-minute film which is about family, among other things, she appears on screen for less than ten seconds

In one way, I understand this. As you get older—more wrinkled, more grey—the idea of being in front of a camera is less appealing. I've felt that way myself, and in fact in my more recent films, my own appearances in front of the camera have diminished in number. But when Marilyn decided she did not want to be in my films *at all*, I felt betrayed. At one point, she told me she did not respect my form of filmmaking anymore. She was, of course, entitled to feel that way, but still, it hurt when she said it. I felt I had always invested my films with obvious affection and love for her, for our children, and for our extended family, including her parents. But for some reason, that no longer mattered. I could not understand why. And now that we're divorced, I confess to being at sea—certainly about my own life and how to move on—but also about my work.

I loved being married, loved having children. In *Time Indefinite, Six O'Clock News, Bright Leaves*, and *In Paraguay*, I felt compelled to film as a way of celebrating the whole wonderful, messy enterprise of having and sustaining a family. Even my most recent film, *Photographic Memory*, which concerns a spring I spent in France long before I married, is set in motion by my maddening relationship with my then-teenage son. Throughout my filmmaking, I have been acutely aware of the murky and miraculous continuity of familial generations—great grandfathers, grandfathers, fathers, and sons; grandmothers, mothers, wives, and daughters. Using this web of generational relationships as my safety net, I was happy to get on a trapeze and reach for answers to those ultimately unanswerable questions of creation and purpose.

But suddenly my family has been reconfigured. Suddenly, my son was living with me, and my daughter was living with my ex-wife. Not one family: two half-families.

When I step back from the emotional trauma of what has happened, I find myself questioning the whole enterprise of autobiographical nonfiction from an almost philosophical and phenomenological perspective. What does it mean to produce these movies in light of the fact that contexts and personal circumstances invariably alter their meanings? *Time Indefinite* devotes many scenes to the preparations leading up to my wedding and the ceremony itself. I've not been able to look at that film since my divorce, but what would it mean for me to view it now? For a viewer who did not know that our wedding vows, uttered with such conviction in the film, have been annulled, the film would play exactly as it always has: funny in some places, occasionally annoying in others (when the filmmaker can't put his camera down), and at its best, sometimes moving and poignant (figure 19).

But if *I* were to watch it now, it would be a completely different film—as different as if it had been re-shot, re-edited, and given a different voice-over.

FIGURE 19 *Adrian McElwee, Ross McElwee, and Marilyn Levine at the Vancouver Film Festival in 1993.*
Source: Courtesy Ross McElwee.

Time Indefinite was made by another Ross living a different life. Like an anthropological film made about a tribe that no longer exists, *Time Indefinite*, at least in terms of my marriage, is an ethnography of extinct emotions.

I have always felt that my films have depended on the viewer's willingness to accept the profundity of generational continuity—what we owe to our parents and grandparents, and for those of us fortunate enough to have had children, what we owe to our progeny. As an autobiographical documentary filmmaker, I am struggling to accept that this continuity, which has always been so important to me, has been at least partially severed. In my worst moments, the family scenes in my films now seem like fictions, a kind of lying. Perhaps there never was any real truth behind the scenes, in the sentiments of my films. Perhaps I should add a message at the end of the credits: "Any resemblance between characters portrayed in this film and actual persons is purely coincidental."

Time Indefinite. Even the title now seems ironic. My ex-wife and I were married on October 10, 1988, and were unmarried on August 25, 2011. There is no longer anything at all *indefinite* about the time frame.

Even if I don't screen *Time Indefinite* for myself anytime soon, I involuntarily carry a version of the film around in my head, as I suspect most filmmakers do with their films. At unpredictable moments during the day, or as I am trying to fall asleep at night, something jogs my interior film projector and a scene from the film runs fleetingly across the movie screen in my mind. The soon-to-be wife preparing for the wedding ceremony, putting flowers in her lovely hair, regarding herself in a mirror. The nervous groom placing a wedding ring on the wrong finger of her hand. These scenes now lacerate— shards of a beautiful stained glass window through which a brick has been thrown.

Perhaps for me the continuity that I have so valued in my life and in my filmmaking has not been severed. Perhaps, as my mother liked to remind me, and as I cite her in the beginning of *Time Indefinite,* everything still does begin and end with family. But I do not know exactly how to begin my next film. I am currently at a cross-road in terms of my work.

MacDonald: In Paraguay seems an homage to what was strong about your family life with Marilyn—made as that life was concluding. Is that how you see it? What exactly has kept that (lovely) film out of circulation?

McElwee: In Paraguay was shot while Marilyn and I were happily married, though under stress due to the fact that it was taking us three months to extract our baby daughter from the Paraguayan court system. I think it's pretty evident from almost all the scenes in the film that we were confident we would eventually succeed, and that while there, we found ways to occupy ourselves. Marilyn took many pages of notes and conducted interviews with other parents who were adopting, for an article about the complications of international adoption. She had a contact at the *New York Times Sunday Magazine* and hoped to publish her article there. My hope, of course, was that some kind of documentary would come from the material I was shooting (I had received an NEA grant to make a film about our experiences in Paraguay) (figure 20).

But the most important thing was that our family would be allowed to return to the US with Mariah in tow. I definitely considered the film an homage to our family life, and especially a valentine to our daughter. For reasons I will never fully understand, Marilyn changed her mind about wanting the film to be made. She consented to the film premiering at the Venice Film Festival, but did not consent for it to be shown anywhere else.

In Paraguay was not, of course, the reason for our divorce. There were deeper problems, and I had long since moved on to the next film, *Photographic Memory,* before we were actually divorced. But it makes me sad that *In Paraguay,* which Adrian says is his dad's "best film," has not been seen by more people. The adoption was never a taboo topic in our family. We discussed it openly with Mariah as soon as she was able to understand the concept. Mariah has often talked about wanting to go back to Paraguay someday to find her birth mother and her siblings. She has a brother and a sister who have also been adopted by American families living in Pennsylvania and New Jersey, and she likes to joke about her adopted siblings possibly being "Yankee fans," and how that might create friction in a family that adores the

FIGURE 20 *Lightscape from* In Paraguay *(2009): as McElwee and Levine await word that they can leave Paraguay with their adopted daughter Mariah, McElwee sometimes allows himself to become fascinated with cinema's ability to capture light and shadow.*
Source: Courtesy Ross McElwee.

Red Sox. Mariah has been totally in acceptance of the reality of her adoption, and would, I am sure, love the film. Nevertheless, I promised Marilyn that I would not show it to Mariah for another year, until she turns 18. I do not know if *In Paraguay* will ever be released, but at the very least, I want Mariah to see it.

MacDonald: *Photographic Memory* is focused on your current life and virtually everything we see was filmed very recently—though the film is also about your experiences in Brittany in the 1970s. How did you happen to be in France during your early twenties?

McElwee: My first trip to Paris, like the trips of 10,000 other American students, was inspired, at least in part, by having read Hemingway's *A Moveable Feast* and by wanting, perhaps, to be a writer.

The genesis of *Photographic Memory* is pretty much described in the film itself. In my concerns about the directions—and lack of direction—I saw unfolding in Adrian's life at that time, I asked myself what *I* was up to at his age. The answer was that I also was lost and trying to figure out who I was and what I wanted to do in life, with the major difference that I was experiencing this confusion in France.

With the encouragement of a French friend, Marie Emmanuelle Hartness, I wrote a proposal which incorporated some photographs I had taken 38 years earlier while in Brittany. That summer, there happened to be a panel at Harvard for some French filmmakers and producers who had done work for Arte, the French/German television consortium. I gave a copy of the proposal to Pierre Chevalier, a somewhat legendary Arte producer. Two months later, I received a call from Paris saying they were interested in helping to make the film. With Marie Emmanuelle as my co-producer, we wedged our way into the Kafkaesque world of French government funding for documentaries.

I made only one trip to Saint-Quay-Portrieux—the month I was there filming. No location scouting, no pre-interviews, no pre-production research. The French footage was shot in September 2010; the film was onlined in Paris in June 2011 and premiered in Venice in September 2011. All amazingly fast, compared to my usual filmmaking pace.

MacDonald: You build suspense into the film through your search for Maurice and Maud. And your meeting up with Hélène and later with Maud provides a moving conclusion to your visit to the past. To what extent did you need to manipulate the order of events to create this suspense?

McElwee: The events unfolded pretty much in the manner depicted in the film. I was unable to find on the Internet any reference to an itinerate wedding photographer in Saint-Quay whose first name was Maurice, but I assumed that once I got there, given how small the town was, someone would be able to lead me to him. That someone, indirectly, was the town planner, whom I met via another man in the bureau of tourism. It took a bit of detective work, and was a dicey way to undertake a documentary production, given that it was being produced with funding from French television. I did become a little nervous when, after being in Saint-Quay for ten days, I could find no trace of Maurice.

I did have a Plan B in case I never found any of the people I was looking for. Plan B would have entailed making a much more atmospheric and meditative movie—more on the order of something by Chris Marker: wall-to-wall narration with no sync sound interactions with any human beings. I could describe it as "Marker-esque" to my French producers, and they would be happy enough. Another alternative was to hire French actors to play Maurice and Maud, which would then allow me to pontificate on the relationship of documentary to fiction, past to present, etcetera. I could label this approach "Godardian" and again appease my French producers. I'm very glad I was not forced to employ either of those approaches.

MacDonald: *Photographic Memory* seems different from your earlier films in one particular way: you seem to have become involved in the project in large measure as a means of improving your relationship with Adrian (figure 21). Sherman's March pretends to be about your search for love, but you're really using that search to generate a feature film. Here, of course, you do want to make a film, but something deeper seems at stake.

McElwee: I'm not sure I agree completely with your notion of the search for love as being a mere MacGuffin in *Sherman's March*. Part of me really was

FIGURE 21 *Ross McElwee filming young Adrian McElwee, imagery recycled into*
Photographic Memory *(2012).*
Source: Courtesy Ross McElwee.

hoping that the right woman would materialize out of the miasmic southern
mist.

What you sense as a deeper filmmaking impulse in *Photographic Memory*
is partially a function of getting older—and having kids, which, of course, is
a life-changer. Perhaps *the* life-changer. In *Sherman's March*, I'm a woebegone
single guy wandering the Southland. In *Photographic Memory*, I'm a father—
one who is worried about his son—but also very aware of the fact that his
own life is creeping towards conclusion. The endgame is much more in focus,
visible now without the aid of a telescopic lens. So, of course, my filmmaking
is going to reflect these changes.

Also, I should say that a year after finishing *Photographic Memory*, I can see
that it's a somewhat "grouchy" film—a little impatient, a little melancholy—
and not just because of thoughts of mortality. Though Marilyn and I were still
married, our marriage was on the rocks, and we both knew it. Also, I had just
had major surgery for removal of a brain tumor. All in all, 2010 was a very bad
year for me—though I will also say that making the film provided a refuge, a
way to escape into something I loved doing, as well as to escape into the much
happier past of my time in Brittany.

MacDonald: Did Adrian agree to perform for you in *Photographic
Memory*—did you sometimes direct him?

McElwee: Adrian was interested and curious about playing a part in *Photographic Memory*. If he had not been, I'd have made a different movie—probably one entirely shot in France. But I did not have to direct him. He was always willing to be filmed, and I would catch him at various moments alone or hanging with his friends or girlfriend, and simply ask if I could film. It was all pretty casual. Sometimes I would be filming something else in the house and would shift to filming him. For instance, when I track into the kitchen, somewhat annoyed, because Adrian has been playing loud music after I asked him not to while I was filming something upstairs, a scene developed spontaneously in which he talks about his "penthouse and helicopter" fantasies.

The moment where I zoom back suddenly and ask him if he thinks that I love him was completely spontaneous. And, in fact, though it may not seem so in some passages, I do love him very much. I know he knows this. The film is a valentine to him, just as *In Paraguay* is a love letter to my daughter.

MacDonald: Has *Photographic Memory* had the effect on your relationship with Adrian that you hoped it might?

McElwee: In some ways it *has* brought us closer together. The divorce and my tumor surgery really shook Adrian up, of course—and our travels together with the film were a way of easing him back into a normalcy of sorts.

Adrian came with me to the premiere at the Venice Film Festival, sat next to me at the press conference, went to the after-parties, wandered the Lido, hung out with young filmmakers and actors. He loved all that. And he's gone to half a dozen similar openings with me in Europe and the US.

Adrian is smart enough to see that he says a few dumb things in the film, and that his behavior could be seen as exasperating. But his view is that the Boston preface to the film was shot when he was 19 and 20 years old and he's more mature now—at least that's what he says in interviews during Q&As. There have been subsequent problems and flare-ups between the two of us, and his life is far from settled [in 2014 Adrian McElwee was living in Colorado], but I'm confident that he'll figure himself out.

MacDonald: Here, as in earlier films, your persona in *Photographic Memory* is easy to identify with (especially for those of us who are older parents!), but more fully than I remember in earlier films, your way of relating to Adrian causes a rift between you and the viewer, or at least this viewer. *You* are often frustrating, overbearing, self-involved—it reminds me of my father's way of dealing with me during and after my adolescence. I assume you mean for us to see the Ross McElwee in *Photographic Memory* as both a frustrated, and frustrating, parent.

McElwee: Yes, of course, I realize that at times I seem overbearing with Adrian. Friends who saw the film as a work-in-progress told me to back off, cut the kid some slack. And I did, believe it or not. Still, the Ross persona in this film is problematical. I guess one of the points I wish to make is that we are all our parents' children—in my case, my father's son; that's why I use the footage of my father in the film. But I fully expect to be lambasted in some quarters for bullying my son with my camera. All I can say is that I'm filming with a great deal of love and concern and affection and hope for this young person's future.

MacDonald: Changes in technology and the kinds of "photographic memory" they can provide are a major theme here. Your imagery of Adrian as a child was shot in 16mm and the more recent imagery in digital video. Your nostalgia for your earlier relationship with Adrian seems connected with the look of your 16mm footage, just as your memories of your time in Saint-Quay seem connected to black-and-white, emulsion-based still photography. I assume you mean to suggest that how we remember the past depends on the kinds of technology we are using.

It's also clear in *Photographic Memory* that memory and memories are, at best, tenuous and full of ambiguity (the title is ironic in this sense).

McElwee: Yes, the ways in which the new digital image-making technology stands in as a metaphor for the difference between my son's generation and mine is an obvious theme, as are fading memories and the passing of time. Getting older and having to master entirely new technical approaches to filmmaking has been daunting—at least for me. Adrian absorbs all of this so effortlessly, while I struggle. As I say in the film, this was the first time I had shot with a camera that only employed memory cards and I was initially distrustful about a technology that did not rely on either videotape or film stock. It often felt as if I were trafficking in vapors. I spent countless hours in Saint-Quay—which was far from Paris with its equipment rental and repair facilities—insecurely checking my memory cards each evening, making multiple copies on external drives of footage I had shot during the day. But as I exported my material and made back-up dubs, I would indeed see the visual evidence that what I thought had transpired actually had and that I had managed to capture a fair amount of it.

MacDonald: Your French is serviceable. I assume you studied French in college and that's partly why you went to France when you were 21. Both *In Paraguay* and *Photographic Memory* involved your filming with people in a different language—though your Spanish seems less sophisticated than your French. As an American I'm impressed that you took this on—in addition to the process of filming itself.

McElwee: "Serviceable" is certainly the correct adjective. My French had become dormant by the time I was preparing to shoot. Marie tutored me off and on while we were working on the proposal, and before I departed for France, I found a French tutor for more intensive sessions. But I am not gifted at languages. I do enjoy *trying* to speak them and I found that most people I filmed were encouraging. Even in Paris, I found the old saw about Parisians turning up their noses at less than perfect French simply isn't true. I cringe when I hear some of the grammatical errors I made in *Photographic Memory*, and my French accent never bothered to show up!

More than one person has said I am "fearless" about trying to speak a language I am not proficient in—a backhanded compliment to be sure, yet I think there is some truth to it. I needed to be unafraid to try. I think that in a larger sense that attitude is completely necessary for making the kinds of documentaries I make. You have to be willing to make mistakes—technical mistakes as well as mistakes in judgment. You have to take risks.

MacDonald: The conclusion of *Photographic Memory* strikes me as the most complex ending in any of your films. You are functioning as Adrian's cinematographer, filming him for *his* movie. But, of course—and this is suggested by your shadow first on him, then on the sand as "the hipster" runs off down the beach—you are also filming Adrian *as* Adrian for *your* film, the one we're watching. Adrian is simultaneously moving *away* from you (literally, and in the sense that he is growing into an adulthood as strange for you as yours was for your father) and *toward* you (he's becoming a filmmaker and using you as his cameraman). The two of you are utterly intertwined—and in part *because* of your making this film.

McElwee: Your analysis is pretty much how I hoped people would read the last scene, with its intertwining of the themes father and son, fiction and documentary, then and now.

I was also quite conscious of the role of the ocean in this film and in other films of mine: *Time Indefinite* and certainly *Bright Leaves*. The last scene in *Bright Leaves* has a four-year-old Adrian running a rescue mission for a fish he's found in a tidal pool. He scampers away from his father, towards the surf, diminishing in size in the frame, which is held constant, his movement perpendicular to the shore line. In the last shot of *Photographic Memory*, he is also running away from his cameraman/father, but this time, he's running parallel to the shore. It's the same beach, the same time of day (the magic hour), but a decidedly different "blocking."

Except, of course, nothing was blocked out in advance. I did not know that little Adrian was going to catch and then try to liberate the fish, but I responded to things as they were unfolding. I did know that big Adrian's script called for the "hipster" to go jogging, but hadn't really mapped out how to film it with him, even though it was a fictional moment. At the very end of the shot, I intentionally shift the camera a bit, compromising the future use of the shot in a conventional fiction by allowing my shadow (the cameraman's shadow) to appear in the lower left corner of the frame. The final shots of *Bright Leaves* and of *Photographic Memory* are both pretty complicated, more in their implications than in their actual execution. And in that last shot of *Photographic Memory*, I get to utilize my Godardian plan B—my fiction ending—after all.

When I look back now and realize that I filmed *Photographic Memory* a scant five months after having had my skull split open, it seems miraculous that I got the damned thing done at all. I spent 26 days in the hospital recovering from the surgery and undergoing physical rehab. When I was discharged, I continued rehab as an out-patient for two months. It was grueling, especially given the fact that my marriage was disintegrating at the same time. I admit I probably would have let this film languish indefinitely had it not been for the pressure being applied by impatient executive producers in Paris. But filmmaking can be a restorative experience, and I guess this was the case for me. It got me up and moving again.

Nina Davenport

Nina Davenport is part of a younger generation of Cambridge personal documentary filmmakers, having studied at Harvard with Robb Moss and Ross McElwee—though her earliest film, *Hello Photo* (1994), was as fully influenced by Peter Hutton's work as by the films of her two mentors. *Hello Photo* is a visual/auditory record of Davenport's sixteen-month stay in India during 1990–92 that intercuts between black-and-white imagery of everyday Indian life and mostly color shots of the Indian film industry at work. Davenport's background in photography (and Hutton's influence) is obvious in her shooting—though the influence of cinema-verite is also obvious in her painstaking post-production syncing of image and sound. *Hello Photo* is an impressive debut film, though it did not predict the direction her subsequent career would take.

Davenport's next film, *Always a Bridesmaid* (2000), was very much in the vein of McElwee's *Sherman's March*, seemingly a conscious attempt to make a McElwee film from a woman's point of view. The subject is Davenport's frustrations with not finding a partner who can commit to an ongoing relationship with her—frustrations exacerbated by the fact that during the late 1990s she supported herself, at least in part, by doing wedding videos. Like McElwee, Davenport depicts herself as a sad sack protagonist, whose hunger to lure her boyfriend into a marriage-level commitment is often as frustrating for viewers as it is for the boyfriend and for Davenport herself. Indeed, as is true in *Sherman's March*, the gap between the filmmaker's dissatisfaction with her personal life and the skill of her filmmaking is the central irony in *Always a Bridesmaid*.

Parallel Lines, completed in 2004, is Davenport's rumination on 9/11, and in some ways a return to the approach of *Hello Photo*. Davenport, whose lower Manhattan apartment had a view of the World Trade Center, was, at the time of the attack, working in San Diego. Her work commitments completed, she was reticent about returning to Manhattan and decided to channel her fear into a road movie during which she would drive across country interviewing people about their feelings/thoughts about the WTC disaster. Davenport's skill as a cinematographer is much in evidence in *Parallel Lines*, as is her willingness to put herself in uncomfortable situations in order to collect the reactions of those she meets on the road. The America she discovers during her wanderings across the West and up through the Deep South to Shanksville, Pennsylvania, Washington, DC, and New York is in some ways not what she might have expected: the overall mood of her trip is evocative of *Easy Rider* (1969)—though her return to Manhattan at the conclusion of the film is entirely upbeat. As an exploration of American life, *Parallel Lines* has much in common with both James Benning's *North on Evers* (1991) and Ellen Spiro's *Roam Sweet Home* (1996).

Perhaps the central irony of Davenport's career as a feature filmmaker is the fact that what may be her most significant film is a project that she had no plans to make. The instigation for *Operation Filmmaker* (2007) was an attempt by producer Peter Saraf and actor/director Liev Schreiber to make a difference in a young Iraqi man's life by offering him a chance to work as a production assistant on their *Everything Is Illuminated* (2005)—an idea inspired by an MTV piece on the destruction of the Baghdad film school that Muthana Mohmed had been attending. Davenport agreed to film this back-story to *Everything Is Illuminated*, never thinking that her involvement with Mohmed would become the focus of a personal-documentary feature, much less a feature in which her subject would rebel against her effort to produce a film about him.

Throughout her work, Davenport has been alert to the resistance of some of those she films. During *Hello Photo* a number of people she meets respond negatively to her presence (indeed, one woman spits at her); one of the central tensions in *Always a Bridesmaid* is her boyfriend's resistance to her desire to instigate discussions about their relationship that she can film; and her experiences on the road in *Parallel Lines* include several encounters during which she is rebuffed, even seems in possible danger. However, in *Operation Filmmaker* this kind of resistance becomes her subject: as her relationship with Mohmed develops, then deteriorates, Davenport becomes increasingly unclear that her project will ultimately lead to a film. Not only does Mohmed refuse to continue participating, but at one point he confiscates some of her footage and refuses to return it.

While friction between filmmakers and their subjects is evident in other films (for instance, in Pincus/Small's *The Axe in the Attic*, made the same year as *Operation Filmmaker*: see pp. 104–108), I know of no more interesting instance of a subject's distrust of a filmmaker becoming the foreground of the action. Nevertheless, as frustrating as Mohmed is—for Saraf, Schreiber, early on, and for both Davenport and the viewer as *Operation Filmmaker* develops—his awareness of his power over Davenport's project and his attempts to exert this power are fascinating and revealing.

For Davenport Mohmed's resistance became a microcosm of the war in Iraq itself, and particularly the insurgency. And just as the insurgency revealed the naïveté of the American assumption that a quick, relatively painless shock-and-awe military victory in Iraq would be appreciated by Iraqis and would instigate a transformation in the Arab world (while having considerable economic benefits for the United States), *Operation Filmmaker* demonstrates the degree to which personal documentary is dependent on the shared assumptions of those filmed and those doing the filming, as well as the fact that the filmmaker's exposure of herself and her subjects is ultimately in the economic interest of the filmmaker alone.

In 2013 Davenport finished *First Comes Love*, a feature about her decision to have and raise a child as a single mother. Much in the vein of *Always a Bridesmaid*, *First Comes Love* is both well-made and candid: the birth of Davenport's son is among the most outrageous depictions of birth in the history of cinema.

My interview began in April 2009, when Davenport came to show *Operation Filmmaker* (2007) to my class in the history of documentary filmmaking at Harvard. Several Nieman Fellows (the Nieman Foundation for Journalism annually hosts several Fellows) were part of this class and I have included one of their questions. The interview was revised and expanded online.

MacDonald: Tell me about your experience studying film at Harvard.

Davenport: It was fantastic. I discovered this whole world I knew nothing about—photography and documentary filmmaking—and the discovery completely changed my life.

I studied still photography first, basic black-and-white street photography of random encounters with people. I liked the way that the camera gave me an excuse to explore worlds I was unfamiliar with. I would wander around Boston with my camera, meeting people and photographing them.

Originally I was a history and literature concentrator, but I switched to VES [the Department of Visual and Environmental Studies] and had to do a ninth term in order to finish my thesis, which was still photographs about Catholic faith-healing services.

I took the first-year filmmaking class with Robb Moss and it was love at first sight, with Robb of course, though I don't really mean *Robb*, but cinema-verite filmmaking. I think the light went on for me when I saw *Chronicle of a Summer* [1961] by Jean Rouch, *Happy Mother's Day* [1963] by Ricky Leacock, and *Diaries (1971–1976)* [1981] by Ed Pincus. I'd never seen *anything* like these films, didn't even know this kind of filmmaking existed. But as time went on, I found it to be the medium that worked the best for what interests me in the world and how I want to express myself.

In 1990 I got a Gardner fellowship, and went to India, where I learned Hindi and traveled around the country shooting what became *Hello Photo* (figure 22).

MacDonald: How long were you in India?

Davenport: From October 1990 through May 1992, but after about one uninterrupted year, I came home for four months.

FIGURE 22 *Nina Davenport's filmmaking as an attraction in her* Hello Photo *(1994).*
Source: Courtesy Nina Davenport.

MacDonald: You shot with a Bolex?

Davenport: Yes. Basically it was all shot silent, but I collected sounds every-where, in some cases sounds that were irrelevant to what I was filming. When I came back, I spent a long time making the film feel like sync sound. I mean you hear every tug of a kite, every clop clop of a water buffalo walking around the corner, the monkeys ringing the bell. . .

When I was showing *Hello Photo*, sometimes people thought the whole film was sync, but if it *were* sync sound, you'd hear *everything*: the micro-phone is not a brain; it just mindlessly records everything. By constructing the soundtrack, I could choose what to accentuate. I think it's more poetic and expressive to work with sound that way—but laborious.

MacDonald: How much did you match the sounds to the places you shot?

Davenport: I was always focused on the image first, and then if I had time, I'd get sounds, but having said that, sound was also a priority, just not the first priority. If you speak Hindi, the soundtrack is much richer, because people beg and sometimes question what I'm doing. One woman tells me, "You have to give something to the poor people!"—her way of saying that since I was taking something, I should be giving something back. Of course, in a sense filming *is* taking something, especially when you're a privileged white person in a country that's largely poor.

MacDonald: Were you mostly alone?

Davenport: I *was* and it was difficult. Looking back, I think I must have been insane. I was influenced to go to India partly by Christopher James, my thesis advisor, who had gone to India with Robert Gardner. I didn't know Gardner or his films at the time, but I did see Christopher's photographs: those and the stories he told me (for example, about his getting cameras stolen by a monkey in a temple) made an impression. A good friend was Indian and my therapist was Indian—these people told me that I *shouldn't* take this on, that I wouldn't be able handle it, it was too hard and too crazy, forget it. . . which, of course, made me go: "You say I can't? Oh, yes I *can*!"

As it turned out, I was sick, really sick, on and off for the first few months. I got dysentery after two days in India and was confined to my hotel for ten days, and sickness continued on and off, one sickness blending in with another and no end to it. My stomach was screwed up for years afterward.

My experience in India was so different from the experience of the other Westerners I encountered; it felt like we had nothing in common. In a weird way I liked being in India and I *wanted* the experience I was having, but it was very lonely. As someone who grew up with every privilege in the world, to see how people lived there was amazing—and I don't just mean the poverty. Everything you use is hand-made and everything happens on the street and the animals coexist with the people—India seemed to me the most amazing place in the world.

Actually, every film I've done has had something incredibly hard about it. Is that just the nature of making a film, or have I been drawn to difficult situations? I don't know.

MacDonald: You thank Robert Gardner at the end of *Hello Photo*. Is that because you were there on a Gardner Fellowship?

Davenport: No: the Gardner fellowship is named after a relative of his; Robert is only one of the people who decides who gets those fellowships.

Because I came into VES so late in my time at Harvard, I was always kind of marginal within the department. At the time I got the fellowship, I had only taken the first year of filmmaking with Robb (VES 50). While everyone else in the Department knew Gardner as this amazing star, I didn't really process that until later. When I accepted the fellowship, I thought I was going to focus on photography. You can tell *Hello Photo* was made by a photographer: there's no plot, no dialogue, no story—making it was my transition from photography to filmmaking.

While I was in India, I sent rushes back to Harvard, and Robert got them developed and looked at them, and he encouraged me to keep working with film, offering to pay for my doing so, and then he just kept giving me more and more money. I thank him because he was my mentor on *Hello Photo*.

MacDonald: Were you familiar with his *Forest of Bliss*?

Davenport: I was not. I saw *Forest of Bliss*, an incredible film, while I was editing *Hello Photo*.

The main influence on the kind of shooting I was doing in India was Peter Hutton. Robb showed his films in VES 50 and Hutton's approach was very important for me [Moss remembers showing Hutton's *New York Near Sleep for Saskia* (1972) and *Florence* (1975) to Davenport, first in class, then again when he knew she was going to India to shoot with a Bolex]. I was already feeling that when cinema-verite filmmakers made the effort to tell stories, the primacy and importance of the image tended to get lost. As a fledgling black-and-white street photographer, the image was very important to me, and Peter's films confirmed what I was feeling and helped me realize that there were other kinds of films, closer to what I was interested in.

MacDonald: I have a couple of questions about the particular places you documented. Late in the film, there's a long passage in what seems to be a mental hospital or a prison for mentally ill criminals.

Davenport: Actually, that's one of a number of similar places that you see throughout India. They're mosques, but Hindus go there too. This particular mosque functions as a home for people who are possessed by spirits. Here it would be called an insane asylum, but I don't think the Indians viewed those people as insane, just as possessed. There's very little money to develop the facilities there, so some of the people are just chained in place.

I spent a fair amount of time with one family, Hindus and Bengali Brahmins of the highest caste, who had a daughter in this mosque. Their daughter was brilliant, spoke five languages, and was about to go to the United States on scholarship, then just went completely crazy, violently crazy: she's the one at the end of that sequence who spits in my direction and walks away. Her parents had tried psychiatrists, everything, with no luck. The father's voice is somewhere in that sequence too.

That mosque is instructive now because of the current American anti-Muslim phobia and racism; it's interesting to know that there are places in India where Hindus and Muslims completely co-exist, in this case, where Hindus worship with Muslims.

MacDonald: Where did you film the erotic sculptures?

Davenport: That's called Khajuraho; it's one of the top tourist spots in India—all these incredibly beautiful temples with erotic statues on them. I was told I couldn't bring a tripod in to film, and I should have bribed people—at that time everything in India was conducted through bribery—but I was young and idealistic and didn't want to participate in that. So I went to Delhi to try and get permission to bring the tripod in, and it took me five days of going to this crazy office with no computers, with papers stacked to the ceiling. I had to sign a form where I agreed that I would be able to film everything at the temples *except* the erotic sculptures, which they viewed as obscene! Here was this incredibly beautiful and sensual cultural inheritance and somehow they'd been brainwashed into thinking it was obscene. That's the influence of Victorian England on India—sad. Needless to say, I defied that agreement.

MacDonald: Funny, because we hear the tour guide saying the tourists should feel free to take pictures.

Davenport: Once you got into the Indian bureaucracy, it was like Kafka. But the tour guides at Khajuraho were amazing—and all local, from the tiny town near the temples; they'd all learned to speak English, Japanese, French, Russian, perfectly.

MacDonald: Throughout *Hello Photo*, you include people, often children, who engage with your camera. At times the film feels a bit like an observational ethnographic film, but you continually keep yourself from seeming a detached observer.

Davenport: When I studied photography in high school, I was obsessed with Diane Arbus who photographed people viewed as freaks by society, but her photographs end up being portraits of her, even though she's not in them. You can feel her in the way her subjects respond to her camera.

I've always found it interesting how people relate to the camera, how they respond to being filmed, and I've always wanted to include that in my films—rather than aspiring to get people to ignore the camera. As a white person with a camera in India, I found that everyone wanted me to photograph them. My film is called "Hello Photo" because little kids would follow me around, saying, "Hello! Photo! Hello, photo!" That interaction felt more real to me and more compelling than my trying to be an invisible observer. It's the dynamic between me and the people I'm filming that I find interesting—not me personally, but me as observer or woman or white person or person-with-a-camera or whatever, in the world.

MacDonald: Your second film, *Always a Bridesmaid*, was very much in the vein of the autobiographical filmmaking of Ross McElwee and Robb Moss.

Davenport: Yes, it was inspired by my having Robb as my teacher, and by working as an assistant editor for Ross on his *Six O'Clock News* [1996].

MacDonald: How much do you plan before you start shooting?

Davenport: Very little. I usually just follow my instincts. The most extreme example is *Parallel Lines*. I had a view of the World Trade Center from my apartment in New York, where I still live, but on 9/11 I was in California, working on a TV show. Somehow, I felt that I should have been in New York, and I needed some way to process this feeling. A month and a half later, when the TV job was done, I got in the car and spent six weeks driving back to New York, filming as I went.

I wanted to connect with people and hoped there might be a film there about 9/11—the plan was that inchoate. I hit the road and started open-ended conversations with the people I met, making sure that at some point our conversation pertained in some way to 9/11. It ended up working as a film focused on how people process tragedy. For the most part, people talked about their own personal tragedies, rather than about 9/11; and yet, 9/11 is in the background of all of these stories because so many people were sad at that point, kind of in shock.

Parallel Lines most clearly exemplifies my methodology, to the extent that I have one: follow your instincts. Which doesn't really sound like a methodology at all, though it has worked for me up to this point. Of course, when you don't know what exactly you're going to do, to a large extent you're going to be making your film in the edit room. I think that's generally more true of documentaries than of fiction films; but I think it's even more true when you're making a journey film or a personal film where you have an open-ended approach to the subject matter.

MacDonald: At what point did you realize that the filming that became *Operation Filmmaker* was not going to result in the kind of simple, heart-warming piece that MTV would have liked?

Davenport: That happened fairly quickly. When I got on the plane to go to the Czech Republic to film Muthana Mohmed's experiences with the American crew, I thought, "Okay, I'm getting paid; I'm going to hang out with Liev Schreiber and some other movie stars for a week, and meet an Iraqi—how bad can it be?" I'm really glad I had the presence of mind to film that first moment when Kouross Esmaeli and Muthana reunite—Kouross had filmed Muthana in Iraq for the MTV special. That was a good beginning for *Operation Filmmaker*. Then Muthana went around introducing us and it seemed like everything was hunky-dory and that he was having a great time.

The editing of the film makes it seem as if I was there from the very beginning of Muthana's time in the Czech Republic, but I wasn't. It took me awhile to raise money, which is a problem with documentary: people who fund documentaries want an idea of what you're going to film, when of course you have *no* idea because you're planning to film real life as it unfolds. I was not there when Muthana arrived at the airport—fortunately, Liev Schreiber had someone film his arrival.

Slowly over the course of that first trip, Kouross and I began to get an inkling that things were not as copasetic as Muthana wanted us to think. By the time I got to Prague, Muthana had already alienated people, and he alienated people even more as time went on. When Kouross and I started to figure this out, we did some interviewing and realized that the fact that people were *not* liking Muthana was interesting. For one thing, it exposed a typical American naïveté: "Let's go out into the world and do this beneficent act and help this young guy"—but with no forethought about what's going to happen afterward and no research about who the guy actually is. So then I thought, okay, this is going beyond what I expected, but it might be an interesting film; it's great that they don't like him, but he'll redeem himself in Act 2, and in Act 3 he'll turn out to be talented and make a great film. Of course, that's not what happened either. If he does kind of redeem himself in Act 2, in Act 3 he turns out to be a failure. I was as naïve as Liev Schreiber and Peter Saraf.

MacDonald: At what point in the filming did you realize that you were going to be a character in *Operation Filmmaker*?

Davenport: At the beginning I had no intention of being in the film; it seemed like the story had nothing whatsoever to do with me. I didn't know any Iraqis; I barely knew anything about Iraq except what I'd read in the paper, which I'm sure was full of distortions. It was a relief, for once, to be making a film that I *wasn't* a character in.

And then, during the shooting, Muthana started asking me for advice: what should he say to Peter Saraf, what should he say to Liev Schreiber, how should he work this situation to his advantage? I found it too hard just to watch him make mistake after mistake, because he was constantly doing the wrong thing. I couldn't bite my tongue; I found myself offering advice—the beginning of a very slippery slope. It soon became, in addition to advice, could he have fifty bucks for this visa application, how about two hundred bucks for that. The demands escalated. The next thing I knew, he wanted ten thousand dollars or whatever it was for film school in the UK.

When I realized that my experience with Muthana was the perfect metaphor for the war itself—we were throwing "good money after bad" into Iraq with no results and no end in sight—I decided that I *needed* to include our interaction in the film (figure 23).

FIGURE 23 *Nina Davenport and Muthana Mohmed during the shooting of Davenport's* Operation Filmmaker *(2007).*

Source: Courtesy Nina Davenport.

Of course, this makes you wonder about all documentaries: what's going on behind the scenes between the filmmaker and the subject—because, of course, once you're filming, you're affecting the situation.

MacDonald: How did you get the Iraqi footage?

Davenport: I didn't go to Iraq. Once I'd gotten involved in this project, I *was* reading a lot about Iraq; I saw all the documentaries about the war; and I felt I had a pretty good grasp on the situation—and yet, of course, it was still unfathomable to me.

Because Muthana looked and acted more and more Western, I found myself almost forgetting what he had come from. I remember thinking, if *I* was forgetting where this guy was from, how would the average viewer make sense of what was going on in the film? I realized that I needed to involve Muthana's friends who were still in Iraq. Getting them to film in Baghdad for me and to actually send something back was a long, drawn-out ordeal, partly because people didn't trust Americans and were angry at Americans.

Another problem was that Muthana's friends wanted to get money from me, and they thought the best way to do this was to give me what they thought I wanted. For example, Nezar told me that he had been threatened by the insurgents, that they'd said to him, "If you don't work for us, we'll kill you, but if you do, we'll pay you seven hundred dollars a week." Nezar shot footage about the insurgents calling him; there was a moment, filmed in black and white, when the cell phone rings and he's talking to them, with a fan spinning behind him; he's smoking a cigarette and sweating, saying, "Give me more time, give me more time." He explains to the camera that he has to flee Baghdad.

At first when he told me about what he was filming, I thought, "This is going to be *great* stuff; this is exactly what the film needs," but when I got the tape, which took forever, it felt fake, and the more I watched it, the more fake it felt. I showed Nezar's footage to an Iraqi friend and she agreed with me that he had probably staged the whole scene.

What I had hoped to show was the boredom and monotony of living in a war zone, how you're just stuck in your house, the power doesn't work, and you can't do anything, you're completely stifled, you begin to feel lifeless. What you see on TV is bombs going off, the scary dramatic stuff. It took forever to get Muthana's friends to understand that I just wanted day-to-day material.

As all of this conflict was playing out, my experience gradually became a nightmare. You have to remember that the war didn't always seem like such a lost cause. It got incrementally more hopeless as time went on, and the worse things got, the more I wanted a happy ending, precisely *because* the war was a disaster and a failure. I wanted this film to be a positive contribution to the world; I didn't want to add to the depressing reality by making a film about an Iraqi who's a failure. Hoping that he would finally succeed was genuine on my part.

I filmed my arguments with Muthana and it wasn't until I stepped back from the footage in the edit room that I realized how funny those scenes are. At the time it was misery. During the editing I also realized that, of course, the film should *not* have a happy ending because the war itself had no end in sight. But it was a long process for me to get to that point.

MacDonald: How long did the editing take?

Davenport: A solid year, but some of the editing was part of applying for money. Every time I would apply for a grant or for funding from a TV station, I would make a trailer. There were a lot of trailers; raising the money took a long time.

Nieman Fellow: It's a rule of journalism that we don't interfere with situations, even though morally it's hard to resist. We're there to get at a truth; we have to be just observers. What kind of film do you think *Operation Filmmaker* would have been if you had been able to maintain your objectivity?

Davenport: Well, I consider myself a humanist, an artist, a filmmaker—but not a journalist. I didn't aspire to that kind of objectivity, that detachment. I did have this nagging feeling that I was supposed to remain objective; it's not like it didn't occur to me, but I also felt that, given the amount of time that I spent with Muthana, an "objective" stance didn't make sense. If you're writing for the newspaper, you're not going to spend anywhere near as many hours with your subjects as I was spending with him; you're going to be asking questions and getting the best answers you can, but you need to stay on schedule; you have deadlines.

When you have to film real events as they evolve, there's a lot of hanging out and trying to get a shot. There were many times when Muthana wouldn't let me film, so I had to come back again and again. Having that much time with someone makes a difference; you can only maintain the façade of objectivity for so long. And he was *so* aggressive in pursuing what he wanted and so manipulative that, given my personality, I couldn't have stayed detached even if I'd wanted to.

Also, Muthana had been brought into this situation somewhat irresponsibly by these Americans, and I felt like I had to pick up the slack, because he had no one. I didn't have the heart to say, "No you can't have the hundred dollars for this visa fee; you'll have to go to the refugee camp." We don't make a lot of money as filmmakers, but a hundred dollars to us is like ten thousand dollars to an Iraqi refugee. Can I spare a hundred dollars? Sure. Is that the difference between Muthana's being able to stay in Prague or go to London versus going to a refugee camp or back to Iraq? It *was* sometimes. As his only ongoing contact with the Western world at that point, I didn't want to watch this guy flounder and do nothing to help. His family couldn't help him; they were in Iraq; and the other Americans had left him in the Czech Republic and had gone home. It was just me and Muthana.

Another thing: if I hadn't helped him, he wouldn't have let me continue filming. In the film we have a fight about his going to the refugee camp; he says, "Over my dead body will you film me going to a refugee camp," and he meant it. In other words, if I hadn't made the decision to help Muthana, I probably wouldn't have a film now.

MacDonald: Was there any point during the process when you considered *not* finishing the film?

Davenport: I fantasized about quitting constantly and about my own "exit strategy." I don't mean that as a joke. As I got into this project, it felt so similar to the war. Like Liev and Peter, I'd begun, thinking the result was going to be one thing, and then it ended up being something completely different. By the time it became totally frustrating, I was halfway finished: I already had funding; I had people expecting the film. I felt my only choice was to continue.

Of course, even after I started to feel that Muthana was becoming unbearable, I didn't know if the film was going to be any good; usually I don't know that for sure until I get pretty far along in the editing. When I was first filming Muthana, he seemed kind of boring to me; and his English wasn't that great so he spoke slowly; as I was shooting, I was thinking, "Oh my god, how am I going to edit this? The guy takes an hour to get a sentence out." But when I saw the footage, I understood why the MTV people cast him; he's great on-camera (MTV interviewed something like fifty guys—and it was actually David Schisgall's editor who looked at the casting tape and said, "This is the guy you want.").

You always need to remind yourself that during the time when something is happening, you don't know how it's going to seem in hindsight. Thank god I filmed all of the scenes of Muthana and me fighting! At the time I didn't think I'd be using them; it was just an insurance policy. And thankfully, *Operation Filmmaker* did turn out alright and was well-received, because otherwise there would have been all of that suffering and nothing to show for it!

I tried to make Muthana seem as good as I could, given the footage that I had. I think he was worse than what you see in the film. But it's more interesting if you feel that there's moral ambiguity there, that maybe I'm to blame, maybe he's to blame, maybe Liev's to blame—really, no one comes out looking great in *Operation Filmmaker*. Everybody has their hands dirty, which is why I think the film is interesting.

I wanted the audience to be torn, to be confused about their allegiance. Whose side are you on? Who's right, who's wrong? Ultimately, the film is a portrait of my going from hope, to confusion, to being overwhelmed by a moral quagmire.

MacDonald: Dwayne Johnson, "The Rock," plays a role in *Operation Filmmaker*. He too seems to assume that Muthana's story will be upbeat. Do you know if he saw the finished film?

Davenport: I saw The Rock on the red carpet at the AFI Film Festival in LA, and he said, "How's our boy Muthana? I hear he's as crazy as ever. I've been hearing great things about your film." I sent him a DVD, but never heard from him, so I don't know what he thought.

Most people tell me that The Rock comes off as a great guy in the film, and very generous. Granted, $12,500 is nothing to him—but still: clearly he didn't have to do anything for Muthana. Was The Rock naïve? Sure. But he was trying to do something good.

Liev saw the film and really liked it, although I think he was hurt by the whole experience of getting burned for doing a naïve thing.

MacDonald: Was Muthana curious about the film?

Davenport: Yeah, he saw it and, as I expected, his view of the film was based on how other people viewed him. At first, he didn't know what to think. Then he found a blog where somebody said he was a jerk, and that was it, he was furious. He threatened to sue us; he got the BBC involved. I had to write letters. He didn't end up pursuing the lawsuit, but it was very stressful for a while.

MacDonald: How much did you test *Operation Filmmaker* on audiences before doing the final version?

Davenport: I always have screenings where I get feedback, and this does lead to changes. A good example is the scene of Muthana and his Czech girlfriend, who was actually a single mother; her baby was in the next room during that whole cuddle scene. At one point Muthana says, "We know each other so well; I know what she's saying," but in fact, when I had their conversation translated, it was clear they could not communicate at all. In one version of the film, I ended that scene with a shot of the sleeping baby, and people felt it raised too many issues so I dropped that shot.

I love the scene where Muthana's trying to translate a text message and his roommate gets involved, while Abu Ghraib is on the TV in the background. That scene went on and on and on, and the misunderstandings were hilarious, but people gave me feedback that it was *too* long. There are a million examples of how the film was influenced by feedback screenings.

MacDonald: Do you know what's going on with Muthana now?

Davenport: He's still in London. David Schisgall talks to him frequently. I stopped speaking to Muthana a long time ago because he'd become very abusive. He blamed me for anything that would go wrong in his life. I gather from David that Muthana is still waiting tables and trying to make films. That he has somehow managed to survive in London is pretty amazing, a testament to his perseverance, considering how expensive that city is.

MacDonald: Are you able to make a living with filmmaking?

Davenport: It's not easy; it's a very insecure career. I never know whether I'm going to be able to get money for the next film. It's easier for me now than it was early on, because I can sometimes get money from television stations without showing them anything, but I'm in my forties—having those opportunities took a while. I used to apply for grants but many of those have dried up and, in any case, the ones that are available offer minimal support. In *Always a Bridesmaid* you see that I was a wedding videographer and photographer for a while. I've worked on television shows. I've helped shoot for other people's films.

I'm now making a sequel to *Always a Bridesmaid*, about having Jasper, my son [*First Comes Love*]. I'm a single mom. I made a decision to ask a friend for his sperm and, lo and behold, it all worked and now at the age of 42 I have a baby! Jasper goes with me wherever I go and will be the star of my film. It won't just be about a baby going goo goo ga ga; it's about single mothers, my mom's death, other issues (figure 24).

Now that I have Jasper, what am I going to do to support him?—no idea. I'll have to figure something out, but the sad truth of the matter is that it's probably not going to be by making my own films. If I could make a different kind of film, the kind that sticks to a preconceived topic, it might be different, but the films I make take you in crazy directions, and don't pay well or win Academy Awards. Nobody making documentary is living high on the hog on their films, but I don't make it easier on myself with my quirky choices.

MacDonald: Have you ever considered making fiction film?

Davenport: It's a huge struggle to get into position to make a fiction film, because you can't just say, "I have this gut feeling that X would be interesting, let me pursue it"; you have to have all your financing in place, the cast and crew contracted, all your ducks in a row, beforehand. I like filmmaking to be

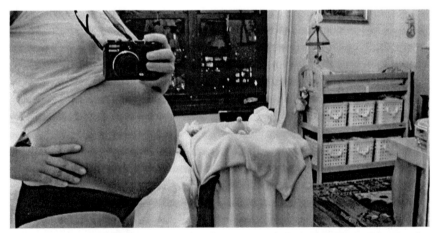

FIGURE 24 *Nina Davenport documenting her pregnant belly in* First Comes Love *(2013).*
Source: Courtesy Nina Davenport.

a process of discovery, to be able to start without anyone breathing down my neck, and to see where the process takes me.

I am inspired by the idea of making something entertaining, something *like* fiction in its intensity and impact, out of real life itself. Even though I'm manipulating this reality and turning it into a three-act structure—the main character fails, then is redeemed, then he fails again, or whatever—underlying that is something real. Sometimes people think of documentary as a stepping stone to fiction, but to me it's not, it's the end itself.

Of course, the fact that it's difficult to make a living as my kind of documentary filmmaker doesn't mean you shouldn't do it. And look what's happened with reality TV, which borrowed a lot of the conventions of observational and personal documentary and perverted them. That's a money-train that we couldn't have imagined twenty years ago. I worked on a couple of reality TV shows—Bravo's *The It Factor* and *Crime and Punishment*, both good shows, real and honest—and the process was fun. But the final products were always frustrating, nowhere near as nuanced and interesting as they could have been. Shooting the scenes and then seeing what they were turned into in the edit room made the whole experience very unfulfilling. Nonetheless, if you hear of someone offering a job in reality TV, let me know!

Leonard Retel Helmrich

Cinema studies academics and some filmmakers are fond of the counterin-tuitive assertion that essentially nothing in traditional, celluloid film actu-ally moves: that is, that the motion picture projector merely projects single, still frames of imagery onto the screen, which are then transformed by the combined mechanisms of persistence of vision and the phi phenomenon into the *illusion* of motion. But this assertion is true only so long as the cinema apparatus is framed in extreme close-up. The long shot reveals that in fact the projector is processing the filmstrip very quickly, so quickly that for the unfortunate projectionist who has not noticed that her take-up reel is stuck, the filmstrip can create a celluloid mountain in no time. Eisenstein's famous metaphor that dialectic editing is like an internal combustion engine that propels the film narrative forward is useful here: the "dialectic" of the still-ness of each frame before the gate and the motion of the filmstrip as the next frame is moved into position powers the motion picture experience. The images arrayed along the filmstrip are, of course, a vestige of still photog-raphy; but the "movies," and all the levels of motion and emotion they rep-resent and create, are made possible by the motion of the projector, which is powered by the continuous flow of electricity.

The assumption that cinema *is* movement has been fundamental for Dutch/ Indonesian filmmaker Leonard Retel Helmrich, both in his choice of subjects and in his manner of representing them. The physical, emotional, psycho-logical, and spiritual development of characters is the focus of his films, but from early on in his filmmaking, Helmrich was committed to the idea that the correct way of representing these forms of movement, whether in fictional narratives or documentaries, involves movement on the part of both film-maker and camera. For a time, Helmrich studied Tai Chi, which helped him move smoothly around his subjects as he was filming. In more recent years he has become widely known for developing a range of devices for facilitating cinematic movement.

Not surprisingly, Helmrich's first subject (at least the first subject of a film that he was in control of—he worked for Dutch television for a time) was Dutch experimental puppetry. His documentation of various means for caus-ing inanimate objects to seem to be alive in *Moving Objects* (2001) helped him come to see the camera as essentially *his* puppet, which is what it became in his second documentary feature, *Jemand auf der Treppe* ("Somebody on the Stairs," 1994). For this film he invented a device that could be suspended from the ceiling, allowing a sound-art performance by Peter Zegveld and Thijs van der Poll to be recorded by a heavy video camera not only in a single, continuous sixty-minute shot (antedating Andrei Sokurov's *Russian Ark* [2002] by nearly ten years), but from within the performance itself.

One of Helmrich's inventions—he calls it "Steadywings"—has allowed him to extend the possibilities of observational documentary. In his Indonesian Trilogy (*The Eye of the Day*, 2001; *Shape of the Moon*, 2005; *Position among the Stars*, 2011) the Steadywings allows him to be in close quarters with people, without the camera's functioning as a physical intrusion. Since Helmrich uses a digital camera that makes no noise, and since he does not edit in-camera— he allows the camera to run continuously so long as something interesting is being recorded, and only decides which sections to use, later on: he calls this "single-shot cinema"—he is able to create an unusual and engaging sense of intimacy. We are with him, *inside* a family and their community, as they are transformed by personal and political events. The Steadywings also allows even complex camera movements to be fluid (figure 25).

FIGURE 25 *Leonard Retel Helmrich shooting with Orbit, his new camera stabilization/ mobilization system (an elaboration of the Steadywings); it allows smooth movement of the camera, even from one camera operator to another.*
Source. Courtesy Leonard Retel Helmrich.

One of the advantages of his mobile camera is Helmrich's ability to move smoothly from one dimension of reality to another: from the cosmic level (*Position among the Stars* ends with shots of the night sky and the Southern Cross), to the macro level of political events playing out across Indonesia (in *Flight from Heaven*, 2003, and *Promised Paradise*, 2006, the growing influence of conservative forms of Islam is a focus), to an individual family's struggle to survive and get along with one another, to the animal life, even the insect life, interwoven with human society (one of the memorable sequences in *Position among the Stars* is the spraying of the Sjamsuddin family's neighborhood with insect-killing gas: we see the event from the point of view of children and adults *and* from the point of view of the cockroaches!). For Helmrich the fabric of experience includes all these levels imbricated with one another, affecting one another.

Helmrich seems to assume that his mission as filmmaker is to help others create more intimate and engaging work, more *moving* films. During production and as he tours with his work, he is always demonstrating how the camera can be mobilized in the cause of humanistic filmmaking and how otherwise expensive effects can be created with home-made devices.

My interview with Helmrich began when I recorded a conversation between Helmrich, myself, and filmmakers Rebecca Baron, Jeff Silva, and J. P. Sniadecki at the Harvard Film Archive in the fall of 2007 (I've included some of their questions). Further recording occurred during the "Nature/Place/ Cinema" symposium hosted by Colgate University and Hamilton College during the spring of 2008. Once I had transcribed and edited the resulting tapes, Helmrich and I exchanged drafts of the interview until we agreed on a final version in the fall of 2008.

MacDonald: How old were you when you became interested in film?

Helmrich: My father had a film camera. He not only made family films, he made fun of them. I remember a little film where my sisters, my brothers, and I were chasing a ball. He filmed so that you didn't see when the ball stopped; it was as if the ball was bouncing and bouncing and bouncing and we were running and running and running. Quite funny, and for me, intriguing. When I was 13, my brother had an 8mm camera with cassettes, and he always talked about making a film, but never did. He left the camera lying around, so I borrowed it, made some films with friends, and began to send them to amateur film festivals. The festivals liked the films. Later when I decided to study filmmaking, I showed that work to the film school and even though I didn't have the right papers, they accepted me.

I was influenced by the films of Sergio Leone and his crazy camera work. People have made satires of Leone, but when I was 17, I wanted to make a film in his style that was *not* a satire. I called it *Escalation* [1976]. It's about two people having a quarrel that escalates until the moment when they kill each other. People who know me from the old days say that was my best film [laughter].

Filmmaking was quickly more than a hobby. When I stood up in the morning, I was thinking of film. When I walked out the door, I was thinking of film. I wanted to become a director.

When I went to film academy, I discovered that there was the camera department, the directing department, the acting department, the documentary department, and it seemed as if any kind of interaction between the departments was frowned upon. This was the 1980s—I don't know how it is now; I haven't filmed in Holland for quite a while. At that time, they wanted the American system where there is a person for every job, even very small jobs. I realized quickly that that was not my kind of thing. I wanted to do fiction films, but not with this kind of infrastructure. One of the reasons I turned to documentary was because in making documentaries you can use a smaller crew and you can work together with them.

MacDonald: When you were at the film academy, did you do documentary as well as fiction?

Helmrich: All fiction. You were not even allowed to *think* in two directions—crazy. I finished film school in 1986, then worked as a storyboard artist and editor, and sometimes as an assistant to the director on a fiction film. Then there was a moment when they needed a director for a documentary, and I applied. The producer said, "Oh, you've had film academy, so you also know how a camera works!" Well, actually, I *didn't* know anything about the 16mm camera, but I said, "Yes, of course!" I did some reading and a friend explained some things, and it all worked out.

MacDonald: What was that first documentary?

Helmrich: *Dag mijn klas, ik mis jullie allemaal* ("Good-bye My Classroom, I Miss All of You") is about a Moroccan family living in a small city in the Netherlands who got a government grant to go back to Morocco. At the time, the Dutch government wanted to get rid of immigrants from Morocco and Turkey, and was offering money to those willing to go back. As it turned out, this family no longer had contacts in Morocco; the children had been born and lived their whole lives in the Netherlands, so they were completely Dutch. In the end the family came back to Holland, but now the government wanted to keep them out, despite the support of lots of people in their old neighborhood.

It was a 25-minute documentary. I directed it, shot it, and oversaw the editing. It was very traditional: narration and interviews. Rudy Cross, a friend who did the interviews and wrote the narration, told me I should always do my own camerawork, "because it will express what you actually want to say."

MacDonald: How many documentaries did you do for TV?

Helmrich: A bunch of short pieces, a few minutes each, for a television series, *Jules Unlimited*—"Jules" being Jules Verne—about new kinds of inventions.

They sent us the subjects and we could decide which we were interested in. Standard television stuff: somebody wants to go rock climbing, so you have a shot of the belt and then a close-up of the hands going into the gloves, an interview with the climber—so predictable.

In 1990, I wrote and directed a fiction film, *The Phoenix Mystery* [1990], about an Egyptian architect whose design for a government building in Tilburg, a middle-sized city in the Netherlands, had been accepted by the city council. The city council had the megalomaniac ambition to make Tilburg the center of Europe once the borders between the states in the European Union would be opened, but the city council had misinterpreted the architect's design, which created the drama in the film.

The funny thing was that what happened in the story also happened in reality during the making of the film. It was clear from the beginning that the Tilburg city council had misinterpreted my script. We told them that we wanted to make a film that showed the reality of the city; in fact, the mayor played himself in the film. The city council thought that my film would create a very positive image of the city and would make people believe that Tilburg could in fact become the "center of Europe." But instead I showed how these bureaucrats were just competing with each other for attention.

The Phoenix Mystery was made in the tradition of the "Minimal Movies Movement" initiated by the Dutch filmmaker Pim de la Parra--a group of filmmakers who were committed to making films outside of the traditional government subsidy system, because of the artistic freedom we wanted. Even though we did make *The Phoenix Mystery* with money from the Tilburg city council, it is still regarded as a "Minimal Movie" because we didn't use the national government funding system.

MacDonald: I came to *Moving Objects* after seeing your later films and learning how you create various gizmos for moving the camera. It struck me that your interest in puppetry makes perfect sense because it feeds into your way of working with the camera.

Helmrich: Actually, the idea for *Moving Objects* came from my sister Hetty and her husband Joris Naaijkens. They lived for a while in Curaçao; they were teachers there, and when their contract was finished, they had to find another job. Since they both liked puppetry, they became puppeteers. When they returned to Holland in the late 1980s, they got jobs as teachers again, but were still interested in puppetry. My sister became my producer and since puppetry had remained her and her husband's passion, they said, "You should look at the world of Dutch puppetry; what the puppeteers are doing is the same thing you're doing: telling stories with images, with gestures." They were right.

MacDonald: The subtitle of *Moving Objects* is "Portraits of Six of Holland's Many Puppet, Object, and Visual Theater Groups." In the film we see seven.

Helmrich: For people who know the Netherlands, Feike Boschma, who you see talking near the beginning of the film, is one of the main people in puppetry. By the time we made *Moving Objects*, the Puppet Institute had already produced a book about him, and they didn't want him to have too much attention in the film. They were providing money for the project, so I thought, okay.

Boschma was the mentor of many Dutch puppeteers, some of whom don't want to acknowledge that they were inspired by him. But I *know* they were and are, and I think these people should acknowledge this. So, while I didn't make a full portrait of Boschma in *Moving Objects*, I put him at the very beginning, talking with Boerwinkel, and came back to him several times—he's the seventh.

I went quite deep in my research for *Moving Objects*. At that time, there was a discussion around the theater scene in Holland and in puppetry conferences about what "puppetry" actually is. Some people wanted to separate mime and puppetry and other related activities, reflecting the fact that funding bodies in the Netherlands were giving funding to these different theatrical disciplines. But as I observed the works of the puppeteers, I saw that they had one thing in common: they all managed to make believe that something that's not alive *is* alive. Often they achieved this through the way they interacted with an object. Many times, they achieved this by moving the object in ways that made the illusion more real, pretending that the puppet had inner emotion and could move on its own. There was even somebody who made believe that a pillar was alive by the way he moved around it.

When I talked with Feike Boschma, he agreed with me and told me that you can only create a successful illusion when you as puppeteer *believe* that the puppet is alive. I asked him to say this in *Moving Objects* and he did, and after that, the discussion was over; everybody agreed with this definition of puppetry. Even the funding bodies in the Netherlands define it that way now.

Later, I made another film that focuses on Boschma: *Als een vloedlijn Englis* ("Like a Shoreline," 2000).

MacDonald: Somewhere between *Moving Objects* and *Jemand auf der Treppe*, you change your approach: the latter film is a 60-minute, single-shot, mobile camera film.

Helmrich: After *Moving Objects*, I was more interested in how film actually worked and what the essence of film is. In film school I had bought Andre Bazin's *What is Cinema 1* and *2*, but didn't catch his meaning; when I read Bazin again after I'd had some experience making film, I thought, Oh, yeah!

In his discussion of how to film a theater performance, Bazin explains that theater and film are actually "false friends." They only *seem* to be related. When you film a theater performance from the position of the audience, adding some close-ups here and there, you never have the theatrical feeling. The only way to recreate the theatrical feeling is to be *with* the actors, to have the camera on the stage. Bazin also talks about shooting at the pace of the reality, that is, in real time. And he says that camera movements should be the main narrative, that the moving camera is actually the essence of cinema. I decided to try to combine these ideas in a film: to be on the stage with the performers, shooting from inside the action in real time without editing, and to let camera movement *be* the action.

I went to lots of theater production houses and asked if they had a performance that was not longer than one hour that I could shoot in one continuous shot. Peter Zegveld, who was also in *Moving Objects*, said he and Thijs van der Poll had such a performance. So I went and saw the performance; in fact, I saw it many times. It was noisy and very contemporary and many people didn't like it—but I liked it very much.

For this project I had the opportunity to shoot with an HD video camera. I wanted the same kind of freedom that I had experienced in 1986 when I directed one scene of a fiction film in the Caribbean. I was an assistant to the director, Pim de la Parra, and when an underwater scene was needed, it turned out that Pim could not scuba dive. He asked, "Can you dive?" and I said, "Yeah." Actually, I couldn't, but I quickly learned how, at least well enough to do the scene. I showed my design for the scene to Jordan Klein, a very good cameraman who did *Flipper* [1963] and several James Bond films, and he said, "Under water, you can approach from any direction you want."

Shooting that scene, I really felt the three-dimensional space; there was no above and below, and from that moment, I wanted to have the freedom of movement you have underwater, on land.

When I was preparing to shoot *Jemand auf der Treppe* in 1994, I was already aware that it's the heavy bulky camera that makes camera movements so limited. We were using an analog HD camera that shot on very thick tape, very heavy, so I developed a special crane that would hang from the ceiling as I shot. The first device I designed had a little pulley with a counter weight; with a smaller camera and lighter counter weights this worked okay, but when we used the big camera—it weighed almost twenty kilos—you needed your whole body weight and sometimes two people to change the camera angle. This caused a crisis. Orkater and Hetty Naaijkens of Scarabeefilms, the producers of both the performance and the film, gave me three months to think of something else. I redesigned the system, using a pair of trusses, so that the device worked like a large mobile. The cameraman [Godert Walter] could just grab the camera and move it. I put a headphone on the cameraman so I could guide him within the performance, and it worked, except for one moment where he misstepped on a little staircase.

MacDonald: How big a crew was in that space as you were shooting? Obviously, the fact that the camera moves around within the performance must have required the crew to be moving to stay out of the image.

Helmrich: We tried to have as few people as possible on the set, but it was quite the choreography. I wish I could have shot it like *Symbiopsychotaxiplasm: Take One* [1968/1972, directed by William Greaves], where everyone is visible!

MacDonald: The audio must also have been a complicated process.

Helmrich: The audio recordist [Frank van der Weij] was clever. He put little microphones in many places and had a panel so that he could control sound levels. The panel also controlled the lights: the key light came from above, where we had a big parachute that softened the light and also kept you from seeing the shadows of the crane. There were little hidden lights, and the lighting crew [Stefan Dijkman, Bart Oomes] could add some light here and drop some there, to keep the performance from looking flat.

Jemand auf der Treppe was shown on television, on "TV Plus"; at that time they were the only station that could broadcast analog HD on widescreen.

MacDonald: I don't know what the title of *Jemand auf der Treppe*, "Somebody on the Stairs," means in connection with the performance!

Helmrich: Me neither! At the end of the performance there's a projection of a staircase and a big ugly face entering the frame. But I should ask Peter Zegveld or Thijs van der Poll about that.

MacDonald: Between *Jemand auf der Treppe* and *Eye of the Day* several years go by. What were you doing in the interim, because again, between those two films, the nature of your filming changes? Your commitment to the idea of mobile shooting remains clear, but your subject becomes Indonesian life.

Helmrich: While working on *Jemand auf der Treppe*, I applied for a grant to go to Indonesia to do research for a documentary. I had visited Indonesia in 1990 for the first time and very much wanted to do something there. I was born in the Netherlands, but my older brothers and sisters were born in Indonesia, and we'd all kept in contact with our family there.

When I finished *Jemand auf der Treppe*, there was money to do research; and—this is also important—a new camera was available: the Sharp View Camera Hi8. It was a consumer camera with an unusual design: from behind it looked like a television screen, quite a big screen, and there was a handlebar with an on/off button. The screen could be moved, so that you could be very free in your movement of the camera. The handlebar design allowed you to hold the camera with two hands, so your movements could be steady.

I bought this camera and when I went to Indonesia, shot with it, and I also constructed some devices to be able to create that three-dimensional feeling I'd felt when I shot underwater. I shot some scenes which I later used to get financing for what became *The Eye of the Day*.

What surprises me is that the Sharp View Camera never became a hit. Maybe it's because people didn't think it looked like a real camera: I remember finding that I could shoot very close to people without them being aware of me. The one thing that did become a hit is the little screen next to the camera, but other cameras that added that kind of screen lost the Sharp View option of being able to hold the camera in both hands—in the newer models the screen was in the way of one hand.

MacDonald: What kind of research did you do in Indonesia?

Helmrich: I was just shooting things to see how they looked. I didn't plan on using any of this material because Hi8 was a consumer format not considered suitable for TV or film; I was thinking of shooting the real film on 16mm, later on. What slowed everything down was that during this research, I got arrested and put in jail, then kicked out of Indonesia because I was filming a student demonstration from the inside. It took us two years to arrange for me to go back.

MacDonald: How long were you in jail?

Helmrich: Only four days—long enough for me! [laughter] Luckily my brother went to the Dutch Embassy in Jakarta, and they made an effort to get me out of jail and Indonesia. I returned in 1998 just at the beginning of the economic crisis that resulted in Suharto's stepping down.

In the meanwhile the DV system came on the market, and it appeared to be very good quality blown up to 35mm. I remember *The Saltmen of Tibet* [*Die Salzmänner von Tibet*, 1997] by Ulrike Koch. She shot the film on 35mm, but when she got to the border, they took her equipment and all her footage. She went back with a DV camera and shot the whole film over again; it was blown up to 35mm and became a hit in Europe. This made me realize that I could shoot on DV instead of film, and I went back to Indonesia with a DV camera.

MacDonald: Did you start filming right away?

Helmrich: Well, when I learned I'd be allowed to go back, I didn't have enough money. Only one funding body had agreed to help, but this wasn't enough. So in order to be able to pay people, I put some nice plants in my attic, plants that we were allowed to grow and sell in Amsterdam in those days—and that turned out to be quite helpful!

Then I went back to Indonesia and into a new period of living and filming.

MacDonald: How much film had you seen by this time, and which filmmakers were important to you? The Netherlands has produced a number of important documentary filmmakers: Joris Ivens is a foundational figure and, like you, somewhere in between what in the US would be called an avant-garde filmmaker and a more conventional documentarian. Johan van der Keuken also.

Helmrich: I met Ivens once at a premiere of his film, *Une Histoire de vent*, in 1988, but he was very old. I only shook his hand. I always liked Bert Haanstra's films very much, even though he uses narration. His cinematography and his observations are so striking. When I'm filming, I often think, is this an Ivens moment, or a van der Keuken moment, or a Haanstra moment?

MacDonald: Are there particular non-Dutch filmmakers you're drawn to?

Helmrich: Sergio Leone is in first place, and Stanley Kubrick, Akira Kurosawa, Tarkovsky. I like Spielberg's earlier films.

Recently, I was inspired by a scene in Spielberg's *War of the Worlds* [2005] with Tom Cruise. Cruise's character is driving a car and the camera goes around the car while he's driving. They're stressed out *in* the car, but the stress doesn't come across. I thought, you have to move with the camera *into* the car so that you can communicate the stress. I decided to make a little scene on video to demonstrate the flexibility of my Steadywings apparatus, a camera mount you hold in your hands and with which you can make all kinds of smooth camera movements. I was able to go *through* a moving car with the Steadywings; my brother Johan was inside the car, helping to move the camera from one side to the other and out.

Bresson's *Pickpocket* [1959] is a fantastic film. It shows how much you can do with only the camera. The actors don't have to act; the *camera* expresses their emotion. Lars von Trier does the opposite of what Bresson does; he doesn't let the camera do anything. He takes the best performances and mixes them together without concerning himself about composition or editing or whatever—and it works, when the acting is good.

MacDonald: You seem quite intimate with the family you shoot in *The Eye of the Day*.

Helmrich: My relationship with the Sjamsuddin family started during my research trip in 1995, when I went to my mother's native village. In those days the Dutch gave money to people interested in making films about their roots. I'd always had contact with my Indonesian family through letters, but I didn't meet my aunts and cousins who live in that village until 1990, when my mother passed away.

While I was there, I met my mother's friend Rumidja (figure 26). In 1995, when I returned with the research subsidy, she was a good contact for me, in part because she knew Jakarta, and because she and Marwan, her late husband, still could speak a little Dutch—they'd had to learn Dutch in the old days of the Dutch occupation. Her son Bachtiar was very willing to help me with anything I needed: in fact, his name means "helpful."

This family felt very badly about my being kicked out of Indonesia in 1995. When I went back at the end of 1997, I told them I wanted to start shooting in Jakarta. I got Bachtiar a driver's license so he could work as my driver and help me make a film about the student demonstrations, and then when the demonstrations developed into the resistance that brought Suharto down, I realized that this family—I mean the whole infrastructure of the family and how these political events were affecting them—should be my focus. In time, they became a kind of second family for me and I myself became a member of their family: the little girl Tari [Theresia Untari] can't remember when I was not part of her world.

MacDonald: How long did you shoot for what became *The Eye of the Day*?

Helmrich: I started shooting in 1998 and finished in 2001. Sometimes I went back to Holland, but most of the time I was in Indonesia. It was only in 2001 that I felt that I had a good beginning middle and end. Yesterday I was asked

FIGURE 26 *Rumidja Sjamsuddin in Leonard Retel Helmrich's* The Eye of the Day *(2001).*
Source: Courtesy Leonard Retel Helmrich.

if my shooting ratio was 1 to 10, 1 to 20? Actually, *The Eye of the Day* is a little bit less than one percent of what I shot: about 200 hours for a 90 minute film, but that does not mean that all the footage I didn't use is rubbish. There's a lot of very interesting stuff.

There's a fantastic film in that material about people living in the huge garbage field, called Bantar Gebang. I lived for two weeks *inside* that garbage field and discovered a hierarchy among the ethnic groups working there: only the Madurees are allowed to get the tin cans and the iron, the metals; then the Indamayu people, a different ethnic group, are allowed to get the plastics; and then the children come and get the paper. It's an infrastructure like you can find in nature with insects and animals: first, the big ones come, then the smaller, all the way down to the bacteria; and everything gets used again in one way or another.

When I'm shooting something that's happening, the moment I have the feeling I have a good beginning, a good middle, and a good ending, I can stop. But as long as there is some tension among people, something emotionally hanging there, I keep shooting. I'm not editing in-camera; I'm simply continuously shooting and reacting to what I see so long as there is something to react to. When that stops, I turn the camera off.

MacDonald: I'm assuming from the finished film that when you were shooting and editing *The Eye of the Day*, you had a double focus: the film is a panorama of Jakarta and rural Java *and* it focuses on this one family's lives.

Helmrich: That is how the film developed, yes. In many scenes in the beginning the family are not in the foreground, but during the film, you can feel the evolution of my interest in them.

Once I had accumulated a certain amount of material for *The Eye of the Day*, I began looking at what I had and, as a kind of self-psychoanalysis, tried to figure out what story I was telling. Later, when I made *Shape of the Moon*, I already knew what my focus was going to be: if something happened that had to do with money and surviving, or with religion, I would shoot it. But when I was shooting *The Eye of the Day*, I didn't know what I would use; editing became a process of figuring that out.

For instance, I filmed the scene of the merry-go-round. . .

MacDonald: An astonishing scene!

Helmrich: . . . because I thought it was amazing how these people moved the merry-go-round manually; dozens of people are sitting *in* the merry-go-round and just a few people are making it go around. I thought, I'll shoot this and find a way to use it when I'm editing. I ended up using it as a metaphor for the euphoria of the people after the fall of Suharto, but a euphoria that might not lead anywhere.

MacDonald: There's a place where you cut from people at a political demonstration to geese being herded along a country road. It seems a metaphor for the demonstrators.

Helmrich: I remember that soon after Suharto stepped down, you thought, Oh, there will be a new era and things will become better. But the unity of the students crumbled, and smaller groups would go and demonstrate here and there about different issues. These groups seemed just like those geese.

But that's not the only way one can interpret that image. Just before that shot, the students are singing the Indonesian National Song; I slowly zoom into this soldier, then I dissolve to the countryside where the geese are being herded. Some people understand that to mean that the *soldier*, who is from the countryside, sees the *students* as geese. Someone else might say that the *soldiers*, including this man, are the geese. All these interpretations fit. I let people make up their own stories. The main thing is that these images express a feeling. That feeling is actually what I "mean," that feeling in *all* its implications.

MacDonald: The Indonesian politics in *The Eye of the Day* are unclear to me.

Helmrich: The yellow party was the old party of Suharto and the red party was one of the opposition groups. I didn't make the details clear in the film partly because I wanted to suggest that in Indonesia, as in other developing countries, there always seems to be a dictator doing a terrible job and people trying to make a new infrastructure. I liked that the groups used bright yellow and bright red—it helps dramatize the situation—but there was another party and another color that I don't show: green; this represented the Muslim party, which was getting more powerful in Indonesia even before 9/11. Later on,

I learned that when Suharto fell, lots of Arabian Muslim missionaries came to Indonesia and preached a fundamentalist interpretation of Islam.

MacDonald: How did your filming modify what was going on in the family? You don't seem to be intrusive, but we don't know how much you're instigating what happens. When you arrive at the family's home, is your camera already running?

Helmrich: Not always. But since I always have it with me and since I never hold the camera in the usual way and since the camera is quiet, I can be shooting without them knowing. They only realize I'm filming when suddenly I lift up and orbit around them, something I try to avoid.

Since I am now a part of the family and of the events I film, I can have interaction with people even without saying something. I can affect the situation just by lifting my eyebrow when the mother is talking to her son. In *The Eye of the Day* there's a scene where Rumidja reacts to me when she has this argument with her son Dwi about the food that she accepted from the Golkar Party. Sometimes she is talking directly to me, explaining that she wasn't bribed but was only trying to get food for the family. Where her interaction with me seemed too much for the film, I just cut it out of the visuals and used the audio. That left big gaps which I filled with the cock fight Bakti had been part of earlier that same day. As long as they don't interact with me within the frame, it's not a problem for me.

Bachtiar and Rumidja know me so well that they often understand what I want to do and decide to help out, and I know them so well that I can help myself out. For instance, when Bakti was arguing with his mother in the apple scene and Rumidja said, "How do you think you can make money?" I was right next to him, filming her, and I said, quietly, "You still have your pigeons." He hadn't thought of that, but that's what he tells her (figure 27). Sometimes you come up with something that the character might say; only in that moment he doesn't think of it. In those instances I see myself as a souffleur, a prompter, the person who sits out of sight of the audience and when the actors forget their lines, reminds them what their lines are. I can only do that because I'm part of that moment and because my person doesn't have a dramatic meaning in the storyline of the film.

MacDonald: One powerful image that becomes a motif in both *The Eye of the Day* and *Shape of the Moon* is the shot of the distant center city of Jakarta and the huge power lines. It seems a metaphor for the situation of the people you focus on: they're on the margins of the central city and the economic power concentrated there, underneath that power.

Helmrich: At the beginning of *The Eye of the Day* you see a man shaking wires, then I cut to the power lines you've mentioned, then to the sun behind the power lines. Three different levels of energy, each related to the other. At the moment I'm shooting, I'm usually not aware of the symbolic meanings I discover during the editing.

FIGURE 27 *Bachtiar Sjamsuddin and his pigeons in Leonard Retel Helmrich's* The Eye of the Day *(2001).*

Source: Courtesy Leonard Retel Helmrich.

MacDonald: In both *The Eye of the Day* and *Shape of the Moon*, you seem very aware of the impact of Islam on Indonesian society and in *Shape* you suggest that this impact is often negative.

Did making *Flight from Heaven* have an impact on *Shape of the Moon*? *Flight from Heaven* is interesting for Americans because it shows us the impact of 9/11 in a very different part of the world. I don't know if I would say it's an anti-Islamic film. In fact, in a way Islam has nothing to do with it: the issue is a certain way of *using* religion. But the film certainly seems against certain aspects of modern Islam as they are playing out in Indonesia.

Helmrich: The people from VPRO television in the Netherlands asked me, "Can you make something for us in Indonesia?" I remembered that a priest who I'd met while shooting *The Eye of the Day*, had said, "If you want to shoot in my Muslim boarding school, you can come film anytime." I told the television people I could shoot in a Muslim boarding school, and that I could show how moderate and open and spiritual Islam is in Indonesia, that Indonesian Muslims are not for Osama Bin Laden or terrorism. That was what I thought at that time.

When I agreed to make the film, I already knew a family in the neighborhood where I was living in Jakarta who were thinking of trying to send one of their boys, Johan, to a Muslim boarding school because he was always fighting with his brother. I decided this might be my focus.

I told the parents that I knew of a Muslim boarding school that was completely free. They said, "We want to send Johan there!" The family agreed to let me film.

MacDonald: So when he's in the school, he actually has a contact (you) with his previous life.

Helmrich: That's true—even though I wanted to stay as far away from him as I could during the filming. But sometimes he would hang on to me, "I want to go home! I want to go home!" I'd have to explain, "I don't have power over that; you have to talk to your teacher and your family."

I was allowed to film at the boarding school, but only as long as I did the same things the other residents did: pray five times a day, read The Koran. I tried to avoid this rule sometimes by saying, "I have to shoot this because otherwise I don't have a film." And they were flexible.

I also remember that at one point Johan and I were talking about why we had to read The Koran in Arabic and not in Indonesian. I said, "You should ask your teacher." So I filmed him questioning his teacher. He was my "Watson"— the person who can ask questions so that things can be explained without narration. For him, as for me, being there was an interesting drama, but we both wanted to go home—though I wanted to film until the moment when he left.

What changed my interest in wanting to make a positive film about Islam in Indonesia was my learning that this boarding school was proud of the fact that they had burned down the local cinema.

MacDonald: One of the characters talks about how the "war" between Islam and the infidels is not a military war, but a cultural war, and that the war is fought with movies. Ironic that you're there making a *movie* as he makes this statement!

Helmrich: [laughter] Since they knew I wanted to make a positive film, they let me record this. But the moment I heard that they'd burned down the cinema and were *proud* of it, I thought, "You're telling a *filmmaker* that you burned down a *cinema*?!" For me, that's the same as telling an Imam that you burned down a mosque. And especially *that* cinema—the cinema where I'd always wanted to show *The Eye of the Day* to the people from the neighborhood. I'd known that somebody had burned it down, but when I heard it was *them*, my attitude changed completely. I even did something that I normally never do: I jumped out of the boarding school drama to an image of that cinema, and to people talking about the loss of it.

I still want the boarding school brought to court.

I had very bad feelings after *Flight from Heaven*. I got back to the city just after the bombing at the Marriott Hotel [the Marriott Hotel in Jakarta was bombed on August 5, 2003], so that ended up in the film—but as a result, the message of the film seems to be that *all* the people in Indonesia are Islamic fundamentalists, which is not true. That's why, later on, I felt I had to make *Promised Paradise*.

MacDonald: There seem to be two things evolving for you at the same time: in *Shape of the Moon* you're developing the story of this family, focusing more and more on their struggles to survive. But, at the same time, during any period of your work, you're also experimenting with different ways of moving whatever camera you're working with. You seem to think your way into particular films by thinking about how camera movement of one kind or another can function in these films. And this leads you to design pieces of equipment.

Helmrich: When I'm thinking of capturing an event, I'm always wanting to shoot within the three-dimensionality of real experience. I'm not always wanting to make machinery; actually, I try to do it as little as possible and as simply as possible. That's why one of the things that I always teach when I do workshops is how people can stand on each other's shoulders to create high-angle shots.

Certain events can only be captured well with certain camera movements. For instance, look outside that window: the trees standing next to each other form a very nice perspective with the lampposts in the background. If you move horizontally, you have the feeling of three-dimensional space more than if you move vertically. I try to be aware of how space works and how you can bring a particular space across to viewers.

MacDonald: The hair-raising bridge sequence in *Shape of the Moon* required a special boom.

Helmrich: Film is a technical medium, but the techniques are usually created by people who are not filmmakers, and the filmmakers feel forced to work with what the technicians design. When you as a filmmaker know what you want, you need to think as a technician, but one who can make exactly what *you* need for *your* film. I've never studied engineering, so my devices are usually very simple.

I saw that fantastic, narrow railroad bridge while I was traveling. Then I saw people walking on it, which I thought was crazy. I went closer and talked to some of the people and they said I could film them. We built a crane from the bamboo growing there: I wanted to use strings so that I could control the camera like a puppeteer. During the shooting, I was sitting on a little dolly that ran on the railroad track, which we rented from a nearby train station. The whole scene is shot from the "dolly," with the crane, except for the moment where you see the man's feet walking: that was filmed by the man himself, wearing a helmet with a camera mounted on it. The helmet, designed by my co-cameraman Ismail Fahmi Lubish, could look down at his feet while the man looked forward so he could see where to walk.

I was inspired to make this sequence by two things. One was an experience I had when I was working for *Jules Unlimited*. We did a film about people climbing over a glacier. On this glacier, there was a very narrow place to walk, very steep on both sides, though it was actually safe: we were all tied together and if one of us would fall down one side, the main man would jump down the other side to keep things in balance. I was the director and a cameraman was holding the camera. I wanted the scene to be shot so that you would feel the vertigo we felt, but I didn't manage to get that feeling into that film. I continued to wonder how I could create the sensation of vertigo—up until I saw *Spiderman* [2002]. Spiderman's movements in the film are great, but there are moments when you should be *feeling* vertigo, but the film cuts away. I decided to do it the right way on the bridge. And I was right, my method works.

MacDonald: The man we see walk across the bridge is actually not one of the characters.

Helmrich: That's why you never see his face.

MacDonald: I had no idea that crossing a bridge was an important metaphor in Islam.

Helmrich: It's called the Sirotolmustakim. In your life you're walking on a very narrow bridge and every decision you make in life is another step on that bridge, and only that bridge leads to Heaven. At the end of your life you will find out if you are still walking on that bridge. If not, you immediately fall into Hell.

J. P. Sniadecki: It's very unusual to have a dream sequence in a documentary.

Helmrich: I felt I could do it because by that time I was very close to these characters.

In my films, I want to record the scenes from reality, but I want to use the same film language that is used in fiction. That is, I want to use the same expressive camera angles and other techniques for the dramas I record as I would for dramas I would write and produce. I work differently than a fiction filmmaker usually does, but both of us are condensing: the fiction filmmaker condenses events that might happen in reality into a script and then shoots according to the script. I record events as they happen in reality in continuous shots, without editing at all, and then after I've collected my footage, I analyze it and find the parts that will allow me to condense what I've shot into a dramatic experience.

When I shoot, I always have a sense of what can be used, and what can't, but I try to be inspired by the moment. Sometimes there are dull parts at one level but there is still something happening on another level. I just need to sense where the energy flows. Take the scene of the apple in *Shape of the Moon*: the lady who has lost the apple comes in, and there is a moment when they're sitting on the bench talking about the apple; at that moment I just floated away, pulled back without losing them in the frame until I had Tari playing with beads and little toys in the foreground, as the women continue to talk, now in the background. I always try to capture a moment as a whole, and the results often look like *Jemand auf der Treppe*. Once I've recorded the whole experience in real time, I can come back and decide which parts I need in the finished film.

MacDonald: You shoot in sync, but you also re-dub sound.

Helmrich: Yes. During the sound editing of *Shape of the Moon*, I wasn't present all the time. The sound editor, Ranko Paukovic̀, had a track record—he's worked for Peter Greenaway—so I thought I'd let him do his thing. In a few places the sound I recorded with the image didn't work and we had to find sound from another part of the shooting to dub over it. In both *The Eye of the Day* and *Shape of the Moon* there are some things on the soundtrack that are too much. For example, Paukovic̀ even made sounds to accompany the little insect cleaning its feet, but of course you wouldn't hear that in reality. That kind of sound is used in nature documentaries, but I think it's too much in my films.

MacDonald: In general, the change in your feeling about Islam that's evident in *Flight from Heaven* seems clear in *Shape of the Moon*. There's a moment when the bats come out. The first bat reminds me of Jean Painlevé's *The Vampire* [1945], where the vampire bat is compared to the Nazis. You have the Islamic call to prayer, then the bats coming out of the bamboo pipes. *Is* this as a way of saying the Muslims in Indonesia are becoming creepy?

Helmrich: Well, no. For me a bat is one of the most fantastic animals. It's a mammal, but its evolution is completely different from the evolution of all the other mammals. I like bats very much.

Muslims in Indonesia believe that at Magrib (dusk), that is, during the evening prayer and the last prayer of the day, all the bad spirits come out, so you *can* read the bats that way. But as I've said, for me an image can be this *and* that, just as in quantum physics, mass is understood as a wave *and* as particles.

It's also true that things are changing in Indonesia and in a direction that scares me. The problem is the indoctrination of the people not from above, not by the government, but from underneath, in the mosques—especially by Muslim missionaries teaching a fundamentalist Arabic Islam. They don't start by saying all Christians are bad, because there are Christians living in the neighborhood, or by saying Indonesian culture is bad. But if they see that someone wants to present the shadow puppet performance called Wayang Kulit, an old and wonderful Indonesian tradition, they say, "Well, as a good Muslim, you'd better not watch this." Even in little villages they approach the Lurah, the person who gives the permission for this performance, and say, "It will be better if you don't let them do this performance." Many Lurahs don't give the permits anymore.

In the village where my mother was born, Javanese dances were tradition-ally taught to the young people every Friday evening. The Muslims now say that those dances are too sexy and shouldn't be permitted. So young people aren't being taught traditional dances. The fundamentalist Muslims want people to play only the rebana, a kind of drum tambourine that you hold in your hand (sometimes there are bells on it) and not other instruments, including traditional Javanese instruments. The richness of Indonesian culture is under attack.

MacDonald: There's a man playing drums at the very beginning *Shape of the Moon* and an old man dancing. Is that a native Indonesian instrument and a native dance?

Helmrich: Yes. The dance is called Kuda Lumping. In many places now, both the drums and the dance are forbidden by local leaders—the reason given is that people who do these dances go into trance. But that's a crazy reason for banning the dance: in Islam most Muslims pray until *they* go into trance.

MacDonald: One of your subjects in the Trilogy is the family struggling to make ends meet in the midst of social change. Do you ever pay people to be part of your process?

Helmrich: No. I learned during the shooting of *Shape of the Moon* that I should not give them money. You remember the scene where the woman comes to get the money for the couch? Rumidja didn't want to pay and you see the woman leave without getting payment, but what actually happened was that I thought it was a pity that she could not pay for the couch, and decided I'd pay. I gave Rumidja the money and said, "When she comes back, pay her." Two months later, Tari came to my office and said, "They're taking away the couch!" I thought, that's crazy, I *paid* for the couch. I went to their home and Rumidja tells me she used the money to pay for Tari's school and for electricity and other things. In the end, I filmed them taking away the couch.

MacDonald: *Shape of the Moon* has several surprising transition moments: when Rumidja is moving to the country, you go into the railroad tunnel, then suddenly we're in a bucket coming out of a well.

Helmrich: To make that shot, I put the camera in the bucket. I wanted a poetic way of showing her arrival in the village. Actually, it's a kind of suicide for her to go back to the countryside to live, because she cannot make a living there. It's as if she jumps into a well. You could also say that the transition represents a kind of time warp: going from the modern city to the countryside is a kind of time travel.

MacDonald: One thing that's clear in the two films is that Bachtiar changes a great deal. He becomes a Muslim and gets married, and seems to become much more adult with his mother. Was part of the reason Rumidja moves to the country the fact that, despite her Christianity, Bachtiar has converted?

Helmrich: Before he converted, Bachtiar didn't go to church, even though he was baptized. For Rumidja it was a greater shame to have a son who was not religious at all, than to have him become a Muslim.

Rebecca Baron: Rumidja mentions Allah when she's praying at her mother's grave.

Helmrich: For her, as for many Indonesians, it's all mixed up and it's all one. That's what I like about Indonesia. She's a Christian but she prays to Allah also.

MacDonald: The house-moving sequence is amazing; it's reminiscent of the barn raising in *Witness* [1985, directed by Peter Weir].

Helmrich: Rumidja comes from that village and in a village everybody is willing to help out. I *was* thinking of *Witness* as I shot that!

MacDonald: You include animal life and even insect life in your films in a manner that's very unusual. I'm thinking in particular of the dragonflies, or the ants carrying the mantis, and the lizards we see during the scene where the couch is being repossessed. Do you go looking for these events?

Helmrich: I rarely know beforehand exactly what I want to shoot. I just try to be inspired by what's around me. For instance, when I saw the butterfly in the spider web that you see near the end of *Shape of the Moon*, I remembered that earlier I'd shot butterflies just flying free. As I shot, I didn't want to have the spider and the butterfly in the same frame right away; it seemed more dramatic to orbit around the web to the spider sitting there on the other side.

Sometimes when I see something beautiful, something that would be beautiful as a still image, I don't even shoot it. I have to be able to *do* something with the image, not just record it. Bergson, the philosopher who inspired Andre Bazin, talks about how information has to develop through a duration of time.

How I reveal an image is more important to me than what I shoot. For instance, in the shot when the ants are carrying the mantis, I begin by following one ant that ends up being part of that shot. I also made a kind of stock shot, quite beautiful, with a fixed camera, so that you see the two antennae coming into the frame with all these ants around it, and slowly you see it become this large insect being dragged through the frame—a beautiful shot, but it didn't fit in that context because it was too slow and still, and if I had used it...

MacDonald: You'd be Peter Hutton.

Helmrich: Yes! [laughter]

MacDonald: How did you decide to make *Promised Paradise*?

Helmrich: It came very much out of my disappointment with my failure in *Flight from Heaven* to show the variety of Islam in Indonesia. I thought that by focusing on Agus [puppeteer/performance artist, Agus Nur Amal], I could show that Indonesian culture is not one thing, and that many Indonesians are not for Bin Laden and terrorism.

MacDonald: You've known him for quite a while?

Helmrich: Yes. Agus was involved in my other films. If I'd say, "Do I have to apply to somebody to get permission to shoot on a railway track?" he'd say, "I have the name of somebody." There are only a few rich people in Indonesia, and they have a network; he's related to these rich people and I make use of his network.

We wanted to get an interview with the Bali bomber. In the film you see Agus finding the footage of the interview in the black market, but actually I got that footage from the person who really did the interview, somebody who had been a student of mine in one of my single-shot-cinema workshops (I can't name him because I don't want him traced). This man tells me, "The police have asked me to make a portrait of one of the Bali bombers [on October 12, 2002, three bombs were detonated in or near popular nightclubs in Kuta, Bali]. What should I ask him?" I made suggestions and said, "When you film him, make sure you make clear he's in prison." He shot the interview through the bars of the prison. The police only wanted him to ask the bomber factual questions like: "What time did you leave to plant the bomb?" and "What ingredients were used in the bomb?" I asked the filmmaker to let the bomber talk about his ideology, which the police didn't care about, so afterward he told them—this was very clever—"Well, I had to make him feel comfortable with me so he would trust me with information; we don't have to use that footage." *They* didn't use the footage but *I* could. And so, in a way, I was able to interview the Bali bomber. And in *Promised Paradise*, I remake the interview so that *Agus* is interviewing him in his funny way.

MacDonald: *Shape of the Moon* ends with Tari being upset that her grandmother is not coming back to Jakarta with her.

Helmrich: Yes. The third film [*Position among the Stars*] will focus more specifically on Tari and the world of young people in Jakarta. It will be more about the future of Indonesia and about how Tari grows and begins to rebel against Bachtiar (figure 28).

FIGURE 28 *Theresia Untari Sjamsuddin in Leonard Retel Helmrich's* Shape of the Moon *(2005).*

Source: Courtesy Leonard Retel Helmrich.

I'll be trying to reach a younger audience. *Shape of the Moon* and *The Eye of the Day* don't sell well because they're not in a conventional television form. These days, television *explains* everything. Even when the things that are happening are quite clear, a narrator is explaining what we are seeing—especially in reality TV. The younger generation expects explanations, and I must adjust to this. I still have to make a living or otherwise I can't continue to make films.

I'm thinking that maybe I can explain the inner thoughts of Tari and her friends by using music. This method is used by the Bollywood movies, which are very popular in Indonesia. The new film will be a documentary and all the scenes will be from reality, but I'll use music to add another level. I was even thinking of having my daughter Angel, who is a very good singer, do the singing. She's friends with Tari and is a character in the film. I'm curious to see how far you can go with this way of filming and still have a documentary.

Of course, it's also true that in *Shape of the Moon* I did not end up doing what I'd planned. I'll be filming from within events and who knows where events will lead?

Jonathan Caouette

I first saw Jonathan Caouette's *Tarnation* (2004) at Upstate Films in Rhinebeck, New York (since 1972, a stalwart independent theater committed to a broad-ranging film exhibition program) during its initial run. I no longer remember what got me to the theater—I was teaching at Bard College at the time, and someone there must have mentioned *Tarnation* or perhaps I'd read a review. But like so many others I was immediately carried into the film and astonished by its energy. It seemed to me one of those rare theatrical features that has both the chutzpah of an avant-garde work and the ability of the best commercial films to engage audiences (other recent instances include Tom Tykwer's *Run Lola Run* [1998] and Todd Haynes' *I'm Not There* [2007], though this mini-tradition goes back at least as far as *The Cabinet of Dr. Caligari* [Robert Wiene, 1920]). *Tarnation*, perhaps the first feature edited on iMovie, is a fantasmagoria of recycled imagery from film and television, clips from fiction films and videos of his family that Caouette made as a child, visual text, family photographs, and early digital special effects—organized into a series of music videos that together create a bildungsroman of how this troubled child came to be a skilled and committed filmmaker.

Tarnation is a personal documentary, part of the tradition nurtured in Cambridge, Massachusetts, by Ed Pincus, Alfred Guzzetti, Ross McElwee, and Robb Moss, but it is far more visceral than any of the films by those filmmakers. Indeed, *Tarnation* is the horror film of personal documentary: Caouette's childhood, as depicted in the film, was often harrowing and Caouette's approach to filmmaking owes much to the revival of the horror film in the 1970s. When I hosted *Tarnation* and Caouette at Hamilton College in 2006, I was initially concerned to see him returning to the projection booth over and over during the opening moments of the film to raise the sound level—but I soon saw the wisdom of this: when Renee Leblanc, Caouette's mother, begins receiving shock treatments, we are jolted—the way effective horror films jolt us—by the impact of this brutal "therapy" on both Leblanc and on Caouette's childhood.

By the time *Tarnation* is over, one cannot help but wonder how Caouette survived his upbringing and how he could be as patient as he seems to have been with the bizarre grandparents who raised him and so loyal and committed to a mother whose mental illness kept her away from him for much of his youth. After the Hamilton screening, when Caouette appeared at the front of Bradford Auditorium to take questions, it was nearly as surprising as *Tarnation* itself to see how unpretentious, gentle, and serene, how *sane*, Caouette seems to have turned out.

There are several "occupational hazards" to making personal documentary. One of these was quickly evident to many of us who saw and admired *Tarnation*: if a film painstakingly reviews the filmmaker's entire life up until the time when he finishes the film, what comes next? This question resulted in the two-part structure of the interview that follows. In the late fall of 2006 I interviewed Caouette about his evolution as a filmmaker and about the production of *Tarnation*, but I didn't finish the interview then, since I wanted to see what in fact would come next for him.

For a time, it seemed as if Caouette's filmmaking career was in hiatus, but in 2010 his surreal short, *All Flowers in Time*, premiered at the New York Film Festival, and in 2012, he completed *Walk Away Renee*, which began as a road movie focused on Caouette's moving his mother from an assisted-living facility in Houston where she has been seriously mis-medicated, first to a facility in the Hudson Valley, and ultimately to his home in Queens. When Renee's meds get lost early in the trip north, *Walk Away Renee* turns into a suspense thriller. As the new, personal feature developed, it expanded, revisiting Caouette's youth, contextualizing the road trip and re-contextualizing *Tarnation* in important ways. *Walk Away Renee* has the youthful energy of *Tarnation* and the earlier film's dynamic style, but through his remarkable patience with his mother's mental illness (and the other demands of family life), Caouette has been able produce a deeply adult film, one that models loyalty and familial love in a way that few other films have.

I interviewed Caouette again, about his life and career since *Tarnation*, at his home in Queens in April of 2012; we expanded and refined the entire interview online in the months that followed, though I present it here in two parts.

Fall 2006

MacDonald: Your consciousness of cinema seems to have developed unusually early. This is clear in *Tarnation*.

Caouette: A lot of people say that they don't remember their childhood, but I have very specific and strong visual memories of being 3 years old. Of course, there's always the risk of false memories and who knows what can happen along the way that can make people believe that they remember their lives that far back, when they don't. But I really *do* remember and I don't know why that is, because my life wasn't particularly traumatic prior to my being 4. I remember how things were before the "trauma" happened. I use quotes

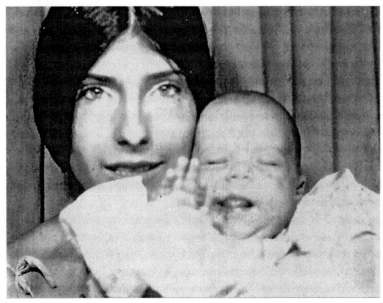

FIGURE 29 *Renee Leblanc and baby Jonathan, in Jonathan Caouette's* Tarnation *(2003).*
Source: Courtesy Jonathan Caouette.

because it's all in retrospect now, and as a child I didn't really think of what happened to me as traumatic (figure 29).

When you grow up in an atmosphere where you're a wild child raised by wolves, you learn that what to you is just normal is socially unacceptable to some people. The "trauma" that did happen to me as a kid happened on such a consistent basis that I guess if I were hard-wired differently, it could have pushed me in a completely different direction. For whatever reason, my experiences made me want to create and to make movies. That was my saving grace.

About the time I turned 5, just after I got out of the foster home system—I was in at least *four* foster homes—I already knew, just *knew*, that I had to be a part of what was happening on television and in the movies. Of course, it was a very nebulous, abstract idea at that point.

The first movie I remember seeing in a theater was *Benji* [1974]. A movie that I remember as a bit traumatizing was *Close Encounters of the Third Kind* [1977]: I'll never forget how I felt when the kid is getting sucked away by that orange light in the door; that imagery still haunts me. Obviously, it had to do with my separation from my mother.

When I was 11 years old, I begged my grandfather to buy me a Super-8 camera from a pawn shop. Even though it was well into the 1980s, you could still get Super-8 film from the electronics department at Target.

When I was first making movies, it was mostly about emulating horror films, my favorite genre. I was always into horror, especially films like *The*

Texas Chainsaw Massacre [1974], *The Exorcist* [1973], and the horror films that were on late night TV in the early 1980s when I was growing up: the original *Stepford Wives* [1975] and *Let's Scare Jessica to Death* [1971]. Those films always seemed to be shot on this wonderful, creepy film stock that isn't used anymore, film stock that gave the films an almost documentary feel, while at the same time being over-lit. And the acting was way over the top.

MacDonald: That was a powerful, regenerative moment for horror film.

Caouette: It really was, because nobody had quite gotten the formula yet: "formula" is a horrible word when it comes to art or cinema. Everything is just a doppelganger of everything else right now.

MacDonald: Also, there was a new level of violence in horror films. One of the great film-going experiences of my life happened at *Dawn of the Dead* [1978]; the audience I was with was completely freaked out by the shocks in the film and we spontaneously became zombies as we left the theater and took over the street.

Caouette: Oh, those Romero films are wonderful; I just got the boxed set. I love *Dawn of the Dead*, which I saw for the first time at midnight on a double bill with *The Warriors* [1979, directed by Walter Hill] at one of the old General Cinemas in Houston. My grandfather and I didn't get home until four in the morning! I loved the whole shopping mall idea in *Dawn*. That was when zombies still moved slowly; now they *run* after you. Nobody has the attention span for zombies anymore.

The first film I made was an imitation of *The Texas Chainsaw Massacre*. You can actually see bits of that film in *Tarnation*: there's a scene where you see a small figure wearing a mask that's turned inside out—I was a would-be Leatherface—and my mother is the Sally Hardesty character.

Around that time I also made *The Ankle Slasher*; the working title was "The Techniques and Sciences of Eva." It was about a girl who could morph into two or three people at the same time and also occasionally into inanimate objects: you wouldn't be able to tell her apart from other objects in the room. Looking back, it's kind of an interesting idea, and maybe also an insight into some disassociative symptoms I experienced at some point— "disassociation" is the key word for all of my upbringing I think, because I tended to disassociate myself from what I really knew. Even at a young age, I think I may have had enough insight to realize that something was a little off kilter in my family and that my life was substantially different from most kids' lives.

Sorry, I keep having to remind myself that interviews are not therapy sessions! You can shut me up when I start ranting. I'm just thinking that when you have a sordid upbringing and you don't really have a strong family foundation—that is, people to set boundaries for you, people to explain things to you, to tell you what's going on in the world—you develop a very abstract version of the world around you.

During the period when I was beginning to make movies, I was enrolled in the Big Brother program in Houston and was lucky enough to be matched up with long time film critic, Jeff Millar. With his illustrator-partner Bill Hinds, Jeff still has a syndicated comic strip called "Tank McNamara." I was Jeff's Little Brother from when I was 11 until I was 15 and have maintained a friendship with him and his family ever since. Jeff was a wonderfully encouraging person. Instead of our going on the typical outings to baseball and football games that most Big Brothers would take their Little Brothers to, I would tag along with Jeff to the first-run screenings that he would review.

When Jeff wasn't around, I'd be at the local Landmark Theater (the River Oaks). I think I must have made friends with most of the people that worked at their snack bar; they let me sneak into films. River Oaks had an amazing repertory calendar, sometimes different films every day, from *Blue Velvet* [1986] to *Au Revoir les enfants* [1987], from the early Merchant Ivory films to John Waters, Peter Greenaway, Jim Jarmusch, Gus Van Sant. At home I was watching Beta and VHS bootlegs of films by Paul Morrissey, Alejandro Jodorowsky, Derek Jarman, John Cassavetes, and enjoying *Repo Man* [1984, directed by Alex Cox], *Andy Warhol's Bad* [1977, Jed Johnson], *The Brother from Another Planet* [1984, John Sayles], *The Garden* [1990, Derek Jarman], *Home of the Brave* [1986, Laurie Anderson]. . . too many to name.

I know this will interest you: when I was about 12, I went to the library and got the John Waters *Trash Trio* book [New York: Vintage, 1988]. I still have it. In the back of *Trash Trio* is "Flamingos Forever," the script for the would-be sequel to *Pink Flamingos* [1972]. For a 12-year-old to be into John Waters would probably not be as amazing now—though it's still *inappropriate*. I think, "Yeegads, I would *never* let *my* kids watch *Pink Flamingos*!" On the other hand, there's so much information available, how could they *not* see it?

MacDonald: Last semester, I pushed one of my classes at Hamilton College to do an "underground" midnight screening of *Pink Flamingos*. The students had heard of the film, but none of them had actually seen it. The film shook them up.

Caouette: It stands the test of time!

MacDonald: In some ways it's *more* powerful now than it was then.

Caouette: You're right. Now, everybody is into looking so pretty and perfect, and everybody in that movie is just god-awful and hideous—and there's the whole dancing asshole thing!

MacDonald: Yes, unbelievable!

Anyway, so you're 12, finding your way into John Waters. . .

Caouette: Yes, I was friends with this teenage drag queen named Kip who did a dead-on impersonation of Divine; he was about three hundred pounds and even sort of looked like Divine. And there was a twenty-something woman friend of mine, named Varna, who kind of looked like Mink Stole.

I was always hanging out with people who were much older than me—again, this goes back to my unstructured upbringing. I didn't know if these people could act, but I told them, "*You're* going to be Mink Stole and *you're* gonna be Divine!"

So I was getting ready to do this film, and Jeff gave me a bit of seedling money for Super-8 film stock. Super-8 was already archaic; people were getting the big VHS video cameras, but somehow I had already realized that film looks better than videotape and I wanted to make things on film. When I would sit in a theater with my grandfather, I loved the snap you hear when the reel changes; I was fixated on film.

A couple weeks before I was ready to shoot *Flamingos Forever*, I wrote to John Waters to ask his permission. I don't know how I found his address; he might have been listed in the Baltimore directory. I was too afraid to do the phone call myself; my friend Joan made the phone call, but John wasn't there. We sent him a handwritten letter asking permission, and a couple of weeks later he wrote back explaining that the lawyers would never go for it (he didn't know how old I was or anything), and he said, "You should make a film with your own script one day and I'm sure it will be great."

I was devastated, but I totally respected his wishes. I ended up using the film stock to make other films, including *The Ankle Slasher*. It's strange how life works: though I couldn't have imagined anything like this at that time, only a few years later I would have the absolute pleasure and honor of actually hanging out with John Waters and Paul Morrissey!

I saw the films of Morrissey and John Waters as license for exploring my own family members, who had always seemed like real-life beautiful characters to me: my grandmother, a southern Ruth Gordon with a few drops of Edith Massey; my mother, a kind of Edie Sedgwick stirred together with the beautiful wackiness of Andrea Feldman. I created these inner mythologies as a way to make sense of my surroundings.

The second camera I got was a dinosaur VHS loaner (from Bill Hinds through Jeff) with the VCR suitcase for the tape that came with it and the attached umbilical cord. I used it periodically as my early interest in horror began to metamorphose into other genres. This was the period where I was staging performances of Southern Gothic battered women, disheveled drug-addicted female folk singers, and down-and-out street kids. I would recite various monologues to the camera in my attic bedroom, and I began to follow my grandparents around the house and film my mother whenever she would visit.

All of this was my "film school."

MacDonald: As far as I can tell, you've always been a performer, but at some point you knew you were making a larger film about your life, and I'm wondering when that was.

Caouette: I was probably cognizant that I was working on something about my life when I was about 14.

You know, I wasn't filming myself or my family as often or as much as people might think. I wasn't obsessive about keeping the camera on all the time or filming things on a day-to-day basis. There *were* periods here and there when there *was* an element of obsession surrounding my filming, but not so many of those. *Tarnation* was created out of only 180 hours of footage, mixed with photos and audio-cassette-tape sound.

When I was 16, something really started brewing. I did a makeshift edit of a lot of what I had done up to that point, and called the result *Sugar Water*. I was always looking at what I'd already done, and I guess at 21 or 22 I began to want to make use of all this stuff; I wanted to *do* something with it, but I didn't know what. When I was 28, I began to write a screenplay that had various working titles: one was "Tarnation"; another was "The Day I Disappeared"; and the third was "Lucid." I wanted to place my footage within the context of this fictitious screenplay that had to do with me and David and my mother all living together in New York. At the time, I could never have imagined that my mother would actually come to live with us!

This screenplay was like a *Twilight Zone* episode. I thought I could utilize my footage in a safe way that didn't need to allude to the fact that these characters were real, as flashbacks and flash-forwards in a story that had to do with parallel universes and different layers of reality, blah blah blah—a very vague script, although I think if it had been tweaked a little, it could have turned into something. I sat with the screenplay and the three titles for awhile, and in the end decided that the screenplay and the footage were two different entities. I put the screenplay away and started thinking more seriously about the footage as its own thing.

Then, jumping ahead again, David's Aunt Vicky bought us an iMac, the bubble-looking computer, which had iMovie, this little editing program that you could use to make movies. Very exciting. I began to obsessively digitize everything I'd shot on Super-8 and on VHS and Betamax, maybe a hundred and forty hours of stuff, including photographs that I'd recorded on Hi8 video. I digitized the audio diaries that I'd kept as a kid when I was in the psychiatric hospital after smoking those joints laced with formaldehyde, and left-over answering machine tapes of people leaving messages—everything I could find. My first masters.

Around this time, I acted in an NYU thesis film that was loosely based on the Malcolm McDowell character in *If. . .* [1969, directed by Lindsay Anderson]. In the film my character is bludgeoned on the head, and on the day that we shot that sequence, I'm in this purple velvet suit covered in blood in an abandoned asbestos-ridden psychiatric hospital. This abandoned hospital was a perfect place to make a movie and I decided that

I wanted to make my own movie in between the takes of the movie that I had agreed to act in. I had secretly called my friends over to the set, and I shot tons of footage of us doing little performances in the electro-shock therapy room and the morgue, covered in blood. David was a big participant in some of the morgue scenes.

I took this hospital footage and coupled it with some childhood stuff, a few photographs, and some footage of my son, Joshua, who is jumping on the bed in front of a little Willie Nelson poster, and I guess the result was really the first version of *Tarnation*.

Gosh, there is so much more to this story—but I'll save the long version for a book. I also made a 30-minute film called *The Hospital* that had something to do with a schizophrenic who has died in a psychiatric facility; his soul is in purgatory and he's slowly realizing that he's dead—sort of *Jacob's Ladder*-y [1990, directed by Adrian Lyne]. Joshua plays me. The soundtrack was by John Denver and Bread. That was the first thing I actually cut on iMovie. Parts of these projects are included in the denouement of *Tarnation*.

MacDonald: When did you have a son?

Caouette: I had Josh when I was 22 years old. He's 11 now. He lives in San Antonio with his mom, Joan. We have a very good relationship and I'm looking forward to the day, which I think is going to be sooner rather than later because David and I are getting into a position where we might be able to get a bigger place, when they can move here and all of us can be together. It could be a little odd, but I think it's do-able. I'm trying to encourage Joan, who wants to be a comedy sketch writer, to get to New York. She's very talented. Josh is an unbelievably bright kid. He was born right around the time my grandmother died...

MacDonald: That's the baby we see with your grandmother in *Tarnation*?

Caouette: Yes, he was just a little button back then.

MacDonald: So what happened next?

Caouette: I began thinking to myself, if I want to tell the story of our lives, what song would I choose to accompany my visuals? I decided I wanted the film to start off as a kind of cheesy wedding video, which is basically what iMovie was designed for.

MacDonald: The "Once upon a time" story at the beginning of *Tarnation*?

Caouette: Yes, "Once upon a time in a small Texas town...." This was well before my mother overdosed on lithium, and before what I was working on was called "Tarnation."

MacDonald: That section of the film is beautifully done. Very few filmmakers handle the pacing of visual text as well as you do.

Caouette: Thank you! That was one of my biggest worries. I wanted to make sure that things happened fast, but not so fast that you wouldn't get it. I wanted to make sure that certain words or phrases, even though they're childlike words and phrases, appeared at certain particularly beautiful moments in the song; it all had to be in syncopation. It's one of my favorite moments in the film. I stuck in a Nick Drake cover by Scott Appel called "Bird Flew By," a great, great song.

So the idea was to start things off with the kind of video you would see at a bar mitzvah, a historical anniversary kind of thing, which would then start to become dark. Bits of story would come in and you would realize, "Hey, I'm *not* watching a cheesy wedding video!" As you know, things get darker as I go through my mother's shock treatments, her marriage to my father, me being born, our horrible trip to Chicago. . .

The original version of the film, which is two-and-a-half-hours long, segues all the way into my mother's second marriage and my half-brother, David. Later in the editing process, a lot of people, and I myself, agreed that the story of my son and of my half-brothers had to become sub-plots in the film or just quiet references. I don't really have a strong relationship with my two half-brothers. David lives in San Diego with his wife and kids; Jason, who I've only met once in my life, is from my father's second marriage. (I think my father has been married many times; in fact he was married to Jason's mother *while* he was married to my mother!). In any case, it became clear that these relationships were going to distract from what the story eventually became.

So I did that first sequence. Then I went a little further with it and created a 35-minute piece that I felt really satisfied with; it was called "Lucid." I took it around and showed it to my grandfather and my mother, and to old friends down in Houston. It was nice to get feedback. I also showed it to Jeff, whose reaction was: "I'd like to see more!" And I thought, "Yeah, so would I!"

I had moved to New York in 1997 and by this time had done various acting jobs. I'd gone to the American Academy of Dramatic Arts, an egregiously expensive thing to be paying for—it was like a grueling psychotherapy session. All in all, not a good experience. I ended up doing a lot of work in rock musicals. I was in a really cool, off-off-Broadway version of *Hair*, hailed in the *Village Voice* as the best *Hair* since the original. James Rado came in and supervised and it was a lot of fun. I was also an understudy for the Frank N. Furter role in *The Rocky Horror Show* in Europe for a couple of years, and I did some commercials, nothing major. I was living hand-to-mouth in New York, barely surviving and getting very, very fatigued.

Then I got a job as a sort of glorified doorman at a place called Mikimoto America on Fifth Avenue, a very subservient job where I had to stand and stare at Trump Tower for eight hours a day. The most torturous thing about it was that there was a clock right in front of me, so I *literally* watched the clock—talk about time slowing down! I took the job because it paid quite a ridiculous amount of money for what it was, and I needed to pay the rent. I'd recently stopped auditioning and was about to throw in the towel—not with life, but with living in New York.

One day I go to a local bodega and pick up a copy of *Backstage*. I didn't realize until I got home that it was the previous week's issue, and I was especially frustrated to learn that John Cameron Mitchell had been holding auditions for "The Sex Film Project." The stipulation for the audition was that you had to create a video and send it in, along with your head shot and resume. It looked like the auditions had already passed and I was devastated; I'd seen an early club version of *Hedwig and the Angry Itch* and the movie [2001], and really liked what John was doing.

I thought, "Maybe I'll just go down and see what's happening." I dug up an old head shot that I thought might get me in the door—it no longer looked like me but I'd held onto it. And I wrote what John now calls my Cry-for-Help letter (ha ha), something to the effect of "Dear John, I saw your ad in *Backstage* and I know a week has passed, and I've never done this under any other circumstance, ever, and I would never, but . . ." I didn't approach him like a groupie or anything like that, though it probably could have been perceived that way. There was something urgently psychic about the writing of this letter. Instead of saying, "Hey, can I still come and audition for you?" I began, "There is a reason that I need to meet you; I don't know what that reason is yet, and it doesn't necessarily have to do with your film."

I immediately set my video camera up, did an interview with myself, and integrated it with this montage of different pop cultural references I was into and with a monologue I did when I was 11. I threw in an older monologue from Eric Bogosian that I'd used in my video, *The Fan*, and I included footage of my boyfriend David and me being intimate together. I stayed up all night, editing all of this together to a Le Tigre song and a Joni Mitchell song—altogether it was about fifteen minutes. The next morning I went to John's *house*. I told him I was an actor and a filmmaker making a film called "Tarnation," and said, "I'm hand-delivering this video. Would it be okay if I actually sat down and watched it with you? I'm really tired."

I wanted to see his reaction to the video because there was some pretty crazy stuff in there. I'm sure it was awkward for him, but I think he liked it. The next day I left for Texas—I don't remember why, something I was going to help my grandfather with. While I was in Texas, John and I corresponded by email: he wanted me to be involved on some level, but he didn't yet know how; he asked me to come to the final call-back when I returned from Texas.

When I got back, I began going to these improvisational workshops with John; it was the coolest, most wonderful audition process I've ever gone through. And John ended up calling me back to audition four or five times. Now, looking back, I don't think he really wanted to cast me; maybe he thought I was a little too complicated: he knew I had a plethora of baggage— we had talked about it and it was probably evident in the auditions. He might have wanted to use me as a stimulus for the other people around me: there were always two other people in the room interacting and when those two would go, two new people would come in, but I would stay. John and I became good friends as a result of the process.

Not long after the auditions, I called my mother. She hadn't called in about three days, and for my mother not to call me in three days was the equivalent of not hearing from a normal loved one for weeks—she usually called every day. Finally, after five days or so, my grandfather picked up the phone in her apartment. He had just gotten over a major car accident and was having major cognitive problems. He told me, "Your mother's here, yes, and I'm not sure what's wrong with her; she's been laying down here for two days with a blank expression on her face and she's not talking to me."

I asked him to put the phone up to her ear, and I remember screaming into the phone, hoping that she would respond, but my grandfather came back on and said, "She's not responding." I ended up calling 911 in Houston. Apparently a first set of ambulance drivers arrived, and my grandfather opened the door and said, "Oh, she doesn't need any help; she's just sick and has a cold, so you guys can go away, I don't know who called the ambulance." My grandfather must have looked savvy enough to turn them away.

I called them again, and said, "Please, could you just go into the house; there's something strange going on. Get on the phone with me once you're there." So when the second ambulance driver called, his exact words were, "Is she always like this? I mean she's just lying here and rolling around on the floor. We tried to get her to sit her up and she collapsed. She's defecated all over herself; does she do this a lot?"

I must have had seventeen heart attacks that night. There's nothing like feeling that disempowered, being on the other side of the world with insane things happening. I thought it might be a stroke. A day later I found out that she had taken too much lithium. It wasn't a suicide attempt; she'd run out of one medication, never filled the prescription for whatever reason, and felt she could over-compensate by popping an extra lithium or two a day. The crazy thing about that medication is that if it goes one notch above the therapeutic level, it can become toxic.

As you know, all this is re-enacted in *Tarnation*.

I continued to document aspects of my mom's recovery. There was a lot I *didn't* film: my mother lying in bed in the hospital, completely aphasic and that kind of stuff. I was also taking care of my grandad. I ended up calling Adult Protective Services to make sure he was safe and had services set up. And once I knew my mom was going to recover, I moved her back into my grandfather's house and remained with them for months.

MacDonald: Was the pumpkin scene in *Tarnation* filmed during the recovery?

Caouette: The pumpkin scene is actually not a result of my mother's post lithium overdose. That was filmed during an earlier time when my mother had been off the lithium and was being re-acclimated to it. But I used the scene to express what my mom's changes were like.

There are a number of little cheats in *Tarnation*, cheats with time, to help the film make sense cinematically. I don't want to give all of them away, but here's one more example: I had filmed my son when he was 4 years old and used that footage as a stand-in for me during the foster home sequence.

I decided to take my mother back to New York. Even though she had accidentally overdosed on lithium, I was scared that she would do it again. I set her up here in my apartment, and David and I continued to take care of her.

During all of this, I'd continued to work on the film. I was telling stories derived from my life and my mother's life, and I thought maybe my mother's overdose and recovery could be a good ending to these stories. I was getting more ambitious about making the film.

Soon after getting back from Texas, I met the new roommate of a dear friend of mine who lived just around the corner. His name was David and he had come from UC-Santa Cruz to be an intern at the Mix Film Festival, a gay and lesbian experimental film festival that was to take place at Anthology Film Archives. By this time, I had about 45 minutes of my film, pretty much in the form you see it in *Tarnation*. The new-neighbor David came over and I showed him what I had. He told me he was working with a guy by the name of Stephen Winter and said, "You should finish this; there's a deadline for submissions for Mix in about three and a half weeks." When I'd shown John Cameron Mitchell my audition tape, John had said, "You should meet my friend Stephen; he's a great guy. He's the programmer for the Mix Film Festival. Maybe you should submit this to him." The chances of John *and* this new roommate of a friend around the corner from me in a city of a gazillion people, *both* saying the same thing to me felt beyond the realm of the coincidental.

I started feverishly piecing the film together. The process of editing on the iMovie 1 program—having the computer crash over and over and over again and having to rebuild sections of the film from scratch—was exhausting. I was using an iMac bubble 1999–2000 computer, without any education—I didn't even know that external hard-drives existed. I'd build a sequence of 10- to 15-minutes—this would take me about 48 hours—and sometimes those sequences would crumble right before my eyes. In time I became savvy about what the computer's threshold was and could stop before that happened and export that chunk digitally to a Hi8 tape. Later I created transitions between all the 15-minute intervals, then re-exported all those chunks and intervals onto two VHS tapes.

During the course of this editing hell, I was in touch with Stephen Winter, begging him to give me extra time—the official deadline had passed: "I can't show you anything yet and I can't even explain what's going on, but please give me a few more days." I ended up rushing to the Mix Festival office with two VHS tapes just before the doors closed. The initial cut was 2½ hours.

Stephen called me around midnight that night to say, "I just got through the first tape; I'm going to take a break to go smoke a couple of cigarettes"—he was being very personal, very emotional; he sounded out of breath. Then he calls me back around 3:00 in the morning and leaves a message on my machine: he's completed the second tape and thinks the film is amazing and wants to centerpiece it for the Festival. He also told me there was no way that they were going to be able to centerpiece a 2½-*hour* film by an unknown filmmaker. The next day we negotiated a two-hour limit, including opening and closing credits.

Stephen notified Brian Cates who had worked with Todd Haynes on one of my favorite films of all time, *Safe* [1995], and Brian came over to watch *Tarnation* with me, and gave me some great notes, as did Stephen. Over the course of two weeks I cut the film down to two hours.

Here's another of the beyond-serendipitous events that were happening during this incredible moment. In the original cut there was a scene where a friend of mine is shaving another friend's head and talking about *Grey Gardens* [1975]. When I taped that conversation I hadn't seen *Grey Gardens*, but by the time I was making *Tarnation*, I knew the Maysles Brothers film and even had the feeling that what I was working on might in some weird, indirect way be compared to *Grey Gardens*. I decided to utilize that scene in the Mix cut because I thought it was an interesting, if indirect point of reference.

At some point during those weeks, another friend was going to perform at a party, and I agreed to let her use some fantasmagoric visual sequences from my film as a backdrop. The night of the party I got into a cab and this cab driver is talkative. He's like, "What do you do?" and I say, "I'm a filmmaker, maybe more of a video artist," and told him about my movie; and *he* says, "I was in a movie." "Oh, what movie?" And he says, "It's called *Grey Gardens*." It was Jerry, the gardener in *Grey Gardens*, driving the cab!

A few days before the Mix Festival premiere, I FedExed a copy of the VHS tape to John who was in Portland, Oregon, tweaking his screenplay for *Short Bus* [2006]. I wanted to see what he thought—maybe he'd be interested in giving the film a quote. Apparently he passed the tape on to Gus Van Sant who was living just around the corner from him and a few days after that, Stephen Winter came over with the news that John and Gus wanted to come on as producers to endorse the film. And Stephen wanted to come on as a producer too to utilize his contacts to help shepherd the film into the world. Stephen helped me find Micky Cattrell, a wonderful publicist (in *My Own Private Idaho* [1991, directed by Gus Van Sant] Micky's the john who makes River Phoenix scrub his house down!). Stephen was also integral in helping me get the film into Sundance.

For Sundance, we were encouraged to tighten the film even further, and we got it down to about 88 minutes.

The ending was changed between the Mix Festival version and the Sundance version. For the current ending I use my grandfather's story about an angel touching people underneath the nose to have them forget their previous lives before their life in this world. I come downstairs, cover my mother with a blanket, and touch her on that spot beneath her nose.

In the Mix Festival ending, I used the scene of my grandfather and me having a heated argument; my mother is in the background. It's where my granddad yells, "Take the camera away! Take the camera away!" as he's reaching into his pocket for a pen. About two weeks after we had that argument, I asked my grandfather and my mom to dress in the same clothes, and I dressed the table in exactly the same way I had filmed it before. I re-shot that moment, this time asking my grandfather to reach into his pocket and pull out the gun that you see earlier in the film, point the gun at me and pull the trigger. He does. The camera drops and the film goes into my point of view as I'm dying: I'm in this white, heavenly looking place that has a weird sort of *Eraserhead* [1977, directed by David Lynch] feeling. I'm naked and David approaches me, wearing angel wings, and puts his finger under *my* nose. In that ending *I'm* the one to forget everything.

Tarnation actually screened that way at the Mix Festival, which was cool and weird but also just awful—I'm *so* glad that's not the ending of the film now.

Spring 2012

MacDonald: When we talked before, the big question for me was, what does somebody do when their first film is their whole life? I know *Tarnation* doesn't cover your *whole* life. . . .

Caouette: It doesn't, and it's funny, a journalist asked me the same exact thing the other day, and I didn't know what to say then either. I've just kept going in whatever way I can. Since we last talked, I did *All Flowers in Time* in 2010; I worked on *All Tomorrow's Parties* [2009], a feature-length concert film—kind of a big anarchic collaborative project about the All Tomorrow's Parties concerts; and I've just finished *Walk Away Renee*, another film about my mother and me.

Two major things happened almost immediately after I finished *Tarnation*. I began to receive loads of scripts and even some flat-out offers to direct "ready-to-go" film projects—all of which I eventually turned down or opted out of either due to unusual circumstances surrounding the projects or because I found that the production infrastructure didn't seem like a fit. I was feeling a sense of paralysis.

Coupled with the what-am-I-gonna-do-after-*Tarnation* feeling came enormous life-changing circumstances. I don't want to delve too much into the details, but I ended up becoming a more or less full-time caretaker for both my grandfather—my grandparents raised me so my grandfather was essentially my father—and for my mother who has schizoaffective disorder.

My boyfriend David was and still is helping me maintain this very unusual scenario, but my entire universe became dedicated to making sure that my mother and grandfather were safe and taken care of and could find some peace and that we could have a bit of normal family life together. It's devastating to see the people you love in institutional settings, even when those settings are "nice." I kept my grandfather with me as long as I could, until his aging issues became too overwhelming to handle even with David's help. I had to place him in a nursing home in Texas, where he passed in 2008. Just after all of this, my 16-year-old-going-on-30 son Josh moved in with me.

So from 2008 on, I was juggling the responsibility of continuing to look after my mother while being a full-time dad!

MacDonald: I saw *All Flowers in Time* at the New York Film Festival. A strange, surreal film. Your grandfather is in it.

Caouette: All Flowers in Time evolved out of another project. A friend who was commissioned to work on "One Dream Rush," a project for 42 Below Vodka, was asking 42 filmmakers that he admired to make 42-second films, based on dreams. He asked me and an amazing group of other filmmakers—James Franco, Harmony Korine, David Lynch, Abel Ferrera, Jonas Mekas, Kenneth Anger, Mike Figgis, Charles Burnett. I was geeked to be part of a project that included those people, humbled and grateful and all of that, so I asked Chloe Sevigny to come to my apartment and we made our 42-second film in one day.

"One Dream Rush" premiered in Beijing and also showed at Cannes. I don't know what became of the series; I don't even know if the website is still up. There was also an installation, which I never saw, something along the lines of 42 LTV screens with all the 42-second films looping and a big vodka bottle in front.

As I was working on my contribution to "One Dream Rush," it occurred to me that some of what I was doing with Chloë was similar to things I had asked my grandfather to do years before for footage I still had. A plethora of my footage, including some that I remembered as being experimental and interesting, had been residing on an external hard drive for years, and being the mildly obsessive person I am, the notion that this footage was just "collecting dust" made me want to do something with it.

I decided to see if these two things—what I'd shot with my grandfather and what I shot with Chloë—somehow complemented each other and could be constructed to feel like a dream-illogical world. Basically, I just mashed the new stuff and the old stuff together and created an elongated version of that surreal 42-second film.

I don't really know where the imagery itself came from—psychically, I mean. I think a lot of it is derived from my own childhood fear of the dark. As you can tell, *All Flowers in Time* is a nod to David Lynch, Brian DePalma, William Friedkin, and Alfred Hitchcock. After it was shown at the New York Film Festival, it went to Sundance, and was at the Short Film Corner in Cannes. It was an experiment that could maybe have been part of something bigger.

MacDonald: How did you become involved with *All Tomorrow's Parties*?

Caouette: The All Tomorrow's Parties festivals had been going on for about ten years and I was asked to work on a documentary. My first inkling was that films about music festivals are a dime a dozen. One of my early ideas was to do something different, a sort of post-punk *Nashville* where we focused in on maybe six different characters and used the festivals as the backdrop for their stories. I don't know if this would have worked, but it would have been more interesting than what we ended up with.

We did some shooting and encouraged people who had been at the festivals to contribute their own footage as well. Ultimately, the process became *so* collaborative that I decided I had to opt out of saying that I was *the* director, and in the end, I only took a co-directing credit. As I worked on the film, I felt that it was becoming less a documentary than an electronic press kit for the festival. The people who were paying for the film wanted their own pick of bands, because a lot of the bands were on their label. And there was just so much footage. I took a stab at editing, then just withdrew from the project—there were too many cooks in the kitchen. I was a gun for hire and eventually had to accept that. That was my first and last concert doc I think.

You know, every project I've worked on since *Tarnation* has been a completely different set of circumstances with different personalities and entities to work with and work around: challenging and in the end not so satisfying. I don't know whether sometime down the road this recent work will seem part of some vast tapestry, or will just be a series of things I regret having done.

I don't feel that *Tarnation* was all that exceptional—though I've been told it is. I *do* think it was unprecedented in some ways, and it's the one project I do feel satisfied with. After *Tarnation* came out, I would joke that someday I was going to make *Reintarnation*, but never did I see myself actually doing another personal film.

MacDonald: How did the idea of making *Walk Away Renee* evolve?

Caouette: The genesis was back in 2004 when I was doing press for *Tarnation*. I met a gentleman by the name of Pierre-Paul Puljiz on the rooftop of the Noga Hilton in Cannes. He had interviewed me for *Tarnation*, and we'd forged a friendship. We worked on a very small project together for French TV and talked about doing something more ambitious one day. At one point, we began working on a project that involved heartfelt stories having to do with emotionally disturbed children. We worked on the project for a number of months, but it turned out that there were unusual legalities involved, as well as some creative control challenges, so he and I opted out. Having already invested time and money in that project, we began to talk about a new project.

During this whole period, I'd been attending film festivals promoting my films and serving on various juries for films in competition. There was an inspiring film festival in Warsaw. I'd been invited as a jury member and had an opportunity to sit through some really amazing, very slow-burn cinema-verite films: *Le Quattro Volte* [2010, Michelangelo Frammartino], *Mama* [2012, Andres Muschietti], *I Travel Because I Have to, I Come Back Because I Love You* [2009, Karim Ainouz, Marcelo Gomez], among them. I was mesmerized by these films. And conversations with Gus Van Sant turned me on to Béla Tarr. I became attracted to idea of slow cinema and wanted to think about a project that could work with that rhythm, as opposed to the frenetic pace of *Tarnation*.

Because of the time constraints around the release of *Tarnation*, many aspects of my story had needed to be cut out. My son is by no means a sub-plot in my life, but there was no place for him in *Tarnation*. Also, I felt that the dynamics between my mother and me hadn't been fully represented. So in early 2010, when my mother, who was in a difficult and lonely situation in an assisted living facility in Texas, was administered the wrong medication, I decided I wanted her here with me and thought: Wouldn't it be cool, just as an experiment, to shoot a real-time road movie with Renee? I was interested in exploring the mundane, the quiet, the solitude of a road trip to New York (figure 30).

FIGURE 30   *On the road in Jonathan Caouette's* Walk Away Renee *(2013).*
Source: Courtesy Jonathan Caouette.

The original idea was that we were just two regular people, one of them taking care of the other. I wanted to show my mother a good time and have her spend a few weeks at my apartment in NYC with me and Josh before I took her to the new assisted living facility upstate. I arranged for a crew of two guys to shoot the road trip sequences, then went down to Texas to move Renee, and we shot the six-day trip. The road movie was going to be all that there was of this film—virtually no back-story.

At one point, the road trip footage was going to be one of several extras for an opulent DVD that would be released for the ten-year anniversary of *Tarnation*—along with a series of self-contained episodes that hadn't been included in the original film, including one about Josh. But the road movie began to snowball into the idea of another feature.

During the time when we were editing the road movie, out of my fear of losing the unused footage I'd recorded years ago, I was digitizing most everything I'd ever shot: Super-8, VHS and Beta, Hi8, MiniDV, HD. This took months. (A sidebar of technological irony: digital editing has evolved so much since 2004 that while I was able to create *Tarnation* in just three and a half weeks on iMovie, it was now taking a *year* to do this the "right way" with a "real" editing program!)

In the end, I felt the road movie needed to be broken up with back story, and that I needed to take five steps backwards (in terms of re-presenting what we learn in *Tarnation*) in order to make ten leaps forward with the "companion piece to *Tarnation*" that was evolving. My biggest challenge was how to review the basic stories without repeating *Tarnation*. I did feel that I needed to re-adopt the same stylistic devices I'd developed for *Tarnation*: explanatory text on screen juxtaposed with montaged imagery cut to popular music, etcetera—this seemed a part of the past that was referenced in the back story. But I wanted to focus whatever I used now *on my mother*, not, as in so much of *Tarnation*, on myself. And the back-stories needed to be less drawn out than in *Tarnation* and then move *past* the year 2004 to hook us into the present of 2010.

My original slow-burn cinema-verite film idea was now just a memory.

The first editor I worked with on the film, Brian McAllister, and I decided to bring in a friend to help out with the story editing. The three of us decided that it would be a cool idea to tell the back-story of my mother in reverse—*that* would be different from *Tarnation*! I thought this was a wonderful idea—at least it sounded good on paper.

But as we developed this approach, I began to waver. I was still optimistic, but more and more, it seemed to me that we had painted ourselves into a structural corner. I should have pulled the emergency break. The film did get into Cannes with that original structure, but my mantra from now on is: Don't ever "finish" a film for the sake of rushing it into a film festival.

By the Cannes screening, I knew this original structure didn't work, and immediately after Cannes, working with Marc Vives—he edited *Putty Hill* [2010; Matthew Porterfield]—I reedited *Walk Away Renee*, making the film more linear, more chronological. The Cannes version included some fictional weirdness that I decided to get rid of. There's some fictional weirdness in the new version too, but it was heavier in the Cannes version. Marc was a dream to work with and had the patience and demeanor of an angel. He and I tackled the final version and brought it home, or at least as close to home as I think this film could go.

MacDonald: What's the fictional weirdness you're referring to?

Caouette: As I did in *Tarnation*, I wanted to include some moments that were obviously fictional, but were still conveying a truth. In *Tarnation*, the "fiction" was the re-enacted scenes that bookend the film and a few other more minor moments. With *Walk Away Renee*, I wanted to create a completely fictitious subplot. I thought, wouldn't it be interesting, perhaps even funny, if I began the film playing a fictitious version of myself who had hit rock bottom and was willing to take any strange job that he could (I'd had several fiction projects fizzle during that time). Suppose a cult had hired me to make a series of PSAs that involved people lip-syncing and dancing to songs, "outreach" videos to lure people into their sect? For this fictional subplot, I created a group who referred to themselves as the Cloudbusters (inspired by the Kate Bush song "Cloudbusting"). The Cloudbusters believed that they were from the 4th dimension and were desperately trying to get home. Wilhelm Reich, their demigod, had invented a machine called the Cloudbuster, a device that accumulated orgone energy from the clouds by producing rainstorms. The irony was going to be that this silly, surreal, over-the-top sect and their orgone therapy would contribute to the healing of my mother.

I'd planned on shooting a very ambitious version of this fictional story that involved about 200 cult members all living inside a former Episcopalian church, and I had asked Harmony Korine if he and his wife wanted to play the cult leaders. Harmony was interested and we had some exciting exchanges about it, but then the Cannes deadline constraints began to overshadow these plans. I ended up shooting a less ambitious version of this fictional plot, an echo of what I was originally going for. It was funny and strange, but only snippets ended up in the Cannes version.

About half way into the current version of *Walk Away Renee*, there's a moment from a TV show where Dr. Michio Kaku is talking about the possible existence of a Multiverse. This moment was going to be connected to the Cloudbusters' theory of the cosmos.

MacDonald: The story of your going from Houston to New York, and the whole struggle about what to do about your mother's meds, is intense. The trip seems to last…

Caouette: . . . forever! *Walk Away Renee* is a suspense thriller. It's also the story of an endless struggle with the most simple-minded bureaucracy—I'm dealing with similar bureaucracy now regarding my mom's apartment and her benefits from Social Security. It's always something.

MacDonald: Your phone conversations with Renee's doctors and the administrators at various facilities are reenactments, right?

Caouette: Are there aspects of those moments that seem like reenactments?

MacDonald: In the credits you list "replacements" for the voices of whoever was on the other end of the phone, so on that level it's clear that they're constructed conversations. But I'm just wondering whether when you get a phone call in the middle of the night, you have your camera ready to go and turn it on, or whether you generally just do what you do and then you come back and re-enact what went on.

Caouette: It's a mash-up. I don't want to say exactly what was mashed up but I can tell you that because of legalities and HIPAA laws you can't use the names and voices of the real doctors.

MacDonald: Your father, Steve Caouette, is a nice presence in *Tarnation*, but in *Walk Away Renee* you block out his face. Has he turned against your work?

Caouette: No, it's a personal thing. He's not as nice as I was coerced into making him out to be in *Tarnation*. I had to make some major sacrifices of the truth to have his likeness in *Tarnation* and other stuff happened after that that wasn't too great. I didn't want to bother interacting with him for *Walk Away Renee.*

MacDonald: Ultimately, of course, the journey you portray in *Walk Away Renee* is more than about you and your mother; it's really about what we do about people we love who are in trouble (figure 31).

Caouette: *Yes!* I think that some people don't understand how challenging it is to attain the kind of footage you see in *Tarnation* and *Walk Away Renee.* It's *hard* to be dealing with something emotionally while you're simultaneously filming and/or being filmed—and all the while trying to deflect the idea that you're part of some cheesy reality TV program. The most frustrating thing is that I'm trying feverishly to communicate a world, a feeling, but am not quite able to do it in *Walk Away Renee* the way I was able to do with *Tarnation*. Even in its umteenth version, the new film feels a little half-baked.

I hope at some point in the future I'll be able, again, to fully endorse *something* I do.

MacDonald: You know, Jonathan, whatever you think about your recent films, I think the thing you *can* say about yourself—and hardly *anybody* can honestly say this—is that through it all, you did the right things as a son, as a grandson, and as a father. *Tarnation* and especially *Walk Away Renee* model courage, persistence, and deep love for family and friends.

FIGURE 31 *Jonathan Caouette and Renee Leblanc in Caouette's* Walk Away Renee *(2013).*
Source: Courtesy Jonathan Caouette.

Caouette: I've *tried*. You know, nobody in their right mind would ever make films like mine to get into the film industry or become famous. Those certainly weren't my reasons for making the films. I am very grateful that, as a result of making the films I've been able to make, I have a mild filmmaking career, but I don't long to be in the limelight. I'm uncomfortable with the whole process of marketing myself and my work. Even with all the excitement in 2004-2005 after *Tarnation* came out, I was relieved when it ended. At the same time, I can't wait to begin a new film!

As is obvious in the films, I don't come from money; I'm no trust fund kid. I don't have anything to sustain me beyond what I can come up with, and I've been helping to provide for other people most of my life. That's not a complaint or a cry for help; it's just the reality. My life circumstances and my hard-wiring have sent me in a particular direction, and I have to engage my circumstances the best that I can. Thank God for cinema because I swear I don't know where I would be had I not had a compulsive love for good movies.

Paweł Wojtasik

"An artist," to quote food critic Anton Ego in Brad Bird's *Ratatouille* (2007), "can come from anywhere." Paweł Wojtasik, who spent his childhood in Poland, then moved to New York City by way of Tunisia, is evidence that an artist can also arrive on the scene at any point in life: Wojtasik emerged as an accomplished video artist during his late fifties, though his work, made in the aftermath of a mystic experience, often has a youthful glow. In fact, the power of his video pieces comes from the unusual combination of Wojtasik's "youthful" excitement at being able to make video and a disposition formed by decades of psychic struggle.

Roughly speaking, Wojtasik has produced two kinds of work: short pieces on highly unusual topics—sewage treatment (*Dark Sun Squeeze*, 2003), naked mole rats (*Naked*, 2005), pigs (*Pigs*, 2010), autopsy (*Nascentes Morimur*—"The moment we're born, we begin to die," 2009)—and large-scale installations on more overtly public issues, designed for gallery situations. For Wojtasik, making motion picture art is about facing fear—the fear of death, of pain, of loss—and the shorter pieces often confront the viewer's own fears, including the fear of seeing certain kinds of imagery on a motion picture screen. Wojtasik's mature films are shot in high-definition video, with a rigorously formal compositional sense; his imagery is as elegant as his topics are disconcerting, even repulsive. Nowhere is this more obvious than in *Pigs* (in several versions, but most recently 2010), which is the inverse of the convention in modern nature film of representing animals in such a way that whatever might repulse us is suppressed. In a sense, Wojtasik is a child of Stan Brakhage, especially that early strand in Brakhage's monumental tapestry dedicated to the confrontation of taboo. Indeed, *Nascentes Morimur* seems to be in conversation with Brakhage's *The Act of Seeing with One's Own Eyes* (1972).

Wojtasik's more publicly oriented work is contemplative in a somewhat different way. *The Aquarium* (2006) focuses on the way in which aquariums can contribute to the illusion that environmental damage to the world's oceans is of minor importance. The large-scale installations—*Below Sea Level* (2009), a 360-degree panoramic work created for MASS MoCA [Massachusetts Museum of Contemporary Art]; *At the Still Point* (2010), a five-screen work designed for Smack Mellon; and *Single Stream* (installed at the Museum of the Moving Image in 2013)—though less shocking than the shorter works, are contemplations of mortality and/or serious global issues. *Below Sea Level*

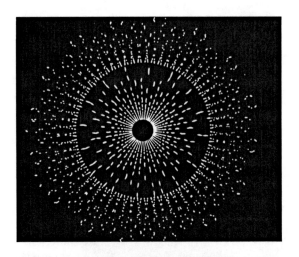

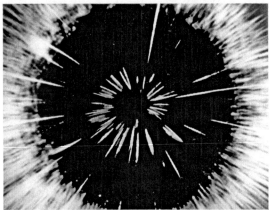

FIGURES 32A, 32B, 32C *Three cine-mandalas: (top) from Jordan Belson's* Allures *(1960); (middle) from Belson's* World *(1970); (bottom) the "ninth gate" in Paweł Wojtasik's* 9 Gates *(2012).*

Source: Courtesy Jordan Belson, Paweł Wojtasik.

focuses on the Katrina disaster within a context of the ongoing environmental struggles in and around New Orleans; *At the Still Point* visits various locations within India, including the Manikarnika Ghat in Benares, where the dead are cremated in a ritualized fashion after being immersed in the Ganges, and the ship-breaking yard in Alang; and *Single Stream* focuses on the immense stream of recyclable refuse created by contemporary capitalist culture.

As this is written, the most recent of Wojtasik's short videos is *Nine Gates*, which confronts taboo in a rather different mood from the earlier work: as a celebration of passionate love. Using Guillaume Appollinaire's "Le Neuf Ports de Ton Corps" ("The Nine Gates to Your Body") as a guide, Wojtasik's camera explores a lover's body, revealing her various orifices in extreme close-up, and (in the final version of the video) transforming the ninth "gate," the anus, into a mandala (figures 32a, 32b, 32c).

This interview was begun at the Robert Flaherty Film Seminar in June of 2010 and expanded and revised online.

MacDonald: You're not young, and yet you're a young filmmaker...

Wojtasik: An "emerging artist"!

MacDonald: So who were you in your previous incarnations and what led to your recent shift to experimental video?

Wojtasik: As you ask me this, I see my life passing in front of my eyes, kind of like when people are dying, you know? I've had several separate chapters to my life and I've often felt like a beginner. The earlier parts of my life were devoted to various pursuits—all designed to help me overcome a certain kind of alienation that I felt as a child.

MacDonald: You grew up in Poland?

Wojtasik: Yes. My father was a surgeon, and my mother was a journalist, a theater critic, but she didn't write according to the government's dictates, so at some point they said, "Okay, that's enough: you don't write at all." Her anger became so profound that she would fall down in the street while walking and would be brought home by ambulance. Her heart experienced tremendous palpitations, but the cardiologists would say, "There's nothing wrong with you. We don't understand." She lived on valium until we left Poland, and the minute we left, all her symptoms stopped.

I had dual ideological input from the communist government and the Catholic Church, and I grew up being accustomed to the relativity of whatever was considered truth. As a child, I was alienated from myself, my friends—did I even have friends?—from my parents, from everybody, by such extreme sensitivity that it kept me unable to speak to people, even to let myself play. The only ray of hope, the most empowering thing that I experienced as a child, was when my parents got me a movie camera, an 8mm Russian camera (it had three lenses on a turret). Maybe I was 14.

For my first roll of film I just looked out the window of my building—it was L-shaped—at the other side of the L, lit by sunlight. I filmed the light and suddenly understood something about visuality; and the world, which previously had seemed alienating and cold, opened up for a moment. Seeing this perceptual phenomenon somehow translated into a momentary feeling of liberation from my interior prison. I've loved filming ever since; having the camera is both protection and a way to open up to the world. After that experience I made some short fiction films and also some simple impressions of things.

My best friend in Poland was the son of the director Jerzy Kawalerowicz, one of two major Polish directors at that time—Andrzej Wajda was the other—and one day my friend invited me to the set of a film Kawalerowicz was making: *Pharaoh* [1966]. It was about ancient Egypt, and I remember the majestic temple they'd built and the pharaoh being pulled on some sort of chariot. I met the director; we shook hands, and I thought, yes, I want to be a filmmaker.

MacDonald: Do your early films still exist?

Wojtasik: In 1982 I destroyed everything I'd done. I lived in an abandoned loft, kind of a squat, with my second wife, Esperanza; and when we had to leave there, I made a decision to leave my past behind. I was still struggling with my identity and thought this would give me a chance to start anew, to be free of the inner sense that I'm defective in some way.

Of course, now I'm thinking, "Oh god, I wish I had those films!"

MacDonald: When did you and your family leave Poland?

Wojtasik: When I was 16 we went to live in Tunisia. I was there for three years. Tunisia is an exotic country—and for a time I thought that changing my environment would change me, but soon realized I had brought my alienated worldview to Tunisia; and it traveled with me again when I came to the United States. My mother, my sister, and I moved to New York in 1972—my father stayed in Tunisia. Once here, I experienced an initial euphoria, then fell into deep depression for three years.

I got a job at Columbia University, shelving books for the medical library. Somehow I gravitated towards the lowest floor where there were no windows, and stayed in that basement as much as I could. They called me "the mole."

I had continued making films in Tunisia, with the 8mm camera; it was a nice camera, but my films were not very ambitious. I didn't really think like a filmmaker. I didn't know how to structure what I shot. One of my first actions after coming to this country, once I'd made some money at the library, was to buy a Beaulieu Super-8 camera, the most beautiful camera I've ever had, with a long, gorgeous, tremendously phallic lens and a small attachment for the film cartridge. My mother was upset with me when she found out how much money I'd spent—$800. I thought I would do great things with that camera, and I did make some films with it, but my mind was still blocked.

Because I was working at Columbia, I could take classes there, so I took Film Analysis—taught by Stefan Sharff, a former assistant to Eisenstein. I began thinking, "Maybe there's a chance for me to become a filmmaker," but because of my sense of alienation, because my personality was so withdrawn, I also knew I couldn't possibly be a director like Kawalerowicz. And my alienation was increasing, to the point where I often felt like I was losing my mind. I tried cocaine and smoking weed, and learned that those things were worthless as far as curing my problems. I tried sex. Nothing worked.

I'm telling you all this to explain why I lost so much time, but maybe the time wasn't exactly wasted. In retrospect, it all seems to make sense, but I couldn't see any logic to it back then.

MacDonald: What films do you remember seeing at Columbia?

Wojtasik: I took a class with a woman (I forget her name) who showed us Maya Deren's *Meshes of the Afternoon* [1943], which blew me away and pulled me out of my alienated state for a moment. Somehow I felt connected to the world in that film, through its dream-like reality inhabited by Maya's erotic presence. There's a special place in my heart for Maya Deren.

In addition to the library job, I was working part-time in a bookstore; and the book *How to Meditate* fell into my lap. I didn't know exactly what "meditate" meant; I thought it meant to *think*, and I hoped that maybe through thinking, I could find a way to get out of the psychic space I was in. But this book was about the practice of focusing on your breath. I was skeptical, but by this time, willing to try anything.

At one point the author said something like, "Okay, reader, you must stop reading and take fifteen minutes or so to just breathe, and count your breaths; then resume reading." I lay down on the carpet and started to do this breathing, and within five minutes this stone, this alienation, this horrific, monstrous demon that had been sitting in my chest was gone. The relief was temporary, but here was a ray of hope. I continued this practice, and my state improved somewhat, though I still wasn't making any films. I'd realized I couldn't be a director and had no interest in standard film jobs.

Because I liked to draw cars, I sent a letter to Ford, GM, and Chrysler, asking them to please hire me as a car designer, and they said, "First, you have to finish school and train to be an industrial designer." So I applied to Pratt, but for some reason checked off architecture on the application form, and became an architecture student for several years. I didn't really like doing architecture, but the professors liked my ideas, so I kept going at it until I couldn't continue, until my body refused to draw those straight lines.

I transferred to painting—because I'd taken a painting class with Professor Max Gimblett, a painter from New Zealand, an introvert who had transformed himself into an extreme extravert—I felt he understood where I was coming from. I made a painting based on a still life Max had set up and when he saw the painting, he said, "Let's talk," and I was amazed to hear him speak very seriously about my work. For the first time I felt validated as an artist, and I began painting a lot. I remember late one night a student opening the door, maybe looking for someone, seeing the painting I was working on, and saying, "Your painting makes me feel good." I thought, "This is *it*, I'm a *painter*." And in fact I enjoyed painting very much and was a painter for some years—until I fell in love with Esperanza Cortes while traveling in Europe and North Africa. But something very important had happened before this, something that allowed me to fall in love.

In 1980 I began to study Buddhism more seriously, and I went to a Tibetan monastery in Vermont, where I meditated every day for ten hours or so, for a whole month. During the third week of my stay, we were instructed to allow our whole being to go out of our bodies with each breath, so one day I'm imagining myself as a cannonball and my body as a cannon and with each breath I'm being fired from this cannon—when suddenly, out of the blue, I'm projected out of the cannon with the out-breath *and I don't return.* Suddenly I'm wandering in space. Everything in the room is *glowing.* All the suffering I'd been feeling all my life was gone, and I realized that the people sitting with me in that room were my brothers and sisters. I felt that I would do *anything* for them, for *any* of them; they were all equally glowing in my perception.

Then I looked for myself—where was *I* in this scheme of things?—and I couldn't find myself. I'd had this ego that was so sore and filled with all kinds of repressions and fears and anxieties, and it was erased, gone, vanished in a flash. All I could see was this shining field with all these people who really were no different from me; they *were* me and there *was* no *me.* I realized that all my negative thinking, even my positive thinking, everything that I'd been taught in school, was irrelevant. Everything had vanished, except for this radiant universe and I wasn't *in* it, I *was* it.

That was the most important experience of my life—I'm always referring to it in everything I make. Of course, at first I thought this intense moment would last forever, but after half an hour or so I began to feel a little bit of *me* coming back. It was kind of weird, feeling the old self returning, and I could see that to the extent that it *was* returning, the suffering and the dissatisfaction with the present moment were also coming back, and I was becoming jealous of *this* person and didn't like *that* person, and after an hour or so I was back where I had been—except that now I had a memory of that new experience, and understood that my older way of being was not Reality.

Later, I had a hard time bringing that moment back and learned you couldn't just manufacture that state. It comes only when you encourage it, but there are no guarantees.

This momentary release from my alienation was strong enough to allow me to fall in love with Esperanza, and I realized myself as a sexual being with her during our travels. Our trip—we traveled with a group—was like a "grand tour" of Europe (one of the highlights was hanging out with Bill Murray in Paris). Italy was especially fantastic.

I insisted that we not stay anywhere longer than three days: the movement of traveling was keeping the demon away. So long as we kept moving, Esperanza and I were on a cloud, and I felt completely free. We ended up in Tunisia, out of money. Lying on my bed one day, I felt the demon come down as if from the ceiling; it descended upon me like a falcon and took possession of me again. And because Esperanza could no longer recognize me, she became a nightmare.

This was a disastrous set-back, but still, I asked Esperanza to marry me, and she accepted. As I grew increasingly alienated from her, I thought our having a child might help, so we had a child—that didn't help either. Back in New York, I was still considering myself a painter, but to support us I was working construction, doing carpentry and house painting and trying to run a small business. I was a terrible house painter because I would stand around forever choosing the right color, and even once the house had been painted and the color was sublime, the clients would say, "You're late!" Also, I was a terrible businessman. One time, when I finished paying everybody I'd hired, I had two dollars!

I loved my wife and daughter, but I couldn't ignore my inner compulsion to be an artist, which was being squashed by my needing to work at this terrible job—terrible for me. Finally I left on a long trip, and when I came back, the locks had been changed.

After the divorce, I had a series of relationships. One of my girlfriends was a student, and I felt jealous of her life, a life of ideas. I decided I should go back to school and in 1991 enrolled in Empire State College: they give you academic credit for your life experience and they pull together all your credentials from different schools—and you can create your own major. My major was The Arts. Even though I was considering myself a painter, I took a course in black-and-white, 16mm filmmaking—and I was drawn back toward film. I got an undergraduate degree within eight months and applied to graduate schools and got accepted to Yale for painting and Columbia for film. I had a terrible time trying to decide between them. Finally a friend of mine said, "Go to Yale to study painting; you'll make better films!" So that's what I did.

I enjoyed myself at Yale. After those years of doing carpentry and house painting, I was like a sponge. Most of my Yale painter friends stayed in their studios and made paintings, but I took all kinds of classes, including drama and religion and the history of Japanese and Chinese art. My schedule was full from morning to night with the classes I audited, but my favorite was Language of Film, taught by Michael Roemer, who's a brilliant professor.

MacDonald: He did a wonderful film.

Wojtasik: Yes, *Nothing but a Man* [1964]; we're going to show it at UnionDocs this coming November. Nan Goldin has promised to introduce it; it's her favorite film. In Michael Roemer's class we made a film every week. I still liked painting, but working with moving image was a liberation.

I used to go to the photographic critiques at Yale. Gregory Crewdson was one of the critics and Tod Papageorge another, and Philip Lorca di Corcia and Nan Goldin—there were great minds in that department. Nan didn't say all that much in class, but what she did say was *so* non-academic. For example, one photography student wanted to do an investigation of prostitution; Nan's advice was that she should turn tricks. The student was appalled, but I admired that answer.

Nan and I were involved for a while, then parted ways. I still love her; she's a great friend. About a month ago, we went to an Anthology benefit: Jonas Mekas was there and Sonic Youth and Lou Reed and most of all, Kenneth Anger, who received a lifetime achievement award. It was a great time.

MacDonald: So at what point did you start making films?

Wojtasik: I did the class exercises for Michael Roemer, who had a lot of wisdom. I remember him quoting Robert Young, his cinematographer on *Nothing but a Man*: "The filmmaking business is not all that complicated; you find an oncoming wave, put the camera in front of the wave, and let it do its thing." When you find "the wave," somehow *the film* tells you what to do and what not to do, where to focus and how to frame.

My sewage-treatment-plant film—*Dark Sun Squeeze*—made itself, framed itself, and edited itself; it set all the parameters, and everything was as it's supposed to be.

MacDonald: Where was *Dark Sun Squeeze* shot?

Wojtasik: In West Haven, Connecticut, at Enthone Omi Inc. The film was a result of a series of investigations, which began with supermarkets. Soon after we arrived in the States, my mother dragged me to a supermarket; she was so excited about America and all these products. I was nauseated by her excitement, but I took my camera and filmed the shelves, the products, all in negative. After that, I wondered, "What's next?" And I thought "Trash!"—because all this stuff ends up as trash, so I went to a garbage transfer station where trucks come in and the trash comes out of their giant bellies. After filming trash, I thought, "What would be another good subject along these lines," and I thought, "Shit." I asked around and found out about this sewage treatment plant in West Haven. I called them, told them what I wanted to do, and they said, "Sure, why not?"

They gave me a tour of the plant, an amazing place. When I came back to film, they told me, "You're on your own; try not to fall into the tanks, because we're not getting you out of there"—there were no guard rails or anything. I said "Great!" and soon I was a man alone in a vast sea of sewage. Very existential. During the time when I was shooting, my girlfriend left me for someone else and I was in a lot of pain, but somehow the smell of this sewage and the experience of documenting this process were very healing. In my mind, that break-up and this film are related.

Dark Sun Squeeze is constructed very logically and builds in intensity. In the end this mass of shit feels unstoppable and it's coming *at* you, but the film begins with close-ups of bubbling. The way the sewage treatment process works is that air is pumped into these thirty-foot-deep tanks; the solid excrement is sitting there and they dump tons of bacteria into the tanks, the same bacteria that process leaves in a forest. The bacteria are actually doing the work, but the process needs air, so they pump air in—that's why there are bubbles.

I made one or two hand-held shots, but everything else was shot on a tripod, very carefully framed. There's a scene near the beginning of the film where I was shooting in wide angle, and you see an expansive image of this tank; you don't immediately know what is *in* that tank, sparkling in the sun, then you begin to see these floating chunks and you understand.

At first I'm pointing the camera at the wide view of the tank and the directional mike picks up the overall sound, which increases in intensity as I point the camera down and the mike gets closer to the flow. I was right there at the foot of this waterfall, the outflow from the tank, and so when I'm pointing the camera all the way down, you can hear the slapping splashes of these chunks of shit, and the sun is sparkling and it all feels kind of unreal because it's so sunny and happy and joyful—you don't know if you should celebrate or deplore the situation.

Each time I worked on the editing of *Dark Sun Squeeze*, I would start from the beginning, reviewing all I had done, then I'd move forward. Whenever I would encounter a problem, I'd fix it before going on. Finally, I started from the beginning and continued to the end with no problems, and I remember thinking to myself, "That's very satisfying; now I can die!" (figure 33).

MacDonald: *Dark Sun Squeeze* seems a metaphor for the fundamental artistic quest: to turn shit into gold.

Wojtasik: Yes, yes, exactly: alchemy. I have a relationship with a Zen master who told me once, "Your role in life is to turn negative into positive."

MacDonald: Was *Pigs* the next film?

Wojtasik: My chronology is messed up because I keep working on some of my pieces. For example, *Pigs* now bears the date 2010, but I originally thought it was finished in 2006. This year I was showing it at a gallery and realized that I wanted to re-work it. The new version is quite different.

But *Pigs* wasn't the next film. The next one was a piece about car crushing that I didn't show because I couldn't get it right. It has also been redone, as *Crush* [2010]. The next film I *did* show was *Naked*, about naked mole rats in a laboratory. The researcher there was hoping I would do some sort of science film about her beloved naked mole rats; she's the world's leading expert and is studying them in order to discover the elixir of youth—by size the mole rats

FIGURE 33 *Portrait of Paweł Wojtasik by Pat Mazzera.*
Source: Courtesy Paweł Wojtasik.

are the longest living animal on the planet. Most tiny animals live very short lives, but the mole rats live up to thirty years. They have a lot of Omega-3; the researcher told me to drink a lot of flax oil because it has Omega-3.

In any case, she was hoping for a science film, which is why she allowed me to be in that lab. She even let me stay after hours; no one was there but me and two hundred mole rats, each mole rat worth twenty thousand dollars— they're very rare. By spending time with these mole rats, I developed tremendous sympathy and empathy for them. I could see they had neuroses and they expressed feelings; they loved each other and had fights.

The plastic tunnels they lived in were a bad imitation of the mole rats' real underground tunnels, and some of them chewed on that plastic desperately— those teeth grinding against the plastic was the main sound in the lab. Even though they were treated well, for laboratory animals, I saw their situation as a metaphor for imprisonment—animals desperately trying to get out and in the process fighting with each other, losing their minds. Of course, *Naked* is probably referring to my own inner state of being, my imprisonment in my *own* plastic tubing. I worked to create a sickly intense color for the film.

When I showed *Naked* to the researcher, she was appalled; she said, "Okay, it's beautiful, but *I* can't show it."

MacDonald: There's an unusual, mysterious sensibility behind your films, almost a frightening sensibility. The opening image of the version of *Pigs* I'm most familiar with is so visceral that for a while I couldn't continue watch it. Also, there's a hysteria in the pigs' voices.

Wojtasik: Especially during the feeding frenzy. The pigs normally make sounds like a dissonant symphony. In the film, we see them as individuals or in small groups for a time; then suddenly, at feeding time, we're seeing a whole mass of them, piling up on each other with the sounds of their voices drowning out everything else.

MacDonald: Frightening.

Wojtasik: Fear—you're on the right track. That *is* the motivating force. And the counter-force to fear, the way I see it, is pure perception, or naked perception. It's William Blake's idea of seeing the world without filters, which many people would claim is impossible, though during my experience at the monastery, I *experienced* the world in its nakedness.

Fear of death is certainly a driving force for me. When I was maybe 9 years old, my grandfather had cancer, but nobody knew he had cancer; they thought he had tuberculosis, and meanwhile the cancer was growing, causing him tremendous pain. I remember passing by his door and hearing his moaning; I think I'm still processing that moaning. I couldn't understand what was going on and no one was talking about it. My grandmother and my mother would go into the room, and sometimes I'd hear them crying and occasionally I would even catch a glimpse of him, getting thinner and thinner, disappearing. I was not terrified at that time, just baffled.

One day in 1961, my sister and I were watching television. I still remember what the movie was: at that time Polish television showed Russian movies—they were forced on us—but this particular movie was great: *Ballad of a Soldier* [1959] by Grigori Chukhrai. There's a scene where the son comes back to the mother and at that very moment I remember hearing crying from my grandfather's room, and it went on and on, this crying. At some point my mother came out of the room and said, "Your grandfather just died." My sister and I looked at each other for a moment, then went back to watching the movie. There was no shock; I didn't feel any pain or remorse or regret;

I was just blank, which baffled me even then, because I sensed that I should have been crying or expressing my grief somehow—but I didn't *feel* any grief.

Later on, I saw that my grandfather's death had had a profound effect, because that scene of watching the television and this crying and my mother's announcement kept returning to me, and, having seen that death is a mysterious force to be reckoned with, I became more and more terrified. Though I was a child, I realized that there was this ultimate punishment waiting for all of us. Death is present among us at all times. Even as we speak now, countless beings are vanishing and transforming, sometimes in situations of extreme cruelty. The horror is unspeakable.

I'm sometimes asked why I choose the subjects I do. I use art, and film, as a tool to discover ways in which I can go *from* fear *to* freedom-from-fear. Each one of my pieces is like a small journey from a state of fear through an experience of accessing and encountering some terrifying reality which speaks ultimately of death, and becoming intimate with it, until I see that there is something beyond death. Having an intimacy with death allows you to be free of it.

MacDonald: *Nascentes Morimur* is your most obvious confrontation of the fact of death. Many people who see *Nascentes Morimur* will have also seen *The Act of Seeing with One's Own Eyes*, Stan Brakhage's visual exploration of autopsy in the Pittsburgh morgue. Not only is your topic the same, but like *The Act of Seeing*, *Nascentes Morimur* is silent, your first silent piece. I wonder if you saw making *Nascentes Morimur* as an engagement with *The Act of Seeing*.

Wojtasik: I was aware of Brakhage's film, which, when I saw it the first time, seemed to me the best film ever made. Or, to put it a different way, all other films shoot at the target, but only *The Act of Seeing* hits the bullseye. Because it goes directly to the essence of what life is about, of what we are. It shows us as meat, animate becoming inanimate, the living and the dead as one. The living hand of the doctor holding the pale bluish hand of the dead patient. Yet somehow there's a sense of transcendence, and that transcendence is through beauty, through perception.

Nascentes Morimur has its own way of dealing with the horror, it's *my* confrontation with death; but at all times while shooting and editing it, I kept Brakhage's film in mind.

MacDonald: Like Brakhage you compose your shots and edit what you've shot into what feels like a coherent structure, but in addition, you use *Nascentes Morimur* to rethink the frame. At the moment I can think of only one other comparable experiment, a film that was shown at Cinema 16: *The Door in the Wall* [1956] by Glen H. Alvey, Jr. It uses variably sized screen images—Alvey called it the "Dynamic Frame Technique"—that echo the kind of action portrayed on-screen (I've only seen stills from this film).

Sometimes you're clearly using the technique as a metaphor: in several instances, your frame-within-the-frame creates a kind of incision within the outer frame that echoes the scalpel cutting flesh during the autopsy.

Wojtasik: Until the Renaissance, the inside of the body was taboo, forbidden territory, in Western culture. A lot of fear associated with the interior of the body persists, and the frame changes are meant to regulate the "dosage" of the horror—they can be seen as a "drawing of the curtains" on the autopsy: these black curtains, slowly opening or closing, protect the viewer.

Brakhage often hides the dead patient by showing the doctor's white coat in the foreground. Only a small, bloody fragment of the body can be seen. But that little bloody fragment is extremely important because we suddenly realize we *want* to see the whole body. In this way Brakhage addresses our voyeurism; we are repelled, yet we want to see the forbidden. So the "curtains" in *Nascentes Morimur* simultaneously hide and reveal—and, hopefully, make viewers aware of the inner contradiction of their wanting both.

I like your comment about the incision of the frame echoing the incision done on the body. I wasn't consciously thinking about this, but now it seems quite obvious.

MacDonald: Do you know Brakhage's line, "The elimination of all fear is in sight. . ." from the first paragraph of "Metaphors on Vision"?

Wojtasik: "In sight"? Oh, "in sight"—it's coming toward us.

MacDonald: Yes, it's in sight, coming toward us, becoming accessible; but also, the end of fear is in *sight*; it has to do with vision. . . *and* it's *insight*.

Wojtasik: Yes, yes, yes. Oh my god, thank you for telling me—that's an amazing line. Earlier, I spent ten minutes trying to say what he said in eight words!

I have a suspicion that perception is only a front to something that lies beyond perception and maybe is the true place of no-fear. When you're making love, the orgasmic experience is beyond life and death; for a moment you're in a space outside of creation or destruction. Somehow, even on a daily basis as I'm walking around as an individual full of fear, I'm also realizing that there is a place of no-fear that just witnesses the world and enjoys all kinds of manifestations of visible reality, including the horrific ones—like what Michael Glawogger shows us in the slaughtering operation in Nigeria [*Workingman's Death* (2005) was shown at the 2010 Robert Flaherty Seminar, programmed by Dennis Lim]. Okay, yes, there is the horror, and the pain of those animals, and there is an aspect of cruelty and terror, and death is very much present, and yet. . .

MacDonald: The experience is exhilarating.

Wojtasik: Precisely. Not that *killing* is exhilarating, but a certain intense kind of *perception* is exhilarating. An artist comes and selects for the viewer certain phenomena to observe more closely than we normally do, and if the artist observes in a particular way, we can move beyond fear.

MacDonald: *The Aquarium* is very different from your other films. It's clearly a political film about the environment.

Wojtasik: *The Aquarium* was a collaboration with the writer, Ginger Strand, whose essay, "Why Look at Fish?" [*The Believer* 3, no. 1 (February 2005)] refers to the John Berger essay, "Why Look at Animals?" Ginger's essay describes the political and sociological economy of aquariums with a witty, cutting kind of intellect.

We were at MacDowell Colony, and Ginger approached me to say that she liked my films and would like to work with me. I read her essay and thought it was brilliant—it helped me understand how aquariums are smokescreens that make people feel good, despite the tragic situation of the oceans. I agreed to collaborate with her.

We didn't know how this collaboration would work, but I knew I wanted to maintain my primary focus on the visual aspect of the experience while approaching the issue from a political/sociological standpoint. I was hoping that even without the information that ended up in the voice-over, the visuals would tell the story—while the voice-over would be adding another, partly informational and partly hypnotic, layer.

I asked Ginger to write a list of statistical data pertaining to the oceans and aquariums. Then I hired a performance artist, Kyle DeCamp, and instructed her to deliver this horrific information in the voice of an airport announcer, so it would seem totally free of emotion, almost pleasant.

This kind of film is not really my forte, but there's one scene in *The Aquarium* that feels like my other work. When I was at the Alaska Sea Life Center, feeding time for the octopus didn't go as planned: the octopus grabbed the hand of the caretaker and wouldn't let go. I zeroed in on this struggle, the latex-gloved hand overtaken by the tentacles. That moment had an abject quality and became symbolic in the way my other films are.

MacDonald: The beautiful, sometimes eerie, landscape/seascape shots remind me of Peter Hutton.

Wojtasik: I admire Hutton's work.

It was Alaska in December, and during the six hours when I could be shooting, changes were creating what looked like a totally different landscape every ten minutes. Of course, this beautiful, constantly changing landscape symbolizes the idealized state of nature before we arrived on the scene, wreaking havoc—and building aquariums.

The Aquarium was a precursor of other projects. I started to expand not only thematically but in terms of the actual presentation of my work, which culminated in the 360° panoramic film/sound piece called *Below Sea Level*, which was shown at MASS MoCA for about a year in 2009–10 and was part of the Prospect 2 Biennial in 2011–12 in New Orleans. I was again dealing with an actual place and a political/sociological/environmental issue: this time, the situation of post-Katrina New Orleans. I'm very interested in ecology; my experience of sensing the whole world as part of me in the monastery is the origin of this interest. I can't tolerate that something is happening in the Arctic that harms the environment; I feel it in my body.

MacDonald: How did the panorama project develop?

Wojtasik: Roughly a year after Hurricane Katrina, Sebastian Currier was commissioned by the Ying Quartet to make a piece about New Orleans. He told me about the commission and I proposed a video—because I had fallen in love with New Orleans when I visited in 2000 (and because my collaboration with Sebastian on *Naked* had turned out well). We submitted a proposal for a 360° digital video cyclorama to Denise Markonish, a visionary, hands-on curator at MASS MoCA. She was interested.

In the nineteenth century, cycloramas were round buildings where one would be immersed in a panoramic painting, of a battlefield, for example. There are still panoramas in Waterloo, Gettysburg, and Wroclaw in Poland, but we were attempting a moving-image panorama, with surround sound. I made many trips to New Orleans, explored numerous sites in the vanishing wetlands area surrounding the city, and met many great people, such as Chief Howard Miller of the Creole Wild West tribe of the Mardi Gras Indians. Many of the individuals we met are featured in the resulting work.

The shooting was done using the Ladybug 2, a panoramic camera on loan from EMPAC [the Experimental Media and Performance Arts Center] in Troy, New York. We also used an HD camera, sometimes with an anamorphic lens. Gian Pablo Villamil, an expert in panoramic technology, became a full-fledged member of our creative team. I quickly realized that 360° footage is quite boring unless the camera is moving, and Gian Pablo came up with ingenious ways to attach the camera to various vehicles, for example the canoe and the airboat that we used to film in the bayous. We also shot from a plane, a helicopter, a river boat, and the ferry crossing the Mississippi, as well as from cars and trucks.

I developed an idée fixe about partially immersing the $20,000 Ladybug 2 in the Mississippi. I thought that would be *the* shot. Everyone advised against it, since an underwater housing for the camera doesn't exist, so I stayed up all night making one out of a sheet of transparent plastic and tape. When I immersed the camera in the brown water of the Mississippi the next day, the Ladybug worked for half an hour, then went dead. I thought, "I've ruined the project!" But, amazingly, when it was sent to be repaired, the Ladybug was working perfectly.

Sebastian worked on the music for the piece, but over time our respective visions didn't coalesce, so I made the difficult decision to start working with sound artist Stephen Vitiello. Stephen's approach was much more "documentary": he built an aural *environment*.

The 360° panorama in *Below Sea Level* is thirty-eight minutes long and runs on a loop within the panoramic gallery space. Two single channel pieces developed from the same material. One is the short film also called *Below Sea*

Level (2010). The other is *Next Atlantis* (2010), a twenty-minute video accompanying a musical composition by Sebastian, who showed great generosity of spirit in asking me to create a video for his New Orleans composition. Since the music for *Next Atlantis* was already fixed, the task was to find appropriate images that would unfold in parallel with the developmental arc of the composition.

There are, of course, major differences in the way each piece is seen. The panoramic footage is spatially curved, so it only appears normal if projected on a curved wall; if we saw panoramic footage of a New Orleans street projected on a flat wall, the buildings would appear distorted. In the single channel pieces, I consciously use that distortion. I even use it in the panorama itself because I feel distortion is consistent with what I am trying to say about the situation in that city.

MacDonald: Both pieces have an elegiac mood, though I'm not entirely clear on how you see *Below Sea Level* and *Next Atlantis* in relation to the Katrina disaster.

Wojtasik: They *are* elegies. *Below Sea Level*, the panorama, was actually envisioned as part of the larger MASS MoCA exhibition called "These Days—Elegies for Modern Times." I once asked Tom Piazza, who wrote *Why New Orleans Matters*, to define the essence of New Orleans; he said: "Elegant and defiant affirmation in the face of mortality." New Orleans lives on the brink of disaster all the time. Aware of death, it lives fully, fabulously. Transmuting terror, slavery, poverty, racism, natural disasters into vibrant, visionary life is the essence of New Orleans. *Below Sea Level* is both elegy and homage to the spirit of the city.

This brings *Below Sea Level* and *Next Atlantis* in line with the rest of my work, which I would say is an attempt at transmuting the abject, repellent, or terrifying—alchemy, as you observed earlier. Both works portray the largely inundated landscape, punctuated by oil rigs, some of them destroyed (a premonition of the BP oil spill?), intercut with scenes of the city, from the bleak emptiness of the Lower Ninth Ward to the ecstatic dance of the Mardi Gras Indians. With the ecological crisis hitting New Orleans so hard, with entire sections of the city, and of the wetlands around the city, vanishing—they are losing a football field's worth of land every forty-five minutes—a depiction of the city *has* to be an elegy, one that refers to a broad view of the ecological and human disaster taking place, of which Katrina is only the best known example.

MacDonald: Like the *Below Sea Level* panorama, *At the Still Point* also takes your work to a larger space.

Wojtasik: *At the Still Point* was created for Smack Mellon, a huge, cavernous space that was formerly a power plant, producing heat for a large part of Brooklyn. Several years ago, all the machinery was taken out and it's now an art gallery, empty except for the support columns, whose presence was a decisive factor in establishing the five-screen configuration of *At the Still Point*.

Actually, it was the filmmaker and anthropologist Toby Lee who realized that the space called for five screens. At Smack Mellon, like in a church, the rows of columns formed a series of naves and I decided that at the end of each nave there would be a video image. The columns and the height of the wall (about twenty-seven feet) dictated that I film with the camera in vertical position. So when I went to India, where the shooting took place, I kept the architecture of the space in mind and shot vertically, which was a new way of seeing, as well as of framing and filming. I found that within each elongated vertical frame, space can be organized like in a Chinese scroll painting, without Western ideas of perspective. A series of horizontal "layers" seem to pile up on each other from the bottom to the top of the frame. When it opened at Smack Mellon in March 2010, *At the Still Point* looked like five tall vertical altarpieces or stained-glass windows; it filled the whole space, which was helped by Stephen Vitiello's surround-sound-scape.

MacDonald: At the Still Point reminds me of the tradition of the City Symphony, where a filmmaker documents a composite day in the life of a city—though here it's more like a day in the life of India. How did this piece develop, and why is it called "At the Still Point"?

Wojtasik: For a long time, I had wanted to film the "ship breaking" operation in India. Of course, there are the photographs by Edward Burtynski and the film *Manufactured Landscapes* [2006, directed by Jennifer Baichwal, about Burtynski], but I wanted to see for myself (I haven't seen Peter Hutton's *At Sea* [2007], which contains a ship-breaking sequence, and at that point I hadn't seen *Workingman's Death*, which also has one).

When I finally went to India in 2009, the experience was a revelation— though at the beginning I didn't leave the hotel for three days. I was staying in Paharganj, a very vibrant and raw neighborhood in Delhi, and when I did try to go out, it was overwhelming. I couldn't even figure out how to cross the street! The movement of humans, animals, and vehicles was incomprehensible and I felt my life was in danger. And yet I wanted to make contact with India.

I would look across from my hotel room and observe the renovation going on in the building opposite from me. I began to film the workers who were doing the construction. I noticed that they and their families ate and slept at their workplace. In the evening I filmed them lighting the stove to prepare the food, crouching around the fire, hanging out, smoking, going to bed, and I was ready with my camera in the morning when they started the day. Of course, I felt guilty about spying on the workers and at some point they noticed that I filmed them; I saw them pointing fingers in the direction of my room and laughing. I was embarrassed.

I left Delhi and traveled to other parts of India. I was able to film at the ship-breaking yard in Alang in the state of Gujarat, but only for three hours. The place is infamous for the dangerous working conditions—Greenpeace has been on their case—and the Indian authorities don't like to let anybody film there. At one point, when I was waiting at a government office, hoping to obtain a permit, the military officer asked why I wanted to go to Alang. I said, "I'm an artist and I find big ships being taken apart picturesque." He said, "Since you're an artist, can you make me a portrait?" I said, "Sure," but thought, "Oh no!"—because I hadn't drawn a portrait in years. He gave me a pencil and paper, and somehow I got "into the zone" and finished the drawing quickly. When presented with the result, the officer said, "I will cherish this for the rest of my life!" and made it possible for me to film the ships. An armed guard was at my side the whole time.

Later on, in Bombay, I encountered an archaic laundry, a huge site in the middle of the city where half-naked men were standing in pools of soapy water and washing the laundry by slapping it against stone walls. Thousands of pieces of cleaned laundry, many stories high, in multi-colored Indian designs, were drying in the sun, waving in the wind, all of it surrounded by skyscrapers and train tracks and highways, symbols of the new India. I kept coming back there to film, often standing in the soapy water (figure 34).

After Bombay I flew to Varanasi [aka, Benares], the holiest and oldest city of India, where I met a group of young men who hung out around hotels. One of them, Babu, was a charismatic 14-year-old orphan. He arranged for me to film at the Manikarnika Ghat, the site where the dead are cremated in a ritualized fashion after being immersed in the Ganges. The fire that burns the bodies is said to have been aflame continuously for 3,500 years. Manikarnika is where Robert Gardner filmed much of *Forest of Bliss* [1986].

When I first went to the site, and saw the funereal pyres with parts of charred bodies among the flames and smoke, the giant quiet river to the side, the huge piles of brown wood for use in cremations, the scorched earth and ash, and the towers of the temples pointing heavenward, I began to sob. It was overwhelming to be part of this incredible confluence of the elements: fire, earth, water, wood, and air; and of death and life—because the place was teeming with life, even though the activity of the hundreds of people revolved entirely around servicing the dead.

Although it is normally forbidden, my connection with Babu (and a bribe) enabled me to film bodies being immersed in the holy river, accompanied by chanting and the sound of countless bells, and then burned on pyres—for half an hour. A person stood next to me with a stopwatch making sure I did not go over my allotted time. At night, Babu and his friends took me out to Hindu festivals of the goddess Durga, amusement parks, food establishments. I filmed and also let them film, taught them how to use my camera. At sunrise, they took me on the boat ride on the Ganges which opens *At the Still Point*.

At the end of my journey, a month later, just before returning to New York, I stayed in the same hotel in Paharganj where my trip began. This

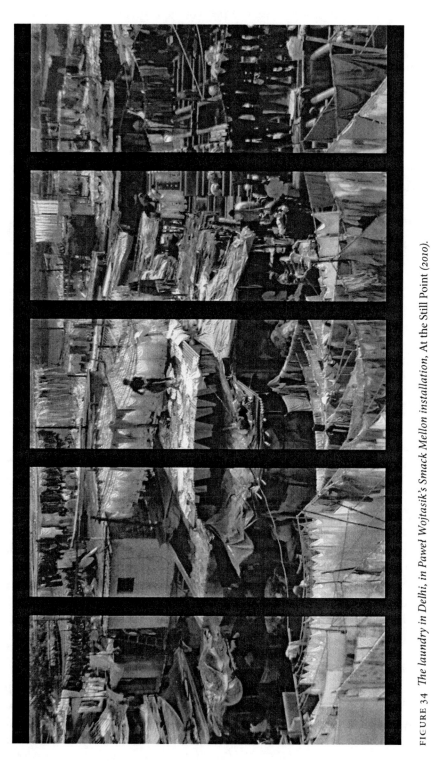

FIGURE 34 *The laundry in Delhi, in Pawel Wojtasik's Smack Mellon installation, At the Still Point (2010).*
Source: Courtesy Pawel Wojtasik.

time I crossed the street, went to the workers, and asked for permission to film. They seemed puzzled that I found what they did interesting, but they demonstrated their skills to me and looked at the camera with a very direct, unforced, unselfconscious gaze. There was no annoyance or impatience in the gaze, nor any attempt to ingratiate themselves. I recognized the stillness in that gaze as the same stillness that meditators in the state of samadhi (absorption) achieve. But here it was part of the whole culture. Having studied Buddhism for many years, I felt like I had arrived home.

In the *Four Quartets* T. S. Eliot says: "And the end to all our exploring will be to arrive where we started and know the place for the first time" [final section of "Little Gidding"]; he also uses the line: "At the still point of the turning world. Neither flesh nor fleshless; / Neither from nor towards; at the still point, there the dance is, / But neither arrest nor movement" ["Burnt Norton," part 2, lines 16–18]. That describes the Indian gaze, which to me represents the fulcrum of the Indian mind, unmoved like the axis of a wheel in the midst of chaos, poverty, the caste system, the humiliation.

MacDonald: The five-image format of the installation allows for both expansive views and interwoven realities. Did you devise rules for the various manipulations of the format?

Wojtasik: I understood the five screens as areas of darkness to be filled with light as the need arose. So sometimes all five screens are dark, sometimes they all contain projected images, but often I am using one, two, three, four out of five, while the rest of the screens remain dark. Often a sequence will begin with complete darkness, then gradually a single expansive view is revealed, starting from the bottom, as if a black curtain were rising on all five screens. It could reveal, for example, the astounding scene of that archaic laundry. After this establishing shot ends, I often introduce single discrete images on some of the five screens: a worker wiping the sweat off his eyebrows, multi-colored clothes drying in the wind, a passing train. I can construct meaning through juxtapositions of images.

Early in *At the Still Point* you see three images: in the middle, a boy rowing, flanked on the left by a shot of bodies being burned and on the right by a shot of the ship dismantling operation: two images representing death flank an image implying continuity or eternity. The presence of death in life, the intermingling of life and death, does not have to be a cause for depression; it is also a cause for celebration. New Orleans is imbued with this idea, and I found it again in India, especially in Varanasi, but at Alang also: the ships were dying but what I saw was the intensity of life.

MacDonald: What are you working on now?

Wojtasik: I'm working on a more chamber-music type of film, *Nine Gates*, which has to do with the nine openings of the body of a lover. The idea arose as a result of viewing many of my films during one week with other people at the Flaherty in 2009. Also, I knew the poem by Appollinaire: "Le Neuf Ports de Ton Corps" (that is, the nine doors, or gates, of your body), written while Appollinaire was fighting in World War 1. Each orifice receives its proper respect. There are two versions of the poem: in one, he names the vagina as the ultimate gate, but in the final version he names the anus. The poem ends with the line, "I am the master of the key." With death all around him, Appollinaire was thinking of his lover in this very carnal way, turning the horror of war into ecstasy.

My sense that presence and perception are a way of dealing with death became very actual for my mother, who had a remarkable experience a few weeks before she passed away. She was living in a nursing home at the time. At some point she stopped watching TV and her interest in social interaction waned. Instead, she began to take note of her surroundings, to really appreciate the sensory quality of the simplest of things. Once she called me over to where she was sitting in her wheelchair, held out a piece of lemon rind and, squeezing it, said, "Smell this!" The scent of the spray from the rind amazed us both. She died saying her last days were the happiest ever.

Michael Glawogger

Vienna has long nurtured a tradition of independent cinema. The accomplishments of such avant-garde cine-pioneers as Peter Kubelka, Kurt Kren, and Valie Export emboldened a younger generation of film artists—Martin Arnold, Peter Tscherkassky, Gustav Deutsch. . .—to make their own contributions. In recent decades, Austrian filmmaking has been identified with a variety of avant-garde approaches: Actionism, formalist experiments with image and sound, recycled cinema; and recently with the challenging feature narratives of Michael Haneke—not so much with a documentary sensibility. But Michael Glawogger, who had roots in the American avant-garde, was, until his untimely death in April, 2014, an exception to this tendency, as is his Viennese colleague, Nikolaus Geyrhalter (*Our Daily Bread*, 2005); the international success of their films has been crucial in establishing Vienna as a nodal point for contemporary documentary.

Glawogger's "Globalization Trilogy"—*Megacities* (1998), *Workingman's Death* (2004), and *Whore's Glory* (2011)—is a landmark. *Megacities* and *Workingman's Death* offer intimate, visceral, sometimes courageous panoramas of working conditions of a wide variety of kinds across the globe and especially in places where the world's dirty work is done. *Whore's Glory* is an exploration of prostitution in Thailand, Bangladesh, and Mexico. Collaborating with cinematographer Wolfgang Thaler, Glawogger functioned as a cine-guide into places and situations that create what he called "knots in the head": complex layerings of shock, beauty, thoughtfulness, empathy. The experience of his films can be exhausting, sometimes horrifying—but exhilarating as well.

Glawogger also made fiction features—the political suspense film *Das Vaterspiel* ("Kill Daddy Goodnight," 2009) and the comedy *Contact High* (2009), for example—but he was that rare feature filmmaker who understood documentary as his calling and feature narratives as enjoyable distractions from more serious labors.

I first saw Glawogger's films at the 2010 Robert Flaherty Film Seminar [programmed by Dennis Lim], at Colgate University, where he showed student films (including the remarkable and prescient *Haiku* [1987]) and the first two parts of the Globalization Trilogy. I interviewed Glawogger (Wolfgang Thaler was present and contributed to the conversation at several points) at

UnionDocs, the center for documentary filmmaking in Brooklyn, New York, on April, 20, 2012; we refined our conversation online.

Glawogger died of malaria in Liberia while shooting material for the project he describes at the end of the interview. A tragic loss for documentary; Glawogger was 54.

MacDonald: Before you went to film school in Vienna, you studied at the San Francisco Art Institute. Has that experience been important for you?

Glawogger: My experience at the Art Institute sharpened my eye for the visual aspect of the art of cinema. My filmmaking has to do with painting, with light and texture, with a haptic approach towards the image that unfolds on the screen. This imagery is the essence of the art of cinema—and language, sound and story are the legs on which this painting-in-motion is standing. The film school in Vienna was industry oriented, unlike the San Francisco Art Institute, but only through experiencing two completely different approaches to filmmaking was I able to find my own style.

MacDonald: *Haiku* [1987] is a powerful short film.

Glawogger: *Haiku* was done in a class at the Vienna Film Academy. There you do one documentary, one feature film, one experimental film—this was the experimental film. In a way, it is a prelude, if I can call it that, to *Megacities* and *Workingman's Death*; it's *Workingman's Death* in three minutes—three minutes, to the second.

MacDonald: The work that you do with sound and image in *Haiku* is reminiscent of Peter Kubelka and *Unsere Afrikareise* [*Our Trip to Africa*, 1966].

Glawogger: That's a very important film. In film school we learned to connect sound to image in very straightforward ways, which is one way of dealing with sound; but I think it's very interesting to also contradict sound with image: sound and image can talk to each other. The potential for working with sound has developed during the time I've been making films—there's so much you can do with sound and sound-and-image—but sometimes it seems like the more technical possibilities we develop to enhance our creativity, the more conservative we get. *Unsere Afrikareise* is important because it opened up that possibility of using sound that contradicts the image you see it with.

MacDonald: When Dennis Lim showed *Haiku* at the Flaherty Film Seminar in 2010, it felt like a wake-up call.

Glawogger: Because the theater was vibrating. That morning I told the projectionist, "I haven't shown this film for twenty years; let's show it the right way. Sound has changed: at the time when the film was made the sound came from one box behind the screen—let's see what will happen with this new system: turn the volume up to *here*." After the Flaherty I restored *Haiku*; I printed it again and it made a tour of the United States.

Haiku was an Eighties film; it was conceived as part of a structural work that would be composed of 33 pieces, each of which would have a different color and a different overall tone. Each would be exactly 3 minutes long. When *I* watch *Haiku*, it's all about the color orange and a particular rhythm. *Haiku* was the only piece of that project that got made.

MacDonald: You mentioned that *Haiku* is a premonition of *Megacities* and *Workingman's Death*, your panorama of people at work. At what point did it strike you that depicting physical labor is something cinema should be doing; and how did the *Megacities* project develop?

Glawogger: More and more, I became interested in the lives of people, in evolving *with* them in making films. That took me in a totally different direction, though I incorporated certain tones and certain rhythms from that earlier period into later work.

MacDonald: There's a structural dimension to the Global Trilogy documentaries. *Megacities* is subtitled "12 Stories of Survival"; *Workingman's Death*, "Five Portraits of Work in the 21st Century"; and *Whores' Glory* is a triptych. In each film it's clear at the beginning what the overall shape of the piece is.

At the beginning of *Workingman's Death*, you pay homage to earlier filmmakers who have worked in a similar way as you do: Georges Franju, in *Le Sang des bêtes / Blood of the Beasts* [1949], Vertov, in *Enthusiasm* [1931].

Glawogger: *Le Sang des bêtes* is one of the best films ever made. Franju is poetic in a realm that is normally not poetic. Dziga Vertov is interesting because he's always considered to be an ideological filmmaker, a filmmaker who helped to promote communism. I think he's not interesting for that; he's interesting for being dedicated to his own playfulness, to his own approach to reality. He probably would have been a filmmaker in whatever system he found himself. When I watch *Enthusiasm* I get a little weary when he shows the destruction of churches—nowadays they are restored again—but when you watch his films, you're always drawn into them more by the force of an artist than by an ideology.

It's interesting to me to have my films reach out for other art forms: music, poetry, painting. . . Hollywood film relies on the 3-act drama which does work very well for certain kinds of commercial film, but culture has way more to offer. The history of cinema has become lame. Somebody said that in the 1970s they made daring films in Hollywood because they didn't know what kind of films they wanted to make. The problem today is that the big studios and the people who put up money in America, and even the people who put up money for television in Europe, know *exactly* what kind of films *they* want to have. That's a problem for creative people because we're trying to *discover* something, to do something new and interesting. We are living in square times and I think nowadays artists have to fight tooth and nail to make daring films.

In America there really is a market for film; many people watch the commercial stuff that gets made, so money comes in; the investor puts up money to make a film he thinks will sell and he gets his money back. In Europe it's different, because the government gives us money, taxpayers' money, to maintain our culture by making interesting work—but there's no market. The governments say there should be a return on their investment, but it's ridiculous: these films can *never* make the money back. The governments could say "We just want to fund art," but for political reasons they don't do that. So they tend to fund the films they think they want to see on television.

MacDonald: Did you know when you started *Megacities*, where that film would take you?

Glawogger: I had no fucking clue. I was very naïve. I remember thinking, "Oh my god, what am I going to do with all this money they've given me," but actually that's a good situation to be in. It's like when you're a painter and finally somebody gives you a grant: you go out and celebrate with your buddies, then you buy some blank canvas, and you look at the blank canvas and think, "What am I gonna paint?" You're reduced to your zero, you're stripped of everything and you stand there naked—and you have to ask yourself, "If I go to an island and nobody gives me money, will I do art with a couple pieces of wood and some stones?" If the answer is yes, then you can move ahead with your movie.

MacDonald: For me the quintessential sequence in *Megacities* is the man sifting the colors for dye. In a health sense, the work he's doing must be horrible—I can't imagine breathing this stuff all day long—and yet at the same time there's a gorgeous element to that sequence. This mixture of horror and beauty is what gives your films their vitality. You're looking at struggle, but there's a glorious element to the struggle that comes through color, through composition, in many ways.

Glawogger: That's really the essence of what I do, but I didn't know it at the time I was shooting that imagery. Plato says beauty is the splendor of truth—I really *believe* that. People accuse me sometimes of *making* things beautiful, but that is utterly impossible: you cannot *make* anything beautiful. Things have beauty or they don't have beauty. If it's not out there, if it's not in the world, we can't film it, and Wolfgang, my cameraman, knows that. We do what we can to enhance the exposure and so forth, but otherwise we don't *make* anything: we just *film* the stuff. The beauty is *out there*, and the beauty is the splendor of the truth that comes across.

I'm interested in situations that are contradictory, like the situation you've described or in the slaughterhouse sequence in *Workingman's Death*, situations that produce what I call "the knot in the head." When you see a scene that's about killing animals, but that also feels beautiful, you say to yourself, "How can that be?" You don't know what to think. And there is no answer to this; there is only the knot in our heads. The borderline between beauty and horror is what my films come down to; I'm always looking for that.

For me the greatest artist is Hieronymus Bosch because in *The Garden of Earthly Delights* he painted all these things that are utterly horrible, but when

FIGURE 35 *Color man in the Darabi neighborhood of Mumbai, in Michael Glawogger's* Megacities *(1998), part 1 of his Globalization Trilogy.*
Source: Courtesy Michael Glawogger.

you look at the scheme of the whole painting, you think, oh my god, that's beautiful!

MacDonald: How did you find your way to the man working with the colors? (figure 35)

Glawogger: I was on the subway in Mumbai and got off because I wanted to see this famous area called Darabi. I walked around there for a day and at one point I came around a corner and saw a green man and thought, "Amazing!" I stood there for a while, watching the green man, and the next day I went back because I thought maybe I'd been dreaming; and the next day he was yellow. The third day he was red.

I think you can make this same kind of discovery in Queens or in Brooklyn; if you're open for it, you can find interesting things anywhere. In *Megacities* there's the scene with the Bioscope Man, a man who has a little machine, almost a little cinema, that he travels around with, showing films to kids. He's like a showman from the time of Méliès. I really liked this guy because he reminded me of my early training at film school. He'd go around to movie theaters that showed Bollywood films, and since the theaters were quite sloppy with the prints, pieces of the films and previews of upcoming films would end up on the floor. The guy would collect them and stitch them together with needle and thread, then run the result through his little projection machine.

When I learned film at film school, I always had film in my hands, and I liked that. In the old books you see images of the filmmaker holding the filmstrip up to the light to see the picture. I miss that hands-on quality of filmmaking. But I don't want to get too nostalgic because now there are computers, and editing is much easier and digital sound, a revelation.

So the Bioscope Man is somebody I met one day and found interesting, but I assumed there were lots of guys doing the same thing and so I didn't worry about finding him again. Mumbai is a city of a fifteen million and when I realized the guy was actually very unusual and decided to film him, he was nowhere to be seen. I even hired a detective. Then entirely by accident I met him again on the street.

MacDonald: Wow.

Glawogger: Yeah, wow. Maybe it was an accident, maybe I was meant to find him. I can get a little religious about this.

MacDonald: The access you have to many of the people you film is amazing. How do you get people to trust you enough to be there with the camera during intimate moments?

Glawogger: If I want something, I approach people and ask. If you do films like mine, you have to reach out, you have to connect with people. For example, remember Mike, the "air-pussy" hustler in *Megacities*? *He* approached *me* on 42nd Street. I said, "Hi, I'm Michael, what's your name?" And he said, "I'm Michael too." I said, "I know you're a scam; you want to sell me a prostitute that doesn't exist; you're not gonna do this with me, but maybe we can make a deal about something else; let's have a drink." Two months later I filmed the scene of him hustling the young gay guy.

To be in a position to do a scene like that involves a lot. It means going up to Harlem, it means buying the guy drugs, it means sharing his life with him to a certain extent. I went with Michael to his parole officer, even got arrested because of him—are you willing to do that or not? It's not easy, but to reveal something about the world means to be connected to people that you normally wouldn't connect to. Nowadays it might be easier, but back then spending weeks working in Harlem was pretty tough. And when the guy gets down, he'll call you at 3:00 o'clock in the morning, and you drive up to Harlem and buy H for him. If you're willing to do that, you get the scene.

But it's not a magical thing or an amazing thing; it's a *human* thing. It's like going to a bar and making friends with some stranger and then deciding if that friendship works for you or not. You cannot be friends with everybody. There are people you can relate to and people you can't. Mike was very intelligent and very interesting and I had a lot of fun, and a lot of horror, with him.

MacDonald: One of the things that's exciting about your work is that not only do you go to places that normally we wouldn't go to, but as a filmmaker, you ignore the documentary debates about whether the filmmaker should be detached or involved, how much the filmmaker can rework material, should an observational documentary include interviews, and so on. At the end of *Megacities* the scene of the gay guy and Mike and the sequence about the radio show are clearly enacted—though much of what we've seen up to that point has been strictly observational. I sense that you're interested in getting your view of the reality of certain kinds of lives onto film and whatever works for doing that is what you want to do.

Glawogger: Very fair. I think if you involve yourself as a filmmaker in theoretical debates, you're lost. Because that's another job. People can debate about my films in whatever way they want; it's none of my business. *My* business is to go out there and see reality and to think about how I can put it on the screen. I didn't become an artist to obey rules. If you read the documentary books and follow the rules, if you do the do's and avoid the don'ts, you're fucked.

As you say, I do whatever I need to do. If observation is the right thing, you do it, and you always *like* to do that because an action or an event is never the same once you have to re-enact it. If a director tells me, "Do that again," I'm now *thinking* about how I'm doing it—so it's not the same. But sometimes observation doesn't work: you see Mike on 42nd Street and think, "Oh my god, this is amazing, he's hustling all these people; I have to film this." But if I'm standing there *with a camera*, I can stand there until the end of my days, because nobody will stop to talk with Mike. So you have to think about different ways to get this reality across, and you may have to overstep the borders of what people think is a documentary.

In the end what you see is an aberration; every film, including every documentary, is an aberration of "Reality." There is no such thing as Reality; there is no objective reality out there that you can capture and put on the screen—that's bullshit. The reality that is "out there" is reality as you see it, and as you bring it to people—*that's* the reality.

MacDonald: Are you still dedicated to film, or have you totally moved into digital?

Glawogger: The distinction is not so important. If you're a painter, you go to a shop for paints and you can buy either oils or acrylics. You use what fits your vision. You can make a film with an iPhone.

I grew up and became a filmmaker liking the warm tones of film, but that's no big deal; it's just that I grew up then and it will take me a long time to get rid of that preference. What you do a long time, you like. But what's available now can be used and used well. I need to change and it will be a challenge for me. The *film* thing is over, but you can still learn an important thing from it: *reduction*.

The danger of the new formats is that because filming doesn't cost anything, you can film everything. Through the older process of filmmaking we learned to reduce what we shot, and that sharpened our vision. If you film everything around you with your iPhone, you end up with so much material that nobody has the time to watch it, and the time needed for

FIGURES 36A, 36B, 36C *Sulfur miners in Indonesia; on page 257, butchers in Nigeria; on page 259, ship breakers in Pakistan, in Michael Glawogger's* Workingman's Death, *part 2 of his Globalization Trilogy*

Source: Courtesy Michael Glawogger.

editing becomes expensive, not to mention the cost of transferring what you've collected to a medium that's going to be seen by other people— *unless* you make something that really works with this particular format. If you do something 5 minutes long and put it on YouTube, a million people might click on it.

Not everything has to be in a movie theater, not everything can work on the Internet. So you need to know what you can do with the "paints" you choose. I make my documentaries to be seen large and loud in theaters. Seen on a computer most of their power disappears.

MacDonald: There's a level of commitment in your work and in Wolfgang Thaler's cinematography that's seems remarkable to me. I get claustrophobic just looking at the miner sequence in *Workingman's Death* and I can't imagine how much you'd need to pay me to go into that mine. It seems clear that when you film somebody doing difficult, dangerous labor, you're committed to participating in the difficulty and danger as a filmmaker.

Glawogger: Yeah, but as we would say in German, "Lassen wir die Kirche im Dorf": "Let's keep the church in the village!"—let's not exaggerate things! We live in times when people wear helmets to bicycle around very safe cities; from that perspective, what Wolfgang and I do may look dangerous, but that perspective doesn't count. Life for most people in the world *is* more dangerous than what we do, but if I were in their circumstances, I would be living the way they do, and so would everybody else.

I didn't consider it to be a horrible thing to go into that mine. In fact, that sequence was easy to do because at the moment those miners realize that you also work with your bodies, you're connected. You go in there, *you* work, *they* work, and you connect. It was much more difficult to do *Whores' Glory* because I don't do sex work and don't have that connection with the girls. But the moment Wolfgang and I crawled into this mine, the miners were with us.

And I trusted those men. I think if you'd been there with me, I wouldn't have had to pay you to go into the mine; you would have done it because, like us, you would have been curious—and also because otherwise you'd have sat outside and been the cry-baby!

MacDonald: Wolfgang, is there anything you want to say about this?

Wolfgang Thaler: You know, I'm generally a very timid person, but the moment I look through a camera, all fear is gone. Somebody has to catch these images. At first, four of us went into the mine: Michael, then me, then my assistant, and the sound man—but in the end it was just Michael and me, and when they said, "Come share a day with us," I trusted them and it wasn't scary to be with them.

Glawogger: They're experienced miners.

MacDonald: But in the film, *they* say *they're* afraid all the time.

Thaler: I can feel when there is *real* danger and I get out of the situation immediately. For example, we were in Pakistan, close to the border of Afghanistan, and I felt there was something going on and that it was time to leave this place, so I told Michael, "Please let's go out now, because this situation is out of control." He didn't believe me, so I said, "Okay, but *I* go. Please take the camera." If the feeling comes from deep inside, I trust it.

MacDonald: At the beginning of the miners' section, you use some mid-1930s Soviet footage about Alexey Stakhanov. I hadn't known about him.

Glawogger: I put Stakhanov into the film because I was amazed that a system could make a worker into a pop star. Nowadays this is not possible. And it's also interesting that from the moment when Stakhanov was made into a worker-hero, he never worked again; he spent the rest of his life drinking with Stalin's son. And, of course, all the other miners hated him because they were forced to work as hard as he did.

I was also amazed by the sculptures of workers that I saw. When we were shooting, a city in the Ukraine still looked a lot like it did during the time of the Soviet Union—things are changing, but there are many holdovers. And some of those holdovers were still affecting contemporary reality. When I asked the Ukrainian workers to behave like those statues, they knew exactly what poses I meant and what I wanted to suggest. They understood the irony (figures 36a, 36b, 36c).

MacDonald: Each of the sections in *Workingman's Death* is very different from the others: you're on a path in the Indonesian sequence; you're on top of

FIGURE 36B
Source: Courtesy Michael Glawogger.

a ship in the ship-breaking sequence. When you and Wolfgang are working together, are you directing him? What's going on between you?

Glawogger: I give him some idea of what the end product should look like, basically a single page of notes. In the case of the sulfur harvesting in Indonesia, I said, "Here's the volcano where they take out the sulfur, here's the path they walk down, and here they weigh the sulfur; I want the film to be that story"—a simple idea, but logistically very difficult to shoot.

Normally the sulfur workers bring their baskets to the weighing station on the same day that they've collected the sulfur, but on a normal shooting day, we might ask them to let us film them all day as they collect sulfur, or as they talk with each other after the work is over—so that day they get no money for their sulfur. To create a sense of the normal working day for the film, we needed to develop almost feature-film behaviors: we had to ask the workers to wear the same clothes every day, to have the same sulfur in the baskets everyday—so we could pretend in the editing that what was shot during a week happened in one day.

Or in Nigeria I would draw for Wolfgang all the circles where important parts of the process of animal slaughter were taking place: the goats come in *here* and they go *here* and they are killed *here* and they are roasted *there* and they are washed *there*—he films one circle every day.

I don't do much while he's filming; I just watch him.

Thaler: Since he's watching me and what I'm doing, he knows more or less what is on the film. At the end of the day, he might ask, "Do you have the feeling we have enough of this?" We know each other very well, and I know what he is expecting from me and which kinds of images he likes.

MacDonald: How much time do you spend just observing before you actually shoot?

Glawogger: It depends on the particular social situation and on how much time you're given—this has to do with money; someone has to fund your life while you're spending time in a factory or in a mine in the Ukraine. I take as much time as I can get because time is key to how good the film will be, but there is no rule. In *Whores' Glory* I couldn't just hang out in a brothel every day and pretend I wasn't there; I was there because people allowed me to be there.

It also depends on how long your life is, because you can film any situation forever. It's also about how much of your life you're willing to sacrifice for a film. In *Whores' Glory*, the research was always enormously longer than the filming because to be actually in a brothel with a camera is very difficult and you have to know what you're doing so you can limit the shooting time. The whole film was shot in 30 days, but my research time was much longer.

MacDonald: Peter Hutton and Carolina Gonzalez went to Bangladesh to film ship-breaking at Chittagong [for what became the third part of Hutton's *At Sea* (2007)], and they were given a single day to shoot. When you went to Pakistan to do the ship-breaking sequence for *Workingman's Death*, did you go to the government to get permission?

Glawogger: No. Actually, I wanted to film in Bangladesh, but couldn't get permission. I fought for it for a year and a half with all the connections I had. I'm not the kind of guy who goes somewhere with a hidden camera; I take too much time to know what I want and cannot stay hidden for so long. Without permission I couldn't film at Chittagong, though I think the ship-breaking there is the most interesting. I shot in Pakistan because by luck a big entrepreneur there said, "I don't give a fuck what the government says, you can do it here." What goes on at Godani is not as impressive as what happens in Chittagong, but I was lucky to be able to film the wrecking of the Sea Giant, one of the biggest ships that's ever been taken apart, and to be able to work without a lot of political pressure.

Sometimes you don't know where to start. I had an absurd situation in Thailand doing *Whores' Glory*. There isn't a place on Earth with so much prostitution as Thailand. You can practically ask any waitress in any restaurant if she wants to sleep with you if you pay her. It's all over the country, but when I approached the authorities about filming, they said, "Prostitution doesn't exist here." How do you apply to a censor board to film something that "doesn't exist"? So you say, "I want to film bar girls," and they consider this for three months, then call you in and say, "What do you mean by 'bar girls'?" It took me *years* to get permission to film in Thailand because the beloved king of Thailand says there is no prostitution!

FIGURE 36C
Source: Courtesy Michael Glawogger.

When I was in Bangladesh for *Whores' Glory*, I first made an agreement with the mothers and the brothel owners to film the girls. That was enormously important because when I approached the government and they said, "They're never gonna let you film them," I could say, "Here's a contract, signed by the women." That made a difference—not immediately, but in the long run.

MacDonald: I assume that people ask you why you're drawn to film such difficult lives.

Glawogger: Yes, but I like to turn that question around. A journalist in Luxembourg asked, "Why do you always film Hell?" And I said, "I don't think I film Hell; these people give me more strength than you can imagine," and he said, "Well, then, what *is* Hell to you?" I said, "Look out of that window: if I had to work, every day, in an office in that building across the street, *that* would be hell." The people I film give me their souls, their lives, and I try and do the same, to connect with them so that my film of their lives is worthy of them. It's not that I'm reaching for something horrible, not at all.

I have a rule based on my experiences filming in many places. When I come to a country that I don't know, I think, "Everything here is so interesting that I could film it!"—but I stay in that country until the very moment when I think, "Everything here is so boring; I should go home." And *that's* the moment when I actually start filming, because when you feel that, then you can connect with the real lives of the people there. When I showed the Nigerian workers the slaughterhouse sequence, they looked at me and said,

"Well, that's all right, but why did you film such a normal thing?" Because that's their everyday life; it looked totally normal to them! When they said that, I knew that I'd succeeded. And that's what I want to show *you*, that even if the world you're seeing in my film might seem exotic, even horrible, it is in fact very normal.

MacDonald: Is it a regular part of your process to share the films, or parts of them, with those you film? If so, what's that experience like?

Glawogger: Not always, but when I promise to do so or if the occasion arises, I do. The experience is nothing very special. Under normal circumstances these screenings are private get-togethers where the main topic is not film criticism, but how happy we are to meet up again. It's like showing photographs to your family: everybody wants to see how he looks and how the other family members come across.

With *Whores' Glory* it was a little different. The Mexican women were interested in the whole film and not only in their own appearance. Actually, they were very grateful to be prostitutes *in Mexico* and not anywhere else. For them Mexico is the most humane place to be a working girl, the place where you can connect best with your clients. They got furious about the Thai situation where the women have to sit behind glass (figure 37). They said, "We need the *animo*"—the direct connection to their guys.

MacDonald: Do you pay the subjects of your films? You mentioned that you bought heroin for Mike and no doubt did other things for him as you were filming with him, but in general do the people you film receive anything from you other than the satisfaction of being in a film?

Glawogger: Oh, yes they do and I am proud of the fact that I am able to compensate them for their time and effort. They open up to me, share their lives and their souls, and the least I can do is to give them something in return. Some people have the twisted notion that the exchange of money alters the truth. Nothing is more wrong than that. Exchange of money or gifts is an act that determines the way people deal with each other in situations of work. And making a film is a working situation. So *not* to compensate your protagonists is nothing but bad behavior.

MacDonald: As you explore locations for a film, what specifically are you looking for?

Glawogger: I look for locations where I can *show* something. Much of *Whores' Glory* is filmed in a place where the johns are in the dark and the women are in the light, and there is a glass wall in between them. That space is perfect for showing the separation between men and women in that kind of brothel. And the moment I myself walked into "the fish tank" where the girls were, I saw that the lighting turns that glass wall into a mirror, which is very interesting and revealing.

When I find places that speak for themselves before anybody starts talking, I know this is film territory. I don't go out there to find something to prove my

FIGURE 37 *Prostitutes in "fish tank" in Thailand, in Michael Glawogger's* Whore's Glory *(2012), part 3 of his Globalization Trilogy.*
Source: Courtesy Michael Glawogger.

ideology, to confirm my theories. I want to find places where I can *show* the world. Otherwise, I'm lost. I wanted to do something about escort services and Internet dating in Europe or the United States, but I had no idea how to do it. What do I show? A woman sitting in an office, taking phone calls?—boring.

MacDonald: How broad was your research in terms of different places where prostitution exists. *Whore's Glory* is a triptych, but it could have been shot in many places.

Glawogger: My choices don't just depend on me. If you want to do a film about Roman Catholicism, you can't just walk into the Vatican and film; there is no documentary that really shows the Vatican because, as an individual filmmaker, you don't have the power to make such a film. You cannot walk into any country's government and begin shooting. There is no documentary about McDonald's, made freely by an independent documentary filmmaker. In the Sixties and Seventies it was possible to film the Rolling Stones the way Robert Frank did in *Cocksucker Blues* [1972], but you couldn't even do that today because there is a public relations power structure between canonical rock groups and filmmakers. Even an agitprop filmmaker like Michael Moore, who focuses on the limits on freedom, can only stand outside with a microphone and say, "I can't film that."

When we filmmakers want to portray the world, we only have so much power, so much persistence, so much money to actually film what we want to film. If you are a filmmaker like me who likes to really go into depth in the spaces where you film, you're often out of luck.

And people have changed a lot since the Seventies. Back then you could walk into a neighborhood and film people in a very open environment. Today if you do a film in America and you go to the Bronx and start filming, people will say, "What kind of show are you doing, man?" "Is this National Geographic? Some kind of reality show? How do you want me to behave?" There's a huge awareness now on the part of many people about what they think reality is supposed to look like. In other places of the world it's less this way, but still, for all these reasons, the world is only available to a documentary filmmaker to a certain degree; it's not a visual supermarket.

I encountered many places I would have *loved* to film for *Whore's Glory*, but political situations, mafia situations—and prostitution is always connected to one mafia or another—would not allow me to film there. I could have spent my life trying to film more examples of prostitution, but in the end, I decided on a triptych and filmed in three different countries where there are three different social status situations and three different religious situations. I think if you take seriously the fact that this is now a globalized world, it doesn't really matter so much *where* you film; what counts is what you film and how you film it.

MacDonald: How did you decide the order of the three sections in *Whores' Glory*? It's clear that while there are three distinct locations, certain elements become motifs through all three. For example, there's the motif of doors closing; throughout the first two parts of the film we don't get to see what's happening behind the doors, but in the final section we do go inside in one instance for what is actually a very sad (literally an anti-climactic) sequence that forces us to reflect on all that has gone before.

Glawogger: When I decided *Whores' Glory* would be a triptych, I decided to follow the order of a Catholic altar triptych if you read the images from left to right, the order Hieronymus Bosch used in *The Garden of Earthly Delights*. On the left is Paradise. In the middle part is the World, and on the right side is death and Hell. It was easy to follow this order because Buddhism has a much more casual approach to sexuality than Islam or Catholicism, and because sexuality in Catholicism is loaded with guilt and death.

MacDonald: Have there been complaints about *Whores' Glory* and the way you depict the women?

Glawogger: Some people accuse me of making a very *male* movie about prostitution, which is actually true—and I hope it *is*, because, after all, I *am* a man who did a film about prostitution. A woman would do a very different film.

It's not so easy for a woman to go into a brothel, because not only would she have the same problems I did in getting permission to film, but she could have a struggle with the girls, who can be very competitive and difficult.

MacDonald: How do you understand the implications of your title?

Glawogger: Actually it's a reference to the American writer William T. Vollman, who wrote a book called *Whores for Gloria* [1994]. I love this book and the approach he takes in it—my title is an homage. It's also a result of the goal I set for myself when I took on the endeavor of making this movie: I said to myself, "Clear your mind of everything you know or think you know about prostitution and brothels, and whatever comes up as you explore this world, *always respect the girls*"—the title is meant to reflect my respect for their work.

MacDonald: Obviously, many people would argue that prostitution is not glorious.

Glawogger: I think we *should* perceive some glory in it, because prostitution always is and always will be, despite our stigmatizing of it: we stigmatize the johns, we stigmatize the girls, but prostitution is an important form of labor in every society. Criminalizing it, as you do in America, is absolutely insane.

MacDonald: I understand the title in a different way from those you've described. One of the themes in *Whores' Glory* is the way in which a spiritual life seems interwoven with this sexual labor. All the women have prayers; they all do spiritual rituals; they all have things they will do and won't do, more or less on religious grounds—and so I see the "glory" in *Whores' Glory* as an evocation of the spiritual dimension of their lives.

Glawogger: That's true, but I wasn't thinking of it when I decided on the title.

MacDonald: How did you explain your project to the women you filmed?

Glawogger: I told them, "Whatever you want to say, say it. I don't do commentary and I won't make you a victim. I won't put out things about you that you wouldn't want known. This film is a stage *for you*, so please use it." The moment they realized that this is really what I wanted, they trusted me and were very open. I had hardly any problems.

MacDonald: Was music part of the original conception for *Whores' Glory?* It's far more central here than in any of your other documentaries.

Glawogger: No. You learn many things when you're filming. Often the things that you *don't* think of when you start filming become the everyday life you show. Two things about prostitution especially struck me. One of them is how much waiting there is—I think prostitution is one of the most boring jobs on Earth, because when you're not having sex, you're just waiting around hour after hour. What the girls do at those times is listen to music—and when I realized that, I knew music had to be a vital part of the film, had to be almost in dialogue with the imagery. They have *their* music; I would have *my* music because in a way I was waiting with them when I made the film.

The other thing that struck me is how hard it is sometimes to get a customer. In the opening sequence the girls are tracking the guys. When you work as a prostitute, it's often very hard to earn your daily bread. In Bangladesh the women actually grab men and pull them into their rooms, because there are 600 girls working, basically in competition with each other. I was in Bangladesh for a month and all the girls did every day is fight for the men.

MacDonald: I hesitate to ask this, but I also hesitate to *not* ask it. Was part of your research into prostitution having sex with prostitutes?

Glawogger: It is strange you would hesitate to ask this. Would you hesitate to ask if I also experienced hard manual labor while filming *Workingman's Death?* Actually nobody ever asked *that*, but many people *have* asked if I had sex with prostitutes. If I thought the answer was in any way relevant to the perception of my film, I would gladly answer your question.

MacDonald: In addition to documentaries, you also make fiction films and do commercial work; do you see this work as relating to your documentaries?

Glawogger: It's fun and a privilege to make fiction films. When I spend four years in brothels or in mines, I've *had* it! I want to have fun and be like the Farrelly Brothers, go a little crazy.

I'm not the kind of filmmaker who brings a documentary sensibility to fiction. For one thing, generally I do very light, sometimes comic fiction films. In some instances I use the method of documentary filmmaking because financially I cannot do otherwise. In *Slumming* [2005], for example, I have a street scene where a guy attacks people on the street. In Europe I could throw my actor into an actual busy street and say, "Attack people," and follow behind him with a steadycam and a small armada of people who could enable the people in the image to sign releases that they were okay with my using the shots they were in. Here, the moment you walk onto Broadway with the steadycam, you have to deal with a union. The first time I shot in New York City, a union guy approached me on the second day and said, "What you are doing! I'm gonna sue you if you don't stop." To do that scene in *Slumming* with professional extras who know what's coming their way, either here or in Vienna, would have required a big effort, and even with that effort I don't think the results would have looked right.

So sometimes I let my two filmmaking worlds collide, but not often. Making the documentaries can be useful for the fiction films. I couldn't decide how *Slumming* should end, and I only came up with a solution because I knew a very special place in Jakarta that I'd visited while doing *Workingman's Death*. It helps to know the world through documentary, because otherwise filmmaking is *only* about storytelling; it's *only* about the three-act script.

MacDonald: Your approach is almost the opposite of the American model where established filmmakers put their primary energy into fiction films, but sometimes make a documentary as a kind of lark.

Glawogger: That's true.

To make a good documentary, you've got to really want to do it, because it's a bitch of a job. It's very difficult to find money and it's not going to make you rich and famous. I wouldn't want to be 20 and trying to make my documentaries; I'd be scared shitless. But I don't want to sound discouraging; real artists do what they have to do and under whatever conditions they're in—but it's not easy.

MacDonald: Do you think it was easier when you began?

Glawogger: In a way easier, in a way harder. When I began, producers didn't trust my generation; they'd say, "If we decide to let you make a film, you'll have to take an experienced cameraman with you." They were patronizing. Now they say, "Well, try it." You get a $100,000; if the film succeeds, your career goes ahead; if it doesn't, you can try again using your credit cards, and if *that* doesn't work, you're fucked and left with no friends and no career. In Europe maybe they give you a couple extra chances. Then if you don't have success, you can go to a supermarket and be a cashier—which might be nice too: there are lots of ways to live.

MacDonald: Are there other documentary filmmakers you particularly admire? Are you familiar with Nikolaus Geyrhalter's films; they're clearly quite different from yours.

Glawogger: Earlier I mentioned Franju and Vertov, who are high on my list. I admire Robert Gardner, Werner Herzog, Viktor Kossakovsky, and some of Joris Ivens's work.

Of course I'm familiar with Geyrhalter's films. I think he's a great filmmaker, a talented visual artist and a truly naïve spirit. I mean that in a good way. He questions the world with his eyes.

MacDonald: Are you working on a new documentary?

Glawogger: Yes, I'm working on a project called "Untitled—The Film without a Name," which has developed out of my thinking about journalism and the six basic questions that need to be answered before a story can be considered watertight: Who was involved? What happened? Where did it take place? When did it take place? How did it happen? And why did it happen? Documentary filmmaking often takes the same approach. A new film project usually starts with questions: What is the story? Where does it take place? Who is in it? Why do you want to make it? And how are you going to structure it? Such questions can be helpful, providing the filmmaker with a framework, but they can also twist your sense of what is happening around you and reduce the actual events to a pre-formulated thesis.

On trips I have taken in order to do research or to shoot, I have repeatedly encountered situations which I perceived as special but was not able to actually film because at the time I was caught up in another subject that demanded my full concentration. I have always seen this as a problem. To a true storyteller the whole world is a potential story and he draws from the things he encounters and tells what he considers worth telling. This new project will be an attempt to work with these ideas.

Susana de Sousa Dias

Susana de Sousa Dias's experience of the fall of the Salazar regime in 1974 when she was 12 years old helped to create a fascination with the nature of the Portuguese experience during the decades before the Carnation Revolution freed the nation from forty-eight years of dictatorship. Once she found her way into the archive that houses the propaganda films produced by the Salazar regime—the PIDE/DGS (Policia Internacional e de Defesa do Estado/Direcção-Geral de Segurança; International and State Defence Police/General Security Directorate)—and saw the photographic evidence of the widespread imprisonment of men and women who resisted the regime, she made a commitment to use filmmaking to explore what most of her countrymen had become comfortable suppressing from the national dialog: the nature of the brutalities that had kept the dictatorship in place for so long.

Processo-Crime 141/53 ("Criminal Case 141/53," 2000) was her first attempt to deal with the history of the Salazar regime. The result is relatively conventional in its reliance on talking heads describing personal experiences, illustrated by archival footage that provides personal and social context—though the stories of the Portuguese nurses struggling for improved conditions and the right to marry within a society that repressed freedom of expression and severely restricted the lives of women are revealing and moving.

In *Still Life* (*Natureza Morta*, 2005) the question was how does a filmmaker transform imagery produced to promote the stability of a brutal dictatorship into an attack on that dictatorship? She found inspiration in the pioneering work of Yervant Gianikian and Angela Ricci Lucchi, especially their *From the Pole to the Equator* (*Dal Pollo all'Equatore*, 1986), where they allow us not merely to *see* documentary imagery recorded nearly a century earlier, but to *see through* it: that is (with the benefit of hindsight) to understand its troubling implications. *Still Life* is a panorama of the history of the Salazar regime using its own imagery, foregrounding de Sousa Dias's sense that the government's production of spectacles of its power and widespread support was accomplished in large measure through the suppression of the individuality of its citizens. A crucial motif in the film is the mugshots of individual political prisoners of the regime, taken for the most part as they began their incarceration.

Nearly all the images in De Sousa Dias's remarkable third feature, *48* (2008), are extended close-ups of the mugshots of political prisoners

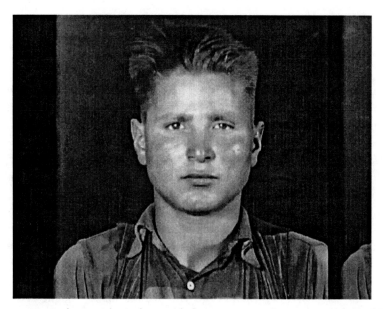

FIGURES 38A, 38B (page 269), 38C (page 271) *Same man at various moments during his incarcerations.*

Source: Courtesy Susana de Sousa Dias.

during which we hear the political prisoners' memories of the humiliations they endured. The visual challenge in *48* was how make a moving film from still photographs. Even more fully than in *Still Life*, de Sousa Dias's in-close framing of the mugshots transforms what were originally small, generic images, useful only for identifying enemies of the regime, into large-scale portraits that reveal the dignity, and often the beauty, of these women and men—half of the prisoners whose stories we hear in *48* are women. Further, de Sousa Dias brings the photographs to life by subtly altering the framing of each image as we listen to the speaker, and in some instances by having one image of a prisoner morph into a second, recorded at a later date (figures 38a, 38b, 38c).

Though we never see the ex-prisoners as they look now, we hear them within the various physical environments in which de Sousa Dias recorded them; their environment becomes ours and it is as if we and the ex-prisoners are sharing a space from which, together, we can contemplate their past. *48* overcomes one problem with *Still Life*: De Sousa Dias's use of the evocative music composed for the earlier film by her brother António de Sousa Dias sometimes tends to over-determine the experience of that film, to tell us how we are supposed to feel about imagery that without the music might be relatively opaque.

The patient pace of *48*—each photograph is on-screen for several minutes as the ex-prisoner recalls her/his experiences—allows us not merely to be appalled at what these women and men went through, but to understand the nuances of their experiences and, in many cases, to have a complex sense of the varied ways in which these individuals have come to terms with what happened to them.

I spoke with de Sousa Dias during her visit to the 58th Robert Flaherty Seminar in June 2012, and we refined this interview online. Thanks to Josexto Cerdán for bringing my attention to her work.

MacDonald: You didn't come to filmmaking as a young person. What were you doing before you became a filmmaker, and what led you to commit to exploring the horrors of oppression during the Salazar regime?

De Sousa Dias: Actually, my beginnings in filmmaking and the dictatorship are interconnected. I went to film school in the 1980s and got a three-year degree, but still couldn't think how to begin making films. I was somewhat stymied by the Portuguese cinema milieu back then. During the 1960s, my father, António de Macedo, was part of a cinema movement that went under the name of Cinema Novo. The Cinema Novo filmmakers opened up a new aesthetic path for Portuguese Cinema, which had been stagnating under the Salazar regime. My father was the first Portuguese filmmaker to make it into the official competition at Cannes.

A film critic once said António de Macedo was the "Maverick of the Portuguese Cinema." My father chose to pursue a very personal path. He experimented with a very wide range of genres, from experimental film and documentary to drama; there was even a detective movie. In the 1980s, he turned to science fiction and fantasy and got savaged by critics and fellow filmmakers. His reputation fell into oblivion. By the 1990s he had been attacked so much that he could no longer find financing and had to give up making films. He was writing books instead. His films are now being rediscovered by a younger generation.

So, when I entered film school, I arrived as the daughter of an important and controversial figure. It even made the newspaper. For many years, I was "the daughter of"; in fact, it was only after *Still Life* that I got the right to my own name. Actually, when I started making *Still Life*, my relationship with my father took on a new dimension. He became one of my favorite interlocutors and we discussed my work a great deal.

These days my father and I seem to be in opposite universes. He lives in a world of fiction, pursuing narrative and endeavoring to make the viewer imagine and long for what is coming next. My work is about subverting narrative; my objective is to ensure that viewers are connected to what they are watching at that moment on the screen and *not* thinking about what is coming next—and that through this process they are accessing their own imaginaries.

MacDonald: So how did you proceed after graduating from film school?

FIGURE 38B
Source: Courtesy Susana de Sousa Dias.

De Sousa Dias: I decided to take another university degree, in painting. Ironically, it was when I was studying Fine Art in my mid-twenties that I received my first invitation to make a documentary, from Portuguese public television. I ended up making three 25-minute documentaries in 16mm.

I had no awareness about what a documentary actually should be, so I watched TV and in the end came to the conclusion that a documentary involved people being interviewed, some images illustrating what they were saying, and so on. I tried to fit the conventional mold, and those were very conventional films.

Later, in the 1990s, I received another commission from public television, to make a film on the Portuguese cinema between 1930 and 1945, the Salazar dictatorship's high water mark. This necessitated my first contact with film archives and discovering cinema history through archival research became an exciting process. Doing this research I came into closer contact with my own country's history.

I became fascinated by the images produced during the regime, especially the documentary footage. The archives provided an immediate connection with those times. One of the ex-political prisoners in *48* very movingly describes the celebration on the 1st of May, 1974, soon after the Carnation Revolution. He refers to all the excitement and to the abundance of red flags. That same moment in 1974 was also the beginning of my interest in the dictatorship. I'd lived under the Salazar regime for 12 years, my age when the Carnation Revolution happened, and I remember all the excitement of that time. Witnessing a revolution is incredible for a young person: one day the country is one thing and the next day everything is different: how people behave, their gestures, their ways of talking and moving, the colors you see within the physical environment—it's all new.

During the couple of years following the Revolution, I went to southern Portugal to work with peasants in the fields and to teach people how to read and write. I stayed in a house without water or electricity, without a toilet. I was told first-hand stories about killings by the police, about repression. I gained some slight insight into what it meant to be a peasant during those times and what fascism was like in the flesh.

Entering the archives of the regime in the 1990s reactivated all those memories.

MacDonald: Were people in your family involved in the resistance?

De Sousa Dias: Actually, no. The brother of my mother's great grandfather, a general in the military, was the first person to try to lead a rebellion against the dictatorship; he ended his days in exile. But that's really a distant memory and only present in the family as a reference. However, some years ago, my mother was working on her thesis for a Master's degree in Women's Studies, about two nurses imprisoned because they had tried to get married (during the dictatorship, there was a law prohibiting public hospital nurses from being married). I found this case very interesting and decided to make a film about it. The result was *Criminal Case 141/53*. Like my earlier films, this one was very conventional; I ended up frustrated with the film's cinematic language and the ways in which, under the pressure of time, I had used archival footage.

I'd become disillusioned with the whole system of film production and decided that from then on I would assume full responsibility for my work, which meant setting up my own production company. Kintop was founded by me, my husband, and a close friend of ours. Our funding has mainly come from two sources: the Portuguese Film Institute and the state television channel. Actually, once we secured the Film Institute funding (a jury-based selection process), state television funding was mandatory.

Two things did happen during the making of *Criminal Case 141/53* that proved crucial for my future work. First, in the political police archive (PIDE/DGS), I found huge albums crammed with pictures of political prisoners. Page after page of mugshots. Just faces—nothing else. I was fascinated by these images. Second, I also went to the army archive; they have materials that document the Portuguese colonial wars. What I was seeing in these archives haunted me—and made me rethink the history of my country.

I began to ask questions: first, what is a documentary? Then, what is history? What is an archival image? What is the aesthetic potential and the historical potential of this kind of material? What problems need to be taken into consideration when dealing with these issues?

Soon, I was completely inside the archive, working on what became *Still Life*. Actually, I consider *Still Life* my first film. The earlier work was my learning process about what cinema was and what I could do with it.

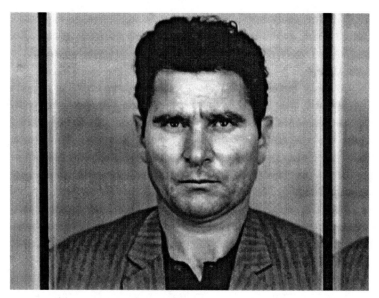

FIGURE 38C
Source: Courtesy Susana de Sousa Dias.

MacDonald: Were you the first person to work with this archival material?

De Sousa Dias: The first to work with it in this way, yes.

MacDonald: It's interesting that your first longer film was about nurses. In both *Still Life* and *48* there are many *women* political prisoners. While it makes perfect sense that both women and men would be involved in underground resistance, I don't remember seeing women in these roles in film.

De Sousa Dias: Well, this *is* a man's world—and men are often not particularly interested in women-related issues.

The role of women in the resistance was completely different from the role of the men; and, in fact, these roles echoed conventional societal roles. When there was a clandestine meeting, the man was usually the one who went to the meeting; the woman stayed at home. At the same time, however, women were very important in keeping resistance activities underground and while they continued to do the many kinds of work women have always done—housework, cooking—they also wrote for and worked on clandestine publications. And some women did become important as political activists.

When I began to show *48*, everybody, even in Portugal, was astonished to see so many women. I do not have an accurate ratio of the numbers of women arrested in comparison with men, but what is clear in the archives is that women played a very important role.

MacDonald: The Italians Yervant Gianikian and Angela Ricci Lucchi and the Hungarian Peter Forgács use an approach similar to yours, especially in *Still Life*. Like you, these filmmakers explore archival materials, re-seeing them in ways quite different from how the original filmmakers would have understood them. Has their work has been of interest to you?

De Sousa Dias: One of my main references for *Still Life* was the Gianikian and Ricci Lucchi films. And I know the work of Peter Forgács, as well. But Gianikian and Ricci Lucchi's *From the Pole to the Equator* [1986] was particularly important for me.

MacDonald: Salazar has a stroke in 1968, loses control over the government, and dies in 1970. This is exactly when many of us who were politically active during the late 1960s and early 1970s were involved in the resistance to the Vietnam War; we had little attention for anything else. This is also when a lot was happening in France. I assume that part of your reason for making your films is an interest in bringing broader international recognition to Portuguese history.

De Sousa Dias: Yes, definitely, but not only *international* recognition— greater awareness *even in Portugal*. Many younger people in Portugal know little about the history of the regime. Usually, the Franco dictatorship and Hitler and Mussolini entirely overshadow Salazar.

The perception of people abroad, to the extent they think about Portugal at all, is that the Salazar regime was a very mild dictatorship. Not many people died, so it could not have been all that bad. It is true that not many people were killed by the dictatorship *in Portugal*. However, if we include the Portuguese colonies in Africa, it becomes a different story: lots of Africans were killed, even though almost nobody speaks about them.

And in any case, we cannot measure dictatorships merely on their numbers of dead. The most powerful facet to the Portuguese dictatorship was its control over the minds of the people. This invisible violence ensured the dictatorship's survival for so many years. Even today, we continue to experience the lingering after effects of this mind control.

In my view, it is absolutely paramount to work on the details of what was rendered invisible during the dictatorship, and especially on the stories of political prisoners. What these people went through in prison has been completely erased from the public consciousness. Partly as a result, we now see attempts by historians to rehabilitate the regime by focusing only on what they say were its *good* aspects.

MacDonald: There's something very American about the "rehabilitation" process you're describing. It seems almost illegal for an American politician to admit that America has ever done anything wrong.

In both *Still Life* and *48* you don't allow viewers to simply look at an image the way it was originally meant to be seen; you use a variety of techniques to force us to look long and carefully. Rather than simply re-presenting the imagery, you create an investigation into it: in *Still Life* you slow the governmental propaganda imagery down; and in *48*, you bring the mugshots of the political prisoners to life by using subtle visual dynamics and sound.

De Sousa Dias: When I started to make *Still Life*, I was faced with a challenge. How do you show the reverse side of the dictatorship using archive footage produced *by* the dictatorship? I started to look very carefully at the images on the flatbed, and slowing the imagery down was a natural process during my viewing. Sometimes the important features were in the details, sometimes in the background. As I looked and looked, I began to understand that within the particulars of certain images, within the message the regime sought to convey, I could see symptoms of a kind of disease. The search for these symptoms became the main *démarche* of the film.

I looked at hundreds of hours of archival footage, and when I finally began editing what became *Still Life*, I had reduced what I was working with to 20 hours. My first version of the film used only 45 minutes of archival footage, and one year later, after going through many other versions, the final 72-minute version of the film incorporates only 12 minutes of the original footage.

I came to understand that it is not necessary to juxtapose several images to communicate; it may be enough to look at one single image more carefully. One of the methods I deployed was montage *within* the shot. This approach involves de-composing the space—the visible space—revealing and juxtaposing various parts of the image in new ways. Basically, I applied three formal principals to expose the most revealing aspects of the images: reframing, slow motion, and fades in/fades out.

MacDonald: How did you decide on the music for *Still Life*?

De Sousa Dias: Early on, when I was still trying to conceive a structure for the film, I was alone in a Paris hotel, listening to some of my brother's music—he's a composer—and suddenly, when I heard his 8-minute electro-acoustic piece called *Sill Life with Bruitage, Special Effects and Clap*, a very spatial music, I decided *Still Life* would be without words and would be based on the notion of "exhibition."

I began arranging the imagery as if creating several abstract rooms, each of which would have its own distinct theme and sound. The film's two structural principles, the principles determining its narrative construction, were to not use words and to not follow a chronology. In other words, I resorted to an-achronism as a fundamental principle of the film. There is a macro-structure with anchor points that place certain key episodes within a historical context, but the images within each sequence actually belong to different times. These principles stem from a concept of history and an idea of image that does not correspond to traditional historical filmmaking. For this, I drew on Aby Warburg, Walter Benjamin, and George Didi-Huberman.

My brother began composing pieces of music that I could use while I was editing; each piece would function as an individual "sound shot." I was able to work with the sound in the same way I was working with the image: I could superimpose sounds, cut them into pieces, combine them in different ways, extend them by changing the speed, and insert punctuation whenever I wanted. Then, after editing the sound alongside the imagery, I would hand everything over to my brother so he could rearrange the sounds and recompose them into a single piece of music. He would return everything to me once more: I'd re-cut his new piece, rearranging it in new ways as I edited the imagery. This process continued for over a year. Finally, when the film was finished, I handed everything over to my brother and he rearranged the various pieces of music into the final version you hear.

MacDonald: A couple of very specific questions: how do you understand the opening shot in *Still Life*, of the monkey?

De Sousa Dias: One of the film's principles is the non-reduction of any image to a single interpretation. The monkey image is very rich; it can sustain a range of readings. However, I can give you my personal motivation for including this monkey. I had two uncles who were in the colonial wars and one of them brought back a little monkey just like the one you see in the film. And when you talk to people from Portugal who were children in those days, you find many memories of little monkeys. The monkey is the moment in the film when my personal memory touches the collective memory.

MacDonald: I speak no Portuguese, so I can't understand the words we are hearing repeated on the soundtrack near the end.

De Sousa Dias: There are two kinds of words: one repeated sentence: "Aqui Posto de Comando do Movimento das Forças Armadas": "This is the Command Post of the Armed Forces Movement," the statement that preceded all press releases issued by the MFA (the armed forces movement that had staged the coup) in the days following the Revolution. The other is taken from "Grândola Vila Morena," the song adopted as a signal confirming the coup was underway. Both were sourced from the original recordings.

MacDonald: The second-to-last shot, of the soldier in the truck, includes the first smile in the film. Are you paying homage to the role of the soldiers in instigating the Carnation Revolution?

De Sousa Dias: I've never seen this as an homage to the soldiers. When I entered the army archive, I understood that I was living a contradiction. Being clearly in opposition to the colonial war, I started watching the images with certain preconceptions. However, in an archive, all our certainties eventually collapse. I was confronted by images of solders, perhaps soldiers eventually involved in the massacres that took place in Guinea-Bissau, Angola, and Mozambique. And I had two uncles, who I was very close to, who fought in the colonial wars. I had always lived as if these were entirely separate realities. In my family, nobody talked about the war—except my mother, who wanted to emigrate to Paris so that my brother could avoid the draft.

Watching the images unfold in the archive, I was thinking that these men could be my brother, my uncles, or even a son of mine. A disturbing thought that obliged me to think much more deeply about the history of my country. I came to realize that there is a reason for the colonial wars having been a kind of taboo in Portugal for the first three decades after the Revolution: the people who had been in Africa fighting in the colonies and conducting the massacres were the very same people who carried out the revolution.

MacDonald: Your final shot, of a *woman* distributing carnations seems to be a final confirmation that while the Salazar dictatorship was on every level *male*, the resistance was a male *and* female process.

De Sousa Dias: I can explain why *I* included that final shot—though mine is only one possible understanding. The woman puts carnations, the revolution's symbol, through a small gap in the door. In the original sequence we can see somebody on the other side receiving them. However, I just show one of the shots of the sequence and I delay the speed on the hand so that we see the carnations disappear as a hand reaches out to try and grasp them. Can *we* still reach them, or is what the Revolution meant forever gone?

Thus far, my life has been lived almost entirely during the Portuguese democracy but, while making *Still Life* and virtually living inside the archive, I was disturbed to find that I had kind of reversed time. The revolutionary moment of the 25th of April, 1974, came to seem very far away, to be *the past*; and the dictatorship was becoming my present. Further, by studying the imagery so closely, I had begun seeing what features of dictatorship exist in contemporary Portugal—and elsewhere because everywhere there are cultures with dictators or at least with forms of repression. Furthermore, some of what are commonly referred to as the revolutionary "conquests of April" (the welfare state, etcetera) are now slowly being undermined.

However, your reading is also fair; it is true that I am always trying to put across a feminine point of view. Unfortunately, sexism is still endemic to Portuguese institutions.

MacDonald: When was the installation version of *Still Life* conceived?

De Sousa Dias: I have to go back a bit. The film was produced in association with a TV channel (Arte France), but when I submitted it to the senior programmers for Portuguese public television, they said *Still Life* was not appropriate for television, so at the time it was not broadcast in Portugal. Later, when the film was released in movie theatres, some Portuguese film critics attacked it ferociously; they didn't think it was cinema.

Finally, one day, I received a telephone call from the artistic director of a well-known contemporary art collection. He had loved *Still Life* and wanted to acquire it but was of the opinion that the film would not be a comfortable fit in the art world. He suggested that I produce an installation version. At that time (2008), I was already hoping to expand the images and the sounds beyond the confines of a movie theatre. By the time the piece was installed, it included three screens and seven speakers.

MacDonald: A three-screen installation creates opportunities for a kind of meta-editing, even a reinterpretation of the film.

De Sousa Dias: You've put your finger on two of the main issues with this project. From my perspective, it's not possible to simply transpose a film to a different exhibition situation. To transform *Still Life*, a single projection in stereo sound, into three screens with 5.1 surround sound required a complete reworking of both time and space, enabling the montage of sounds and images to acquire new meanings. During this process, I dropped shots from a number of sequences and made use of images incorporated into earlier versions of the film but that had not made it into the final version.

I decided that I would think of the installation as a triangle. The central panel would be the vortex and the locus of power: whenever Salazar appears, it is within this screen. However, this panel does not always assume the role of main screen. At times, it is left in total darkness. A key factor in constructing the installation is the interrelationship between screens with and without images, as well as between sound and silence. Each panel can acquire full autonomy or, on the contrary, be contaminated by others, not only by means of montage but also literally: there are images that extend from one screen onto the others. It was also fascinating to craft a spatial soundtrack and create an entire geography of sounds. The changing of listening points (sometimes we are immersed in the sound space, on other occasions we have only a single sound that comes from behind the screens) allowed me to work in ways I had never before imagined.

MacDonald: How long did it take you to make *48*?

De Sousa Dias: I started thinking about the film in 2003, received the funding to make it in 2006 and began shooting in 2007, though most of the shooting was done in 2008. In 2009 I went to Mozambique to film the African ex-prisoners. I spent ten months editing.

MacDonald: How did you decide who to interview and who to track down? And how many of the people that you were able to track down were willing to talk?

De Sousa Dias: I first had the idea of doing *48* when preparing for the shooting of *Still Life*. I'd thought it would be easy to film inside the archive, as I had already been filming there for *Criminal Case 141/53*. The problem was that in the meantime the archive's management had changed and the new director had decided to apply the "right of image" to the political prisoner mugshots: that is, I had to get permission from the subjects to use their images. Very ironic, given the fact that the subjects had no control over the *making* of the images! So, I had to find the prisoners. When I did find them, I took the opportunity to talk with them about their lives and their experiences in prison.

During my meeting with one of the women, Conceição Matos, she began talking about her own mugshot: "Did you notice my hair is tousled? And I grew a bit of a hairy lip." The photograph had been taken only 17 days after she was imprisoned, she explained. And at one point, she told me, the clothes she was wearing in the photograph—a light pullover and a dark shirt—had been used during torture to clean the floor covered in her own excrement. This was the precise moment when I got the idea for *48* (figure 39).

During my first period of doing research in the political police archive, I found the picture of a child imprisoned along with his parents, actually the only mugshot of a child photographed along with his imprisoned mother. In 2001, I had already begun to research the story of this family and, in 2002, managed to talk with the child for the first time, a man in his late forties by then. Later, I expanded my research to other children of prisoners and got in touch with many former political prisoners. I started shooting interviews with them. So, when I actually began making *48*, I had already interviewed many people.

Still Life was a very important film for building the confidence of the former prisoners in me and my project, because in that film they saw that for the first time someone was recognizing them *as political prisoners*. One man interviewed in *48* told me that this was the first time in thirty years that he had talked to anyone about his experiences: "I will talk with you for *48*," he said, "because I loved *Still Life*."

I think people were also willing to talk because, three decades after the fall of the dictatorship, they felt less constrained. They also realized that I genuinely wanted to listen to them, that I was not some journalist trawling for a few quotes for a brief article.

In the end, all of the ex-prisoners I was able to make contact with were willing to talk with me for the film.

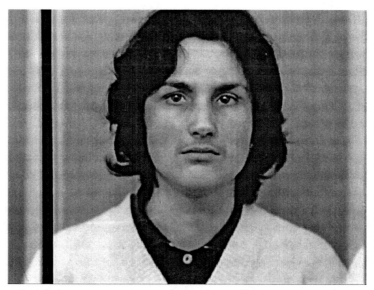

FIGURE 39 *Mugshot of Conceição Matos, from Susana de Sousa Dias's 48 (2009).*
Source: Courtesy Susana de Sousa Dias.

MacDonald: What was it that the political prisoners did or allegedly did in their resistance to the regime? Was theirs a violent resistance?

De Sousa Dias: Actually, no. Throughout many years, the Communist Party was practically the only force of organized resistance and its main goal was nonviolent activities to provoke the overthrow of the system from within. The party did organize an armed group at the end of the 1960s and detonated some bombs, and there were some radical left-wing organizations in the 1970s that defended armed struggle. But the resistance was mainly pacific, in defense of worker rights in the factories and the fields, against repression and for better working conditions, which later, during the 1960s, also included an end to the colonial wars.

MacDonald: In *48* the interviewees speak for a very limited amount of time—for as long as their photographs are on-screen. How long were your interview sessions with them?

De Sousa Dias: Hours and hours. I spent several days with some of them and so the problem was deciding just what and how much to include.

Having decided on what I would like to include, I then had to decide where to place each excerpt in relation to the others and within the structure of the film as a whole. One of the decisions I made was that each prisoner would talk only once. The problem was that sometimes part of what a prisoner said only made sense during the first half of the film and another part only during the second half.

Cutting the testimonies was very painful. I usually say *48* is a film of renunciation, not a film of choice. I was in constant mourning for the sequences I had to set aside.

MacDonald: From the conversations in *48*, it seems as if much of the torture the people endured was less a means of getting specific information, than torture for torture's sake (rather like Abu Ghraib). Were there people you talked with who felt that they had provided information that had been to the detriment of colleagues in the field? It's one thing to be humiliated by yourself; it's another to know that you've contributed to further humiliations endured by others.

De Sousa Dias: That's a very complex problem and one I decided not to deal with in *48*. In Portugal, people ask, "Why did you choose to include only people who didn't talk in prison?" But in *48* there *are* people who talked, who gave information to the police. There are people who talked, but who did not exactly betray anyone. There are people who betrayed others only because of the pain and they subsequently tried to warn those named. Then again, there were people who betrayed in the full sense of the word, real traitors.

Some of the prisoners of African origin told me, "We told the police everything!" One African told me that the only way to deal with the police was to bow your head, but another male prisoner said, "The only way of dealing with the political police was to raise your head and look them in the eye"—but of course *he* could say this because he was white and Portuguese, and not black and African.

One reason I went to the ex-colonies was because in Africa, the torture and killings were much more savage. The Portuguese normally portray themselves as a people of gentle habits and customs, even during the dictatorship, but the reality is far starker. We have only just begun to remove the veil from Portugal's colonial past.

MacDonald: So you're not really trying to portray a panorama of heroes— just people who endured a terrible experience.

De Sousa Dias: They're just people with strengths and fragilities. From time to time, I do wonder if some of them are not made of the same material as heroes—they had ideals and the strength to try and attain them and a generosity regarding the collective that has become pretty rare in these neo-liberal times. I have great respect for them because they are willing to tell their stories, sometimes undergoing great pain so that we all can understand something of our past.

MacDonald: At some point you must have decided that in *48* you would present the individual photographs in basically the same way, within a very formal composition, but that you would subtly modulate the compositions so that each photograph would come alive and be different from the others.

De Sousa Dias: All the images were shot directly from the albums in the PIDE/DGS Archive. At first, I thought filming the prisoner photographs would be easy, so easy that I could film the project in 35mm. I thought I could shoot at almost a one-to-one ratio. But when I looked at the first shot, I understood that this was completely impossible—when faced with motionless images, we give up looking. The viewer absorbs the information quickly and the image vanishes from consciousness; we are no longer *seeing* it. I realized that I needed some form of motion, something to keep the eye and mind alert. I asked the cameraman to make some camera movements within the photos. And I decided to make the film in video because I realized I had to shoot much more footage than I had originally thought and would have to work on the speed digitally.

During the editing phase, I slowed the movements down. The objective was to nurture the ambiguity between movement and stillness. It proved a long process. Dropping the speed from 10% to 7%, and then upping it back to 10% again, sometimes shifting from 3% to 2%. Adding one more frame to the shot, cutting two, adding three; changing the length of a fade in or a fade out. Actually, if I were to play the images in *48* at the right speed, the film, which is 92 minutes long, would not last longer than 7 minutes. Sometimes it felt as though I was working on a musical composition.

MacDonald: Though we don't see imagery of the prisoners in the present as they are speaking to you in *48*, you allow us to feel what seems to be the sound environment in which your interviewees are speaking. Were those sound environments created later, after you recorded the interviews, or were they part of your original recordings?

De Sousa Dias: Everything was recorded at the time of the interviews. At the beginning, I thought it would make sense to interview people in a proper sound studio. But, luckily, I did not have the money for that so I decided to ask where they would prefer to be interviewed and most chose their own homes.

I started off asking them to avoid any movements that might cause noise, like the creaking of chairs, fidgeting with hands, and so forth, because I thought these inadvertent noises would become a distraction. However, after some months of interviews, I began understanding how important these sounds were for the film.

One of the principles of *48* was not to show the faces of the former prisoners in the present. I wanted the viewer to be confronted only with the *prisoner* (the person portrayed in the mugshot) not with the *former* prisoner (the person in the present). I wanted to avoid this fracture between present and past and instead work with the co-presence of heterogeneous times.

However, I did face one problem: would it be *fair* not to show the faces of the people as they are today? At some point in the process, I started to grasp that I would be able to embody the interviewees through the sounds connected with their bodies (hand movements, rustling of clothes, whispers, the way of breathing) along with the surrounding ambient sounds. In the editing room, I introduced many cuts into what the people said, so it was useful to have continual background sound. One of the most important aspects was working with silence. There are silences that people make simply because they pause while speaking. On other occasions, I created a silence so that there is time to observe the image and to consider what has been said.

MacDonald: The prisoners often speak about the particular photographs we are looking at; this connects what we hear to what we see in a dramatic way.

De Sousa Dias: Yes. At a certain point during each interview, I showed the person a copy of the mugshot. Some had already seen their pictures while others were seeing them for the first time. The reactions were quite diverse, even contradictory.

The connections between what we see and what we hear in the film, as well as the general structure, were quite complex to achieve. From my perspective, it is important to discover the "vertical structure" of whatever film I am working on: that is, the fundamental concepts that inform my thinking. In *Still Life* this vertical structure was in place before I began the editing process and the difficulty came with working on the "horizontal structure": that is, deciding on the order of what would be seen. In *48*, I started editing without any vertical structure, that is, without effective guiding concepts. In time, having decided on the formal approach, general theme, and basic issues, I decided to focus on the specific theme of torture—but it was necessary to go deeper.

In *Still life* the tutelary figure was the dictator; in *48*, the authoritarian *system* is at stake. At the deepest level, the structure of *48* is a function of guiding concepts: identity, mask, power, similarity, recognition, etcetera. This "vertical" structure of concepts anchors the horizontal sequence of image and sound.

MacDonald: The long passage of dark imagery near the end of *48* is a surprise—you confront the viewer with the materiality of the filmstrip; it has the impact of a minimalist abstract painting (figure 40).

De Sousa Dias: When I went to Africa to interview the people who had been political prisoners there, I had no idea there were no surviving images of those prisoners. I was shocked—because *48* is a film that relies on *faces*. I did not know what to do. In the end I decided to incorporate this absence into the film. While, on the one hand, this black image with the tiny flecks of light does, as you've suggested, refer to the filmstrip, it also represents night—the darkness before the appearance of the tree. When the landscape appears, it is not a landscape we look into—there is no Alberti "window" here—but rather a landscape inscribed into a surface.

MacDonald: On one level you're making finished films, but also, a series of ongoing chapters of an epic story, each of which refers to the others, builds on the others. If a viewer knows *Still Life*, then sees *48*, the viewing of *48* has a variety of evocations that might not be evident to a viewer who has not seen

FIGURE 40 *Blasted tree in African landscape at conclusion of Susana de Sousa Dias's* 48 *(2009).*

Source: Courtesy Susana de Sousa Dias.

the earlier film. This works both in terms of content and form. For example, we meet some of the same people in *48* that we see in *Still Life*; and on a more formal level, in *Still Life* we see you develop the device of having a photograph of a prisoner as a younger person transform into a photograph of that same person, older—a device you do much more with in *48*.

As you've worked on *Obscure Light*, have you been assuming that the new film should make sense on its own, but should also—for those who know *Still Life* and *48*—function as a companion piece to those earlier films?

De Sousa Dias: Ultimately, this is inevitable. Each film should make sense in its own right; however, when we do see it in connection with the other films, we will definitely gain an enlarged view about the general political system and the private lives of the people appearing in each film.

MacDonald: Your ongoing project has much in common with Claude Lanzmann's *Shoah* [1985], which is also about memory. Like the survivors of the extermination camps in *Shoah*, the ex-political-prisoners are getting older and if they don't tell their stories to someone, their experiences, and a certain history, die with them.

De Sousa Dias: Yes. But also important is precisely *how* they tell their stories. I interviewed one woman who had talked a lot about her time in prison after the revolution; she'd told her story to journalists, writers, to everyone. By the time I began talking with her, she was not telling me her memories, she was narrating a constructed discourse on the past, almost as if reciting, rather than remembering it. It was very difficult to get into the deeper memories hidden within the constructed and ordered speech, the actual background to her story which her story enabled her to suppress or at least control. During the interview process, one challenge is to try to find the key to unlocking the memory, which differs from one person to another. It is a simultaneously painful and fascinating process.

MacDonald: As you look forward, do you assume your exploration of the Salazar regime and its after effects is going to be your life's work as a filmmaker?

De Sousa Dias: Yes, I think so. Making *Still Life* gave me lots of ideas, ideas for at least ten different films. I had to choose one of them to actually make, which was *48*—but doing *48* gave me *another* ten ideas! Then, while making modifications in the editing of *Obscure Light*, which is still not finished, I started working on *another* film, about three sisters, collecting interviews with them and doing archival research about their criminal cases. One of the sisters is the first woman who appears in *48*.

It's become a huge process, exponential. A never-ending archive that I am continually exploring and rethinking. Of course, what gets done depends a lot on what I find the financing for.

Amie Siegel (on *DDR/DDR*)

Amie Siegel's *DDR/DDR* (2008) is a rumination on the history and demise of the Deutsche Demokratische Republik (DDR, what Americans call East Germany): in particular, two aspects of the DDR's cinematic history: the relentless surveillance of its own population by the Stasi [the nickname for the Ministerium für Staatssicherheit, the East German Ministry for State Security] and the widespread popularity within the DDR of the movie Western and of going Native-American (in the DDR, the Indians, the "redskins," were the "good guys," and, at least in theory, ideologically simpatico with the "reds" of the DDR).

Within her investigation, Siegel considers the commonalities between forms of cinema that usually seem quite distinct. At one point, a tracking shot follows a truck from which various pieces of equipment are being thrown to the side of the road, a metaphor explained in one of Siegel's voice-overs: "The history of the Stasi is simultaneously a history of media technology in the second half of the twentieth century. Their surveillance efforts begin with silent, small-gauge film, 8mm, then 16mm throughout the Sixties. In the Seventies black-and-white video is introduced, accompanied by silence. In the Eighties, 16mm film is abandoned entirely for sound color video, and this lasts until 1989. The Stasi are entirely analog, encapsulating the period before digital, the wall falling before the advent of digital video, mini-DV, HDV, and HD." This metaphor and historical review reveals suggestive connections between East German surveillance and the modern history of American documentary and avant-garde film and video.

DDR/DDR has particular relevance now, in the wake of the Wikileaks revelations about the NSA. Near the conclusion of the film, Frank Döbert, standing in front of the Zeiss headquarters in Jena (Zeiss, the legendary German, then East German, now German manufacturer of fine optical equipment) suggests that since 9/11, America has become like the DDR: "I think personal freedoms are being twisted and the system seems very familiar to us. And we're really sorry, here in the GDR, that America has gone in this direction. And as a tourist it's very stressful and complicated, the whole state control—biometrics, surveillance: you can't believe it." Siegel asks Döbert if traveling to the United States gave him "a feeling like in the DDR," and he responds, "Yes, very strong."

My interview with Siegel was conducted, revised, and refined online in 2011. During what follows I have distinguished between "East Germans," that is, citizens of the DDR, and "east Germans," people who originally lived in the DDR, but are now Germans living in reunified Germany.

MacDonald: What instigated *DDR/DDR*? Did you begin with the idea of a feature film?

Siegel: In 2003 I was invited to Berlin by the DAAD [Deutscher Akademischer Austauch Dienst] Berliner-Kunstlerprogramm, a residency that brings foreign artists to Berlin. I was aware of works produced by the many artists, filmmakers, and writers who had had prior DAAD residencies, ranging from Marcel Broodthaers and Walter Abish to Yvonne Rainer and Ernie Gehr. So I came to Berlin first through the veneer of its representation in art and cinema and only in 2003 began to know it directly. For me Berlin was, from the beginning, an uncannily layered visual space.

I began to research the surveillance and observation videos in the Stasi archive. But since much of my work in cinema is pre-occupied with ethical boundary crossings, especially those that define dominant non-fiction film practices, I became engaged with a paradoxical question: how does one make a film—an activity involving cameras and microphones—about a culture defined in part by the surveillance of its citizens with cameras and microphones? I'm often interested in how human activity instigated in the guise of betterment veers off into unethical and/or harmful practices—this comes up in *Empathy* [2003], my film about psychoanalysis, and in *DDR/DDR*.

From the beginning I knew *DDR/DDR* would likely be a feature-length work and, perhaps even more than *Empathy*, a ciné-constellation of elements that I felt were connected: private and public spaces, psychoanalysis, modernist architecture, recording devices, victims and perpetrators, east German "Indian hobbyists," authority and control, and so on. In this sense *DDR/DDR* is not a typical feature film where the production follows a prearranged scenario, but was realized as a kind of cine-collage; I was insistent during both the production and the editing, on the shared, unfolding, associative montage of its images and ideas.

I don't write formal scripts. When I make a long film, I generate a scene layout/choreography in no particular order, shoot those scenes and various accompanying improvised ideas, moments and interviews, then *find* the film in the editing room. I filmed *DDR/DDR* over the course of a year, and kept filming while I was editing the early material; it took a little under two years to make.

MacDonald: Am I correct that little in the film is candid, even the "accidents"? For example, early on there's the "awkward" moment when your first interviewee attempts to hold the mike after you ask her how things were after the Wall came down, and you refuse to let her hold the mike. It's a tiny gesture that I read as a subtle metaphor for what you and she are talking about: the

East Germans' brief grab at freedom after the *Wende*, only to be met with new forms of limitation.

Siegel: Actually, quite a bit in the film *is* candid, if candid means offhand, improvised and unscripted. The scene you mention is one for which I wrote very loose dialogue, an amalgam of the things that people I talked with tended to say about the period after the *Wende*.

The woman in blue is Christiane Ziehl, an east German actress. She and I worked on the interview dialogue in front of the camera, trying out different things, but agreed we might throw each other unscripted events. That scene was done in two shots—far and medium—and for each I had two-to-three takes of almost the entire bit. I chose to use the one with her grab for the microphone, something she only did once, as I loved its implications, which are as you've described—though I saw it not so much as enacting a grab for freedom as expressing the anxiety about the control one didn't have in the GDR *and* the control one doesn't have as an interview subject—an interview subject is at the mercy of the filmmaker. The microphone and recorder allude to recording devices as a means to power, a method of control (figure 41).

That scene also underscores the recording equipment itself, which is quite outmoded—my ever-present sound man with his 1970s silver headphones and reel-to-reel Nagra. Later in the film, for the sequence where I as the filmmaker and author am onscreen visibly performing the voice-over into a microphone on a stand, and talking about analog versus digital, the reel-to-reel Nagra used by my sound man was exchanged for a fancy LED-lit digital recorder. That scene underscores the transition from analog to digital, a period that begins only after the fall of the Berlin Wall. The Stasi were entirely analog.

FIGURE 41 *Amie Siegel interviewing German actress Christiane Ziehl, in* DDR/DDR *(2008).*

Source: Courtesy Amie Siegel.

But the presence of the microphone, *and* the more general issue of the interchangeability of Stasi equipment and other film production recording equipment, as well as the unstable ethics of the whole enterprise of recording "non-fiction" and of image-making in general, returns again and again throughout the film.

MacDonald: What exactly do you mean by "*unstable* ethics"?

Siegel: Unstable ethics are inherent in non-fiction filmmaking. So many documentary films purport to represent singular, objective truths, rather than an entire messy world of subjective gray zones. Often, little attention is paid to the coerced or scripted performance of documentary film subjects, or to the use of third-world subjects for the benefit of a privileged first-world western gaze, or to the claim that fly-on-the-wall cinema-verite filmmaking removes the maker from the mix, when in fact cinema-verite is really an exaggerated subjectivity on display (the best of the verite bunch recognize and even play to this), or to the complex web of projection and identification the viewer experiences: that is, how watching a film's horrific events and human conditions "there" can unconsciously reify one's sense of privilege, of being safely, comfortably "here."

It's not that I don't love cinema; I am passionately attached to so much about cinema. But for me this attachment does not exclude a critical eye on its formulaic governing and even unconscious practices. For me, the fact that the Stasi used the same film cameras and reel-to-reel sound recorders as other filmmakers of their time, from feature filmmakers to amateur home movie-makers, posed questions about recording, documenting, privacy and public space, permission and access. And it raised the question, what *is* the boundary between filming as an art and film as an act of surveillance and control?

I included in the film many of the "accidents" and candid moments that other filmmakers/artists would be likely to leave out. For example, one can often see the microphone intruding into the frame or reflected in the glass of a picture on the wall. Or when the woman psychoanalyst switches from talking about her patients' experiences to talking about her own experiences, she moves from her analyst's chair to the analysand's couch—something that I asked her to do, but left it to her to claim the particular moment.

Scripted or unscripted, candid or staged—often the film uses an unfair mixture of the two, which is of course part of what interests me.

MacDonald: "Unfair"?

Siegel: "Unfair" in that I don't play by the rules of traditional documentary film, or even fiction film. "Unfair" because these differences between moments that are staged or scripted and moments that are not (that are "candid," to use your word) are not disclosed, and therefore one must parse and really consider the status of what is "real" and what is "fiction" and why this distinction is of consequence. It's not unfair at all by *my* standards of spectatorship, but certainly within the context of dominant film practice, my film agitates for a more open form.

DDR/DDR is a feature-length film, but at 135 minutes it's longer than the marketable, pre-packed lengths of 90 or 120 minutes, a gesture meant to subvert expectation.

MacDonald: You intercut between interviews with two sets of doubles: the woman and the man psychoanalysts, the two men who worked for the Stasi. Did you record interviews you didn't use?

Siegel: I don't think very much about shooting ratios and such, the amount of film or video shot versus the amount that ends up in a film. The things that sometimes keep me up at night are the many tangents that could have been included, but were eliminated during the shooting or editing. Though *DDR/DDR* is a broad constellation of intertwined ideas, many things that felt relevant, including things that got said in interviews, didn't become part of the finished film; they haunt me.

I love your construction of the interviews as sets of doubles. I see that too. I wonder if doppelgangers, binaries and doubles don't unconsciously suggest roads not taken, choices we could have made. Certainly this arises towards the end of *DDR/DDR* where the Stasi psychologist confesses that what he really wanted to do was be a filmmaker, or where another former Stasi operative admits that there were things they did—*he* did—that shouldn't have been done.

But of course the largest double at play here is that of East and West. What would my life have been, had I been East German? Or West German? I suspect that this sense of a parallel world—and a fantasized, projected alternate self—played a large role in the psychic life of both East and West Germans. They were "other" to each other.

MacDonald: What was the nature of your access to Stasi documents?

Siegel: It took a long time to get access to the films and videotapes made by the Stasi—their training films, observation and surveillance films, propaganda films, and so on. I just persisted and was supported by particular east Germans (which is the way to get things done in the former east; ask a west German to advocate for you and you're nowhere). And they liked that I was employing some young east German assistants on the project. I called and checked in so often that finally they had to take me seriously.

One of the most extreme, and interesting, characteristics of the Stasi material was that very, very little of it could be explained or contextualized. It was like a dictionary of illustrations without corresponding definitions, so one had to parse and interpret quite subjectively. This is not discussed enough in relation to the Archive. In fact it concerns me the way many journalists and writers have rather blindly relied on Stasi files and documents to reflect a so-called factual history, with little acknowledgement of the conditions under which these documents were produced, and often faked or coerced.

The Stasi struck me as a highly neurotic and often psychotic organization, caught in endless self-regard, a kind of infantile extended mirror phase of looking for evidence of its own power through the frightened actions of its citizens. A power that paradoxically remained invisible because the operatives and informants had to remain "unknown" to one another. It took a long period of watching the films and tapes to begin to understand their objectives, which, it seemed to me, were often more about the narcissism of, and later desperation for, power and control than any real interest in the subjects they were surveying or interrogating.

I looked for things that demonstrated the subjectivity of the Stasi operative as an individual person behind the camera—voices, hands, a brief glimpse of a camera turned on at home, the aesthetic pretensions of an operative concentrating his camera on the abstraction of light refracting through a glass lamp post. These men were *filmmakers*, and my own film sought out moments that acknowledged this as a way to draw what might be uncomfortable parallels between filmmakers of all kinds, myself included, and the ethics of all our activities.

MacDonald: In the film, the title is presented as "DDR" combined with the mirror version of those letters, which of course makes sense—*DDR/DDR* argues that East Germany and West Germany (and the Capitalist West in general) were mirror images of each other. But in normal word-processing the mirroring is replaced by a repetition. Was this part of your thinking when you came up with the title? There's a suggestion near the end of the film that post-9/11 America is a kind of repeat of the DDR, at least in terms of the current level of surveillance.

Siegel: The film's title is *DDR/DDR*, not *DDR*. Representing the double mirror image typographically was a challenge that became apparent when the first printed materials on the film came out. The film's title was always supposed to be a visual mirror, or something along the lines of a Rorschach ink blot: the present (remains) of the DDR looking back at its past self, and reading into the DDR what is now imagined about it.

Your suggestion that what was once opposite has become the same thing all over again is interesting, but not something I had in mind. I've come to rather like the doubling of DDR typographically, since much of my work (*Berlin Remake* [2005], *Deathstar* [2006], *Black Moon and Black Moon/Mirrored Malle* [2010]) engages doubles and multiples—but I continue to think of the mirrored version of the title as correct.

MacDonald: What's the song the rock group plays midway through the film?

Siegel: The band is a Polish group called Los Trabantos, which is a funny "Spanish-ization" of the well-known East German car, the Trabant, driven widely within former East European countries, including Poland. Los Trabantos sing in Polish. They wrote the song they perform, which is called

"Rabatky"; it's about the past. I wanted to allude to another former communist country, another *Wende*, at some point in *DDR/DDR*.

However, I was also fond of the song, so I invited the group to perform in the film, making the sound-track "live." It interests me to take music that would traditionally be placed on top of the film as accompaniment and integrate it as a performance within the film. It could be argued that this performance is an intermission of sorts—but one you wouldn't want to miss. I think of it as connective tissue from one part of the film to the next: watching it, one is "delivered" into both a new architectural space and a new set of concerns.

The same song is played later in the film in the outdoor bar scene where Kurt Nauman stops for a beer along the Spree at dusk, the silver Berlin TV tower visible in the background, next to the bar's hanging disco ball. Kurt Nauman was the star of the last East German film studio film, *The Architects* [1990], discussed and seen in clips earlier in *DDR/DDR*. He is seen walking along the line of the former Berlin Wall throughout the film, and he turns up in the daybed with me in one of the film's final shots. He is playing himself *and* enacting my fantasized projection of who he is in present-day, post-communist circumstances.

MacDonald: What is that location where the band performs?

Siegel: It's the former East German radio station complex and recording hall in what was East Berlin, a proto-example of East German modernism. Part of the complex is a ruin—as you can see in the first half of the scene; the other part (where the band plays) has been renovated. It has no direct Stasi connection other than once being a state-run facility and therefore an organ of DDR propaganda. My interest was in the complex as simultaneous ruin and restoration, as well as a place for creating and recording—and therefore surveilling—sound, a recurrent thread in the film.

MacDonald: Why do you wear white coats in the film?

Siegel: There are two white coats—one is my rain jacket, in the opening scene with Christiane Ziehl. Then later in the film I have on my white puffy winter coat, particularly as I do the backward-walking voice-recording scene.

The white coats were intuitive; they just seemed right at the time, but later I realized that I must have been thinking of a doctor's white coat or a scientist's lab coat—a uniform of "diagnosis." I'm stepping into the frame of a culture and a past that are not mine; I am a foreign body, performing the role of a doctor, an analyst, a scientist—representing but also interpreting. On some level I was also thinking of the many East German films I've seen where scientists, doctors, or technicians enter a factory in their lab coats and consort meaningfully, if a bit dryly or dictatorially, with laborers who wear quite different uniforms.

With regard to the white puffy coat, I do recall thinking about science fiction, a huge East German film genre I didn't get into in *DDR/DDR*—since

I wanted to stay grounded somewhere in the real, even during the perform-ance rituals of the Indian hobbyists.

I think my white coat and status as "other" become nicely contradicted when I'm among the Indian hobbyists and you see me, and my crew, dressed as "one of them" (there's a rule that everyone must wear Native American dress in order to be present at these gatherings). In ethnographic terms we've "gone native," though the "native" in this instance is already a performed simulation of going native. A more typical western ethnographic film would be looking at a native culture's rituals, performances, tribal structures, and kinship. *DDR/DDR* works against the grain of those practices by looking at a "race" (Germans) that was historically a colonizer, not an untouched na-tive population that was colonized. Beginning in the 1970s, the East Germans enjoyed a hobby that involves performing or impersonating a native cul-ture—a form of native drag if you will (within which their own East German culture, as well as their white Protestant background, shows through). This is still a popular hobby (figure 42).

The hobbyists perform an identification that foregrounds correspon-dences between the so-called communal, anti-government, anti-materialist ways of Native Americans (as the East Germans have articulated them) and the collective, anti-capitalist, progressive Leftist values of their own com-munist upbringing. They romanticize a loss of Native American culture, and see Native Americans as victims of western capitalist aggression. Their views have considerable truth, but this identification process also allows these

FIGURE 42 *Native American enthusiast in German encampment, in Amie Siegel's* DDR/DDR *(2008).*

Source: Courtesy Amie Siegel.

Germans—whose relatives fought in and lived through World Wars I and II just like other Germans—to identify as victims, rather than perpetrators.

The fact that I, an American woman of Jewish background and recognizable as such, had to dress in their image of a Native American, with braids and belt and beads, compressed both the victim they seek to identify with—the Native American—and the victim they avoid acknowledging—the Jew—into one being.

Of course, any ethnographic filmmaker would have absolutely refused to "go native," as this would give the lie to his supposed "objective" distance. My dressing up also questions my own complicity in the very activity my camera is supposedly recording/critiquing.

And of course the final irony is that in a sense the East Germans actually *did* lose their land; and their own culture, as many of them see it, *has* been colonized by the west in the process of German "re-unification."

Alexander Olch (on *The Windmill Movie*)

Like Nina Davenport, Alexander Olch is a "third generation" Cambridge filmmaker who studied with Robb Moss and Ross McElwee, though his interests as a fledgling filmmaker did not jibe with those of his teachers: while the Harvard filmmaking courses were geared toward cinema-verite documentary of one kind or another, Olch's interest was in fictional narrative. Nevertheless, Olch adapted, survived the program, and became a filmmaker. At Harvard Olch achieved an early student-film success with his *No Vladimir* (2000), produced during his junior year by McElwee and Chantal Akerman; and he forged a friendship and what looked to become a working collaboration with Richard P. Rogers, another of his Harvard teachers and an accomplished filmmaker, who, unlike Moss, McElwee, and Akerman, was happy to nurture Olch's interest in storytelling. Olch planned to work with Rogers on a film about Orson Welles as a young man in Spain, but when Rogers was diagnosed with cancer in the summer of 2001, Olch abandoned the project.

Not long after Rogers's death, his widow, the photographer Susan Meiselas, asked Olch to assist her in dealing with Rogers' personal archive, which included not only papers and artifacts relating to his early experimental films: *Quarry* (1970), *Elephants* (1973), and *226-1690* (1984); his work on a series of political films about the Nicaraguan revolution (see the Guzzetti interview in this volume, pp. 126–132), and his work for public television, but also considerable footage presumably shot for an autobiographical film about Rogers's life in the Hamptons. Rogers was never able to complete the film he labeled "Wind Mill" (a private club at Georgica Pond to which Rogers's family belonged includes an old wooden windmill)—apparently because he was embarrassed about the idea of a privileged white man making his personal life, including his troubles and frustrations, the focus of a film. As Olch worked through Rogers's archive, he became increasingly interested in the possibility of an unusual "collaboration" between a filmmaking student and his deceased mentor, a collaboration that would, on one hand, do something like justice to the personal film Rogers never completed, and on the other, would allow Olch to meld the personal documentary approach with imaginative fiction.

The result was *The Windmill Movie* (2008), an engaging "personal documentary" of Rogers, partly shot by Rogers, but *directed by Olch*, who not only shot additional "Rogers footage," but channels Rogers in a voice-over during which he (as Rogers) speaks excerpts from what purports to be Rogers's filmmaker's diary. *The Windmill Movie* imbricates documentary and fiction so thoroughly that when the film is over, viewers feel that they've experienced a Rogers film, even though within *The Windmill Movie* Olch is entirely open about his fabrication of this faux personal documentary.

In recent years, Olch has become well-known known as a fashion designer. At Alexander Olch New York (olch.com), he designs ties, handkerchiefs, scarves, and other accessories, which are sold at Bergdorf Goodman, Barneys, and other high-end men's stores. It remains to be seen whether he will be able to meld his success in fashion with a filmmaking career.

This interview was recorded on November 14, 2010, when Olch visited Hamilton College to present *The Windmill Movie*. It was expanded and revised online.

Olch: In the years when I was at Harvard, 1996–99, relatively few film students had the intention of becoming professional filmmakers. Most were learning about film as an elective while majoring in other things. I was somewhat unusual, having always known I wanted to be a director.

Historically, the Department of Visual and Environment Studies saw filmmaking as an outgrowth of still photography, as opposed to drama. So there was not the kind of education you would find in a traditional film school: no writing classes, no lighting classes, no editing classes. Sophomore year, it was, "Here's a camera, make a film." Junior year, "Here's a camera, make a longer film." Thesis year, basically the same thing. We were taught documentary photography quite extensively, but anything connected to artifice—drama, writing, working with actors—was not in the curriculum. In searching for subject matter, we were encouraged to find situations already taking place in real life that could make for good films, which pretty much means documentary. I had always thought about film as an outgrowth of theater and literature, so I rebelled as best I could, taking independent study across campus with Robert Brustein at his American Repertory Theater and learning editing technique with visiting filmmaker Grahame Weinbren.

When attempting to do something narrative, you had to develop a flexible attitude: there weren't a lot of lights and dollies, none of the typical tools of fiction filmmaking, but I still wanted to tell a story using what we had available—working hand-held, trying to create a style based on documentary techniques that could be used with fiction. A narrative fiction filmmaker like Andrew Bujalski [*Funny Ha Ha* (2002), *Mutual Appreciation* (2005), *Computer Chess*, 2013], who was a year ahead of me in the department, was powerfully affected by this dynamic.

At the same time, the teachers were remarkable. I had amazing experiences with Robb Moss, Ross McElwee, and Chantal Akerman, and then finally with

Dick Rogers. What was especially important for me was that these grown-ups seemed to think I knew what I was doing enough to try it for real when I left college. I remember Ross saying at some point during my senior year, "Well, I would imagine you can do this professionally." Chantal and Dick said the same thing. That kind of support will fuel a young filmmaker for years.

So whatever limitations I felt in the curricular approach were balanced by the hands-on encouragement of the faculty. It's important for a filmmaker coming out of school to have the energy and confidence to say that *this* is what I'm going to do with my life. For that, I'll be forever grateful.

The Harvard environment also made me bump up against a set of concerns which continue to fascinate me: particularly the differences and relationships between documentary and fiction. My thesis film, *Artemin Goldberg: Custom Tailor of Brassieres* [2000], was a fake documentary about the world's most famous custom tailor of brassieres: kind of an old-fashioned New York comedy, fully scripted, starring a large cast of actors, staged and filmed hand-held, as if it were a documentary made by a film student.

MacDonald: When you left Harvard, did you have a next film in mind?

Olch: I was going to make a film about the summer that Orson Welles spent in the south of Spain when he was 17 years old—the working title was "Orson's Summer." My idea was based on a footnote in the Peter Bogdanovich book, *This Is Orson Welles*, which indicates that Welles's ashes were scattered in a town three hours outside of Seville. I thought, "Of all places, why would Welles want his ashes spread *there*?"

Very much in the spirit of Ross McElwee, I was going to go to that town with my camera, and let whatever happened, happen. With the help of a small Harvard grant, I'd done my research at the Welles archive at Indiana University and had come up with what I thought was a pretty interesting story. As a young man, Welles had a romance with bullfighting, even got involved with bullfighting himself, and later in life, he was close with some of the most famous matadors.

What was special about his seventeenth summer is that it was the last moment when he was just a regular guy. That fall, he went up to Dublin and talked his way into the Gate Theatre and became the *actor* Orson Welles. My feeling was that this summer in Spain must have stood out in his mind all his life as a kind of last innocent moment.

MacDonald: Rosebud.

Olch: Exactly. So I thought I had a great little movie going, even before I'd shot a frame. And so did Dick Rogers. Dick and I applied for and won one of the larger Harvard grants, so there was now actual money to start shooting. And I had some momentum because *No Vladimir* [2000], the junior year short I had made with Ross and Chantal as my producers, had gotten some attention; it was playing in festivals and had been sold to Bravo and IFC.

I moved out of my apartment in Cambridge, came down to New York, and that's when I first heard that Dick was ill. I also found out that a Spanish documentary was being shot about Orson Welles's time with the bullfighters. Nowadays, as a somewhat more seasoned person, I understand that neither of these developments should have stopped me from making *Orson's Summer,* but at the time, fresh out of school, I was frightened to begin a project that already seemed taken, and I felt insecure about doing such a big film without Dick there as a guide. So I stayed in New York, putting off the trip to Spain month after month.

Dick got more and more sick and passed away the July before September 11, 2001, and I was a bit lost. At the time, none of the projects I was working on felt right. One day I get a phone call from Susan Meiselas, Dick's widow, asking me if I have time to come by and help her clean up their loft, which was filled with Dick's film equipment. Susan said his Avid editing computer seemed to be broken; she didn't know how to make it boot up. So I stopped by and figured out how to plug everything in; it turned out that each of Dick's hard drives was named after someone from Watergate: there was an Erlichman drive, a Haldeman drive, and so on.

I managed to plug in all the Watergate culprits, and up came these images of the Hamptons, beautiful 16mm film images of girls on the beach, ocean waves, people playing tennis. I asked Susan, "What *is* all this?" and her answer was, "I don't really know. What are you doing for the rest of the day?" So I stuck around, cut together a couple of things, showed her, and we were both intrigued. Susan said, "What are you doing for the rest of the week?" And one week led to a month, led to three months.

I had wanted to make a film with Dick, and I still wanted to collaborate with him somehow. At the very least I thought I could just cut his footage together and make something for his friends. I figured this would take a couple of months—like many documentary filmmakers, at the beginning I totally underestimated what the project would require. Then, as I began to work regularly with Dick's material, another thing started to happen: I found that I was demanding of the project that it work *as a film,* not just as a memorial to Dick. This forced me to assess the footage and make editing decisions in a different way, and started me down a road that was significantly more interesting than any script that I could think of at the time and any other project that I could potentially get hired for.

I realized that if this was going to be a movie about Dick, then it was best to be unconventional. If you've seen his *226-1690,* the answering machine film, and any of his other short experimental films, you would likely agree that he was interested in pushing narrative and formal boundaries.

MacDonald: Yes, early on he was as much an avant-garde filmmaker as a documentarian.

Olch: So Susan used Dick's life insurance policy to start financing a production, and I started working full-time on what became *The Windmill Movie*. At the beginning, neither of us had any idea where the project was going, which was an amazing way to collaborate. Susan is an artist and knows that there's not a lot to be gained by coming up with contrived explanations of what you *think* you're going to do; you just *do* it and look at it and see if it works.

Working through three-hundred hours of footage was a challenge. There was no narrative focus in what Dick left behind. There were hints of intelligent and interesting ideas that Dick was exploring, but not anything you could call a coherent plan. What it first appeared to be was a story about Georgica, a town in the Hamptons—about the place and the people in what, over the course of Dick's life, had become the wealthiest community in the US. But by the time I was a year into looking at the footage, it was clear that the reason he couldn't figure out how to finish that movie is that it was not really a film about that community; it was a film about himself (figure 43).

Once I knew the focus was Dick, I also knew the film would need to get personal, and that's where issues arose in terms of working with Susan, and working with Nonie, Dick's lover and friend. I was dealing with limited information about Dick's life, and it was hard to get the real stories out of his friends. I began showing rough cuts to Susan and Nonie as way to develop their trust. I'd show them a cut of the film up to say 1985, and then stop and ask, "Well, what happened next?" And each time they would open up a little more. It was a weird process of using the filmmaking to do more filmmaking.

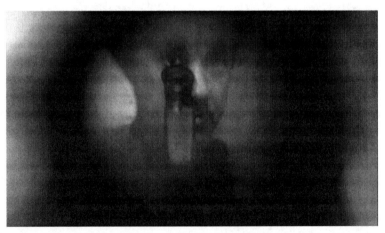

FIGURE 43 *Filmmaker Richard P. Rogers filming himself in the mirror, in Alexander Olch's* The Windmill Movie *(2008).*

Source: Courtesy Alexander Olch.

It took some time for Susan and Nonie, and everybody else, to trust me with the real stories. But once I had convinced them that I was going to portray Dick not necessarily in an easy-to-swallow way, but at least in an honest way, we were all able to work together.

MacDonald: How accurate is the finished film?

Olch: The dates were verified by all parties concerned; there was fact-checking. But Dick kept no diaries during the years covered in the film. I immersed myself in the footage and tried to imagine, based on the footage, what his thoughts might have been. If the result feels genuine, then I've done a good job. I had no interest in creating a kind of fact versus fiction dynamic as to what exactly happened or didn't happen, whether or not Dick said that or said this—that's not the point (and that idea is better suited to a film like *The Thin Blue Line* [1988], where the veracity of the details of each event is in question). The point was to present the remains of this man's attempt to tell a story about himself *and* the attempt of the student who cared for him to somehow tell his story. Hopefully, the tension between those two elements is evocative and interesting.

MacDonald: Was there resistance at some point from Susan about certain material, and were there people you might have wanted to include in the film who didn't want to be included?

Olch: Everything I wanted in *Windmill* is there. There are a number of people who are *not* in the final cut who wished they were. Dick interviewed many members of the Georgica community, especially when he was structuring the film as a story about that town. Of those interviews only the one with Mrs. Hayes remains.

MacDonald: How much of what we see did you shoot?

Olch: Early on in the film you see Dick say that it would be interesting to make a film that deals with the difference between documentary and fiction filmmaking, and that was what excited me. There are some tricks I'd prefer to keep between me and Dick. Suffice it to say that 15 to 20% of the footage in the film was shot after Dick's death.

MacDonald: There are a number of moments when neither you nor Dick is shooting. Were you always able to find out who shot the material you used?

Olch: Yes. Cory Shaff was shooting in the hospital. David Grubin shot all the footage of Dick in the blue polo shirt. Scott Kennedy, who was also Dick's student, shot the footage at the wedding party where Dick gives the toast. The party material where Dick is wearing the poncho was shot in New York by Rick Rosenthal. And Alfred Guzzetti shot the footage of the wedding ceremony in the courthouse.

MacDonald: Did you always assume you would use your own voice as the voice-over?

Olch: I didn't consider using voice-over for probably three years. I thought the actors were going to be the center of the movie. In time, I came across the

FIGURE 44 *Actor Wallace Shawn, playing Richard P. Rogers, in Alexander Olch's* The Windmill Movie *(2008).*

Source: Courtesy Alexander Olch.

little one-minute clip where Dick is talking to the camera about his issues with making a film about his own life, and I thought, well, if he were still here, he would probably do the whole movie with his own voice-over; why don't I give voice-over a try.

I tried writing in Dick's voice, and at first it didn't work; I wasn't confident that I knew him well enough to pull this off. But then someone told me a story about how Dick had taken Susan to Bergdorf Goodman or Barney's to buy her an outfit because he didn't like the way she dressed, and for some reason that story resonated with me and I thought, "Okay, I think I'm *getting* who Dick is now," and from then on I could let my imagination go to work.

As to using my own voice for the voice-over, from the beginning I was adamant that I would *not* be in the film. All of my writing was imagined for Wally Shawn, who would speak in the first person as his deceased friend (figure 44).

MacDonald: Shawn has a remarkably distinctive voice.

Olch: I thought using Wally was a great idea. But being a busy writer and actor, Wally has limited time. There was no way I was going to be able to have him first record what I had written, and then when it didn't work, have him come back to re-record it, and come back again and again. So, as I was writing the voice-over, I was using my own voice to test out what I had written so I could get to versions which were good enough for Wally to try. I started showing those test cuts to my producers, David Grubin and Susan, and from the very first time they watched the material with my voice, they said, "*You're the voice.*"

I told them they didn't know what they were talking about. I recorded the voice-over with Wally, but, when you heard him doing it, somehow it felt less intimate than what I had done. So in the end I had to admit my producers were right.

Writing voice-over is difficult. Coming up with what sounds natural is unbelievably time-consuming. That's a lesson I learned from Ross when I was making short films at Harvard—it becomes vastly more daunting at feature length.

MacDonald: When students see McElwee's films, often they assume that he just talks, but obviously the writing takes him a long time, and then once he's got it written, he practices a monolog or a voice-over until he's got a recording that he's comfortable with. Is that what you did?

Olch: Yes. I had a microphone in the edit room and I created a set-up where I could perform voice-over directly into the editing computer and cut it instantly, and I would just keep doing takes until I found something that I liked. I guess the proper way to do voice-over would be in a recording studio, though that often removes some of the spontaneity. There are certain lines in *Windmill* that are first takes. Maybe from a sound engineer's point of view, they're not quite the way they should be, but I thought it was important to convey a little bit of the student in me. Mine isn't the perfect voice-over voice or delivery, there's something fallible and searching—the voice of the young student trying to make sense of this footage.

MacDonald: We see a number of Dick's Harvard colleagues at the wedding and in other scenes: Guzzetti at the party and Robert Gardner at the wedding.

Olch: I tried to get all the great Cambridge characters involved in some way.

MacDonald: But not McElwee and Moss—at least they're not visible in the film.

Olch: I guess that's true on screen, but they were definitely involved. I sent them many rough cuts. Aside from the producers, Ross and Robb were the two people I consulted the most.

In fact, Ross solved a key issue for me. Once I had the voice-over written, and it was clear that it worked, the question was how to transition into it from the section I had of Dick talking to the camera. I tried to do separate scenes of myself in the editing room or where you'd see me writing. I tried every cocka-mamie idea you can think of, and none of it was working, so I sent my cut to Ross, saying, "Ross, I'm lost here," and with the aplomb and style so characteristic of him, Ross emailed back in about a week, suggesting a fix, and it was genius and it worked: the implicit transition from Dick's voice to mine seems so effortless that some people don't even notice it.

That's great from my point of view because *then* when you're thinking about the film afterwards, you're confronting the question that I want you to confront, which is what *is* the difference between documentary and fiction?

Windmill is *Dick's* autobiography, that *I* wrote; it's mostly *Dick's* footage, but it's *my* film, etcetera. There are logical conundrums there that really interest me. I've not seen another film that tries to explore these questions in this way, and that's exciting to me.

MacDonald: The transitional passage you mentioned is

> At this point we're running out of narration. The scenes with Richard's voice are working, but I have nothing like that for the story of his life with Susan. But remembering his director's diary, "How does not being me help me tell a story about me," I start thinking, maybe there's a way to build on that. So, using the boxes we could find, what his friends have told me, what he told me, the things Susan will reveal to me, I begin to write a kind of script in Dick's voice, a way to take this footage and tell the story for him.

You've created several levels of "present" (something typical of Ross's best work): there's the present of Dick's statement; the present of Susan's exploration of the closet in the synced visuals; the evolving "present" of your realizing that you might be able to build on Dick's comments and beginning to write a script; the implicit present of your editing the film; and the experiential present of your narrating this story to us sitting in the theater.

Olch: Absolutely. I'm very interested in the way movies can shift both between present and past but also more figuratively between verb tenses, as it were. That was one of the exciting things about working with both old and new footage and thinking about ways to frame the footage within this story.

Another exciting thing was the idea of sampling and re-mixing existing work, which had become so popular in music. A few artists whose work I'd seen were exploring this idea in cinema, but pretty much using stock images, material that was not particularly personal for them. What was interesting with the *Windmill* project was that I had a trove of frighteningly personal material that I was in effect sampling and re-mixing to create something new.

MacDonald: Do you know Alan Berliner's work? In some ways *The Windmill Movie* seems close to his *Nobody's Business* [1996] and *Intimate Stranger* [1991].

Olch: I'm a huge Alan Berliner fan, and have tremendous respect for his work. I was very fortunate to be shown his films in class at Harvard. He's an amazing editor and he creates wonderful image-sound moments that I absolutely was thinking about while working on *Windmill*.

MacDonald: It seems to me that there were two different traditions developing, at least for a time, largely in ignorance of each other: the history of avant-garde personal film—Mekas, Brakhage, Schneemann, and, later on, Berliner and Su Friedrich—and the history of personal documentary: Ed Pincus and Miriam Weinstein, McElwee, Moss in *The Tourist* [1991] and *The Same River Twice* [2003]. You're the beneficiary of knowing both these traditions and being able to work with both.

Olch: I've never distilled that thought as succinctly as you've just done, but I think that's exactly right. Stylistically I owe a debt to Berliner, and the engineering of the writing and the voice-over is what I learned from Ross.

MacDonald: Is the sense we get of Dick Rogers from your film an accurate reflection of your experience of him as a person?

Olch: In some ways, no. In real life Dick was one of the most charming people anyone ever met. He was the life of any party he went to. But when he turned the camera on himself, in all of the hours of footage I watched, he always tended to become very serious—by and large, overly serious. There are a couple of moments in *Windmill* where you see him light up a bit, but those are just the tip of the iceberg of how he really was. In fact, the original idea of bringing Wally Shawn into the film was to try to evoke that missing comic side.

MacDonald: When you and Dick were shooting the imagery in the surf at Wainscott Beach, the imagery that ends the film, how did you understand Dick's reason for making this imagery? You use it as a metaphor for both his death and the conclusion of your project, but do you think *he* was seeing it as a metaphor for his oncoming demise?

Olch: There are many different tapes/rolls of footage shot on the beach—some by Dick, some by others under his direction. His father had also photographed many images of the waves in 8mm. The beach and waves were a key focus for Dick—similar to the tennis courts, the houses, the softball game, sailing—image ideas/categories that he returned to over and over again as he shot more and more in the Georgica/Wainscott community over the years.

The specific footage used at the end of *Windmill* felt exciting to me for the visceral quality of pounding the camera into the waves, and the humor of Dick's voice directing. It was part of hours of footage which also included floating in the water and swimming back up to the beach. His shooting was never overly calculated or planned out. He shot very much as a cameraman—making great images; the meaning, use, and direction of those images he usually left until later. That's why I had so many interesting editorial options, because of the strength of his photography: his best images feel pregnant with so much mystery and potential meaning.

MacDonald: How much did you and Dick talk about his mortality? Did you and he ever talk about your making a film for him? Near the end of *The Windmill Movie* you come back to Dick's early comment about personal documentary, the cliché of the filmmaker shooting himself in the mirror (as enacted by Wally Shawn). This time, that passage continues with Wally speaking as Dick, saying the bit about oncoming death solving the problem of the future. I'm assuming that you wrote that.

Olch: Wally's passage is a mix of my own writing and memories Wally had of things Dick said to him when he was ill—performed in many takes, Wally improvising in the mirror.

The video footage Dick shot of himself in the mirror toward the beginning of the film is from 1990–92, well before any illness. His preoccupation in that original footage, which was shot in Los Angeles while he was shooting an episode of *Life Goes On* for ABC television, is about the making of a personal film. Out there, the contrast between working on large Hollywood sets and making more personal, small budget films was quite striking for Dick.

As for talking about mortality, Dick was open and honest with me. He taught me about life and by consequence death, just as much as he taught me about filmmaking. My thesis film, *Artemin Goldberg*, which we made together, had a weirdly similar dynamic to *Windmill*; it's about a film student whose documentary subject ends up dying on him.

MacDonald: Did you create the scene of Wally and Susan in the cemetery, or did you just film a visit they decided to make (I assume the former, since Wally is dressed as Dick).

Olch: We were shooting a scene between Wally and Bob Balaban at the cemetery, at Dick's mother's gravesite. Bob was playing David Grubin, Dick's friend who shot the original DV interview with Dick in the blue polo shirt. My idea was to construct some additional fictional versions of this interview during which Wally and Bob would be going in and out of character. I also made sure to have Susan come by to watch. I knew that something interesting would happen, and made sure that all three of our cameras were rolling to catch it. After I yelled cut for one camera (the others still rolling), Wally and Susan took a moment to walk over to Dick's grave. This was exactly what I had been hoping for. I didn't follow them, gave them their space—and fortunately the shot worked. It's a real moment between Susan and Wally. And yet, of course, Wally is in costume. Somewhere between documentary and fiction.

MacDonald: It's a film about Dick Rogers, but it's *your* film about Dick Rogers. In what senses do you see the film as being about *you*? Was part of what kept you at work on this project for seven years your own issues about success?

Olch: *Windmill* is quite personal for me. My background is different from Dick's in that I come from an immigrant Jewish family, and unlike Dick, I have a supportive mother, the most encouraging parents. But aside from that, I grew up on 74th Street in a building *next door* to the building that Dick grew up in; we both went to the Collegiate School for Boys; we both went to Harvard and made our first films there; and weirdly enough, I ended up renting an apartment down the block from Dick's loft on Mott Street where I lived during the making of *Windmill* (I still live there).

As an ambitious young filmmaker from New York who had big plans to be a fiction filmmaker but was not moving in that direction, and whose friends were getting *their* movies made and into festivals and theaters, I definitely had an affinity for Dick's doubts about success. I'd run into friends at cocktail parties who'd say, "You're *still* working on that doc?!" In fact, every single person I know told me to quit the film at some point, that it was just a disaster, that I was wasting my life. I had tremendous insecurities about whether the movie was going to exist, much less be good, and these insecurities certainly paralleled Dick's, or at least the version of him I was creating.

MacDonald: When someone decides to be an independent documentary filmmaker, there's always the economic question. I understand you've entered the fashion world to support yourself.

Olch: After I finished *Artemin Goldberg*, I planned to make a souvenir for the members of the crew; in the end, I decided on a necktie (seemed more memorable than a T-Shirt or a baseball cap). Later, learning how to make a tie became a kind of hobby during the time after I didn't go to Spain to do the Welles movie and was looking at different film projects. It took about a year to make a tie that I liked and when my friends, recent Harvard grads in New York working as bankers and lawyers, saw the tie, they said, "Cool tie, could I buy one?" and I said, "Sure!" I sold four ties, and made some more, sold eight, sold sixteen, and by the time I was editing *Windmill*, I was having sales appointments where I'd lay the ties out on a table and people would come by.

To make a long story short, the neckwear collection ended up at Bergdorf Goodman in 2007, and has since grown to become an accessories company making scarves, notebooks, and bags. We now have about fifty accounts worldwide. It's been very fortunate in that it allows me to develop and work on my film projects without outside pressure.

MacDonald: Do you have a new film in mind?

Olch: Two, actually. One fiction, the other documentary.

Arthur and Jennifer Smith (on *Ice Bears of the Beaufort*)

"Avant-garde film," "experimental film," even "critical cinema," the term I've used in my other interview collections, are problematic and become increasingly problematic as the years go by and the history/geography of cinema continues to develop and expand. It is particularly difficult to makes sense of these terms once they are used to describe new contributions to what have become traditional approaches to making film—as often seemed the case, for example, in the screenings presented at "Views from the Avant-Garde," the long-time sidebar to the New York Film Festival curated by Mark McElhatten and Gavin Smith. Can a new work made by painting and scratching onto 16mm film or a new surrealist montage really be "avant-garde"? For all practical purposes, "avant-garde," and even "experimental," are no longer descriptive terms, but are simply conventional ways to refer to time-honored traditions that may have been, or at least seemed to most cineastes, "avant-garde" or "experimental" when they were first attempted. Of course, particular works may be experimental, if indeed they experiment; and these approaches may still be "critical" in the sense I use the term in the Critical Cinema series: that is, they may implicitly critique conventional media and the audience that has developed for it.

Our use of such terms is problematic in other ways as well, since there are, in fact, approaches to filmmaking that can be understood as "avant-garde"—if not "experimental" or "critical"—in a more traditional sense. Arthur and Jennifer Smith live, year round, in a tiny, largely Iñupiat town called Kaktovik (Qaagtuvigmiut, in Iñupiaq), on the north shore of Barter Island off the *north* coast of Alaska. They live there because they love Alaska's North Slope, a place they find beautiful and energizing, and admire the people who make Kaktovik their home; but also because they are committed to the ongoing documentation of the local polar bear population, and especially the way that the lives of the local bears and the human residents of Kaktovik are imbricated and have been imbricated for thousands of years.

After the Bush administration opened the Arctic National Wildlife Refuge, within which Kaktovik sits, to oil drilling, the Smiths' photography and filmmaking became imbued with the mission of demonstrating the beauty of the polar bears and of their complex social structure, in the desperate hope that if a substantial number of filmgoers could be convinced not only that polar bears can be lovely to look at, but that they (and their Iñupiat neighbors) live together in a way that deserves to be an environmental model, their filmmaking might play a role in forestalling the seemingly inevitable drilling that will destroy the bears' habitat and the traditional Iñupiat way of life. The Smiths are masterful cinematographers who make gorgeous, often meditative imagery of their surroundings—imagery comparable to the work of filmmakers like Peter Hutton, James Benning, Sharon Lockhart, and Leighton Pierce. As people committed to a life in a most challenging place, whose work is literally at the forefront of resistance to environmental change, they and their films strike me as "avant-garde" in more than the rather flabby sense in which we cineastes have come to use that term.

Since *Ice Bears of the Beaufort*, the Smiths have made two shorter, more overtly polemical videos—*What Do Polar Bears Dream While They're Dying* (2011) and *Once There Were Polar Bears* (2012)—again arguing for the right of the local polar bears in and around Kaktovik to live among humans as neighbors—as they have for so many generations—and not to be exterminated in order to facilitate US industrial development. In all their videos the Smiths use the beauty of their imagery and the elegance of their timing as an implicit metaphor for the bears themselves.

I spoke with the Smiths in November 2009, when they visited Hamilton College to show *Ice Bears of the Beaufort* (2009). We refined the conversation online during 2010.

MacDonald: In *Ice Bears of the Beaufort*, you ignore many of the conventions of nature filmmaking. Normally, a nature film does the cycle of the year, focusing on mating, raising the young animals, and the struggle for food. You don't focus on mating; and there's virtually no predation. Your film is mostly polar bears hanging out, apparently having a good time. Also you don't use narration and instead use intertitles to provide information; it's almost as if we're back to Robert Flaherty and *Nanook of the North* [1921]. What led you to those choices?

Arthur Smith: I've still never seen *Nanook of the North*! *Ice Bears* is just what made sense to me. I came to the film with an understanding that before I came to live in Kaktovik, I had no idea what polar bears *were*, and that after six years—and I'm not saying this to boast or lay claim to anything; there's still a lot I don't know—I suspect that few other individuals have spent more time in the presence of polar bears than I have. Jennifer and I have filmed polar bears during all twelve months of the year.

The current science of polar bear biology rests largely upon helicopter tracking and satellite telemetry. I understand the necessity for this research, but those methods alone are not enough. Observation from helicopters as the bears are chased down and darted offers no insight as to the true nature of these animals. In our rush to technology, we've lost the art of observational biology.

The other day, when we flew from Seattle to Chicago, we watched *Into the Storm*, a Ridley Scott film about Winston Churchill's role in World War II. I watched it because I'm interested in who Churchill was and what he represented at that time and place in history. The film didn't center upon how much he weighed or his shopping at the grocery store or eating at restaurants. Do we have to reduce natural history to an asinine, infantile representation? Does it make us feel superior to think that animals can only kill and eat and reproduce, as if they don't have any higher function, as if they're not intelligent, not cognizant?

I've seen polar bears exhibit qualities that most humans would be hard-pressed to emulate: the way the sows and the cubs interact and the way the bears take care of each other and how expressive they are. Polar bears have a social structure. There's a sow in *Ice Bears* who ran half a mile across the ice to meet a boar—she recognized him from that far away; their affectionate interaction is in the film. But this wasn't breeding season; it was October; they're not mating, so what *are* they doing? (figure 45).

These animals have a capacity that we *completely* underestimate. Absent observational biology, modern science does not address an important aspect of their being. I mean if I were to put a satellite collar on you and track your movements from an office three thousand miles away, what would that tell me about who you are and what you do and the quality of your life?

MacDonald: This is interesting to me because Claude Nuridsany and Marie Pérennou, the French nature filmmakers who did *Microcosmos* [1996], suggest much the same thing about insects.

The commitment you two have made to living in Kaktovik year round to film the environment there is unusual and impressive. I'd like to know how each of you got to Kaktovik and into filmmaking. Arthur, you've been at this the longest.

Arthur Smith: My dad hunted big game in Alaska in the 1950s, and he shot 16mm Kodachrome film during his hunting trips. He used to show his films locally, so I'd imprinted on Alaska by the time I was 2. Hunting and fishing with my dad in the Adirondacks confirmed my connection with the wild. At age 10, I picked up his Bell & Howell movie camera and his Polaroid Land Camera. I did a Polaroid of a white-tailed deer standing on a logging road in the Adirondacks, and a couple of other things, and that turned my interest away from hunting to filming.

I grew up near Watkins Glen, New York, when it was the home of the International Grand Prix, and I still have hundreds of feet of film of the Grand Prix from that era.

MacDonald: A lot of young men hunt in the Adirondacks and some make movies and photographs, but you ended up on the *north* coast of Alaska.

FIGURE 45 *Second year polar bear cub, in Arthur and Jennifer Smith's Ice Bears of the Beaufort (2010).*
Source: Courtesy Arthur Smith.

Arthur Smith: Once I'd become a professional photographer, I got an assignment on the Arctic coast for an agency, Grant Heilman Photography. I set up camp about fifty miles east of Prudhoe Bay, and the first night I was there, a polar bear went through camp. I knew it from the tracks (I know the difference between a polar bear track and a grizzly track), and at first I thought, "How come that polar bear didn't kill me? Why did I even get to wake up?" I was working from the received wisdom about polar bears, the conventional storyline: polar bears are solitary and threatening; they kill everything they pass. In time I learned that the polar bears in that area are well-fed; they're in a healthy environment and don't look at people as a food supply.

I guess going to Alaska was part of my attempt to understand what life is—in and of itself—apart from our influences and our assumptions; and to try to understand what's become of the natural environment under our stewardship. In Alaska there are places that are completely undisturbed and intact. If you sit in the middle of a hundred thousand caribou or watch bears charging salmon up a stream, and recognize the perfection of what life, left to its own, *is*—well, once I'd seen that, there was no turning back.

I've been an Alaska resident since 1992, but for a while I still traveled full-time, coast to coast, making photographs. During the past few years I've worked only in Alaska.

MacDonald: Jennifer, how did you get involved in filming polar bears?

Jennifer Smith: Well, I fell in love.

MacDonald: With the Arctic, the bears, or with Arthur?

Jennifer Smith: Well, first with the Arctic and then with Art. I grew up outside of Chicago and graduated from DePaul University with an English degree. Right out of college, I found a city apartment, a city job, and spent the next year working overtime and commuting—for what? "I'm too young for this," I thought, "I've got to travel." I went off to India, then to Thailand where I did a bit of volunteer teaching—I just wanted to immerse myself in a completely different culture from my own. My plan was to have a lot of experiences in Asia, then go to Alaska and make some money in the fishing industry. At that time you heard stories about people making ten thousand dollars in a summer.

So, I went up to Alaska. I didn't make any money, but I discovered the *place*. Not only was it exotic—geographically and culturally—it was *wild*.

I decided to stay for a journalism degree at the University of Alaska. Once I had my Masters, I figured I'd globetrot some more as a "travel writer" and spend my downtime snug in a Fairbanks cabin. Fate happens, though. I met my ex-husband during that time, and he got me into wilderness guiding in the Brooks Range. We ran an ecotourism business together for about eight years—fly-in trips of eight to ten days—taking clients into the Alaska's most pristine roadless areas: Gates of the Arctic National Park, the NPR-A

(National Petroleum Reserve, in the western arctic), the Arctic National Wildlife Refuge.

Soon I'd lost my appetite for wandering south of the Arctic Circle. The only writing I did—for *Alaska* magazine and newspaper Sunday sections—was about the North. I was hooked. But it was also frustrating. By itself, the pen just doesn't measure up to this place. The 3:00 a.m. midnight sun douses the rolling tundra, shadows hang in creek valleys, space overwhelms you. In many respects, you have to see the Arctic to believe it. At that time, my palette didn't include the visual arts, so I found myself mostly just soaking things up, through my own experiences and those of my clients. Here they were, spending thousands of dollars to sleep in tents, eat cup-a-soup, get snowed on, watch caribou, drag rafts, and maybe spot a grizzly. Then, when they would get on the plane to leave, no matter how hard the trip had been and whether they'd seen any animals or not, there'd be tears in their eyes.

Through these clients, I realized that being able to live and work in wild Alaska was a gift; in fact, when I left my first marriage, I still wasn't willing to leave the Arctic. None of my trips had allowed for real exchange with the people of the Alaskan arctic—the Iñupiat—plus, I'd never over-wintered up north. So, I took a job in the village of Kaktovik, thinking, let's see what comes of it. That's when Art and I met.

MacDonald: I can already see that I'm working totally out of stereotype: all my questions assume that you're sacrificing yourselves by living in Kaktovik to do this work.

Arthur Smith: Oh, it's no sacrifice: if there's an Eden left on this planet, Kaktovik is it. We have the Arctic Ocean out our front doorstep, and behind us, thirty-five miles or so, some of the highest peaks in the Brooks Range; you add the drama of the Arctic weather and the diversity of life—there aren't many places in the world where whales and polar bears and caribou and grizzlies all come together in a habitable environment that you can call your backyard. Before you step off your front porch up here, you've got to look both ways and it's not for traffic! We had a bear on our porch this past September; I stepped out at five o'clock in the morning, just at daylight, and we greeted each other: "You punchin' in?" We both went to work; I went out to film and he went off to be a polar bear in my film. Kaktovik is a pretty intense place to be.

And the people are great. I have deep respect and admiration for our neighbors and our friends, for what the Iñupiat do and how they do it; the community that exists in Kaktovik is remarkable. I'm impressed with how well the Iñupiat take care of each other, how unified they are. The closest thing to it in my experience, and this is a horrible analogy, is when you go to a college football game and everybody is united in support of the home team. Imagine that being not just a moment at a game—but a real, functioning, year-round community. This is their reality, and I'm convinced that at one time that's what we all had; we've let real community erode.

We love it in Kaktovik. We live in a four-hundred-square-foot space, but we don't feel deprived; nobody competes there. Iñupiat culture is based on an entirely different standard from the culture down here: a lot of people we know in Kaktovik work to be able to have time to be with each other, and go out fishing and hunting—doing what they've been doing for thousands of years. The Iñupiat are not working to pay for all the junk that we pay for; they work to buy time.

MacDonald: The Kaktovik website says 291 people live in town. How many are Iñupiat?

Arthur Smith: Well, not counting the school teachers, who are only there in the school season, and the missionaries, who also come and go, there are fewer than a dozen whites, including us.

MacDonald: I know you've provided footage and done camerawork for major broadcasters and other organizations. Is *Ice Bears* the first film that you call yours?

Arthur Smith: Yes. Selling motion-picture and still imagery of polar bears and other aspects of the Far North is how I've been able to live and make films that bear witness to an arctic ecosystem painted, now, with a political bull's eye. There's a lot at stake up there, and at the same time, so many misinterpretations. I remember some producers putting together a show on Alaska, asking me, "What's the apex predator in the Arctic?" Of course, they wanted it to be the polar bear.

But if you want to understand the Arctic and the dynamics of the balance there, a balance that's existed during the thousands of years that humans have been part of the environment, you have to know that the Iñupiat Eskimo is the apex predator in the Arctic. These human beings are still a natural part of an intact ecosystem. And that's a beautiful thing to witness. It makes no sense to carve "nature" into little niches; we humans are part of it and the animals are part of it.

Jennifer Smith: Or to designate as "wilderness" only places where humans are *not* living. In Kaktovik, while the land status isn't wilderness *per se*, the very fact that the Iñupiat are still there on the coast, subsisting, makes this place—for me—more wild and whole than any place I've ever been.

MacDonald: How did *Ice Bears of the Beaufort* happen to get finished; you've been shooting for years, but not finishing films.

Arthur Smith: A transition from standard definition to high definition allowed us to make *Ice Bears* and get it out. In 1999, Sony introduced the F900, a high definition camera that cost over $100,000, not including lenses and editing equipment. Three years later, George Lucas shot *Star Wars Episode II: Attack of the Clones* [2002] with the F900. At that time, shooting a movie digitally wasn't feasible unless you were already plugged into Hollywood or a major broadcast organization. Over the last ten years, the rapid advancement in digital technology enabled a two-person team like us to afford an HD camera and finish a high-definition movie.

Now, as digital cinema has evolved, the bar has been raised beyond HD, and some would argue, we are now able to match 35mm film quality standards. In 2009, Jennifer and I started shooting with the RED ONE, a digital camera that has four times the resolution of high definition. With this camera, and several dozen terabytes of hard drive space, we're able to generate a better product than we could if we were shooting 35mm film—partly because of the ease of working with a smaller camera that handles cold weather well: we're often shooting at 20 degrees below zero. Now, we change compact flash cards instead of rolls of film, and we don't have to worry about the physical properties of film in those temperatures. Also, sometimes we're over-cranking at a hundred frames per second (to get slow motion); in 35mm that would mean a thousand feet of film in ten minutes. Physically handling all that film would be virtually impossible for a self-funded, two-person crew.

Jennifer Smith: With the new equipment, we can handle the workflow from concept all the way through a finished edit, in-house. The end product is so good it can be shown theatrically, straight out of our edit suite. Shooting with the RED means that despite our limited financial resources, the work we're doing meets the highest technical standard, so that feels good.

MacDonald: When you go out shooting, how do you divide the labor?

Arthur Smith: Jennifer is on the monitor, focus-checking and making sure everything's right.

Jennifer Smith: And Art is shooting and working as my wind-breaker! He gets the colder part of the job.

MacDonald: How does *Ice Bears* fit into the larger project you're envisioning now, which will deal with the human component of your environment? And how close is the new piece from being done?

Arthur Smith: We're waiting for music. When you're an independent, self-funded filmmaker, music is a real son of a gun.

MacDonald: Patrick O'Hearn again?

Arthur Smith: I wish; I was really happy to be able to use his *Glaciation* in *Ice Bears*.

MacDonald: Did you always assume *Ice Bears* would have a music track?

Arthur Smith: Absolutely, from the very beginning.

MacDonald: Has *Ice Bears* found its way to audiences?

Arthur Smith: It hasn't achieved a substantial audience. For broadcast types, this film doesn't translate into a commercial product, and we're not inclined to transform it into what they might think *is* a commercial product. It was shown at a few festivals.

Jennifer Smith: A lot of the film festivals that we thought might be a good fit, environmental festivals or wildlife festivals, wouldn't touch it. We're wondering if that had something to do with our claim in the film that Alaska's polar bears might survive global warming if their habitat isn't damaged by oil drilling. This might be seen as a heretical message. A lot of NGO fundraising rests on doomsday scenarios.

Arthur Smith: It's a tendency for most festivals to consider this a "wildlife film" and to dismiss it. That's where I say, "No, you need to *get* this; this film is about the balance of life on the planet. It is a film where the polar bears are the characters, but it's about a balance and a perfection that we humans need as a model.

MacDonald: Have there been particular filmmakers or films that have been models for your thinking about your work?

Arthur Smith: I think Michael Mann's *The Last of the Mohicans* [1992] was visually stunning; he did some remarkable things with a forest environment and natural light--but most of what I admire in film has come from learning to make good photographs, learning to support myself as a professional photographer.

I've just tried to be technically proficient, to know what the state of the art is in image-making, and what level my work has to achieve in order to have a chance of having some impact. This new film isn't *Ice Bears* by any stretch; it's more about the Iñupiat, though the bears are still very much a part of it. We've got the visual material and we've started cutting it; I have a script—it's all there, but this year we ran out of time. Last year, we edited probably 80% of the time and were out shooting 20%; this year, we were out shooting 80% of the time. We've had our cameras in front of Pete Domenici, Lisa Murkowski, Gale Norton, Dirk Kempthorne, Samuel Bodman when he was energy secretary; they showed up to tell the Iñupiat that they were going to drill the ocean, like it or lump it. It was contemptible. I have more respect for polar bears than for these guys—I feel safer in the bears' company!

The press that came along with the panel had already predetermined the story; and they totally misrepresented what the Iñupiat think about all this. To see firsthand the distortion by the media and the political process, to be on the front line where this war of resources is being waged—it's scary. Go into an area that's been drilled, with the flaring of the gas wells and toxins in the air, and tell me you want to live there.

The three dollars a gallon you're paying at the pump is not the true cost of your gasoline; if people were paying the true cost, they wouldn't stand for it. But the process gets located so far from where most people are living that the reality isn't understood.

Jennifer Smith: Art has on-camera what the local Kaktovik people were saying—footage of the signs and the protests—but the media went back and broadcast the complete opposite of what happened.

Arthur Smith: There have been multiple occasions when I've been thought to be a spy for an environmental group, sent in and paid to promote their agenda. We're not against oil. And nobody has to fund me! Because we're *for* preserving the environment here doesn't mean we're *against* oil. That's false logic. Obviously we're all dependent upon fossil fuels and that's not going away anytime soon, but still, there needs to be a balance on the planet. We have to conserve natural areas so there's space for components of civilization that don't have dollar signs attached to them. Not everything that's important to our being human can be wrung up on a cash register.

Jennifer Smith: A picture *is* worth a thousand words and can translate into a judgment call that makes the difference between protecting a place or letting it go.

Arthur Smith: For the new material, I got pretty daring with the bears. We took the opportunity to look at bears on a more micro scale.

Jennifer Smith: Although a full-frame bear feels pretty *macro*!

Arthur Smith: The bears don't freeze and pose; they're always moving, sensing and reacting and assessing and doing things, but at a hundred frames per second, a pause that may only last one second is four seconds in play-back. Shooting at this frame rate gave us the possibility of being able to move with these bears and capture details that I don't think have ever been recorded before.

I showed some of the new footage to my parents, and my mom was screaming; she's convinced that we're going to be eaten!

In this recent material, there's a sequence of the northern lights that we shot in time lapse. We had set up facing the bluffs of the island, looking out over the ocean, and the northern lights fired off. We were shooting a one-frame exposure each second, and this new chip was clean enough at a high ASA that we were able to fully capture the display—not easy to do. There was a full moon off-camera, and a polar bear, fully illuminated by the moonlight, walked into the image, sat down on the bluff under the northern lights, looking around as if it were watching the lights, then stood up and walked out of the image.

Our job, as we see it, is to get people to pay attention, open up, and drop their preconceived notions for a minute; we hope that if the doors of perception do open just a little bit—poom—they'll *get it*; they'll *see* the reality of this place. And the next time they hear some moron characterize the Arctic as a wasteland, no good for anything but drilling, maybe they'll think, "You know what? We know better. We know that isn't the truth."

Betzy Bromberg (on *Voluptuous Sleep*)

Betzy Bromberg has been making 16mm films since the 1970s, but little in the first thirty years of her filmmaking career could have predicted her *Voluptuous Sleep* (2011), an impressive contribution to a distinguished tradition within both avant-garde and documentary cinema that begins in the 1920s with Henri Chomette's *Cinq minutes de cinéma pur* (1925), Ralph Steiner's *H2O* (1929), and Henwar Rodakiewicz's *Portrait of a Young Man* (1931); or perhaps even earlier, during cinema's first decades, with experiments in filming after dark: Edwin S. Porter's *Coney Island at Night* (1905), for example. In more recent decades, Kenneth Anger's *Eaux d'artifice* (1953), much of the work of Jim Davis, sections of Marie Menken's *Notebook* (recorded from 1962 to 1964), and Stan Brakhage's many films devoted to the nuances of light moving in time— *The Text of Light* (1974) most obviously—are premonitions of *Voluptuous Sleep*.

The particular spaces we see in *Voluptuous Sleep* do not exist in the physical world, at least not as we see them in the film. Bromberg's way of recording what are, in fact, familiar, mundane locations transforms them into *cinematic* spaces, places that can only be recorded by the mechanism of a 16mm camera and can only be truly *seen* within a movie theater. Her film was produced by and produces an adventure of perception, to use Brakhage's phrase; it evokes a retrieval of a kind of visual innocence.

The two parts of *Voluptuous Sleep*, "Language Is a Skin" and "And the Night Illuminated the Night" are distinct from one another both in structure and tone, and reveal Bromberg's interest in exploring the micro world she has discovered. "Language Is a Skin" is a visual panorama that begins with black-and-white imagery of a wide variety of textures and forms of motion, gradually adds color, ultimately climaxing with extravagant color compositions, then gradually moves back toward a more restrained palette and to black-and-white imagery similar to what is seen at the beginning. The visuals in "Language Is a Skin" are accompanied by a range of sounds and pieces of music composed by Bromberg. As its title suggests, "And the Night Illuminated the Night" is a cine-nocturne; it works primarily with

---

˙ The mini-tradition of "cine-nocturne" is analogous to, and to some extent inspired by, the traditions of the musical nocturne established by composers John Field and Frédéric Chopin, and the nocturne in painting (James McNeill Whistler was the first to call paintings "nocturnes," and Ralph Albert Blakelock made the painterly nocturne widely popular at the end of the nineteenth century). Distinguished instances of the modern cine-nocturne include *Kristallnacht* [1979] by Chick

black-and-white and a very narrow range of muted color, accompanied by a musical composition by Robert Allaire.

I was in touch with Bromberg, who is Director of the Program in Film and Video at California Institute of the Arts, during the summer of 2012, when I sent her questions about *Voluptuous Sleep*. We developed the interview online.

MacDonald: Voluptuous Sleep is simultaneously familiar and mysterious. It's clear that you're filming water in motion, light on water, and sometimes rocks and plants—but your procedure for re-framing what we see so that it seems to exist outside our normal sense of space and time is not obvious.

Bromberg: The act of shooting the two parts of *Voluptuous Sleep* was entirely mysterious. You're absolutely correct about what I was shooting, and the fact that the images, in the end, function outside of our normal sense of space and time is not something I can easily explain. I honestly don't know how they become so abstract, other than the fact that I try not to press the camera trigger until what I'm seeing through the viewfinder becomes some other reality. It's not easy to shoot this way. The variables that need to come together are very elusive. I'm not yet able to pinpoint why some shoots become almost mystical and others bomb. But this has always been the case for me.

When I was shooting for *Voluptuous Sleep*, there were times when I would look through the lens and think, "Holy Shit, look at *this*! I hope it records this way on film!" Both parts were entirely shot in my yard—with infinite help from my husband whose gardening has created a wonderland! At some point a few years ago, he got tired of my complaining about noisy neighbors and strategically placed a number of fountains around our yard to replace noise with the flow of water. There is also a small star-shaped pond that dates back to 1928. These are my water sources.

Also, the film looks the way it does because it was shot on Kodak Vision II 50D and 250D. 250D is not a great looking stock, but I needed a high-speed daylight stock and I've never been a Fuji lover: Fuji is a little too cool for me and I prefer Kodak's reds and yellows. I think I made the most out of the 250D. Vision II 50D is a gorgeous stock (now no longer available and replaced with Vision III 50D). I'm a strong believer that the look and content of a film necessarily emerges from its technical parameters.

Strand, with whom Bromberg studied at California Institute of the Arts; Peter Hutton's *In Titan's Goblet* (1991); "Moon and Swamp," from *Five (for Ozu)* (2003) by Abbas Kiarostami; *Glow in the Dark: January–June* (2002) by Rebecca Meyers; and many of Phil Solomon's films—Solomon is the master of this mode. See my "Gardens of the Moon: The Modern Cine-Nocturne," in Kenneth I. Helphand and Michael G. Lee, eds., *Technology and the Garden* (Washington, DC: Dumbarton Oaks Research Library and Collections, 2014): 201–229.

I love the act of shooting film. The world through a lens is often entirely different from the world seen through the naked eye. My filmmaking has evolved very slowly towards the abstract, but I think my dedication to the art of cinematography has been clear in all my films. I began as a documentarian, a recorder of my external reality, and slowly I've become more and more fascinated with interior reality and with finding ways to visualize the inner world.

At this point I'm most interested in light. I can't really predict when and how I'm able to get an image that blows my mind. In my yard, I'll see an area that might be interesting and I set up tripod and camera. So many elements have to come together for a great shot: the sun, the angle, the framing, the color, the movement or stillness. It's like waiting for the perfect storm. I often find myself twisted into a pretzel, uncomfortable and unable to attain anything, until a magic portal opens and a series of shots unfold; then, just as stunningly, the portal closes and there are no more good shots to be gotten. Very mysterious. And very hallucinogenic. What I love most about shooting is the exquisite high I get looking through a camera—leaving this world and entering an alternative (figure 46).

Voluptuous Sleep developed out of my previous film, *a Darkness Swallowed* [2005]. In a way, *a Darkness Swallowed* is a film about time, and *Voluptuous Sleep*, a film about light. The water footage in *a Darkness Swallowed* was shot with an intervalometer, which allowed me to shoot long exposures, anywhere from 1/16th of a second to 4 or 6 seconds for each frame. What I really was

FIGURE 46 *Lightscape in Betzy Bromberg's* Voluptuous Sleep *(2011).*
Source: Courtesy Betzy Bromberg.

recording was the sun's movement over time. Each of the water shots in *a Darkness Swallowed* took anywhere from three to seven hours to shoot.

With *a Darkness Swallowed* I entered the close-up world, which necessitated the use of a tripod. In terms of content, I felt that I was ready to make a film about a subject matter that I had attempted to talk about earlier in my filmmaking, but lacked the sophistication and skill to properly address. I decided that *a Darkness Swallowed* would begin with a verbal prologue, and then plunge the viewer into a purely visual and aural experience, leaving the external world behind and entering and embodying an internal landscape. *Voluptuous Sleep* was a natural next step.

When I began to shoot *Voluptuous Sleep*, I used the intervalometer, but the results were clearly less interesting than what I was recording in real time without any manipulation at all. Isn't that fantastic? And I could never explain why! Though it's hard to believe, even for me, all of the imagery in *Voluptuous Sleep* was shot in real time (except for one shot and one triple exposure).

MacDonald: How long and how often did you shoot for *Voluptuous Sleep*?

Bromberg: I shot *Voluptuous Sleep* relatively quickly, probably three or four times a week for about five months.

The laboratory turn-around for what I shoot is about 24 hours. I usually drop film off late at night, hoping to pick it up the following evening so that I can project the dailies and see what's complete, what I need to shoot more of, and what I should abandon. In general, I shoot as much as I feel is necessary and I don't really care if it's excessive. Of course I beat myself up when I shoot badly or when I make stupid errors. But because I'm often discovering the visual articulation of my ideas as I shoot, I have no qualms about shooting a lot of film.

But for *Voluptuous Sleep, Part I*, I shot very little film and used much of what I shot: a ratio of about 3 to 1 overall. And for *Part II*, I used just about everything I recorded.

MacDonald: Before becoming an independent filmmaker, you worked in Hollywood, doing special effects. On a certain level this isn't surprising—*Voluptuous Sleep* feels like an elaborate special effect—but nevertheless that trajectory from the industry to the kind of work you're doing now seems unusual. Could you talk a bit about your experiences in the industry?

Bromberg: Your phrase, "like an elaborate special effect," makes me wince. The imagery that I've created is completely organic and natural. I've applied no artificial manipulation to the image at all. I've only recorded what is truly there, what I actually see through the lens. I've made a very conscious decision *not* to use "special effects" in my filmmaking, which is not about trickery, but about exposing that which the eye fails to see.

The twenty years that I spent working in the film industry were invaluable in terms of my technical growth as a filmmaker. Optical effects are extremely challenging and difficult, but it was great fun to be able to handle 35mm film every day and to have to find ways to matte and layer and compose shots from multiple sources. I was never much interested in the content of most of the films that I worked on, but it didn't really matter since my job was to work with individual shots and sequences, to brainstorm and problem solve and figure out ways to manipulate and combine many elements together in complex ways. All of the work I did in the industry was post-shooting, optical printer work (except for *Tron* [1982], for which I shot on an animation stand), first as a camerawoman, then as a supervisor who prepared and figured out technically how to make happen what needed to happen in a given shot.

In the industry I had marvelous teachers who were/are genius with their craft, and I was able to learn much that I could then apply to *my* craft (personal filmmaking). What I learned in the industry about emulsion and its response to light is the very basis of filmmaking, and I use what I learned every time I pick up my camera, every time I handle film, and every time I interact with a lab. I enjoyed the professionalism and the collaboration that had to happen with the many talented people I worked with—not the executives and directors and producers, but the eccentric group of special effects workers, many of whom are artists and filmmakers in their own right.

I always kept my own filmmaking and my occupation entirely separate. When I was laid off or between jobs, I would have the time to physically work on my own films, but even as I was toiling away on industry projects, my films were always present in my mind.

MacDonald: What led you to leave special effects work?

Bromberg: I left the industry because the industry left Hollywood. And it all went digital—I had no desire to spend countless hours sitting in front of a computer. Working in analog, I was very active. I'd be looking at exposure wedges over a light table, then running into the camera-room to check on an element; then I would need to talk to someone in the animation department, then run somewhere else. I'm pretty hyper and the constant movement suited me. Sitting at a computer had no appeal, didn't seem like it would be fun.

I had already been teaching part and full time on and off since 1990: *on* for my pleasure and *off* because the industry afforded me enough money to make my films—teaching, at that point, did not. In 2001, as analog effects work was drying up, I had the opportunity to become Director of the Program in Film and Video at CalArts. This was good timing because overseeing a program is demanding and I could not have done that job and continued to work in the industry.

MacDonald: Voluptuous Sleep is part of a distinguished tradition in avant-garde film, beginning in the 1920s, and revived in later decades by Jim Davis, Bruce Baillie, Stan Brakhage—*The Text of Light* and *Commingled Containers* seem particularly close to *Voluptuous Sleep*—Chick Strand, in *Kristallnacht*, and the films/videos of Andrew Noren and Leighton Pierce. How fully involved with this tradition do you feel?

Bromberg: I appreciate the filmmakers you've mentioned and I like some of their work a great deal, but I don't recognize myself or my filmmaking as part of any specific tradition. To be honest, the films that most inspired me when *Voluptuous Sleep* was still just a seed of an idea were silent films by Germaine Dulac: *Thémes et variations* [1928], *Disque 957* [1928], and especially *Étude cinématographique sur une arabesque* [1929]. First seeing these films (in 2009) was a revelation. I recognized the female root that I'd been longing for without realizing that I had been longing for it.

There are very few films which have deeply entered my psyche and affected my soul. Certainly most of Chick Strand's films—Chick was a great mentor and an even greater friend, and a brilliant, wildly sensuous and profound filmmaker. And I also adore Patrick Bokanowski's work, especially *L'Ange* [1982], and his wife Michele's extraordinary sound compositions and soundtracks.

What I have always appreciated about avant-garde filmmaking is its personal approach, the way that the eccentric sensibilities of its makers are instilled within the films, plus the freedom to combine and manipulate both sound and image to create one's own language. I see myself as yet another eccentric filmmaker working within the realm of the avant-garde.

MacDonald: In the title credit of *Voluptuous Sleep*, you say "Voluptuous Sleep *series*." This suggests that Part I ("Language Is a Skin") and Part II ("And the Night Illuminated the Night") are the first two parts of an ongoing project. Is that true?

Bromberg: It is true. Originally I thought there would be quite a number of parts, maybe seven or nine; but now I'm thinking maybe there's only a Part III, which I'm currently working on. I had put footage aside for the additional parts, and am finding that some of that footage will work in the current project and some will not. And as usual, I've felt a need to shoot additional footage, which again has turned into a larger shooting episode than I had expected. It's so much fun to shoot!

We'll see, at least *one* more part.

MacDonald: The challenging length of *Voluptuous Sleep* and the relative consistency of the imagery make it easy to get lost in the film—at least this was my experience during early viewings. But in fact, as I've looked more carefully, your shaping of the experience of each section has become clearer, as has my sense that the two parts are different from one another.

Bromberg: "Language is a Skin" has basically a 5-part structure (although I actually refer to its last sections as 4a and 4b, which are separated by the emerald green section). What's peculiar about its arc is that in at least one sense—in terms of the amount of movement you see—it works in reverse. It would be normal for the film's movement to build and in the third part, crescendo, then wind down. However, in this case, the center or, the third and most colorful part, becomes almost entirely still. This was extremely tricky in terms of editing. It's challenging for a viewer when a film becomes very quiet

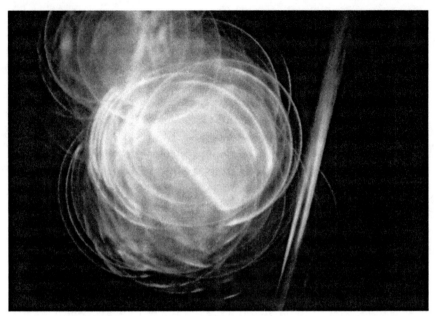

FIGURE 47 *Circles of light in Betzy Bromberg's* Voluptuous Sleep *(2011).*
Source: Courtesy Betzy Bromberg.

and still at its center, yet that structure was essential here and always clear to me. I'm glad that it works.

Part I ends exactly where it began, with the ephemeral circular lens image, the light circles. As soon as I saw the footage of these shots projected, I knew they would bookend Part I (figure 47).

At the beginning of making a film, I usually have an intrinsic under-standing of the content and form. The form evolves, and all the strands and details have to be developed, but the essence and the structure are gener-ally clear from the start. There was a period when I thought that "And the Night Illuminated the Night," might actually not be a separate part, but be embedded towards the end of Part I. I toyed with this concept throughout the shooting, but once I began to edit, it was clear to me that Part II was its own entity.

MacDonald: Part II is a nocturne, and feels more consistent, less modu-lated—partly because it's accompanied by a single, more consistent piece of music. Was Part II finished after or before Part I?

Bromberg: I edited Part II before Part I. The reason for this was that it was, as you suggest, very self-contained. Much of it came from one day's shoot (a spectacular day it was!). As I formulated *Voluptuous Sleep* in my mind, I wanted this part to be almost black and white, and to have a solid emotional gravity. Part II is also very flickery and I was concerned about whether or not an audience would be able to endure such a long duration of flicker. I myself can have great difficulties with traditional flicker films, so I wanted to edit Part II first to see if it could be watchable at all.

While editing Part II, I found myself often leaving large sections of footage as they were shot because there was a natural progression and rhythm that I thought was more interesting than any editing I could do. This also held true for Part I. I shoot in 100-foot loads, approximately 3 minutes worth of film each, and *Voluptuous Sleep* contains many complete 100-foot rolls from start to finish. This also made the negative cutting less laborious and saved the footage from additional film handling, another ploy of mine to keep the film as clean as possible.

I wasn't sure what the overall length would be when I began editing, but as I was shooting and plotting the edit, it became clear which shots would make up Part I and which would make up Part II. When I completed the edit for Part II, it timed in at 35 minutes, and I realized that Part I would probably be about an hour. This realization about the lengths of the two sections helped me understand the necessity of a cohesive accompanying track for Part II. I decided to work with a real composer (as opposed to me, a wannabe composer). Fully picture edited, the cut could be shown to Robert Allaire, who I rightly suspected would write an amazing score. Once I was able to get Bob involved, I was able to concentrate on Part I, first editing the picture, then doing the sound myself.

I wasn't able to hear Bob's composition until he had the piece finally performed and recorded; he felt that it would be best for me to wait until the musicians had practiced and properly recorded the actual piece. I knew all along that Bob was composing a string quartet, so I was able to incorporate strings into my soundscape for Part I, almost like a premonition or a foreshadowing. Everything worked out in the end, because Bob and I were on the same wavelength.

MacDonald: By the 1970s when you began making films, the idea that 16mm filmmaking was a *visual* art, a visual art to be enjoyed in silence—as in so much of Brakhage—had been replaced by a wholesale return of voice, sound effects, and music, and part of the exuberance of your early films includes your exploration of the uses of sound. *Voluptuous Sleep* is basically visual imagery accompanied by music. . .

Bromberg: . . . I *don't* think of *Voluptuous Sleep* as "visual imagery accompanied by music"! The soundscape for Part I is very complex, and I feel strongly that the experience of watching the film comes as much from the sound as it does from the visual imagery.

My original plan was that Part I would have an incredibly subtle soundtrack. At first I thought that "subtle" would mean "minimal," but I came to understand that that wasn't true. There is an enormous amount of sound in Part I. Because it *is* subtle, one would never know how many layers of sound and how many hours of sound work were required. Dane Davis, great friend and sound designer extraordinaire, generated many hours of raw sound material and sent it my way. I then spent months manipulating and treating that raw material, in addition to manipulating and treating a lot of material that I had recorded, then layering it all together in a complex weave, which Dane brilliantly mixed. In addition, there are segments of Zack Settel's music and a knock-out percussion piece by Jean-Pierre Bedoyan. Jean-Pierre's piece was performed and recorded as we projected a section of the edited work print in his living room.

For me, it is the combination of sound and visuals that creates *Voluptuous Sleep*. However, the sound functions very differently in each of the parts. In Part I, it is almost as if the images are generating the sound, as if these images would make those sounds. In Part II, the music and soundscape create a space for the imagery to live.

I guess the point you were making, really, is that I've abandoned any use of words in my recent soundtracks. I think I've come to avoid words because I'm more interested in creating alternative realities. At this point we're so thoroughly bombarded with verbiage and information that I'm in full retreat from the onslaught. I'd rather be elsewhere. I'm much more interested in creating dreamscapes and places of the interior. While I was working on *Voluptuous Sleep*, I spent a lot of time looking at Mark Rothko paintings and listening to Morton Feldman's music.

MacDonald: The final shot in "And the Night Illuminated the Night" seems to be a tiny waterfall. On first seeing that image, I understood it as a kind of punch line: as a revelation of the particular place where all of "And the Night" was filmed.

Bromberg: Both parts were shot in just a few small places! But the actual shooting place is no clearer in that last shot than in any of the other shots—meaning there is no small waterfall. You could walk around my yard for a century and never find where I was filming: it's not evident with normal sight, and as I mentioned earlier, all the elements have to come together—the light, the sun's trajectory, the shrubbery, the water. I love that last shot because, after so much movement, it's so seductive and mysterious and still.

I have a shot that does reveal much about the scale and place where I'm shooting, an amazing shot that I might use in Part III. But the "punch line" aspect makes me *not* want to use it!—though I think I've concocted a cut that might make the shot transcend its punch-line nature.

MacDonald: I understand the title "The Night Illuminated the Night" but am confused by "Language Is a Skin."

Bromberg: "Language is a Skin: I rub my language against the other. It is as if I had words instead of fingers, or fingers at the tip of my words. My language trembles with desire"—Roland Barthes, *A Lover's Discourse*. Images are also a language. *Voluptuous Sleep* is in some measure a film about sexual desire; its imagery is rich with cracks and crevices.

MacDonald: Like Peter Hutton and Tacita Dean, you've stuck with 16mm—even as opportunities for presenting 16mm prints have become less widespread. I'm one of those who feel that the *option* of screening 16mm prints must be kept alive—and that it is the obligation of those who identify themselves as Film Studies people to understand 16mm exhibition as an essential part of the infrastructure of the field—but I'm wondering about the nature of your commitment to 16mm. Do you plan to continue making celluloid cinema or is *Voluptuous Sleep* a swansong?

Bromberg: Presently I only shoot 16mm (in other words, I do not work with video or digital) and I continue to edit on a flatbed with 16mm work print. It is essential now more than ever for me to cut on film. *Voluptuous Sleep* has so much to do with the film image—meaning light projected through emulsion—that it would be impossible for me to cut digitally. If the final product were digital, it might not be a problem, but since I'm going to make film prints, I need to make all of my editing decisions based on the actual 16mm.

For *Voluptuous Sleep*, it became necessary to continuously project the film as I was editing it. The images read very differently projected large than if seen on the smaller screen of the flatbed where they lack depth and proper scale. I would cut on the flatbed for a couple of nights and then project, back to the flatbed, and then back to the projector, and so on.

For sound, I work digitally. I love Pro-Tools and having the ability to work with sound in extremely complex ways. I had no problem switching from cutting magnetic track on a flatbed to using Pro-Tools, once I was sure my sync would be accurate. I do find it essential to hear my sound with the actual film image to make sure I'm getting it right.

The sound mix for *Voluptuous Sleep* turned out to be much more difficult than anticipated. This was due to the inherent limitations of a 16mm mono optical track. The stereo mix went very well, but when Dane began to transform the stereo mix into a 16mm mono mix, it was, at first, a disaster. Because of the nature of the sounds used, Part I more easily converted to 16mm mono; but Part II was initially a mess. The luscious buttery sound of violins, I now know, is due to high-end harmonics. 16mm is not able to reproduce these high pitches; its range is limited. What is left is the miserable scratchy sound of a bow on a string. Dane and his engineer, David McRell, spent hours figuring out a way to simulate (fake) the thick lush violin sound onto 16mm optical. We ran sample tests from mix to release print to determine the exact capabilities of the 16mm optical. Genius that they were able to make the 16mm track sound so good.

Technically, the most difficult part of 16mm filmmaking is dealing with the laboratory. My expectations are always very high. From years of dealing with industry labs and having to produce extremely high quality work, I know the machinery and lab processes quite well. Too well! I'm obsessed with all things technical, obsessed about every dirt particle and imperfection that appears on the film surface! I try to convince myself that this is part of the beauty of film, of its physicality, but it doesn't seem to soothe my neurotic quest for the perfect film image.

I imagine I'll continue to work in film until either *I'm* done or *it's* done. Whichever comes first. There's no doubt that celluloid is on its way out. I'm lucky to live in Los Angeles where it's still possible for me to work. Within an hour's drive there's Kodak, Fuji, the lab, DaneTracks, 16mm theaters. But eventually, the feasibility of 16mm will be over. I'm already pushing the limit, in terms of the lab and 16mm optical track capabilities.

My filmmaking certainly reflects the fact that I'm working in a medium that's almost at its end. This inevitability has given me license to make the most of the medium, to saturate the film with as much light and color and sensuality as possible. The films I'm making now could not be made in any other medium, which is why I'm shooting them on film, while I still can.

Jennifer Proctor (on *A Movie by Jen Proctor*)

The differences between Betzy Bromberg's *Voluptuous Sleep* (2011) and Jennifer Proctor's *A Movie by Jen Proctor* (2012) are the differences between genera-tions. *Voluptuous Sleep* is a landmark instance of a long tradition of films about light, as well as a vestige of an earlier sense of avant-garde cinema: shot and distributed/exhibited in 16mm, it is a big film, a kind of perceptual epic, and *serious* in the sense that Brakhage's films were serious. Jennifer Proctor is a child of the 1990s and 2000s and while she is certainly attuned to the history of avant-garde filmmaking—she studied hands-on 16mm filmmak-ing and video at the University of Iowa—her work, including *A Movie by Jen Proctor*, requires no special screening situation and is easily accessed through her website and on Vimeo. Proctor is serious about her work and about the history it is part of, but her instinct is less to accomplish another remarkable film than to rethink the history she has inherited and in some instances to see it as raw material for her own work. Her *A Movie by Jen Proctor*, for example, is a nearly shot-by-shot remake of one of the most canonical of avant-garde films: Bruce Conner's *A Movie* (1958).

Of course, remakes are endemic to Hollywood, though what is remade in nearly all instances is a particular story, not a specific filmic rendition of that story. The lone exception I am aware of is Gus Van Sant's remake of Hitchcock's *Psycho* (1960/1998), which is remarkable and interesting, even if it fails to have anything like the impact of the original (in large measure because of its casting: the power of Hitchcock's film has to do with Anthony Perkins's performance as a young man who seems so unthreatening that an intelligent young woman, and the Hitchcock audience, would have no clear sense of the violence within him). The surprises in Van Sant's *Psycho* are not created by the plot, by the surprise of Norman Bates's double nature (and its implicit mirroring of the schizoid nature of Hitchcock's audience: harmless citizens by day, movie-goers hungry for mayhem in the darkness of the the-ater at night). Rather, the "shocks" in the remake are those few instances when Van Sant deviates from his otherwise rigorous shot-by-shot strategy: Norman masturbating as he peeks through the peephole at Marion, changes in the shower scene montage. . . Van Sant's is a kind of postmodern shock.

Shot-by-shot remakes have, until recently, been nearly as rare in inde-pendent cinema. In her *What Farocki Taught* (1998), Jill Godmilow remade

Harun Farocki's *Inextinguishable Fire* (1969), shot by shot, in order to retrieve the Farocki documentary from obscurity. James Benning remade his *One Way Boogie Woogie* (1977) in *One Way Boogie Woogie/27 Years Later* (2006), filming the same urban spaces in Milwaukee from the same positions decades later, and has often shown the two films together. There is also Kerry Tribe's live restaging of Hollis Frampton's *Critical Mass* (1971), where actors perform a simplified, de-cinematized approximation of the reworked argument at the center of the film. But these are exceptions that prove the rule.

What makes *A Movie by Jen Proctor* interesting is not simply its being a careful and inventive remake, but its way of simultaneously paying homage to a remarkable film and re-seeing both *A Movie* and Conner's way of producing it from within an entirely new technological context. While Conner collected prints of a wide range of films and edited them together with relatively simple splicing equipment, Proctor used her web browser to search out clips within the vast world of imagery archived online, then edited the results on her computer. Hers is a digital work recycling the essence of a 16mm film, transforming a quintessential filmic experience into a quintessential digital experience.

Further, while Van Sant's *Psycho* cannot begin to recreate the shock of Hitchcock's *Psycho*, the particular accomplishment of *A Movie by Jen Proctor* is Proctor's recreation of a sense of the impact that *A Movie* must have had in 1958, when its combination of materials and its diverse moods—its bizarre juxtapositions of humor and horror—would have seemed new. By the end of the twentieth century, the imagery in *A Movie* was so antiquated that images that might have seemed powerful in 1958 (nuclear detonations, for example) had become virtually generic. In her choices and juxtapositions of imagery, Proctor doesn't merely mimic *A Movie*, she retrieves something of its original power.

Proctor has made many kinds of work, from hand-processed autobiographical films and self-portraiture to sponsored projects to what she calls "voodles"—video doodles. While her work is sometimes presented as public screenings, mostly it is accessed through her website.

The following conversation was developed online during the summer of 2012.

MacDonald: In the films and videos you did before *A Movie by Jen Proctor*, you were trying your hand at a range of approaches, and it's clear that you particularly enjoyed working hands-on with the filmmaking process, in part, as you've said in interviews, because it allows for surprise since one can't predict precisely how a hand-made, hand-processed film will look. And yet, *A Movie by Jen Proctor* is a nearly shot-by-shot remake of a canonical avant-garde film: that is, a project that *is* relatively predictable, even constraining.

Proctor: I am certainly interested in—and embrace—constraints in my work (handmade films, while unpredictable, are nonetheless confined to whatever accidents are produced in the process, and you have to find a way to work with them), so the idea of working within the boundaries of a pre-existing film appealed to me. I knew it would also be a way to expand my own style and cinematic vocabulary—I get very bored and frustrated with being "me" cinematically; I find it much more interesting to step into someone else's shoes (or give up control, as with my handmade work). As much as I adore popular narrative film. I have no interest in being totally in control of the process of creating something.

Over the years I've also thought about a writing assignment I did in high school—a popular kind of assignment, I'm sure—in which I had to rewrite an author's essay using the same grammatical structure but with different words, on a different topic. It was the first time I truly experienced an alternative to my native style of writing, and it blew open possibilities; the same is true with a careful film remake.

MacDonald: Were the film/video production faculty at the University of Iowa important for you?

Proctor: Yes, of course. Leighton Pierce opened me to a new way of listening. I adore Franklin Miller's 1970s films; like Michael Snow's work, they have a fantastic sense of humor but also conceptual rigor and aesthetic vision (*Cold Cows* [1977] is a favorite). And Sasha Waters Freyer uses found footage in inventive ways, blending aesthetic experimentation with documentary.

MacDonald: While remaking earlier narrative fiction features is quite normal in Hollywood, the idea of a shot-by-shot remake is nearly unprecedented in the industry and, until very recently, rare in independent film.

Proctor: During grad school I collaborated on a shot-by-shot remake of *Ballet Mechanique* [1924], filmed on 16mm and optically printed, but with footage of contemporary machinery/electronics. Neat film, but with technical issues, so it didn't have a life beyond the classroom.

More recently, I've been inspired by previous avant-garde remakes: Jill Godmilow's superb *What Farocki Taught* and especially Ben Coonley's fantastic *Wavelength 3D* [2003] which remakes Snow's work as a contemporary 3D video (perhaps more prank than full-fledged remake, but delightful nonetheless, and in keeping with what I see as Snow's wonderful and pun-tastic sense of humor). Also, I've contributed to *Man with a Movie Camera: The Global Remake* [ongoing], an online, global, crowd-sourced remake of the Vertov film [http://dziga.perrybard.net/].

After making *A Movie by Jen Proctor*, I came to realize that I was taking part in a rather widespread movement of using digital technologies to remake avant-garde films, which now includes Evan Meaney's *Ceibas: Epilogue—The Well of Representation* [2011], a remake of Frampton's *Gloria!* [1979]; Bill Brown's *Kustom Kamera Kommandos* [2008], his remake of Anger's *Kustom Kar Kommandos* [1965]; and Eric Fleischauer's remake of Hans Richter's *Rhythmus 21* [1921] as *Rhythmus 21st Century* [2011]. Meaney is also working on a kind of remake of *Decasia* [2002; Bill Morrison], and of course I've remade McCall's *Line Describing a Cone* [1973]. I'm doing some writing on this trend.

At a recent screening, someone in the audience asked what I thought about the idea that avant-garde filmmakers, who were expected to be ground-breaking and pioneering—forward-looking—are now turning to the past. Of course, all art springs from the past, but it was an interesting question. I don't have a fully formed answer yet, but there is certainly a sense of the loss of *film* as a medium that I think a number of these makers are exploring by trans-lating filmic works into digital forms as a way of looking at the differences between them.

And, of course, the explosion of digital expression, just the sheer volume and variety of digital work, entails a different kind of loss; it's become, in some ways, more difficult to *be* avant-garde. These days, some of the most interest-ing unconventional work is coming out on YouTube and/or is generated by accident or by people unfamiliar with the context of film history just goofing around. I love that—but I also think a lot of us are looking back, trying to make sense of what's come before in order to understand where we are now.

MacDonald: What led you to a remake of *A Movie* in particular?

Proctor: The impetus to remake *A Movie* came from repeated viewings in the intro film classes I teach and watching how students react. I find Conner's titles absolutely hysterical and I've always been amused by the idea that while most students have no idea who Conner is, they understand the humor in those titles. Of course, the film also contains tropes still popular today—the "America's Funniest Home Videos"/YouTube compilations of pratfalls, goofy bicycles, and boneheaded accidents. Perhaps in that way my students responded more as original audiences might have: that is, without the context of Conner's lifetime body of work. To see *A Movie* now, *knowing* Conner's achievements, means that the film has more echoes and layers than it might originally have had (figures 48a, 48b).

So I started thinking about what it would mean if a real nobody—someone like me—put her name in huge letters on the screen: "A MOVIE BY JEN PROCTOR." It's ridiculous, especially because it seems to place me on the same level as someone now recognized as one of the great artists of the twen-tieth century. And I'm a woman—given how few of us get our names in huge letters as directors of mainstream films, the ridiculousness is even more pro-nounced: it would throw into relief what Conner was after, retrieving the element of prank from a film that is now canonical. When a film that sets out to jam culture and poke authority in the eye enters the canon, its subversive-ness is largely removed; the prank turns highbrow.

In the past few years, my creative interests have also shifted away from film and into the online realm. I'm fascinated by the way that our experiences with moving image and sound have made their way onto the computer, a tiny screen often watched in isolation with tinny speakers or earbuds. And I'm

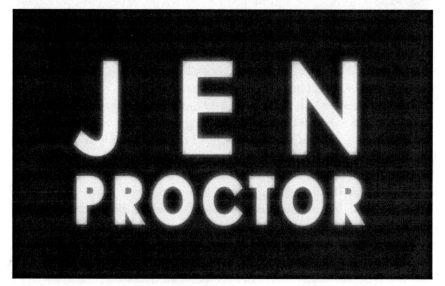

FIGURES 48A, B *(above) Title "A MOVIE" in Bruce Conner's* A Movie *(1958); and (below), in Jennifer Proctor's* A Movie by Jen Proctor *(2012).*

Source: Courtesy Bruce Conner and Jennifer Proctor.

especially interested in the access we now have to visual databases that are growing at a rate of thousands of hours a day on sites like YouTube and Vimeo. The mashup, of which *A Movie* is a pioneer, has taken off, and I couldn't help but think about what *A Movie* might look like in this online context.

This was swirling around in my head as I watched *A Movie* with my students, semester after semester, but I couldn't decide whether such a remake would be cheap and gimmicky or actually meaningful until I started putting the footage together—and then, the power and logic of the film's structure became apparent. The structure of *A Movie*—even if somewhat random, based on the footage Conner was able to find—is beautifully taut.

I came to feel that if you followed his thread through the film, you could switch footage every year and the film would still be powerful.

MacDonald: How long did you work on *A Movie by Jen Proctor*? At any point were you in contact with Conner?

Proctor: Sadly, this piece was set in motion after Conner's death, so no, I was never in correspondence with him. Because his estate has been rather protective of his work, part of me was nervous about remaking *A Movie*, so I haven't been in direct contact with anyone associated with him.

The bulk of the video took about three weeks to make—as often seems the case, the piece that I spent the least amount of time on has gotten the most attention! Someone rightly mentioned that the video doesn't ever have to be "finished"—up until now an approach I've been uncomfortable with: when a work is done, I like to feel that it's *done*. But I've taken that comment to heart with this piece, and have returned to "fix" a couple parts that never felt right. Of course, I could continue to update it forever—I don't think I'll do that, but for right now, I date the video as 2010–2012 to account for the revisions.

I should mention that *A Movie by Jen Proctor* is not a perfect shot-for-shot remake; I was working from a bad bootleg copy of the original, and having seen a good print of the film recently, I realized there were a number of details and a few flash frames that I missed because they weren't visible in the bootleg. But, of course, that's part of the mediated process of a digital remake.

MacDonald: The decision to do a shot-by-shot remake must have led to other decisions. What rules did you set for yourself in the process of finding the imagery that you ended up using?

Proctor: There are more shots in my piece per original shot in Conner's, in part to play with the idea of the increased pace of editing in digital film. But yes, I did have some rules. Mainly, I started by looking for images that were parallel to the original images, but that bore the mark of contemporary culture. So the Hindenburg becomes a blimp advertising Ron Paul; military parachuting becomes BASE jumping; oversized and tiny makeshift bicycles become Lombard Street tricycle races and Red Bull "flugtag" competitions; the woman removing her garter becomes several women doing so, including what appears to be a kinky man in a mask; bombs dropping are now portrayed in infrared, and the woman on the other side of the periscope is in FLIR [infrared recording]. The sexual metaphor of the submarine missile being deployed remains, but in the remake it's impotent—the missile slides out and falls to the ground: a statement about contemporary military technology.

As I started searching for these images, I also discovered interesting aesthetic shifts. For example, much of the chase scene at the beginning of the remake is in first-person point of view, a result of new small, mountable cameras. A mark of contemporary culture is the absurdity of images afforded by ubiquitous and highly mobile cameras: dogs or cows running down the side of the road are uploaded to YouTube alongside archival images of 9/11.

One of the key differences in my process from Conner's is that he was working with images he had truly *found*; he worked with what he had. By comparison, I was searching an enormous database with nearly infinite options, and that introduced distressing ethical problems for me. For instance, I found myself searching for images of suffering and destruction, but having to judge which clips did or didn't work with the piece. Not only was I watching a lot of tragic footage, but I was having to reject a lot of it for rather superficial aesthetic reasons, which didn't sit well.

The section in *A Movie* that includes footage of starving, weeping Africans was what did me in; I couldn't bear actively searching for the "right" footage of starving, suffering people. So I shifted to a very different kind of image, one rather popular on the confessional outlet of YouTube: crying teenagers. This actually became one of my favorite sections of the remake because it's such a visceral comment on our contemporary media ecosystem that images of (what appear to be) privileged adolescents weeping are more ubiquitous than images of real victims of natural disaster or war, and that such images are largely performed explicitly for the camera (a shift from observational footage to direct address). Indeed, I found a meme of YouTubers demonstrating their ability to cry on command for the camera. This kind of media consciousness on the part of the subjects of the found footage is largely absent from Conner's piece, and becomes one of the key markers of the remake. *But* it's also funny—and funny partly because whatever these kids might be crying about is trivial compared to the images around them— we can't help but scoff at them, even as we might recognize that we've been there ourselves.

A couple of the most powerful (and perhaps controversial) departures are my use of video game footage and the inclusion of imagery of the 9/11 attacks, particularly the images of the people who jumped from the towers. *A Movie* includes footage of a firing squad, while the remake offers live-action paintball shooting and clips of a video game firing squad. Many clips of war dead and bombs in the original are replaced by unrated footage of gory video-game zombie kills ("unrated" means the game contains ultra-violence).

MacDonald: Near the end we see a terrifying image of someone on fire; is that from a video game?

Proctor: Yes, unrated.

MacDonald: Wow, I thought it was real! I've had almost no experience with videogames since the era of Ms. Pac-Man!

Proctor: These particular deviations from *A Movie* are less about their content and more about media representation: all of these alternative, fictional representations of death are readily at our fingertips, alongside and on equal footing with images of *actual* war. Indeed, we're less likely to see raw footage of war and war dead now, even as we regularly watch digital bodies ripped to pieces. Even audiences unfamiliar with the original can take from the remake a critique of contemporary media culture and, particularly, Western obsessions with violence. Eisensteinian montage is itself, of course, a violent editing strategy.

The inclusion of the 9/11 footage has elicited the most criticism (and support) because that imagery is so loaded. The original didn't contain anything nearly as inflammatory as that footage. But it struck me as a serious omission not to include it—that imagery is perhaps more imprinted on modern memory than any other. And now, of course, we rarely see that footage anymore—we don't really need to because it's so present in our minds. The footage of the Hindenburg in *A Movie* functioned this way to some degree; it was a rare recording of tragedy that became notorious because the images and sound were seared into public memory. While the Hindenburg tragedy is certainly not on par with the 9/11 attacks, my video makes us confront that WTC footage again, makes it visible again. And the footage of the people who jumped, in particular, makes us confront what we will and won't accept for popular consumption, with all its contradictions and hypocrisy.

Interestingly, because this video is made up of material readily available on YouTube and LiveLeak (and LiveLeak is important; it's a less-censored YouTube, popular with military uploaders), it also introduces the question of what it means to be a passive viewer, as for example with television news— we don't quite know what's coming, so we rely on newscasters to maintain certain boundaries of taste for us—versus active viewing that requires us to search out footage. So the imagery of the 9/11 jumpers is "inappropriate" for the passive TV experience, but perfectly acceptable if you desire to search it out on YouTube: it's right there on the Internet. And, of course, so is everything else you could want (including Conner's *A Movie*!).

Having said all this, I should say that for me, my remake is endlessly haunted by the original, and forever made more interesting by its relationship with Conner's work.

MacDonald: My guess is that *A Movie* was more jolting in its time than you seem to think. Remember, Conner's film was made during an era where there was virtually no violence in movies or on television. Seeing a live-action firing squad actually killing someone would have had much more power for many viewers back then. And nuclear detonations were becoming frightening; the era was full of demonstrations against the arms race and the Bomb.

These days it's easy to read the Hindenburg disaster as a premonition of the fall of the Third Reich. Is your use of the World Trade Center imagery, at least on one level, a mordant commentary on American empire?

Proctor: In addition to the WTC collapse, I include lots of footage of controlled demolitions of buildings, which of course echo the fall of the WTC. And that's purposeful, again as a kind of comment about our fascination with destruction: we've turned building demolitions into planned public spectacles to which audiences are invited. And they *are* exhilarating—I would line up to watch one too.

There *is* definitely a comment on empire in my piece (see the impotent missile launch mentioned above), and not just American, but Western empire (which is evident in the Conner version, augmented by the use of Respighi's *The Pines of Rome*, also used in my remake). To some extent *A Movie by Jen Proctor* is about privilege and power and the absurd and petty behavior of the citizens of wealthy nations. Here, again, point of view becomes important: much of the thrill of the chase at the beginning is in first-person POV, all about ME, documenting MY point of view, giving it priority. And, of course, almost all of those clips are of sports only available to the privileged—race boats, motorbikes, four-wheel driving, mountain biking, etcetera. The footage of tragedy, on the other hand, is all observational, filmed by outsiders. So there is a comment there about the distance that the "developed world" places between itself and "developing countries" within media representation.

And yet—and this is important—there's still a primal, visceral delight in watching all those people in costumes on their funny bicycles and miniature motorcycles and crashing on water skis and inner-tubes. And, I would argue, there's also genuine compassion and humanity in viewing the scenes from Katrina and Haiti. So while there is a critique contained in my remake, it's not a monolithic, seamless message. I can't fully read it as any kind of prediction about empire and its impending collapse. And my video, like Conner's film, ends optimistically, looking out from the dark abyss of the sea to the hopeful light above: the promise of ascension.

MacDonald: I read that final image in *A Movie* differently, as an image seen from a momentary and futile hide-out by someone so terrified by the potential destructiveness of modern culture that he can only try to hide at the bottom of the ocean.

How much research did you do on the material you included?

Proctor: I did want to make sure that I had a strong sense of the origins of the video images: some are from home-videos, others are TV recordings that someone uploaded. Still others were commercially produced and posted. I also wanted to make sure that as much as possible I had some sense of the context of the video so that I didn't include an image that had political implications I didn't understand. But the imagery wasn't researched beyond that.

As with so much of my work, my interest in remaking *A Movie* stemmed largely from what I would learn in the process; that the film works as a final product is just the icing on the cinematic cake. It was an experiment in the true sense of the word: what happens if I do *this*? And what happens if I do THIS instead? That's the joy of working with a template like Conner's original film.

MacDonald: I've also seen *Spline Describing a Phone* [2012], your "remake" of Anthony McCall's *Line Describing a Cone* [1973]. Could you describe the ways in which it comments on the McCall film?

Proctor: I'm still thinking of this piece as a work-in-progress because I'm not sure that it's all the way there conceptually, but my first experience participating in McCall's original piece—set up in a performance space in Austin, Texas, about ten years ago—absolutely took my breath away, and that sensation has been on my mind ever since.

I'm always watching to see what new portable image technologies are coming out, and I was struck by the advent of tiny video projectors—pico projectors—which got me thinking about how they might work to produce sculptural light. Remakes have been on my mind, obviously, and in some ways, ideas start as a play with the titles of the original work, so a little punning led to "Line Describing a Phone," with an iPhone attached to a pico projector, which led to the idea of miniaturizing McCall's piece.

What once required a 25-pound mechanical hulk to project the light can now fit in one's pocket. The miniature functions as an intimate condensation of reality and, in a sense, an evocation of memory (I'm thinking, in particular, of Joseph Cornell's memory boxes—and Vivian Sobchack's writing about them). The miniature is precious and we may long to be small to be able to partake in it.

I'm also focused on ghosts and haunting these days, and the unattainability of the miniature renders it ghost-like—both there and not-there. Much of my thinking about remakes right now is about the way that they are, on some level, inextricable from their sources, which always haunt the background. Of course, the texture of smoke illuminated by light is itself ghostly—visible but nearly untouchable. And there's the notion of interactivity: allowing viewer/participants to reach in and become part of the installation, to shape it themselves—to *play*, which is such a huge part of creative experimentation. Remaking McCall's piece gave me an opportunity to play with these concerns.

I remember you asking me at the Ann Arbor Film Festival about my decision to use color in the piece, and I've been thinking about that—indeed, that's where I think the piece needs punching up. The use of the almost ridiculously saturated colors afforded by a laser pico projector comes with a smack of kitsch and always an "oooh" from spectators—confirming the notion of the miniature as something child-like and wonderful. And that's what struck me so much about McCall's original, the sense of wonder at something so elemental: just light, smoke, and time.

I've also been thinking about the role of humor in my work (and life!); in some respects humor—or at least tongue-in-cheekiness—is a built-in element of a remake, particularly an experimental film remake, which should seem impossible: how does one *remake* something that is meant to be wholly original, personal, inimitable?

MacDonald: Conner became increasingly concerned, as the media world changed around him, about having not gotten permissions to use the imagery and music in his films. Indeed, as a result, he worked very hard to keep his work off the Internet and available only as 16mm prints. You made *A Movie by Jen Proctor* during an era when copyright issues have become downright scary. How did the current media climate play into making your video and into your distribution strategy for the piece?

Proctor: Certainly, copyright was a concern from the get-go, but I'm a fervent supporter and practitioner of the Fair Use exception to copyright law, and I would argue that this film with all its copyrighted work (Conner's film, the YouTube/LiveLeak footage, the music) falls under Fair Use. While the legal climate with regard to copyright *is* scary, there's also a powerful coalition of Fair Use advocates and defenders, so while I'm on guard about my use of copyright, I'm also quite confident. I do give careful thought to each piece of copyrighted material to ensure that it *is* a fair use, and I feel able to defend my choices (not that it would stop my being issued a cease and desist or from being sued, but I'll deal with that should the time come).

MacDonald: Your piece is a video, not a film—though I assume you consider both films and videos *movies*. Did you consider calling the piece "A Video by Jen Proctor"?

Proctor: I thought of a *lot* of titles: "A Movie: The Sequel," "A Movie Part II," "The Movie," "Another Movie"—all bad. It did occur to me to call it "A Video," but you're right, it's not a video, it's a *movie*—just like *A Movie* isn't "A Film."

I didn't want to make the piece explicitly about format. To distinguish it from the original, and to punch up the humor, I added my name to the title. One thing's for sure: when your movie title has your name in it, people get to know who you are at film festivals! And yet the joke of the title is about nobody knowing who I am.

Jane Gillooly (on *Suitcase of Love and Shame*)

There are filmmakers who find their métier early in their careers and continue to work in a generally predictable way for a lifetime; Frederick Wiseman and Peter Hutton can serve as examples. And there are filmmakers whose approach seems to change with every project. Over the past twenty years Jane Gillooly has completed three feature-length documentaries, each of which involved a different production process and has a different kind of impact. *Leona's Sister Gerri* (1995) is an activist film focusing on a photograph of a woman dead from a botched abortion, which became an important symbol in the struggle for abortion rights. Gillooly explores the personal history behind this photograph and its political history, using talking-head interviews with family members and friends, photographs, and filmed images of demonstrations for women's reproductive rights.

For *Today the Hawk Takes One Chick* (2008), Gillooly traveled to the Lubombo region of Swaziland, which was suffering from the world's highest incidence of HIV and lowest life expectancy, to document grandmothers taking care of young children whose parents have died and who are, in some cases, suffering the ravages of AIDS. The film focuses on those who are working to support these grandmothers and to do what they can to alleviate suffering, both in clinics and in remote villages. *Today the Hawk Takes One Chick* is generally observational.

In 2013 Gillooly finished *Suitcase of Love and Shame* in which excerpts of audiotapes made by two lovers involved in an illicit love affair during the early 1960s create an ongoing narrative and a window into that era. In *Suitcase*, Gillooly reverses the usual deployment of sound and image in cinema: here, the soundscape becomes the foreground of the experience, and the imagery, which is more characteristic of avant-garde filmmaking than conventional documentary, the accompaniment. The experience of the film is virtually unprecedented in the annals of either documentary or avant-garde cinema, and is both revealing and somewhat harrowing.

My conversation with Gillooly, who is on the graduate faculty of the school of the Museum of Fine Arts, Boston, was conducted online during the spring and summer of 2013, as *Suitcase of Love and Shame* was making its way around the festival circuit.

MacDonald: How did you came to be in possession of the tapes that form the basis for *Suitcase of Love and Shame*?

Gillooly: I was looking for collections. I'd been researching a film about "time" with S. A. Bachman, an artist friend. One thought was to work with a collection of objects that had been assembled over a long period—the concept being to trace the sources and significance of the objects and interpret their imbedded meanings within a contemporary context. This was partially inspired by my coming across a collection of my own, a box of all the birth control I've used in my life. Unsurprisingly a vast amount of information can be extracted from the contents of that box: medical, personal, political, societal, and sexual—it conjures so much.

My friend Albert Steg, who knew what I was thinking about, discovered the suitcase on eBay in December of 2009. He shared the discovery with me and asked if I wanted him to place a bid. I did, of course, and no one bid against me.

MacDonald: What was in that suitcase? How much tape material, and what else?

Gillooly: Approximately 60 hours of audio material—most of it was Tom and Jeannie, but there were a few audio newsreels, which I suspect they were going to tape over if they ran out of stock—they did that on occasion. A few of the tapes were events they recorded: an American Veterinary Medical Association lecture, for example; and there were also recordings of record albums, of one Red Foxx Comedy Hour; of someone's wedding. And there were photographs and slides in the suitcase, and letters, phone bills, photo processing and audiotape receipts, name tags, matchbook covers, a bottle opener.

MacDonald: At what point did it occur to you that these tapes might be reworked into a piece, and in particular, a film?

Gillooly: I knew immediately this would be a film. The fact that the collection was primarily audiotape gave me instant access to narrative. And the fact that it was reel-to-reel audio was intriguing. I have a history of working with audiotape; my first two nonfiction projects, *No Applause* [1984] and *So Sad, So Sorry, So What* [1988-90], were audiotape-and-slide pieces, using three and four projectors. Each of these works was audio driven and in each, as in *Suitcase of Love and Shame*, the imagery was minimal.

The audiotapes arrived in a hard-bodied suitcase, the one you see in the film. I already knew from the initial eBay ad that the tapes chronicled an affair. The very first impression was the smell: it smelled like mildew—not a good sign as far as preservation is concerned. I was also struck by how well organized the material was. The tapes and the reel-to-reel boxes were labeled, dated, and in some cases notated clearly with other details.

MacDonald: What were your thoughts as you first listened to the tapes?

Gillooly: I never knew what I was going to hear, and I was constantly surprised. And I was as uncomfortable listening to some of the tapes as I imagine some audience members are when they experience *Suitcase of Love and Shame*.

However, unlike what you hear in the film, what I heard was often completely baffling. I listened to the tapes randomly, trying to make some sense of how what I was hearing might relate to the themes that were beginning to emerge: the obsession with technology, the use of personal performance and how that differed if Jeannie and Tom were alone or together; the idea of the "memory library," as Jeannie referred to the tapes; the daily grind—they regularly informed each other of the trials and tribulations of their separate lives; Jeannie's recurring "pressuring-but-loving" lectures trying to convince Tom to leave his wife and his equally loving demands for more time.

By disregarding the chronology of the tapes, I gave myself the freedom to re-present the material. I decided early on that I would reconstruct their story according to what I imagined could have happened, "writing" the narrative as I listened and eventually listening for content that supported the narrative I was imagining.

The feeling that I was eavesdropping was something I wanted to retain in the film. When I was digitizing a tape, I couldn't stop the tape recorder for fear of damaging the tape, so I listened to many extremely banal conversations, as well as to Tom's and Jeannie's expressions of the excruciating pain they were in. At times I was so affected by what one of them was doing that I physically had to move away from my desk. In the film I spared the audience the full-on experience of the emotional trauma as well as the dreadfully boring repetitions. No one needs to hear Jeannie cry for 30 minutes straight to know she was despondent, or hear Tom read her every hourly event in his date book to know he was a busy man. With that said, it was exciting every time I sat down to digitize another tape.

So, what unfolds in *Suitcase* is not the actual beginning, middle, end of the affair. I chose from among the more interesting scenes or events or in some cases created scenes from multiple tapes made months apart or sequenced a series of events in an order to increase the suspense.

MacDonald: Once you knew what you had, what kinds of research did you do relating to this material?

Gillooly: Investigation is such a satisfying part of filmmaking. This is the third film I've either directed or produced that involved researching people who lived in the Sixties. I approached all three films in a similar way—sleuthing the way any private detective might. I have to know as much about my subjects as possible before I can begin to think about structuring a film. What I learn helps inform what I do with the material—in this case how I was going to portray Jeannie and Tom, how their personalities would be reflected in the locations I devised for each of them.

I know, but am not comfortable revealing, specifically where Jeannie and Tom lived. I want to protect their anonymity, but I also don't feel that knowing this is important. I believe the film is much stronger for your *not* knowing—*Suitcase of Love and Shame* represents a way of life that was not exclusive to Tom and Jeannie or to any particular American location.

I do know their last names and have post office box numbers in various towns where I presume they lived. I did web searches and found a list of people that could have been them. I traveled to the Midwest and went to various locations that had been mentioned on the tapes and looked through court records and city directories. Starting from what I believed were their last known addresses, I worked my way forward in time. When I do research, I always establish relationships with the librarians, clerks, or record keepers in the state depositories or courthouses where I'm working, and return to the same person as I need follow-up information. I find most people eager to be helpful.

There were many clues on the tapes themselves. Given a street name or post office box associated with Tom or Jeannie, I could cross-reference those addresses with a business or a hotel they might have mentioned. I found my way to one city that way. I also made some informed guesses. Once I knew Jeannie's age and had established what I believed to be her last home, I got a list of nursing homes in the area and guessed correctly which one she would be in. I walked in and asked for her.

I came prepared to tell her everything I knew, and I did. As it turned out, Jeannie was very communicative although she has dementia. I told her I had her tapes, which had been sold at an estate sale or an auction and ended up on Ebay. I explained that I knew a lot about her from listening to the tapes. She remembered recording audiotape as part of her job as some kind of veterinary technician. When I told her that the tapes I had were intimate tapes she had made with a doctor, she remembered Tom and spoke about him in a professional way, then changed the subject.

As you might imagine, talking to someone with dementia was peculiar and disjointed. She recalled certain things about that period of her life, but I don't know how selective her memory was.

MacDonald: Tell me more about the process of working from the original tapes to the story you end up telling.

Gillooly: I wanted the contents of the film to be drawn from the contents in the suitcase. If it was spoken or recorded on one of the tapes, then it could be considered for inclusion. In time I had an ongoing assembly of material that fit a conventional narrative arc of an illicit love story.

There was far more material than I could include. Fortunately, it became a process of my choosing from among fascinating yet similar material. There was much more about the personal toll this was taking on each of them than you hear in *Suitcase*, more detailing of their relationships with their families, and more explicit descriptions of their sexual exploits. And the tapes were rich with identifiable background sounds and atmosphere, filled with historical detail and references to mid-century popular culture.

MacDonald: I saw several different versions of *Suitcase* during the years you were working on it, and as I remember, each version included more imagery than the previous one.

Gillooly: The amount of imagery evolved over time. At first, I was reluctant to add images because I wanted to create what I imagined as a listening environment. I wanted to heighten the sense that the audience was eavesdropping, as well as provide a visual void that listeners could project into. If you lived at that time or recognize the Fifties–Sixties references, the audio is sometimes remarkably "visual."

My first cut was 30 minutes long and had no images at all. I debated releasing an audio-only version and decided against it—I do plan to release *Suitcase* in a primarily audio version for gallery exhibition; I'm working on that now.

Slowly, I began to add imagery. The first images were abstract and impressionistic. In fact, that first version had the advantage of coaxing the viewer to look more deeply to consider what each image *was*. I liked the idea that the audience would sometimes feel as if they were taking in an image, but not really watching a film—though I grew concerned that the abstract, blurry imagery, which I loved, would begin to feel gratuitous.

I had also begun imagining where Tom and Jeannie were when they made the tapes, which led to designing or finding locations that I could associate with each of them. His were more internal and claustrophobic and hers, more about waiting and longing. Obviously by positioning the camera I could satisfy my initial idea of positioning the *audience* (including me) as eavesdroppers. We are outside the window or on the other side of the door.

Discovering or creating one set of images would lead to other ideas. For those who notice, we (my director of photography, Beth Cloutier, and my co-editor Pam Larson) were very deliberate in how the tape recorders were filmed. Whether a tape recorder was on play or record complicates the issue of who is operating the deck. In time you come to discover that other people, besides Jeannie and Tom, were listening to the tapes.

The slow pace of the film was working for me so I began to add motion picture images of what at first appear to be extended static shots. In one instance, you're looking down from a window at a street corner and only realize that the shot is a motion picture, when the color of the pavement shifts from red to green after an off-screen stoplight changes.

Some ideas came purely from my proximity to the material. I kept a slide projector in my studio and would periodically cycle through the slides that belonged to Jeannie and Tom. I decided to project the slides into a corner of my room so that I could crop them in a way that would provide glimpses of the couple without revealing what they looked like, as well as to take advantage of details in the images: the 8-Ball toy, the food at a picnic, etcetera.

MacDonald: At times, we'll hear sound events that *may* have been happening on the tapes or might have been recorded by you and added to the mix later; is *all* the sound we hear from the tapes?

Gillooly: For the most part I used the sounds I found on the tapes, but some of the sound is designed. Often I took recognizable background sounds (footsteps, talking in hallways, doors closing, intercoms, mike-cable noise, coughs) and used them as Foley in other places or layered them to build up a sound bed.

I wanted to fatten the machine noise that was audible on the original tapes. I managed to locate working vintage tape recorders of the kinds that Tom and Jeannie mentioned using. As reflected in the imagery, Tom's is the green/brown Webcore and Jeannie's, the white Wollensak (figures 49a, 49b). With the help of Rob Todd, I made additional recordings of machine noise (the hum of the recording deck motors and the whirling of the reels, etcetera). This allowed us to thicken the aural atmosphere, create additional room tone with the sound of the tape recorder associated with each person.

There is also a small amount of illustrative sound: a running shower, a lawn mower, and sync sound recorded in the locations where I shot. The nature sounds were recorded in the Midwest in the towns where Tom and Jeannie lived. The sound of the elevator in the hotel was added, but that *was* the elevator in the very hotel where that tape was made. As far as TV, radio, singing along to record albums, all of that was recorded by Tom and Jeannie, except for the NASA Radio Program from 1963 (that was a tape I had of my father, who worked in the aeronautics industry, being interviewed about the Gemini Space Craft).

MacDonald: Ultimately *Suitcase* is a case study of illicit love during a certain moment of American history. The way the lovers talk with each other and the kinds of things they think to say seem largely a function of the culture that surrounded them.

Gillooly: Certainly their behavior and manner of speech reflected their era and their class. They were middle class, with some disposable income, and were consumed by the popular culture of the time—diet drinks had just come out, for instance, and they might refer to a drink as if they were actors in a commercial. They discussed what they wore, what they ate, the movies and TV shows they watched, their hobbies and pastimes.

I was particularly interested in material that challenged what we think of as typical of the Sixties. This was a decade that would soon spawn the sexual revolution, which we associate with youth culture. These lovers were a generation older than college students but they were living their own sexual revolution secretly. Yet, I also wanted the film to address the morals laws, societal mores, and inhibited lives of adult Americans in the Sixties. They had a real fear of being charged with adultery.

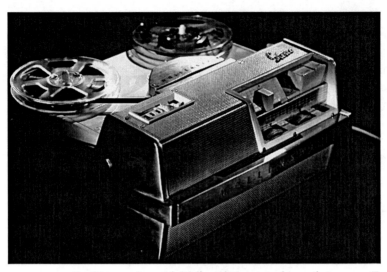

FIGURES 49A, 49B *On this page, Jeannie's Wollensak tape recorder; on facing page, Tom's Webcore.*

Source: Courtesy Jane Gillooly.

To me it was obvious that Jeannie encouraged the sexual relationship as much or more than Tom. I wanted it to be apparent that she was in control of her sexual life, and of all aspects of her life, in a pre-feminist time. It was difficult to emphasize this in the film, but she is the one who stages the sex scenes: the one who sets the recording levels, decides the placement of the microphone, and checks the tapes afterward.

MacDonald: Suitcase is harrowing to sit through, both alone and especially with an audience. What has been your experience of the audiences who have seen the film?

Gillooly: I find myself admitting to audiences that I felt as uncomfortable listening to the tapes the first time, as I make them feel. The material is so startlingly real that it can be unsettling. Tom and Jeannie were often performing for the tape recorder but at the same time they were inventing a form.

There is also a very sad quality that comes across as Tom and Jeannie become resigned to the inevitable end of the affair. I know the audience relates to the human emotion in the recordings and the fact that the couple does not disguise the pain they are in. And in those moments I do not cut away. The recordings were made in a uniquely unselfconscious state with the goal of reaching out to another human being—the lover—so much so that we listeners, a half century later, can feel as though they are speaking directly to us, that we are in the room with them. Yet we know that Tom and Jeannie never expected these tapes to be heard by anyone. In these moments of pure despondency, when they do not mask their feelings of utter misery, *my* heart at least is breaking for them.

FIGURE 49B
Source: Courtesy Jane Gillooly.

I believe it is this, the sadness of it all, coupled with the way the film forces the audience to face, within a public sphere, their own feelings about privacy and regret that causes some audience members to challenge my use of the tapes.

MacDonald: The performance element of the tapes sometimes verges on the surreal: at one point Jeannie is talking to Tom via tape (a tape he will hear, but not until later) as she is waiting at a hotel for him to join her. The phone rings; she stops talking to the tape recorder to answer and talk to Tom, who is the caller; then, when the phone call is over, continues her *taped* conversation with Tom, who presumably has been held up and may not make the rendezvous. The taping seems the *real* connection with Tom; the phone call, an interruption of it.

In another instance, Tom and Jeannie both speak to the tape recorder, describing their visit to Chicago. Their affair is secret; do they expect to get together and listen to themselves? And yet, of course, why not—I think we do assume they listen to the tapes of their sexual interaction.

Gillooly: The moments you mention so fascinated me that they shaped my approach to the edit. Sometimes the tape recorder seems not only a witness but a participant. There's a scene where they've just made love and Jeannie speaks to the tape recorder: "I don't know if you were able to pick up on all that." I wanted these moments to illustrate the ménage à trois of Jeannie, Tom, and the Wollensak, as well as to call into question the location of the listener—who *is* Jeannie speaking to?

Tom and Jeannie did listen to the tapes, especially the sexual ones. They made copies of the recorded sexual encounters so they both could have them. They also listened to the tapes when they were lonely for one another. In another cut of the film, I used a comment that Jeannie made about placing her earphones on the pillow next to her as she played Tom's tapes and pretended he was there.

The Chicago tapes were special to them because it was one of the few times they met up outside of a work-related trip and were completely free to be out in public together. I thought of those four tapes as their "audio snapshots." The only photo from Chicago is the two of them holding hands on the street; it must have been taken by a passing stranger.

I love that you described Jeannie's taped conversation as the real connection with Tom and the phone call, an interruption. I often wondered if the tapes allowed them to create an alternate "ideal relationship," at least as much of one as was possible, rather than admit their actual relationship would never come to fruition.

MacDonald: There is also a performance element in some of *your* imagery—not only in its timing, but in its evocations of a particular moment and sometimes in its very abstraction (the use of blur calls attention to itself as device and conscious metaphor). And there are visually arresting moments—the lightning bug shots, most obviously—that, on one hand, help to create the mood of that time and the mood of the relationship at its happiest, but also demonstrate your ability to make a gorgeous image. Do you think of your minimalist approach as a form of self-reflexivity?

Gillooly: To varying degrees, once I decided to invent imagery, there was no avoiding self-reflexivity. As I mentioned, initially I tried to imagine the edit without imagery, and the visuals were added slowly and sparingly; I didn't want them to distract too much from the audio. Gradually I decided to include images throughout the film, all the while keeping them minimal and/or abstract. Sometimes I draw audience attention to the screen without expecting them to know what they're looking at or why they're looking at it. The minimalism is intended to provide space for listeners/viewers to imagine, to see with their ears.

MacDonald: *Suitcase of Love and Shame* seems quite different from your earlier work—except in the sense that you have often been interested in intimate revelations. *Leona's Sister Gerri* takes what had become a generic photographic image and reveals its particular context, re-animating our sense that this was a real person whose painful death was not just a statistic, but the conclusion of a very human story.

How different did the process of working on *Suitcase* seem from your earlier projects?

Gillooly: In almost all ways, there is a big difference between my last film, *Today the Hawk Takes One Chick*, and *Suitcase of Love and Shame*—but I do see overlap between *Leona's Sister Gerri* and *Suitcase*. I used to say that Gerri Santoro didn't die of an illegal abortion, she died of shame. Not that I'm always drawn to "shame" as a topic, but Gerri Santoro and Jeannie in *Suitcase* were women living lives they were made to feel ashamed of. They also happened to live at the exact same moment in history.

In hindsight I also see obvious similarities in my approach as an interpreter of tragedy. Some are obvious: for example, the device of using the purse in *Leona's Sister Gerri* closely resembles how the contents of the suitcase are visually investigated in *Suitcase of Love and Shame*. And both films are shot in a highly stylized, minimal way. Coming from a fine arts background, I approach film from a studio practice: keenly observing materials, collecting physical components, making things by hand, working out ideas by collaging and composing.

I am not sure if this makes sense, but in a way possessing the objects that belonged to the subjects inspired the structure of both *Suitcase of Love and Shame* and *Leona's Sister Gerri*. When I was working on *Leona's Sister Gerri*, Gerri Santoro's family loaned me her purse, which I kept in my studio. Pouring over its contents (tissues, receipts, snapshots of friends, scribbles on the backs of pictures in the wallet, shopping lists, a letter) revealed clues about what happened and led me to people who had information. For example, I discovered that one reason Gerri took the huge risk to have an illegal abortion at 6 months was because her estranged and sometimes violent husband was coming for an unannounced visit. And I use the purse as proof that the infamous photograph was in fact Gerri Santoro. Once I found my way to a copy of the police file photo that was not cropped, I could see Gerri's purse in a corner on the hotel room floor. How that information is communicated visually in that film was something that, in hindsight, I can see I was doing again in *Suitcase of Love and Shame*.

But there are also important differences. With *Leona's Sister Gerri* I felt compelled to reconstruct the sequence of events that led to Gerri's death with as much accuracy as possible. I relied heavily on archival research and interviews. Gerri Santoro's family entrusted me with her story. They had never spoken publicly about it and in fact, at first, they were not at all happy with how I had structured the film.

In *Suitcase of Love and Shame* I felt I could take the liberty of inventing imagery. I was not concerned with being factual—either with the particulars of how the audio was assembled or how the imagery was associated with the audio. The details of the love story were not important to me. I wanted to use what seemed *historically* significant to me, representative of an era.

MacDonald: As a filmmaker, you seem to change the kind of film you make and your approach with each new project. Is this a function of your interest in trying new things, or of the difficulty of finding financing, or both?

Gillooly: I never get much financing for my films, and I've abandoned projects for the lack of financing. I would never have attempted to make a film in Swaziland [*Today the Hawk Takes One Chick*] if the pre-production trip hadn't been unexpectedly and very generously funded, after which everything fell into place.

Most of my work is feature length and on average it takes me about four years to complete a film. What audiences do not see is the research for abandoned projects on similar subjects. By the time I finish something, I often feel as if I've made a series of films and am ready to move on. The next film often finds me during that fallow time. *Leona's Sister Gerri* found me when a close friend of mine confided that it was her aunt whose body was in the now famous photo.

I suppose you could say I am open to certain types of content; obviously I become committed to films which have a social issue origin. But my films are not didactic. I'm more dedicated to my pursuits as a filmmaker than I am to any of the causes that I make films about—if that makes sense. I'm not an *activist filmmaker*, even though I consider myself an activist.

With that said, *Suitcase of Love and Shame* came about because I wanted to go back to my earlier studio-art roots. I welcomed the freedom to work with images and sound to re-present a moment in time, as opposed to representing a subject. What had begun as a search for a way to look at time by critically examining a collection became an experimental documentary about a moment in history that reflects the current obsession, on Facebook, on Twitter, with recording and sharing intensely private moments.

Godfrey Reggio (on *Visitors*)

In the arts, developments/accomplishments that come to seem outmoded, things of the past, have a way of reasserting themselves back into artistic practice, often without being recognized as reassertions. The traditions of nineteenth-century American landscape painting and of the diorama and panorama have been periodically revived by a range of filmmakers, as have the Lumière Brothers' Cinématographe shows that provided early cinema audiences with arresting cine-documents of local and exotic people and places. During recent decades, Godfrey Reggio and Ron Fricke have directed a series of features that often evoke these earlier forms. They collaborated on one of the more popular and influential avant-docs, *Koyaanisqatsi* (1984; Reggio directed, Fricke saw to the cinematography) before going their separate ways: Reggio, to complete what he called the "Qatsi Trilogy" (*qatsi* means life in the Hopi language), with *Powaqqatsi* (1988) and *Naqoyqatsi* (2002); Fricke, to make the IMAX film *Chronos* (1985) and the theatrical feature *Baraka* (1992). Both Reggio and Fricke have used technical means unusual for feature filmmaking—complex forms of time-lapse in *Koyaanisqatsi, Chronos,* and *Baraka*; elaborate slow motion in *Powaqqatsi*—to create panoramas of cultural sites and practices that attempt to evoke a global consciousness.

Reggio and Fricke work slowly. Twenty years passed between *Baraka* and the release of Fricke's *Samsara* in 2012; and after *Naqoyqatsi* Reggio didn't finish a new feature until *Visitors* (2014). These substantial gaps in time are necessitated in part by the filmmakers' commitment to making technically advanced films for large-scale theatrical exhibition—money for these sorts of projects is not easy to come by—and presumably by the meditative sensibility that seems to infuse their films. *Visitors*, like Reggio's earlier features, was developed in collaboration with composer Philip Glass, but while it sometimes evokes the Qatsi Trilogy, it is distinct both formally (*Visitors* was shot in elegant black and white on 3K and 5K high-definition video and released in 4K) and in terms of its subject matter: Reggio's focus is on portraits of individuals, nearly all of them in close-up, interspersed with panoramic imagery filmed in areas of Louisiana that had been, five years earlier, devastated by Katrina.

Reggio's black-and-white close-ups in *Visitors* evoke Warhol's *Screen Tests* of 1964–66 (figure 50), in their composition, as well as in their meditative

FIGURE 50 *Portrait of young girl in Godfrey Reggio's* Visitors *(2012).*
Source: Courtesy Godfrey Reggio.

pace (the *Screen Tests* were shot at 24 frames per second, but were meant to be shown at 16 frames per second)—though the kinds of gaze that interest Reggio are quite different from the gazes of the Factory visitors at Warhol's 16mm camera. *Visitors* seems part of a contemporary revival of interest in the cinematic portrait, shared by Susana de Sousa Dias, whose extended meditation on mugshots of political prisoners incarcerated during the forty-eight years of the Salazar regime in *48* (2009—see the de Sousa Dias interview) uses some of the same visual strategies as *Visitors*; and by Stephanie Spray and Pacho Velez, veterans of Harvard's Sensory Ethnography Lab, whose *Manakamana* (2013) is a series of portraits of visitors to the holy site of a Nepalese goddess, filmed on the cable car that transports them to the top of a mountain where the site is located—a meditation on the ongoing transformations of ancient and modern culture (see the Spray/Velez interview).

Visitors is not for everybody. For a good many sophisticates the ambiguities of Reggio's imagery and the pomp of its mood will seem mindless and pretentious—and Glass's music, which seems to have its own legion of detractors, will exacerbate this reaction. But for those who can enjoy the experience of looking at Reggio's stunning imagery within the context created by Glass's elegant composition, and who can appreciate an experience of cinema akin to the experiences enjoyed by the original audiences for the Cinématographe, for nineteenth century moving and still panoramas, and for Louis Daguerre's Diorama shows, *Visitors* can be powerful and meaningful.

I spoke with Reggio about *Visitors* in December of 2013; an earlier interview about his work up through *Powaqqatsi* was published in *A Critical Cinema 2* (Berkeley and Los Angeles: University of California Press, 1992).

MacDonald: It's been more than a decade since you finished *Naqoyqatsi*. How long has *Visitors* been germinating?

Reggio: What has become *Visitors* went through a series of progressions. I started the process in 2003, just after *Naqoyqatsi*, but it was seven-plus years before there was any funding for the film. My first thought was a film called "The Border." I had become interested in working with Butoh Theater, especially with the emotive expression of human faces. I tried to get traction for the project—I even had some help, but I couldn't get the funding I needed to make the film.

"The Border" transformed into "Savage Eden." An image of primates in a pew came to me. I did a whole scenario for "Savage Eden"; it dealt with "isms": scratch the surface and there's an "ism" within us all. It was to be an anarchic, comedic piece dealing with the ideology of books, flags, walls, and screens.

Then in 2005 Katrina happened. Being from New Orleans, this affected me deeply; a lot of what's in *Visitors* is a result of Katrina. I went down to Louisiana to see the debacle, which enforced my idea of "Savage Eden," but then I took it in another direction, which I called "Evidence." Again, I couldn't get anything more than a documentary amount of money—about a million dollars—for the project. I know it sounds ridiculous to refuse so much money, but I know how to budget what I want to do, and I didn't want to shoot a doc. At the time, other people were doing docs about Katrina (I'd seen Spike Lee's *When the Levees Broke* [2006]).

So "Evidence" transformed into "holy see." I visited Louisiana a lot during the four years after the hurricane, to see, to observe; and I noticed that while what I had first seen was the evidence of an enormous storm, a catastrophe, as these places moldered over several years, this evidence was becoming like a visage, like a huge set for the ruins of modernity, a modern Pompeii—in other words, more aesthetically articulate. This gradual transformation revealed something that I could not have seen had I taken the money just after the hurricane.

"holy see" was the working title of *Visitors* throughout most of the making of the film, but my feeling is, "When in doubt, cut it out." While I loved "holy see" as a title, I didn't want it to get confused with the Vatican or be too obtuse or misunderstood. For me the phrase was like "holy smoke!" "holy shit!" "holy moly!". . . "holy see!": to *see* is what *Visitors* is about—to see that which the eye cannot see, to make the invisible visible, to see that which is hidden in plain sight.

MacDonald: How did you finally arrange the funding?

Reggio: One executive producer is my angel from *Koyaanisqatsi* and on into the present moment: Dan Noyes. I think when Dan sees me coming, he must want to run in the other direction! But Dan did something remarkable for love of the project: he said he would put up half the money, but wouldn't give it to me until I had arranged for the other half—"Being first in," he said, "I'll be the last out"—clearly the action of an angel.

During the fall of 2010, I had occasion to be introduced to a theatrical attorney in Montreal, Dean Chenoy. Dean had liked my previous films and we brainstormed where we might get financing for this one. He came up with people he thought would be the best to approach, people who had responded to the films and loved Philip Glass's music: Phoebe Greenberg and Penny Mancuso, who head the Phi Center in Montreal. It was arranged for me to meet them, and after a few minutes of my pitch, I saw that Phoebe was smiling, which made me a little nervous. Then she said, "Godfrey, just stop; we've already decided: it's our pleasure to give you the money."

So again, *angels*, people who were into the art of the project, rather than hard-line business investors, came to the rescue. Dan Noyes, Phoebe Greenberg, the Phi Group, and then Phoebe's family were our supporters.

MacDonald: What was the final budget?

Reggio: Just over 4.6 million, most of which is the below the line: that is, it's all going into the film. The funding started mid-to-late summer 2010. Dan Noyes let us shoot a bit in Louisiana before we actually had the rest of the money, then we regrouped again in February of 2011 and worked through May of 2011, doing some more shooting in New York; then we regrouped again in March of 2012 and worked through the end of the year and three months into 2013. Altogether, within a three-year period, about two years of work.

MacDonald: At what point did Philip Glass become involved?

Reggio: Well, in all my projects, I keep him informed—when I'd go to New York, I'd usually sleep on his kitchen floor and we'd talk. He's been involved in *Visitors* since 2003.

We began shooting *Visitors* in New Orleans and in the Louisiana swamps during the autumn of 2010. I asked Philip to come down with one of his producers to join us. Philip likes to experience firsthand what the camera will see. He was also at the Bronx Zoo when we first shot the gorillas—that was very moving to him, I think. And he came to the studio where we were shooting the people who were playing video games, watching TV. By coming to the locations, he gets an original hit, a connection to the project.

I always ask Philip not to write a note until he's really marinated in the ethos of the film, in its emotive atmosphere. He came and saw all the film selects (we shot over 630,000 feet for *Visitors*) and talked with us about creating a dance of music and image, so that one wouldn't overwhelm the other, so that music and image would blend into one synergetic movement.

Normally when composers work on theatrical films, they do musical cues that can be anywhere from fifteen seconds to a few minutes at most. Here, we were asking for a full orchestral score: in effect, a narrative for the film, an emotive armchair in which to view the images. That process takes time. Philip's first writings were beautiful, but they were too symphonic and tended to overwhelm the images. Being someone who can function in a critical forum, Philip understood our feedback—and started over. At one point he had a Eureka moment and said, "What you're asking is that I write for the attention of the audience; I get it." He went back to his studio and we got two pieces of music in less than a week, and they were spot on. Philip's activity in terms of writing and then recording the score took about six months.

MacDonald: The earliest shoot was in Louisiana?

Reggio: Yes, towards the end of 2010 we shot for almost six weeks. The building that has "Novus Ordo Seclorum" ("New Order of the Ages") on it— we came up with that name—is an art deco building from the 1930s. It had a "VISITORS" sign embedded in the wall, and my colleague Ray Hemenez and I were really keen on shooting it—and that ended up as our title. It's not important that the audience knows this, but tattooed on the masonry that makes up "VISITORS" are at least six bullet holes.

I came to feel that that's really what *we* were, and are, "visitors," and I liked the ubiquity of the word because you can interpret it in any way you wish.

MacDonald: The Art Deco of the building and the opening titles suggests the first half of the twentieth century, the era when America came to see itself as leading the world.

Reggio: That monolithic building has a real presence. I thought it could stand in for modernity itself. Its voice fills the frame.

MacDonald: Is the abandoned amusement park imagery also from Katrina?

Reggio: Yes, that was the Six Flags franchise, built on platforms above the swamp, with cement-slab sidewalks. When the hurricane came across, the water swamped the park and now it's full of alligators and snakes—and is used pretty regularly for photography. The hurricane was in 2005; we shot at the end of 2010; the imagery has a ghostlike feel.

MacDonald: It's unusual to do the kind of extended close-ups—portraits— so important in *Visitors*, in a theatrical film. I was reminded of the Andy Warhol *Screen Tests*.

Reggio: I've not seen the Warhol films, but that reference has come up before.

MacDonald: In *Visitors* there seem to be at least two different kinds of facial close-ups, plus a sequence of close-ups of hands mimicking gestures used with modern digital technologies. At the beginning the faces seem to be looking at *us*, they seem to be conscious of the project they're part of.

Reggio: Those portraits are what I call "from the inside-out"; the people were consciously sitting for portraits. All my effort involves getting organized in the *hope* that spontaneity is going to take over. And it does, usually. As a crew we discovered the virtue of an inhumanly slow move into the face so that the face you see at the beginning of the shot is not the face you see at the end. This face may be a mirror of the face within us all.

After the fingerplay section and the beginning of the Six Flags movement, which is called "Off Planet/Games," we go to a little girl who's signing, then to another little girl who has the longest single shot in the film, then to four children each watching television, followed by the Big Clown face at Six Flags, then to a whole other series of portraits of young people playing video games. All of these young people knew they were being filmed, but they weren't sitting for portraits; they were asked to do what they normally did when they played these games. As soon as that digital screen came on, it was like a tractor beam; each person went out of a self-conscious state and became entranced by the virulent presence and demands of the game. We could record their entrancement by filming directly through the mirror that was reflecting the video game screen. I call these portraits "from the outside-in."

You don't see the screen they were actually paying attention to, which was bounced onto a two way mirror that we could shoot through. I had used that technique for a little film called *Evidence* (1995) that I did in Rome. And Errol Morris uses his version of it for his interviews. It's used on television all the time.

MacDonald: Early on, right after we see a boy and a girl on a merry-go-round, we see a man who looks like he's screaming. Is this Edvard Munch screaming about the arrival of modernity?

Reggio: Well, it could be. That's up to the viewer. Your specific reference wasn't in my mind.

Because my wife does yoga, I know about "laughing and crying yoga." Of course, everything's available in New York, so I had someone check out who was doing laughing-crying yoga and found a group of people. I shot about twenty-five of them, and chose this person, at a point where you don't know if he's screaming or laughing. He was laughing, but it's like that wonderful Baudelaire line about humor being the stigmata of Original Sin. Humor and tragedy, twins, same mother—an insight into consciousness.

MacDonald: How did you eliminate all the details of the space around the faces you filmed?

Reggio: We shot all the portraits on what I call "the blackground"—something that was part of the original motivation of the project. My interest in using "the blackground" created quite a discussion early on. I wanted to do the film in black-and-white and in infrared. Color contemporizes the film image and would have been less emotive. In some cases this can be useful, but for *this* film I didn't want to represent the contemporary; I wanted to put *Visitors* in an otherworldly zone.

Further, during the making of *Naqoyqatsi*, I'd realized I wanted to do a film that involved split screen, but I wanted a way to use split screening that would be hidden in plain sight, and using the blackground was important for this; it allowed me to put multiple faces next to each other in pans and dolly shots *in the editing room*, and without any visual distraction from the intensity of the faces. Every portrait was done separately—except for the sports bar where people are clearly in a group.

There's only one bit of color in *Visitors*, the blue of the earth at the end.

MacDonald: How did you get the moon shots?

Reggio: The moon shots are based on precise maps from NASA. I did see a shot of the moon that I loved from JAXA, the Japanese equivalent of NASA—they did a run over the moon in 2005. But that image was in 1080 resolution, which couldn't work on a big screen, so we used a 3-D program, and over four-plus months we built three different moons. Quite a task.

The moon needs to be seen in relation to the building: the moon has no atmosphere; it's in the blackground. The building and the structures in the amusement park were all shot in infrared, so the sky disappears and when clouds are present, they're ghostlike. For me, seeing the building after the opening shot of the moon puts the building and us squarely *on* the moon. We are the "Man in the Moon," as it were.

Of course, in any art, and particularly in the case of—dare I say—poetic cinema, much more is suggested than is intended by those who make it. *If* it has a presence, a film takes on a life of its own; it outsmarts the art that was intended.

Obviously I don't use a logical conceptual design in *Visitors*—there's no traditional story to follow; what it "means" is almost a non-sequitur. If there are ten people in the theater (and they stay!), there're going to be ten different experiences.

The *meaning*, in this case, the subject of this film, is the person *watching* the film. I wanted to avoid a didactic piece, but I came to realize that what I was making was an *autodidactic* film. *Visitors* has no intrinsic meaning, all meaning is in the eye of the beholder. Each member of the audience must become the storyteller, must become the character and plot of the film.

The films I intend are beyond the limits of my capacity to achieve. The process I employ is collaborative. I always work with people more talented than I. Jon Kane and the young crew of Optic Nerve (in Red Hook, Brooklyn) were my principal collaborators, and together with Philip Glass we made *Visitors*. For what I do, *I* is *we*.

MacDonald: All your films have felt like emotional warnings, more or less to the effect that we'd better learn to be *human*, to be *gentle*, while there's still time—it's a "Look, let's get *serious*" message.

Reggio: Yeah, it is. It is. And as you say, I've had that "message" through all the work I've done. I can see *Visitors* as a requiem. However, I know that we'll all see the film differently.

MacDonald: What went into your decision to use Triska, the gorilla (figure 51)?

Reggio: I looked at a lot of representations of gorillas, most of which are gorillas as monsters—maybe in some films they represent the interior of who we are, but always they're a violent presence. In reality, gorillas are sedentary. I've worked with chimpanzees and, compared to gorillas, they're on steroids. The reason I chose Triska, a lowland gorilla, is that, in the great primate line-up, the face of the female lowland gorilla is most similar to ours.

FIGURE 51 *Triska the gorilla, as "the adult in the room," in Godfrey Reggio's* Visitors
(2012).

Source: Courtesy Godfrey Reggio.

I was out at the gorilla exhibit in the Bronx Zoo for almost three weeks, a mind-blowing experience. Literally tens of thousands of people came to see the gorillas; it's a very popular site. We had to shoot on a platform above the crowds. People go *nuts* trying to get the *gorillas* to go nuts! Unbelievable.

Loren Eiseley has said that we have not seen ourselves until we've seen ourselves through the eyes of another animal. And there's Rene Dubos's beautiful book: *So Human an Animal* [New York: Scribners, 1968]—we have a lot to learn from those we're here with. As the gorillas see us, we're the real monsters, hanging by our "tales" from the trees. In that long pan shot past five human faces, leading to Triska, she becomes the adult in the room.

MacDonald: I assume you mean to allude to the original *King Kong* at the very end, when Triska is on the movie screen in the movie theater within our theater.

Reggio: Well, not really. The last shot is a key to the autodidactic nature of *Visitors*: here we are, looking at a screen, and a screen is looking back at us. Throughout, the film has been about this reciprocal gaze.

Also, I believe in bookends. As soon as you put a frame around anything that is (or is posing as) art, people have the propensity to conjure meaning, *because* of the limit that is offered. Beginning and ending with Triska is a kind of framing.

MacDonald: *King Kong* seems an appropriate reference because the scene of King Kong on the stage near the end of the original film, being seen by the audience and photographed by the journalists, remains powerful: the issue of the enslavement of the environment (and the people of certain environments), implied there, is still relevant.

The New Orleans material causes *Visitors* to seem more personal than some of your other works.

Reggio: I've wanted to film in Louisiana for a long time but had never had the opportunity. I grew up around the swamp you see in the film. My father was born less than two miles away, in a place called Olivia, between New Iberia and Jeanerette on the Bayou Tesch, and I spent a lot of my adolescence in that swamp. I know its power, and felt it would be the perfect companion for what I was trying to suggest with the moon. The contrariety of the swamp has a palpable primordial presence; it's otherworldly.

Knowing the swamp, I knew that had we filmed in the summer, it would be full of beautifully colored flowers and magnificent greens—but the water levels could be as high as twelve feet in the place we shot, so you wouldn't see the root structure of the trees. Also I wanted the imagery to have a unified look, so shooting at the end of November was the best time—in November the water was inches deep in some of the places we were filming (figure 52).

MacDonald: With the mist and the grey scale, those shots seem very Edenic.

Reggio: The camera is showing us something our eyes can't see. I'm told our first dreams come in black-and-white.

A lot of words go into creating the shooting script of a film like this, deciding on the point of view, getting everybody on the same page and into one breath, one heartbeat—but at the end of the day we're making a pictorial composition, a syntax for the eye. It's not about *text*; it's about *texture*. Until the film is shot, it's just words on paper; once the film is shot, the paper goes out the window and we're left with the material qua material of the medium—the image-in-time—and *that's* what we have to work with.

Essentially, the people in *Visitors*, be they humans looking "at you" or people playing games, are the proverbial doubles of who *we* are. In daily life we see ourselves as doubles through shadows, reflections, through spirits, but

FIGURE 52 *Louisiana swamp in Godfrey Reggio's* Visitors *(2012)*.
Source: Courtesy Godfrey Reggio.

we can also see ourselves through other people. Their gaze brings us into a dialogue with ourselves, but the specific nature of the dialogue is up to the viewer. My films may not offer the kind of clarity text can provide, but they do offer the aesthetic triplets of sensation, perception, and emotion. The film becomes a meta-language that is not dependent on textual metaphor.

MacDonald: Steven Soderbergh's name is on the film as a presenter.

Reggio: On March 19th, 2000, two of the *qatsi* films and *Anima Mundi* [1991] were shown in New York. Philip Glass had had too much publicity around that time for the *New York Times* to do a feature on his music, so they asked if they could do something on me, and I said yes, but only if I could pitch the *next* film. At the time, John Rockwell was the Arts & Leisure editor; I'd known him from way back. He liked *Koyaanisqatsi* and assigned film critic Ty Burr to do the feature and I was able to talk about the next film, rather than the films I'd already done.

That afternoon, Soderbergh's producer calls Philip Glass to ask how they can reach Godfrey: "We want to talk about his new film." And that evening I talked to Soderbergh, who asked if I could come out to LA in the next couple of days. My producer Larry Taub and I went out to LA, where Steven asked me, "Do you have the emotional fortitude to *do* this project now that you've been trying to find the money for 11 years?" I said, "Of course!" And he gave us money for *Naqoyqatsi* and got Harvey Weinstein involved.

Soderbergh is also the presenter of *Visitors*. Upon completion of the film I invited him to see the result. His response was palpable. He volunteered to do whatever it took to make sure the film got distribution. Through his efforts the Toronto International Film Festival premiered *Visitors* with the Toronto Symphony Orchestra. Steven chairs our committee of distribution, communicates with the North American distributor, Cinedigm, and the live performance agent, CAMI. He joins Dan Noyes and Phoebe Greenberg as angels in deed. The making of *Visitors* and its distribution have taken flight on their wings.

Todd Haynes

Todd Haynes has worked back and forth between experiment and commerce, between fact and fiction. *Superstar: The Karen Carpenter Story* (1987) is a faux documentary that uses Barbie dolls for characters. Because Haynes's use of Barbie and of the Carpenters' music made it a magnet for legal action, *Superstar*'s exhibition life remained underground until the advent of the Internet. On the other hand, Haynes's *Far From Heaven* (2002) is a remarkably effective evocation of the super-commercial Douglas Sirk weepies of the 1950s; it earned Julianne Moore an Academy Award nomination for Best Actress and Haynes a nomination for Best Screenplay (Moore, Haynes, and Dennis Quaid won Golden Globes).

But Haynes's career does not seem to be tracing a simple trajectory from early experiment to commercial success. His *I'm Not There* (2007) is a remarkably challenging feature; indeed, its combination of modes is demanding in ways similar to many canonical avant-garde films. *I'm Not There* assumes our awareness of a wide range of cinematic approaches (including both documentary and avant-garde approaches) and demands a willingness to make sense of a wildly fractured narrative that defies conventional senses of film time—while proposing to be a revelation of, and a comment on, a moment in the life of Bob Dylan, one of the best-known celebrities of our era. It is simultaneously a postmodern comment on modern film history (including the advent of cinema-verite documentary) and an avant-garde commercial feature.

Once I had seen *I'm Not There*, I decided to try to arrange for an interview with Haynes. I wanted to test my sense of his work as being, at least partly, rooted in avant-garde cinema. The interview that follows is an expansion of a conversation that took place at the Portland Art Museum in Portland, Oregon, where Haynes lives, in front of an audience. The interview was arranged by Portland's Cinema Project, a micro-cinema that provides a variety of services to the Portland film community, including regular screenings of avant-garde film and experimental documentary. This event, co-sponsored by the Northwest Film Center, was the kick-off of "Expanded Frames," a five-day celebration of Cinema Project's five-year anniversary. I had chosen a series of excerpts from Haynes's films that, in my view, demonstrated connections with avant-garde film history—one excerpt each from *Superstar*, *Poison* (1991), *Dottie Gets Spanked* (1993), and *Velvet Goldmine* (1998)—and used these clips to raise cine-historical issues. At the end of the evening, Haynes took questions from the audience. After the event, I transcribed the conversation, edited it, and returned it to Haynes for corrections and with some additional questions.

MacDonald: I've been interested in talking with you about your awareness of avant-garde cinema for several years. My interest was piqued once again when I saw *I'm Not There* in a packed downtown Boston theater last fall. Early in the film a few people left—something that happens at most any screening of avant-garde films attended by more than avant-garde aficionados—but after that, as far as I could see, nobody left. And at the end, when the credits were rolling, I looked around and everybody was still sitting there, talking. I thought, "Wow! Todd Haynes has made an avant-garde feature that has kept nearly this entire audience in their seats."

You earned a B.A. from Brown and then studied at Bard College, which has long been identified with avant-garde filmmaking.

Haynes: I never got a degree from Bard; I was there only briefly, during the first summer of their cool three-year MFA program offered during summers at the Milton Avery Graduate School of the Arts. I had the concept and the script for *Superstar* with me when I arrived at Bard.

My sense of being a filmmaker was modeled on the people I had met at Brown, people like Leslie Thornton, an experimental filmmaker I greatly admired, who joined the staff during my last two years there. At the time, she was just beginning her amazing collection of "Peggy & Fred" films. Leslie, along with my film theory mentors Michael Silverman and Mary Ann Doane, advised and participated in my thesis film, *Assassins: A Film Concerning Rimbaud* [1985].

I looked at the work of the filmmakers at Brown and at the work of filmmakers I studied there, and felt sure that my sensibility and my interests were never going to put me into mainstream filmmaking. I figured I should get a degree and teach. That's what they had done, and they seemed able to balance their own filmmaking with their academic lives. So with that plan in mind, I went to Bard, where it was just me and one other filmmaker (Marcelle Pecot); at that point, the Bard program was mostly painters and sculptors.

I spent that summer in the sweaty, mosquito-ridden heat of Annandale-on-Hudson making the sets and props for *Superstar*. At the very end of the summer I got my friends together and we shot the film there. Then I moved to New York and cut *Superstar* in my Brooklyn apartment that fall.

I was soon involved in a new venture, with my friend Barry Elsworth, who I went to college with, and Christine Vachon, who has been the producer of all my feature films. Barry had received an endowment and wanted to form a nonprofit organization that helped emerging filmmakers, and together the three of us started Apparatus Productions in 1987–88.

Apparatus was our reaction to what seemed to be happening around independent/experimental film at this time. I had been exposed to classic experimental film, best exemplified by Stan Brakhage—that is, a basically non-narrative, abstract, and personal cinema—in high school and in college. A very influential high school teacher and poet, Christina Adams, first exposed me to films by Brakhage, Michael Snow, Ken Jacobs, James Benning, and others.

But during my college years, the early 1980s, there started to be something of a shift in the kinds of subject matter and experimental approaches that were considered interesting. I remember Sally Potter's *Thriller* [1979] as a turning point (Sally went on to make *Orlando* [1992]), and *Riddles of the Sphinx* [1977] by Laura Mulvey and Peter Wollen—feature-length, but experimental in every other way. We studied *Riddles*, and both Peter and Laura came to Brown at various times to discuss their work.

These films were beginning to engage with commercial genres and to make direct references to popular culture using the experimental vernacular. Of course, to describe this moment as a shift is to overlook whole traditions of experimental film that preceded Potter and Mulvey/Wollen, including Warhol and the Kuchar Brothers and others who, earlier on, were also interested in referencing Hollywood and genre filmmaking. But in the late Seventies and early Eighties this was happening in a specific way that interested me, and Christine and Barry, tremendously.

We three began to think of ourselves as experimental narrative filmmakers, and what was of particular interest to us, as Apparatus Productions, was a difference in the way in which experimental film was produced before and after the shift I've described. If you were in the tradition of Stan Brakhage, you were making your films alone, experimenting on an individual level with the nature of image and cinematic time. You didn't need any help; you could make your films by yourself. But as soon as you were employing references to genre and commercial style in your work, you needed people to help you, and we figured that that's where our organization could be of use.

We thought that emerging experimental narrative filmmakers coming out of college and moving to New York City had no chance of getting grants from the New York State Council on the Arts or the National Endowment for the Arts, and that Apparatus would provide production support and financing during this delicate transition period. Christine had to teach Barry and me the hierarchy of film production practice and we learned and experimented with this new way of working in the films we were helping to get made.

Apparatus was never going to be about our own work, and we did have three years of some success in getting interesting projects completed [Apparatus helped produce seven films: *Cause and Effect* (1988) by Susan

Delson, *Muddy Hands* (1988) by Even Dunsky, *American Lunch* (1988) by Julian Dillon, *He Was Once* (1989) by Mary Hestand, *La Davina* (1989) by M. Brooke Dammkoehler, *Oreos with Attitude* (1990) by Larry Carty, and *Anemone Me* (1990) by Suzan-Lori Parks and Bruce Hainley].

As *Superstar* started to take off and gain attention, our experience with Apparatus, with the hands-on, New-York-based practice of working with small crews and local craftsmen and creative people, led to our collaborating on my first feature, *Poison* [1991].

MacDonald: I think you're correct that there was a kind of pivot at the end of the Seventies and during early Eighties, *from* filmmakers whose films looked more or less the same from beginning to end, or expressed a certain very particular kind of structure from beginning to end, *to* films that started to mix things up. *Superstar* was made almost simultaneously with Su Friedrich's *Damned If You Don't* [1987] and Marlon Riggs's *Tongues Untied* [1989], and each of these films combined approaches common to both documentary and fiction, plus performance, poetic experiment, and found footage into a single work.

Haynes: Yes, there was less focusing on formal questions and the material status of the image and more commentary about cultural and political issues and on the debates that were occurring around us.

MacDonald: There was also a striving for a larger audience; by the late Seventies it was clear that certain forms of avant-garde film were probably not going to have anything like a substantial audience, at least not any time soon.

Haynes: I guess that was true. But though *Superstar* certainly generated a bigger audience than most experimental films, a larger audience wasn't something that I set out for, at least as I recall.

In my mind, *Superstar was* an experimental film, but unlike early films by Su Friedrich and Abigail Child and Marlon Riggs, and others—and maybe this is *not* true for all those filmmakers; I'm not sure—it wasn't immediately accepted into the venues for experimental film.

MacDonald: I understand that the Collective for Living Cinema wouldn't show *Superstar*.

Haynes: The Collective refused to show it. The Whitney and MoMA people didn't want to show it. Millennium refused to show it. We had to rent Millennium's theater ourselves for something like seventy bucks a night (which at that point felt like a lot) to show *Superstar* and *Assassins*. Karen Cooper at Film Forum loved *Superstar* and *wanted* to show it, but was worried about the legal issues.

With *Superstar* we had three years of freedom before the lawsuits came. And I knew they were coming; I knew our days were numbered. *Superstar* did have a robust life, mostly due to the good fortune of getting a *Village Voice* review: J. Hoberman singled it out, which helped arts museums and galleries and art centers and colleges around the country start booking it.

Superstar was shown at the New Museum in a theme series on video (during that first year it was almost always shown as a video film in museums and galleries) and at clubs. It was part of "Karen Carpenter Night" at the Pyramid Club, following fantastic drag performances of Karen Carpenter songs. Pyramid was *packed* with people just standing around talking, and I was afraid that they wouldn't stop talking to watch the film, but once the film started, everybody was frozen watching it and drinking their beer—amazing. That was one of my all-time favorite screenings.

So, *Superstar* occupied a hybrid position between the more traditional experimental film venues, which had rejected it, and other, broader arts and semi-theatrical venues. Then eventually it became a kind of coveted bootleg object that circulated illicitly. As a result of this circulation of the prints and video copies, the *texture* of the film changed, and *Superstar* bore the marks of that illicit circulation. One writer said that the disappearing image on the surface of the bootleg *Superstar* tapes was like the disappearing Karen Carpenter body in the movie [Lucas Hilderbrand, "Grainy Days and Mondays: *Superstar* and Bootleg Aesthetics"—see bibliography].

MacDonald: Of course, the most unusual aspect of *Superstar* is the use of Barbie Dolls to do the leading roles. When I try to think of a cinematic predecessor to this approach, the only film I can think of is *A Town Called Tempest* [1963], an 8mm film by George and Mike Kuchar. It's about a tornado coming through a Midwestern town and as I remember (the film is no longer in circulation), some of the characters are little plastic people. What was fascinating about that film was that even though George and Mike were using obviously primitive means, the brothers knew enough about genre film to effectively mimic Hollywood visual grammar. On some crazy level, the sequence works.

Did you know their work before you began making films?

Haynes: I can't remember when I first saw Kuchar Brothers' films. It's very likely that I did see some before making *Superstar*, but I was much more conscious of Laurie Simmons. She's a visual artist who at the time was working with dolls. I'm sure there are others who preceded her, but she became known for her beautiful photographs of dolls. I don't know if she ever made films.

I've never felt that anything I've done was particularly original. My work is about appropriating and responding to cultural influences and stimuli and ideas, and recombining those elements in ways that make you think about them or see them differently.

The whole *Superstar* project started innocently and goofily, when one day Cynthia Schneider, my best pal from Brown, said, "Let's make a movie together!" *She* said, "Let's have it be with pets!" and *I* said, "No, let's have it be with dolls!" I'd studied narrative theory in college and was very interested in doing a genre piece where I would very carefully follow all the rules of narrative structure, but use dolls instead of live actors. Would an audience feel the same emotional connections with the story that they feel when it's Meryl

Streep up there? I wanted to see if the form has as much to do with how we connect with a film, as the content does.

But at first, we didn't have a content. We just knew that we weren't going to work with real people. One day I was sitting at Café Dante in the West Village, where they were playing Seventies retro music, and I heard Karen Carpenter singing "every sha-na-na, every woewoewoe." Karen had died just three or four years earlier, and hearing that music and that voice after her death and after the new insight into this popular figure that the nature of her death had given us, was suddenly very powerful.

She had become a figure of ridicule, even cruel ridicule, in some intellectual circles (I'll never forget that Grammy Awards where Bette Midler introduced Karen Carpenter and *had* to say some nasty thing about her). Earlier you'd make fun of that deep, lilting voice and think, "Ah, she's just a crock; what does *she* know about pain and suffering!" But now, when I listened to it again, the song had other levels. I called Cynthia, and I was like, "We gotta do the Karen Carpenter story!" and she was like, "Okay, okay, we'll use dolls!"

MacDonald: Were you sued first by the music people or by the Barbie people?

Haynes: The Barbie people were the first to emerge. They sniffed around at what we were doing, even to the degree that I received in the mail copies of their patents on the Barbie Doll body. The patents were all for separate body parts! There was a page for just the torso; turn the page, an arm; turn the page, another arm—demonstrating, as if there were any question, their legal jurisdiction over Barbie's body, which, of course, echoes what *Superstar* is about!

We talked to a lawyer about how to defuse the issue, because Mattel had a long history of going after products that were mimicking their originals. Many of the dolls that we used in *Superstar* were knock-offs that came from thrift stores, not Mattel products, so there was already some ambiguity. Mattel backed off; I think they saw that the music rights were a more severe legal obstruction heading my way fast, one that would also take care of their problem just fine. And it did.

MacDonald: The use of montages, of course, is common to commercial film, as well as avant-garde film, but the montages in *Superstar* remind me of avant-garde work, including certain Brakhage films and some of Bruce Conner's work, especially *Report* [various versions, 1963–67], his film about the assassination of JFK.

Haynes: I've seen some of Bruce Conner's films, but I'm not certain I was thinking about his work in particular at that time, though you're right, the montage work in *Superstar* comes out of experimental traditions. It *also* comes out of narrative and genre traditions, although I think I was taking it to some extremes: I use references that explode out of, or can't be contained within, a narrative explanation of Karen Carpenter's bad emotional state.

MacDonald: That's what reminds me of *Report*: at the end of that film Conner moves away from the death of Kennedy into a kind of free-form montage of the commercial context within which all political events play out in this country.

How fully were you trying to be funny in *Superstar*? Aside from the Barbie Dolls, it comes across as a relatively conventional documentary about a serious subject.

Haynes: At the time, there was always a question about the film's attitude toward Karen Carpenter. Was I being a little too ironic or campy or something like that. Of course, as soon as you deal with dolls as a vehicle for telling a story or with a character as over-determined as Karen Carpenter—particularly if you're a gay filmmaker, identified with traditions of camp sensibility and humor—you're going to create those questions. And they were fair questions I thought. But in fact, Cynthia and I had an almost childishly earnest desire to understand this character *against* the grain of the criticism and the dismissal of her as not a serious singer or subject. We thought of ourselves as trying to rescue Karen Carpenter from her family.

Superstar was also our way of trying to understand anorexic behavior, which, as we learned, often occurs within very controlling families, and in Karen Carpenter's case, was compounded by the extraordinary pressures on a young girl who was suddenly in the spotlight and whose every change in body fat was being discussed worldwide. Her desire to take back control over her life was something that we understood and tried to create some sympathy for.

MacDonald: In the *Superstar* montages there are images of spanking. Spanking is a motif in your work for a while, and I'm wondering what spanking means to you. The way it's positioned in the films leads me to think that, among other things, you see spanking as a re-direction of repressed sexual energy, maybe repressed gay male sexual energy.

Haynes: There's a fantastic essay by Freud called "A Child Is Being Beaten." It looks at mostly female subjects who told him about their fantasies or memories of witnessing little boys being spanked in the schoolyard, and how this event would create tremendous pleasure, sexual and otherwise, for them.

MacDonald: You've included that idea in *Dottie Gets Spanked*; the sister clearly enjoys seeing a boy getting spanked.

Haynes: Absolutely. What I found so interesting, and useful in terms of anorexic behavior, is the tremendous pleasure some female subjects have in orchestrating a sado-masochistic spectacle for themselves, where they are basically controlling all aspects of the situation. Freud sees it as a clitoral stage where girls are empowered and feel a freedom of expression and agency that they don't feel later when they're vaginally oriented.

I remember reading accounts that made clear that to an anorexic, control over the body brings great pleasure and is, in fact, part of the addiction.

Anorexics would say, "I hear a voice telling me, don't eat, don't eat, and another voice, telling me, okay, okay, I won't." This suggests the double role of being victim and punisher at the same time: a miniature sado-masochistic drama is going on in the anorexic subject's head.

In *Superstar* the only time you see human hands is when hands make one doll spank another. There I was referring to the way kids use dolls to play out their fantasies, sexual and otherwise. But the spanking in *Dottie* is more personal, more weirdly rooted in my early childhood memories and in a dream that I had as a child, which is actually replicated in the film.

At one point I was back at my parents' house. They'd put aside a box of my childhood drawings for me, and as I was sorting through the images, I was reminded of how obsessed I was as a kid with Lucy [Lucille Ball], and Elizabeth Montgomery, and the Flying Nun and Alice in Wonderland and Cinderella—all that girl stuff. It started with *Mary Poppins* [1964], the first film I remember seeing. I would draw these women endlessly, and I especially remember loving to draw the eyeliner and the big nails and the lipstick; in my drawings all the women look like whores! [laughter].

I grew up in Los Angeles and I think my parents met Lucille Ball on a vacation somewhere, so I was able to go to her show as a kid. I visited during the run of *Here's Lucy* [1968–74]. As in *Dottie Gets Spanked*, I made her a book and handed it to her when we visited the set. We all know that the television "Lucy" she portrayed was a sort of child-woman, so it was phenomenal to watch the real-life Lucille Ball controlling the entire production like a general. There was a sort of mock director standing to the side, but Lucy was clearly in charge of everything, and then suddenly she'd be back in character, crying "Waaaaaaa!"—the child-woman again. That duality was fascinating to me, partly because it mirrored a different duality in my life and my fantasy world.

At a certain point, PBS, through ITVS, was trying to get independent filmmakers and experimental filmmakers involved in television; they wanted to produce short films dealing with issues of family. I decided to work with my childhood fascination with Lucy and to focus on the spanking issue—even though my parents didn't believe in spanking.

MacDonald: That's talked about in the film.

Haynes: Right, because the boy *doesn't* get spanked, and he notices that other kids *do*, and so it creates curiosity and desire around spanking.

Another part of this project came from that dream I had as a child. I must have been 3 or 4—very young; the dream ended with a spanking that I received from the strongest man in my world: my Uncle Barry. At the time, my grandmother was studying art, and she had all these instructional books that featured the musculature of the human body. In the dream, at the point of the spanking, I experienced a flood of images; I saw a rapid-fire montage of these drawings and experienced a kind of orgasm.

MacDonald: This orgasmic moment expressed itself as a montage?

Haynes: A cinematic montage. Right out of Bruce Conner!

I find spanking a fantastic theatrical ritual in the family setting. There's something interesting about *desiring* spanking, *desiring* subjugation: it unseats the power dynamic, because you're not supposed to want to be spanked. To desire spanking is to undermine the father's control.

What's so interesting about *He Was Once*, Mary Hestand's evocation of the *Davey and Goliath Show* (an Apparatus film that I performed in), is that it's almost *Superstar* in reverse. Mary wanted to have actors playing dolls, so we shot the whole thing moving in half-speed motion, and under-cranked the camera so that our movements seemed to be at normal speed. We did a slow-motion pantomime to the prerecorded dialogue. I love that *He Was Once* ends with the *father* being spanked, being completely undermined in the power dynamic.

MacDonald: At one point in the dream sequence from *Dottie Gets Spanked*, the father is standing behind the mother who is standing behind the boy who is sitting in front of the TV set watching Dottie. This brings back something in my own life. When I was the boy's age, my favorite television personality was Liberace, which made my parents nervous. I didn't get spanked for it and they didn't tell me to turn the show off, but when I was enjoying Liberace, I could always feel them behind me, worrying about what this might mean, or worrying whether they *should* be worried, and I always felt defiant of their concern.

Haynes: It's amazing how kids understand shame before they even understand the word! They *feel* it, and that's a lot of what *Dottie* is about. Near the end of the film, the boy carefully folds up his drawing of Dottie getting spanked, wraps it in tinfoil and buries it in his backyard. It's as if he's preserving something for the future.

MacDonald: You were born in 1961. I'm surprised at how well you seem to know the Fifties and what it was like for my generation growing up, in *Dottie* and in *Far From Heaven*.

Haynes: Well, I learned about the Fifties from the *films* of the Fifties. During the production of *Far from Heaven* I was very rigid about the idea that we were recreating a Hollywood sound stage experience from the Fifties. In fact, when we were looking for extras, many of the people we considered looked too much like *real* people, not like the sort of patrician, handsome, blonde, *movie* people that you see in the background of those Sirk films. So everything about *Far from Heaven* was filtered through a very self-conscious *cinematic* depiction of the period. It says a lot about the Fifties if my movie connects you to real memories and experiences.

MacDonald: I remember going to see Sirk's *Imitation of Life* [1959] at the huge Fox Theater in St. Louis. The climactic scene is the mother's funeral, where the daughter returns full of regret that she'd disowned her mother for so long, and throws herself on the coffin. During this scene, the theater was in a paroxysm of crying, but for my friend and me, the scene seemed utterly preposterous, ridiculously over the top. Actually, my friend Jerry burst into laughter and I thought we might have to fight our way out of the theater! But as a result, I never took Sirk seriously, at least until you brought him back to me with *Far from Heaven*. For me your film is actually New Improved Sirk, Sirk made credible.

When you were first seeing Sirk, did you take the films seriously?

Haynes: I was first presented with Sirk in an entirely different context, an already elevated context—in college. I didn't have the experience of seeing the films when they first came out, or even of watching Sirk on late night television like so many people did. My first experiences with Sirk were positioned as something of intellectual value—but I know exactly what you mean; even understanding the intellectual defense of Sirk, his films are difficult to watch. For me *Imitation of Life* is one of the more emotionally accessible Sirk films.

There's something about melodrama that is unsatisfying, over-determined and under-explained. The characters in melodrama do not come to knowledge about their predicament; they are pushed along by the forces and mores of their societies, and ultimately they crumble under the pressure, against their own desires. You're supposed to want them to comply, because you know that that's the way movies get resolved, but you also feel, "No! Wait a minute! I thought you were in *love* with this person!" For many people this is exactly what makes melodrama radical: melodramatic films are not about people who are free agents, who are in control of their destiny; they're not like the protagonists of Westerns or gangster films, more male-associated genres where men have a kind of infinite freedom. Often the female subjects in melodramas are trapped, and so, even though they live in these hyper-artificial-looking environments, the characters are more like ordinary people, who don't, in the end, have the strength to be heroes.

MacDonald: The characters in *Far from Heaven* do seem to learn and they do seem to change their lives.

Haynes: They do and they don't. All three of the central characters are suffering in one way or another. I felt that it was really interesting to compare different levels of oppression in a particularly codified, repressed era. And ironically it's the gay man, Frank Whitaker, who has the most freedom, and who gets closest to satisfying his desires—through hiding. He's not as intensely visible as Raymond the gardener, who has to move. But Cathy is at the bottom of the hierarchy; she gives up the love object, loses the husband, and is left with the responsibility for the children.

As I was getting ready to shoot *Far from Heaven*, I thought, "How the hell are these actors going to deal with these roles?" and I remember Julianne Moore saying that Cathy was easy to perform because everything about her *is* on the surface; she really has no deeper psychological dimension. There's no Aristotelian conflict in these characters who are too innocent and ill-equipped to deal with the big issues they confront. Julianne found that freeing.

MacDonald: You've made it clear, even in the opening credits, that *Poison* is based on three Jean Genet novels, but I can't help but see a connection to Genet's *Un Chant d'amour* [1952].

Haynes: *Un Chant d'amour* is just so amazing, so radical. It's from 1949, right?

MacDonald: 1952.

Haynes: 1952—so it came *after* Kenneth Anger's *Fireworks* [1947]! Oh, *that's* amazing, too.

Un Chant d'amour is Genet's one film, and uses a prison setting. It has one of the most erotic and understated moments in all of cinema, the scene of one inmate putting a reed through the stone wall dividing him from his neighboring inmate and blowing smoke through this narrow reed so that the smoke comes out in the other inmate's cell where the neighbor inhales it (figure 53). It's simple, but so beautiful and powerful. And the film is an incredible, frank depiction of nudity and homoerotic imagery. It's exquisite. So yeah, *Un Chant d'amour* was a kind of ghost text that inspired me in *Poison*. I didn't want to re-enact any of it; its influence needed to be implicit, not amplified.

MacDonald: The scene of the men getting married in the "Homo" section of *Poison*, which I assume is a fantasy scene, evokes for me the fantasy sequence in *Un Chant d'amour* where the men frolic in the woods.

FIGURE 53 *Prison inmate imbibing smoke from adjacent cell, in Jean Genet's* Un Chant d'amour *(1952).*

Haynes: That scene in *Poison* isn't a fantasy, actually. All the scenes depicted in and around that rustic courtyard refer to Genet's depictions of Mettray, the Penal colony he romanticizes in *Miracle of the Rose* and contrasts with the scenes of adult prison life at Fontenal—though Genet's romantic inversions have all the investment and desire of fantasy.

MacDonald: One of the early screenings of *Un Chant d'amour* in this country was in San Francisco; it was shut down by the police, who confiscated the film. Saul Landau, who later was involved with the San Francisco Mime Troupe, wrote a brilliant defense of the film. It was the first important essay to be published in what would become a key publication for those interested in avant-garde cinema from the mid-1960s into the 1980s: the *Canyon Cinemanews*. Landau had courage; one of the first things he did after the brouhaha about the first screening was to show the film again, this time as a benefit for Kenneth Anger.

When did you first see *Fireworks* and also *Inauguration of the Pleasure Dome* [1954], a film that is about identity being multifarious and composite, a theme in much of your work?

Haynes: I think I was first seeing Kenneth Anger films in college, or maybe even in high school. I forget which one I saw first, probably *Scorpio Rising* [1963]. The story behind *Fireworks* is so interesting. It was made in 1949, right?

MacDonald: 1947.

Haynes: Unbelievable. His parents are gone for the weekend and he and his friends make this radical, homoerotic, crazy, *beautiful* film.

MacDonald: The earliest openly gay film that I'm aware of. Kinsey was at the first public screening for the film, and, according to Anger, Kinsey bought the first print.

Haynes: Then that film traveled to Europe, and Genet and Jean Cocteau and all those dudes had their screening of this Los Angeles teenager's film. Pretty remarkable.

MacDonald: Like *Scorpio Rising* and some other avant-garde films—Jack Smith's *Flaming Creatures* [1963] is a notable instance—*Poison* ran into trouble with "moral guardians," particularly because of its depiction of homosexuality.

Haynes: The production of *Poison* was given a $25,000 grant by the National Endowment for the Arts. After the film was finished and won the prize at Sundance, there was a review by *Hollywood Reporter* that mis-described the film. *Poison* is made up of three stories—"Homo," "Hero," and "Horror." The review described the whole movie as if it were "Homo," as if the entire film was about anal sex in prison. Somehow, Donald Wildman of the American Family Association heard about the film and took up the cause, and several senators got involved. This was not long after the controversy about the "NEA Four": Karen Finley, Tim Miller, Holly Hughes, and John Fleck, performance artists who were given grants and then charged with inappropriate use of tax-payer money. In the end, their grants were rescinded.

Poison became the next in line for that kind of fame. All of a sudden I was on *Larry King* and all these other shows, and *no* politicians were supporting my position. Sometimes it was me and Dick Armey, or later, me and Ralph Reed, the head of the Christian Coalition. Many of the people attacking *Poison* hadn't even seen the film; they were just arguing that money shouldn't be put into public art that might offend American sensibilities. It wasn't a fair discussion: I was just the artist who made the film with a grant; and they were opposing the whole notion of giving artists grants. If we were going to have a discussion about the *film*, I could have spoken to that, I suppose; but since the issue was public funding of the arts, it would have made more sense to have a politician in favor of public support for artists, defending that position.

The best thing was that they had to have special screenings of *Poison* wherever Senators and Congresspeople go to see movies, so they could see what the controversy was about. In the *Washington Times* I was called "the Fellini of Fellatio"—a proud moment! [laughter] One senator's wife said that watching *Poison* made her want to "bathe in Clorox." Pretty good press! I think this was the first time, or one of the first times, a *film* was the subject of questions about public support of the arts.

MacDonald: The controversy over Marlon Riggs's *Tongues Untied* predates the flap over *Poison*.

Haynes: That's true. These controversies are almost always about gay-related stuff.

At some point during the flap over *Poison*, Robert Redford wrote a letter to John Frohnmayer, the head of the NEA; it went something like: "Hey, John, I just want to speak up in favor of this homo-y movie that you have such problems with. . .." I think because of Redford's support and because *Poison* had the sanction of the Sundance Award, Frohnmayer finally had the nerve to stand up and defend the film.

That's been my only big controversy, and really I'm happy to be part of the tradition of controversial films like *Un Chant d'amour*, *Scorpio Rising*, *Flaming Creatures*, and *Tongues Untied*.

MacDonald: In *Velvet Goldmine* the character of Jack Fairy is pretty obviously an allusion to Jack Smith, who is increasingly considered not only an important avant-garde filmmaker (his *Flaming Creatures* is a crucial Sixties film), but the initiator of what's now called performance art—as well as a major influence on Warhol and many others. Am I correct that you too see Smith that way?

Haynes: Oh, absolutely. I love the famous stories of his performance pieces that would go on for days. They were like Eastern traditions where you watch a NŌ play for twelve hours or whatever. And I love the way his performing was woven into his life; living and performance weren't separated by a curtain or a proscenium.

MacDonald: I remember a Smith performance at the Times Square Show in 1980. Smith arrives and seems to be getting things ready for his performance, putting things where they need to be. The audience waits for what's going to happen. Half an hour goes by, and he's still getting ready; then it's an hour. Finally we realize that this *is* the performance: the process of seeming to get ready to perform *is* the performance.

Haynes: Exactly—the line between life and art is erased. In so many ways that crazy intersection of experimental filmmaking, erotic film (it wasn't called porn in the mid-Sixties), and feature filmmaking—that crazy commingling of all those traditions—produced a moment when people would line up around the block to see *Chelsea Girls* [1966]. All the categories were in a state of flux. This produced not only extraordinary filmmakers, but active and essential audiences. We don't have audiences like that today.

MacDonald: One major theme, if not *the* major theme of your work, has been the quest to be free of identity, or at least of a simplistic sense of what identity is. This is reflected in your quest to be free of *cinematic* identity, your refusal to be restricted to one genre, one kind of presentation—a tendency obvious as early as *Superstar*. *I'm Not There* may be the ultimate instance. I sense that *I'm Not There* was an attempt to pay homage not just to Dylan's career and to *his* defiance of simple definitions of identity, but to the expansion of the American sense of film history that took place during the 1960s and 1970s. You evoke so many dimensions of the cinema scene of that era. *I'm Not There* is a brilliant synthesis of commercial *and* documentary *and* avant-garde attitudes and approaches (figure 54).

Haynes: Well, thank you. I had an extraordinary period at my disposal for that film (even though, of course, Bob Dylan's career has continued well past that era); there were *so* many formal and visual, cinematic and otherwise, experiments going on during that time, experiments that produced a remarkable array of work and so many possibilities.

The subject of Dylan was clearly an expansive one, and one that doesn't stop growing, given his profuse and unending output. In addition to this I was applying a *structure* that was expansive—the opposite, in my mind, of the traditional biopic's determination to reduce and simplify. So I knew from the start that I would need to impose some conceptual limits on the thing. And since most of the characters I'd developed had their roots in the Sixties, an era as seminal to Dylan as he was to it, I decided to take that as my conceptual and stylistic sourcebook—though as creative limits go, the Sixties provided anything but. At the very least I could be guaranteed distinct and contrasting cinematic references for each of the stories that would all, still, come out of a period defined by experimentation, in effect the Vietnam years: 1964 through 1973.

FIGURE 54 *Cate Blanchett as Bob Dylan, re-enacting the "Subterranean Homesick Blues" trailer for D. A. Pennebaker's* Don't Look Back *(1967). The Pennebaker trailer was reenacted by all the major characters in* I'm Not There; *these unreleased trailers are on the Collector's Edition DVD of the film.*
Source: Courtesy Todd Haynes.

MacDonald: How early in the process of conceiving *I'm Not There* did you know you would use a composite of many different kinds of filming, a weave of various cinematic approaches?

Haynes: From conception. The specific cinematic references—the visualization of the film—was something I felt needed to be considered from the start, and would determine not only how the film would look, but how the script would be written.

MacDonald: During the Cate Blanchett story, you remind us of the Warhol Factory and the various forms of image-making that went on there. In other instances, you remind us of the hand-held, gestural 8mm and Super-8mm filmmaking of that era. In still others, you show your awareness of breakthroughs in documentary work (Pennebaker's observational cinema work in *Don't Look Back* [1967], most obviously). How fully were you thinking of particular makers of one kind or another as you conceived the film? Or were you just channeling the general zeitgeist of that moment?

Haynes: All of the references you mention were influences, along with many others. In the end the guiding cinematic references were not necessarily those that Dylan himself was directly associated with (like Pennebaker), but those that, to me, most closely illustrated what Dylan's music was doing at the time. For instance, the Jude story—Cate Blanchett's section—I'd initially pictured like *Don't Look Back*, in verite black-and-white. But this story was about the electric Dylan of late 1965 and 1966, the Dylan of *Highway 61* and *Blonde on Blonde*—a period in his music that was about as far from "social realism" or early cinema-verite as one could get. So Fellini—and particularly *8½* [1963], a film whose rich baroque and urban ironies became the perfect conduit to *Blonde on Blonde*—replaced Pennebaker as the leading stylistic reference for that story (with some Richard Lester, Pennebaker, and William Klein thrown in). Elsewhere the references are nearly as specific: early Godard for the Robbie [Heath Ledger] story; the hippie westerns of the late 1960s and early 1970s for Billy [Richard Gere]; black-and-white experimental minimalism for Arthur [Ben Wishaw]; leftist studio filmmaking—from *Face in the Crowd* [1957, directed by Elia Kazan] to *Bound for Glory* [1976, directed by Hal Ashby] for Woody [Marcus Carl Franklin].

Of course, the ways in which one particular artist has dodged the fixing of identity that the culture always seems to demand (and that so many people still struggle to fulfill) is certainly not confined to that particular era. There was more of an audience for experimenting with identity in the Sixties, but the issue itself hasn't changed much. Of course, I knew from the beginning that whatever happened to *I'm Not There* in today's world market couldn't be the same as what was happening then, couldn't be—and that was fine. But I also didn't want to limit the range of possibilities suggested by *I'm Not There* because of today's different audience; as fully as possible, I wanted to honor the exuberance of that time and make it accessible. *I'm Not There* had fantastic actors and that helped to root a lot of people within the narrative fracture of the film, and the music gives a lot of people access as well.

MacDonald: I'm Not There didn't do as well as we might have hoped.

Haynes: I was completely satisfied with the reception. Critically it was well-received, more than I expected, and that felt bizarre and exciting. All in all, it was a surprising year for American film, and *I'm Not There* was in the company of a lot of interesting work. If the film was going to get such generous critical reaction, it would probably have done better in a less exciting year. But I was happy to see great commercial films by interesting directors coming out for the first time in what seemed like a decade—and then look what happened! In one year four major independent film companies folded.

Also, the ancillary possibility for DVD sales is disappearing: people download now. This is a really curious time for independent filmmaking. Fassbinder's films have been hugely influential on me and they still amaze and exhaust me. I just bought the great Criterion collection of *Berlin Alexanderplatz* [1983]; I hadn't seen it since the late 1980s, when it was being shown around. It's become interesting to me again, in part because I'm just now thinking about doing something in an episodic format, a long, multiple-part piece for television [this would become *Mildred Pierce* (2011)].

"Sensory Ethnography"

In recent decades the "truth claim" of documentary film has come to seem to some commentators more dangerous than fiction itself. No one *believes* that narrative melodrama is true; we understand that we are watching stories performed by actors. On the other hand, by the 1920s the history of documentary had developed a range of techniques—most obviously, the expert "voice-of-god" narrator (expressed in visual intertitles or, later on, vocally)—precisely in order to convince viewers of the veracity of whatever claim the specific documentary was making. During the 1960s cinema-verite filmmaking challenged the classic informational mode of documentary presentation, and some of its early practitioners seemed convinced that this new approach to shooting as events unfolded before the camera re-established the legitimacy of documentary's truth claim, at least until a series of faux documentaries—Stanton Kaye's *Georg* (1964), Jim McBride's *David Holzman's Diary* (1967), Mitchell Block's *No Lies* (1973)—demonstrated that cinema-verite shooting could be used to delude viewers as well as to enlighten them. More recently, *Bontoc Eulogy* (1995, directed by Marlon Fuentes and Bridget Yearen) did the same for a certain kind of informational documentary about colonialism.

The expansion of postcolonial studies during the past twenty-five years offered particular challenges to the tradition of documenting Other cultures. The proposition that filmmakers from one culture, using equipment and techniques of representation developed in that culture, could provide a fair and insightful depiction of a culture not their own came to seem increasingly absurd. One result was the reframing of our understanding of ethnographic film, including its classic progenitors. Clearly, Robert Flaherty's representation of Inuit culture in *Nanook of the North* (1922) and Merian C. Cooper and Ernest B. Schoedsack's depiction of the annual migration of the Bakhtiari tribes in *Grass* (1925) were more about these filmmakers' own assumptions, their *own* cultures, than about the cultures they pretended to reveal. The same came to seem true of John Marshall's *The Hunters* (1957)—even to Marshall himself!—and Robert Gardner's *Dead Birds* (1964), the first two ethnographic films to be included in the Library of Congress's National Film Registry. And as early as 1979, Tim Asch's *The Ax Fight* demonstrated a variety of problems with the representation of the Yanomami in the films he made with Napoleon Chagnon, including the fact that an unedited, direct-cinema view of an altercation is almost inevitably misconstrued by audiences not already familiar with the culture in which the altercation occurs.

These challenges to ethnographic filmmaking did not negate interest in the genre—though it did help a new generation of filmmakers interested in depicting unfamiliar cultures and cultural practices to come to grips with the limitations of their process. As these filmmakers reconsidered the process of documenting the Other, some of them mounted their own critique of anthropology itself—at least to the extent that anthropology was focused on the production of written texts that codified what was learned by anthropologists working in the field. These filmmakers and theorists saw filmmaking not as a poor substitute for serious anthropological study or as mere illustrations of its conclusions, but as a means of recording at least some of the sensory elements of culture and of evoking the complex, multifaceted experience of being present within that culture—an experience that for all practical purposes is erased in the transition to textual codification.

Among the most important proponents of what has come to be called "sensory ethnography" is Lucien Castaing-Taylor, who established Harvard's Sensory Ethnography Lab (SEL), a collaboration between the Departments of Anthropology and Visual and Environmental Studies, in 2006. The Lab has revived Cambridge's significance in the history of ethnographic filmmaking, nurturing a cadre of accomplished and adventurous filmmakers—most notably, John Paul Sniadecki, Stephanie Spray, Véréna Paravel, and Pacho Velez—interested in using cinema to provide sensory experiences of cultural practices in the process of transformation. After all, in a world where the population explosion has necessitated constant migration and technological development, any culture and virtually any cultural practice is no longer a "traditional way of life," but an experience of change—and the films coming from the Sensory Ethnography Lab are in most instances attempts to pay careful visual and auditory attention to the ongoing processes of transformation in all their complexity.

Castaing-Taylor and fellow anthropologist Ilisa Barbash provided one model of sensory ethnographic cinema in their documentary *Sweetgrass* (2009). Beginning in 2001, Barbash and Castaing-Taylor immersed themselves in the experiences of the sheep ranchers of Big Timber, Montana, and Castaing-Taylor accompanied the cowboys as they herded thousands of sheep into the mountains at the beginning of summer and down from the mountain pasturing at the end of the summer—a practice that had been going on for a century, but was now coming to an end as a result of a variety of economic and environmental factors. *Sweetgrass* was shot by Castaing-Taylor in the direct-cinema fashion—with considerable invention with image and sound (often epic long shots of the cowboys at work are accompanied by auditory "close-ups") and without entirely suppressing his own presence. Though the sheepherding project began before Barbash and Castaing-Taylor's move to

Harvard, the project evolved along with the Sensory Ethnography Lab, and *Sweetgrass* became the Lab's first critical success.

A second result of Barbash and Castaing-Taylor's sheepherding research was a series of gallery installations focusing on particular elements of the annual round of birthing, pasturing, and shearing the sheep. Perhaps the most noteworthy of these shorter pieces is *Hell Roaring Creek* (final version, 2010). For twenty minutes, Castaing-Taylor's camera—positioned in the middle of Hell Roaring Creek facing the flow of the water just before dawn—records the sheep, cowboys, and their dogs amassing on the right side of the creek, then crossing the creek (and the widescreen film frame) from right to left. *Hell Roaring Creek* alternates between sound alone, and image and sound; and the surrounding landscape revealed by the gradual coming of dawn provides a ground against which the endlessly distinct actions of the sheep are figured.

The following interview is divided into five parts. In the first, Barbash and Castaing-Taylor talk about their first collaboration, *In and Out of Africa* (1992), a film about the transnational market for African art, and about the process of producing, shooting, and editing *Sweetgrass* (this conversation began in the fall of 2009, when the filmmakers visited my class on the History of Documentary at Harvard, and continued online during 2010–11). During the second part, Castaing-Taylor and I discuss his installation pieces; and, during the third, the theoretical assumptions behind the Sensory Ethnography Lab.

The fourth and fifth sections focus on two recent noteworthy contributions of the SEL. In the fourth, developed online during the fall of 2012, Castaing-Taylor and Véréna Paravel discuss the collaboration that resulted in *Leviathan* (2012), their remarkably visceral and sensual depiction of ocean fishing on boats shipping out of New Bedford, Massachusetts. In the fifth, Stephanie Spray and Pacho Velez discuss *Manakamana* (2013), their engaging meditation on pilgrims on the Manakamana cable car in Nepal, going to visit or coming from visiting the temple of the goddess Bhagwati (our interview was developed online in January 2013).

Ilisa Barbash and Lucien Castaing-Taylor (on *In and Out of Africa* and *Sweetgrass*)

MacDonald: In and Out of Africa *was your first film; how did that project develop? And what accounts for the fifteen-year gap between it and your re-entry into filmmaking with* Sweetgrass?
Barbash: I grew up loving the movies, but it never occurred to me that an ordinary person could make them. When I got out of college, I was interested in journalism, but this was during the cable-channel boom in New York City, and it was easier to get a freelance job in television production than at a newspaper. At a certain point I realized that I didn't want to climb the ladder to be

a small part of a large production organization, so I went back to school, to the Master's Program in Visual Anthropology at the University of Southern California, where I learned some of the technical skills necessary to be part of a small film crew. There I met Lucien who was escaping his own insular world in England. We were part of a cohort of about eleven students, and Lucien and I started working together. *In and Out of Africa* was our thesis video, a discursive collage on authenticity, taste, and racial politics in the transnational African art market.

We had originally intended to make a single-channel video about the cultural effects of tourism on the Dogon of Mali. We'd been there a few times and had a number of contacts, both African and European. But about three months before we were to shoot, there was a coup d'état in Mali, which of course meant no tourists. So we shifted gears. At the time, Lucien was editing the journal *Visual Anthropology Review*, and had published an article by a doctoral student, Chris Steiner, whose dissertation research was on Hausa Muslim art traders in the Ivory Coast. We called him up and asked if he knew any who were trading between the Ivory Coast and New York. Chris introduced us to Gabai Baare in New York, and that summer Chris, Lucien, and I met up on the Ivory Coast to film. Of course, there were obvious differences between our original ideas and our final project. But what we were really interested in exploring—the ways in which Africans and Europeans/Americans see each other, the ways in which they represent themselves to each other and the ways in which they internalize all these representations—remained the same.

The gap between *In and Out* and *Sweetgrass* was much longer than we'd have liked. The reasons are mundane. Having vowed never to return to academia, Lucien did a doctorate in anthropology! For that we lived in Martinique for two and a half years, during which time we wrote *Cross-Cultural Filmmaking* and collaborated with Isaac Julien on the film *Frantz Fanon: Black Skin White Mask* [1996]. We moved twice, because of new jobs, started a family, and wrote and edited a number of books. I had a six-month battle with head and neck cancer, which consumed all our energy for a year or more.

Both of the films were informed by a long period of reflection and revision, about what we liked and didn't like in documentary, what we knew and didn't know, and what we thought might be possible. I'm not sure whether we'd have been able to make *Sweetgrass* soon after making *In and Out of Africa*, even if all the funding and logistics had been in place. It takes us a long time not just physically to make a film but also to be ready to try something new.

MacDonald: I've seen *Sweetgrass* in various forms over the past couple of years. You've been working on it for nearly a decade. Could you talk about how this project has evolved?

Barbash: We were living and teaching in Boulder, Colorado, when the project came to us. There was a New Jersey/Wisconsin newspaper owner, Bill Heaney, who was leasing land to Lawrence Allestad, the owner of the sheep in the film, at a point when Lawrence's deeded land was drying up because of drought and changing weather patterns. Lawrence would graze this land during fall and spring, and then follow an 80-year-plus tradition of trailing his sheep into the Beartooth-Absaroka range near Yellowstone each summer. He had a family permit that had been passed down through four generations of Norwegian descendants. One day the sheep owner said to the land owner, "This is the last time I'm ever going to do this; someone should make a film about me," and word traveled, eventually to us in March of 2001, and we thought it sounded like a wonderful project. We had small children so we didn't want to travel very far. That summer, we went up through Wyoming to Montana with the family, and a babysitter and her dog, and started shooting.

Castaing-Taylor: As Lisa said, we were living in the Rockies and were interested in the so-called New West (the *wunderkind* scholar Patti Limerick was a colleague in Boulder [Limerick established the Center of the American West in Boulder in 1986]), especially the changes wrought by yuppification, with all the neo-homesteaders—rich hobby farmers—moving in and buying up the land as a playground for their kids and guests for a few weeks every summer.

It was a chance, or a challenge, for us to engage anew with "salvage ethnography"—how to represent a world on the wane—something that had been considered totally retrograde within anthropology since the 1960s. Could we acknowledge a historical loss without falling prey to all the pitfalls of patronizing romanticism and nostalgia?

MacDonald: When you say that the tradition of salvage ethnography has been intellectually discredited, to what extent do you feel that that negates the value of the films of crucial contributors to cinematic salvage ethnography like John Marshall and Robert Gardner?

Castaing-Taylor: Maybe it does negate their value. But is that all wrong? They remained committed to visual salvage anthropology long after written anthropology, critical theory, and art practice had moved on and turned their attention to hybridizing, globalizing cultural formations in various states of emergence and becoming.

Marshall's early sequence films among the !Kung are still remarkable, not least for their unselfconscious structural rigor in a filmmaker who never, to my knowledge, had any interest in the avant-garde. *A Joking Relationship* [1962] is extraordinary in its coupling of the erotic and the ethnographic. But Marshall was an uneven cinematographer and a rather sloppy filmmaker. His magnum opus, *A Kalahari Family*, is all over the place, stylistically and substantively.

MacDonald: In 1973 I took a one-week intensive course on ethnographic film from Marshall; to my surprise, he opened that course with Peter

Kubelka's flicker film, *Arnulf Rainer* [1960]. He did have some awareness of avant-garde filmmaking.

And Gardner?

Castaing-Taylor: Gardner lost interest in anthropology early on, and has never really done ethnographic fieldwork of his own, but in a typical cinematic division of labor, has borrowed from the anthropological expertise of others—among the Dani, the Hamar, the Wodaabe, and also in Benares. His one masterpiece, for me, is *Forest of Bliss* [1986], and I doubt it will seem any less of an achievement a century from now.

But the anachronistic discourse of *Dead Birds*, its divine cinematographic omniscience—if not falling afoul of the pathetic fallacy, then at least exemplifying a kind of pathetic infallibility—has been an embarrassment to anthropologists for decades. The purple-prose voice-over imprisons the Dani within some sublimated, dehistoricized, deeply racialized Stone Age formaldehyde that was concocted in Cambridge, Massachusetts. Even Gardner's later *Deep Hearts* [1979] and the cinematographically mind-blowing *Rivers of Sand* [1974] display almost no evidence of modernity, or of any coevality between the Hamar, the Peul, and their imagined spectators.

Barbash: I disagree, Lucien. I don't think the developments you mentioned negate the value of these films at all. Certainly the Marshall family was aware that they were filming a world on the wane and were careful not to film things like Coke bottles (a la *The Gods Must be Crazy* [1980]) in their work. In retrospect, we can criticize them for not being more upfront about their subject positions and the effect of their presence on their communities in their 1950s–1970s films and ethnographies. But that's applying contemporary standards to work done fifty-odd years go. And since then, John, Lorna, and Elizabeth Marshall have acknowledged the changes in the lives of the !Kung that were occurring as they did their research—John, especially, in his *Kalahari Family*.

Nobody sees these films outside of a classroom any more, and there they remain valuable approximations of what life was like for hunter-gatherers in the 1950s. Were the !Kung "untouched" when the Marshalls arrived? No. Are these real !Kung in their films? Yes. Is this pretty close to what their lives were like? Probably.

What's delighted me about anthropology since I first started studying it is that at least since the mid-1980s we've learned that we can't look at any kind of representation without being critical of it, and without second-guessing the ideological inclinations and personal motivations, conscious and unconscious, of the author. I'm not sure other disciplines reflect on themselves to the same degree.

A close examination of the work of Gardner taught me that a work of ethnography emerges from the originating culture, that of the filmmaker, and is inevitably a product of its time. If you are looking for a single truth, you are not going to find it in one of Gardner's films. But that doesn't mean you're not going to get anything of value from them.

MacDonald: When did you begin shooting what became *Sweetgrass*?

Castaing-Taylor: In 2001-2002. We became so engrossed that we, all of us as a family, spent three summers there. I was on a sabbatical during this period, so during 2001-2002, I was spending three or four days out of every week or two, year round, up there—all the winter sequences, the shearing and the lambing, were shot during that time. We shot in Montana between 2001 and 2007, but far more intensively in the early years before we moved to Boston. Had we not moved east, we'd probably still be shooting!

Barbash: The majority of the footage you see in *Sweetgrass* was shot that first summer—the whole trajectory of going up into the mountains and coming back down. In retrospect, this surprises me because you would think that as you get to know people better, you're going to get more interesting, more intimate footage. Instead, what happened was that, summer by summer, we had to work harder and harder to get useful material.

Also, over the three summers the hired hands working with the sheep changed, and that made it difficult to integrate the three years. The first summer's footage had John and Pat, the two herders you get to know in the film; during the second summer Pat worked with someone else and was becoming discouraged with the whole sheep-herding endeavor. He was exhausted, homesick, had a girlfriend back home he missed, and he was doing the bulk of the work himself. That's when he went up to the top of the mountain and complained to his mother that he just couldn't handle it anymore. So that sequence is from the second summer. There's almost nothing in the film from the third summer. All the birthing and shearing and the hay being spewed out onto the landscape was shot between the first summer and the second summer.

MacDonald: How often did you need to have the herders, or others, re-enact things they did?

Castaing-Taylor: I don't think we staged anything. We didn't interview anybody either, at least when the camera was rolling—though when I wasn't shooting I probably drove them spare with my asinine questions. But it would have been antithetical to both the aesthetics and the ethics we were after to have asked anyone to re-enact anything for the camera. Sometimes something happened and I missed it and I would pray that they would do it again— invariably in vain—but we never directed action, even in cases where it might look as if we did.

Barbash: The one scene for which we most prepared was the shot of the sheep going through town. For that we had two cameras going the first year. I was on the roof of a Land Rover shooting down the street from above and Lucien was on the ground shooting tracking shots. I focused way down the street toward the railroad tracks to catch the sheep coming up onto the horizon and crossing the tracks. It seemed to take forever. And then as the sheep came closer I spied Lucien in the corner of the frame, wearing his harness, walking and shooting alongside Lawrence. Of course, we could not do a second shot with three thousand sheep in the middle of town!

Jump cut to the next summer. Again on or around July 5 we got up at 4:30 in the morning, got both cameras ready, quickly drove to the center of town to set up the shot, and then I realized that in our rush, I'd forgotten my camera! Lucien filmed down from the Land Rover roof and that's the shot in the film.

MacDonald: Lucien, what was your relationship with the herders; they seem amazingly at ease around you, and yet, you must be kneeling on the ground right in front of them as you're filming. They do mention you when you're in the tent at one point; and at the end of the phone call scene, Pat seems to talk to you about his "phone booth," but generally your presence is not remarked by John and Pat.

Castaing-Taylor: There's a weird moment when we're all in the cook tent. After you hear a snore, John tells Pat that it's so hot in the tent that "Lucien fell asleep." Technically, even epistemologically, that's so bizarre as to be borderline incomprehensible. It's definitely thought-provoking. How can the camera operator *of what you're seeing* have fallen asleep? Well, as it happens, I really *had*, but the camera was on my lap and my right hand was still on the handle, and the camera was just mindlessly recording away. It's a reflexive moment, but not your garden-variety documentary *mise-en-abîme*.

Another moment that bowls me over is right after Pat's phone conversation with his mother, when his cell battery gives out. He turns to me and says "I love to torment her." That remark speaks volumes, and you immediately have to rethink the whole sequence you've just seen. Was his vulnerability with his mother not genuine? Was he hamming it up for attention, and if so, hers, or mine, behind the camera? Or is he making light of it to cloak his vulnerability? I rather think the latter, which only adds more pathos to the scene. There are various other moments when I'm acknowledged, explicitly or implicitly, but you're right that, stylistically, we chose not to belabor them.

Most of our subjects knew each other well, which affected how comfortable they were around the camera. And being at eleven or twelve-thousand feet in the mountains for two–three months, looking after three thousand sheep, controlling where they graze and trying to protect them from predators, tending camp day in day out, with nobody but two guys and the animals to talk to, you get intimate. We had extended conversations about Uncle Snooks and Aunt Edna; John and Pat mapped their conjugal relations; I would tell them about growing up in Liverpool and life in Europe. Pat and I are about the same age, and have kids the same age, but I was a foreigner who had never set foot in Montana before starting this project; John is maybe twenty years older, has spent more time herding sheep, and is a Vietnam Vet. We had more than enough to talk about—there were some fantastic conversations that didn't get into *Sweetgrass*.

I think a number of things contributed to their apparent indifference to the camera. One is that when I wasn't filming, when I didn't have the camera on me, I was working as they were, or at least trying to help out as best I could. I was a greenhorn; I didn't know sheep, had never ridden a horse before, and so on—so I was their apprentice in many ways. Obviously I had to learn fast. And I was not only a greenhorn, but a foreigner with a funny, barely comprehensible British accent. I must have seemed like an alien to them, and my project might have seemed as alien as I was.

I remember when I first went out there, during the lambing in 2001, I was on the phone with Lawrence Allestad, the rancher who owns the sheep and the grazing allotment, and I could tell he wasn't understanding a word I was saying. Finally he said, "Hold on a second, I'll get my wife; she speaks English. I'm a 'Wegian." Since the Second World War, as their family-oriented ranching culture has withered away, rural Montanans of Norwegian descent have felt more and more displaced by political-economic developments, and they have sometimes internalized a sense of their own inferiority. It's terribly sad when a culture or subculture that perceived itself as the center of its own universe gets progressively marginalized. One of the later scenes to end up on the cutting room floor was a story about a 'Wegian kid who believed it was illegal for 'Wegians to go to college.

Also, the camera was a gargantuan shoulder-mounted monstrosity that was suspended from a spring and aluminum bar that came up my spine and extended over my head—to help lower the center of gravity and take some of the pressure off my arms. It cut off 180 degrees of my vision and blocked out half my face. And because I almost never lowered it from my shoulder, even when eating around the fire or herding the sheep, it became almost a prosthetic extension of my body, and I, I suppose, a kind of cyborg. Paradoxically, because it was *so* visible, with no possibility of dissimulation, the camera became part of the fabric of our daily lives and everyone tended to ignore it.

Contrary to what you'd expect, the effect is almost the inverse of what happens with small home-video cameras, especially now that they have fold-out LCD screens—you can tell immediately whether these new cameras are recording or not, which results in this self-conscious performativity on the part of subjects. We were mostly interested in ways our subjects would reveal dimensions of themselves when they weren't explicitly or exclusively acting out for the camera.

Barbash: The Montanans we worked with are used to going on trail-riding expeditions and hunts with East Coast dudes, and they make fun of how lame they are. I think the fact that Lucien walked up the mountain, for the most part holding a heavy camera, while other people were riding, was a kind of endurance test that he passed; they could see that he was not some wimpy East Coaster.

Castaing-Taylor: I don't know about that.

Another thing is that when I did have the camera on me and was shooting, I wouldn't interact with them; I wouldn't talk or answer any questions. Because they knew I was working in my own way, and because they had a respect for work, they stopped trying to interact with me. If we were bedding the sheep down or something, we'd exchange a minimum of information through the walkie-talkies we all carried—which ended up being acoustically prominent in the sound track of *Sweetgrass*—but they soon realized I wasn't very good company when I was holding the camera.

MacDonald: One thing that troubles me about *Sweetgrass* is a technological issue. When I saw the blow-up to 35mm at the Flaherty seminar and again, at the New York Film Festival, the epic landscape shots often seemed to break down a bit. I didn't notice this when I originally saw the material on DVD before the blow-up, and I assume it's a function of the limitations of the video technology you had in the early 2000s. Could you talk about your struggles to get this film looking its best?

Castaing-Taylor: You're such a snob! But I agree, it was unwatchable in Alice Tully Hall: the screen is too large and it's also a multi-purpose space, with red lights from the aisles shining on the screen. Incredible! But it looked fantastic at Film Forum, where the cinema screens are probably smaller than some people's private plasma screens on the Upper East Side.

What can I say? We had no money. With our kind of uncontrolled, unscripted methodology, we knew we'd end up with a high shooting ratio. We had no choice but to shoot it on standard definition NTSC digital video. We used three cameras, but almost all of it was shot on a 3 2/3" CCD DVCam camera, a then-excellent model that no student today would touch with a ten-foot barge pole. "Standard" definition video has 480 lines of horizontal resolution—actually two interlaced fields of 243 lines. High definition, which wasn't yet available, has 720, 1080, or more.

Blowing up a standard-def NTSC signal to 35mm is never straightforward. Pedro Costa's Lisbon trilogy, and a number of his other works, were shot on PAL DV, which is superior to NTSC, but still a far cry from the resolution of analog 35mm film, which is usually reckoned as somewhere around 15,000–18,000 pixels. Costa is often shooting in low light, with very high contrast ratios, yet his work looks out of this world. He told me about his colorist, Patrick Lindenmaier, based in Zurich, who has hand-built the most advanced digital-to-film transfer facilities in the world.

I sent Patrick a rough cut of *Sweetgrass* on DVD, and when he saw the shot of the newly shorn sheep shivering in the snow, he agreed to work with us, but warned that he could only do so much. To the extent that *Sweetgrass* is watchable at all is in large part due to his efforts. We spent two long weeks in Zurich and Bern doing final post-production and film-out. But when *Sweetgrass* premiered in Berlin, on the largest screen in that obscene shrine to unfettered post-unification global capital, Potsdamer Platz, I looked at Patrick halfway through the screening, and he had his head in his hands. Even 35mm film resolution doesn't hold up at that size. Big Sky is God's country, and it wasn't made to be rendered on standard def. But beggars can't be choosers.

Barbash: I would add that I don't think that anyone with a 35mm camera rig would have gotten up into those mountains and been able to film all that went on, so from the get-go it was obvious that there would be some technical compromises.

MacDonald: Lucien, I've heard you say that *Sweetgrass* is more interested in the sheep than the humans (figure 55). Could you talk about this?

Castaing-Taylor: Oh, I don't trust anything I say about the film. The other day at a Q&A, I even found myself reciting something from a review as if it was my own take on the film! If we could say in words what the film, the *vilm*, is about—our collaborator Ernst Karel prefers "vilm," as an umbrella term to encompass video and film, analogous to "photograph," which doesn't discriminate against digital or analog—we wouldn't have had to make it.

But I think *Sweetgrass* is interested in both the sheep and the people, or more precisely their intertwined naturecultures within the context of their larger ecological fold. Sheep and humans have existed uneasily with each other since we first domesticated them in Mesopotamia ten-thousand-odd years ago in the Neolithic Revolution; sheep were quite possibly the first domesticated livestock animal. They gave humanity our first staple proteins: milk

FIGURE 55 *Bellwether ewe, in Ilisa Barbash and Lucien Castaing-Taylor's* Sweetgrass *(2009)*.

Source: Courtesy Barbash and Castaing-Taylor.

and meat. Not to mention their skins, for shelter—and a couple of thousand years later, also their wool. They wouldn't exist without us, and couldn't survive without us, because of the way we've bred them (to maximize both birth weight and the number of live births) over the millennia. So I don't think you can distinguish between "people" and "sheep." It's more that we're so many variations of sheeple.

It's true that while we started off more interested in the herders and their relationships to their animals and land, the sheep slowly crept up on us and in a way stole the film. I hadn't given much thought to the aesthetics of sheep before, never mind their lifeworld, the phenomenology of sheep. Come to think of it, the Christian iconography of lambs and sheep (don't forget, Jacob, David, Isaac, Abraham, Moses, and of course Mohammed, were all shepherds) had probably inured me to sheep as a subject. But it's hard not to spend countless hours herding and filming them in the back of beyond without starting to think about their subjectivities and also of course their objectivities—their appearance. I find their bodies fascinating to look at.

Western thought from the Greeks on, and especially after Descartes, has been hell bent on setting humanity apart from animalia. Linnaeus was the one exception—as he put it in his *Systema naturae* in reference to the Cartesian conception of animals as so many soulless *automata mechanica*, "Cartesius certe non vidit simios": evidently Descartes never saw a monkey! Linnaeus was dead right. The same has held true ever since, from Heidegger, for whom animals inhabited an "environment," but never a "Welt," a world, through Benjamin, Levinas, Lacan, even Derrida—who tried harder than anyone to turn the theoretical tables on the human/animal dyad in his last book, *L'animal que donc je suis,* but failed miserably. His efforts to extend ontological density to animalia never went any further than the disquiet he felt before his cat—his *chatte,* his pussy, as he insists—as she beheld his limp *bitte* in his Parisian apartment.

In any event, in some way *Sweetgrass* does seek to anthropomorphize sheep, and simultaneously to bestialize humanity. I think Dewey was right in *Art as Experience* where he insisted that the best art recouples us with our base, bestial selves, and yokes culture back to nature and the human to the live animal. Most social theory now supposes that "nature" is just some secondary elaboration, a cultural construction—Bruno Latour has argued that the concept of nature has been coopted by the singular authoritative voice of capital-S Science and should therefore be abolished altogether—but that's pure poppycock, postmodernism of the most parochial kind.

Barbash: I'd like to propose that the *dogs* are the unsung heroes and heroines of the film. They function on all sorts of levels, as real helpmates, as physical extensions of the herders, and as their psychological mirrors. There are at least two kinds of dogs in the film. There are the herders—border collies. They're working dogs but are like pets and have names: Coco, Breck, Tommy

Dog, Lena, and my favorite, Maybe. They take commands, as many as two in order. And they can be directed to round up masses of sheep, corral strays, push a herd forward. These dogs seem to function as emotional extensions of the people. When all is chaotic, Lena seems to be running out of control, Breck won't follow John the way he would like. When Pat is at the end of his tether, Tommy Dog needs an affectionate pat and a drink of water.

Then there are the big white dogs, five Great Pyrenees and one Turkish Akbash. These are the guard dogs. They are raised with the sheep and are not treated like pets. They don't have names; in many ways, they're almost feral. They live and sleep with the sheep and will protect them as long as the sheep are alive and healthy. In fact, you may notice that they even allow the sheep to push them around a bit. They will fight to the death defending their flock against a bear. But right after the cell phone call, when we know that things are falling apart, we see the white dogs snarling at each other, tearing apart the carcass of a sheep. They're always hungry, and the moment one of their charges is dead, she becomes meat. They reflect the dramatic, and sometimes very dark, tenor of the film, and remind me of the three old witches at the beginning of *Macbeth*.

MacDonald: In what ways did your thinking about humans and animals affect the structuring of *Sweetgrass*?

Castaing-Taylor: In both filming and later editing *Sweetgrass*, we became more and more invested in nature, both our identity within it and our experience of it. It's no accident that the film begins in the domain of the sheep, and humans enter the fray only later and gradually. One of the most trenchant qualities invoked by philosophers and anthropologists as evidence of our separation from the animal kingdom has been our putative monopoly of language, which is why, when humans eventually do appear in *Sweetgrass*, they do so largely non-verbally. Other than AC/DC's "Highway to Hell" lyrics, which I worry are read as overtly allegorical, or as editorializing on our part, there are no intelligible spoken words during the shearing sequence.

The first spoken human word in *Sweetgrass* is the call of the shepherd trying to get the sheep to follow him into the shearing pen. He yells something unintelligible to non-locals, "Coom biddy." When I first heard this, I asked what it meant. The Norwegians told me it was a bastardization of old Norwegian that their grandparent homesteaders had brought with them. The local Irish thought it was a corruption of "Come, Paddy!" They were both wrong. In certain valleys in the south of England in Stuart and Tudor days, when you let your ducks out of their coop in the morning, you would call for them to follow you so you could feed them grain, "Coom biddy, coom biddy"—a contraction of "Come, I bid thee!" So to my knowledge these twenty-first-century Montanans are the last people on earth to speak this Stuart and Tudor vernacular (I've certainly never heard any rural Brits use it) (figure 56).

FIGURE 56 *The opening moment in the "Coom biddy" sequence in Ilisa Barbash and Lucien Castaing-Taylor's* Sweetgrass *(2009), and in Lucien Castaing-Taylor's installation version of this event,* Coom Biddy *(2012).*
Source: Courtesy Barbash and Castaing-Taylor.

The next human enunciation in *Sweetgrass* is in my favorite shot of the movie—when the woman in the night lambing shed is trying to coax the ewe to acknowledge and follow its lamb into a "jug," a pen. She's mimicking the sound of the lamb, and if you're not a sheep person, you probably can't be sure in this shot which sounds are ovine and which human. Mimicry, of course, is behind all communication, and is a much more profound form of commensality than propositional language. So here we have proto-language, uttered by a human imitating an animal, but we're still delaying the introduction of language per se.

It's interesting how slowly these "ideas," or idea-images, if that is what they are, came to us. While nature loomed ever larger in my mind, not to mention my body, as we were filming, the structure of the film, which now seems so self-evident and conventional—basically just reflecting the narrative of the sheep drive to and from the mountains—was created only at the very end of the editing. Originally all the snow footage that you see at the beginning, the sheep eating the cake, the unraveling of the hay bale, the shearing, came at the end. But very late in the editing we shifted that material to the beginning. After the release of the journey down the mountain and the semi-closure of the train tracks and stock yards, it seemed too grueling for the spectator to be submitted to the shearing, and we wanted to end the film back in the domain of the sheep, relegating humanity to the periphery, beyond figure, even beyond ground (figure 57).

FIGURE 57 *John, on the move, at the end of Ilisa Barbash and Lucien Castaing-Taylor's* Sweetgrass *(2009)*.

Source: Courtesy Barbash and Castaing-Taylor.

But this then left us ending on John and the other guy driving away in the pick-up, which was initially very hard for me to be reconciled to—ending on *humans*, I mean, the obsessive subject of cinema since its invention—after all we had done to try to relativize them and relocate them within a larger matrix of nature. And it seemed to hint at a kind of closure that was both specious (this human's future is in fact so uncertain, totally open-ended) and clichéd. But, by extending the shot for as long as possible, and thereby minimizing the significance of the already laconic dialogue in it, and then by extending it acoustically for as long again after the hard cut to black, I came around to it.

And it was important that after the main credits we return to the mountains, the view of the Beartooths from the Absarokas, but with a totally different soundscape: it's fall, elk are bugling (an eerie sound that most city folks can't identify), the domesticated animals are gone, the humans are gone. In a sense, nature has returned.

MacDonald: Your use of sound in *Sweetgrass* is fascinating, not just because of the sounds of the sheep, but because of the way the sound-scape of the film is constructed: we're often *hearing* in close-up, extreme close-up, as we're *seeing* in long shot, even extreme long-shot. Could you talk about how you did this and what led to this approach? Kiarostami's *The Wind Will Carry Us* (1999) works with sound this way.

Barbash: The discrepancy between what you hear and what you think you should hear in sync with an image emerged in the editing room rather than being planned. Initially, we just wanted to get the best sound possible, and it was clear that we had to do that with radio microphones. As we edited, we had to think about which sounds we'd privilege and then these odd pairings began to emerge, but Lucien can speak more to the actual recording process.

Castaing-Taylor: When I was recording up in the mountains, I would put up to eight wireless mikes on people—and occasionally on a horse, a dog, or a sheep, though the mikes were expensive and the cables tore easily, so we couldn't afford that as much as we'd have liked—I think we ended up spending more money on mikes than we did on the camera! I could only record four tracks at any one time, two through the camera and two through a tape recorder, so I would be listening through headphones to the different sound sources and deciding which to plug in and record. My experience of being high in the mountains, with these incredible views, but of listening all the while to these sound sources had a huge effect on the final film. In the first place, because lavaliere mikes are so close to the sound source, they result in this very subjective, guttural, highly embodied sound. Roland Barthes spoke not of the mouth, but of the animalic muzzle—the *museau*, not the *bouche* or even the *gueule*—and I thought a lot about what he meant when I was recording the sound.

If we succeed in adequately bestializing humanity in *Sweetgrass*, I'd guess it's in large part due to the sound. Exclamations, heavy breathing, non-propositional fragments of language half mumbled under someone's breath, tailing off into song or a cough or a cry. This *is* how we speak, these *are* the sounds we all make. But documentary has almost entirely turned a deaf ear to them. Also, documentary conventions of naturalism are such that acoustical and optical perspectives are generally made to appear to be one and the same. If someone is close to the camera they should sound close; if they're far away, they should sound far away. Fiction films are not nearly so literal-minded. When we were editing, the aesthetic tension between the perspective and spatiality of the sound and picture really came to the fore, and we often tried to push the discrepancy as far as we could.

The danger of lavalier mikes is, of course, twofold: you privilege speech over other kinds of sound, which is probably documentary's greatest failing, and you collapse the space. But we wanted to combine the intimate eavesdropping the lavs allowed us with the monumental magnitude of the mountains, often filmed with long lenses, compressing and pictorializing and in a sense de-realizing the space.

One other quality of recording with so many lavs that jumped out at me while shooting was the absurd, often completely surreal synchronicities that would result. The transmitters we used were 250 milliwatt, the most powerful that are legal in the US, which would transmit a signal to me from up to a mile and a half away. So I could be simultaneously recording with four lavs up to three miles away from each other, none of which might suggest anything whatsoever in common with what the camera was recording. Other times, when I'd hear something interesting through a lav, I'd see if I could locate where it was, and try to turn the camera onto it.

MacDonald: Was everything shot in sync?

Castaing-Taylor: A few times we moved a word or two a few seconds one way or another so it would be intelligible, but basically all the speech is sync. At times, though, we really wanted people to wonder whether the sound *was* sync or not. For example, during the first night-time scene, above the timber-line, up in the basins—what we call the lullaby scene—it's getting dark and John goes into a kind of reverie as he tries to round the sheep up and get them to settle on the bed ground next to his teepee for the night. He has to go all the way around the sheep to get them close enough to give him a chance of protecting them from bears and wolves, and so he rides up to the horizon.

The scene is almost surreal because, even when John is perhaps three-quarters of a mile away from the camera, his lovely, subjective, gut-tural voice gets recorded and feels very intimate. A litany of "girly, girlies," almost a soliloquy, gently cascades from his mouth, and then he starts sing-ing these half-remembered fragments of old-time Western songs. And when he and his horse ride along the horizon, you feel like you're being subjected to a classic, over-mythologized Western stereotype—it's almost too good to be true. It's such a cliché that you might doubt the nonfiction status of the image. At the very least, you lose confidence for a moment in the filmmakers for peddling a corny stereotype of the cowboy. But when he breaks from his song, halfway along the horizon, to bark "Get back, Breck!" at his dog, and you faintly make out his dog responding, it clicks, and you know, as impos-sible as it may seem, that this was being recorded in sync. Moments like that are scattered throughout.

The sound was edited and mixed by Ernst Karel, an experimental musician, phonographer, sound artist—even an anthropologist. A jack-of-all-trades. He designed a highly orchestrated multi-track soundscape that layered many different kinds of sound, especially of ambience and of the sheep. My own on-camera mono microphone couldn't begin to do justice to the vastness of mountain acoustics. He eventually mixed his composition down into two versions, a 5.1 surround sound mix for the Dolby SRD, and a stereo version for the analog optical track. I'm almost completely tone deaf, so it was a god-send to find him.

MacDonald: Did the route of the seasonal migration take you into Yellowstone National Park? Pat brings the environmentalist issue up when he and John are talking about the "problem bears" that are not afraid of humans. Did the environmental issue play into the demise of this sheep migration?

Castaing-Taylor: Yes and no. The grazing permits in the area date back to the early part of the twentieth century (long after the park was established back in 1872) and were for the Bureau of Land Management and National Forest lands just to the north. In 1975 the area was designated a federal "wil-derness" area (preserves of putative "wildness" that, etymologically, impose their extra-human will on you), which prohibits all "development," and since then the Forest Service, under pressure from various self-identified environmentalist constituencies, has sought to phase out all herding allotments. The Allestads' was the last grazing permit to go.

They will tell you it was because of pressure from environmentalists, and that's half true. But it was also economic and cultural. This kind of transhumance is extraordinarily labor-intensive and costly. As a system, capitalism will substitute commodities for people, and machines for people's labor, whenever and wherever it can. And it can on ranches, down on the plains. For the cost of a new pick-up, you could probably pay the salary of three or four old-time hired hands. Every rancher I know would prefer the pick-up. But you can't get pick-ups into the mountains. And finding qualified help to herd sheep and defend them against protected predators like grizzly bears and re-introduced grey wolves is no easy feat.

In *Breakfast* [2010], one of the installation pieces that came out of this project, Pat casually lets slip his contempt for "backpackers, granolas, and environmentalists." The words slide out of his mouth almost unthinkingly and virtually devoid of affect. It's an amazing line, there's a whole worldview contained within it, and a whole unwritten history of dispossession of rural folk by educated urbanites patronizing them about how to be proper custodians of the land.

Barbash: Even while we were in Big Timber, the locals had already started dealing with other kinds of environmental issues with perhaps more significant consequences. The Stillwater Mining company had recently opened up a new corridor into the US's only palladium and platinum mine. Some of the people in our film worked there—Pat's brother–in–law for example—in four twelve-hour shifts a week. In 2001 I filmed a town meeting called to discuss the mine, but that material didn't make it into the final cut.

The people who attended seemed pretty divided about the impact of the mine on their town. While some of the year-round Big Timber population saw the employment benefits of the mine, others were concerned about the effect of drainage from the mines going into the Boulder river and changing its temperature and chemistry. And there were also people worried about the social and economic impact of suddenly adding new families to the local area. By 2008, the mine was the county's largest employer and paid about 40 percent of the county's tax revenue, and when they started to lay people off because of a mining bust, it hit the community hard. The mine has had other problems more recently during the downturn in the auto industry as the metals it produces are used in catalytic converters—to screen out auto pollution, of all things.

MacDonald: Your end credits say "Produced by Ilisa Barbash" and "Recorded by Lucien Castaing-Taylor." Lisa, I'd be interested in knowing what was involved in producing the film. And, Lucien, why the unusual "Recorded by"? You both have editing credit, but no one is listed as "Director" or "Filmmaker."

Barbash: I'm not entirely comfortable with dividing the credits in this way. I think elaborate titles make more sense when there's a larger crew and a need to make sure the division of labor is clear and that the credit for doing various kinds of work is evident. I'd say that we're both the "filmmakers," and I'd almost have been happy leaving it at that. We both conceived the film, edited it, and dealt with all the production logistics. But Lucien did more, having shot all of footage that ended up in this film, and he "directed" himself as a cameraman. No one "directed" the participants, except perhaps the ranch owner, Lawrence Allestad!

Castaing-Taylor: "Directed" just seemed all wrong. We're not out to disavow our agency or anything, but what or who did we direct? We never interviewed anyone. We never told anyone what to do, or to do anything again, however much I sometimes wished they would. I was a parasite, along for the ride. Anything that made it into the film did so through contingency, happenstance, serendipity. At its best, cinema-verite works through a unique combination of anticipation and accident, and although our engagement with aesthetics is very unlike verite's—remember the old quip that verite makes up in immediacy what it lacks in appearance?—our renunciation of directorial control rendered us dependent on the accidental and correspondingly elevated the importance of our capacity to anticipate action before it happened. "Directed by" smacks of a documentary inferiority complex, fiction-film envy. It's both epistemologically dubious and ethically duplicitous.

MacDonald: I wonder how much you were thinking of particular westerns—*Red River* [1948], for example—as you shot or edited *Sweetgrass.*

Barbash: I grew up watching *Gunsmoke* [1955-75] and *Bonanza* [1959-73], and when I first met the people who ended up in *Sweetgrass*, they reminded me of characters from these shows and from Western movies. Pat's intonation always reminds me of John Wayne. One of the characters has a brother whose nickname is Festus, as in *Gunsmoke.* When we started this project I bought a whole bunch of DVDs of Westerns, and we kept intending to watch them, but ended up not doing that kind of homework. What's interesting to me is how accurately in some ways and how inaccurately in others Hollywood has portrayed the West. Our film confirms some of what you see in Hollywood Westerns and perhaps corrects other things.

The people in *Sweetgrass* really do wear cowboy hats. $350 a shot, pure beaver pelt. One of them came to visit us and wore his cowboy hat on the T and in Sever Hall at Harvard; all the groomsmen wore cowboy hats at his wedding. On the other hand, the people we filmed were really good at riding four-wheelers (often on just two wheels!) and at using cell phones and communicating by walkie-talkie, so in a way, *Sweetgrass* is meant to show you what the Old West has become. But *I* definitely meant for our film to refer back to films like *Red River*, though we weren't informed by *Red River* in particular.

Castaing-Taylor: I grew up in Liverpool, a post-industrial detritus of a city. We didn't have television at home and we never went to the movies. I've never seen *Red River*, though Lisa's told me about it; I've seen hardly any Westerns. In fact, when it comes to cinema, I'm pretty illiterate. To be honest, I don't really like movies: most are so audio-visually intrusive, all about spectacle and distraction. I resent them. Literature at once gives freer rein to and intrudes less on your imagination. It's less sensorially stimulating and less coercive—it seems more intellectually democratic. Not that I have the concentration to read either!

MacDonald: You've described the sheep-herding project as salvage ethnography, which in many senses it is, of course; but sometimes it seems as close to James Benning's films and the work of other avant-garde filmmakers, as to traditional documentaries. In *Sweetgrass* what is normally thought of as avant-garde film history and documentary history seem to merge. Did your working in Boulder have an impact on the way you think of yourselves as filmmakers? Stan Brakhage and Phil Solomon are thanked in the end credits.

Barbash: At every point during the editing, because of our anthropological training, we, or at least I, thought about both ethnography and aesthetics, or art; and when the two concerns didn't seem to mesh, we'd incline one way or the other. I don't think we put our chips in one particular camp.

I do think we could have made the film more "ethnographic" if we had provided more information within the film. A friend of ours showed a film of his to Clifford Geertz, an eminent anthropologist, and Geertz's response was something like, "Well, how many people lived in that village? Your film doesn't even show me that." We could have told you how many people lived in Big Timber; at the very beginning, we could have explained that this was the last sheep drive, but we decided not to impart information in what felt like an artificial or extraneous way. If we end up showing *Sweetgrass* to anthropologists who are disgruntled that we don't give them enough information, we'll have to defend ourselves. But we're happy with the choices we made.

I never studied Stan Brakhage's work but came to know it when we were colleagues in Boulder, and I showed his films in my classes. Stan would go to a café on Pearl Street every day and paint directly on celluloid, which was how he was making his films at the time. One Christmas he generously gave us a few frames as a gift.

I think Stan's attention to detail, to the frame itself, in fact to parts within the frame, was influential on our thinking about film, and even about video—which for Stan, of course, was toxic waste. Each tiny element, each frame, each sound needs to be carefully considered. But while he would build up a frame by painting or gluing layers upon layers, we would deconstruct what we'd shot on video, pulling bits apart, separating sound from video at times, then reconstructing it all back together.

MacDonald: One final question about *Sweetgrass*: Is the title a reference to the Merian C. Cooper, Ernest B. Schoedsack film, *Grass*? There too, domesticated animals climb over a mountain.

Barbash: By calling it *Sweetgrass*, I think we make it fairly clear that we are referencing *Grass*, but we don't expect that most people who see our film will have seen *Grass*. When we were thinking about our project as a kind of salvage ethnography, we thought back to films we'd seen and studied and taught, and about ways in which we might respond to this history in our work, either by doing some kind of imitation or some kind of contradiction. Certainly *Grass* was foremost in our minds because it is about this huge seasonal migration of animals.

Castaing-Taylor: "Sweet Grass" is the name of one of the counties where we shot, where the town of Big Timber is. "Sweetgrass" was Lisa's title, and the tilt of the hat to Cooper and Schoedsack was hers. I wanted "Sweetgrass Beartooth," which I now realize is too much of a mouthful. *Grass* is an amazing work in its own way—though it's also classically Orientalist—in its representation of the Bakhtiari, much closer to the racializing and patronizing colonial travelogues of the period than *Nanook* [1921], which incarnated a kind of humanism that seems to me totally without precedent. In any case, *Sweetgrass* is not predicated on anyone getting that reference. I see *Sweetgrass* as a revisionist riff on the pastoral, an age-old form in literature and painting.

Barbash: And now that *Sweetgrass* is finished, we're going to depart from the pastoral and make our own version of *King Kong* [1933]!

Seriously, I do think it's interesting that after exploring the intensity of a mass migration of animals, Cooper and Schoedsack delved further into animality by exploring the dark, bestial nature of man.

Lucien Castaing-Taylor (on his Installation Work)

MacDonald: I first became aware of your sheepherding project when you projected the short installation pieces at Hamilton College in 2008, and for me they were as evocative and beautiful as *Sweetgrass* itself. Am I correct that the installation pieces were completed before the final cut of *Sweetgrass*?

Castaing-Taylor: In very rough form, yes. Long before. But the sound work was all done after, in the fall of 2009 with Ernst Karel, and for me they're more sound pieces than image pieces. And I also fiddled with the picture, making hundreds of changes even after I'd exhibited earlier versions with just rough and ready stereo sound patched in.

MacDonald: Only two of the installation pieces are made up exclusively of material that didn't get into the final cut of *Sweetgrass*: *Hell Roaring Creek* and *Bedding Down* [2012]. For me *Hell Roaring Creek* is the gem of the project, and very closely related to avant-garde work, especially to the films of James

Benning and Peter Hutton, and in a different way, to J. J. Murphy's *Sky Blue Water Light Sign* [1972].

Castaing-Taylor: I've never seen the Murphy film.

MacDonald: In the version I've seen projected, *Hell Roaring Creek* is made up of three shots, each separated from the next by moments of black. Why those breaks?—it's clear that for the second shot, you've moved the camera closer (or have readjusted your zoom lens) and that you move back to the original position after the second pause—does each visual pause represent a break in time? The two caesuras do function to refresh one's attention.

Castaing-Taylor: I think the whole effect of *Hell Roaring Creek* is predicated on the viewer's not knowing anything about it, so hopefully nobody will read this who's not seen it.

I don't really know how to talk about this work yet. It wasn't shot as a conceptual piece, but it's become one for me, at least in part. One answer to your question is that I made a mistake. It was my first time in the mountains and my first year with that many sheep. We were trailing in, we'd set up camp, bedded the sheep down, and then Lawrence, the rancher, showed me where we'd cross the creek the next morning.

I knew we'd be getting up about 4:00, and would cross the creek around 5:00 or a little later. I guessed where the sun would come up. And then I guessed how long it would take for the band of sheep to cross. I was thinking three–four minutes. I decided I'd stand in the creek and film the crossing in a single shot. The sun would be coming up behind and it would be beautiful. I thought it might make a great three-minute pre-title sequence to what would become *Sweetgrass*, and alert viewers to the durational qualities of the film and the kind of patience it would demand.

Well, what did I know? It took them *thirty* minutes, not three, to cross. I could only guess at the time while I was shooting, but I knew it wouldn't work in the way I'd imagined. I was thinking on the fly and I lost confidence in the idea of a single-shot, just enough to screw it up. After about ten minutes, I slowly zoomed in, to change the camera angle. I instinctively knew not to stop shooting, to hold on to that conflation between real and cinematic time, but I was still thinking about *Sweetgrass*, and felt the need to change focal length so we'd have the option of cutting later. But after twenty minutes the crossing was still going strong, seemingly infinite, like Rabelais's "moutons de Panurge" in *Pantegruel*. And I started fretting about the zoom-in, and what that had done to the shot, so I slowly zoomed out again, as if that might somehow rectify my original sin. And still the crossing took another ten minutes.

Had I not zoomed in and out, my guess is that I would have left it as this structural single-shot. I wanted to stick with the shot as a whole, including the zooms, but I found them too distracting. I'm a biped, not a tripod, and even though I was trying to hold the camera as still as if it were on a tripod, all the little movements tell you that it's hand-held, they made it too much about *me*.

I also wanted to subvert or somehow move beyond all the macho heroics of structural filmmaking, which seem dated now and can often be epistemologically pretty naïve. Benning's *RR* [2007], which I love, feels so impatient as almost to be impetuous in its complete exclusion of the before and after, those periods of transformation that are so much more revealing than the restricted times the trains take to traverse the frame.

So I cut out the two zoom movements, and for years—honestly, *years*—played with how to combine the truncated shots that were left, from straight cuts to using as many minutes of black as I'd cut out. Every time I thought I'd got it right, I'd watch it again, and it would feel all wrong. In the end I settled on two sections of ten seconds, and another of a minute (or two of thirty seconds, if you don't see it as a loop within the installation).

With the surround sound composition that Ernst and I built, *Hell Roaring Creek* feels about right to me now. Maybe it'll feel all wrong in five years. As I see it, the stretches of black ask you to question what you think you're seeing. You might even wonder, when you return to the image, if this is the same crossing, or if it was shot at another time. Or if you trust that it's one and the same, you still have to ask yourself what was cut out, and why, or wonder if there was more than one camera, because of the shift in focal length combined with apparent infinity of Panurge's sheep. The first ten-second section of black is hell, a killer, a complete violation of the temporal fusion you've been experiencing, and of the unconsummated anticipation of an event that's only just beginning, but the second period of black, or rather the return to the sheep and the creek at the end of the second stretch of black, recontextualizes that.

It also returns humans to the ecological fold, somewhat bestialized after the 3,000 head of sheep, and you're jerked out of the almost atemporal synchronicity of the middle section, which has no beginning or end, where you're engaging essentially aesthetically, rather than narratively, your attention fluctuating between the vertical stream of water and the horizontal movement of sheep, between the sheep as a collectivity and all of their individual particularities—the ewes and the lambs, the shorn and the unshorn, the arthritic and the athletic, the fearful and the fearless. You're jerked out of these ruminations, and forcibly plunged back into the narrative temporality of the crossing, with the end now in sight.

MacDonald: I've never quite understood why you would want these pieces seen in a gallery, where your unusually patient sense of timing seems sure to get lost on nearly everyone strolling through. It's true that some avant-garde filmmakers (I don't know that this is the case with documentary makers) have moved toward gallery installation partly because of the surreal disparity in potential financial reward between installation work and works made for theatrical projection. Can you help me understand the value of seeing these pieces as installations?

Castaing-Taylor: Hell Roaring Creek might seem patient to you, as a spectator, though I kick myself for my impetuousness when shooting it, but you can hardly call *The High Trail* [2010] or *Bedding Down* or *Into-the-jug* (*"Geworfen"*) [2010] patient or durational in any meaningful way. They all bombard you with different kinds of frenetic, tactile intensity.

Basically, in the course of editing the material we had shot, around two hundred hours, various sequences jumped out at me as having a kind of structural integrity or some kind of aesthetic autonomy or value that would be eclipsed or at least radically attenuated if they were included in the single-channel documentary. I remember Umberto Eco a long time ago describing film as being constituted by so many "syntagmatic chains imbued with argumentative capacity." This is not only a potential strength, but also a weakness, a foreclosing of aesthetic possibility. Documentary is even worse than so-called narrative cinema in this regard because of its explicit concern with expository argumentation or logical propositionality. As Gabriel Marcel once said, you don't go to the movies to hear a lecture on the "doctrine of Kant" or to "listen to explications." Yet often times with documentaries that's about all you get!

As much as we sought to resist this in *Sweetgrass*, the film still has a narrative structure, an ostensibly very simple one, and hence all the limits that narrative entails. The other works assumed their rough shape before we finished *Sweetgrass*, and early versions of a few of them were installed at Marian Goodman Gallery in 2007 and at CUNY's James Gallery in 2008—but I only got around to finishing most of them in 2010.

These pieces explore different structures and also quite different stylistic registers from *Sweetgrass*. It feels to me like they made themselves, in a sense. I didn't have an exhibition space in mind when they were being edited. But your question points to a real conundrum. I'd be staggered if there weren't as many starving self-appelled artists as starving self-appelled filmmakers, so I'm not at all sure that financial motivation is often a factor. In fact, for many, the obscenity of the recent high capitalization of the art world might be more a source of repulsion than of attraction.

I know in my case, and I'd guess also for many working in so-called film or video art, the motivating factor is a desire to get more from your audience, a deeper and a different kind of spectatorial attention to the work, one less attuned to narrative chains of meaning than to sheer manifestations of being and to forms of figural expressivity that are more ambiguous and opaque than narrative's proclivity for discursive clarity usually allows.

I think that Lyotard got it pretty much dead right in *Discours/figure*: figuration is much more unruly, much more of a provocation and an intervention, than discourse, which, in its self-sufficiency and capacity to say essentially anything, its faith in lucidity and transparency, constantly threatens to control and manipulate the messy material world which we inhabit, and which mercifully will always have a magnitude far in excess of our representations of it.

Discourse is about signification, its space is essentially flat; the figural is about sense and the sensorial, and its space is deep. Of course, everything, even discourse, is, in the end, figural (if you take the metaphor and metonymy out of language there's not much left), but this is an attenuated, almost ashamed, figuration, which is perhaps why it's constantly trying to colonize and control fuller figuration.

But you point to a very real problem that I think all film and video artists, and art curators, struggle with, and which is never going to go away: how best to exhibit time-based figural media in a gallery or art context? In reality, of course, *any* site, theater, studio or street, public or private, has its own specificity. But when Sharon Lockhart's recent *Lunch Break* [2008] was installed at Barbara Gladstone gallery in New York, I think they made a mistake in simply recreating a black box within the white cube of the gallery (they also left the rear wall white, reducing the contrast ratio of the projection by over 50 percent). Had the film been installed in a long dark tunnel mirroring the corridor that is the subject of the piece, as I imagine Sharon would have liked, it would have been something else entirely.

The biggest problem seems to me the temporal one, and the aesthetic of a loop, which *has* to be an aesthetic of the fragment, a metonymic aesthetic whereby a part, *any* part, has to be able to work on its own terms and also to stand in for the whole. Even if you want a richer and less circumscribed kind of attention when showing work in an art context, you also get *less*, at least temporally, as people walk in and out of a loop willy-nilly.

Hell Roaring Creek—my favorite of the installation pieces, except maybe for *Bedding Down*—consists of seven movements if you see it linearly, but only six if you experience it as a loop in a gallery situation and stay with it all the way through: three periods of black with sound and three of picture with sound. The three periods of picture are all excerpts from what originated as a single shot, a fusion of real and cinematic time. There's a temporality, and a narrativity, to the whole, with the first period of black and then the first of picture setting up the expectation of an event, which only begins to take form towards the end of the first shot. The "event" turns out to be both seemingly infinite, in the second shot, and then, in the third, to become something of a non-event (dawn is past, the sky is overcast, the creek has returned to its undisturbed self).

But the piece is also made to be seen *in part*. To be sure, what you get by experiencing one ninety-second fragment is not the same as what you get from another, so within the gallery situation there's a renunciation of authorial control, but this can be liberating and part of the open-endedness of the work.

Another thing, which for me is important: I call all of these pieces "audiovideo" works, because they have five discrete channels of sound. Few theaters are equipped to play back 5.1 or 7.1 (or any other format of) surround sound, and fewer still from HD video, rather than 35mm film. So to show these pieces in a non-surround theater, which is the norm for avant-garde and documentary screenings, is like cutting off half their limbs and privileging a kind of ocularcentricity which the works themselves oppose.

Two more points, then I'll shut up. James Benning has given up on film, or so he says, because he can't deal with the nightmare of 16mm processing any more. Who can blame him? But, for all of the putatively "lossless" infinite clonability of the digital, and its subversion of the distinction between original and copy, video projection is fickle and mercurial and downright complex, far more unreliable than even 16mm projection. It's an unmitigated nightmare. But if you install a work in an exhibition space, you potentially have much more control over the playback of the picture—as well as the sound.

Lastly, the site-specificity of theatrical projection spaces is essentially repressed, or a given—if you're present, you might fiddle with the sound level, or ask for a new bulb for the projector, but your choices are very limited; and if you're absent, you have no control at all. We haven't the foggiest inkling about the theatrical spaces where *Sweetgrass* is showing. But gallery installation engages with the space directly and unavoidably. *Hell Roaring Creek*, for instance, is designed to be projected onto a hanging, translucent screen, so you can view it from either side. You can't walk through it, into the stream itself, but you can walk around it, in effect along either bank of the creek, and watch and listen to it from either side. The five-channel surround is also to be installed on both sides of the screen, so you're effectively dealing with ten channels of sound, all situated spatially in relationship to a two-sided screen. A far cry from a cinema theater, or worse, a classroom.

MacDonald: It's interesting to see how *Sweetgrass* sometimes includes a substantial portion of the relevant installation piece (*Coom Biddy*, for example, and *Daybreak on the Bedground* [2010] and *Turned at the Pass* [2010]) and sometimes uses very little of the installation piece (*The High Trail, Into-the-Jug ("Geworfen")*).

Castaing-Taylor: In a sense *Sweetgrass* quotes from some of the audiovideo pieces, but not actually that much, and with the shorter shot lengths and recontextualization within *Sweetgrass*, even the quoted shots feel quite different to me. *Coom Biddy* is a triptych, with the two formal, static images sandwiching the long interior tracking shot. There's no way that tracking shot could have been sustained within *Sweetgrass*, because of the narrative thrust propelling the film forward and excluding other kinds of aesthetic engagement.

Bedding Down is about the real in a totally different register from the other works, with nothing but jump cuts, its low-res handheld horseback video, and initially unlocatable sync soundtrack. As the piece proceeds, it increasingly channels an agonistic, diabolic descent into a kind of violent interiority.

The picture seems in places to decompose, moving in amorphous waves as the rider rises and falls. It's at once at the threshold of the visible and at the threshold of the technological, pushing the camera's sensors and automation beyond their capabilities.

It's true that some of these pieces can be seen as reframing or elaborating a sequence that appears in *Sweetgrass* (the dialogue-heavy *Breakfast*, for example), but for me the installation works are quite separate.

MacDonald: Where does the title of *Into-the-Jug ("Geworfen")* come from?

Castaing-Taylor: The small pens that newborn lambs and their "mothers" are kept in for the first few days of the lambs' lives are called "jugs." Don't ask me why, unless a jug is just a symbol of containment. I've asked a few people and they don't know either.

I suppose that if it weren't for the roving, fallible camera, that this is the one piece—an eleven-minute single shot, limited in dutiful Bazinian fashion to the duration of the various births it depicts—that might be seen to give itself over to some of the indulgences of structural film. For me, it proceeds through slow disclosure and progressively defamiliarizes and reframes its subject as it goes along. Birth, especially, of course, of innocent, harmless, soon-to-be-gamboling lambs, is as over-determined as anything could ever be, and the births we're witness to are so tactile, so viscous, so acoustically overbearing, and so physically intense that it's hard not to avert your gaze. As Susan Sontag once put it, we're not blessed with earlids—so unless you leave the room you can't altogether avert your consciousness.

In *Into-the-Jug ("Geworfen")*, sound is even more a vector of the abject than the picture. But it's hard to give the piece your full attention on an initial viewing. And even if you do, it probably takes anyone other than a sheep rancher the full eleven minutes to figure out what exactly is going on: to realize that the lambs are being mixed and matched and that the ties of kinship being created are fictive, not biological, and mediated through and through with the well-nigh omnipotent agency of the man pulling them out.

MacDonald: Why is the man doing this?

Castaing-Taylor: Basically, mothering ewes have different amounts of milk, and some can support two (very occasionally, three) lambs, and some (especially many two year-olds) just one. But once you start mixing and matching, you create this pool of "bum" lambs. And you only have about a twenty-four-hour window when you can convince an ewe that a lamb that is not her biological offspring *is* hers, by covering it in the caul and amniotic fluid of her own newborn (or the flayed skin of her stillborn). So you automatically take the biological lamb away from her because you have others who have been alive for going-on twenty-four hours and who need a mother bad—the clock's ticking. The man, in short, is a *deus ex machina*, even if he's down on his knees in the jug grunting and groaning with his bloody arm stuck up the vagina of a mother in labor.

What kind of "nature" is this? "Domesticated" doesn't seem the right word for it; it's not about *taming*. It's more precisely a form of unholy alchemy that we don't have a word for. Within the space of these eleven minutes, the whole ideological edifice and opposition between Nature and Culture collapses in a pool of impure interspecies nascency on the floor of the strawed jug. In any event, as for the title, this piece evokes for me Martin Heidegger's core concept, his neologism *Geworfenheit*, which is usually translated as "Thrownness" or "Thrown-into-the-World" in English. It was his principal revision to Husserlian phenomenology and Husserl's notion of the *Lebenswelt*—immediate, intuitive, unreflective lived experience—as opposed to the *Weltanschaung*, one's worldview, which is a matter of metaphysics, of belief, of rationality, of ideology.

Heidegger wanted to emphasize the way our lot in life, our *Dasein*, the flux of our Being-in-the-world is constrained and structured and in many ways a function of all the variables and contingencies that lie outside of our control, beyond our grasp, that predate us, and so on. For me, *Into-the-Jug ("Geworfen")* is an absolutely literal exemplification of that *thrownness*, that *Geworfenheit*—all these newborn lambs being thrown around with such abandon but also with such attention. And their being paired up with mothers, not willy nilly, because the rancher is processing a mass of calculations as he chooses who to couple with whom, but in ways and for reasons unknown to the lambs but which will go a long way to determining the kind of life they'll lead.

In everyday, colloquial German, *Geworfen* (without the nominalizing suffix) is used to describe both whelping and foaling. Quite possibly also, though not so far as I know, lambing. Metaphorically, then, being born is being thrown. What more perfect image of *Dasein* is there than this moving, messy image of liquid, liminal entry into life?

Lucien Castaing-Taylor (on "Sensory Ethnography")

MacDonald: You've developed the Sensory Ethnography program at Harvard. I assume you're using *sensory* ethnography as opposed to *verbal* ethnography: writing about cultural practices in essays, books, or in screenplays for documentaries that use a lecture format. Your interest in filmmaking seems *experiential* in the sense that John Dewey talks about artworks being concentrations/intensifications of lived experiences, rather than informational presentations and/or theoretical conjectures; and your sense of "ethnographic film" seems much broader than what that term has been traditionally taken to mean.

Tell me about the thinking that resulted in the Sensory Ethnography program.

Castaing-Taylor: Well, you've pretty much said it all. Juxtaposing perspectives from the sciences, the arts, and the humanities, the aim of the Sensory Ethnography Lab is to support innovative combinations of aesthetics and ethnography, especially with work conducted through audiovisual media (video, sound, film, photography, and "new" hypermedia), that are at an angle to dominant conventions in anthropology, documentary, and art practice.

I suppose it's worth situating the Sensory Ethnography Lab both within the provincial domain of Harvard and within larger trajectories. Harvard has long been intellectually timorous about the arts—happy to exhibit them (in the Fogg), commodify them (make the odd purchase—though these days neither the Fogg nor the Peabody has a significant acquisition budget), and perform them (undergraduate orchestras and dramatic groups), but not to actively produce them within the academic belly of the beast. What is really the art department has a name—Visual and Environmental Studies (VES)—that does its level best to disavow the art-making that goes on there and which corresponds to no disciplinary nomenclature outside the university.

The same is true, in a way, of the History of Consciousness program at University of California Santa Cruz, but because of the distinctiveness of the work that came out of there, especially during the early decades, it achieved a kind of totemic status, and was recognized within the humanities and the human sciences. That's not really the case for VES, until recently an undergraduate-only program which has signally failed to conjugate the "visual" and the "environmental" in any systematic way.

But all this is now changing. Drew Faust, Harvard's President, has three big agendas—global health, environmental consciousness, and art practice and creative work. Her first significant act as President was to create a Task Force for the Arts, chaired by Stephen Greenblatt, which recommended integrating art-making into the cognitive life of the university across the board and especially in the graduate and undergraduate curricula. The sequel to the Task Force, a new Committee on the Arts (HUCA), is now deciding how to implement the recommendations, and what kind of graduate art-making programs to establish.

The Sensory Ethnography Lab; the Graduate School of Design's new degree in Art, Design and the Public Domain; the practice-based Ph.D. in Media Anthropology; and the new fellowship program at the Film Study Center (Harvard's one Center devoted to art-making or creative work), all have to be understood within this new commitment to take art-making as seriously as traditional scientific and humanistic forms of academic scholarship.

As for situating the Sensory Ethnography Lab within the larger trajectories of visual anthropology, documentary, and contemporary art, your reference to Dewey seems right on. On the one hand, the SEL's ethnographic imperatives mean that the work coming out of it is generally more committed to the "real" than most art is (especially conceptual and post-conceptual art), as well as to a form of expression that is somehow adequate to the magnitude of human experience. Or, if that's too much, at least to working within (as well as against) various species of realism.

Dewey seems crucial here, especially *Art as Experience*, which has somehow been neglected by anthropologists of art. I would guess there are at least two reasons why. In the first place, Dewey takes as his subject, although he does not use the term, the phenomenology of aesthetic experience—experience that surely is at the heart of human existence if anything is, but which is something that anthropologists of art have actually not been very interested in, concerned instead to reduce being to mere meaning and art to so many epiphenomena of one or another culture, to mere "material culture," or to something analogous to ritual, and so on and so forth.

In the second place, Dewey is deeply invested in "nature," to recursively coupling aesthetic experience not simply with everyday experience, but also with its infra-human animalic sources, and the at once sub- and supra-cutaneous interaction between what he called—three decades or more before the coinage of "cyborgs"—the co-constituting "live creature" and its "environment." For social and cultural anthropologists, talk of "nature" has long been something of an embarrassment—to be disavowed, immediately transformed into "second nature," mediated through-and-through by culture, a mere social construction, or (as with Bruno Latour) a dangerous political or scientific ideology to be actively combated.

Like Dewey, the SEL is concerned not with analyzing, but with actively producing aesthetic experience, and of kinds that reflect and draw on but do not necessarily clarify, or leave one with the illusion of "understanding," everyday experience. The SEL also seeks to transcend what is often considered the particular province of the human: that is, to re-conjugate culture with nature, to pursue promiscuities between animalic and non-animalic selves and others, and to restore us both to the domain of perception, in all its plenitude—rather than be satisfied with the academic game of what Dewey called "recognition," of naming, that he derided as a barely conscious endeavor— and to the fleshy realm, of "wild being," in Merleau-Ponty's phrase, in which the invisible, far from being the negation or contradiction of the visible, is in fact its "secret sharer," its *membrure. . .*

MacDonald: Not only *Sweetgrass* and the related installation works, but the films I've seen by Sensory Ethnography Lab students J. P. Sniadecki (*Songhua*, 2007; *Demolition/Chaiqian*, 2008), Stephanie Spray (*Kale and Kale*, 2007; *Monsoon Reflections*, 2008; *As Long As There's Breath*, 2009), Sniadecki and Véréna Paravel (*Foreign Parts*, 2010), and Spray and Pacho Velez (*Manakamana*) seem to fit within two traditionally distinct historical paradigms: they are documentaries of cultural places, moments, and practices; but they are also contributions to the strand of avant-garde filmmaking that includes Bruce Baillie, James Benning, Peter Hutton, Nathaniel Dorsky, and

Sharon Lockhart. Am I correct that you've jettisoned the distinction between "documentary" and "avant-garde"?

Castaing-Taylor: Yes. Not deliberately, I don't think, or in some kind of dogmatic way. But just because the distinction seems indefensible, and it would never occur to me to invoke it. The distinction is also unfortunate: documentarians as a result often don't see any reason to engage with so-called "experimental" or "avant-garde" traditions, and on the flip side, a category like "experimental" implicitly sets itself off against a domain that is thereby defined as non-experimental, as if all documentarians just follow genre rules and regulations by rote. But all genres have their conventions, are in a constant state of flux and de- and re-formation.

I think Bourdieu overstated his case that artists, like intellectuals, are forever in competition with their fellows as they seek to carve out a niche in which to inscribe their authority in a particular field of cultural production. It's not, of course, that artists are any less self-interested than anyone else, but rather that many are often willfully ignorant of what others are doing even within their own "field" (a term that only makes sense to me if the root metaphor is a multi-dimensional electromagnetic field, rather than a planar agricultural one).

For my part, I know that when I'm working on a project, I often feel the need *not* to know about or experience work that is in some sense "related," lest it compromise my efforts to find the proper form for whatever it is *I'm* doing. In any event, consigning the works of such different film- and video-makers as, say, Jana Sevcikova, Dorothy Cross, Sergei Dvortsevoy, Pedro Costa, Rosalind Nashashibi, Sharon Lockhart, Alexandr Sokurov, Steve McQueen, or Phil Collins exclusively to either the avant-garde, or documentary, or contemporary art makes no sense.

As you've suggested, the works emerging from the SEL are more concerned with issues of aesthetics and form than documentary usually is, and are for the most part opposed to conventional documentary on a slew of specific counts. These include the journalistic use of interviews or of featuring subjects merely talking about their lives *ex post facto*, rather than actually living them; the reductive range of dramaturgical narrative structures documentary typically deploys and their linearity and predilection for resolution and closure; as well as the narrow repertoire of styles that are sanctioned by the gatekeepers of documentary practice. I'm referring in particular to the ongoing hegemony of a kind of lazy and lax cinema-verite and the continuing consecration of a frequently unseeing and unsensing, putatively "observational," aesthetic within the ethnographic film world and its dismissal of anything experimental, structurally rigorous, or stylistically demanding as provincially "avant-garde" or unduly self-reflexive or self-indulgent. It is as if the custodians of the sacred flame of ethnographic cinema are oblivious to any developments in art or in film since Jean Rouch's experiments in ethno-fiction in the 1960s and 1970s.

Lastly, I think it's true that the SEL is also opposed, though this time in the name of art and its inherent exegetical ambiguity—in the name, that is to say, of the figural and its opacity, over against the discursive and its desire for transparency—to the clarity and interpretive self-sufficiency toward which anthropology and academia typically tend. The SEL is much more invested in what John Keats, in his famous letter to his brother, characterized as "negative capability": the quintessentially human capacity to be, as he put it, "in uncertainties, Mysteries, doubts without any irritable reaching after fact & reason."

In regards to anthropology, this inclination to the perceptual first and the conceptual second implicitly entails a relativization of the "cultural textology," in Barbara Stafford's phrase, bequeathed by the hermeneutic turn of Clifford Geertz; and a renewed interrogation of core abstractions like culture, society, and the self (or at least, representations of the self) and a return to the primacy of the individual, the body, and above all inter-subjective and inter-corporeal experience—as the ground of what is thought and what is said, as the ground of both meaning and symbolism.

There are more than enough precursors for this move, in addition to Dewey, Keats, and Merleau-Ponty. This is the domain, in part, of what Mead and Bateson (in *Balinese Character*) called "kinaesthetic learning." In existential anthropologist Michael Jackson's more recent expression, it is "practical mimesis." It is also, to be sure, the realm of the non-verbal and the non-discursive, or, in Foucault's neo-Kantian terms, the "seeable" (though why privilege sight—why not simply *sensible*?), but "un-sayable." Works in film, video, and sound have a particular purchase on the experiential that differs quite fundamentally from that of our written representations, particularly, as Vivian Sobchack emphasized, in their deployment of acts of moving, hearing, and seeing as at once the originary structures of embodied existence *and* the mediating structures of discourse.

Lucien Castaing-Taylor and Véréna Paravel (on *Leviathan*)

MacDonald: I understand that originally the two of you thought you were making a more broad-ranging film about the fishing industry in and around New Bedford. At what point did you know you wanted to film on fishing boats, and were there difficulties in having the opportunity to do that?

Castaing-Taylor/Paravel: Filming in New Bedford, in and around the harbor, started, occasionally and intermittently, during the summer and fall of 2011, and in earnest during the winter. The initial idea was to make a film about fishing, and the ocean more broadly, without ever seeing, or at least recognizing, a fishing boat or the sea. We first went out to George's Bank on a dragger in March 2012. After that first trip, we quickly lost interest in the land; it seemed altogether too familiar.

Most captains we met in port were very welcoming, intrigued by our interest, and happy for us to go out with them.

MacDonald: It must have been obvious to both of you, almost from the beginning, that you weren't going to make a documentary about industrial ocean fishing, or a TV-like melodrama about the men who work on fishing boats, but something very different—something that would be less informational in the usual sense than experiential, a kind of virtual voyage.

Castaing-Taylor/Paravel: Fishing is perhaps the most fully represented endeavor in the history of photography and cinema—from Octavius Hill and Robert Adamson, Robert Flaherty and John Grierson, all the way up to Allan Sekula, Discovery Channel's *The Deadliest Catch*, and *The Cove* [2009]. The vast majority of this tradition indulges in the kinds of sentimentality and romanticism that one knows all too well, or else fits smugly into the agit prop liberal public television victimhood tradition, both of which we knew from the get-go we had to avoid.

MacDonald: In *Sweetgrass*, the subject was the interplay between cowboys and sheep, what Lucien has called "sheeple"; and in *Foreign Parts*, the focus is the personalities within an industrial space. In *Leviathan* the focus seems to have a double level: first, you focus on a modern or late modern version of a centuries-old industrial process; and second, you seem to be focusing on a new kind of documentary experience. Did your assumption that you were going to be working in a new way develop quickly once you were out on the fishing boats?

Castaing-Taylor/Paravel: We weren't hell-bent on creating a new kind of "documentary experience," any more than we were interested in slavishly following or subverting the dominant rules and regulations of filmmaking. We were trying, largely in vain, to grapple with the magnitude of what we were confronted with, both inside and outside ourselves, when out at sea.

Does filming fishing demand anything more than filming anything else? Subject doesn't dictate style. One's style is borne out of one's encounter with one's subject. Yet many films, especially nonfiction films, seem to go to great pains to render that encounter invisible. Neither of us is interested in cinema as sheer spectacle, a distraction, a form of enter- or info-tainment. We're interested in the world, and how to render the world's aesthetic due, whether or not that ends up conforming to the norms and forms of cinematic or other artistic conventions as they congeal at any one point in time.

If *Leviathan* represents for some people a new kind of cinematic experience, as you've suggested, this is perhaps simply because the film returns us to some of the imperatives of cinema at its inception, allowing us to apprehend the world anew, to shake us out of our dogmatic and perceptual slumbers, to rid us momentarily of the habitual blinkers and moralistic alibis which burden our socially sanctioned everyday lives.

MacDonald: I know from talking with the two of you over the past couple of years that the labors of recording the material for *Leviathan* were considerable—if not as grueling as working as fishermen, difficult in other ways. Could you each talk about what you physically and psychologically went through while shooting the film?

Paravel: The boat contained many of my deepest fears, if not phobias: being trapped in a highly claustrophobic space with no possible way to escape either from the men or the unrelenting engine noise, or the menacing, dark sea, constantly sensing the deep and unknown below me (figure 58). Despite all that, I felt pretty much at ease to move about on the boat. Unfortunately after several days of rough seas, my body could no longer handle the pressure and on each trip I ended up covered with bruises and immobilized, having put my back out.

Castaing-Taylor: I had never been seasick before and didn't anticipate having any problem with it, even though Véréna had an intuition that I would. I basically puked my guts out for the first 24–48 hours of each trip. I tried various anti-emetics, which induced different degrees of stupor in me, and even made me see double, which didn't particularly help matters.

The boat was also all-imposing, oddly claustrophobic, with no relief anywhere—very loud, not especially sea-worthy, no real privacy.

MacDonald: It seems clear from both your earlier films—particularly the approach used in *7 Queens* by you, Véréna, and Lucien, your cinematography in *Sweetgrass*—that each of you brought different tendencies and skills to the production.

FIGURE 58 *Prow of fishing boat in Lucien Castaing-Taylor and Véréna Paravel's* Leviathan *(2012).*

Source: Courtesy Castaing-Taylor and Paravel.

How did you two develop your collaboration? From the beginning did you assume both of you would shoot and edit? Was the collaboration a struggle at any point?

Castaing-Taylor/Paravel: We were clueless; we never really had any fixed idea of what the collaboration would be. We'd collaborated before in various ways in the Sensory Ethnography Lab, co-teaching and so on, but we'd never made a long-form film together. There was never any division of labor. We just worked intuitively, discussing at once nothing and everything. We brainstormed together, sulked together, shot together, re-shot together, edited together. It was all more or less instinctive and unpredictable. One day, one of us would argue against the other; the next, the positions would be reversed, or one of us would be arguing with him- or herself.

Part of this was borne out of necessity: the boat was very unstable and we had to look out for each other both so that we didn't fall overboard or get hit on the head with a cable or a hook, but also to take turns holding one another when the other was filming, to help stabilize the image and make sure neither of us fell.

MacDonald: How many trips did you take? How much film did you shoot?

Castaing-Taylor/Paravel: We took six trips out to sea of between nine days and three weeks. We never knew how long they would last, any more than the captain did—it would depend on the weather, their catch, whether the gear broke, and fluctuating fish prices. Maybe two or two-and-a-half months out at sea, altogether.

Between land and sea we probably shot around 250 hours of footage. None of it on film. Once we'd lost interest in land, we jettisoned maybe 100 hours of footage.

MacDonald: What cameras did you use, and how did your shooting process evolve?

We started filming with our own cameras, quite heavy and shoulder-mounted, but one was stolen in New Bedford and the others were lost to the waves. So we resorted to progressively smaller DSLRs and tiny GoPro cameras which we both handheld ourselves and attached to the fishermen's bodies: to their heads, chests, and wrists. From the second trip on, we also attached a couple to the end of two 8-foot poles that were fastened together, giving us about a 16-foot reach, so we could film underwater and from above the sea and the boat.

It wasn't until the last trip that our curiosity and sense of wonder about what we were witnessing began to wane, and that we felt that our accumulated footage had begun to do justice to everything we'd experienced on the boat.

MacDonald: What were the struggles during the editing process?

Castaing-Taylor/Paravel: Editing was weirdly easy and intuitive. Our main struggle was where to situate humanity in the cosmos we were constructing.

For all of the inherent anthropomorphism of cinema, we had a kind of post-humanist ambition to relativize the human in a larger physical and metaphysical domain of both inter-species bestiality and of animate-inanimate promiscuity, one in which humans, fish, birds, machines, and the elements would have a kind of restless ontological parity (figure 59). We felt this, instinctively, in most of our images, but we did struggle with how to structure them, whether to begin in the familiar domain of the recognizably human and end somewhere much more inchoate and abstract, or to begin in the realm of undomesticable nature and proceed progressively towards the human.

In the final edit of the film, there is perhaps a gradual, if far from seamless, trajectory that leads towards the human-as-we-know-it, culminating in the shot of the fisherman in the galley falling asleep in front of *The Deadliest Catch* on satellite television, but this is subsequently blown asunder in the apocalyptic ending: the encounter with the Leviathan rolling below the boat and the sublime of the nighttime sky.

MacDonald: Like so many of the Sensory Ethnography films, *Leviathan* is as much a sound work as an image work. I assume this was partly inevitable, given the realities of ocean fishing.

Castaing-Taylor/Paravel: Initially, both in New Bedford and out in the Atlantic, we were shooting with a Sony EX3 and an EX1, each with a stereo Sanken microphone mounted on it. We were also recording wild sound onto a Sound Devices T788 recorder, both from a super stereo microphone (another Sanken model) and various Lectrosonics wireless lavaliers. Though we lost these cameras, and ended up discarding all the images except one that we'd

FIGURE 59 *Gulls following fishing boat in Lucien Castaing-Taylor and Véréna Paravel's* Leviathan *(2012).*

Source: Courtesy Castaing-Taylor and Paravel.

shot with them, we kept the sound—as well as all the wild sound we recorded on the Sound Devices: the nets, the winches, the cutting tables, the scallop shucking basins, inside the bridge, etcetera. Then we started recording on DSLRs, with smaller stereo mikes mounted on them, and with the tiny automated cameras with their inbuilt mono microphones, which were no great shakes, and even more compromised when enclosed in a waterproof housing.

MacDonald: You also went for surround sound and worked both with Ernst Karel and, later on, Jacob Ribicoff. Could you talk about the decision to put the sound-design through a two-step process?

Castaing-Taylor/Paravel: The sensorial intensity of life on the boat is as acoustic as it is visual—the engine is relentless and renders dialogue all but unintelligible—and it never occurred to us not to afford equal billing to sound and picture.

Paravel: Except at one point early in the editing when Lucien had the ridiculous notion to make the whole film silent!

Castaing-Taylor/Paravel: In many ways, sound is also less coded and reducible to putative meaning than picture, more evocative, imaginative and abstract. As choreographed as the film is, both of us are drawn to the uncoded and the uncontrolled. But while we are both obsessed with and highly opinionated about sound, we are also more or less tone deaf. And we have, as you say, collaborated with our friend and colleague Ernst Karel in all of our work.

Ernst's ears are the most delicate and discerning we know. While we were editing the film, the sound track was unremitting, often over-modulating, an overbearing monotony somewhere between punk rock, grunge, and heavy metal. We were interested in continuing something of this aesthetic over into the final mix, but we also knew it would have to be rendered much more variegated and multidimensional. Ernst came up with a wonderful 5.1 mix that had subtleties and modulations we could barely imagine, and Jacob then reworked this into something more cinematic.

MacDonald: The color palette of the film is impressive, partly I think because we see the yellow slickers, the red blood, mostly against black—much of what we see was filmed at night. Were you filming day *and* night, or mostly at night? Did the footage shot at night just look more interesting?

Castaing-Taylor/Paravel: Day *and* night, and yes, the footage at night seemed more evocative of our experience at sea and our sense of wonder before what we were witnessing. At night you lose all your bearings, and if the sea is rough and you're out on deck, half the time you don't know up from down, or sea from sky. And, of course, sea and sky are both pitch black, unless the moon is up, and the only source of illumination comes from the ferocious lights illuminating the deck where the hauling back and gutting of the fish continues around the clock. So there's a huge latitude between the brightest and darkest parts of the frame, and the oranges and greens and reds of the slickers, the nets, and the blood are fluorescent, even psychedelic at times.

The owl of Minerva takes flight at twilight, and art and cinema do too. Nonfiction films, to their own impoverishment, tend not to, being beholden to the dazzling discursive clarity of daylight.

MacDonald: Faye Ginsberg, who saw *Leviathan* at the New York Film Festival, complained to me that the fishermen were stereotypes.

Castaing-Taylor/Paravel: You could argue that they're barely *mono*types! To the degree that stereotype means a culturally conditioned and conditioning cliché that does a disservice to its object's nuance or complexity, the fishermen don't seem, to us, to be represented in this way. To be sure, we don't round them out as characters, or through narrative emplotment, in recognizably dramatic and human ways. We shied away from this for the same reason that we shied away from shore and that we shied away from light.

The way in which the toiling bodies are portrayed in the film as part of the scenarios of life and death playing out on the boat seems to us quite faithful to the realities we witnessed. But we never had the slightest interest in depicting the fishermen in any way that would dissociate their labors from their being and their niche in the larger psychophysical naturecultural ecological fold that we momentarily inhabited.

We don't share the humanistic concerns of the documentary tradition. Marx fetishized work no less than capitalists do, as the be-all and end-all of life. But work is embodied and is finally inextricable from our being-in-the-world.

Stephanie Spray and Pacho Velez (on *Manakamana*)

MacDonald: How did the Manakamana project evolve, and what led you to each other as collaborators?

Spray: The initial idea for *Manakamana* evolved from filming I was doing in Nepal, in a village just outside of Pokhara, where over the years I'd made *Monsoon-Reflections, As Long As There's Breath,* and *Untitled* [2010]. I was looking for new film contexts for my subjects, taking them to various locales where I'd have some control over the shoot. I'd heard about the Manakamana cable car and the Manakamana temple, although I'd never been there myself. I invited Bindu Gayek (the woman in the second shot of *Manakamana*) and her son Kamal to ride with me on the cable car in September 2010, thinking that the confines of the small space would allow for a productive, albeit forced, intimacy between the film subjects and the camera—I'd never been on a cable car and wasn't quite sure what to expect. Later, viewing the footage, I realized that the duration of the trip would allow for intimate exchanges to unfold.

I'd been thinking about this project for months and had written treatments for it when I returned to Cambridge in January 2011. Toward the end of my stay, I met with Pacho at a pub to catch up.

Velez: Stephanie and I had known each other for several years. We'd met in Lucien Castaing-Taylor's first Sensory Ethnography class, back in 2006: I was Lucien's teaching assistant and Stephanie was a graduate student. Stephanie continued in the Harvard program, and I went to study at CalArts with James Benning, Thom Andersen, Rebecca Baron, then returned to Harvard with my MFA.

Spray: There had already been examples of productive collaboration in the SEL, namely *Foreign Parts* [2010, co-made by Véréna Paravel and J. P. Sniadecki], which was doing exceptionally well at that point. I'd never collaborated on a film before, but knew that Pacho had successfully collaborated with others and felt confident he'd be a good partner. He'd already been thinking about a film about public transportation. In March 2011, Pacho got in touch and said he was interested in the project, and it was his brilliant idea to shoot on 16mm, knowing that a 400-foot roll of film at 24 frames per second would be roughly equivalent in cinematic time to the duration of the cable-car trip.

Velez: We were drawn in by the conceptual logic that the string of cable cars pulled along on a wire "rhymes" with the frames of 16mm film pulled along through a motion picture camera.

Spray: We became conscious of the parallels between the two technologies, their related evolutions, and the constellation of associations they might produce. There was also the parallel of the frame of the film image and the framing of the landscape by the cable car windows—both motion pictures— with viewing spectators coming along and marveling at the ride.

MacDonald: Filming in a cable car suggests an idea that seems fundamental to the Sensory Ethnography Lab: that culture is always in a process of transformation, on the move.

Velez: *Manakamana* presents the audience with a collection of time-and-space-limited encounters. Throughout the film, groups of characters are on the move, and the repetitiveness of the structure, combined with the lengths of the shots, lets each group's quirks reveal themselves. During these long tracking shots, the characters' attention is also shifting around: absorbing the landscape, reflecting on inner thoughts, and contemplating the goddess Manakamana. Since the film is so much about these flows, "movement" begins to take on an ideological and maybe a metaphoric aspect as well. These people are on the move, and so is their way of life.

But while the camera is constantly moving, it also never moves at all. Both movement and stasis are important to the film. As we built the film, we thought in terms of binary propositions: portraiture/landscape, nature/culture, man/animal, east/west, speech/ambient noise. Maybe the film makes an experiential claim that culture is a moving target, but it's a moving target locked inside an enclosed box.

Spray: My relationship to Nepal, where I've done most of my work, and the people there, preceded my training in filmmaking and in anthropology.

I began filmmaking in 2006 as an art practice that might allow me to explore the world in ways that were not merely discursive. In 2007, I began training in anthropology; I was attracted to its traditional emphasis on long-term, deep engagements with people and place and, especially, learning the local languages. For me, humanistic aims trump any interest in illustrating concepts such as culture or culture-in-flux. I hope *Manakamana* conveys how artificial distinctions (call them cultural, religious, political, or whatever) between ourselves and presumed Others fall short of what James Agee calls "the cruel radiance of what is" or what Buber refers to as "I and Thou."

Concepts such as "culture" function as frameworks for how we perceive the behaviors and values of others. *Manakamana* gives you fleeting glimpses of the world being filmed, without satisfying the desire to fully know the human subjects or the mountainous landscape they traverse. This is conveyed through units that appear temporally whole, shots that offer up simulacra of both realtime and reel-time.

Manakamana also provides commentary on the cinematic frame: the window behind the passengers is reminiscent of the ways in which the image's frame both reveals and misconstrues our vision. The cinematic frame is therefore a metaphor for any conceptual frame that we bring to viewing Others.

MacDonald: Am I correct, Stephanie, that your seeing James Benning's *13 Lakes* [2004] and, Pacho, your studying with Benning at CalArts had some influence on the structuring of the film?

Spray: Yes, Benning's films made a strong impression. *13 Lakes* was the first I saw and is a favorite. As a kind of homage to *13 Lakes*, I've been working on a sound project about the lakes of the Pokhara Valley, but with a twist: I'm primarily interested in what lies under the surface—literally, as well as metaphorically and acoustically (I use hydrophones). I plan to compose the pieces with references to local stories about drownings and malevolent water spirits. *7 Lakes* will be the dark twisted sister of *13 Lakes*.

Pacho: At CalArts, I was very interested in structural films, works like *13 Lakes*—but even more, Jørgen Leth's *66 Scenes from America* [1982] and Alan Clark's *Elephant* [1989]. I found a freshness in structures that supported narrative elements without fully giving themselves over to the conventions of story-telling. I had recently directed some theater experiments (for lack of a better term), and I was particularly intrigued by the "doubleness" of acting: actors' studied non-attention to their audience. This interest carried over into *Manakamana*—I'm watching the subjects' awareness of their world, and how it shifts to acknowledge the passing landscape, other passengers, and private thoughts, before occasionally, obliquely returning to the camera, which is so clearly staring at them yet is never explicitly addressed.

MacDonald: When was the film shot? How much time did you spend filming?

Velez: The film was shot over two summers, 2011 and 2012. The bulk of the work was done that first trip. The second trip was necessary to collect some things we'd been unable to finagle during the first trip (like the goat shot). The first summer we worked for 5 weeks and the second summer, 3 weeks.

MacDonald: What was the division of labor during the shoot? When the folks we meet in the film looked your way, what did they see?

Spray: Pacho selected the stock, loaded and unloaded the magazines, and shot the film. We borrowed the Aaton camera Robert Gardener used to shoot *Forest of Bliss* from the Film Study Center. We're both admirers of Gardener's films and handled his camera with reverence and glee, conscious of how our film participated in the history of ethnographic filmmaking and commented on *Forest of Bliss* in particular.

We hired carpenters in Nepal to build a wooden platform to anchor the Hi-Hat tripod for the camera. We measured the exact location of this tripod platform in the cable car before shooting, so that the framing would be consistent throughout. I recorded sound using a shotgun stereo microphone encased in a zeppelin on a boom pole and recorded the sound on a two-channel sound recorder, the Sound Devices 702.

Velez: There were a number of practical reasons why 16mm film was right for us. It has a great exposure latitude and we wanted to capture both our characters and the bright backgrounds behind them. Also, 16mm has very deep focus, and we wanted to be sure that the distant backgrounds, as well as our characters, were crisp. The look we wanted runs counter to the standard look today, when everything is shot on DSLRs with big chips and little depth-of-field.

We shot in 16mm and ended up with a 2k DCP [Digital Cinema Package]. We had dreams of going to 35mm, but just couldn't afford it.

Spray: But we also decided against 35mm because we were convinced by Patrick Lindenmaier, who worked on our image and color in post-production, that it would in no way add to our film aesthetically.

We were aware of the nostalgia indexed by the grain of 16mm film and the 16mm film camera—especially the camera we were using. We thought about how within the state-of-the-art digital technology of the "developed" world, our use of 16mm might reflect the "developing" country of Nepal, where the majority of cable-car riders go to worship a goddess requiring blood sacrifice.

Velez: Our production situation was unusual. Because of the intermittent power supply, we didn't have a good way to charge our camera batteries during the day. We were very much at the mercy of our conditions and had to move forward quite slowly and deliberately. It was also very hot; the cable cars became mobile greenhouses in the midday sun. We usually shot about four rides in a day, then went to the nearby town for two-three days of recovery, recharging, reloading, etcetera. In total, we probably shot for about nine days on the cable car. We filmed 36 trips.

The nicest, easiest part of the shoot was dealing with the people. I think we said the same things that many observational documentarians say to their subjects: "Please ignore the camera; just do what you would normally do." I don't think we interfered any more than Drew Associates or the Maysles Brothers in their early work. Of course, fly-on-the-wall observation is impossible to achieve. In fact, the ways in which we most clearly failed to be flies-on-the-wall add an interesting texture to the film. Stephanie knew some of the characters from her earlier fieldwork, but for many it was their first time in front of a camera, and also on the cable car.

Spray: While we did shoot a number of individuals neither of us knew at all, the majority of the subjects we ended up including in *Manakamana* had known me upwards of a decade. They'd been subjected to my camera and field recordings for years. In fact, I had "kinship" relations with most of these subjects: I'd been adopted by one family, one of the matriarchs in the third shot (Khim Kumari Gayek, the woman in red who tells the rambling story about the ascetic and Kalika) adopted me as her daughter in 2004 after I'd been visiting her family for several years, because all of her daughters had died. Her co-wife, Chet Kumari Gayek, seated in the middle, later came to adopt me as well, perhaps a form of competitive co-adoption—they share a husband, why not an American "daughter." Bindu Gayek (in the second shot) is Chet's daughter-in-law and came to call me her "younger sister." So they needed little prepping before sitting before a camera; whereas those subjects we did not know as well tended to be either awkward and stiff or more obviously performative.

We didn't tell our film subjects much about our project, other than to say we wished to film them on their journey to and from the Manakamana temple in the cable car. We gave them free rein to talk about whatever they pleased, but asked that they not stare at the camera. This creates a productive tension, for subjects do indeed glance at the camera or at us from time to time. I suppose *Manakamana* is the inverse of Andy Warhol's *Screen Tests* [1964–66], in which subjects were instructed to gaze directly at the camera. In either case, the subject is aware of the camera, as is the audience (figures 60a, 60b, 60c).

MacDonald: What's the history of the Manakamana cable car?

Velez: It was built about fifteen years ago by a Nepali businessman, after receiving a concession from the Royal family. A lot of the technical know-how comes from India, though the cable cars themselves are Austrian. It's been in continuous operation since it opened, except for repairs after the Maoist insurgency tried to blow it up.

MacDonald: Ernst Karel worked with you on sound. Ernst had done *Swiss Mountain Transport Systems* [2011], sound pieces of a variety of forms of mountain transport, including cable cars. At what point did he become involved in *Manakamana*?

FIGURES 60A, B, AND C *Pilgrims traveling by cable car to visit the Hindu goddess Bhagwati in Stephanie Spray and Pacho Velez's* Manakamana *(2013).*

Source: Courtesy Spray and Velez.

Velez: Ernst consulted with us from the beginning about strategies for documenting sound in the cars. And he received reports about our progress while we were in the field.

But we used different techniques to record than he did. He was interested in the ambient sounds in the cable cars. We did want to record those, but we also knew it was important to have clean, intelligible recordings of the dialogue. So we were using a very different style of microphone and a different placement strategy.

During post-production, Ernst mixed and sweetened our sound, and he built the two-minute-long sound piece (featuring the temple bells) at the film's mid-point.

Spray: Ernst has been crucial to nearly all SEL films; he informs our way of thinking about sound in cinema and sound more generally. In post-production, he worked with us to make the 5.1 sound mix, for all of our recordings were stereo. He spatialized the sound, helped us emphasize particular frequencies over others for a very subtle sci-fi effect in some of the earlier shots. That said, with the exception of some additional wind rustling in the goat shot, we did not foley any of our sound, as many presume; we stuck with the original stereo recordings. As a phonographer who frequently edits and works with field or location recordings, Ernst encouraged us to be confident in doing so.

MacDonald: How did you choose the eleven trips you included in the final version? What factors led to the 6/5 organization?

Velez: We spent a long time figuring out the film's shape, starting from a much more rigid, structural idea of how the film should look. Early cuts featured eighteen rides: nine up, nine down, and for each ride the camera would switch positions in the cable car: facing forward, backward, forward, backward. It was a very precise and clean edit, without loose ends or mysteries. In many ways, it felt like a Benning film. And that was a problem for us. Somehow, the balance was tilted too much towards conceptual precision and away from small human revelations. We had to find a balance between structuralism and ethnography, these two huge traditions we were trying to synthesize.

We ended up with a more playful structure, one that borrowed ideas from structuralism, but also from classical Hollywood cinema, like the shift at twenty-five minutes from "Act 1" to "Act 2." In *His Girl Friday*, that's the moment when Walter Burns (Cary Grant) convinces Hildy Johnson (Rosalind Russell) to stay in town and write the newspaper article; in *Psycho*, it's the moment when Marion Crane meets Norman Bates; in *Manakamana*, it's the moment when characters begin to talk. And it totally shifts the audience's expectations.

We also added a two minute space of black in the middle of the film, between the rides up and the rides down. During this time, the audience can hear the temple bells and the bustle of pilgrims, and come as close as the film allows to the experience of seeing the temple. It's a moment for the film's characters to have an experience with the goddess. Stephanie and I could not figure out how to visually represent that religious experience in a way that conveyed its deeper meanings, so we settled on black and sound.

The glib explanation for six shots up but only five down is that the goats that you see going up are sacrificed, and don't make the return trip. But we gave a lot of thought to the film's end. For a while, it finished with the two musicians (now shot 10) riding into the station. But then we realized that we had a character arc with the older couple who ascend with a live chicken, then descend at the very end. When I watch their descent, I find myself drawn to the woman's face. I see her fear at the shaking car, her interest in the beautiful landscape, but also what I would call her spiritual satisfaction. She looks fulfilled to me. And it's something I don't think I've ever really felt, living my comfortable, rational, agnostic existence; I envy her for it. That's why it should be the last shot.

{ FILMOGRAPHIES }

The following listing, organized alphabetically and sequentially by date, includes title, date of completion, gauge or format; length to the quarter-minute; color/black-and-white; sound/silence; and (in parentheses, distributors). DV means Digital Video; HDV, High Definition. Within the individual filmographies, I provide detailed information about a distributor only the first time that distributor is listed in that filmography. When a film is not in distribution or even available from the filmmaker, I indicate that it is not available: NA.

Several distributor abbreviations are used with some regularity: CC (Canyon Cinema: http://www.canyoncinema.com/); DER (Documentary Educational Resources: http://www.der.org/); VDB (Video Data Bank: http://www.vdb.org). When DVDs of films are widely available, I use "Amazon."

In a few instances, filmmakers have websites that include quite complete filmographies with detailed annotations; in those instances I have directed readers to the websites.

Betzy Bromberg

Petit Mal. 1977. 16mm; 18 minutes; color; sound (CC).
  Ciao Bella. 1978. 16mm; 13 minutes; color; sound (CC).
  Soothing the Bruise. 1980. 16mm; 21 minutes; color; sound (CC).
  Marasmus. 1981. 16mm; 24 minutes; color; sound (CC).
  Az Iz. 1983. 16mm; 37 minutes; color; sound (CC).
  Body Politic. 1988. 16mm; 40 minutes; color; sound (CC).
  Divinity Gratis. 1996. 16mm; 59 minutes; color; sound (CC).
  a Darkness Swallowed. 2005. 16mm; 78 minutes; color; sound (CC).
  Voluptuous Sleep. 2011. 16mm; 95 minutes; color; sound (Bromberg: bromberg@calarts.edu).

Ilisa Barbash/Lucien Castaing-Taylor

Made in USA. 1990. 16mm; 10 minutes; color; sound (Barbash: barbash@fas.harvard.edu).

In and Out of Africa (co-made with Gabai Baare, Christopher Steiner). 1992. 16mm; 59½ minutes; color; sound (Berkeley Media: http://www.berkeleymedia.com; Royal Anthropological Institute: http://www.therai.org.uk).

Frantz Fanon: Black Skin, White Mask (photography, consultants; directed by Isaac Julien). 1996. 35mm; 73/52 minutes; color; sound (California Newsreel: http://www.newsreel.org).

Sweetgrass. 2009. 35mm; 101 minutes; color; sound (Cinema Guild: http://www.cinemaguild.com; Mandragora International: info@mandragora-sales.com; Dogwoof: dogwoof.com; Arsenal: http://www.arsenal-berlin.de; Kinosmith: http://www.kinosmith.com; 791.cine: info@791cine.com).

Jonathan Caouette

Tarnation. 2004. DV/35mm; 85 minutes; color; sound (Amazon).

Fat Girls (actor; directed by Ash Christian). 2006. 35mm; 82 minutes; color; sound (Amazon).

Short Bus (actor: cameo; directed by John Cameron Mitchell). 2006. 35mm; 101 minutes; color; sound (Amazon).

All Tomorrow's Parties (co-directed by Caouette and others). 2009. DV; 82 minutes; color; sound (Amazon).

All Flowers in Time. 2010. 35mm; 14 minutes; color; sound (PHI Films: http://www.phi-montreal.com).

Walk Away Renee. 2012. DV; 88 minutes; color; sound (Caouette: jonathan-caouette@gmail.com; Sundance Selects).

Lucien Castaing-Taylor

[See also listing for Ilisa Barbash and Castaing-Taylor]

Fine and Coarse (Castaing-Taylor). 2007. DV; 8 minutes; color; sound (since re-worked as *Coom Biddy*).

Breakfast. 2010. 35mm; 10¼ minutes; color; sound (Castaing-Taylor: lucien-castaingtaylor@gmail.com).

Daybreak on the Bedground. 2010. 8¼ minutes; color; sound (Castaing-Taylor).

Hell Roaring Creek. 2010. 35mm/Dolby SRD, digital audio-visual installation (5 channel audio; single-channel video); 19¾ minute; color; sound (Castaing-Taylor).

The High Trail. 2010. 35mm/Dolby SRD, digital audio-visual installation (5 channel audio; single-channel video); 7¼ minutes; color; sound (Castaing-Taylor).

Into-the-Jug ("Geworfen"). 2010. 35mm; 11 minutes; color; sound (Castaing-Taylor)

Turned at the Pass. 2010. 35mm; 10 minutes; color; sound (Castaing-Taylor).

The Quick and the Dead/Moutons de Panurge. 2010. 4-channel video installation; color; silent (Castaing-Taylor).

Bedding Down. 2012. 35mm/Dolby SRD, digital audio-visual installation (5 channel audio; single-channel video); 6½ minutes; color; sound (Castaing-Taylor).

Coom Biddy. 2012. 35mm/Dolby SRD, digital audio-visual installation (5 channel audio; single-channel video); 7¾ minutes; color; sound (Castaing-Taylor).

Leviathan (co-made with Véréna Paravel). 2012. High-definition HDV; 87 minutes; color; surround sound (Cinema Guild: http://www.cinemaguild.com).

Still Life (co-made with Véréna Paravel). 2013. HDV; 28 minutes; color; sound (Castaing-Taylor).

Nina Davenport

[Nina Davenport has worked as a freelancer on two reality television shows: Bravo's *The "It" Factor* and NBC's *Crime & Punishment*; on the PBS show, *Greater Boston Arts*; and in minor roles on several films, including Darren Aranofsky's *Pi* (1998).]

Hello Photo. 1995. 16mm; 56 minutes; black-and-white/color; sound (DER).

Always a Bridesmaid. 2000. 16mm; 98 minutes; color; sound (New Video: http://www.newvideo.com).

Parallel Lines. 2003. Mini-DV; 98 minutes; color; sound (DER).

Operation Filmmaker. 2007. Mini-DV; 92 minutes; color; sound (Amazon; Davenport: nina.davenport@gmail.com).

First Comes Love. 2012. HDV; 108 minutes; color; sound (Amazon; Davenport).

Susana de Sousa Dias

Rotas do Extremo Ocidente: os Livros de Pedra (director). 1988. 16mm; 26¼ minutes; color; sound (RTP Archive—Portuguese public television channel).

Rotas do Extremo Ocidente: o Tempo e as Jóias (director). 1988. 16mm; 25 minutes; color; sound (RTP).

Rotas do Extremo Ocidente: por Muitos e Altos Montes (director). 1988. 16mm; 25¼ minutes; color sound (RTP).

Uma Época de Ouro: Cinema Português 1930–1945 ("A Golden Age: Portuguese Cinema 1930–1945"). 1997. Betacam SP; 57¼ minutes; color; sound (Portuguese Cinematheque—ANIM [National Archive of Moving Images]).

Processo-Crime 141/53: Enfermeiras no Estado Novo ("Criminal Case 141/53: Nurses in Fascist Portugal"). 2000. Betacam SP; 52¼ minutes; color; sound (Kintop: http://www.kintop.net)

Natureza Morta—Visages d'une Dictature ("Still Life"). 2005. Digibeta; 72 minutes; black-and-white/color; sound (Kintop).

Natureza Morta/Stilleben ("Natureza Morta/Still Life"). 2010. 3-screen installation; 33 minutes; black-and-white/color; sound (Kintop).

48. 2009. Digibeta; 93 minutes; black-and-white/color; sound (Kintop).

Robert Gardner

[An annotated, illustrated filmography of Robert Gardner's work is available at his website: http://www.robertgardner.net.]

Jane Gillooly

No Applause. 1984. Multi-image slide presentation; 20 minutes; color; sound (Gillooly: http://www.janegillooly.com).

White House Shuttle. 1987. Interactive slide performance, designed for stage with music by Bob Moses (Gillooly).

So Sad, So Sorry, So What. 1988. Multi-image slide and video presentation; 27 minutes; color; sound (1990 video release: Gillooly).

Shrine to Ritualized Time (co-made with Karen Aqua). 1990. Multi-media 16mm and 35mm, 8-projector installation; 5 minutes; color; sound (Gillooly).

Leona's Sister Gerri. 1995. 16mm; 57 minutes; color and black-and-white; sound (New Day: http://www.newday.com; New Video/DocuramaFilms: http://www.newvideo.com/docurama/leonas-sister-gerri/).

Theme: Murder (co-producer, co-writer; directed by Martha Swetzoff). 1998. 16mm; 57 minutes; color; sound (New Day).

Dragonflies the Baby Cries. 2000. 16mm; 10 minutes; black-and-white; sound (http://www.transitmedia.net/shop/index.lasso?fsid=Dragonflies_The_Baby_Cries).

Upstairs, Downstairs. 2004–2006. DV; 10 minutes; color; sound (Gillooly).

Splendor. 2006. DV; 2 minutes; color; sound (Gillooly).

Today the Hawk Takes One Chick. 2008. DV; 72 minutes; color; sound (DER).

Suitcase of Love and Shame. 2013. HDV; 70 minutes; color; sound (Gillooly).

Michael Glawogger

[Glawogger website: http://www.glawogger.com/]

Pacific Motion. 1981. 16mm; 7 minutes; color; silent (office@filmmuseum.at).

Street Noise. 1982. 35mm; 9 minutes; color; sound (office@filmmuseum.at).

Death of a Person Reading. 1984. 16mm; 15 minutes; color; sound (office@filmmuseum.at).

Haiku. 1987. 35mm; 3 minutes; color; sound (office@filmmuseum.at).

Changing Places. 1989. 16mm; 30 minutes; black-and-white/color; sound (office@filmmuseum.at).

War in Vienna (Krieg in Wien). 1989. (office@filmmuseum.at).

Ant Street (Die Ameisenstrasse). 1995. 35mm; 87 minutes; color; sound (office@dor-film.at).

Movies in the Mind. 1996. 35mm; 87 minutes; color; sound (office@dor-film.at).

Megacities. 1998. 35mm; 90 minutes; color; sound (Amazon).

France, Here We Come (Frankreich, wir kommen). 1999. 35mm; 80 minutes; color; sound (office@lotus-film.co.at).

State of the Nation (Zur Lage: Österreich in sechs Kapiteln). 2002. 35mm; 85 minutes; color; sound (office@lotus-film.co.at).

Slugs (Nacktschnecken). 2004. 35mm; 86 minutes; color; sound (Amazon).

Workingman's Death. 2004. 35mm; 122 minutes; color; sound (Amazon).

LKH. 2004. Digital; 20 minutes; color; sound (office@dor-film.at).

Mai Thai. 2005. 35mm; 1 minute; color; sound (Michael.glawogger@draxler.co.at).

In Heaven. 2006. Digital; 12 minutes; color; sound (pepo@befilm.ch).

Slumming. 2006. 35mm; 100 minutes; color; sound (Amazon).

Kill Daddy Goodnight. 2009. 35mm; 110 minutes; color; sound (Corinth Films: http://www.corinthleasing.com).

Contact High. 2009. 35mm; 98 minutes; color; sound (Amazon).

Whore's Glory. 2012. 35mm; 114 minutes; color; sound (http://shop.film-laden.at/; Amazon.de).

Alfred Guzzetti

[Guzzetti website: http://www.alfredguzzetti.com/]

Film segment for stage production of Pirandello's A Dream or Perhaps Not. 1964. 16mm; c.2 minutes; black-and-white; silent (NA).

Coffee. c.1966. 8mm; c.6 minutes; color; silent (NA).

Film segments for stage production of Shakespeare's Coriolanus (collaboration with Thomas Babe). c.1965. 16mm; c.25 minutes; black-and-white; sound (NA).

Film segment for production of Ionesco's Rhinoceros. c.1966. 16mm; c.3 minutes; black-and-white; silent (NA).

A-P-A. 1966. 16mm; c.15 minutes; color; sound (NA).

The Sickness Unto Death. c.1967. 16mm. Unfinished.

Leaf Film. c.1966. 16mm; c.2 minutes; color; sound (NA).

Rock. c.1966. 16mm; c.2 minutes; black-and-white; silent (NA).

Nightcap. 1968. 16mm; 3½ minutes; black-and-white; sound (NA).

Film segments for stage production of Shakespeare's Coriolanus. 1968. 16mm; c.15 minutes; black-and-white; sound (NA).

Two-screen segment for stage production of Thomas Babe's A Winter's Tale in Georgia. 1968. 16mm; c.3 minutes; black-and-white; silent (NA).

Film segments for stage production of Pinter's The Basement (cinematography). 1969. 16mm; c.15 minutes; black-and-white; sound (NA).

Notes on the Harvard Strike (collaboration with Frederick Steadry). 1969. Open-reel Sony videotape transferred to 16mm; 39 minutes; black-and-white; sound (NA).

Exercises en route (collaboration with Earl Kim). 1971. 16mm; c.5 minutes; black-and-white; silent (NA).

Air. 1971. 16mm; 18 minutes; color; sound (Guzzetti: http://www.alfredguzzetti.com).

Evidence. 1972. 16mm; 16 minutes; color; sound (NA).

Gestes: esquisse d'un repertoire des gestes-signes français/French Gestures: A Preliminary Repertory (collaboration with Laurence Wylie). 1974. 16mm; 30 minutes; black-and-white; sound (NA).

Family Portrait Sittings. 1975. 16mm; 103 minutes; black-and-white/color; sound (Guzzetti).

Sky Piece (collaboration with Ivan Tcherepnin). 1978. 16mm; 10½ minutes; color; sound (Guzzetti).

Scenes from Childhood. 1980. 16mm; 77¾ minutes; color; sound (Guzzetti).

Living at Risk: The Story of a Nicaraguan Family (collaboration with Susan Meiselas and Richard P. Rogers). 1985. 16mm; 58 minutes; color; sound (DER).

Chronological Order. 1986. 16mm; 4 minutes; color; sound (NA).

Beginning Pieces. 1986. 16mm; 40¾ minutes; color; sound (Guzzetti).

July, 1986. 1986. 16mm. Unfinished.

The Fourth of July Parade in Wellfleet, Massachusetts. c.1988. 16mm. Unfinished.

The House on Magnolia Avenue. 1989. 16mm; 40 minutes; color; sound (Guzzetti).

Pictures from a Revolution (collaboration with Susan Meiselas and Richard P. Rogers). 1991. 16mm; 92 minutes; color; sound (Docurama: http://www.docurama.com/docurama/pictures-from-a-revolution/).

Rosetta Stone ("Language Lessons 1"). 1993, revised 2001. Hi8 videotape; 7½ minutes; color; sound (Guzzetti).

Seed and Earth (collaboration with Ákos Östör, Ned Johnston, and Lina Fruzzetti). 1994. 16mm; 36 minutes; color; sound (DER).

The Curve of the World ("Language Lessons 2"). 1994, revised 1999. Hi8 videotape; 5¾ minutes; color; sound (Guzzetti).

Variation. 1995. Hi8 videotape; 5¼ minutes; color; sound (Guzzetti).

The Stricken Areas ("Language Lessons 3"). 1996, revised 1999. Hi8 videotape; 7½ minutes; color; sound (Guzzetti).

What Actually Happened ("Language Lessons 4"). 1996. Hi8 videotape; 9¼ minutes; color; sound (Guzzetti).

Under the Rain. 1997. DV Tape; 10½ minutes; color; sound (Guzzetti).

The Ghost Violin. 1998. DV Tape 8 minutes; color; sound (Guzzetti).

A Tropical Story. 1998. DV Tape; 9½ minutes; color; sound (Guzzetti).

Santiago's Story (collaboration with Richard P. Rogers and Susan Meiselas). 1999. DV videotape; 15 minutes; color; sound (NA).

Khalfan and Zanzibar (collaboration with Ákos Östör and Lina Fruzzetti). 1999. DV Tape; 25½ minutes; color; sound (DER).

Une Histoire tropicale (French version of *A Tropical Story*). 1998. DV Tape; 9½ minutes; color; sound (Guzzetti; Heure Exquise!: http://www. exquise.org/).

The Tower of Industrial Life. 2000. DV Tape; 15¼ minutes; color; sound (Guzzetti).

La Tour de la vie industrielle (French version of *The Tower of Industrial Life*). 2001. DV Tape; 15½ minutes; color; sound (Heure Exquise!).

Down from the Mountains. 2002. DV Tape; 8¾ minutes; color; sound (Guzzetti).

Sous la pluie (French version of *Under the Rain*). 2003. DV Tape; 10½ minutes; color; sound (Heure Exquise!).

Calcutta Intersection. 2003. DV Tape. 10¼ minutes; color; sound (Guzzetti).

History of the Sea. 2004. DV Tape; 14½ minutes; color; sound (Guzzetti).

América Central. 2004. DV Tape; 6¾ minutes; color; sound (Guzzetti).

América Central (Spanish version). 2004. DV Tape; 6¾ minutes; color; sound (Guzzetti).

Night Vision. 2005. DV Tape; 2½ minutes; color; sound (Guzzetti).

Passages (collaboration with Kurt Stallmann). 2005. HDV and DV Tape; 9½ minutes; color; sound (Guzzetti).

Singing Pictures: Women Painters of Naya (principal cinematographer). 2005. DV Tape; 40 minutes; color; sound (DER).

Reframing History (collaboration with Susan Meiselas and Pedro Linger Gasilgia). 2006. DV Tape; 12½ minutes; color; sound (Docurama).

Reframing History (version for two-channel installation; collaboration with Susan Meiselas and Pedro Linger Gasilgia). 2006. DV Tape; 7 minutes; color; sound (Guzzetti).

Breaking Earth (installation in collaboration with Kurt Stallmann). 2008. HDV Tape; 30 minutes; color; sound (Trigon Music Press: http://www.trigon-music.com/).

Songs of a Sorrowful Man (principal cinematography). 2009. DV Tape; 36 minutes; color; sound (DER).

Still Point. 2009. HDV Tape; 14½ minutes; color; sound (Guzzetti).

Moon Crossings (co-made with Kurt Stallmann). 2011. HDV Tape; 15½ minutes; color; sound (Guzzetti; Trigon Music Press).

The Barrios Family Twenty-Five Years Later (collaboration with Susan Meiselas). 2011. HDV Tape; 20 films totaling 131 minutes (one of the 2 DVDs in "A Family in History"); color; sound (DER).

Time Exposure. 2012. HDV; 11 minutes; black-and-white/color; sound (Guzzetti).

Time Present (collaboration with Kurt Stallmann). 2013. DV; 17 minutes; color; sound (Guzzetti).

Todd Haynes

Assassins: A Film Concerning Rimbaud. 1985. 16mm; 20 minutes; color; sound (Haynes).

Superstar: The Karen Carpenter Story. 1987. 16mm; 43 minutes; color; sound (Haynes).

Disappearer (music video for Sonic Youth). 1990. 35mm; 4½ minutes; color; sound (YouTube).

Poison. 1991. 16mm; 85 minutes; color; sound (Amazon).

Dottie Gets Spanked. 1993. 16mm; 27 minutes; color; sound (YouTube).

Safe. 1995. 35mm; 119 minutes; color; sound (Amazon).

Velvet Goldmine. 1998. 35mm; 124 minutes; color; sound (Amazon).

Far from Heaven. 2002. 35mm; 107 minutes; color; sound (Amazon).

I'm Not There. 2007. 35mm; 135 minutes; color; sound (Amazon).

Mildred Pierce (5-part TV miniseries). 2011. HDV; 300 minutes; color; sound (HBO; Amazon).

Leonard Retel Helmrich

Escalation. 1977. 8mm; 31 minutes; color; sound (Helmrich: leonardretelhelmrich@gmail.com).

Dag mijn klas, ik mis jullie ("Good-bye My Classroom, I Miss All of You"; director, screenplay, camera). 1988. 16mm; 25 minutes; color; sound (NOS 3 Television, Amsterdam).

Het Phoenix Mistery ("The Phoenix Mystery"; screenplay, director). 1990. 16mm; 93 minutes; color; sound (Helmrich).

Moving Objects (screenplay, director, camera) 1991. 16mm; 50¾ minutes; color; sound. (Scarabeefilms: http://www.scarabeefilms.com.)

Jermand auf der Treppe ("Somebody on the Stairs"). 1994. HD; 50 minutes; color; sound (Scarabeefilms).

Art Non-Blok (screenplay, director, camera). 1994. BetaSP; 40 minutes; color; sound (Helmrich).

Closed Circuit. 1996. Performance with DV-BetaSP (Workshop on Single Shot Cinema); 15 minutes; color; sound (Helmrich).

Als een vloedlijn ("Like a Shoreline"; screenplay, director, camera). 2000. DV-digi-Beta; 50 minutes; color; sound (Scarabeefilms).

The Body of Indonesia's Conscience (screenplay, director, camera). 2000. DV-BetaSp; 20 minutes; color; sound (Scarabeefilms).

The Eye of the Day/De Stand van de Zon. 2001. DV-digi-Beta; 94½ minutes; color; sound (Scarabeefilms).

Flight from Heaven/Vlucht uit. 2003. DV-digi-Beta; 50 minutes; color; sound (Scarabeefilms).

Shape of the Moon/Stand van de Maan. 2005. DV/35mm; 92 minutes; color; sound (Scarabeefilms).

Aladi (co-made with Pim the la Parra; screenplay, director, camera). 2006. HDV; 135 minutes; color; sound (SFA Surinam).

Promised Paradise. 2006. HD; 52¼ minutes; color; sound (Scarabeefilms).

Jadwiga's laatste reis ("Jadwiga's last journey"; editing and coaching). 2006. DV-Cam; 50 minutes; color; sound (NPS Television, Scarabeefilms).

In My Father's Country (Director of Photography). 2006. HDV; 90 minutes; color; sound (Mayfan Films, Sydney, Australia).

Contract Pensions/Djangan Loepah (Director of Photography). 2007. HDV; 90 minutes; color; sound (Scarabeefilms).

Beautiful Crazy (Director of Photography). 2007. HDV; 90 minutes; color; sound (Chi Company, Taiwan).

The Burning Season (Director of Photography). 2007. HDV; 90 minutes; color; sound (Hatchling Productions, Australia).

Position among the Stars/Stand van de Sterren. 2011. HDV; 110½ minutes; color; sound (Scarabeefilms).

Buitenkampers ("Outside-prisoners"; cinematographer). 2012. HDV; 90 minutes;
color; sound (Holland Harbour, Netherlands).

Hollandse Nieuwe ("Dutch New"; director, screenplay, camera). 2012. HDV; 90 minutes;
color; sound (EO tv and In-Soo productions).

Moving Curves (Director, Screenplay, Stereographer) 2013. 3-D; 30 minutes, color; sound; (NYU, Abu Dhabi).

Ross McElwee

[McElwee website: http://www.rossmcelwee.com/]
   20,000 Missing Persons. 1974. 16mm; 30 minutes; color; sound (NA).
   68 Albany Street. 1976. 16mm; 24 minutes; color; sound (NA).
   Energy War (some cinematography; directed by D. A. Pennebaker, Pat Powell, Chris Hegedus). 1977. 16mm; 300 minutes; color; sound (Pennebaker: http://phfilms.com).
   Charleen. 1978. 16mm; 59 minutes; color; sound (First Run Features: http://www.firstrunfeatures.com; Institute of Contemporary Arts/ICA Films: http://www.ica.org.uk; Rezo Films: http://www.rezofilms.com).
   N!ai: Portrait of a !Kung Woman (some cinematography; directed by John Marshall). 1978. 16mm; 60 minutes; color; sound (DER).
   Space Coast (co-made with Michel Negroponte). 1979. 16mm; 90 minutes; color; sound (DVD: McElwee).
   Resident Exile (co-made with Alexandra Anthony, Michel Negroponte). 1981. 16mm; 30 minutes; color; sound (FR).
   Backyard. 1984. 16mm; 40 minutes; color; sound (Amazon; First Run; ICA Films; Rezo Films).
   Sherman's March: A Meditation on the Possibility of Romantic Love in the South during an Era of Nuclear Weapons Proliferation (aka *Sherman's March*). 1986. 16mm; 155 minutes (Amazon).
   Something to Do with the Wall (co-made with Marilyn Levine). 1990. 16mm; 88 minutes; color; sound (McElwee).
   Time Indefinite. 1993. 35mm; 114 minutes; color; sound (Amazon; First Run; ICA Films; Rezo Films).
   Six O'Clock News. 1996. 35mm; 103 minutes; color; sound (Amazon; First Run; ICA Films; Rezo Films).
   Bright Leaves. 2003. 35mm; 105 minutes; color; sound (Amazon; First Run; ICA Films; Rezo Films).
   In Paraguay. 2009. 35mm; 78¾ minutes; color; sound (McElwee).
   Photographic Memory. 2011. DV; 84 minutes; color; sound (Marie Emmanuelle Hartness, St. Quay Films: mhartness@stquayfilms.com).

Alexander Olch

Soaked. 1992. 16mm; 8 minutes; color; sound (Olch: olch@olch.com).
   Overexposed. 1993. Super8mm; 45 minutes; color sound (Olch).
   No Vladimir. 2000. 16mm; 6 minutes; black-and-white; sound (Olch).
   Artemin Goldberg: Custom Tailor of Brassieres. 2000. 16mm; 29 minutes; color; sound (Olch).

The Windmill Movie. 2008. 35mm; 80 minutes; color; sound (The Film Desk: http://www.thefilmdesk.com; HBO; Amazon).

Véréna Paravel

7 Queens. 2008. DV; 19 minutes; color; sound (Paravel: verena.paravel@gmail. com).
   With Such a Wistful Eye (Interface Series #1). 2008. DV; 15 minutes; color; sound (Paravel).
   Habitat (Interface Series #2). 2008. DV; 12 minutes; color; sound (Paravel).
   I Only See Problems (Interface Series #3). 2009. DV; 11 minutes; color; sound (Paravel).
   Presented with Severe Pain (Interface Series #4). 2009. DV; 23 minutes; color; sound (Paravel).
   I Have No Friends (Interface Series #5). 2010. DV; 16 minutes; color; sound (Paravel).
   Foreign Parts (co-made with J. P. Sniadecki). 2010. DV; 80 minutes; color; sound (Kino Lorber: http://www.kinolorber.com).
   Leviathan (co-made with Lucien Castaing-Taylor). 2012. HDV; 87 minutes; color; surround sound (Cinema Guild: http://www.cinemaguild.com).
   Still Life (co-made with Lucien Castaing-Taylor). 2013. HDV; 28 minutes; color; sound (Paravel).

Ed Pincus

Mrs. Smith. 1965. 16mm; unfinished (NA).
   Black Natchez. 1967. 16mm; 62 minutes; black-and-white; sound (Lucia Small: http://pincusandsmallfilms.com/); and/or Harvard Film Archive (HFA).
   One Step Away (co-made by David Neuman). 1968. 16mm; 58 minutes; color; sound (Small; HFA).
   Harry's Trip (co-made with David Neuman). 1969. 16mm; 16 minutes; color; sound (Small; HFA).
   Portrait of a McCarthy Supporter (co-made with David Neuman). 1969. 16mm; 16 minutes; color; sound (Small; HFA).
   The Way We See It (co-made with David Neuman). 1969. 16mm; 57 minutes; black-and-white; sound (Small; HFA).
   Panola. 1970. 16mm; 21 minutes; black-and-white; sound (Small; HFA).
   Life and Other Anxieties (co-made with Steve Ascher). 1977. 16mm; 90 minutes; color; sound (Small; HFA).
   Diaries (1971–1976). c.1980. 16mm; 200 minutes; color; sound (Small; HFA).

The Axe in the Attic (co-made with Lucia Small). 2007. DV; 110 minutes; color; sound (IndiePix: http://www.indiepixfilms.com/; Cinema Guild: http://www.cinemaguild.com/).

One Cut, One Life (co-made with Lucia Small). 2014. DV; 100 minutes; color; sound (hello@onecutonelife.com).

Jane Pincus

Abortion (co-made with Catha Maslow, Mary Summers, Karen Weinstein). 1971. 16mm; 23 minutes; black-and-white; sound (Jane Pincus: aggiesmee@tds.net).

Jennifer Proctor

[Jennifer Proctor's moving-image work is available online at her website: http://www.cargo.jenniferproctor.com. Proctor distinguishes between her more substantial work and what she calls "voodles" (i.e. video doodles).]

Surfacing. 2003. 16mm; 2½ minutes; black-and-white; sound.

Margo. 2003. DV; 1 minute; color; sound.

Hickory Hill. 2004. mini-DV; 2 minutes; color; sound.

Alternative Forms of Energy. 2005. Super-8mm; 4½ minutes; color; sound.

(dis)placement (sound design; image by Aaron Valdez). 2005. 8mm; 5 minutes; color; sound.

Groundless. 2006. DV; 5¼ minutes; color; sound.

invisibilities. 2006. 16mm/Super-8mm; 10½ minutes; color; sound.

Smackem Yackem (co-made with Aaron Valdez for Video Race hosted by Iowa City Microcinema). 2006. DV (voodle); 2 minutes; color; sound.

Flow. 2006. DV (voodle); 4¼ minutes; color; sound.

Self-portrait in Rotoscope. 2006. DV (voodle); ½ minute; color; sound.

Testing the Undertow. 2007. 16mm; 13 minutes; color and black-and-white; sound.

Evening Lights (from Videoblogging Week 2007). 2007. DV (voodle); 1¼ minutes; color; sound.

Pere Marquette. 2007. DV (voodle); 2 minutes; color; sound.

Lonely Balloon. 2007. DV (voodle); 1¼ minutes; color; sound.

Weird Science. 2007. DV (voodle); 2¾ minutes; color; sound.

A License to Write: The Iowa Workshop Experience. 2008. DV; 18 minutes; color; sound.

Still Life with Hand and Rice, on Glass (from Videoblogging Week 2008). 2008. DV (voodle); 1½ minutes; color; sound.

Done Moshed Some Data (from Videoblogging Week 2008). 2008. DV (voodle); 1½ minutes; color; sound.

Grand Rapids in Miniature (from Videoblogging Week 2008). 2008. DV (voodle); 1¼ minutes; color; sound.

Ants (from Videoblogging Week 2008). 2008. DV (voodle); 2¾ minutes; color; sound.

Pillow Fight. 2008. DV (voodle); 1½ minutes; color; sound.

Chicken Flavor (for Suppendapo series). 2008. DV (voodle); ¾ minute; color; sound.

House of Cards. 2008. DV (voodle); 1¼ minutes; color; sound.

Star Wars Uncut Scene 427 (for starwarsuncut.com project). 2009. DV (voodle); ¼ minute; color; sound.

A Movie by Jen Proctor. 2010–2012 (various versions). DV; 12 minutes; color; sound.

Spline Describing a Phone. 2012. Installation with 10-minute video loop; silent.

Godfrey Reggio

Koyaanisqatsi. 1983. 35mm; 87 minutes; color; sound (Criterion: http://www.criterion.com).

Powaqqatsi. 1988. 35mm; 99 minutes; color; sound (Criterion).

Anima Mundi. 1991. 35mm; 29 minutes; color; sound (World Wildlife Fund: Vimeo: vimeo.com).

Evidence. 1995. 35mm; 8 minutes; color; sound (Reggio c/o Ray Hemenez: ray@qatsi.org; YouTube).

Naqoyqatsi. 2002. 35mm; 89 minutes; color; sound (Criterion).

Visitors. 2013. 3K and 5K high-definition video; 87 minutes; black-and-white/color (Cinedigm: http://www.cinedigm.com/).

Amie Siegel

[An annotated, illustrated filmography of Amie Siegel's work is available at her website: http://www.amiesiegel.net.]

Lucia Small

The Blinking Madonna and Other Miracles (producer; directed by Beth Harrington). 1996. 16mm/video; 60 minutes; color; sound (ITVS: http://www.itvs.org).

The Jew in the Lotus (producer; directed by Laurel Chiten). 1998. 16mm; 60 minutes; color; sound (ITVS).

The Mississippi: River of Song (one of several co-producers; produced/directed by John Junkerman). 1999. Beta; 4-part PBS series.

American Wake (co-producer; directed by Maureen Foley). 2004. 16mm; 95 minutes; color; sound (Amazon).

My Father the Genius. 2005. 16mm; 84 minutes; color; sound (Small: http://www.smallangstfilms.com).

The Axe in the Attic (co-made with Ed Pincus). 2007. Video; 110 minutes; color; sound (IndiePix: http://www.indiepixfilms.com/; Cinema Guild: http://www.cinemaguild.com/).

Love and Other Anxieties (editor; directed by Lyda Kuth). 2011. DV Tape; 66 minutes; color; sound (Kuth: naditaproductions@gmail.com).

One Cut, One Life (co-made with Ed Pincus). 2014. DV; 100 minutes; color; sound (hello@onecutonelife.com).

Arthur and Jennifer Smith

Ice Bears of the Beaufort. 2010. HDV; 57 minutes; color; sound (Polar Art Productions: http://www.arthurscsmithiii.com; 907-640-6037).

What Do Polar Bears Dream While They're Dying? 2011. HDV; 33¼ minutes; color; sound (Polar Art Productions).

Once There Were Polar Bears. 2012. HDV; 6¼ minutes; color; sound (Polar Art Productions).

Stephanie Spray

[An annotated, illustrated filmography of Stephanie Spray's work is available on her website: http://www.stephaniespray.com.]

Pacho Velez

[An annotated, illustrated filmography of Pacho Velez's work is available at his website: http://www.pachoworks.com/.]

Paweł Wojtasik

[Wojtasik's videos are often shown publicly in various versions before Wojtasik decides on a final version. The dates listed below are the (current) final versions. Wojtasik website: http://www.pawelwojtasik.com/.]

Dark Sun Squeeze. 2003. DV video; 10 minutes; color; sound (VDB).

Firehole. 2005. Single or 2-channel DV video (two versions); 7½ minutes; color; sound (Wojtasik: http://www.pawelwojtasik.com).

The Aquarium. 2006 (with writer Ginger Strand). HDV; 22¼ minutes; color; sound (VDB).

Naked. 2007. DV video; 10¾ minutes; color; sound (VDB).

Landfill. 2007. HDV single or 2-channel video installation; 10 minutes (loop); color; sound (Wojtasik).

Nascentes Morimur. 2009. HDV; 28 minutes; color; sound (VDB).

Below Sea Level. 2009 (with sound artist Stephen Vitiello) 2009. 360° panoramic installation video; 38 minutes (loop); color; sound (Wojtasik; Massachusetts Museum of Contemporary Art [MASS MoCA], producer, http://www.massmoca.org/contact.php).

Next Atlantis. 2010 (with composer Sebastian Currier) 2010. HDV; 19¾ minutes; color; sound (Wojtasik; Boosey & Hawkes: http://www.boosey.com/).

Pigs. 2010. DV video; 7¾ minutes; color; sound (VDB).

At the Still Point. 2010 (with sound artist Stephen Vitiello) 2010. 5-channel HD video installation; 29½ minutes; color; sound (Wojtasik).

Crush. 2010. DV video;15 minutes; color; sound (VDB).

Nine Gates. 2011. HDV video installation; 15 minutes; color; sound (Wojtasik).

Nine Gates. 2012. HDV; 12 minutes; color; sound (Wojtasik).

{ SELECTED BIBLIOGRAPHY }

General References

Angell, Callie. *Andy Warhol Screen Tests: The Films of Andy Warhol Catalogue Raisonné, Volume 1*. New York: Abrams and the Whitney Museum of American Art, 2006.

Anker, Steve, Kathy Geritz, and Steve Seid, eds. *Radical Light: Alternative Film & Video in the San Francisco Bay Area, 1945–2000*. Berkeley and Los Angeles: University of California Press, 2010.

Barnouw, Erik. *Documentary: A History of Non-Fiction Film*. New York and Oxford: Oxford University Press, 1993.

Beattie, Keith. *Documentary Display: Re-Viewing Nonfiction Film and Video*. London: Wallflower Press, 2008.

Bruzzi, Stella. *New Documentary: A Critical Introduction*. London: Routledge, 2000.

Cubit, Sean, Salma Monani, and Stephen Rust, eds. *Ecocinema Theory and Practice*. New York: Routledge/AFI, 2013.

Dewey, John. *Art as Experience*. New York: Perigee, 1980 (originally published 1934).

Frampton, Hollis. *On the Camera Arts and Consecutive Matters: The Writing of Hollis Frampton*. Ed. Bruce Jenkins. Cambridge, MA: MIT Press, 2009.

Gaines, Jane M., and Michael Renov, eds. *Collecting Visible Evidence*. Minneapolis: University of Minnesota Press, 1999.

Grant, Barry Keith, and Jeannette Sloniowski, eds. *Documenting the Documentary: Close Readings of Documentary Film and Video*. Detroit, MI: Wayne State University Press, 1998.

Heider, Karl G. *Ethnographic Film*. Austin: University of Texas Press, 1976.

Holmlund, Chris, and Justin Wyatt, eds. *Contemporary American Independent Film: From the Margins to the Mainstream*. London: Routledge, 2005.

Kahana, Jonathan. *Intelligence Work: The Politics of American Documentary*. New York: Columbia University Press, 2008.

Lane, Jim. *The Autobiographical Documentary in America*. Madison: University of Wisconsin Press, 2002.

Leacock, Richard [and Valerie Lalonde, ed.]. *The Feeling of Being There: A Filmmaker's Memoir*. Meaulne, France: Semeïon Editions, 2011.

Levin, G. Roy. *Documentary Explorations: Interviews with Film-Makers*. Garden City, NY: Anchor Press, 1971.

MacDonald, Scott. *Adventures of Perception: Cinema as Exploration*. Berkeley and Los Angeles: University of California Press, 2009.

———. *American Ethnographic Film and Personal Documentary: The Cambridge Turn.* Berkeley and Los Angeles: University of California Press, 2013.

———. *Cinema 16: Documents Toward a History of the Film Society.* Philadelphia: Temple University Press, 2002.

MacDougall, David. *Transcultural Cinema.* Ed. Lucien Taylor. Princeton: Princeton University Press, 1998.

Murphy, J. J. *The Black Hole of the Camera: The Films of Andy Warhol.* Berkeley and Los Angeles: University of California Press, 2012.

Nichols, Bill. *Engaging Cinema: An Introduction to Film Studies.* New York: Norton, 2010.

———. *Introduction to Documentary.* Bloomington: Indiana University Press, 2001.

———. *Representing Reality.* Bloomington: Indiana University Press, 1991.

Renov, Michael. *The Subject of Documentary.* Minneapolis: University of Minnesota Press, 2004.

———, ed. *Theorizing Documentary.* New York: Routledge/AFI, 1993.

Rothman, William. *Documentary Film Classics.* New York: Cambridge University Press, 1997.

———, ed. *Three Documentary Filmmakers: Errol Morris, Ross McElwee, Jean Rouch.* Albany: SUNY Press, 2009.

Ruby, Jay. *Picturing Culture: Explorations of Film & Anthropology.* Chicago: University of Chicago Press, 2000.

Russell, Catherine. *Experimental Ethnography: The Work of Film in the Age of Video.* Durham, NC: Duke University, 1999.

Sitney, P. Adams. *Eyes Upside Down: Visionary Filmmakers and the Heritage of Emerson.* New York: Oxford University Press, 2008.

———. *Visionary Film: The American Avant-Garde, 1943–2000.* Oxford and New York: Oxford University Press, 2002.

Stubbs, Liz. *Documentary Filmmakers Speak.* New York: Allworth Press, 2002.

Vaughan, Dai. *For Documentary.* Berkeley and Los Angeles: University of California Press, 1999.

Wahlberg, Malin. *Documentary Time: Film and Phenomenology.* Minneapolis: University of Minnesota Press, 2008).

Warren, Charles, ed. *Beyond Document: Essays on Nonfiction Film.* Middletown, CT: Wesleyan University Press, 1996.

Young, Paul, and Paul Duncan, eds. *Art Cinema.* London: Taschen, 2009.

Zimmermann, Patricia R. *States of Emergency: Documentaries, Wars, Democracies.* Minneapolis: University of Minnesota Press, 2000.

Ilisa Barbash/Lucien Castaing-Taylor

Barbash, Ilisa, and Lucien Taylor, eds. *The Cinema of Robert Gardner.* Oxford: Berg, 2007.

Barbash, Ilisa, and Lucien Taylor. *Cross-Cultural Filmmaking: A Handbook for Making Documentary and Ethnographic Films and Videos.* Berkeley and Los Angeles: University of California Press, 1997.

MacDonald, Scott. *American Ethnographic Film and Personal Documentary: The Cambridge Turn.* Berkeley and Los Angeles: University of California Press, 2013, 314–324.

Betzy Bromberg

Murray, Nick. Interview with Betzy Bromberg. *Cinemad*, 2009. http://www.cinemad. iblamesociety.com/2007/07/betzy-bromberg.html.

Jonathan Caouette

Saunders, Dave. "*Tarnation* (Jonathan Caouette, 2003): Performance and Autobiography." In *Documentary*, ed. Dave Saunders, 186–206. London: Routledge, 2010.

Lucien Castaing-Taylor

Castaing-Taylor was the founding editor of the American Anthropological Association's journal, *Visual Anthropology Review* (1991–1994).
Leimbacher, Irina. "The World Made Flesh—The Sensory Ethnography Lab: Toward a Post-Humanist Cinema." *Film Comment* 50, no. 2 (March/April 2014): 36–39.
MacDonald, Scott. *American Ethnographic Film and Personal Documentary: The Cambridge Turn*. Berkeley and Los Angeles: University of California Press, 2013, 324–327, 334–337.
MacDougall, David. *Transcultural Cinema*. Ed. Lucien Taylor. Princeton: Princeton University Press, 1998.
Taylor, Lucien, ed. *Visualizing Theory: Selected Essays from V.A.R. 1990–1994*. New York: Routledge, 1994.

Nina Davenport

Erickson, Steve. "Nina Davenport: 'I've Never Encountered Anyone Quite Like Him Before'," an interview with Nina Davenport. http://www.greencine.com/central/ ninadavenport.
MacDonald, Scott. *American Ethnographic Film and Personal Documentary: The Cambridge Turn*. Berkeley and Los Angeles: University of California Press, 2013, 279–291.

Susana de Sousa Dias

Susana de Sousa Dias's website—http://www.kintop.net—includes a listing of reviews of her films.

Robert Gardner

Barbash, Ilisa, and Lucien Taylor, eds. *The Cinema of Robert Gardner*. Oxford: Berg, 2007.

Cooper, Thomas W. *Natural Rhythms: The Indigenous World of Robert Gardner.* New York: Anthology Film Archives, 1995.

Gardner, Robert. "The Impulse to Preserve." In *Beyond Document: Essays on Nonfiction Film*, ed. Charles Warren, 169–180. Middletown, CT: Wesleyan University Press, 1996.

———. *The Impulse to Preserve: Reflections of a Filmmaker.* New York: Other Press, 2006.

———. *Just Representations.* Ed. Charles Warren. Cambridge, MA: Peabody Museum Press/Studio7Arts, 2010.

———. *Making* Dead Birds: *Chronicle of a Film.* Cambridge, MA: Peabody Museum Press, 2007.

Gardner, Robert, and Ákos Östör. *Making* Forest of Bliss: *Intention, Circumstance, and Chance in Nonfiction Film: A Conversation between Robert Gardner and Ákos Östör.* Cambridge, MA: Harvard Film Archive, 2001.

Gardner, Robert, and Karl G. Heider. *Gardens of War: Life and Death in the New Guinea Stone Age.* New York: Random House, 1968.

MacDonald, Scott. *American Ethnographic Film and Personal Documentary: The Cambridge Turn.* Berkeley and Los Angeles: University of California Press, 2013, 61–110.

Ruby, Jay. *Picturing Culture: Explorations of Film & Anthropology.* Chicago: University of Chicago Press, 2000, 95–113.

Michael Glawogger

Michael Glawogger's website—http://www.glawogger.com—includes a listing of reviews of his films.

Alfred Guzzetti

Guzzetti, Alfred. *Two or Three Things I Know about Her: Analysis of a Film by Godard.* Cambridge, MA: Harvard University Press, 1981.

Lane, Jim. *The Autobiographical Documentary in America.* Madison: University of Wisconsin Press, 2002, 95–104.

MacDonald, Scott. *American Ethnographic Film and Personal Documentary: The Cambridge Turn.* Berkeley and Los Angeles: University of California Press, 2013, 151–182.

Rothman, William. "Alfred Guzzetti's *Family Portrait Sittings.*" In *The "I" of the Camera*, ed. William Rothman, 304–320. New York: Cambridge University Press, 2004.

Todd Haynes

Camera Obscura special issue on Haynes: Vol. 19, no. 3 (2004). Includes Mary Ann Doane, "Pathos and Pathology: The Cinema of Todd Haynes"; Mary Desjardins, "The Incredible Shrinking Star: Todd Haynes and the Case History of Karen Carpenter"; Lucas Hilderbrand, "Grainy Days and Mondays: *Superstar* and Bootleg Aesthetics"; Laura Christian, "Of Housewives and Saints: Abjection, Transgression, and Impossible Mourning in *Poison* and *Safe*"; Susan Potter, "Dangerous Spaces: *Safe*"; Edward R. O'Neill, "Traumatic Postmodern Histories: *Velvet Goldmine*'s Phantasmatic Testimonies"; and Lynne Joyrich, "Written on the Screen: Mediation and Immersion in *Far From Heaven.*"Morrison, James, ed. *The Cinema of Todd Haynes: All That Heaven Allows*. London: Wallflower Press, 2007.

Leonard Retel Helmrich

Anderson, John. "A Master of Impossible Camera Angles." *New York Times*, September 9, 2011, AR12.

Ross McElwee

Cuevas, Efrén, and Alberto N. Garcia, eds. *Landscapes of the Self: The Cinema of Ross McElwee/Paisajes del yo: El cine de Ross McElwee*. Madrid: Ediciones Internacionales Universitarias, 2007. Includes Stephen Rodrick's "The Meaning of Life," 21–33; Efrén Cuevas's "Sculpting the Self: Autobiography According to Ross McElwee," 37–69; Josep Maria Català's "The Man with a Movie Camera," 97–133; Dominique Bluher's "Ross McElwee's Voice," 135–149; James H. Watkins's "Sword Holes in the Sofa: Documenting the Autobiographical in Ross McElwee's *Sherman's March*," 153–179; Paloma Atencia's "*Time Indefinite* and the Narrative Structure of the Self," 181–201; Gonzalo de Pedro's "*Six O'Clock News*: Based on a Real News Broadcast," 203–221; Gary Hawkins's "Life Studies: Ross McElwee's Art of Slowing Time," 223–235; Ross McElwee's "Finding a Voice," 239–279; and "Talking with McElwee: 'Collage' Interview," 281–313.
Fischer, Lucy. "Documentary Film and the Discourse of Hysterical/Historical Narrative: Ross McElwee's *Sherman's March*." In *Documenting the Documentary: Close Readings of Documentary Film and Video*, ed. Barry Keith Grant and Jeannette Sloniowski, 333–343. Detroit, MI: Wayne State University Press, 1998.
Lane, Jim. *The Autobiographical Documentary in America*. Madison: University of Wisconsin Press, 2002, 69–77.
MacDonald, Scott. *American Ethnographic Film and Personal Documentary: The Cambridge Turn*. Berkeley and Los Angeles: University of California Press, 2013, 183–237.
———. "Interview with Ross McElwee." In *A Critical Cinema 2: Interviews with Independent Filmmakers*, ed. Scott MacDonald, 265–282. Berkeley and Los Angeles: University of California Press, 1992.
Rothman, William, ed. Dossier of essays on McElwee in *Three Documentary Filmmakers*. Albany: SUNY Press, 2009. Includes Diane Stevenson's "Coincidence in Ross McElwee's Documentaries," 63–71; Marian Keane's "Reflections on *Bright Leaves*," 73–82; Jim Lane's "Drifting in Time: Ross McElwee's *Time Indefinite*," 83–90; Charles Warren's "Surprise and Pain, Writing and Film," 91–102; and Rothman's "Sometimes Daddies Don't Talk about Things like That," 103–121.
Stubbs, Liz. *Documentary Filmmakers Speak*. New York: Allworth Press, 2002, 93–108.

Annette Michelson

Michelson was founding editor of *October* and has remained one of its editors, contributing in a wide variety of ways to the journal. Allen, Richard, and Malcolm Turvey, eds. *Camera Obscura, Camera Lucida: Essays in Honor of Annette Michelson.*

Amsterdam: Amsterdam University Press, 2003. Includes a detailed bibliography of Michelson's prolific writing career, along with essays by Malcolm Turvey, Mikhail Iampolski, Allen S. Weiss, Tom Gunning, Stuart Liebman, Edward Dimendberg, Noël Carroll, Peter Wollen, Richard Allen, Noa Steimatsky, William G. Simon, Guiliana Bruno, and Babette Mangolte.

Michelson, Annette, ed. *Andy Warhol*. Cambridge, MA: MIT Press, 2001. Includes essays by Benjamin H. D. Buchloh, Thomas Crow, Hal Foster, Rosalind E. Krauss, an interview with Warhol by Buchloh, and Michelson's "'Where Is Your Rupture?' Mass Culture and the *Gesamtkunstwerk* (1991)."

———. "'Anemic Cinema': Reflections on an Emblematic Work." *Artforum* 12, no. 2 (October 1973): 64–69.

———. "Bodies in Space: Film as 'Carnal Knowledge,'" *Artforum* 2, no. 6 (February 1969): 54–63.

———, ed. Catalog for New Forms in Film, Montreux, Switzerland, August, 1974. Includes Michelson's introductory essay "Film and the Radical Aspiration" and her "Yvonne Rainer: 'Lives of Performers'" and "Camera Obscura: The Cinema of Stan Brakhage," and essays by Stan Brakhage, Rosalind Krauss, George Landow, Jonas Mekas, Louis Mendelson, Yvonne Rainer, Paul Sharits, Rimydas Silbajoris, Bill Simon, Elena Pinto Simon, P. Adams Sitney, Michael Snow, and Joyce Wieland.

———, ed. *Kino-Eye: The Writings of Dziga Vertov*. Berkeley and Los Angeles: University of California Press, 1984.

———. "'The Man with a Movie Camera': From Magician to Epistemologist." *Artforum* 10, no. 6 (March 1972): 60–72.

———. "Rose Hobart and Monsieur Phot: Early Films from Utopia Parkway." *Artforum* 11, no. 10 (June 1973): 45–57.

———, ed. Special avant-garde film issue of *Artforum*: 10, no. 1 (September 1971). Includes her forward, "Forward in Three Letters," and essays by Paul Arthur, Wanda Barshen, Regina Cornwell, Hollis Frampton, Joan Jonas, Stephen Koch, Max Kozloff, Barbara Rose, Richard Serra, Robert Smithson, and Michael Snow.

———, ed. Special "Eisenstein/Brakhage" issue of *Artforum* 11, no. 5 (January 1973). Includes Michelson's "Camera Lucida/Camera Obscura," "Eisenstein on Mayakovsky," essays on Eisenstein by Roland Barthes, Noël Carroll, Rosalind Krauss, and essays on Brakhage by Paul Arthur, Phoebe Cohen, Fred Camper, plus an interview with Stan and Jane Brakhage by Hollis Frampton and a Brakhage filmography.

———. "Yvonne Rainer, Part One: The Dancer and the Dance." *Artforum* 12, no. 5 (January 1974): 57–63.

———. "Yvonne Rainer, Part Two: 'Lives of Performers.'" *Artforum* 12, no. 6 (February 1974): 30–35.

Alexander Olch

The website for *The Windmill Movie*—http://www.windmillmovie.com—includes a listing of reviews of the film. Alexander Olch's own website—http://www.olch.com—includes information about Olch's involvement in men's fashion.

MacDonald, Scott. *American Ethnographic Film and Personal Documentary: The Cambridge Turn*. Berkeley and Los Angeles: University of California Press, 2013, 300–307.

Paravel, Véréna

Leimbacher, Irina. "The World Made Flesh—The Sensory Ethnography Lab: Toward a Post-Humanist Cinema." *Film Comment* 50, no. 2 (March/April 2014): 36–39.
MacDonald, Scott. *American Ethnographic Film and Personal Documentary: The Cambridge Turn*. Berkeley and Los Angeles: University of California Press, 2013, 332–337.

Ed Pincus

Lane, Jim. *The Autobiographical Documentary in America*. Madison: University of Wisconsin Press, 2002, 52–62.
Levin, G. Roy. *Documentary Explorations: Interviews with Film-Makers*. Garden City, NY: Anchor Press, 1971, 329–371.
MacDonald, Scott. *American Ethnographic Film and Personal Documentary: The Cambridge Turn*. Berkeley and Los Angeles: University of California Press, 2013, 138–151.
Pincus, Ed. *Guide to Filmmaking* (assisted by Jairus Lincoln). New York: New American Library, 1969 (paperback). Washington, DC: Regnery, 1972 (hard cover).
———. "New Possibilities in Film and the University." *Quarterly Review of Film Studies* 2, no. 2 (May 1977): 159–178.
Pincus, Ed, and Steve Ascher. *The Filmmaker's Handbook*. New York: Plume, 1984.
———. *The Filmmaker's Handbook: A Comprehensive Guide for the Digital Age*. New York: Plume, 1999. Revised edition, 2007.

Jennifer Proctor

Baron, Jaimie, "On the Experimental Remake." *Framework* 53, no. 2 (Fall 2012): 467–490.
Proctor, Jennifer, River E. Branch, and Kyja Kristjansson-Nelson. "The Woman with the Movie Camera Redux: Revisiting the Position of Women in the Production Classroom." *Jump Cut* 53 (Summer 2011): available at *Jump Cut*'s website: http://www.ejumpcut.org.

Godfrey Reggio

Catalog for Criterion DVD release of the Qatsi Trilogy, 2012, includes Scott MacDonald, "Celebration and Warning," 7–13; Bill McKibben, "Geologic Scale and Human Scale," 27–31; and John Rockwell, "Counterpoint and Harmony," 16–23.
Dempsey, Michael. "Qatsi Means Life: The Film of Godfrey Reggio." *Film Quarterly* 42, no. 3 (Spring 1989): 2–12.
Holden, Stephen. "Staring at You, Staring at Me." *New York Times*, January 24, 2013, C13.

MacDonald, Scott. "Interview with Godfrey Reggio." In *A Critical Cinema 2*, ed. Scott MacDonald, 378–401. Berkeley and Los Angeles: University of California Press, 1992.

Amie Siegel

Siegel's website (http://www.amiesiegel.net) includes an annotated listing her writings and other contributions to books and journals, as well as an annotated listing of reviews of her work.

MacDonald, Scott. *American Ethnographic Film and Personal Documentary: The Cambridge Turn*. Berkeley and Los Angeles: University of California Press, 2013, 307–313.

Stephanie Spray

Castaing-Taylor, Lucien, and Véréna Paravel. Interview with Spray and Pacho Velez. *Manakamana* website: http://www.manakamanafilm.com.

Leimbacher, Irina. "The World Made Flesh—The Sensory Ethnography Lab: Toward a Post-Humanist Cinema." *Film Comment* 50, no. 2 (March/April 2014): 36–39.

MacDonald, Scott. *American Ethnographic Film and Personal Documentary: The Cambridge Turn*. Berkeley and Los Angeles: University of California Press, 2013, 328–332.

Pacho Velez

Leimbacher, Irina. "The World Made Flesh—The Sensory Ethnography Lab: Toward a Post-Humanist Cinema." *Film Comment* 50, no. 2 (March/April 2014): 36–39.

Paweł Wojtasik

Barliant, Claire. "*The Aquarium*." *Artforum* 54, no. 9 (May 2006): 294.

MacCash, Doug. "Prospect.2 New Orleans. Best of the Show: 5 Exhibits that Should Not Be Missed." New Orleans *Times-Picayune*, November 13, 2011.

Shuster, Robert. "Pawel Wojtasik's 'At the Still Point.'" *Village Voice*, March 30, 2010.

Wojtasik, Paweł. *Like a Shipwreck We Die Going into Ourselves*. Catalogue for a show of photographs and video at Martos Gallery, New York City, September 18th to November 1st, 2008. Includes an interview with Wojtasik by Denise Markonish.

{ INDEX }